Lecture Notes in Computer Science 12858

T0202805

More information about this subseries at http://www.springer.com/series/7409

Leong Hou U · Marc Spaniol ·
Yasushi Sakurai · Junying Chen (Eds.)

Web and Big Data

5th International Joint Conference, APWeb-WAIM 2021
Guangzhou, China, August 23–25, 2021
Proceedings, Part I

Springer

Editors
Leong Hou U (ID)
University of Macau
Macau, China

Marc Spaniol (ID)
University of Caen Normandie
Caen, France

Yasushi Sakurai
Osaka University
Osaka, Japan

Junying Chen (ID)
South China University of Technology
Guangzhou, China

ISSN 0302-9743 ISSN 1611-3349 (electronic)
Lecture Notes in Computer Science
ISBN 978-3-030-85895-7 ISBN 978-3-030-85896-4 (eBook)
https://doi.org/10.1007/978-3-030-85896-4

LNCS Sublibrary: SL3 – Information Systems and Applications, incl. Internet/Web, and HCI

This Springer imprint is published by the registered company Springer Nature Switzerland AG
The registered company address is: Gewerbestrasse 11, 6330 Cham, Switzerland

Preface

This volume (LNCS 12858) and its companion volume (LNCS 12859) contain the proceedings of the fifth Asia-Pacific Web (APWeb) and Web-Age Information Management (WAIM) Joint Conference on Web and Big Data, called APWeb-WAIM. With the increased focus on big data, the new joint conference is expected to attract more professionals from different industrial and academic communities, not only from the Asia-Pacific countries but also from other continents. The objective is to enable the sharing and exchange of ideas, experiences, and results in the areas of the World Wide Web and big data, thus covering web technologies, database systems, information management, software engineering, and big data.

The fifth APWeb-WAIM conference was held in Guangzhou during August 23–25, 2021. As an Asia-Pacific flagship conference focusing on research, development, and applications in relation to Web information management, APWeb-WAIM builds on the successes of APWeb and WAIM: APWeb was previously held in Beijing (1998), Hong Kong (1999), Xi'an (2000), Changsha (2001), Xi'an (2003), Hangzhou (2004), Shanghai (2005), Harbin (2006), Huangshan (2007), Shenyang (2008), Suzhou (2009), Busan (2010), Beijing (2011), Kunming (2012), Sydney (2013), Changsha (2014), Guangzhou (2015), and Suzhou (2016); and WAIM was held in Shanghai (2000), Xi'an (2001), Beijing (2002), Chengdu (2003), Dalian (2004), Hangzhou (2005), Hong Kong (2006), Huangshan (2007), Zhangjiajie (2008), Suzhou (2009), Jiuzhaigou (2010), Wuhan (2011), Harbin (2012), Beidaihe (2013), Macau (2014), Qingdao (2015), and Nanchang (2016). The APWeb-WAIM conferences were held in Beijing (2017), Macau (2018), Chengdu (2019), and Tianjin (2020). With the fast development of web-related technologies, we expect that APWeb-WAIM will become an increasingly popular forum that brings together outstanding researchers and developers in the fields of the Web and big data from around the world.

The high-quality program documented in these proceedings would not have been possible without the authors who chose APWeb-WAIM for disseminating their findings. A total of 184 submissions were received and, after the double-blind review process (each paper received at least three review reports), the conference accepted 44 regular papers (23.91%), 24 short research papers, and 6 demonstrations. The contributed papers address a wide range of topics, such as graph mining, data mining, data management, topic model and language model learning, text analysis, text classification, machine learning, knowledge graphs, emerging data processing techniques, information extraction and retrieval, recommender systems, and spatial and spatio-temporal databases. The technical program also included keynotes by M. Tamer Özsu (University of Waterloo, USA), Huan Liu (Arizona State University, Tempe, USA), X. Sean Wang (Fudan University, China), and Xiaokui Xiao (National University of Singapore, Singapore). We are grateful to these distinguished scientists for their invaluable contributions to the conference program. As a joint conference, teamwork is particularly important for the success of APWeb-WAIM. We are deeply thankful to the Program Committee members and the external reviewers for lending their time and expertise to the conference. Special thanks go to the local Organizing Committee led by Yi Cai. Thanks also go to the workshop chairs (Yunjun Gao, An Liu, and Xiaohui Tao), demo chair (Yanghui Rao), industry chair (Jianming Lv), tutorial chair (Raymond Chi-Wing Wong), publication chair (Junying Chen), local arrangement chairs (Guohua Wang and Junying Chen), and publicity chairs (Xin Wang and Jianxin Li). Their efforts were essential to the success of the conference. Last but not least, we wish to express our gratitude to the Webmaster (Jianwei Lu), for all the hard work, and to our sponsors who generously supported the smooth running of the conference.

We hope you enjoy the exciting program of APWeb-WAIM 2021 as documented in these proceedings.

July 2021

Yi Cai
Tom Gedeon
Qing Li
Baltasar Fernández Manjón
Leong Hou U
Marc Spaniol
Yasushi Sakurai

Organization

Organizing Committee

General Chairs

Yi Cai — South China University of Technology, China
Tom Gedeon — Australia National University, Australia
Qing Li — Hong Kong Polytechnic University, China
Baltasar Fernández Manjón — UCM, Spain

Program Committee Chairs

Leong Hou U — University of Macau, China
Marc Spaniol — Université de Caen Normandie, France
Yasushi Sakurai — Osaka University, Japan

Workshop Chairs

Yunjun Gao — Zhejiang University, China
An Liu — Soochow University, China
Xiaohui Tao — University of Southern Queensland, Australia

Demo Chair

Yanghui Rao — Sun Yat-sen University, China

Tutorial Chair

Raymond Chi-Wing Wong — Hong Kong University of Science and Technology, China

Industry Chair

Jianming Lv — South China University of Technology, China

Publication Chair

Junying Chen — South China University of Technology, China

Publicity Chairs

Xin Wang   Tianjin University, China
Jianxin Li   Deakin University, Australia

Local Arrangement Chairs

Guohua Wang   South China University of Technology, China
Junying Chen   South China University of Technology, China

Webmaster

Jianwei Lu   South China University of Technology, China

APWeb-WAIM Steering Committee Representative

Yanchun Zhang   Victoria University, Australia

Senior Program Committee Members

Feida Zhu   Singapore Management University, Singapore
Lei Chen   Hong Kong University of Science and Technology,
                          China
Mizuho Iwaihara   Waseda University, Japan
Peer Kroger   Christian-Albrechst-University Kiel, Germany
Reynold Cheng   The University of Hong Kong, China
Wolf-Tilo Balke   TU Braunschweig, Germany
Xiang Zhao   National University of Defence Technology, China
Yunjun Gao   Zhejiang University, China
Zhiguo Gong   University of Macau, China

Program Committee Members

Alex Delis   University of Athens, Greece
An Liu   Soochow University, China
Aviv Segev   KAIST, Korea
Baoning Niu   Taiyuan University of Technology, China
Bin Cui   Peking University, China
Bo Tang   Southern University of Science and Technology, China
Bohan Li   Nanjing University of Aeronautics and Astronautics,
                          China
Bolong Zheng   Huazhong University of Science and Technology,
                          China
Carson K. Leung   University of Manitoba, Canada
Cheqing Jin   East China Normal University, China
Chih-Hua Tai   National Taipei University, China

Panagiotis Karras	Aarhus University, Denmark
Peiquan Jin	University of Science and Technology of China, China
Peng Wang	Fudan University, China
Qingbao Huang	Guangxi University, China
Raymond Chi-Wing Wong	Hong Kong University of Science and Technology, China
Rong-Hua Li	Beijing Institute of Technology, China
Sanghyun Park	Yonsei University, Korea
Sangkeun Lee	Oak Ridge National Laboratory, USA
Sanjay Kumar Madria	Missouri University of Science and Technology, USA
Senzhang Wang	Central South University, China
Shaoxu Song	Tsinghua University, China
Sheng Wang	New York University, USA
Shengli Wu	Jiangsu University, China
Shuyue Hu	NUS, Singapore
Taketoshi Ushiama	Kyushu University, Japan
Tao Wang	King's College London, UK
Tieyun Qian	Wuhan University, China
Ting Deng	Beihang University, China
Tingjian Ge	University of Massachusetts, Lowell, USA
Vincent Oria	NJIT, USA
Wee Siong Ng	Institute for Infocomm Research, Singapore
Wei Lu	Renmin University of China, China
Wei Song	Wuhan University, China
Wei Wang	University of New South Wales, Australia
Wen Zhang	Wuhan University, China
Xiang Lian	Kent State University, USA
Xiangmin Zhou	RMIT University, Australia
Xiaochun Yang	Northeastern University, USA
Xiaohui Tao	The University of Southern Queensland, Australia
Xiaokui Xiao	National University of Singapore, Singapore
Xiaowei Wu	University of Macau, China
Xike Xie	University of Science and Technology of China, China
Xin Cao	University of New South Wales, Australia
Xin Huang	Hong Kong Baptist University, China
Xin Wang	Tianjin University, China
Xingquan Zhu	Florida Atlantic University, USA
Xudong Mao	Xiamen University, China
Yafei Li	Zhengzhou University, China
Yajun Yang	Tianjin University, China
Yanghua Xiao	Fudan University, China
Yanghui Rao	Sun Yat-sen University, China
Yang-Sae Moon	Kangwon National University, South Korea
Yaokai Feng	Kyushu University, Japan
Yijie Wang	National University of Defense Technology, China
Yingxia Shao	BUPT, China

Yongpan Sheng	Chongqing University, China
Yongxin Tong	Beihang University, China
Yu Gu	Northeastern University, USA
Zakaria Maamar	Zayed University, United Arab of Emirates
Zhaonian Zou	Harbin Institute of Technology, China
Zhixu Li	Soochow University, China
Zouhaier Brahmia	University of Sfax, Tunisia

Keynotes

Approaches to Distributed RDF Data Management and SPARQL Processing

M. Tamer Özsu

David R. Cheriton School of Computer Science, University of Waterloo, Canada
tamer.ozsu@uwaterloo.ca

Abstract. Resource Description Framework (RDF) has been proposed for modelling Web objects as part of developing the "semantic web", but its usage has extended beyond this original objective. As the volume of RDF data has increased, the usual scalability issues have arisen and solutions have been developed for distributed/parallel processing of SPARQL queries over large RDF datasets. RDF has also gained attention as a way to accomplish data integration, leading to federated approaches. In this talk I will provide an overview of work in these two areas.

Striving for Socially Responsible AI in Data Science

Huan Liu

School of Computing and Augmented Intelligence,
Arizona State University, USA
huanliu@asu.edu

Abstract. AI has never been this pervasive and effective. AI algorithms are used in news feeds, friend/purchase recommendation, making hiring and firing decisions, and political campaigns. Data empowers AI algorithms and is then collected again for further training AI algorithms. We come to realize that AI algorithms have biases, and some biases might result in deleterious effects. Facing existential challenges, we explore how socially responsible AI can help in data science: what it is, why it is important, and how it can protect and inform us, and help prevent or mitigate the misuse of AI. We show how socially responsible AI works via use cases of privacy preservation, cyberbullying identification, and disinformation detection. Knowing the problems with AI and our own conflicting goals, we further discuss some quandaries and challenges in our pursuit of socially responsible AI.

Democratizing the Full Data Analytics Software Stack

X. Sean Wang

School of Computer Science, Fudan University, China
xywangcs@fudan.edu.cn

Abstract. Data analysis and machine learning is a complex task, involving a full stack of hardware and software systems, from the usual compute systems, cloud computing and supercomputing systems, to data collection systems, data storage and database systems, data mining and machine learning systems, and data visualization and interaction systems. A realistic and highly efficient data analytics and AI application often requires a smooth collaboration among the different systems, which becomes a big technical hurdle, especially to the non-computing professionals. The history of computing may be viewed as a technical democratizing processing, which in turn brings huge benefit to the society and its economy. The democratizing process for data analysis and machine learning has started to appear in various aspects, but it still needs research and development in multiple directions, including human-machine natural interaction, automated system selection and deployment, and automated workflow execution and optimization. It can be expected that this democratizing process will continue, and the research and development efforts by the computer scientists are much needed.

Efficient Network Embeddings
for Large Graphs

Xiaokui Xiao

School of Computing, National University of Singapore, Singapore
xkxiao@nus.edu.sg

Abstract. Given a graph G, network embedding maps each node in G into a compact, fixed-dimensional feature vector, which can be used in downstream machine learning tasks. Most of the existing methods for network embedding fail to scale to large graphs with millions of nodes, as they either incur significant computation cost or generate low-quality embeddings on such graphs. In this talk, we will present two efficient network embedding algorithms for large graphs with and without node attributes, respectively. The basic idea is to first model the affinity between nodes (or between nodes and attributes) based on random walks, and then factorize the affinity matrix to derive the embeddings. The main challenges that we address include (i) the choice of the affinity measure and (ii) the reduction of space and time overheads entailed by the construction and factorization of the affinity matrix. Extensive experiments on large graphs demonstrate that our algorithms outperform the existing methods in terms of both embedding quality and efficiency.

Contents – Part I

Text Analysis

Text Classification

Machine Learning 1

Contents – Part II

Emerging Data Processing Techniques

Information Extraction and Retrieval

Recommender System

Spatial and Spatio-Temporal Databases

Demo

Graph Mining

Co-authorship Prediction Based on Temporal Graph Attention

Dongdong Jin[1], Peng Cheng[1(✉)], Xuemin Lin[2], and Lei Chen[3]

[1] East China Normal University, Shanghai, China
ddjin@stu.ecnu.edu.cn, pcheng@sei.ecnu.edu.cn
[2] University of New South Wales, Sydney, Australia
lxue@cse.unsw.edu.au
[3] Hong Kong University of Science and Technology, Hong Kong, China
leichen@cse.ust.hk

Abstract. The social network analysis has received significant interests and concerns of researchers recently, and co-authorship prediction is an important link prediction problem. Traditional models inefficiently use multi-relational information to enhance topological features. In this paper, we focus on the co-authorship prediction in the co-authorship knowledge graph (KGs) to show that multi-relation graphs can enhance feature expression ability and improve prediction performance. Currently, the main models for link prediction in KGs are based on KG embedding learning, such as several models using convolutional neural networks and graph neural networks. These models capture rich and expressive embeddings of entities and relations, and obtain good results. However, the co-authorship KGs have much temporal information in reality, which cannot be integrated by these models since they are aimed at static KGs. Therefore, we propose a temporal graph attention network to model the temporal interactions between the neighbors and encapsulate the spatiotemporal context information of the entities. In addition, we also capture the semantic information and multi-hop neighborhood information of the entities to enrich the expression ability of the embeddings. Finally, our experimental evaluations on all dataset verify the effectiveness of our approach based on temporal graph attention mechanism, which outperforms the state-of-the-art models.

Keywords: Co-authorship prediction · Temporal KGs · Graph attention

1 Introduction

Recently, social network analysis has attracted great interest from researchers, such as social recommendation [31], influence analysis [9] and sentiment analysis [25]. Co-authorship prediction [26] is an important problem of social network analysis, i.e., predicting the possibility of collaboration between two authors in the future, which can be regarded as academic user recommendation. Traditional

© Springer Nature Switzerland AG 2021
L. H. U et al. (Eds.): APWeb-WAIM 2021, LNCS 12858, pp. 3–19, 2021.
https://doi.org/10.1007/978-3-030-85896-4_1

co-authorship prediction models [4,23] often ignore or underutilize the information of various relations, such as the conference of papers, the topic of papers, and the affiliation of authors. These information are very important for the co-authorship prediction. For example, the authors in the same affiliation are more likely to collaborate in future.

To utilize the relational information, we apply knowledge graphs on co-authorship data. As a multi-relational graph widely used in many fields, knowledge graphs (KGs) can integrate multiple relations to significantly improve performance such as semantic analysis [16], question answering [15] and recommendation systems [30]. A KG consists of triples in the form of (*head entity*, *relation*, *tail entity*), where entities are nodes, a relation is a directed edge from the entity e_i to the entity e_j and e_i is called head entity as the starting point of the edge, e_j is called tail entity as the end of the edge. It is promising for co-authorship prediction to use KGs considering various relations in a holistic way. Currently, most existing works apply KG embedding learning for link prediction in KGs [2,5,7], where entities and relations are mapped into the low-dimensional continuous embedding spaces through embedding models. Unfortunately, most of them are time independent [5,22], while many real-world KGs (e.g., Wikidata [10] and YAGO3 [21]) carry rich temporal information (e.g., the valid timestamp of triples). With the temporal information, the performance of KG embedding models in link prediction tasks can be effectively improved [6,11].

In this paper, we integrate the temporal information into KGs to predict the potential co-author relations (collaborations) among authors, which can provide valuable suggestions for the collaborations of papers or projects and facilitate the exchange of ideas. To illustrate the effect of the temporal information on the entities, we provide an example in Fig. 1. Each triple has its establishment time, such as the time when two authors collaborated. With time information, for author entity A_1, the difference in its relationships with two 1-hop neighbors (A_4, A_5) is easier to distinguish. We can find that author A_1 was closer to author A_5 in 2013, and was closer to author A_4 during 2015 to 2016. The future co-authors of an author depend on his current state, such as the research fields, affiliation and existing co-authors. For instance, author A_1 and $A5$ published papers at a same conference K_1 in 2012 and 2010, respectively. Then, A_1 and A_5 had collaboration in 2013 since they have similar research fields. Another example is that in 2014 A_3 had collaborations with A_1 and A_4, which promoted the subsequent collaborations between A_1 and A_4 in 2015 and 2016. In summary, there are many interactions with temporal attributes among the entities.

Therefore, encapsulating the temporal information of triples of entities as their embedding can generate better signals in model learning [11]. In order to reasonably obtain the expressive embeddings, especially the embeddings of author entities, we have the following challenges: 1) capturing the temporal interactions between neighbors; 2) effectively aggregating representation of entities at different distances (time and space) in KG.

Inspired by the success of the recurrent neural networks (RNNs) [14] in the graph attention mechanism [34], we propose a novel temporal graph attention

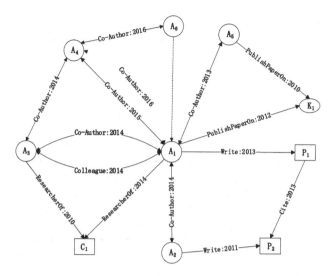

Fig. 1. A knowledge graph of temporal co-authorship, where the double arrow indicates the bidirectional relation between entities, the solid lines represent the actual relations.

network based on Bi-LSTM [12] to solve these challenges and obtain the embeddings of entities and relations. We first serialize the triples related to an entity, then send them to the attention layer to compute the corresponding attention coefficient and aggregate triples representation. When calculate the attention coefficient of a neighbor j to the entity i, we encapsulate the influence of subsequent neighbors (the interaction time with i is later) and previous neighbors (the interaction time with i is earlier) on them. By stacking the temporal graph attention layers, we can implicitly aggregate representation of entities at different distances in the KGs. In addition, we set up a constrained neighborhood strategy to obtain the information of multi-hop entities more directly. Our model is consisted of three parts: (a) considering the importance of the natural semantics of the entities such as paper topic, we use a Semantic Encoder to initialize the embeddings of entities; (b) the temporal graph attention network based Embedding Encoder is used to learn the embeddings of entities and relations; (c) multi-scale convolution kernels are added to ConvKB [5] as a Decoder to predict the author's future co-authors.

Our main contributions are as follows:

- We utilize the time and semantics information to enhance the expressive ability of embeddings in KGs to predict future co-authors.
- We propose a temporal graph attention network to model the temporal interactions between neighbors. Combining the temporal graph attention network and the neighborhood strategy, we effectively aggregate the neighborhood information of different distances into a low-dimensional space in Sect. 4.

- We conduct extensive experiments on three real-world co-authorship datasets in Sect. 5. The results show the clear superiority of our model compared with several state-of-the-art models.

2   Related Work

Firstly, we review some of the existing work on co-authorship prediction. Path-Predict [26] is the first work for heterogeneous co-authorship networks. It constructs several meta-paths between authors to capture topological features and makes prediction through supervised learning. Existing work studies the impact of different topological features between authors in medical co-authorship networks on the results, and uses supervised models to learn the best weights associated with different topological features [23]. LDAcosin [4] incorporates the content of the paper into the similarity measure between authors, and proposes a new metric for evaluating similarity. However, the features extracted by these models are relatively weak in expression, which is insufficient for high-quality learning and prediction.

And the widely used knowledge graphs can obtain the powerful expression for the author nodes through embedding learning. The existing KG embedding learning models in the KGs are mainly aimed at static and temporal KGs. We first introduce several excellent embedding learning models for static KGs. TransE [2], DistMult [33], and ComplEx [27] are three translation-based models. TransE is the first work to take the translation of entities and relations in the embedding space as an optimization goal; DistMult is a simple expression of bilinear model and ComplEx introduces the complex space into the KG embedding. ConvE [7] and ConvKB [5] are two convolution-based models. They both use two-dimensional convolution to mine the global relationships between entities and relations. R-GCN [24] and KBGAT [22] are two models based on graph neural networks (GNNs) [1,18,29]. They use the neighborhood of each entity to learn the embeddings. The difference between the two lies in the way of treating node neighbors. R-GCN assigns the same weight matrix to neighbors that have the same relation type with an entity and KBGAT treats every neighbor differently. Although the above embedding learning models have achieved good results, none of them take into account the temporal information in the KGs.

Embedding learning models for temporal KGs are also important. TAE [17] takes the time order as a constraint to improve the quality of embedding representation. However, it does not use the exact time information of triples, but mines the time order of relations from the occurrence time of triples. TTransE [19] models the establishment and expiration time of the relations between the head and tail entities, and predicts the valid time of unlabeled triples. TA-TransE [11] strengthens the expressive ability of embeddings by learning the time-aware representation of relation types. It can directly act on the current common scoring functions for link prediction, and enable them to obtain better performance and robustness on the temporal KGs. HyTE [6] explicitly merges the time information into the space of entities and relations by associating each time stamp with the corresponding hyperplane. These temporal KG embedding models have excellent performance in link prediction, but the drawback is that they are unable to model the temporal interaction between entities.

3 Problem Description

Given a temporal co-authorship KG $G = [E, R]$, where E is the entity (node) set, R is the relation (edge) set. G is composed of many temporal triples of the form $(h, r, t, time)$, which means that an interaction of type r has occurred between entity h and entity t at time $time$. For example, in Fig. 1, the triple $(A1, Write, A2, 2011)$ means that the authors $A1$ and $A2$ have formed a co-author relation at time 2011. For the purpose of observing the time and frequency of interactions between entities, unlike the general case where the same relation between an entity pair is only considered once, we record all interactions with time information. Link prediction in the temporal co-authorship KGs is to predict whether a co-author relation will be established between two existing authors in the future. We consider that author i and author j form a co-author relation if and only if they jointly write and publish a paper.

In particular, we are only interested in possible co-author relation between two authors who have never collaborated before, and repeated co-authors are not within our forecast.

4 Our Approach

4.1 Semantic Encoder

For KG embedding learning, most methods of initializing entities, such as random and TransE, ignore the semantic information of entities. We apply a pre-trained language model BERT [8] to initialize the embeddings, which can generate word embeddings with semantics. Specifically, an entity e is defined by a sequence of words, i.e., $e = s = [w_1, \ldots, w_L]$, where w_l is the l-th word of sequence s and L is the number of the words. We feed the word sequence s into BERT to obtain the word embeddings, denoted as $[\mathbf{w}_1, \ldots, \mathbf{w}_L] = \text{BERT}([w_1, \ldots, w_L])$, where $\mathbf{w}_l \in \mathbb{R}^{d_{BERT}}$ represents the word embedding of w_l and d_{BERT} represents the dimension of the word embeddings. We apply an averaging strategy and a fully connected layer FC_s to get the low-dimensional representation of s and use it as the initial embedding of e:

$$\mathbf{e}_{init} = \text{FC}_s(\text{Average}(\text{BERT}(s))) = \text{FC}_s(\frac{1}{L}\sum_{l=1}^{L}\mathbf{w}_l) \qquad (1)$$

4.2   Embedding Encoder

Graph attention networks (GATs) [29] introduced the attention mechanism into graph-structure data, and KBGAT better integrated the graph attention mechanism into KGs since GATs ignore the information of the relations. However, as we mentioned before, their models are time-unaware and unable to model the temporal information of triples.

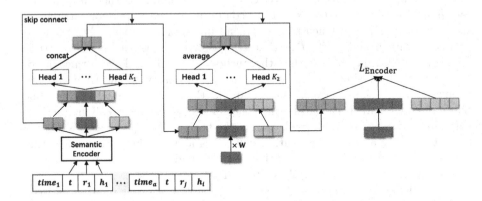

Fig. 2. Semantic Encoder and Embedding Encoder with two temporal graph attention layers. The form of the triples is reversed for convenience. The colored squares indicate the embeddings of entities and relation at different layers in the two Encoders. The arrows represent the input and output of each module or the operations on embeddings. (Color figure online)

Therefore, we propose a temporal graph attention network to encode the time-aware triples. We introduce a single temporal graph attention layer, and the attention network can be implemented by simply stacking multiple attention layers, as shown in Fig. 2. We show the process of updating the embedding of entity t (indicated by the blue square) from the perspective of entity t as the tail entity. The input of each layer is the embeddings of entities and relations, and the output is the new embeddings learned by the layer.

To obtain the new embedding of an entity t, the attention coefficient will be calculated for each triple associated with t (the triples with t as the tail entity). We serialize the triples and denote them as $V = [v_1, \ldots, v_Y]$, where $v_y = [h_i, r_j, t, time_a]$, Y represents the number of triples in V and these triples are sorted in ascending order of time. The process of calculating the normalized attention coefficient of each triple in V is shown in Fig. 3. We first apply a linear transformation to each triple v_y with a weight matrix $\mathbf{W}_1$:

$$\mathbf{v}_y = \mathbf{W}_1[\mathbf{e}_{h_i} \| \mathbf{e}_{r_j} \| \mathbf{e}_t] \tag{2}$$

where $\|$ represents concatenation operation, $\mathbf{e}_{h_i}$, $\mathbf{e}_{r_j}$ and $\mathbf{e}_t$ represent the embeddings of head entity h_i, relation r_j and tail entity t, respectively. The obtained vector set is denoted as $\mathbf{V} = [\mathbf{v}_1, \ldots, \mathbf{v}_Y]$.

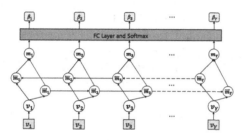

Fig. 3. The process of attention calculation. The input is a sequence of triples related to the entity t, and the output is the normalized attention coefficient of each triple v_y.

We choose Bi-LSTM [12] as an important part of the attention layer to capture the information of the past and future triples and model the temporal interactions between neighbors. A Bi-LSTM layer consists of two LSTM layers [14], which calculate the forward sequence and the reverse sequence respectively, called forward-layer and backward-layer. Specifically, $\overrightarrow{\mathbf{m}}_{y-1}$ and $\overleftarrow{\mathbf{m}}_{y-1}$ are the hidden states of forward-layer and backward-layer at the previous time-step $y-1$, then the hidden states $\overrightarrow{\mathbf{m}}_y$ and $\overleftarrow{\mathbf{m}}_y$ of two layers and the hidden state $\mathbf{m}_y$ of Bi-LSTM layer at the current time-step y are calculated as:

$$\overrightarrow{\mathbf{m}}_y = \text{forward layer}(v_y, \overrightarrow{\mathbf{m}}_{y-1})$$
$$\overleftarrow{\mathbf{m}}_y = \text{backward layer}(v_y, \overleftarrow{\mathbf{m}}_{y-1}) \tag{3}$$
$$\mathbf{m}_y = [\overrightarrow{\mathbf{m}}_y \parallel \overleftarrow{\mathbf{m}}_y]$$

Then we obtain the attention value of the triple v_y by a fully connected layer:

$$\alpha_{v_y} = \text{FC}_a(\mathbf{m}_y) = \sigma(\mathbf{W}_2 \mathbf{m}_y + b) \tag{4}$$

where the weight matrix $\mathbf{W}_2$ and the bias b are trainable parameters, σ is the activation function such as LeakyReLU. Such a structure can provide the attention value with complete past and future contextual information. We apply a softmax function to compute the normalized attention coefficient of triple v_y:

$$\beta_{v_y} = \text{softmax}(\alpha_{v_y}) = \frac{\exp(\alpha_{v_y})}{\sum_{n=1}^{Y} \exp(\alpha_{v_n})} \tag{5}$$

The entity t obtains a new embedding representation by weighted aggregation of the associated triples in V:

$$\mathbf{e}'_t = \sigma\left(\sum_{y=1}^{Y} \beta_{v_y} \mathbf{v}_y\right) \tag{6}$$

To ensure the stability of the attention mechanism and focus on different aspects of the neighborhood, similar to GATs, we employ the multi-head attention [28], which can be described as:

$$\mathbf{e}'_t = \overset{K}{\underset{k=1}{\parallel}} \sigma\left(\sum_{y=1}^{Y} \beta_{v_y}^k \mathbf{v}_y^k\right) \tag{7}$$

where $\beta_{v_y}^k$, $\mathbf{v}_y^k$ are calculated by the k-th independent attention head, K is the number of attention heads, and $\|$ represents the concatenation of the output of each attention head. If the current temporal graph attention layer is the final layer, then the entity embeddings output by the multi-head attention will not be concatenated but averaged to achieve better results as done in GATs:

$$\mathbf{e}_t' = \sigma \left(\frac{1}{K} \sum_{k=1}^{K} \sum_{y=1}^{Y} \beta_{v_y}^k \mathbf{v}_y^k \right) \tag{8}$$

To prevent the problem of gradient dispersion and degradation as well as the disappearance of semantic information due to the deepening of the network depth, we adopt the skip connection [13] in each attention layer, represented as:

$$\mathbf{e}_t = \mathbf{W}_3 \mathbf{e}_{t_{init}} + \mathbf{e}_t' \tag{9}$$

where $\mathbf{e}_{t_{init}}$ is the embedding of the entity t output by the Semantic Encoder. To facilitate the subsequent training process and model design, we use a weight matrix $\mathbf{W}_4$ to transform the embedding space of the relations, where $\mathbf{W}_4$ is a shared parameter, independent of a specific relation r_j.

One of the advantages of graph attention networks is that they can naturally get the information about multi-hop neighbors by stacking attention layers. For example, as shown in Fig. 1, in the first attention layer, entities A_1 and A_4 aggregate the information of their 1-hop neighbors. And when A_1 aggregates the information of neighbor A_4 again in the second layer, it gets the information of all 1-hop neighbors of entity A_4, such as entity A_6. Therefore, a network with n layers can get n-hop neighborhood information through iterative accumulation.

To get the multi-hop neighborhood information more directly, we artificially construct the additional relations between an entity and it's multi-hop neighbors [20,22], for example, the dashed line between entity A_1 and A_6 in Fig. 1. We set the time information of the additional relation to be the same as the latest time on the multi-hop path. In addition, the most important entities and relations in the temporal co-authorship KGs are the author entities and the co-author relations. Therefore, it is unnecessary to construct additional relations for all multi-hop neighbors. We develop a neighborhood strategy, the first is to construct additional relations between each entity and all their 2-hop neighbors; the second is that for an 3-hop neighbor, an additional relation is constructed only if they are both author entities.

4.3 Decoder

Similar to KBGAT, we build the Decoder based on ConvKB [5]. However, unlike KBGAT which uses ConvKB directly, we use the multi-scale convolution kernel strategy instead of the same-scale strategy to capture more information of triples, as shown in Fig. 4. Given a triple (h, r, t), $\mathbf{e}_h$, $\mathbf{e}_r$ and $\mathbf{e}_t$ represent the embedding of h, r and t output by the Embedding Encoder, respectively. The input of the

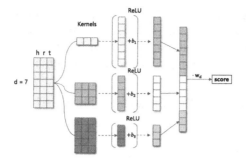

Fig. 4. The process involved in our Decoder based on ConvKB (with the embedding size $d = 7$, the number of multi-scale filter set $M = 1$)

Decoder is a matrix $\mathbf{A} = [\mathbf{e}_h, \mathbf{e}_r, \mathbf{e}_t] \in \mathbb{R}^{d \times 3}$, where d represents the embedding dimension of entities and relations.

In the convolutional layer, we use three convolution kernels of different sizes, denoted as $\boldsymbol{\Omega} = [\boldsymbol{\omega}_1 \in \mathbb{R}^{1 \times 3}, \boldsymbol{\omega}_2 \in \mathbb{R}^{3 \times 3}, \boldsymbol{\omega}_3 \in \mathbb{R}^{5 \times 3}]$. The convolution kernels convolve on the triple matrix independently to generate the feature maps $[\boldsymbol{\tau}_1, \boldsymbol{\tau}_2, \boldsymbol{\tau}_3]$, where $\boldsymbol{\tau}_i \in \mathbb{R}^{c_i \times 1}$ represents the feature map output by $\boldsymbol{\omega}_i$ and c_i represents the dimension of $\boldsymbol{\tau}_i$. After feature extraction by the convolutional layer, the output feature maps are concatenated, i.e., $\mathbf{p} = [\boldsymbol{\tau}_1 \| \boldsymbol{\tau}_2 \| \boldsymbol{\tau}_3] \in \mathbb{R}^{c \times 1}$, $c = c_1 + c_1 + c_3$.

We apply M convolution kernel sets to stabilize the process of feature extraction, denoted as $\boldsymbol{\Omega}' = [\boldsymbol{\Omega}_1, \ldots, \boldsymbol{\Omega}_M]$ and the outputs of M filter sets are concatenated into a single vector, i.e., $\mathbf{P} = [\mathbf{p}_1 \| \ldots \| \mathbf{p}_M] \in \mathbb{R}^{Mc \times 1}$. Finally, we define the scoring function f of Decoder based on ConvKB as:

$$f(h, r, t) = \left(\overset{M}{\underset{m=1}{\|}} \sigma([\mathbf{A} * \boldsymbol{\Omega}_m + \mathbf{b}]) \right) \cdot \mathbf{w}_d = \mathbf{P} \cdot \mathbf{w}_d \tag{10}$$

where $*$ represents the convolution operator, $\mathbf{b}$ is the bias, $\mathbf{w}_d$ is the weight vector and $\cdot$ represents the dot product.

4.4 Optimization

Encoder. The basic idea of the translation-based model [2] is that given a golden triple (h, r, t), the sum of the embedding $\mathbf{e}_h$ of h and the embedding $\mathbf{e}_r$ of r is as close as possible to the embedding $\mathbf{e}_t$ of t, i.e., $\mathbf{e}_h + \mathbf{e}_r \approx \mathbf{e}_t$, where the embeddings are learned by the model. Here the "close" can be measured with $d_{(h,r,t)} = \|\mathbf{e}_h + \mathbf{e}_r - \mathbf{e}_t\|_{l1/l2}$, where $l1$ represents L1-norm and $l2$ represents L2-norm. We borrow this idea and minimize the loss L_{Encoder} to train the Semantic Encoder and Embedding Encoder jointly:

$$L_{\text{Encoder}} = \sum_{(h,r,t) \in \Delta} \sum_{(h',r,t') \in \Delta'} [d_{(h,r,t)} - d_{(h',r,t')} + \gamma]_+ \tag{11}$$

where $[x]_+$ represents $\text{Max}[x, 0]$, γ is the safety margin distance, Δ and Δ' indicate positive and negative training sets, respectively. Additionally, a constraint of the entity embeddings is added that the L2-norm is 1 (no such constraint on the relations) to prevent the training process from trivially minimizing L_{Encoder} [3].

Decoder. The Decoder optimizes model parameters by minimizing the soft-margin loss:

$$L_{\text{Decoder}} = \sum_{(h,r,t)\in\{\Delta\cup\Delta'\}} \log\left(1 + \exp\left(l_{(h,r,t)} \cdot f(h,r,t)\right)\right) + \frac{\lambda}{2} \parallel \mathbf{w}_d \parallel_2^2 \quad (12)$$

where $l_{(h,r,t)} = \begin{cases} 1 & \text{for}(h,r,t) \in \Delta \\ -1 & \text{for}(h,r,t) \in \Delta' \end{cases}$ and $\frac{\lambda}{2} \parallel \mathbf{w}_d \parallel_2^2$ is the L2 regularization on the weight vector.

5   Experiments

5.1   Datasets

Table 1. Datasets Statistics where $|\mathbf{E}|$ and $|\mathbf{R}|$ represent the number of entities and relation types. And we give the number of authors and co-author relations in parentheses after the size of the entity set $|\mathbf{E}|$ and the size of the triple training set, respectively.

Datasets	$|\mathbf{E}|$	$|\mathbf{R}|$	Triples			
			Training	Valid	Test-full	Test-2hop
Management	16327 (1241)		39952 (12314)	1450	640	464
Computer	18454 (2233)	9	54276 (17092)	2998	1104	888
Physics	59100 (13863)		365046 (126290)	5900	10786	7452

We verify the superiority of our model on three temporal co-authorship datasets. We extract three academic relationships of different disciplines with a time span of 2013–2016[1], and process them into three temporal co-authorship KGs. We delete the authors who publish only one paper in each dataset since they contribute less to our task and are not within our prediction range. We use the data of the first three years as the training sets, the new co-author relations of the last year as the test sets, and filter the most recent part of the co-author relations from the training set as the validation sets. We set up two test sets for each dataset according to different purposes. One is a complete test set used to predict all new collaborations, denoted as Test-full. And in the other, to avoid

---

[1] http://cdblp.ruc.edu.cn/.

the excessive calculations between unrelated authors, we only test the new collaborations between two existing authors who are 2hop neighbors in the KGs, denoted as Test-2hop. The number of positive and negative samples in all test sets is balanced. For Test-full, we randomly construct non-existent co-author relations as negative triples; for Test-2hop, we construct negative triples with authors who are 2-hop neighbors to each other. The specific statistical information of the datasets is given in Table 1.

5.2   Training Protocol

We use the *"bern"* method [32] to generate negative triples for training. Given a golden triple, it sets different replacement probabilities for the head and the tail to generate negative triples. This method implies the mapping property of the relation r, i.e., 1-N, N-1, or N-N. The training process consists of two steps. The first is jointly training the Semantic Encoder and the Embedding Encoder to obtain the embeddings of entities and relations, and the second is training the Decoder to predict future co-authors. The input of the Embedding Encoder is the semantic embeddings of the entities and relations outputting by the Semantic Encoder (the dimension size is 50), and its output is the new embeddings (the dimension size is 200). The Embedding Encoder contains two temporal graph attention layers, where each attention layer has four attention heads, and the dropout probability set for each layer is 0.2. We choose ELU as the activation function when aggregating neighborhood information. The margin distance in the loss function and the training epoch are set to 5 and 4500 in the Physics, 1 and 3500 in other datasets. The input of the Decoder is the embeddings of entities and relations learned by the Embedding Encoder, and the output is the score of the triples. The dropout is set to 0.3, and the number of multi-scale convolution kernel sets M is 50. As for training epoch, all datasets are set to 180 except for the Physics which is 300. We choose RELU as the activation function, and the L2-regularizer λ in the loss function is 0.001. Finally, we use Adam optimizer to update all model parameters, where the initial learning rate is $1e^{-3}$ and the decay rate is $1e^{-5}$.

5.3   Evaluation Protocol

The goal of future co-authorship prediction task is to predict whether the author entities h and t will collaborate in the future, i.e., whether a triple (h, r, t) is correct (r is fixed as the co-author relation). Specifically, if the score of a triple output by the Decoder is higher than the threshold, then we consider it to be a golden triple that will occur in the future, otherwise a wrong triple that will not occur in the future. The threshold here is obtained by testing on the validation set. We do training and testing separately on each dataset. Two main metrics are compared for them, i.e., the accuracy of binary classification (ACC), and the area under the ROC curve (AUC).

5.4   Results and Analysis

We choose six models to compare with our model, where PathPredict [26] is a model specifically aimed at co-authorship prediction, TransE [2], DistMult [33], ComplEx [27] and KBGAT [22] are static KG embedding learning models (without considering the temporal information) for link prediction, and TA-TransE [11] is a temporal KG embedding learning model for link prediction.

Results on Test-Full. The results of all models on the Test-full of three datasets are given in Table 2. The results show that our model has achieved significant improvements on each dataset. For example, on the Management, our model has an improvement of 2.65% on ACC compared to the sub-optimal model (TA-TransE), and 2.23% on AUC compared to the sub-optimal model (KBGAT). In addition, we find that the models based on GNNs (our model and KBGAT) are obviously better than other models. For example, our model and KBGAT have achieved the optimal and sub-optimal performance on the Computer and Physics, which reflects the superiority of GNNs in graph structured data and the role of graph attention mechanism in aggregating neighborhood information. Table 2 shows that our model outperforms KBGAT in every computed measure, which illustrates the importance of considering time information and modeling the temporal interactions between neighborhood entities. As a temporal KG embedding learning model, TA-TransE is not competitive compared with other models such as TransE. Since most of the triples in the temporal co-authorship KGs are co-author relations with time information and they are always effective. Meanwhile the unique temporal interactions also makes the performance of TA-TransE more mediocre. PathPredict achieves acceptable results on Management, but performs poorly on the other two data sets. Although it considers multiple types of nodes, and designs several meta-paths to capture the topological features between author node pairs, the features are only between two author nodes, without considering the influence of other authors on them. We also conducted experiments on the unbalanced test set of Physics, with a ratio of positive and negative samples of 1:10. The results in Table 2 show that the performance of all models has improved, and our model maintains optimality.

Results on Test-2hop. If two author entities that have never collaborated are 2-hop neighbors (we call it related authors) such as they have all collaborated with the same author, then they will be more likely to form a new co-author relation. We summarize the comparison results among these models on the Test-2hop of three datasets in Table 3. From the results, our model still achieves better results in all metrics. In addition, the results on most datasets have a certain degree of improvement compared with the Test-full, especially on the Physics. Therefore, predicting relevant authors can achieve better results and is more suitable in application.

Table 2. Experimental results on the Test-full of all datasets. All results are displayed in percentage. The best score is in bold and second best score is underlined. Physics* represents the unbalanced test-full of Physics, where the ratio of positive and negative samples is 1:10.

Methods	Management		Computer		Physics		Physics*	
	ACC	AUC	ACC	AUC	ACC	AUC	ACC	AUC
PathPredict	90.16	93.83	90.31	92.52	81.32	85.42	89.65	87.02
TransE	88.91	92.33	92.03	94.38	83.06	86.74	92.97	86.85
DistMult	89.38	90.59	92.03	92.93	83.47	86.20	93.89	86.12
ComplEx	90.63	92.85	91.30	94.56	83.23	86.65	93.73	86.70
KBGAT	90.31	<u>94.00</u>	<u>93.39</u>	<u>95.37</u>	<u>85.63</u>	<u>90.39</u>	<u>94.06</u>	<u>92.07</u>
TA-TransE	<u>90.94</u>	93.03	92.39	94.40	83.91	88.48	92.56	88.91
Ours	**93.59**	**96.23**	**95.11**	**97.22**	**86.98**	**92.10**	**94.76**	**94.30**

Table 3. Experimental results on the Test-2hop of all datasets. All results are displayed in percentage. The best score is in bold and second best score is underlined.

Methods	Management		Computer		Physics	
	ACC	AUC	ACC	AUC	ACC	AUC
PathPredict	90.30	94.86	88.18	93.06	88.59	94.11
TransE	88.58	94.06	91.33	96.36	91.43	95.55
DistMult	88.36	94.23	90.77	93.61	91.68	95.89
ComplEx	90.30	94.18	88.63	91.10	91.73	95.84
KBGAT	<u>91.59</u>	<u>95.91</u>	<u>93.47</u>	<u>96.50</u>	<u>92.37</u>	<u>96.78</u>
TA-TransE	89.44	94.68	89.86	93.26	90.98	94.40
Ours	**94.61**	**96.59**	**94.59**	**97.00**	**93.58**	**97.51**

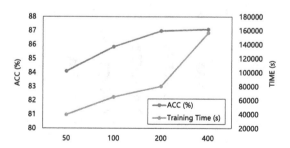

Fig. 5. The influence of the embedding dimension on the accuracy and training time of the model. The experimental results come from Test-full of Physics.

Embedding Dimension Test and Author's Frequency Test. We study the influence of the embedding dimension of entities and relations outputting by the Embedding Encoder on the accuracy and the training time of our model. We test the embedding dimensions of 50, 100, 200 and 400 on Physics, and the results are shown in Fig. 5. From the figure, we can conclude that the larger the embedding dimension is, the more expressive it is, which effectively improves the capability of our model. However, when the embedding dimension reaches 200, continuing to increase the embedding dimension no longer improves the accuracy significantly, and the training time will increase dramatically.

We analyze the effect of the frequency of author collaboration on prediction accuracy. We divide the authors in the test set into several groups according to their current collaboration frequency, and give the test set size for each group. The results are shown in Fig. 6. It should be noted that a test sample may be divided into two groups since the two authors belong to different groups. Therefore, the number of test samples in the figure will be larger than that in Table 1. As a whole, as the number of current collaborations of an author increases, the performance of predicting becomes worse. The results on other datasets are consistent with Physics. This is reasonable as the number of potential co-authors of the author also increases.

5.5 Ablation Study

Our model is a joint learning model composed of several modules. To explore the contribution of each module, we conduct the following ablation studies from three aspects. Table 4 shows the results of two evaluation metrics (ACC and AUC) on the Computer and Physics.

- (Ours-SEMANTIC) We study the effectiveness of integrating the semantic information of the entities into the embedding learning. We use the TransE instead of the Semantic Encoder to generate the initial embeddings of the entities. As shown in Table 4, our model achieves a more accurate prediction

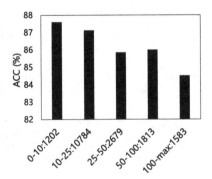

Fig. 6. The influence of the author's collaboration frequency on the accuracy. The experimental results come from Test-full of Physics.

Table 4. Ablation learning results on computer and physics. All results are displayed in percentage and the best score is in bold.

Methods	Management		Computer		Physics	
	ACC	AUC	ACC	AUC	ACC	AUC
Ours-SEMANTIC	92.97	95.38	94.66	96.41	85.93	91.56
Ours-TGA	91.88	93.38	93.39	96.07	85.71	91.15
Ours-MSCK	92.66	94.91	94.29	95.67	86.01	91.69
Ours	**93.59**	**96.23**	**95.11**	**97.22**	**86.98**	**92.10**

than the variant, indicating that it is effective to consider the entity semantic information.

- (Ours-TGA) We analyze the impact of the temporal graph attention mechanism in the Embedding Encoder. We replace it with the attention mechanism used in KBGAT. In Computer, the ACC value of our model is 95.11, almost 2 points higher than the variant, which reflects the importance of capturing the temporal interactions between neighbors. In addition, the variant still has better performance than KBGAT, which also directly demonstrates the superiority of other modules in our model.
- (Ours-MSCK) Finally, we analyze the impact of the multi-scale convolution kernel strategy in the Decoder. We fix the number of convolution kernels of size $\omega \in \mathbb{R}^{1 \times 3}$ instead of multi-scale convolution kernels. From the results, our model is significantly better than this variant, which demonstrates the effectiveness of the multi-scale convolution kernel strategy in capturing multi-dimensional features.

6   Conclusion and Future Work

In this paper, we study the problem of predicting possible future co-authors between existing authors in the temporal co-authorship KGs. Aiming at the temporal interactions among the neighbors of each entity, we propose a temporal graph attention network to encapsulate the current state of an entity. Moreover, we apply the extended temporal graph attention network and neighborhood strategy to capture the multi-hop neighborhood information of entities. Experimental results show that our model with multiple modules outperforms other state-of-the-art models. In the future, we will make slight modifications to this model and extend it to other types of temporal KGs.

Acknowledgements. Peng Cheng's work is partially sponsored by Shanghai Pujiang Program 19PJ1403300. Lei Chen's work is partially supported by National Key Research and Development Program of China Grant No. 2018AAA-0101100, the Hong Kong RGC GRF Project 16207617, CRF Project C6030-18G, C1031-18G, C5026-18G, AOE Project AoE/E-603/18, Theme-based project TRS T41-603/20R, China NSFC No. 61729201, Guangdong Basic and Applied Basic Research Foundation

2019B151530001, Hong Kong ITC ITF grants ITS/044/18FX and ITS/470/18FX, Microsoft Research Asia Collaborative Research Grant, HKUST-NAVER/LINE AI Lab, Didi-HKUST joint research lab, HKUST-Webank joint research lab grants.

References

1. Abu-El-Haija, S., et al.: MixHop: higher-order graph convolutional architectures via sparsified neighborhood mixing. In: ICML, pp. 21–29 (2019)
2. Bordes, A., Usunier, N., Garcia-Duran, A., Weston, J., Yakhnenko, O.: Translating embeddings for modeling multi-relational data. In: NeurIPS, pp. 1–9 (2013)
3. Bordes, A., Weston, J., Collobert, R., Bengio, Y.: Learning structured embeddings of knowledge bases. In: AAAI, pp. 301–306 (2011)
4. Chuan, P.M., Ali, M., Khang, T.D., Dey, N., et al.: Link prediction in co-authorship networks based on hybrid content similarity metric. Appl. Intell. **48**(8), 2470–2486 (2018)
5. Dai Quoc Nguyen, T.D.N., Nguyen, D.Q., Phung, D.: A novel embedding model for knowledge base completion based on convolutional neural network. In: NAACL-HLT, pp. 327–333 (2018)
6. Dasgupta, S.S., Ray, S.N., Talukdar, P.: HyTE: hyperplane-based temporally aware knowledge graph embedding. In: EMNLP, pp. 2001–2011 (2018)
7. Dettmers, T., Minervini, P., Stenetorp, P., Riedel, S.: Convolutional 2d knowledge graph embeddings. In: AAAI, pp. 1811–1818 (2018)
8. Devlin, J., Chang, M.W., Lee, K., Toutanova, K.: BERT: pre-training of deep bidirectional transformers for language understanding. In: NAACL, pp. 4171–4186 (2019)
9. Embar, V.R., Bhattacharya, I., Pandit, V., Vaculin, R.: Online topic-based social influence analysis for the Wimbledon championships. In: SIGKDD (2015)
10. Erxleben, F., Günther, M., Krötzsch, M., Mendez, J., Vrandečić, D.: Introducing Wikidata to the linked data web. In: ISWC, pp. 50–65 (2014)
11. Garcia-Duran, A., Dumančić, S., Niepert, M.: Learning sequence encoders for temporal knowledge graph completion. In: EMNLP, pp. 4816–4821 (2018)
12. Graves, A., Schmidhuber, J.: Framewise phoneme classification with bidirectional LSTM and other neural network architectures. Neural Netw. **18**, 602–610 (2005)
13. He, K., Zhang, X., Ren, S., Sun, J.: Deep residual learning for image recognition. In: CVPR, pp. 770–778 (2016)
14. Hochreiter, S., Schmidhuber, J.: Long short-term memory. Neural Comput. **9**(8), 1735–1780 (1997)
15. Huang, X., Zhang, J., Li, D., Li, P.: Knowledge graph embedding based question answering. In: WSDM, pp. 105–113 (2019)
16. Jain, N.: Domain-specific knowledge graph construction for semantic analysis. In: Harth, A., et al. (eds.) ESWC 2020. LNCS, vol. 12124, pp. 250–260. Springer, Cham (2020). https://doi.org/10.1007/978-3-030-62327-2_40
17. Jiang, T., Liu, T., Ge, T., Sha, L., Li, S., Chang, B., Sui, Z.: Encoding temporal information for time-aware link prediction. In: EMNLP, pp. 2350–2354 (2016)
18. Kipf, T.N., Welling, M.: Semi-supervised classification with graph convolutional networks. arXiv preprint arXiv:1609.02907 (2016)
19. Leblay, J., Chekol, M.W.: Deriving validity time in knowledge graph. In: WWW, pp. 1771–1776 (2018)
20. Lin, Y., Liu, Z., Luan, H., Sun, M., Rao, S., Liu, S.: Modeling relation paths for representation learning of knowledge bases. In: EMNLP, pp. 705–714 (2015)

21. Mahdisoltani, F., Biega, J., Suchanek, F.: YAGO3: a knowledge base from multilingual Wikipedias. In: CIDR (2014)
22. Nathani, D., Chauhan, J., Sharma, C., Kaul, M.: Learning attention-based embeddings for relation prediction in knowledge graphs. In: ACL, pp. 4710–4723 (2019)
23. Qi, Y., Chao, L., Yanhua, L., Hongfang, S., Peifeng, H.: Predicting co-author relationship in medical co-authorship networks. PLOS ONE 9(7), e101214 (2014)
24. Schlichtkrull, M., Kipf, T.N., Bloem, P., van den Berg, R., Titov, I., Welling, M.: Modeling relational data with graph convolutional networks. In: Gangemi, A., et al. (eds.) ESWC 2018. LNCS, vol. 10843, pp. 593–607. Springer, Cham (2018). https://doi.org/10.1007/978-3-319-93417-4_38
25. Severyn, A., Moschitti, A.: Twitter sentiment analysis with deep convolutional neural networks. In: SIGIR, pp. 959–962 (2015)
26. Sun, Y., Barber, R., Gupta, M., Aggarwal, C.C., Han, J.: Co-author relationship prediction in heterogeneous bibliographic networks. In: ASONAM (2011)
27. Trouillon, T., Welbl, J., Riedel, S., Gaussier, É., Bouchard, G.: Complex embeddings for simple link prediction. In: ICML, pp. 2071–2080 (2016)
28. Vaswani, A., et al.: Attention is all you need. In: NeurIPS, pp. 5998–6008 (2017)
29. Veličković, P., Cucurull, G., Casanova, A., Romero, A., Liò, P., Bengio, Y.: Graph attention networks. In: ICLR (2018)
30. Wang, X., He, X., Cao, Y., Liu, M., Chua, T.S.: KGAT: knowledge graph attention network for recommendation. In: SIGKDD, pp. 950–958 (2019)
31. Wang, X., Lu, W., Ester, M., Wang, C., Chen, C.: Social recommendation with strong and weak ties. In: CIKM, pp. 5–14 (2016)
32. Wang, Z., Zhang, J., Feng, J., Chen, Z.: Knowledge graph embedding by translating on hyperplanes. In: AAAI, pp. 1112–1119 (2014)
33. Yang, B., Yih, W., He, X., Gao, J., Deng, L.: Embedding entities and relations for learning and inference in knowledge bases. In: ICLR (2015)
34. Zhang, C., Yao, H., Huang, C., Jiang, M., Li, Z., Chawla, N.V.: Few-shot knowledge graph completion. In: AAAI, vol. 34, pp. 3041–3048 (2020)

Degree-Specific Topology Learning
for Graph Convolutional Network

Jiahou Cheng[1], Mengqing Luo[1], Xin Li[3], and Hui Yan[1,2(✉)]

[1] School of Computer Science and Engineering, Nanjing University of Science
and Technology, Nanjing 210094, China
yanhui@njust.edu.cn
[2] The Key Laboratory of Intelligent Perception and Systems for High Dimensional
Information of Ministry of Education, Nanjing 210094, China
[3] School of Internet of Things, Nanjing University of Posts and Telecommunications,
Nanjing 210003, China

Abstract. Graph Convolutional Networks (GCNs) have gained great
popularity in various graph data learning tasks. Nevertheless, GCNs
inevitably encounter over-smoothing with increasing the network depth
and over-fitting specifically on small datasets. In this paper, we present
an experimental investigation which clearly shows that the misclassification rates of nodes with high and low degrees are obviously distinctive.
Thus, previous methods such as Dropedge that randomly removes some
edges between arbitrary pairwise nodes are distant from optimal or even
unsatisfactory. To bridge the gap, we propose the degree-specific topology
learning for GCNs to find a hidden graph structure that augments the
initial graph structure. Particularly, instead of training with uncertain
connections, we remove edges between the high-degree nodes and their
first-order neighbors with low similarity in the attribute space; besides,
we add edges between the low-degree nodes and their connectionless
neighbors with high similarity in the attribute space. Experiments conducted on several popular datasets demonstrate the effectiveness of our
topology learning method.

Keywords: Degree-specific · Over-smoothing · Over-fitting ·
Dropedge

1 Introduction

Graphs or networks which consist of an edge set and a node set are widely used
to describe complex relationships among objects, such as citation relationship
among papers in citation networks, the relationship among users in social network, etc. GCN [15] and their numerous variants, have shown to be successful
in graph representation learning tasks [1–4], such as node classification, graph
classification, and link prediction.

Despite their strong task performance, most of existing methods have two
major obstacles [5,6,9–11]: (1) *Over-smoothing.* GCNs transmit information

© Springer Nature Switzerland AG 2021
L. H. U et al. (Eds.): APWeb-WAIM 2021, LNCS 12858, pp. 20–34, 2021.
https://doi.org/10.1007/978-3-030-85896-4_2

(a)   (b)

Fig. 1. Receptive field of nodes with different degrees. Target node is colored in red, and the 1-st, 2-nd, 3-rd, 4-rd order neighboring nodes are colored in orange, blue, green, yellow and purple, respectively. (Color figure online)

through edges, and thus they can be approximately understood that the representations of the central nodes are obtained by averaging their first-order neighbor nodes. Since the information of low-order neighbor is not enough in the shallow model, deep GCNs have merged, where more and more layers are stacked. Unfortunately, by repeatedly applying Laplacian smoothing too often, the final embeddings of all nodes will converge to the same values extremely. (2) *Over-fitting.* GCNs, like other deep models, may suffer from over-fitting problem which is generally caused by a model fitting a distribution with insufficient training data. It leads to fitting the training data very well but generalizing poorly to the test data with such over-parameterized model learned.

There exist a variety of methods to address the aforementioned problems. For example, [13] uses linear combination of the multi-order adjacency matrix instead of the original adjacency matrix to expand the receptive field. IDGL [31] adjusts the adjacency matrix iteratively and increases the range of the receptive field by adding edges to learn the graph structure. [27] proposes that high-order graph convolution can help model capture the global structure of graph. And inspired by convolutional neural networks (CNNs), [26] builds deep GCN model by adding residual or dilation convolution which construct graph in the attribute space. Very recently, Dropedge [8] reduces part of the information transmission by randomly selecting some edges to remove in each training procedure. As a widely used method, Dropedge mitigates the over-fitting and over-smoothing problems.

Since randomly removing some edges improves the performance, we take the degree of the node into consideration and formulate a set of rules to add and delete some edges, the performance of GCNs may be further improved. On the one hand, low-degree nodes may possess high sparsity. Once their corresponding edges are removed, the sharp reduction of their receptive field may weaken the performance of the model. On the other hand, high-degree nodes are more likely to be the authoritative or active individuals that have an important effect in networks and communities, and are often bridges or hubs in connecting different communities. Compared with low-degree nodes, their receptive fields are larger, leading into more redundant and noisy neighbor nodes. Therefore,

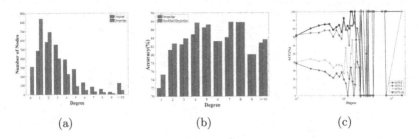

Fig. 2. (a) The degree distribution of original Cora and that after Dropedge. (b) The node classification accuracy of Dropedge and modified Dropedge where we perform Dropedge only for high-degree nodes. (c) The node classification accuracy of nodes with different degrees on different number of layers of GCN.

these statistically-significant nodes are often wrongly divided [17]. As shown in Fig. 1(a), the red target node with one degree requires five times convolutions to cover the entire graph, while in Fig. 1(b), the degree of the red target node is 7, and it only takes three times convolutions of the neighborhood to expand to the entire graph. Intuitively speaking, for shallow GCNs model, the performance of the low-degree nodes is poor because of the insufficient information [12]; while when stacking many layers, over-smoothing is more likely to occur for the high-degree nodes.

In addition, deleting edges gives rise to the change of degrees of nodes. Figure 2(a) illustrates that degree distribution in the original Cora dataset and that after removing some edges. It shows after randomly removing some edges, the number of zero-degree nodes, i.e., isolated nodes, increases. Intuitively, the more nodes with zero degree, the worse performance of GCNs. In addition, we compare the node classification rates on Cora dataset between Dropedge [8] and the modified Dropedge where we merely randomly remove some edges for high-degree (>7) nodes in Fig. 2(b). The results show that modified Dropedge consistently outperforms Dropedge for nodes with different degrees, specifically for low-degree nodes. The results indicate there still exists some room for improvement of Dropedge.

Motivated by the above observations, we hope to remove some redundant and noisy edges, which may severely hinder the capability of GCNs, for high-degree nodes; for low-degree nodes, we hope to add some potential edges to expand their receptive fields. In this paper, we propose degree-specific topology learning for GCN to find a hidden graph structure that augments the initial graph structure.

The main contributions of this paper are summarized as follows:

- We present an experimental investigation which clearly shows that the misclassification rates of nodes with high and low degrees are obviously distinctive.
- We propose a degree-specific topology learning method, acting like a data augmenter, which consists of a message passing reducer for high-degree nodes and a message passing enlarger for low-degree nodes.

- We conduct experiments on five popular datasets and then these experiments demonstrate the effectiveness of our topology leaning method.

2   Related Work

GCN. The success of CNNs to data in Euclidean space (e.g. images and videos) motivates researchers to design deep learning techniques to process data in non-Euclidean space (e.g. graphs or manifolds) [20–25]. Existing methods can be classified into spatial methods and spectral methods. The graph convolution operation in spatial methods constructs each node embedding by a weighted average function over its neighboring nodes [27–29]. For instance, GraphSAGE [27], a framework for inductive representation learning on large graph, defines various aggregators over neighboring nodes. Graph attention network (GAT) [28] proposes learning the importance of different neighbors for the central node via self-attention mechanism. Spectral methods define graph convolution via convolution theorem. For example, ChebyNet [30] adopts a polynomial function of the diagonal matrix of eigenvalues as convolution kernel. Kipf and Welling [16] propose GCN via a localized first-order approximation to ChebyNet.

Drop Edge in the Topology Space. Despite the successes of Graph Neural Networks (GNNs), they can not go very deep due to over-smoothing and over-fitting phenomena. A variety of methods have proposed to address these problems. For example, Dropedge randomly ignores some edges during training, and then the topology used is slightly different, i.e. reducing the dependence on the topology, so that the model can learn a better representation. Additionally, the topology becomes sparser, which may alleviates the over-smoothing problem. However, our experiments show that the network itself is relatively sparse, Using only Dropedge may lead to the learned representations are not good enough especially for the nodes with relatively small degrees.

Construct Edges in the Attribute Space. [14] proposes a random walk on the attribute graph via adding attributed edges between nodes if the nodes contain the same attributes. Thus the nodes can walk through the edges in either or both of the topology space and the attribute space. In fact, when the number of random walk is large enough, it can be equivalent to GCN [15]. [13] uses node attributes to calculate the attention coefficient, the information of higher-order nodes is mainly used, which shows that expanding the receptive field can improve the performance of GCN. Chen et al. [31] propose an end-to-end graph learning framework for jointly and iteratively learning the graph structure and the GNN parameters that are optimized toward the downstream prediction task.

3   Notations and Preliminaries

3.1   Notations

Given an undirected attributed graph $G = \{V, E, X\}$, where $V = \{v_1, v_2, \cdots, v_N\}$ denotes a set of nodes with $|V| = N$, and $E \subseteq V \times V$ is a set of edges. $X = [x_1, x_2, \cdots, x_N]^T$ represents an attribute matrix of all nodes, where $x_i \in R^F$ is a real-valued attribute vector of node v_i. In addition, we use the adjacency matrix $A \in \{0,1\}_{n \times n}$ to represent the observed graph structure, i.e., if an edge $(v_i, v_j) \in E$, $A_{ij} = 1$; otherwise, $A_{ij} = 0$.

3.2 Graph Convolutional Network

An L-layer GCNs [16] consist of L graph convolution layers and each of them is formulated as:

$$H^{(l+1)} = \sigma \left(\widetilde{D}^{-\frac{1}{2}} \widetilde{A} \widetilde{D}^{-\frac{1}{2}} H^{(l)} W^{(l)} \right) \tag{1}$$

where $H^{(l)} \in R^{N \times f_l}$ is the embedding of N nodes in the l-th GCNs layer, and $H^{(0)} = X$. $W^{(l)}$ is the learnable weight matrix of the l-th graph convolution layer. $\sigma(\cdot)$ is the nonlinear activation function, such as Softmax or Relu. $\widetilde{A} = A + I_N$, where I_N is the identity matrix. $\widetilde{D}$ is a diagonal matrix which denotes the degree of nodes, i.e., $\widetilde{D}_{ii} = \sum_j \widetilde{A}_{ij}$.

In other words, the embedding of node v_i at the $(l+1)$-th layer is

$$H_{i,:}^{(l+1)} = \sigma \left(\sum_j \frac{\widetilde{A}_{ij}}{\sqrt{\widetilde{D}_{ii} \widetilde{D}_{jj}}} H_{j,:}^{(l)} W^{(l)} \right) \tag{2}$$

where $H_{i,:}^{(l+1)}$ is the i-th row of $H^{(l+1)}$. Semi-supervised node classification is a popular application of GCNs. By minimizing the cross-entropy in Eq. (3) between the predictions and given labels, the parameter in Eq. (1) can be obtained.

$$\mathcal{L} = - \sum_{i \in V_l} \sum_{c=1}^{C} Y_{ic} \log \left(H_{ic}^{(L)} \right) \tag{3}$$

where V_l contains n labeled nodes; $Y \in \{0,1\}_{n \times C}$ denotes the ground-truth labels and C is the number of classes. $H_{ic}^{(L)} = 1$ if and only if node v_i belongs to the c-th class.

4   Degree-Specific Topology Learning for GCNs

4.1 Methodology

Many researchers [13] expand receptive field of nodes by aggregating high-order neighbors to improve the performance of GCN. However, as shown in Fig. 2(c), as the number of GCN layers increases, the total classification accuracy is decreased, while the classification accuracy of one-degree nodes decreases slightly. This demonstrates that stacking more GCNs layers can significantly reduce the performance of high-degree nodes.

Ideally, the size of receptive field of nodes with different degrees may be the same like CNN [15]. Instead of stacking more GCNs layers, we expand the receptive field of low-degree nodes by adding edges. For high-degree nodes, we inherit the merit of Dropedge and remove some edges with low similarity for high-degree nodes to shrink their receptive field.

To sum up, our goal is to modify the adjacency matrix in GCNs according to the degree of nodes. For high-degree nodes, removing some irrelevant edges in the attribute space may filter the noise introduced by topology and it is not harmful to the performance of high-degree nodes due to their sufficient neighbors. For low-degree nodes, adding some similar nodes in the attribute space as their potential linked neighbors can supplement the insufficient topology information. If we denote the resulting adjacency matrix as A_{Opt}, then its relation with A becomes

$$A_{Opt} = A - A^- + A^+ \tag{4}$$

where A^- is a sparse matrix consisting of the edges between the high-degree nodes and their direct linked nodes with low similarity in the attribute space. A^+ is also a sparse matrix consisting of the edges between the low-degree nodes and those nodes with high similarity in the attribute space. After we get the adjacency matrix A_{Opt} by Eq. (4), we substitute A_{Opt} into A of Eq. (1) to get the output embedding of all nodes at the $(l+1)$-th GCNs layer. In the following parts, we will give the detail to get A^- and A^+.

4.2   Remove Edges for High-Degree Nodes

We remove some edges between high-degree nodes and their direct linked nodes with low similarity to shrink their receptive fields. Based on experiments, we find that when d_{high} is the average degree of the nodes, the performance is the best. It means that the nodes whose degrees are higher than d_{high} are called high-degree nodes. $H_{high}^{(l)}$ consists of the embeddings of the nodes whose degrees are larger than d_{high}.

The similarity is computed via inner product as

$$\left[S^-\right]^{(l+1)} = H_{high}^{(l)} \, H^{(l)^T} \tag{5}$$

where H^l is the input of l-th GCN layer, $H_{high}^{(l)}$ is the embedding of the high-degree nodes. And after calculating $[S^-]^{(l+1)}$, we normalize its each row to guarantee the elements in S^- are between 0 and 1.

Then we modify the adjacency matrix of high-degree nodes as follows:

$$\left[A^-\right]_{ij}^{(l+1)} = \begin{cases} 1, [S]_{ij}^{(l+1)} \leq \varepsilon_{high} \ \text{and} \ A_{ij} = 1 \\ 0, \text{otherwise} \end{cases} \tag{6}$$

where ε_{high} is the threshold to determine whether the edges of high-degree nodes are irrelevant.

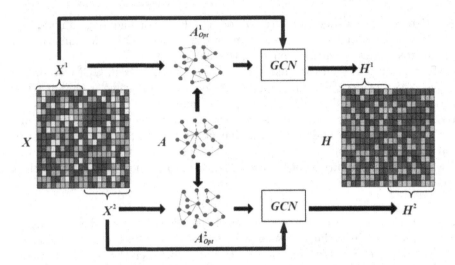

Fig. 3. The framework of degree-specific topology learning for GCN.

4.3 Add Edges for Low-Degree Nodes

We denote d_{low} as the threshold of low degrees, i.e. the nodes whose degree is smaller than d_{low} are low-degree nodes. And in experiments, we generally set d_{low} as 50%–60% of the average degree. And we define ε_{high} as the threshold to determine whether the edges of low-degree nodes are relevant. $H_{low}^{(l)}$ which is also a part of H^l, consists of the embeddings of the nodes whose degrees are smaller than d_{low}.

The similarity of low-degree nodes in the attribute space is computed as

$$[S^+]^{(l+1)} = H_{low}^{(l)} H^{(l)^T} \tag{7}$$

where $H_{low}^{(l)}$ is the embedding of the low-degree nodes. And after calculating $[S^+]^{(l+1)}$, we normalize its each row so that $[S^+]_{ij}^{(l+1)} \in [0, 1]$.

Then we modify the adjacency matrix of low-degree nodes as follows:

$$[A^+]_{ij}^{(l+1)} = \begin{cases} 1, [S^+]_{ij}^{(l+1)} \geq \varepsilon_{low} & \text{and } A_{ij} = 0 \\ 0, & \text{otherwise} \end{cases} \tag{8}$$

4.4 Framework

If we directly compute the similarity between pairwise nodes in the original attribute space, we find it has little correlation between node labels and node attributes. If we compute the similarity between pairwise nodes in the transformed attribute space, we would introduce more parameters to be learnt, i.e.,

Table 1. Dataset details.

Dataset	#Nodes	#Features	#Edges	#Class	#Average degree
Cora	2708	1433	5429	7	4
Citeseer	3327	3703	4732	6	5
Pubmed	19717	500	44338	3	6
Texas	183	328	1703	5	4
Wisconsin	262	530	1703	5	4

attribute transformation weights, resulting in aggravating over-fitting. Alternatively, we could compute the similarities at each attribute dimension, separately, and then combine them. However, the number of attributes is usually high. Thus, we introduce attribute channels to balance the computation complexity and effectiveness inspired by [26]. Specially we divide the attributes into C_{attr} different groups, and regard one group as an attribute channel to improve the calculation speed. Take $C_{attr} = 2$ as an example, the attribute matrix X can be divided as two groups along the dimension of attributes as follows:

$$X = \left[X^1, X^2\right] = \left[X_{:,1:K/2}, X_{:,K/2+1:K}\right] \tag{9}$$

After division, we feed X^1 and X^2 into two attribute channels, respectively, then learn individual A_{Opt} and then use GCN in Eq. (1) to obtain the embedding H^1 and H^2 in each channel. Finally we concatenate the embedding at all attribute channels to obtain the final embedding of nodes. The framework is illustrated in Fig. 3.

5 Experiments

5.1 Datasets and Baselines

We conducted experiments on three citation networks(Cora, Citeseer and Pubmed) and two webpage graphs (Texas and Wisconsin) for semi-supervised classification tasks. The detailed descriptions of these datasets are shown in Table 1. In the experiments, we use accuracy (ACC) as the metrics for semi-supervised node classification.

Our proposed method is a plug-and-play module. We add the module to two widely used models, GCN and GAT, and name them GCN-HLD and GAT-HLD respectively. Then we compare them with ChebyNet [30], JKNet [32], IncepGCN [8], SGC [33], GAT [28], DropEdge [8], ALaGCN [34], and GCN [16]. Due to memory limitations, GAT can not be run on the Pubmed dataset, and only the 4-head version of GAT can be run on the Citeseer dataset.

5.2 Comparison with the Existing Methods

The performance in terms of accuracy is shown in Table 2. The best performance of each column is highlighted in boldface. The performance of our proposed

Table 2. Comparison of prediction accuracy, The dash symbol indicates that reported results were unavailable or we were not able to run the experiments due to memory issue.

Method	Cora	Citeseer	Pubmed	Texas	Wisconsin
ChebNet	81.20	69.80	74.40	64.13	47.70
JKNet	80.20	68.70	78.00	64.21	62.38
IncepGCN	77.60	69.30	77.70	63.04	60.55
SGC	81.00	71.90	78.90	57.61	60.55
DropEdge	82.80	72.30	79.60	65.21	58.71
AlaGCN	82.90	70.90	79.60	**68.48**	56.88
GCN	80.70	70.23	79.50	63.04	56.88
GCN-HLD	82.90	**72.70**	**79.82**	64.44	**63.30**
GAT	83.15	69.00	-	64.18	46.79
GAT-HLD	**84.60**	70.00	-	65.31	48.15

Table 3. The percentage of edges removed and added

Dataset	N_{high}/N	N_{low}/N
Cora	79.6%	6.8%
Citeseer	76.3%	2.2%
Pubmed	65.3%	8.3%
Texas	78.5%	7.3%
Wisconsin	77.3%	5.5%

method is reported based on the average of 20 measurements. From Table 2 we can see GCN-HLD performed best on the three datasets: Citeseer, Pubmed and Wisconsin, and GAT-HLD performs best on the Cora dataset. Compared with GCN, the performance of GCN-HLD on these five datasets has a certain improvement. From the experiments result we can find GCN-HLD and GAT-HLD performs the best on 4 of 5 datasets, which demonstrates the effectiveness of the degree-specific topology learning method.

We denote N_{low} as the edges added and N_{high} as the edges removed. Table 3 shows the percentages of the total number of edges that we add and remove on the GCN model. The removed edges accounted for 60% to 80% of the total edges for every dataset, and the percentage of added edges is less than 10%.

5.3   Ablation Experiments

In order to explore the effects of adding and removing edges, we conduct an ablation experiments on 3 datasets including Cora, Citeseer and Pubmed. Original GCNs [16] (GCN), GCNs with dropout [18] (GCN-DO) and GCNs with Dropedge [8] (GCN-DE) are defined. GCN-HD represents merely removing edges with

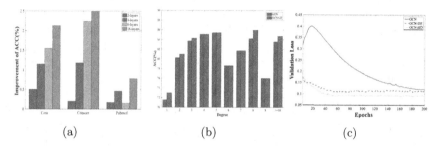

(a)   (b)   (c)

Fig. 4. (a) The improvement of GCN-HD compared with GCN-DE vary with number of layers. (b) The performance of low-degree nodes on GCN and GCN-LD on Cora. (c) The validation loss of GCN, GCN-DE and GCN-HD with 4-layers on Cora.

Table 4. Ablation experiments. The dash symbol indicates that reported results were unavailable or we were not able to run the experiments due to memory issue.

Method	Cora	Citeseer	Pubmed
GCN	80.70	70.23	79.50
GCN-DO	81.50	70.48	79.30
GCN-DE	81.50	71.20	79.60
GCN-HD	82.40	71.80	79.77
GCN-LD	81.45	71.30	79.42
GCN-HLD	82.90	**72.70**	**79.82**
GAT	83.15	69.00	-
GAT-DO	84.00	68.80	-
GAT-DE	83.90	69.20	-
GAT-HD	83.45	69.40	-
GAT-LD	83.45	68.90	-
GAT-HLD	**84.60**	70.00	-

low similarity for high-degree nodes, GCN-LD represents merely adding edges with high similarity in the attribute space for low-degree nodes. Original GAT [28] (GAT), GAT with dropout (GAT-DO) and GAT with Dropedge (GAT-DE) are defined. GAT-HD represents merely removing edges with low similarity for high-degree nodes, GAT-LD represents merely adding edges with high similarity in the attribute space for low-degree nodes.

Table 4 shows the ACC results of the test set of each method for the semi-supervised node classification experiment. From Table 4 we can draw three conclusions. First, when edges are removed by using our rules, the accuracy is improved relative to randomly removing edges. For example, the performance of GCN-HD is better than GCN-DO on the three datasets. The performance of GAT-HD is also very close to that of GAT-DO and GAT-DE. Second, adding edges to low-degree nodes on the GCN and GAT models outperform the original model. This shows that increasing the receptive field of low-degree nodes also improves performance. Third, we can see a significant performance drop consistently on all datasets by turning off the plug-and-play module, which demonstrates the effectiveness of the proposed degree-specific topology learning method for the graph learning problem.

GCN-HLD performs better than GCN-HD and GCN-LD and it can be applied to a variety of datasets. For datasets that contain lots of noisy topology information, the filtering of noise in the topology of graph can be controlled by adjusting d_{high} and ε_{high}; for datasets which is relatively sparse, the graph sparseness can be controlled by adjusting d_{low} and ε_{low}. Besides, It can be seen that the performance of GAT-HLD on the Cora and Citeseer datasets is better than GAT and the other 4 variants of GAT.

5.4   Effect of Nodes with Different Degree

Remove Edges for High-Degree Nodes. To validate the effect of removing edges for high-degree nodes, we vary the number of GCN layers in $\{2, 4, 8, 16\}$ on Cora, Citeseer and Pubmed. As shown in Fig. 4(a), GCN-HD performs better than GCN-DE. Because Dropedge may remove some edges of low-degree nodes whose neighborhood is relatively small and thus influence the performance of these nodes. And due to the use of attribute channels, the topology used in each attribute channel is distinctive which helps model learn more robust information than GCN-DE. In addition, we show the curve of validation loss of GCN, GCN-DE and GCN-HD with 4 layers on Cora in Fig. 4(c), and the results show the effectiveness of GCN-DE and GCN-HD for alleviating over-fitting.

Practically, if the value of is small enough, GCN-HD can be seen as a special case of GCN-DE which chooses edges to remove according to the similarity of nodes. And GCN-HD with greater value means that the we restrict that removing edges only occurs at nodes with high degrees and it cannot influence the nodes with low degrees. And in our experiments, we find that the best value of d_{high} is about the average degree of nodes in datasets as Fig. 5(a). As for the effect of d_{high}, we vary the value of d_{high} as $\{1, 2, 3, 4, 5, 6, 7, 8, 9, 10\}$ due to the maximum value of average degree of those three datasets is 6 and the average degree is the best value for Large-Scale Learnable Graph Convolutional Networks (LGCN) in [15], and adjusted other parameters for the best results.

Add Edges for Low-Degree Nodes. To validate the influence of adding edges, we perform GCN-LD and original GCN with 2 layers on Cora and compared the node classification accuracy of low-degree nodes. The results is shown in Fig. 4(b). The accuracy of low-degree nodes in GCN-LD is higher or just the same as that in GCN, which means adding edges for low-degree nodes improve their performance in shallow GCN model. And as the average degrees of Cora, Citeseer and Pubmed are 4, 5, and 6, respectively, we set $d_{low} = 2$ for both Cora, besides Citeseer and $d_{low} = 3$ for Pubmed in our experiments as about 50%–60% of average degrees.

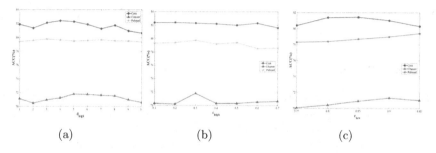

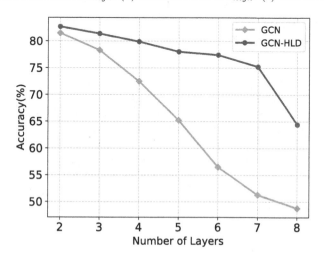

Fig. 5. (a) The influence of d_{high}. (b) The influence of ε_{high}. (c) The influence of ε_{low}

Fig. 6. The performance of GCN-HLD with deeper layers.

5.5   Parameters Sensitiveness

The parameters such as learning rate and L2 regularization factor are adjusted to obtain the best results. And we only use 2 attribute channels in our method due to the memory limitations. We run 20 times for each model and take the mean as the result of the experiments.

We vary the value of ε_{high} as $\{0.1, 0.2, 0.3, 0.4, 0.5, 0.6, 0.7\}$ and fix the value of d_{high} as the average degree of nodes in each dataset, and the corresponding results are shown in Fig. 5(b). When $\varepsilon_{high} = 0.3$, 2-layer GCN-HD reaches the best results on Citeseer and Pubmed, and performs best on Cora when $\varepsilon_{high} = 0.2$.

As we can see from Fig. 5(b), that when the value of ε_{high} is 0.2 the performance of GCN-HD on Cora is best; when $\varepsilon_{low} = 0.9$, the performance of GCN-LD on Citeseer is best and the performance of Pubmed is best if $\varepsilon_{low} = 0.95$. To validate the influence of ε_{low}, we tune the value of ε_{low} in $\{0.75, 0.8, 0.85, 0.9,$

0.95} in 2-layers GCN-LD, and fix $d_{low} = 2$ for Cora and Citeseer $d_{low} = 3$ for Pubmed, the results are shown in Fig. 5(c).

5.6 Classification Performance with Deeper GCN

In Fig. 6 we show the performance of our proposed GCN-HLD framework with different number of layers on the CORA dataset. From Fig. 6 we can observe that when increasing the number of layers, GCN perform worse while GCN-HLD shows stable performance improvements with different depth; GCN-HLD shows performance improvements on GCN with different depth. Our results suggest that augmentation can be a tool which facilitates deeper GNN training, as performance improvements for GCN demonstrate quite large performance improvements when compared to standard implementations.

6 Conclusion

In this paper, we rethought the over-fitting and over-smoothing problems in GCNs from two aspects. First, we empirically show that the misclassification rates of nodes with high and low degrees are obviously distinctive. Second, we propose a degree-specific topology learning method, acting like a data augmenter, which consists of a message passing reducer for high-degree nodes and a message passing enlarger for low-degree nodes. Comparative experiments and ablation experiments on several popular datasets prove the effectiveness of our proposed method.

References

1. Jin, D., Liu, Z., Li, W., He, D., Zhang, W.: Graph convolutional networks meet Markov random fields: semi-supervised community detection in attribute networks. In: 33th AAAI Conference on Artificial Intelligence, Honolulu, Hawaii, USA, pp. 152–159. AAAI Press (2019)
2. Pan, S., Hu, R., Long, G., Jiang, J., Yao, L., Zhang, C.: Adversarially regularized graph autoencoder for graph embedding. In: 27th International Joint Conference on Artificial Intelligence. IJCAI, Stockholm, Sweden, pp. 2609–2615 (2018)
3. He, D., Zhai, L., Li, Z., Jin, D., Yang, L., Huang, Y., Yu, P.S.: Adversarial mutual information learning for network embedding. In: 29th International Joint Conference on Artificial Intelligence, pp. 3321–3327. ijcai.org (2020)
4. Gao, H., Ji, S.: Graph U-nets. In: 36th International Conference on Machine Learning, California, USA, pp. 2083–2092. PMLR (2019)
5. Li, Q., Han, Z., Wu, X.-M.: Deeper insights into graph convolutional networks for semi-supervised learning. In: 32th AAAI Conference on Artificial Intelligence, New Orleans, Louisiana, USA, pp. 3538–3545. AAAI Press (2018)
6. Xu, K., Li, C., Tian, Y., Sonobe, T., Kawarabayashi, K., Jegelka, S.: Representation learning on graphs with jumping knowledge networks. In: 35th International Conference on Machine Learning, Stockholm, Sweden, pp. 5449–5458. PMLR (2018)

7. Li, G., Müller, M., Thabet, A.K., Ghanem, B.: DeepGCNs: can GCNs go as deep as CNNs? In: 2019 International Conference on Computer Vision, Seoul, Korea, pp. 9266–9275. IEEE (2019)
8. Rong, Y., Huang, W., Xu, T., Huang, J.: DropEdge: towards deep graph convolutional networks on node classification. In: 8th International Conference on Learning Representations, Addis Ababa, Ethiopia. OpenReview.net (2020)
9. Abu-El-Haija, S., et al.: MixHop: higher-order graph convolutional architectures via sparsified neighborhood mixing. In: 36th International Conference on Machine Learning, Long Beach, California, USA, pp. 21–29. PMLR (2019)
10. Cao, S., Lu, W., Xu, Q.: GraRep: learning graph representations with global structural information. In: 24th ACM International Conference on Information and Knowledge Management, Melbourne, VIC, Australia, pp. 891–900. ACM (2015)
11. Zhang, X., Liu, H., Li, Q., Wu, X.: Attributed graph clustering via adaptive graph convolution. In: 28th International Joint Conference on Artificial Intelligence, Macao, China, pp. 4327–4333. ijcai.org (2019)
12. Tang, J., Qu, M., Wang, M., Zhang, M., Yan, J., Mei, Q.: LINE: large-scale information network embedding. In: 24th International Conference on World Wide Web, Florence, Italy, pp. 1067–1077. ACM (2015)
13. Wang, C., Pan, S., Hu, R., Long, G., Jiang, J., Zhang, C.: Attributed graph clustering: a deep attentional embedding approach. In: 28th International Joint Conference on Artificial Intelligence, Macao, China, pp. 4327–4333. ijcai.org (2019)
14. Huang, X., Song, Q., Li, Y., Hu, X.: Graph recurrent networks with attributed random walks. In: 25th ACM SIGKDD International Conference on Knowledge Discovery, Anchorage, AK, USA, pp. 732–740. ACM (2019)
15. Gao, H., Wang, Z., Ji, S.: Large-scale learnable graph convolutional networks. In: 24th ACM SIGKDD International Conference on Knowledge Discovery, London, UK, pp. 1416–1424. ACM (2018)
16. Kipf, T.N., Welling, M.: Semi-supervised classification with graph convolutional networks. In: 5th International Conference on Learning Representations, Toulon, France. OpenReview.net (2017)
17. Jin, D., et al.: Incorporating network embedding into Markov random field for better community detection. In: The 33th AAAI Conference on Artificial Intelligence, Honolulu, Hawaii, USA, pp. 160–167. AAAI Press (2019)
18. Srivastava, N., Hinton, G.E., Krizhevsky, A., Sutskever, I., Salakhutdinov, R.: Dropout: a simple way to prevent neural networks from overfitting. J. Mach. Learn. Res. **15**(1), 1929–1958 (2014)
19. Yann, L.C., Leon, B., Yoshua, B., Patrick, H.: Gradient-based learning applied to document recognition. Proc. IEEE **86**(11), 2278–2324 (1998)
20. Defferrard, M., Bresson, X., Vandergheynst, P.: Convolutional neural net-works on graphs with fast localized spectral filtering. In: Conference and Workshop on Neural Information Processing Systems, pp. 3837–3845 (2016)
21. Duvenaud, D.K., et al.: Convolutional networks on graphs for learning molecular finger prints. In: Conference and Workshop on Neural Information Processing Systems, pp. 2224–2232 (2015)
22. Niepert, M., Ahmed, M., Kutzkov, K.: Learning convolutional neural networks for graphs. In: 33th International Conference on Machine Learning, New York, USA, pp. 2014–2023. JMLR.org (2016)
23. Hamilton, W.L., Ying, Z., Leskovec, J.: Inductive representation learning on large graphs. In: Conference and Workshop on Neural Information Processing Systems, Long Beach, CA, USA, pp. 1025–1035 (2017)

24. Scarselli, F., Gori, M., Tsoi, A.C., Hagenbuchner, M., Monfardini, G.: The graph neural network model. IEEE Trans. Neural Netw. **20**(1), 61–80 (2009)
25. Xu, K., Hu, W., Leskovec, J., Jegelka, S.: How powerful are graph neural networks? In: 7th International Conference on Learning Representations, New Orleans, LA, USA. OpenReview.net (2019)
26. Hasanzadeh, A., et al.: Bayesian graph neural networks with adaptive connection sampling. In: International Conference on Machine Learning (2019)
27. Hamilton, W., Ying, Z., Leskovec, J.: Inductive representation learning on large graphs. In: Advances in Neural Information Processing Systems, Long Beach, CA, USA, pp. 1024–1034 (2017)
28. Velickovic, P., Cucurull, G., Casanova, A., Romero, A., Lio, P., Bengio, Y.: Graph attention networks. arXiv preprint arXiv:1710.10903 (2017)
29. Monti, F., Boscaini, D., Masci, J., Rodola, E., Svoboda, J., Bronstein, M.M.: Geometric deep learning on graphs and manifolds using mixture model CNNs. In: Conference on Computer Vision and Pattern Recognition, Honolulu, HI, USA, pp. 5425–5434 (2017)
30. Defferrard, M., Bresson, X., Vandergheynst, P.: Convolutional neural networks on graphs with fast localized spectral filtering. In: Advances in Neural Information Processing Systems, Barcelona, Spain, pp. 3837–3845 (2016)
31. Chen, Y., Wu, L., Zaki, M.J.: Iterative deep graph learning for graph neural networks: better and robust node embeddings. arXiv preprint arXiv:2006.13009 (2020)
32. Xu, K., Li, C., Tian, Y., et al.: Representation learning on graphs with jumping knowledge networks. In: 2018 International Conference on Machine Learning, pp. 5453–5462. PMLR (2018)
33. Wu, F., Zhang, T., de Souza Jr., A.H., Fifty, C., Yu, T., Weinberger, K.Q.: Simplifying graph convolutional networks. arXiv preprint arXiv:1902.07153 (2019)
34. Xie, Y., Li, S., Yang, C., et al.: When do GNNs work: understanding and improving neighborhood aggregation. In: 29th International Joint Conference on Artificial Intelligence and 17th Pacific Rim International Conference on Artificial Intelligence, JCAIPRICAI 2020 (2020)

Simplifying Graph Convolutional Networks as Matrix Factorization

Qiang Liu[1(✉)], Haoli Zhang[2], and Zhaocheng Liu[3]

[1] Department of Computer Science and Technology, Tsinghua University,
Beijing, China
[2] National University of Singapore, Singapore, Singapore
[3] Kwai Inc., Bengaluru, India

Abstract. In recent years, substantial progress has been made on Graph Convolutional Networks (GCNs). However, the computing of GCN usually requires a large memory space for keeping the entire graph. In consequence, GCN is not flexible enough, especially for large scale graphs in complex real-world applications. Fortunately, for transductive graph representation learning, methods based on Matrix Factorization (MF) naturally support constructing mini-batches, and thus are more friendly to distributed computing compared with GCN. Accordingly, in this paper, we analyze the connections between GCN and MF, and simplify GCN as matrix factorization with unitization and co-training. Furthermore, under the guidance of our analysis, we propose an alternative model to GCN named Unitized and Co-training Matrix Factorization (UCMF). Extensive experiments have been conducted on several real-world datasets. On the task of semi-supervised node classification, the experimental results illustrate that UCMF achieves similar or superior performances compared with GCN. Meanwhile, distributed UCMF significantly outperforms distributed GCN methods, which shows that UCMF can greatly benefit complex real-world applications.

Keywords: Graph convolutional networks · Simplification · Matrix factorization · Graph embedding

1 Introduction

Nowadays, works on graph convolutional networks (GCNs) [10] have achieved great success in many graph-based tasks, e.g., semi-supervised node classification [13,18,22], link prediction [26] and recommendation systems [19,24]. However, as the computing of GCN requires to store the entire adjacency matrix of a graph [3], it is hard to perform GCN on large scale real-world complex graphs, where we usually have a constrained memory size and need distributed computing. Accordingly, GCN is not flexible enough, and needs to be simplified while retaining the high performance. For example, various sampling methods have been proposed [2,7,24] to simplify GCN via reducing the number of edges in the graph. These methods can be performed in mini-batches, but need to sample

© Springer Nature Switzerland AG 2021
L. H. U et al. (Eds.): APWeb-WAIM 2021, LNCS 12858, pp. 35–43, 2021.
https://doi.org/10.1007/978-3-030-85896-4_3

high-order neighbours of each node and require a high computational cost that exponentially grows with the number of graph convolution layers, as pointed in [3]. Accordingly, we need a simplified alternative to GCN, which is flexible enough for distributed computing in real-world applications, and can achieve similar or superior performances compared with the original GCN model.

Besides GCN, for transductive graph representation learning, graph embedding methods [6,14,17] are also widely applied. According to previous work [15], graph embedding methods have been successfully unified as Matrix Factorization (MF). Meanwhile, compared with GCN, MF-based methods are extremely flexible and suitable for large scale distributed computing [5,25]. Consequently, if we can simplify the GCN model as a special form of MF, large scale and complex real-world applications will greatly benefit from this.

In this paper, we analyze the connections between GCN and MF, and simplify GCN as matrix factorization with unitization and co-training. Here, the unitization indicates conducting vector unitization on node representations, i.e., forcing the norm of each node representation to one. And the co-training process means co-training with the classification task of labeled nodes, as in some previous works [20,23]. Then, according to our analysis, we formally propose an alternative model to GCN named Unitized and Co-training Matrix Factorization (UCMF). We have conducted extensive experiments on several real-world graphs. Under centralized computing settings, UCMF achieves similar or superior performances compared with GCN and SGC [21] on the task of semi-supervised node classification. Experiments under distributed computing settings are also conducted, where UCMF significantly outperforms distributed GCN methods. These results clearly show that, we can use our proposed UCMF model as a simplified alternative to the original GCN model for transductive graph representation learning in real-world applications.

2   GCN as Unitized and Co-training MF

According to the definition in [10], we can formulate each layer of GCN as

$$\mathbf{H}^{(l+1)} = \sigma \left(\widetilde{\mathbf{D}}^{-\frac{1}{2}} \widetilde{\mathbf{A}} \widetilde{\mathbf{D}}^{-\frac{1}{2}} \mathbf{H}^{(l)} \mathbf{W}^{(l+1)} \right), \tag{1}$$

where $\widetilde{\mathbf{A}} = \mathbf{A} + \mathbf{I}_N$ is the adjacency matrix of the graph G with added self-connections, $\mathbf{I}_N$ is the identity matrix for N nodes in graph G, $\widetilde{\mathbf{D}}$ is a diagonal degree matrix with $\widetilde{\mathbf{D}}_{i,i} = \sum_j \widetilde{\mathbf{A}}_{i,j}$, $\mathbf{H}^{(l)}$ is the representation of each node at layer l, $\mathbf{W}^{(l+1)}$ is a layer-specific trainable weight matrix, and $\sigma(\cdot)$ denotes an activation function (such as $\mathrm{ReLU}(\cdot) = \max(0, \cdot)$).

For node classification task, we can obtain a classification loss

$$l_c = \mathrm{CrossEntropy}\left(\mathbf{Y}, \mathrm{softmax}\left(\mathbf{H}^{(-1)} \right) \right), \tag{2}$$

where $\mathbf{Y}$ is the ground truth labels for the classification task, $\mathbf{H}^{(-1)}$ is the representation of each node at the final layer of GCN. Via optimizing Eq. (2), the cross-entropy error of the node classification task can be minimized, and the GCN model can be learned.

In [13], GCN has been proved to be a special form of Laplacian smoothing. As the GCN model goes deeper and we have more layers of graph convolution, the representations in Eq. (1) have a termination condition as

$$\mathbf{H}^{(-1)} = \sigma\left(\tilde{\mathbf{D}}^{-\frac{1}{2}}\tilde{\mathbf{A}}\tilde{\mathbf{D}}^{-\frac{1}{2}}\mathbf{H}^{(-1)}\mathbf{W}^{(-1)}\right), \tag{3}$$

where $\mathbf{H}^{(-1)}$ is the final representations on the last layer of GCN. In the simplification discussed in SGC [21], nonlinear activation function is ignored. Meanwhile, according to the implementation in some previous works [10,18,22], there is no activation function on the last layer of GCN. Thus, Eq. (3) can be rewritten as

$$\mathbf{H}^{(-1)} = \tilde{\mathbf{D}}^{-\frac{1}{2}}\tilde{\mathbf{A}}\tilde{\mathbf{D}}^{-\frac{1}{2}}\mathbf{H}^{(-1)}\mathbf{W}^{(-1)}. \tag{4}$$

An approximate solution of Eq.(4) can be obtained as

$$\begin{cases} \mathbf{H}^{(-1)} = \tilde{\mathbf{D}}^{-\frac{1}{2}}\tilde{\mathbf{A}}\tilde{\mathbf{D}}^{-\frac{1}{2}}\mathbf{H}^{(-1)} \\ \mathbf{W}^{(-1)} = \mathbf{I}_N \end{cases}. \tag{5}$$

More specifically, for each node i in graph G, the approximate solution of the corresponding final representation is

$$h_i^{(-1)} = \sum_{j \in I} \frac{1}{d_i}\sqrt{\frac{d_i+1}{d_j+1}}\,\mathbf{A}_{i,j}\,h_j^{(-1)}, \tag{6}$$

where I denotes the set of all the nodes in graph G, and d_i is the degree of the node i.

According to above analysis, to train an approximate GCN model, which can simultaneously model the structure of graph convolution and the node classification task, we can minimize the following loss function

$$l = \alpha\, l_c + (1 - \alpha)\, l_s, \tag{7}$$

where α is a hyper-parameter to control the balance between the two losses, and the structure loss l_s refers to

$$l_s = \sum_{i \in I} dis\left(h_i^{(-1)}, \sum_{j \in I} \frac{1}{d_i}\sqrt{\frac{d_i+1}{d_j+1}}\,\mathbf{A}_{i,j}\,h_j^{(-1)}\right), \tag{8}$$

where $dis\,(\cdot, \cdot)$ is a distance measurement. Here, we adopt the commonly-used cosine distance, and obtain

$$l_s = -\sum_{i \in I} \frac{h_i^{(-1)}\left(\sum_{j \in I} \frac{1}{d_i}\sqrt{\frac{d_i+1}{d_j+1}}\,\mathbf{A}_{i,j}\,h_j^{(-1)}\right)^{\top}}{\left\|h_i^{(-1)}\right\|\left\|\sum_{j \in I} \frac{1}{d_i}\sqrt{\frac{d_i+1}{d_j+1}}\,\mathbf{A}_{i,j}\,h_j^{(-1)}\right\|}. \tag{9}$$

Then, to simplify the form of Eq. (9), we conduct vector unitization on the learned representations $\mathbf{H}^{(-1)}$, and thus each representation $h_i^{(-1)}$ has similar l2-norm. As a result, through unitization, Eq. (9) is equivalent to

$$l_s = -\sum_{i \in I} \sum_{j \in C_i} \frac{1}{d_i} \sqrt{\frac{d_i+1}{d_j+1}} \, \mathbf{A}_{i,j} \, v_i \, v_j^\top, \tag{10}$$

where C_i denotes all the nodes that node i is connected to, and $v_i = h_i^{(-1)}$ for simplicity. Moreover, for better optimization, we can incorporate negative log likelihood and minimize the following loss function equivalently to Eq. (10)

$$l_s = -\sum_{i \in I} \sum_{j \in C_i} \frac{1}{d_i} \sqrt{\frac{d_i+1}{d_j+1}} \, \mathbf{A}_{i,j} \log\left(\lambda\left(v_i \, v_j^\top\right)\right), \tag{11}$$

where $\lambda\left(\cdot\right) = \operatorname{sigmoid}\left(\cdot\right)$.

Usually, in graph embedding methods [6,14,17], negative sampling of edges is used, for better convergence. Thus, we can randomly sample negative edges for each edge in graph G. Following previous works in unifying word embedding [11] and graph embedding [15] as implicit matrix factorization, we can rewrite Eq. (11) as

$$\begin{aligned}l_s = &-\sum_{i \in I} \sum_{j \in C_i} \beta_{i,j} \, \mathbf{A}_{i,j} \log\left(\lambda\left(v_i \, v_j^\top\right)\right) \\ &-\sum_{i \in I} k d_i \mathbb{E}_{j' \sim P_G}\left[\beta_{i,j'} \log\left(\lambda\left(-v_i \, v_{j'}^\top\right)\right)\right],\end{aligned} \tag{12}$$

where $\beta_{i,j} = d_i^{-1}\left(d_i+1\right)^{1/2}\left(d_j+1\right)^{-1/2}$, k is the number of negative samples for each edge, and P_G denotes the distribution that generates negative samples in graph G. For each node i, $P_G\left(i\right) = d_i / |G|$, where $|G|$ is the number of edges in graph G. We can explicitly express the expectation term as

$$\mathbb{E}_{j' \sim P_G}\left[\beta_{i,j'} \log\left(\lambda\left(-v_i \, v_{j'}^\top\right)\right)\right] = \sum_{j' \in I} \frac{\beta_{i,j'} \, d_{j'}}{|G|} \log\left(\lambda\left(-v_i \, v_{j'}^\top\right)\right), \tag{13}$$

from which we have

$$\begin{aligned}\mathbb{E}_{j' \sim P_G}\left[\beta_{i,j'} \log\left(\lambda\left(-v_i \, v_{j'}^\top\right)\right)\right] = &\frac{\beta_{i,j} \, d_j}{|G|} \log\left(\lambda\left(-v_i \, v_j^\top\right)\right) \\ &+ \sum_{j' \in I \setminus \{j\}} \frac{\beta_{i,j'} \, d_{j'}}{|G|} \log\left(\lambda\left(-v_i \, v_{j'}^\top\right)\right).\end{aligned} \tag{14}$$

Then, we can obtain the local structure loss for a specific edge (i,j) as

$$\begin{aligned}l_s\left(i,j\right) = &-\beta_{i,j} \, \mathbf{A}_{i,j} \log\left(\lambda\left(v_i \, v_j^\top\right)\right) \\ &-\frac{k \, \beta_{i,j} \, d_i \, d_j}{|G|} \log\left(\lambda\left(-v_i \, v_j^\top\right)\right).\end{aligned} \tag{15}$$

To optimize above objective, we need to calculate the partial derivative of $l_s\left(i,j\right)$ with respect to $v_i \, v_j^\top$

$$\frac{\partial \, l_s\left(i,j\right)}{\partial\left(v_i \, v_j^\top\right)} = -\beta_{i,j} \, \mathbf{A}_{i,j} \lambda\left(-v_i \, v_j^\top\right) + \frac{k \, \beta_{i,j} \, d_i \, d_j}{|G|} \lambda\left(v_i \, v_j^\top\right). \tag{16}$$

Via setting Eq. (16) to zero, we can obtain

$$e^{2\,v_i\,v_j^\top} - \left(\frac{|G|\,\mathbf{A}_{i,j}}{k\,d_i\,d_j} - 1\right) e^{v_i\,v_j^\top} - \frac{|G|\,\mathbf{A}_{i,j}}{k\,d_i\,d_j} = 0, \tag{17}$$

which has two solutions, $e^{v_i\,v_j^\top} = -1$ and

$$v_i\,v_j^\top = \log\left(\frac{|G|\,\mathbf{A}_{i,j}}{k\,d_i\,d_j}\right). \tag{18}$$

Accordingly, the GCN model can be simplified as the following matrix factorization

$$\mathbf{V}\mathbf{V}^\top = \log\left(|G|\,\mathbf{D}^{-1}\mathbf{A}\mathbf{D}^{-1}\right) - \log(k), \tag{19}$$

co-trained with the classification loss l_c, where node representations in $\mathbf{V}$ are unitized. $\mathbf{D}$ is a diagonal degree matrix with $\mathbf{D}_{i,i} = d_i$. According to previous analysis [4,11,15], the matrix factorization in Eq. (19) is as the same as common implicit matrix factorization. In summary, we successfully simplify GCN as matrix factorization with unitization and co-training.

3   The UCMF Architecture

In this section, we formally propose the UCMF architecture. We first need to deal with node features, which can not be directly handled in the original implicit matrix factorization. Let x_i denote the feature vector of node i, and $f_1(\cdot)$ denote the Multi-Layer Perception (MLP) for feature modeling. According to our analysis, given x_i and $f_1(\cdot)$, we conduct vector unitization to obtain v_i, i.e., the representation of node i, as

$$v_i = \frac{f_1(x_i)}{\|f_1(x_i)\|}. \tag{20}$$

Then, following our previous analysis, UCMF consists of two losses: the structure loss l_s and the classification loss l_c. The structure loss l_s can be formulated as implicit matrix factorization with k negative samples for each edge

$$\begin{aligned}
l_s = &-\sum_{i\in I}\sum_{j\in C_i} \log\left(\lambda\left(v_i\,v_j^\top\right)\right) \\
&-\sum_{i\in I} k d_i \mathbb{E}_{j'\sim P_G}\left[\log\left(\lambda\left(-v_i\,v_{j'}^\top\right)\right)\right].
\end{aligned} \tag{21}$$

Meanwhile, the prediction on node classification can be made as

$$\hat{y}_i = \mathrm{softmax}\left(f_2\left(v_i\right)\right), \tag{22}$$

where $f_2(\cdot)$ is the MLP for making predictions. As in GCN, the classification loss l_c can be obtained as

$$l_c = \sum_{i\in I_L} \mathrm{CrossEntropy}\left(y_i, \hat{y}_i\right), \tag{23}$$

where I_L is the set of labeled nodes in the graph, and y_i is the ground-truth label of node i. Co-training the two losses as in Eq. (7), we obtain the final loss function of the proposed UCMF model.

Furthermore, following some previous works on semi-supervised node classification [20,23], during co-training, the two losses l_s and l_c are alternately optimized. To be more specific, we first optimize the structure loss l_s with b batches of samples, then we optimize the classification loss l_c with one batch of samples. We repeat this process until convergence. Here, the parameter b is the balance parameter between the two losses.

4   Experiments

In this section, we empirically evaluate the performance of the UCMF model.

4.1   Experimental Settings

We evaluate our proposed model on five real-world datasets, i.e., Cora, Citeseer, Pubmed, BlogCatalog and Flickr. Cora, Citeseer and Pubmed [16] are three standard citation network benchmark datasets[1], which are widely used in previous works [3,10,18]. BlogCatalog and Flickr [8] are two social network datasets[2]. For the splitting of Cora, Citeseer and Pubmed, we follow the classical settings in previous works [10,23]. And the splitting of BlogCatalog and Flickr is the same as in [22]. Specifically, on BlogCatalog and Flickr, we randomly select 10% and 20% of the nodes for training and validation respectively, and the rest 70% as our testing set. Moreover, these datasets can be categorized into two types: sparse datasets (Cora, Citeseer and Pubmed) and dense datasets(BlogCatalog and Flickr). In our experiments, we run each model 10 times with random weight initialization, and report the average evaluation values. When we implement UCMF and its extended variations, we set batch size as 256, the dimensionality of node representation v_i as 10% of the dimensionality of original node features on each dataset, the dropout rate as 0.5, the l2 regularization as 0.002, and tune the learning rate in $[0.001, 0.005, 0.01]$. The first MLP $f_1(\cdot)$ for feature modeling is with one layer, which outputs the node representations. And the second MLP $f_2(\cdot)$ for making predictions is with two layers, where the number of hidden neurons is set as 128.

4.2   Results and Analysis

To verify the effectiveness of UCMF, we conduct experiments on semi-supervised node classification utilizing node features. Besides **UCMF** and **GCN** [10], we involve **Planetoid** [23] as a baseline. And two simplified GCN models, i.e., **fast-GCN** [2] and **SGC** [21], are also compared. Performance comparison is shown

---

[1] https://github.com/tkipf/gcn.
[2] https://github.com/xhuang31/LANE.

Table 1. Performance comparison on semi-supervised node classification in terms of classification accuracy (%) utilizing node features.

Compared model	Cora	Citeseer	Pubmed	BlogCatalog	Flickr	Average
Planetoid	75.7	64.3	77.2	84.7	70.9	74.6
GCN	**81.2**	70.3	79.0	65.2	62.8	71.7
fastGCN	78.8	68.8	77.4	64.2	61.6	70.2
SGC	**81.0**	**71.9**	78.9	58.8	37.2	65.6
UCMF	**81.4**	71.5	**80.4**	**91.6**	**77.8**	**80.5**

in Table 1. It is obvious that, GCN outperforms fastGCN on all five datasets. This indicates that the edge sampling method may lead to somewhat performance loss. We can also observe that, UCMF, SGC and GCN achieve competitive performances on Cora, Citeseer and Pubmed. This shows that, the two simplified GCN models inherit the effectiveness of GCN. Moreover, on BlogCatalog and Flickr, both GCN and SGC have poor performances. As mentioned above, BlogCatalog and Flickr are relatively dense compared with the other three datasets. That is to say, models based on graph convolution perform poor on dense graphs. This may cause by the over-smoothing of graph convolution as mentioned in [1,13], and this becomes more serious on dense graphs. Meanwhile, UCMF can balance the smoothing of neighbours and the classification of labeled nodes through the co-training process. It is also worth to notice that, on BlogCatalog and Flickr, GCN outperforms SGC. This may indicates that, SGC aggravates the degree of over-smoothing of GCN. In summary, UCMF achieves the best performances on all datasets except Citeseer. On Citeseer, UCMF performs very closely to SGC. Meanwhile, on BlogCatalog and Flickr, the advantages of UCMF are extremely large. In average, UCMF relatively outperforms GCN, fast-GCN and SGC 12.3%, 14.7% and 22.7% respectively. These results clearly illustrate the effectiveness of UCMF.

Then, to test the performances under distributed computing settings, we compare **UCMF** with several distributed GCN models on semi-supervised node classification. In the comparison, we involve the state-of-the-art distributed GCN model **Cluster-GCN** [3], as well as the baseline model **Random-GCN** in the corresponding paper. Moreover, **SGC** [21] is also involved in the comparison, for it is actually a linear model and can be distributed implemented. We also run **fastGCN** [2] in mini-batches via sampling high-order neighbours of each node in the graph, though this causes exponential complexity with the number of layers as pointed in [3]. Under distributed computing settings, parameters of each model are learned with the Parameter Server (PS) architecture [12], where we have 1 server and 2 workers. Each graph is partitioned into two sub-graphs for computing on the two workers. For Cluser-GCN, following [3], the partition is conducted with the METIS algorithm [9]. And for Random-GCN, fastGCN, SGC and UCMF, the partition is randomly conducted. Performance comparison under distributed settings is shown in Table 2. Recalling the results in Table 1, it is clear

Table 2. Performance comparison on semi-supervised node classification in terms of classification accuracy (%) under distributed computing settings.

Compared model	Cora	Citeseer	Pubmed	BlogCatalog	Flickr	Average
Random-GCN	71.7	61.9	71.8	55.2	53.9	62.9
Cluster-GCN	77.1	64.8	76.6	59.8	57.5	67.1
fastGCN	77.6	68.7	77.1	64.1	61.2	69.7
SGC	**80.8**	**71.5**	78.6	58.4	36.9	65.2
UCMF	**81.2**	71.3	**80.3**	**91.5**	**77.6**	**80.4**

that both Cluster-GCN and Random-GCN greatly suffer performance loss. Via sampling high-order neighbours of each node, fastGCN stays the performances as in Table 1. Meanwhile, inherit from the capacity of linear model and MF, SGC and UCMF are extremely flexible for distributed computing, and both achieve very similar performances as in Table 1. However, the performances of SGC are still poor on BlogCatalog and Flickr, because of the over-smoothing problem. In average, under distributed settings, UCMF relatively outperforms Cluster-GCN, fast-GCN and SGC 19.8%, 15.4% and 23.3% respectively. Overall, UCMF enlarges its advantages under distributed settings. These results strongly demonstrate the flexibility of UCMF.

5 Conclusion

In this paper, we simplify GCN as unitized and co-training matrix factorization, and the UCMF model is therefore proposed. We conduct thorough and empirical experiments, which strongly verify our analysis. The experimental results on semi-supervised node classification show that UCMF achieves similar or superior performances compared with GCN. Moreover, due to the MF-based architecture, UCMF is exceedingly flexible and convenient to be applied to distributed computing for large scale real-world applications, and significantly outperforms distributed GCN methods. Extensive experimental results clearly show that, we can use UCMF as an alternative to GCN for transductive graph representation learning in various real-world applications.

References

1. Chen, D., Lin, Y., Li, W., Li, P., Zhou, J., Sun, X.: Measuring and relieving the over-smoothing problem for graph neural networks from the topological view. In: AAAI (2020)
2. Chen, J., Ma, T., Xiao, C.: FastGCN: fast learning with graph convolutional networks via importance sampling. arXiv preprint arXiv:1801.10247 (2018)
3. Chiang, W.L., Liu, X., Si, S., Li, Y., Bengio, S., Hsieh, C.J.: Cluster-GCN: an efficient algorithm for training deep and large graph convolutional networks. In: KDD (2019)

4. Du, L., Wang, Y., Song, G., Lu, Z., Wang, J.: Dynamic network embedding: an extended approach for skip-gram based network embedding. In: IJCAI (2018)
5. Gemulla, R., Nijkamp, E., Haas, P.J., Sismanis, Y.: Large-scale matrix factorization with distributed stochastic gradient descent. In: KDD (2011)
6. Grover, A., Leskovec, J.: node2vec: scalable feature learning for networks. In: KDD (2016)
7. Hamilton, W., Ying, Z., Leskovec, J.: Inductive representation learning on large graphs. In: NeurIPS (2017)
8. Huang, X., Li, J., Hu, X.: Label informed attributed network embedding. In: WSDM (2017)
9. Karypis, G., Kumar, V.: A fast and high quality multilevel scheme for partitioning irregular graphs. SIAM J. Sci. Comput. **20**(1), 359–392 (1998)
10. Kipf, T.N., Welling, M.: Semi-supervised classification with graph convolutional networks. In: ICLR (2017)
11. Levy, O., Goldberg, Y.: Neural word embedding as implicit matrix factorization. In: NeurIPS (2014)
12. Li, M., et al.: Scaling distributed machine learning with the parameter server. In: OSDI (2014)
13. Li, Q., Han, Z., Wu, X.M.: Deeper insights into graph convolutional networks for semi-supervised learning. In: AAAI (2018)
14. Perozzi, B., Al-Rfou, R., Skiena, S.: DeepWalk: online learning of social representations. In: KDD (2014)
15. Qiu, J., Dong, Y., Ma, H., Li, J., Wang, K., Tang, J.: Network embedding as matrix factorization: Unifying DeepWalk, LINE, PTE, and node2vec. In: WSDM (2018)
16. Sen, P., Namata, G., Bilgic, M., Getoor, L., Gallagher, B., Eliassirad, T.: Collective classification in network data. AI Mag. **29**(3), 93–106 (2008)
17. Tang, J., Qu, M., Wang, M., Zhang, M., Yan, J., Mei, Q.: Line: large-scale information network embedding. In: WWW (2015)
18. Veličković, P., Cucurull, G., Casanova, A., Romero, A., Lio, P., Bengio, Y.: Graph attention networks. In: ICLR (2017)
19. Wang, X., He, X., Wang, M., Feng, F., Chua, T.S.: Neural graph collaborative filtering. In: SIGIR (2019)
20. Weston, J., Ratle, F., Mobahi, H., Collobert, R.: Deep learning via semi-supervised embedding. In: ICML (2012)
21. Wu, F., Zhang, T., Souza Jr, A.H.d., Fifty, C., Yu, T., Weinberger, K.Q.: Simplifying graph convolutional networks. arXiv preprint arXiv:1902.07153 (2019)
22. Wu, J., He, J., Xu, J.: DEMO-Net: degree-specific graph neural networks for node and graph classification. In: KDD (2019)
23. Yang, Z., Cohen, W., Salakhutdinov, R.: Revisiting semi-supervised learning with graph embeddings. In: ICML (2016)
24. Ying, R., He, R., Chen, K., Eksombatchai, P., Hamilton, W.L., Leskovec, J.: Graph convolutional neural networks for web-scale recommender systems. In: KDD (2018)
25. Yu, H.-F., Hsieh, C.-J., Si, S., Dhillon, I.S.: Parallel matrix factorization for recommender systems. Knowl. Inf. Syst. **41**(3), 793–819 (2013). https://doi.org/10. 1007/s10115-013-0682-2
26. Zhang, M., Chen, Y.: Link prediction based on graph neural networks. In: NeurIPS (2018)

GRASP: Graph Alignment Through Spectral Signatures

Judith Hermanns[1]($\boxtimes$), Anton Tsitsulin[2], Marina Munkhoeva[3],
Alex Bronstein[4], Davide Mottin[1], and Panagiotis Karras[1]

[1] Aarhus University, Aarhus, Denmark
{judith,davide,panos}@cs.au.dk
[2] University of Bonn, Bonn, Germany
tsitsulin@bit.uni-bonn.de
[3] Skolkovo Institute of Technology, Moscow, Russia
marina.munkhoeva@skolkovotech.ru
[4] Technion, Haifa, Israel
bron@cs.technion.ac.il

Abstract. What is the best way to match the nodes of two graphs? This *graph alignment* problem generalizes graph isomorphism and arises in applications from social network analysis to bioinformatics. Existing solutions either require auxiliary information such as node attributes, or provide a single-scale view of the graph by translating the problem into aligning node embeddings.

In this paper, we transfer the shape-analysis concept of functional maps from the continuous to the discrete case, and treat the graph alignment problem as a special case of the problem of finding a mapping between functions on graphs. We present GRASP, a method that captures multiscale structural characteristics from the eigenvectors of the graph's Laplacian and uses this information to align two graphs.Our experimental study, featuring noise levels higher than anything used in previous studies, shows that GRASP outperforms state-of-the-art methods for graph alignment across noise levels and graph types.

1 Introduction

Graphs model relationships between entities in several domains, e.g., social networks, protein interaction networks, email communication or chemical molecules. The structure of such graphs captures rich information on how people are connected, how molecules function, or how proteins interact.

At the same time, the expressive nature of graphs also implies complexity, which renders some fundamental problems hard. For instance, the *graph isomorphism* problem, which is to determine whether two graphs share the same structure is neither known to be polynomially solvable nor **NP**-complete. Problems that generalize graph isomorphism occur frequently in the field of graph analytics. One of those is *graph alignment*, which aims to find the best (exact or inexact) matching among the nodes of a pair of graphs; a solution to this

© Springer Nature Switzerland AG 2021
L. H. U et al. (Eds.): APWeb-WAIM 2021, LNCS 12858, pp. 44–52, 2021.
https://doi.org/10.1007/978-3-030-85896-4_4

(a) Karate club; Red edges removed.   (b) Alignment by GRASP (left) and REGAL (right).

Fig. 1. With a few removed edges, REGAL [9], an alignment method based on *local* features, fails to correctly align the distorted Karate club graph to the original; GRASP identifies most of nodes (correctly aligned nodes in green). (Color figure online)

problem is sine qua non in tasks such as identifying users in different social networks [11], matching objects in images by establishing feature correspondences and comprehending protein response in the body [12].

We propose GRASP, short for **GR**aph **A**lignment through **SP**ectral Signatures, a principled approach towards detecting a good alignment among graphs, grounded on their spectral characteristics, i.e., eigenvalues and eigenvectors of their Laplacian matrices [5]. We transfer the methodology of matching among shapes based on *corresponding functions* [18] to the domain of graphs: we first extract a mapping of node-evaluated functions grounded on the graph's heat kernel, and then apply this mapping to the matching on nodes. Figure 1 shows an example alignment of the Karate club with a deteriorated version obtained by removing some edges; GRASP correctly aligns most of the nodes, while REGAL [9] based on local descriptors fails to do so.

In short, we propose GRASP, a graph alignment method based on spectral graph characteristics and show its effectiveness in recovering real-graph alignments, with higher accuracy as the state of the art.

2   Related Work

We discuss related work in two main categories: **restricted alignment**, which requires ground-truth mapping or other additional information, and **unrestricted alignment**, which requires neither supervision nor additional information.

Restricted Alignment: *Restricted* methods incorporate non-structural information; a restricted method can be *supervised* or *assisted*.

Supervised methods exploit pre-aligned pairs of seed nodes to construct a first alignment. *Percolation graph matching* (PGM) [11,23] propagates ground-truth alignments across the network. *Representation learning* approaches, such as IONE [16] and DeepLink [26], learn a low-dimensional embedding of the graph nodes and map the node embeddings of one graph to another. Overall, supervised methods rely on prior knowledge, which may not be available.

Assisted methods utilize auxiliary information or structural constraints. FINAL [25] aligns nodes based on similarity of topology and attributes. GSANA [24] lets pairwise distances to seed nodes guide the matching. Another variant matches *weigthed* matrices using their spectra [22]; that is inapplicable to the unweighted case. Overall, restricted methods cannot handle cases where the only given information is graph structure.

Unrestricted Alignment: *Unrestricted* methods require neither prior knowledge of ground-truth pairs nor other information on the input graph. Klau [12] presents a Lagrangian relaxation for the integer programming problem posed by network alignment; the resulting algorithm is polynomial, yet still impracticable for large networks. REGAL [9] constructs node embeddings based on the connectivity structure and node attributes ; we classify REGAL as an unrestricted method since it can work without attributes. CONE-Align [4] realigns node representations, without prejudice to the representation used. IsoRank [20] aligns multiple protein-protein interaction networks aiming to maximize the overall quality across all input networks. EigenAlign [8] formulates the problem as a Quadratic Assignment Problem that considers both matches and mismatches and solves it by *spectral decomposition* of matrices. Building thereupon, Low-Rank EigenAlign [17] solves a maximum weight bipartite matching problem on a *low-rank* version of a node-similarity matrix. NetAlign [2] solves a *sparse* graph alignment variant by message passing.

Shape Matching: Our work is inspired by shape matching methods that employ spectral properties [14,18]. Functional maps [18] generalize the matching of points to the matching of *corresponding functions* among shapes, by revealing a common decomposition of such functions using the eigenvectors of the Laplace–Beltrami operator; the graph equivalent of that operator is a graph's Laplacian matrix. An Extension of this method matches non-isometric shapes by aligning their Laplace–Beltrami operators' eigenbases [14].

Spectral Methods: Graph spectra [5] facilitate graph analysis, image partitioning, and machine learning [19]. NetLSD [21] uses Laplacian spectral signatures to detect graph similarity, *but not to align graphs*, in a multi-scale fashion. LaplMatch [13] derives a permutation matrix for shape matching from Laplacian eigenvectors, without considering multiscale properties. Recent work proposes a fast approximation via spectral moments estimated through random walks [6].

3   Background and Problem

Graph Alignment. Consider two undirected graphs, $G_1 = (V_1, E_1)$ and $G_2 = (V_2, E_2)$, where V_* are node sets, $E_* \subseteq V_* \times V_*$ are edges, and[1] $|V_1| = |V_2| = n$. A graph's *adjacency matrix* $A \in \{0, 1\}^{n \times n}$ is a binary matrix where $A_{ij} = 1$ if there is an edge between nodes i and j and $A_{ij} = 0$ otherwise.

---

[1] Solutions to the problem of aligning graphs with unequal numbers of nodes can rest on solutions to this basic problem form.

Definition 1. *A graph alignment of two graphs $G_1 = (V_1, E_1)$ and $G_2 = (V_2, E_2)$ is an* injective *function $R : V_1 \to V_2$ that maps nodes of G_1 to nodes of G_2.*

Functional Maps. The operator $T_{\mathcal{F}} : (V_1 \times \mathbb{R}) \to (V_2 \times \mathbb{R})$ maps functions f on the nodes in G_1 to functions g on the nodes in G_2, i.e. $T_{\mathcal{F}}(f) = f \circ \tau^{-1} = g$, with τ being the ground truth function $\tau : V_1 \to V_2$ that returns the correct alignment between the nodes V_1 in G_1 and the nodes V_2 in G_2. The operator $T_{\mathcal{F}}$ is linear in the function space, i.e., $T_{\mathcal{F}}(c_1 f_1 + c_2 f_2) = (c_1 f_1 + c_2 f_2) \circ \tau^{-1} = c_1 f_1 \circ \tau^{-1} + c_2 f_2 \circ \tau^{-1} = c_1 T_{\mathcal{F}}(f_1) + c_2 T_{\mathcal{F}}(f_2)$. In addition, let $\phi_1, ..., \phi_n$ and $\psi_1, ..., \psi_n$ denote orthogonal bases for the space of functions on G_1's nodes, $V_1 \times \mathbb{R}$, and that on G_2's nodes, $V_2 \times \mathbb{R}$, respectively. Since those functions produce n-dimensional vectors, we can represent them as linear combinations of their basis vectors, $f = \sum_{i=1}^{n} a_i \phi_i$ and $g = \sum_{j=1}^{n} b_j \psi_j$. By the linearity of $T_{\mathcal{F}}$,

$$T_{\mathcal{F}}(f) = T_{\mathcal{F}} \left(\sum_{i=1}^{n} a_i \phi_i \right) = \sum_{i=1}^{n} a_i T_{\mathcal{F}}(\phi_i) = \sum_{i=1}^{n} a_i \sum_{j=1}^{n} c_{ij} \psi_j = \sum_{j=1}^{n} b_j \psi_j$$

where $T_{\mathcal{F}}(\phi_i) = \sum_{j=1}^{n} c_{ij} \psi_j$. It follows that each coefficient b_j is the dot-product $\sum_{i=1}^{n} a_i c_{ij}$ between the coefficients $(a_1, ..., a_n)$ of functions in G_1 and the coefficients $(c_{1j}, ..., c_{nj})$ of the operator $T_{\mathcal{F}}$. In order to align real-valued functions on the nodes of two graphs, we need to find a *mapping matrix $C \in \mathbb{R}^{n \times n}$*; such a mapping matrix C maps functions from G_1 to G_2, even when the ground–truth mapping τ is unknown. GRASP obtains such a C for a set of well-chosen functions and applies that C to mapping the indicator function δ from G_1 to G_2, thereby constructing a node alignment. The main question we need to answer is what orthogonal basis and functions we should use to construct our mapping matrix C. The next section answers this question.

4   GRASP

We start out with an appropriate choice of an orthonormal basis and a set of functions.

4.1   Choice of Basis: Normalized Laplacian

As a basis for representing functions as linear combinations of base functions, we use the eigenvectors of the graph's *normalized Laplacian* $\mathcal{L} = I - D^{-\frac{1}{2}} A D^{-\frac{1}{2}}$, where D is a diagonal degree matrix $D_{ii} = \sum_{j=1}^{n} A_{ij}$ and A is the adjacency matrix; its eigendecomposition is $\mathcal{L} = \Phi \Lambda \Phi^{\top}$, where Λ is a diagonal matrix of eigenvalues $\{\lambda_1, ..., \lambda_n\}$, i.e., the graph's *spectrum*, which encodes structural information, such as communities, and Φ is a matrix of eigenvectors, $\Phi_{\mathcal{L}} = [\phi_1 \phi_2 ... \phi_n]$. The eigenvectors form an orthogonal basis, which we use as a standard basis. We use ϕ (ψ) to indicate the eigenvectors of the Laplacian of graph G_1 (G_2).

4.2   Choice of Functions: Heat Kernel

We build our *corresponding functions* f_i, g_i, from the time-parameterized heat kernel [21] at different time steps t:

$$H_t = \Phi e^{-t\Lambda}\Phi^\top = \sum_{j=1}^n e^{-t\lambda_j}\phi_j\phi_j^\top \tag{1}$$

where $H_{t[ij]}$ measures the flow of heat from node i to node j at time t, as it diffuses from each node's neighborhood to the whole graph. Let $F \in \mathbb{R}^{n \times q}$, $F = [f_1, \ldots, f_q]$ be the matrix containing the diagonals of the heat kernel of G_1, $H_t^{G_1}$, over q time steps[2], $f_i = \sum_{j=1}^n e^{-t_i\lambda_j}\phi_j \odot \phi_j$, where $\odot$ denotes the element-wise vector product. Likewise, the matrix $G \in \mathbb{R}^{n \times q}$, $G = [g_1, \ldots, g_q]$ contains the diagonals of $H_t^{G_2}$, the heat kernel of G_2. While the q *columns* of F and G contain the same time-dependent heat-kernel-diagonal functions, their n *rows* (i.e., nodes) are not aligned. We need to obtain such a node alignment.

4.3   Mapping Matrix

We approximate each function f_i using only the first k eigenvectors, as done, by analogy, on shapes analysis [3], and thereby calculate the corresponding function matrices F and G. F and G can be thought as coefficient matrices used to produce linear combinations, $F^\top\Phi$ and $G^\top\Psi$, of the Laplacian eigenvectors of G_1 and G_2, respectively. With a slight abuse of notation, we denote with Φ and Ψ the first k eigenvectors, hence $F^\top\Phi$ and $G^\top\Psi$ are in $\mathbb{R}^{q \times k}$. In the projection of the functions on the first k eigenvectors, we would like the corresponding functions to be equal up to a coefficient matrix $C \in \mathbb{R}^{k \times k}$, as it holds on isomorphic graphs.

   Matrix C is diagonal in the case of isomorphic graphs and deviates from a diagonal form as graphs diverge from isomorphism; for simplicity, we assume a diagonal C, and obtain the diagonal entries by solving a least squares problem as in [14]. In Sect. 4.5 we delve into the case of non-isomorphic graphs.

4.4   Node-to-Node Correspondence

We consider the delta function $\delta_i(\cdot)$ as corresponding function; these functions yield an $n \times n$ identity matrix. We express such a function as a vector of coefficients, since the vector of δ_i is the ith row of the heat kernel at $t = 0$:

$$\delta_i = H_{i,t=0}^{G_1} = \sum_{j=1}^n \phi_{ij}\phi_j$$

   The computation for delta functions on G_2 follows equivalently using Ψ in place of Φ. We may match the coefficient vectors of these corresponding indicator functions as, ideally, for two matching nodes $v_i \in V_1$ and $v_j' \in V_2$, the coefficients of δ_i and δ_j for Φ and Ψ should be identical. In particular, the coefficients expressing δ_i as a linear combination of the first k eigenvectors are $\phi_{i1}, \ldots, \phi_{ik}$. We set $\Phi^\top$ and $C\Psi^\top$ in $\mathbb{R}^{k \times n}$ as coefficient matrices of the delta functions, aligned by C.

---

[2] In our experiments we select $q = 100$ values evenly spaced in the range $[0.1, 50]$.

The alignment problem now amounts to a *linear assignment problem*; we apply an off-the-shelf algorithm for matching the columns, such as **nearest neighbor search** or **Jonker-Volgenant (JV)** [10], to obtain a one-to-one matching between the columns of $\Phi^\top$ and $C\Psi^\top$, and hence an alignment of nodes.

4.5 Base Alignment

We have hitherto assumed that the graphs to be aligned are isomorphic, hence their eigenvectors correspond to each other up to sign changes and an orthogonal diagonal mapping matrix C exists. Still, if the graphs are not isomorphic, then their eigenvectors diverge and the diagonal matrix C, which we enforce, cannot capture their relationship well. In this case, we need to *align* the two eigenvector bases before aligning corresponding vectors and, eventually, nodes. We express this *base alignment* [14] in terms of an alignment matrix M. We obtain M by solving the following minimization problem, with regularization μ^3:

$$\min_{M \in S(n,n)} \mathsf{off}(M^\top \Lambda_2 M) + \mu \|F^\top \Phi - G^\top \Psi M\|_F^2 \tag{2}$$

The terms in Eq. 2 balance two different objectives. The term $\mathsf{off}(M^\top \Lambda_2 M)$ aims at keeping the aligned eigenvector matrices orthogonal, while the term $\|F^\top \Phi - G^\top \Psi M\|_F^2$ ensures the alignment of the eigenvector matrices such that $\phi_i \approx \tau \circ \psi$ for the unknown ground truth correspondence $\tau : G_1 \to G_2$. The set $S(n,n)$ is the set of all orthogonal matrices of size $n \times n$. Eq. (2) leads to a manifold optimization problem, which we solve by trust-region methods [1].

After obtaining M, we use the eigenvectors in $\bar{\Phi}$ and the aligned eigenvectors $\hat{\Psi} = \Psi M$ in the next step for the final alignment of nodes. Our approach effectively trades off graph alignment with a proxy problem of manifold optimization, which we solve with reasonable accuracy and scalability.

5 Experiments

We experiment on three different networks. As in [9], we randomly permute the node order and inject noise by deleting edges with probability p. We align a graph to 5 noisy graphs, with p ranging from 0.05 to 0.25; we measure alignment accuracy as the average ratio of correctly aligned nodes; note that none of the noisy graphs in a pair is a subset of the other.

Baselines. We compare against the following established state-of-the art baselines for *unrestriced* graph alignment.

- **REGAL** [9]: A method based on embeddings utilizing local structural features. REGAL allows one-to-many matchings. We let REGAL provide one-to-one matchings using the JV linear assignment algorithm, as GRASP does; we confirmed that, doing so, it fares better than using nearest neighbors.

---

[3] $\mu = 0.132$ in our experiments.

– **Low Rank EigenAlign (LREA)** [17]: A spectral method that yields one-to-one matchings via the minimization of edge mismatches.

We eschew a comparison with IsoRank [15,20] and other methods for the alignment of biological networks [7], since REGAL and LREA significantly outperform those methods.

Parameter Tuning. After experimenting with different settings, we set $k = 20$ eigenvalues and $q = 100$ corresponding functions, which yield best accuracy.

Justifying Algorithmic Choices: We evaluate the impact of (i) the choice of algorithm for node-to-node assignment (Sect. 4.4) and (ii) base alignment (Sect. 4.5). Figure 2 shows that both the JV linear assignment algorithm and base alignment bring a substantial advantage over their rudimentary counterparts, consistently across datasets. In the following experiment, we settle on the variant of GRASP equipped with base alignment.

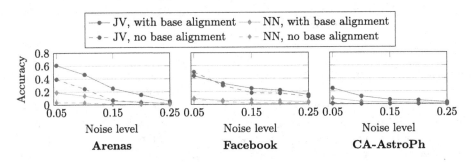

Fig. 2. Accuracy of nearest neighbor and JV matching algorithms.

Comparison to Previous Methods: Figure 3 shows that GRASP outperforms others by a large margin, achieving 62% accuracy in Arenas and 43% in Facebook with 5% noise, and fares at comparably well as REGAL on CA-AstroPH.

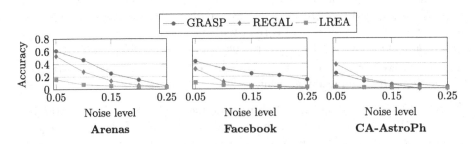

Fig. 3. Accuracy compared to REGAL and LREA

6   Conclusion

We proposed a graph alignment method using Laplacian eigenvectors. We establish a functional correspondence among pre-aligned eigenvectors, capturing multiscale graph properties, and extract a linear assignment among matrix columns, attaining superior alignment quality over the state of the art. To our knowledge, this is the first work to apply a functional alignment primitive to graph alignment. We plan to extend our method to partial correspondences and examine to what extent our representations can be employed within the framework of [4].

References

1. Absil, P.A., Baker, C.G., Gallivan, K.A.: Trust-region methods on riemannian manifolds. FoCM **7**(3), 303–330 (2007)
2. Bayati, M., Gleich, D.F., Saberi, A., Wang, Y.: Message-passing algorithms for sparse network alignment. TKDD **7**(1), 3:1–3:31 (2013)
3. Belkin, M., Niyogi, P.: Convergence of laplacian eigenmaps. In: NeurIPS, pp. 129–136 (2006)
4. Chen, X., Heimann, M., Vahedian, F., Koutra, D.: Cone-align: consistent network alignment with proximity-preserving node embedding. In: CIKM, pp. 1985–1988 (2020)
5. Chung, F.R., Graham, F.C.: Spectral graph theory. No. 92, American Mathematical Soc. (1997)
6. Cohen-Steiner, D., Kong, W., Sohler, C., Valiant, G.: Approximating the spectrum of a graph. In: KDD, pp. 1263–1271 (2018)
7. El-Kebir, M., Heringa, J., Klau, G.W.: Natalie 2.0: Sparse global network alignment as a special case of quadratic assignment. Algorithms **8**(4), 1035–1051 (2015)
8. Feizi, S., Quon, G., Mendoza, M., Medard, M., Kellis, M., Jadbabaie, A.: Spectral alignment of graphs. IEEE Trans. Netw, Sci (2019)
9. Heimann, M., Shen, H., Safavi, T., Koutra, D.: REGAL: representation learning-based graph alignment. In: CIKM, pp. 117–126 (2018)
10. Jonker, R., Volgenant, A.: A shortest augmenting path algorithm for dense and sparse linear assignment problems. Computing **38**(4), 325–340 (1987)
11. Kazemi, E., Hassani, S.H., Grossglauser, M.: Growing a graph matching from a handful of seeds. PVLDB **8**(10), 1010–1021 (2015)
12. Klau, G.W.: A new graph-based method for pairwise global network alignment. BMC Bioinf. 10(S-1) (2009)
13. Knossow, D., Sharma, A., Mateus, D., Horaud, R.: Inexact matching of large and sparse graphs using laplacian eigenvectors. In: GdR International Working, pp. 144–153 (2009)
14. Kovnatsky, A., Bronstein, M.M., Bronstein, A.M., Glashoff, K., Kimmel, R.: Coupled quasi-harmonic bases. Comput Graph Forum. **32**, 439–448 (2013)
15. Liao, C.S., Lu, K., Baym, M., Singh, R., Berger, B.: IsoRankN: spectral methods for global alignment of multiple protein networks. Bioinformatics **25**(12), i253–i258 (2009)
16. Liu, L., Cheung, W.K., Li, X., Liao, L.: Aligning users across social networks using network embedding. In: IJCAI, pp. 1774–1780 (2016)
17. Nassar, H., Veldt, N., Mohammadi, S., Grama, A., Gleich, D.F.: Low rank spectral network alignment. In: WWW, pp. 619–628 (2018)

18. Ovsjanikov, M., Ben-Chen, M., Solomon, J., Butscher, A., Guibas, L.J.: Functional maps: a flexible representation of maps between shapes. ACM Trans. Graph. **31**(4), 30:1–30:11 (2012)
19. Shi, J., Malik, J.: Normalized cuts and image segmentation. IEEE Trans. Pattern Anal. Mach. Intell. **22**(8), 888–905 (2000)
20. Singh, R., Xu, J., Berger, B.: Global alignment of multiple protein interaction networks with application to functional orthology detection. PNAS **105**(35), 12763–12768 (2008)
21. Tsitsulin, A., Mottin, D., Karras, P., Bronstein, A.M., Müller, E.: NetLSD: hearing the shape of a graph. In: KDD, pp. 2347–2356 (2018)
22. Umeyama, S.: An eigendecomposition approach to weighted graph matching problems. IEEE Trans. Pattern Anal. Mach. Intell. **10**(5), 695–703 (1988)
23. Yartseva, L., Grossglauser, M.: On the performance of percolation graph matching. In: ACM COSN, pp. 119–130 (2013)
24. Yasar, A., Çatalyürek, Ü.V.: An iterative global structure-assisted labeled network aligner. In: KDD, pp. 2614–2623 (2018)
25. Zhang, S., Tong, H.: FINAL: fast attributed network alignment. In: KDD, pp. 1345–1354 (2016)
26. Zhou, F., Liu, L., Zhang, K., Trajcevski, G., Wu, J., Zhong, T.: Deeplink: a deep learning approach for user identity linkage. In: INFOCOM, pp. 1313–1321 (2018)

FANE: A Fusion-Based Attributed Network Embedding Framework

Guanghua Li, Qiyan Li, Jingqiao Liu, Yuanyuan Zhu$^{(\boxtimes)}$, and Ming Zhong

School of Computer Science, Wuhan University, Wuhan, China
{guanghli,qiyan.li,clock,yyzhu}@whu.edu.cn

Abstract. Network embedding, which learns a low-dimensional representation for each node in a network, has been proved to be highly effective for a variety of downstream tasks. In this paper, we propose a novel **F**usion-based **A**ttributed **N**etwork **E**mbedding framework (FANE), which consists of two modules. The first is the feature-learning module, in which we propose a general and scalable method SparseAE to embed different types of information (structure, attribute, etc.) into separate low-dimensional vectors. The second is the feature-fusion module, which learns the fused embedding vector to capture the underlying relationships between different types of information for downstream prediction tasks. Extensive experiments on multiple real-world datasets show that our method can outperform several state-of-the-art methods in many downstream tasks, including node classification and link prediction.

Keywords: Feature learning · Network embedding · Attributed network

1 Introduction

Networks are ubiquitous in real-world applications. Network embedding, which aims to learn a low-dimensional representation for each node in a network, has been proved to be highly effective for a variety of downstream tasks, such as node classification [1,17], link prediction [4,15], network visualization [3,8], etc.

In the literature, numerous network embedding methods have been proposed, such as Node2vec [5], LINE [18], SDNE [21], etc. The above works only focus on the structure information of the network. Some recently proposed methods such as GraphSAGE [6] and ASNE [12] have been devoted to integrate the structure information and attribute information. However, most of these methods either learn the embedding in a joint framework by combining the loss functions for different types of information by weighting coefficients, or simply project the embedding vectors of different types of information into a common vector space, and thus cannot well capture the complicated underlying relationship between different types of information.

L. H. U et al. (Eds.): APWeb-WAIM 2021, LNCS 12858, pp. 53–60, 2021.
https://doi.org/10.1007/978-3-030-85896-4_5

These limitations prompt us to rethink: how to design a general and scalable model to integrate multiple types of information in the network for different downstream tasks? In this paper, we propose a fusion-based attributed network embedding framework FANE, and our main contributions are summarized below.

- We propose a general graph embedding framework FANE to embed different types of information by separating feature extraction and feature fusion.
- In the feature-learning phase, we design a new general embedding model SparseAE for different types of information.
- In the feature-fusion phase, we automatically capture the complicated relationship between different types of features for different downstream tasks.
- We have done extensive experiments which validated that our method can outperform several state-of-the-art methods in many downstream tasks.

2   Related Works

In terms of the availability of node attributes, existing methods can be divided into two categories: plain network embedding and attributed network embedding.

Earlier works on plain network embedding are mainly based on random walks. DeepWalk [16] first generates random walk node sequence, and then maps them into a vector space using skip-gram. Node2Vec [5] gives a more flexible definition of network neighborhood based on biased random walk. LINE [18] defines the first-order and second-order proximities and tries to preserve both. SDNE [21] uses the deep autoencoder model with multiple nonlinear layers to discover the high nonlinearity while preserving proximity for sparse networks. [19] proposes DRNE to learn network embeddings with regular equivalence.

Besides structure information, rich attribute information is also exploited. ASNE [12] proposes a generic framework to preserve the structure proximity and attribute proximity by two components. GraphRNA [10] first generates walk paths considering node attributes and then feeds node sequences into a graph recurrent network. GCN [11] introduces the convolution operation to graphs and optimizes the node representation in a semi-supervised learning framework. GraphSAGE [6] samples a fixed number of neighbors for each node to aggregate features from them. GAT [20] utilizes the attention mechanism to learn different weights of neighbors before aggregation. Recently, some efforts are devoted to revise the structure of GNN to make it deeper [13] or simpler [7]. On top of node attributes, techniques are developed to embed graphs with other kinds of information. [22] learns the embeddings of dynamic and heterogeneous networks. [14] embeds graphs with multiple dimensions of relations.

However, the above methods simply project the embedding vectors for different types of information into a common vector space, or concatenate them together, which cannot well capture the complicated relationship between different types of information.

3   Proposed Method

In this section, we will first formalize the problem and then present our methods.

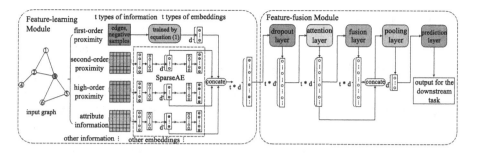

Fig. 1. Overall framework of FANE

3.1 Problem Definition

Let $G = (V, E, \mathbf{X})$ denote an *attributed network*, where $V = \{v_1, v_2, \ldots, v_{|V|}\}$ is the set of nodes, $E \in V \times V$ is the set of edges, and $\mathbf{X} \in \mathbb{R}^{|V| \times l}$ represents the attribute matrix, where l is attribute dimension number. The i-th row $\mathbf{x}_i$ in $\mathbf{X}$ is the attribute vector of the corresponding node v_i. Let $\mathbf{A} \in \mathbb{R}^{|V| \times |V|}$ be the adjacency matrix, where $a_{ij} = 1$ if nodes v_i and v_j are connected $((v_i, v_j) \in E)$ and $a_{ij} = 0$ otherwise. *Attributed network embedding* is to learn a mapping $f : \{\mathbf{A}, \mathbf{X}\} \rightarrow \mathbf{P}$ where $\mathbf{P} \in \mathbb{R}^{|V| \times d}$ is the low-dimensional representation of nodes in the network, such that the structure and attribute proximity of the network can be well preserved by $\mathbf{P}$.

3.2 Overall Framework

In this section, we present a novel **F**usion-based **A**ttributed **N**etwork **E**mbedding (FANE) framework to integrate multiple types of information. As shown in Fig. 1, FANE consists of two modules: the feature-learning module and the feature-fusion module.

In the feature-learning module, we aim to learn feature vectors for different types of information of the network. Here we consider both structural information (first-order proximity, second-order proximity, and high-order proximity) and attribute information.

Two connected nodes are considered to have *first-order proximity*. Following [18], we define the joint probability of each pair of nodes as $p_f(v_j, v_i) = \frac{1}{1+exp(-\mathbf{u}_i^T \cdot \mathbf{u}_j)}$ where $\mathbf{u}_i, \mathbf{u}_j \in \mathbb{R}^d$ are the low-dimensional representation vectors of nodes v_i and v_j. The loss function to train feature vectors for first-order proximity is defined as:

$$L_f = \frac{1}{|E|} \sum_{(v_i, v_j) \in E} \left(-a_{ij} \log p_f(v_i, v_j) + \sum_{i=1}^{K} E_{v_n \sim P_n(v)}(1-a_{ij'}) \log(1-p_f(v_i, v_{j'})) \right) \quad (1)$$

where $a_{ij} = 1$ when nodes v_i and v_j are connected and $a_{ij} = 0$ otherwise. The first term models truly connected samples, and the second term models the negative samples drawn from the noise distribution $P_n(v)$. Following [18], we set $E_{v_n \sim P_n(v)} \propto d(v)^{3/4}$ and K to 5.

For other types of information, we propose SparseAE to independently generate low-dimensional representation vectors for different types of information. SparseAE is an unsupervised model aiming to capture the sparsity and nonlinearity of these proximities, which is inspired by the autoencoder that has been widely used in many machine learning tasks [2,21]. Our SparseAE consists of two parts: an encoder and a decoder. It maps the input data to a low-dimensional representation in the encoder, and then uses the decoder to reconstruct the data from the representation. Given the input $\mathbf{z}_i$, the hidden representation for each layer is shown as follows:

$$
\begin{aligned}
\mathbf{h}_i &= f(\mathbf{W}_m^{(1)}(\cdots f(\mathbf{W}_1^{(1)}\mathbf{z}_i + \mathbf{b}_1^{(1)})\cdots) + \mathbf{b}_m^{(1)}) \\
\hat{\mathbf{z}}_i &= f(\mathbf{W}_n^{(2)}(\cdots f(\mathbf{W}_1^{(2)}\mathbf{h}_i + \mathbf{b}_1^{(2)})\cdots) + \mathbf{b}_n^{(2)})
\end{aligned}
\tag{2}
$$

where $\mathbf{z}_i \in \mathbb{R}^{d_1}$ is the i-th input data, $\mathbf{h}_i \in \mathbb{R}^{d_2}$ is the low-dimensional vector representation of $\mathbf{z}_i$ in the hidden layer, and $\hat{\mathbf{z}}_i \in \mathbb{R}^{d_1}$ is the reconstructed data point from the decoder. d_1 and d_2 are input and output dimension numbers, respectively (d_2 is smaller than d_1). f is the non-linear activation function. m and n represent the number of layers of the encoder and decoder, respectively. $\theta = \{\mathbf{W}_1^{(1)}, \ldots, \mathbf{W}_m^{(1)}, \mathbf{W}_1^{(2)}, \ldots, \mathbf{W}_n^{(2)}, \mathbf{b}_1^{(1)}, \ldots, \mathbf{b}_m^{(1)}, \mathbf{b}_1^{(2)}, \ldots, \mathbf{b}_n^{(2)}\}$ are model parameters.

The target of SparseAE is to minimize the reconstruction error of the output and input. Real-world graphs are usually very sparse and can be considered as binary matrices. We can treat the reconstruction as binary classification and use sigmoid function as activation function and cross-entropy as loss function to avoid gradient divergence. Due to the sparsity of graphs, the number of non-zero elements is far less than that of zero elements. To address the imbalance, we impose more penalties on the non-zero elements' reconstruction error. Thus, the loss function of sparseAE is:

$$
L_{CE} = -\frac{1}{|V|} \sum_{i=1}^{|V|} \sum_{j=1}^{d_1} (C \cdot z_{ij} \log \hat{z}_{ij} + (1 - z_{ij}) \log(1 - \hat{z}_{ij}))
\tag{3}
$$

where d_1 is the number of dimensions of the input data and C is a penalty parameter determined by the sparsity of the network.

Here we use sparseAE to learn the representation of the second-order proximity, the high-order proximity and the attribute information. Two nodes are considered to have *second-order proximity* if their neighbors are similar. To preserve the second-order proximity, we take the adjacency matrix as input and minimize the cross-entropy in SparseAE. The loss function is defined as follows:

$$
L_s = -\frac{1}{|V|^2} \sum_{i=1}^{|V|} \sum_{j=1}^{|V|} (C_s \cdot s_{ij} \log \hat{s}_{ij} + (1 - s_{ij}) \log(1 - \hat{s}_{ij})).
\tag{4}
$$

Here, s_{ij} is the lable smoothing result of a_{ij} so that we can avoid the overfiting, i.e., $s_{ij} = (1 - \epsilon)a_{ij} + \frac{\epsilon}{|V|}$ where ϵ is a smoothing parameter between 0 and 1. $\hat{\mathbf{s}}_i \in \mathbb{R}^{|V|}$ is the reconstruction of $\mathbf{s}_i \in \mathbb{R}^{|V|}$.

Similar to the second-order proximity, the *high-order proximity* considers whether two nodes' k-hop neighbors are similar. We can approximately compute such a high-order proximity matrix by truncated random walks (DeepWalk [16], Node2vec [5], etc.). By replacing the adjacency matrix with a high-order proximity matrix, we can get the loss function for high-order proximity as:

$$L_h = -\frac{1}{|V|^2} \sum_{i=1}^{|V|} \sum_{j=1}^{|V|} (C_h \cdot h'_{ij} \log \hat{h}'_{ij} + (1 - h'_{ij}) \log(1 - \hat{h}'_{ij})). \tag{5}$$

Similarly, we can get the loss function for attribute representation by taking the node attribute matrix X as the input of sparseAE:

$$L_x = -\frac{1}{|V|} \sum_{i=1}^{|V|} \sum_{j=1}^{l} (C_x \cdot x'_{ij} \log \hat{x}'_{ij} + (1 - x'_{ij}) \log(1 - \hat{x}'_{ij})). \tag{6}$$

The feature-fusion module aims to fuse vector representations obtained from the feature-learning module for the downstream tasks in a supervised way. It is composed of a dropout layer, an attention layer, a fusion layer, a pooling layer and a fully-connected layer, as depicted in Fig. 1. The dropout layer is used to avoid over-fitting. An attention layer is then used to express the different importance of different kinds of information. The fusion layer fuses t types of vectors using a fusion model like CNN or Bi-LSTM. Then we combine the fused vector and the output from the attention layer together, and use a pooling layer to reduce the embedding dimensions. Finally, we use a fully-connected layer to predict the downstream tasks. The output dimensionality of the fully-connected layer depends on the downstream tasks to be solved. It will be 2 if the downstream task is a link prediction problem, and will equal to the number of classes if it is a node classification task. The loss function is:

$$L_{FUSION} = -\frac{1}{|V|} \sum_{i=1}^{|V|} y_i \log \hat{y}_i \tag{7}$$

where y_i is the ground truth of the class label that the i-th node belongs to, and the predicted value is $\hat{y}_i = \arg \max_{1 \le j \le c} prob_{ij}$ where $prob_{ij}$ is the probability of the i-th node belonging to the j-th class.

4   Experiments

We compare our model with the representative state-of-the-art network embedding methods on two classic downstream tasks, node classification and link prediction, which have been widely used in the literature to evaluate network embeddings [3,6,9,12,21].

Table 1. Dataset Statistics

Datasets	Nodes	Edges	Features	Labels
Citeseer	3312	4732	3703	6
Cora	2708	5429	1433	7
PubMed	19717	44338	500	3

Table 2. Node classification results (Macro-F1)

Method	Citeseer			Cora			PubMed		
	60%	70%	80%	60%	70%	80%	60%	70%	80%
LINE	0.470	0.484	0.476	0.719	0.744	0.725	0.678	0.678	0.678
SDNE	0.393	0.394	0.499	0.384	0.378	0.410	0.322	0.320	0.318
Node2Vec	0.610	0.598	0.619	0.846	0.851	0.823	0.804	0.804	0.805
LINE+Attri	0.668	0.645	0.648	0.781	0.794	0.796	0.854	0.860	0.861
SDNE+Attri	0.616	0.625	0.636	0.692	0.737	0.710	0.814	0.842	0.849
Node2Vec+Attri	0.618	0.614	0.587	0.840	0.861	0.852	0.846	0.835	0.851
GCN	0.655	0.656	0.658	0.725	0.714	0.722	0.777	0.777	0.779
ASNE	0.577	0.603	0.499	0.762	0.771	0.788	0.854	0.859	0.857
GraphRNA	0.525	0.598	0.637	0.663	0.702	0.697	0.860	0.864	0.863
GraphSAGE	0.682	0.692	0.689	0.834	0.850	0.854	0.814	0.817	0.805
FANE	**0.699**	**0.713**	**0.723**	**0.871**	**0.879**	**0.874**	**0.883**	**0.887**	**0.891**

4.1 Experimental Settings

Datasets. We conducted experiments on three real-world attributed networks Citeseer, Cora and Pubmed ([17]). Data statistics are shown in Table 1.

Baselines. Our baselines are selected from two genres. LINE [18], SDNE [21] and Node2vec [5] only utilize network structure information. We also use the output of SparseAE to enhance their embedding results and denote the enhanced versions as LINE+Attri, SDNE+Attri, Node2vec+Attri respectively. GCN [11], GraphSAGE [6], ASNE [12], GraphRNA [10] take advantage of both network structure and node attributes. For intepretation about these baselines, please refer to Sect. 2.

Parameter Setting. SparseAE uses five fully-connected layers, and their dimensionalities are [D, 512, 256, 512, D], respectively, where D is the input size. The label smoothing parameter ϵ is set to 0.001. We generate 100 random walks with length 5 for each node. The dropout rate is 0.2. We use the Bi-LSTM model as the default fusion layer. The merge-mode of Bi-LSTM is set as "concat". We report the average results by repeating each process five times.

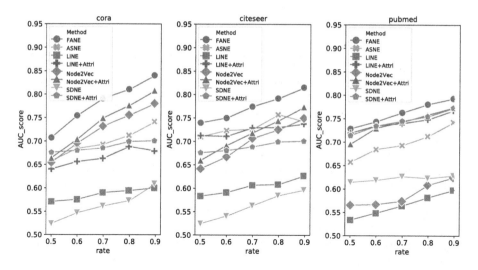

Fig. 2. Link prediction results on Citerseer, Cora and Pubmed

4.2 Experiment Results

Results of node classification and link prediction are shown in Table 2 and Fig. 2, respectively.

For node classification, we experiment with different training set ratios ($\rho \in \{60\%, 70\%, 80\%\}$). We can see that our model FANE achieves the best results on all the datasets. The performance of methods that originally ignore attributes (Node2Vec, LINE, and SDNE) can be significantly improved through a simple connection with the attribute information obtained by SparseAE.

For link prediction, we randomly keep a certain proportion of edges as the training sets and randomly add the same number of negative samples. Since FANE successfully captures the lower-order proximity, high-order proximity, and attribute information, it performs much better than these baseline methods.

5   Conclusion and Further Work

In this paper, we propose a new framework FANE for attributed network embedding, which contains a feature-learning module and a feature-fusion module. Experiments show that our method can outperform state-of-the-art methods in various downstream tasks. In the future, we will try to include more types of information to further boost the performance.

Acknowledgement. The work was supported by grants of the Natural Science Foundation 61972291, and the National Key Research and Development Project of China 2020AAA0108505.

References

1. Bhagat, S., Cormode, G., Muthukrishnan, S.: Node classification in social networks. In: Social Network Data Analytics, pp. 115–148 (2011)
2. Cao, S., Lu, W., Xu, Q.: Deep neural networks for learning graph representations. In: AAAI (2016)
3. Cui, P., Wang, X., Pei, J., Zhu, W.: A survey on network embedding. TKDE **31**(5), 833–852 (2018)
4. Du, D., Wang, H., Xu, T., Lu, Y., Liu, Q., Chen, E.: Solving link-oriented tasks in signed network via an embedding approach. In: 2017 IEEE International Conference on Systems, Man, and Cybernetics, SMC, pp. 75–80 (2017)
5. Grover, A., Leskovec, J.: node2vec: scalable feature learning for networks. In: SIGKDD, pp. 855–864. ACM (2016)
6. Hamilton, W., Ying, Z., Leskovec, J.: Inductive representation learning on large graphs. In: NeurIPS, pp. 1024–1034 (2017)
7. He, X., Deng, K., Wang, X., Li, Y., Zhang, Y., Wang, M.: Lightgcn: simplifying and powering graph convolution network for recommendation. In: SIGIR, pp. 639–648 (2020)
8. Herman, I., Melançon, G., Marshall, M.S.: Graph visualization and navigation in information visualization: A survey. TVCG **6**(1), 24–43 (2000)
9. Huang, X., Li, J., Hu, X.: Label informed attributed network embedding. In: WSDM, pp. 731–739. ACM (2017)
10. Huang, X., Song, Q., Li, Y., Hu, X.: Graph recurrent networks with attributed random walks. In: SIGKDD, pp. 732–740. ACM (2019)
11. Kipf, T.N., Welling, M.: Semi-supervised classification with graph convolutional networks. In: ICLR (2017)
12. Liao, L., He, X., Zhang, H., Chua, T.: Attributed social network embedding. TKDE **30**(12), 2257–2270 (2018)
13. Liu, M., Gao, H., Ji, S.: Towards deeper graph neural networks. In: SIGKDD, pp. 338–348 (2020)
14. Ma, Y., Ren, Z., Jiang, Z., Tang, J., Yin, D.: Multi-dimensional network embedding with hierarchical structure. In: WSDM, pp. 387–395 (2018)
15. Martínez, V., Berzal, F., Talavera, J.C.C.: A survey of link prediction in complex networks. ACM Comput. Surv. **49**(4), 69:1–69:33 (2017)
16. Perozzi, B., Al-Rfou, R., Skiena, S.: Deepwalk: online learning of social representations. In: SIGKDD, pp. 701–710. ACM (2014)
17. Sen, P., Namata, G., Bilgic, M., Getoor, L., Gallagher, B., Eliassi-Rad, T.: Collective classification in network data. AI Mag. **29**(3), 93–106 (2008)
18. Tang, J., Qu, M., Wang, M., Zhang, M., Yan, J., Mei, Q.: Line: large-scale information network embedding. In: WWW, pp. 1067–1077 (2015)
19. Tu, K., Cui, P., Wang, X., Yu, P.S., Zhu, W.: Deep recursive network embedding with regular equivalence. In: SIGKDD, pp. 2357–2366 (2018)
20. Velickovic, P., Cucurull, G., Casanova, A., Romero, A., Liò, P., Bengio, Y.: Graph attention networks. In: ICLR (2018)
21. Wang, D., Cui, P., Zhu, W.: Structural deep network embedding. In: SIGKDD, pp. 1225–1234. ACM (2016)
22. Wang, X., Lu, Y., Shi, C., Wang, R., Cui, P., Mou, S.: Dynamic heterogeneous information network embedding with meta-path based proximity. TKDE (2020)

Data Mining

What Have We Learned from OpenReview?

Gang Wang[1,2], Qi Peng[1,2], Yanfeng Zhang[1,2(✉)], and Mingyang Zhang[1,2]

[1] School of Computer Science and Engineering, Northeastern University,
Shenyang, China
[2] Key Laboratory of Intelligent Computing in Medical Image, Ministry of Education,
Shenyang, China
{wanggangneu,ffpengqi}@stumail.neu.edu.cn, zhangyf@mail.neu.edu.cn,
theremay@outlook.com

Abstract. Anonymous peer review is used by the great majority of computer science conferences. OpenReview is such a platform that aims to promote openness in peer review process. The paper, (meta) reviews, rebuttals, and final decisions are all released to public. We collect 5,527 submissions and their 16,853 reviews from the OpenReview platform. We also collect these submissions' citation data from Google Scholar and their non-peer-reviewed versions from arXiv.org. By acquiring deep insights into these data, we have several interesting findings that could help understand the effectiveness of the public-accessible double-blind peer review process. Our results can potentially help writing a paper, reviewing it, and deciding on its acceptance.

Keywords: Peer review · OpenReview · Opinion divergence

1 Introduction

Peer review is a widely adopted quality control mechanism in which the value of scientific paper is assessed by several reviewers with a similar level of competence. The primary role of the review process is to decide which papers to publish and to filter information, which is particularly true for a top conference that aspires to attract a broad readership to its papers. The novelty, significance, and technical flaws are identified by reviewers, which can help PC chair make the final decision.

Anonymous peer review (no matter single-blind or double-blind), despite the criticisms often leveled against it, is used by the great majority of computer science conferences, where the reviewers do not identify themselves to the authors. It is understandable that some authors are uncomfortable with a system in which

---

Electronic supplementary material The online version of this chapter (https://doi.org/10.1007/978-3-030-85896-4_6) contains supplementary material, which is available to authorized users.

The original version of this chapter was revised: Affiliations 1 and 2 have been corrected. The correction to this chapter is available at
https://doi.org/10.1007/978-3-030-85896-4_39

their identities are known to the reviewers while the latter remain anonymous. Authors may feel themselves defenseless against what they see as the arbitrary behavior of reviewers who cannot be held accountable by the authors for unfair comments. On the other hand, apparently, there would be even more problems if letting authors know their reviewers' identities. Reviewers would give more biased scores for fear of retaliation from the more powerful colleagues. Given this contradiction, opening up the reviews to public seems to be a good solution. The openness of reviews will force reviewers to think more carefully about the scientific issues and to write more thoughtful reviews, since PC chairs know the identities of reviewers and bad reviews would affect their reputations.

OpenReview[1] is such a platform that aims to promote openness in peer review process. The paper, (meta) reviews, rebuttals, and final decisions are all released to public. Colleagues who do not serve as reviewers can judge the paper's contribution as well as judge the fairness of the reviews by themselves. Reviewers will have more pressure under public scrutiny and force themselves to give much fairer reviews. On the other hand, previous works on peer-review analysis [10, 13, 14, 17, 20, 22] are often limited due to the lack of rejected paper instances and their corresponding reviews. Given these public reviews (for both accepted papers and rejected ones), studies towards multiple interesting questions related to peer-review are made available.

Given these public reviews, there are multiple interesting questions raised that could help us understand the effectiveness of the public-accessible double-blind peer review process: a) As known, AI conferences have extremely heavy review burden in 2020 due to the explosive number of submissions [2]. These AI conferences have to hire more non-experts to involve in the double-blind review process. How is the impact of these non-experts on the review process (Sect. 3.1)? b) Reviewers often evaluate a paper from multiple aspects, such as motivation, novelty, presentation, and experimental design. Which aspect has a decisive role in the review score (Sect. 3.2)? c) The OpenReview platform provides not only the submission details (e.g., title, keywords, and abstract) of accepted papers but also that of rejected submissions, which allows us to perform a more fine-grained cluster analysis. Given the fine-grained hierarchical clustering results, is there significant difference in the acceptance rate of different research fields (Sect. 3.3)? d) A posterior quantitative method for evaluating papers is to track their citation counts. A high citation count often indicates a more important, groundbreaking, or inspired work. OpenReview releases not only the submission details of accepted papers but also that of rejected submissions. The rejected submissions might be put on arXiv.org or published in other venues to still attract citations. This offers us opportunities to analyze the correlation between review scores and citation numbers. Is there a strong correlation between review score and citation number for a submission (Sect. 3.4)? e) Submissions might be posted on arXiv.org before the accept/reject notification, which might be the rejected ones from other conferences. They are special because they could be improved according to the rejected reviews and their authors are not anonymous. Are these submissions shown higher acceptance rate (Sect. 3.5)?

In this paper, we collect 5,527 (accepted and rejected) submissions and their 16,853 reviews from ICLR 2017–2020 venues[2] on the OpenReview platform as

---

[1] https://openreview.net/.

[2] International Conference on Learning Representations. https://iclr.cc/.

Table 1. Statistics of ICLR reviews dataset

Year	#Papers	#Authors	Accept rate	#Eeviews	Review len.
2017	489	1,417	50.1%	1,495	295.11
2018	939	2,882	49.0%	2,849	372.07
2019	1,541	4,332	32.5%	4,733	403.22
2020	2,558	7,765	26.5%	7,766	407.08
Total	5,527	16,396	39.5%	16,843	369.37

our main corpus. By acquiring deep insights into these data, we have several interesting findings and aim to answer the above raised questions quantitatively. Our submitted supplementary file also includes more data analysis results. We expect to introduce more discussions on the effectiveness of peer-review process and hope that treatment will be obtained to improve the peer-review process.

2 Dataset

ICLR has used OpenReview to launch double-blind review process for 8 years (2013–2020). Similar to other major AI conferences, ICLR adopts a reviewing workflow containing double-blind review, rebuttal, and final decision process. After paper assignment, typically three reviewers evaluate a paper independently. After the rebuttal, reviewers can access the authors' responses and other peer reviews, and accordingly modify their reviews. The program chairs then write the meta-review for each paper to make the final accept/reject decision according to the three anonymous reviews. Each official review mainly contains a review score (integer between 1 and 10), a reviewer confidence level (integer between 1 and 5), and the detailed review comments. The official reviews and meta-reviews are all open to the public on the OpenReview platform. Public colleagues can also post their reviews on OpenReview. We will present the collected dataset of submissions and reviews from OpenReview, these submissions' citation data from Google Scholar, and their non-peer-reviewed versions from arXiv.org[3].

Submissions and Reviews. We have collected 5,527 submissions and 16,853 official reviews from ICLR 2017–2020 venues on the OpenReview platform. We only use the review data since 2017 because the submissions before 2017 is too few. Though a double-blind review process is exploited, the authors' identities of the rejected submissions are also released after decision notification. Thus, we can also access the identity information for each rejected submission, which is critical in most of our analysis. Some statistics of the reviews data are listed in Table 1, in which **review len.** indicates the average length of reviews.

---

[3] These datasets and the source code for the analysis experiment are available at https://github.com/Seafoodair/Openreview/.

Citations. In order to investigate the correlation between review scores and citation numbers, we also collect the citation information from Google Scholar for all the 1,183 accepted papers from 2017 to 2019. Since the rejected submissions might be put on arXiv.org or published in other venues, they might also attract citations. We also collect the citation information for 2,054 rejected submissions that have been published elsewhere (210 for 2017, 324 for 2018, 493 for 2019, and totally 1027 rejected papers). All the citation numbers are gathered up to 20 Jan. 2020. We do not collect citation information of ICLR 2020 papers because they have not yet accumulated enough citations yet.

Table 2. Statistics of different confidence level reviews

	2017–2019					2020			
	level1	level2	level3	level4	level5	level1	level2	level3	level4
#Reviews	74	455	2,330	4,612	1,600	1,104	2,554	2,659	1,449
Fraction	0.80%	5.01%	25.67%	50.81%	17.71%	14.22%	32.89%	34.24%	18.66%

arXiv Submissions. In order to investigate whether the submissions that have been posted on arXiv.org before notification have a higher acceptance rate, we also crawl the arXiv versions of ICLR 2017–2020 submissions if they exist. We record the details of an arXiv preprint if its title matches an ICLR submission title. Note that, their contents might be slightly different. We totally find 1,158 matched arXiv papers and 948 among them were posted before notification (178/150 for 2017, 103/79 for 2018, 420/303 for 2019, and 457/416 for 2020) up to 18 Feb 2020.

3 Results Learned from Open Reviews

3.1 How Is the Impact of Non-expert Reviewers?

Due to the extensively increasing amount of submissions, ICLR 2020 hired much more reviewer volunteers. There were complaints about the quality of reviews (47% of the reviewers have not published in the related areas [2]). Similar scenarios have been observed in other AI conferences, such as NIPS, CVPR, and AAAI. Many authors complain that their submissions are not well evaluated because the assigned "non-expert" reviewers lack of enough technical background and cannot understand their main contributions. How is the impact of these "non-experts" on the review process? In this subsection, we aim to answer the question through quantitative data analysis (Table 2).

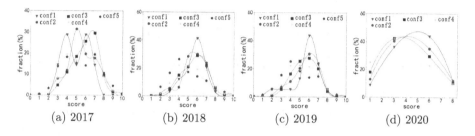

Fig. 1. The review score distributions of different confidence level (conf) reviews

Review Score Distribution. For ICLR 2017–2019, reviewer gives a review score (integer) from 1 to 10, and is asked to select a confidence level (integer) between 1 and 5. For ICLR 2020, reviewer gives a rating score in $\{1, 3, 6, 8\}$ and should select an experience assessment score (similar to confidence score) between 1 and 4. We divide the reviews into multiple subsets according to their confidence levels. Figure 1 shows the smoothed review score distributions for each subset of reviews. For 2018–2020, we consistently observe that the scores of reviews with confidence level 1 and 2 are likely to be higher than those reviews with confidence level 4 and 5. The trend of ICLR 2017 is not clear because it contains too few samples to be statistically significant (e.g., only 7 level-1 reviews). In 2017–2019, the lowest confidence level reviews has an average review score 5.675, while the highest confidence level reviews has an average review score 4.954. In 2020, the numbers for the lowest and highest confidence level reviews are 4.726 and 3.678, respectively. Our results show that the 'low-confidence reviewers (e.g., level 1 and 2) tend to be more tolerant because they may be not confident about their decision, while the high-confidence reviewers (e.g., level 4 and 5) tend to be more tough and rigorous because they may be confident in the identified weakness.

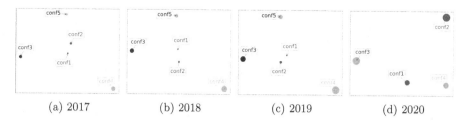

Fig. 2. The visualized layout of groups of reviews with different confidence scores. Each point indicates a group of reviews with a specific confidence level (abbrv. conf). The size of point indicates the relative number of reviews in that group. The distance between two points indicates the divergence of review scores between two groups.

Divergence Reflected by Euclidean Distance. On the other hand, peoples are worrying that non-expert reviewers are not competent to give a fair evaluation of a submission (e.g., fail to identify key contributions or fail to identify flaws) and will ruin the reputation of top conferences [2]. Particularly, these non-expert reviewers may have different opinions with the expert reviewers regarding the same paper. Actually, opinion divergence commonly exists between reviewers in the peer-review process. Each paper is typically assigned to 3 reviewers. These 3 reviewers may have significantly different review scores. In order to illustrate the difference between the reviews with different confidence scores, we first compute the euclidean distance $DIS(l_i, l_j)$ between between group l_i and group l_j as follows. Let R_{l_i, l_j} be the set of paper IDs, where each paper concurrently has both confidence-l_i review(s) and confidence-l_j review(s). Let $\overline{s_p^i}$ be paper p's average review score from l_i-confidence reviews. Then, the distance between the group of confidence-l_i reviews and that of confidence-l_j reviews is:

$$DIS(l_i, l_j) = \sqrt{\sum_{p \in R_{l_i, l_j}} \left(\overline{s_p^i} - \overline{s_p^j}\right)^2}. \tag{1}$$

After computing the distance between each pair of groups, we can construct a distance matrix. According to the distance matrix, we use t-SNE [15] to plot the visualized layout of different groups of reviews of each year in Fig. 2. For ICLR 2017–2019, we can see similar layout, where conf1 reviews are close to conf2 reviews in the central part and the groups of conf3, conf4, and conf5 locate around. The group of conf4 reviews is far apart from the most professional reviews (conf5). In ICLR 2020, there are 4 confidence levels. Surprisingly, we observe that the most professional reviews (conf4) and least professional reviews (conf1) are closest to each other. Conf2 reviews and conf3 reviews are both far apart from conf4 reviews.

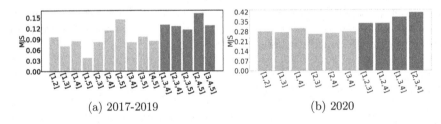

(a) 2017-2019   (b) 2020

Fig. 3. MJS divergence of different combinations of different confidence level reviews

Divergence Reflected by Jensen-Shannon Divergence. By using euclidean distance, we can only measure the divergence of two sets of different level reviews. Inspired by Jensen-Shannon Divergence for multiple distributions (MJS) [4], we design the MJS metric to measure the divergence between multiple sets of reviews. The MJS of m sets ($m \geq 2$) of different confidence reviews is defined as follows:

$$MJS(l_1, \ldots, l_m) = \frac{1}{m} \sum_{i \in \{l_1, \ldots, l_m\}} \left(\frac{1}{|R_{l_1, \ldots, l_m}|} \sum_{p \in R_{l_1, \ldots, l_m}} \overline{s_p^i} \cdot log\left(\frac{\overline{s_p^i}}{s_p^{[1,m]}}\right) \right), \tag{2}$$

where $R_{l_1,...,l_m}$ is the set of paper IDs, where each paper concurrently has reviews with confidence levels $l_1, \ldots, l_m$, $|\cdot|$ returns the size of a set, $\overline{s_p^i}$ is paper p's average review score of l_i-confidence reviews, and $\overline{s_p^{[1,m]}}$ is paper p's average review score of reviews with confidence levels $l_1, \ldots, l_m$. The bigger the MJS is, the significant the opinion divergence is. A nice property of MJS metric is that it is symmetric, e.g., $MJS(i,j) = MJS(j,i)$ and $MJS(i,j,k) = MJS(k,j,i)$. We measure the MJS divergence of different combinations of confidence levels and show the results in Fig. 3. Note that, the results of combinations that contain less than 10 reviews are not shown since they are too few to be statistically significant. In 2017–2019 the MJS divergence between conf1 reviews and conf5 reviews is the smallest. In 2020, it shows bigger divergence than 2017–2019 on different combinations but relatively similar divergence results among different combinations. In addition, a combination of three different confidence levels is likely to result in bigger divergence than a combination of two confidence levels.

How is the Impact of Non-expert Reviewers? All these facts demonstrate that the opinion divergence is not greater after introducing more non-expert reviewers. We also observe that the opinion divergence between non-expert reviewers and other reviewers is often relatively small. The reason behind might be that the non-expert reviewers often have a more neutral opinion rather than clear yes or no. They are more cautious to give positive or negative recommendations.

3.2 Which Aspects Play Important Roles in Review Score?

Reviewers often evaluate a paper from various aspects. There are five most important aspects, i.e., novelty, motivation, experimental results, completeness of related workers, and presentation quality. Some conferences provide a peer-review questionnaire that requires reviewer to evaluate a paper from various aspects and give a score with respect to each aspect. Unfortunately, ICLR does not ask reviewers to answer such a questionnaire. Then a question arises accordingly. Which aspects play more important roles in determining the review score? We aim to answer this question by analyzing the sentiment of each aspect.

Corpus Creation. For each review, we first extract the related sentences that describe different aspects by matching a set of predefined keywords. The keywords "novel, novelty, originality, and idea" are used to identify a sentence that describes novelty of the paper, "motivation, motivate, and motivated" are used to identify a sentence related to motivation, "experiments, empirically, empirical, experimental, evaluation, results, data, dataset, and data set" are used to identify a sentence related to experiment results, "related work, survey, review, previous work, literature, cite, and citation" are used to identify a sentence related to the completeness of related work, and "presentation, writing, written, structure, organization, structured, and explained" are used to identify a sentence related to presentation quality. We have collected a corpus containing 95,208 sentences which are divided into five subsets corresponding to the five aspects. Specifically, we have 11,916 sentences related to "novelty", 5,107 sentences related to "motivation", 62,446 sentences related to "experimental results", 8,710 sentences related to "completeness of related work", and 7,029 sentences related to "presentation quality".

Automatic Annotation. In order to train a sentiment analysis model, we need to first annotate enough number of sentences with sentiment label (i.e., positive, negative, and neutral). However, this workload of manual annotation is huge due to the large size of review corpus. Fortunately, we find a possibility of automatic annotation after analyzing the reviews. A large number of reviewers write their positive reviews and negative reviews separately by using the keywords such as "strengths/weaknesses", "pros/cons", "strong points/weak points", "positive aspects/negative aspects", and so on. We segment the review text and identify the positive/negative sentences by looking up these keywords. The boundaries are identified when meeting an opposite sentiment word for the first time. By intersecting the set of positive/negative sentences with the set of aspect-specific sentences, we obtain a relatively large set of sentiment-annotated corpus for each aspect. Particularly, we have 2,893 sentiment-annotated sentences for "novelty", 1,057 for "motivation", 8,956 for "experimental results", 1,402 for "completeness of related work", 1,644 for "presentation quality", and 15,952 in total. We also manually annotate 6,095 sentences including 1,227 corrected automatically annotated sentences since some neutral sentences are incorrectly annotated with positive or negative sentiment. Finally, we have 20,820 labeled sentences[4], i.e., 21.87% of the total number of sentences (95,208) in corpus. Note that, there might be more than one sentences describing one aspect but having different sentiments. In such a case, we label the sentiment by a majority vote.

Sentiment Analysis. Given these five datasets including the labeled data, we perform sentiment analysis for each aspect using a pretrained text model ELECTRA [7] which was recently proposed in ICLR 2020 with state-of-the-art performance. The results demonstrate that ELECTRA achieves better contextual sentiment analysis compared to the CSNN [11] model. The detailed hyperparameter settings of ELECTRA are described in our support materials. We split the annotated dataset of each aspect into training/validation/test sets (8:1:1), and use 10-fold cross validation to train five sentiment prediction models for the five aspects. We obtain five accuracy results 93.96%, 88.46%, 94.99%, 85.12%, and 93.38% for novelty, motivation, experimental results, completeness of related workers, and presentation quality, respectively. We then use the whole annotated dataset of each aspect to train the corresponding sentiment analysis model and use this model to predict the sentiment of the other unlabeled sentences of each aspect. Finally, for each review, we can obtain the sentiment score of each aspect. Note that, some individual aspects might not be mentioned in a review, which are labeled with neutral.

---

[4] All of the annotated data including manually annotated ones are publicly available at at https://github.com/Seafoodair/Openreview/.

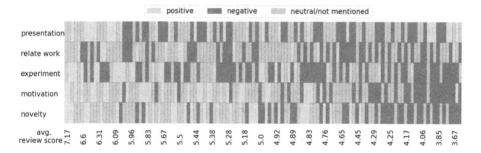

Fig. 4. The sentiment of each aspect vs. the review score. Each column represents a group of reviews with the same combination of aspect sentiments. These groups are sorted in the descending order of the average review score of a group of reviews.

Sentiment of Each Aspect vs. Review Score. Given the sentiment analysis results of all aspects of each review and the review score, we perform the correlation analysis. We group the reviews with the same combination of aspect sentiments and compute the average review score of each group. The groups that receive less than 3 reviews are not considered since they have too few samples to be statistically significant. We visualize the result as shown in Fig. 4. We can see that the higher review score often comes with more positive aspects from a macro perspective, which is under expectation. We observe that most of the reviews with score higher than 6 do NOT have negative comments on novelty, motivation, and presentation, but may allow some flaws in related work and experiment. The reviewers that have overall positive to the paper are likely to pose improvement suggestions on related work and experiment to make the paper perfect. The presentation quality and experiment seem to be mentioned more frequently than the other aspects, and the positive sentiment on presentation is distributed more evenly from high-score reviews to low-score reviews. This implies that presentation does not play important role in making the decision. It is also interesting that there is no review in which all aspects are positive or negative. It is unlikely that a paper is perfect in all aspects or has no merit. Reviewers are also likely to be more rigorous in 'papers and be more tolerant with poor papers.

Causality Analysis. In order to explore which aspect determines the final review score, we perform causal inference following [9]. Besides the above five aspects, we also include the factor of reviewer confidence. The process of causal analysis includes four steps: modeling, intervention, evaluation, and inference. In the modeling process, we use multivariate linear regression method [3] to perform regression task on the ICLR reviews dataset, where the six evaluated parameters are the sentiment scores of the five review aspects and a reviewer confidence score, and the regression label is the review score. Each parameter is standardized to $[-1,1]$. To avoid randomness of model training, we launch 1000 times of training and obtain the average MSE (Mean Square Error) 0.24. The intervention process removes each factor x one by one and performs multiple times of model evaluation to obtain multiple average MSE results, each corresponding to an x-absence model. In the absence of overfitting, the MSE value of any x-absence model should be larger than 0.24. The MSE value of the x-absence model implies the causality. A larger MSE value of an x-absence model implies that the factor x is more dominant in determining the final score, and vice versa. In the inference process, we compare the MSE values to infer the causality. The average MSE values of the reviewer confidence, novelty, motivation, experiment, related work, and presentation are 0.84, 0.77, 0.34, 0.86, 0.33, and 0.34, respectively. We observe that the factors of reviewer confidence, novelty, and experiment change the MSE greatly, so they are more dominant in determining the final score.

3.3   Which Research Field Has Higher/Lower Acceptance Rate?

AI conferences consider a broad range of subject areas. Authors are often asked to pick the most relevant areas that match their submissions. Area chair could exist who makes decisions for the submissions of a certain research area. Different areas may receive different number of submissions and also may have different acceptance rates. Program chairs sometimes announce the number of submissions and the acceptance rate of each area in the opening event of a conference, which could somehow indicate the popularity of each area. But, the classification by areas is coarse. A more fine-grained classification that provides more specific information is desired. Thanks to the more detailed submission information provided by OpenReview, we utilize the title, abstract, and keywords of each submission to provide a more fine-grained clustering result and gather the statistics of acceptance rate of each cluster of submissions.

We first concatenate the title, abstract, keywords of each ICLR 2020 submission and preprocess them by removing stop words, tokenizing, stemming list, etc. We leverage an AI terminology dictionary [1] during the tokenizing process to make sure that an AI terminology containing multiple words is not split. We then formulate term-document matrix (i.e., AI term-submission matrix) by applying TF-IDF and calculate cosine distance matrix. The size of the term-document TF-IDF matrix for ICLR 2020 is 12436 × 2558, and the size of the cosine distance matrix is 2558 × 2558. We then apply the Ward clustering algorithm [12] on the matrix to obtain submission clusters. Ward clustering is an agglomerative hierarchical clustering method, meaning that at each stage, the pair of clusters with minimum between-cluster distance are merged. We use silhouette coefficient to finalize the number of clusters and plot a dendrogram to visualize the hierarchical clustering result as shown in Fig. 5.

From Fig. 5, we observe three aspects of insights. **(a) Overall Structure of Deep Learning Research**. We observe the correlation between research topics. For example, the submissions in the left part belong to reinforcement learning field (20), which is far apart from all the other research topics (because it is the last merged cluster and its distance to the other clusters is more than 27). Another independent research field is Graph Neural Networks (GNNs) (49), as a promising field, becomes really hot in only 2–3 years, which distinguishes

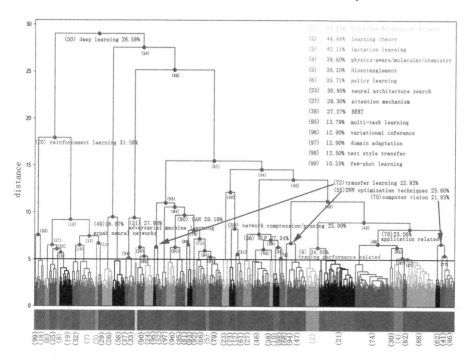

Fig. 5. Visualized hierarchical clustering result of ICLR 2020 submissions. Each leaf node represents a submission. Cosine distance 5 is selected as the threshold to control the granularity of leaf-level clusters. There are 99 clusters in total, including both fine-grained clusters and coarse-grained clusters. Clusters are numbered in the order of their acceptance rate. The color of keywords indicates the acceptance rate of that cluster. Light green means a high acceptance rate, while light red means a low acceptance rate. The keywords of some typical clusters are labeled. (Color figure online)

itself from others by focusing on graph structure. Adversarial Machine Learning (31) is also an independent research field that attempts to fool models through malicious input and different from others. The next independent subject is Generative Adversarial Networks (GANs) (80). But GANs is not completely independent since we found that many submissions on NLP (36) and CV (75) are mixed with GANs as well. We also observe that Transfer Learning (72) is close to GANs, since some works have applied transfer learning to GANs. Most of the submissions in the right part are applications related (e.g., vision, audio, NLP, biology, chemistry, and robotics). They are mixed with DNN optimization techniques since many optimizations are proposed to improve DNN on a specific application field. **(b) Popularity Difference between Clusters**. We observe that multiple areas attract large amount of submission. For example, Reinforcement Learning (20), GNNs (49), GANs (80), NLP (36), and Computer Vision (75) have attracted more than 50% of the submissions, which are really hot topics in today's deep learning research. **(c) Acceptance Rate Difference between Clusters**. There exists significant difference on acceptance rate

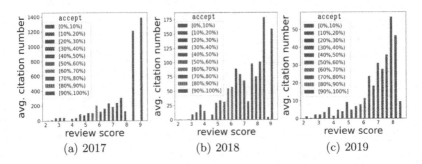

Fig. 6. The histogram of citation numbers against 0.3-intervals of average review score

between clusters, say ranging from 53.33% to 10.53%. The cluster of submissions on "Black-Box Adversarial Attacks" has the highest acceptance rate (53.33%), which is a subject belongs to "Adversarial Machine Learning" area. The top-6 highest acceptance rate topics are listed in the figure. The cluster of submissions on "Few-Shot Learning" has the lowest acceptance rate (10.53%), which is a subject belongs to "Reinforcement Learning" area. The top-5 lowest acceptance rate topics are listed in the figure. We also list some typical topics in the figure. For example, the cluster on "Graph Neural Networks (49)" has an acceptance rate of 26.67%. The cluster on "BERT (38)" has an acceptance rate of 27.27%. The cluster on "GANs (80)" has an acceptance rate of 20.18%. The cluster on "Reinforcement Learning (20)" has an acceptance rate of 31.58%.

3.4 Review Score Vs. Citation Number

The citation number quantitatively indicates a paper's impact. In this subsection, we show several interesting results on the correlation between review scores and citation numbers.

Is There a Strong Correlation between Review Score and Citation Number? OpenReview releases not only the submission details and reviews of the accepted papers but also that of the rejected submissions. These rejected submissions might be put on arXiv.org or published in other venues and still make an impact. We collect the citation number information of both accepted papers and rejected papers and study the correlation between their review scores and their citation numbers. We plot the histogram of average citation numbers of ICLR 2017–2019 submissions as shown in Fig. 6. The papers are divided into multiple subsets according to their review scores. Each bin of the histogram corresponds to a subset of papers with similar review scores (with an interval of 0.3). Then the average citation number of each subset is calculated. The color of bin indicates the acceptance rate of the corresponding subset of papers. From the figure, we can observe that the papers with higher review score are likely to have higher citation numbers, which is under expectation.

We further investigate the citation numbers of individual papers as shown in Fig. 7. Each point represents a paper. Green color indicates an accepted paper and red color indicates a rejected one. The papers are sorted on the x-axis in the ascending order of their review scores. The distribution of citation numbers is messy. We can see that many rejected papers gain a large number of citations (i.e., red points in the top-left part), which is a bit surprised. Generally speaking, the accepted papers will attract more attentions since they are officially published in ICLR. However, the rejected papers may be accepted later at other venues and still attract attentions. In addition, a few papers with high review score are rejected (i.e., red points on the right side). We observe that the reject decision does not impact their citation numbers. Though rejected, the papers with higher review score are still likely to have higher citation numbers.

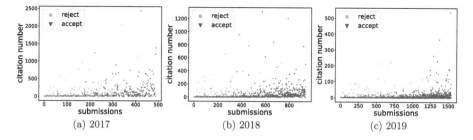

(a) 2017   (b) 2018   (c) 2019

Fig. 7. The distribution of citation numbers of individual papers, where the papers on the x-axis are sorted in the ascending order of their review scores (Color figure online)

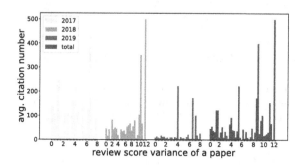

Fig. 8. Review score variance of a paper vs. average citation number

Do Great Papers Gain More Diverse Review Scores? People always have diverse opinions on the breakthrough works. Reviewer A thinks it novel and is happy to give higher scores, but reviewer B may think it too crazy or unrealistic and reject it. There might be a big debate between reviewers. But it is usually hard to reach consensus. We investigate the relationship between the variance of review scores of a submission and its citation number. We group papers according to their review score variances and calculate the average citation number of each group. Figure 8 shows the statistical results of the submissions of ICLR 2017–2019. We observe that the papers that have large number of citations are indeed more likely to gain diverse review scores. Note that a paper that has diverse review scores (big review score variance) does not necessarily have high review scores.

3.5 Do Submissions Posted on ArXiv Have Higher Acceptance Rate?

We found 1,083 submissions that have been posted on arXiv before accept/reject notification[5], which account for about 19.59% of the total submissions. The arXiv versions are not anonymous, which bring unfairness to the double-blind review process. We refer to the submissions that have been posed on arXiv before notification as "arXived submissions". We investigate the acceptance rates of the arXived and non-arXived submissions. The acceptance rates of the arXived submissions in 2017, 2018, 2019, and 2020 are 59.33%, 62.39%, 45.36%, and 30.48%, respectively. The acceptance rates of the non-arXived submissions in 2017, 2018, 2019, and 2020 are 45.88%, 41.23%, 26.37%, and 17.22%, respectively. We observe that the arXived submissions have significantly higher acceptance rate than the non-arXived submissions (49.39% vs. 32.68% on average).

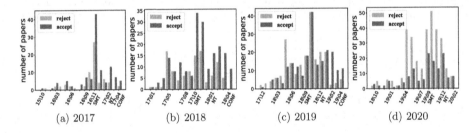

(a) 2017   (b) 2018   (c) 2019   (d) 2020

Fig. 9. The number of accepted/rejected arXived submissions posted on arXiv by month. SMT means the submission deadline. NT means the notification date. CONF means the conference date.

We think the reason should be not only anonymity but also that the arXived ICLR submissions have higher quality. These arXived submissions might attract more feedbacks from colleagues, according to which the authors can improve their manuscripts. The arXived submissions might also be the rejected ones from other conferences and might have been improved according to the rejection reviews. We also observe that some arXived submissions are posted on arXiv one year before the submission deadline. Figure 9 shows the number of arXived submissions posted on arXiv by month, including both accepted ones and rejected

---

[5] We compare paper creation date on arXiv with ICLR official notification date.

ones. We can see that the papers posted on arXiv are more and more when approaching the submission deadline. There are also a large number of papers posted on arXiv between the submission date and the notification date. From the aspect of acceptance rate, we observe that the earlier the papers are posted on arXiv, the more likely they are accepted. In addition, the papers posted on arXiv after notification date have a higher acceptance rate. The reason might be that the authors cannot wait to share their research results after their papers are accepted.

4 Related Work

There exist many interesting works related to peer-review analysis. We list several related works as follows.

Ivan Stelmakh's Blog [19] shares a lot of interesting findings: First, reviewers give lower scores once they are told that a paper is a resubmission. Second, there is no evidence of herding in the discussion phase of peer review. Third, A combination of the selection and mentoring mechanisms results in reviews of at least comparable and on some metrics even higher-rated quality as compared to the conventional pool of reviews. Nihar B.Shah et al. [18] analyzed the influence of reviewer and AC bid, reviewer assignment, different types of reviewers, rebuttals and discussions, distribution across subject areas in detail. Homanga Bharadhwaj et al. [5] provide an analysis on whether there is a positive impact if his/hers paper is upload on arXiv before the submission deadline. They suggest that the paper arXived will have a higher acceptance rate. David Tran et al. [21] analyzed ICLR conferences and quantified reproducibility/randomness in review scores and acceptance decisions, and examined whether scores correlate with paper impact. Their results suggest that there exists strong institutional bias in accept/reject decisions, even after controlling for paper quality. They analyzed the influence of scores among gender, institution, scholar reputation in detail. Emaad Manzoor et al. [16] proposed a framework to nonparametrically estimate biases expressed in text. The authors leveraged the framework to accurately detect these biases from the review text without having access to the review ratings. Birukou et al. [6] analyzed ten CS conferences and found low correlation between review scores and the impact of papers in terms of future number of citations. Gao et al. [8] predict after-rebuttal (i.e., final) scores from initial reviews and author responses. Their results suggest that a reviewer's final score is largely determined by her initial score and the distance to the other reviewers' initial scores. Li et al. [14] utilize peer review data for the citation count prediction task with a neural prediction model.

In this paper, we investigate ICLR 2017–2020's submissions and reviews data on OpenReview and show more different interesting results, e.g., the effect of low confidence reviews, the sentiment analysis of review text on different aspects, the hierarchical relationships of different research fields, etc., which have not been studied before.

5 Conclusion

We perform deep analysis on the dataset including review texts collected from OpenReivew, the paper citation information collected from GoogleScholar, and the non-peer-reviewed papers from arXiv.org. All of these collected data are publicly available on Github, which will help other researchers identify novel research opportunities in this dataset. More importantly, we investigate the answers to several interesting questions regarding the peer-review process. We aim to provide hints to answer these questions quantitatively based on our analysis results. We believe that our results can potentially help writing a paper, reviewing it, and deciding about its acceptance.

Acknowledgement. This work was supported by the National Natural Science Foundation of China (62072082, U1811261), and the Key R&D Program of Liaoning Province (2020JH 2/10100037).

References

1. Artificial-intelligence-terminology (2020). https://github.com/jiqizhixin/Artificial-Intelligence-Terminology
2. Some metadata for those curious about their #iclr2020 (2020). https://twitter.com/cHHillee/status/1191823707100131329
3. Allison, P.D.: Multiple Regression: A primer. Pine Forge Press, Thousand Oaks (1999)
4. Aslam, J.A., Pavlu, V.: Query hardness estimation using Jensen-Shannon divergence among multiple scoring functions. In: ECIR, pp. 198–209 (2007)
5. Bharadhwaj, H., Turpin, D., Garg, A., Anderson, A.: De-anonymization of authors through arxiv submissions during double-blind review. arXiv e-prints pp. arXiv-2007 (2020)
6. Birukou, A., et al.: Alternatives to peer review: novel approaches for research evaluation. Front. Comput. Neurosci. **5**, 56 (2011)
7. Clark, K., Luong, M.T., Le, Q.V., Manning, C.D.: Electra: Pre-training text encoders as discriminators rather than generators. In: ICLR (2020)
8. Gao, Y., Eger, S., Kuznetsov, I., Gurevych, I., Miyao, Y.: Does my rebuttal matter? insights from a major NLP conference. In: NAACL-HLT, pp. 1274–1290 (2019)
9. Gelman, A., Hill, J.: Causal inference using regression on the treatment variable. In: Analytical Methods for Social Research, pp. 167–198. Cambridge University Press (2006)
10. Ghosal, T., Verma, R., Ekbal, A., Bhattacharyya, P.: Deepsentipeer: Harnessing sentiment in review texts to recommend peer review decisions. In: ACL, pp. 1120–1130 (2019)
11. Ito, T., Tsubouchi, K., Sakaji, H., Yamashita, T., Izumi, K.: Contextual sentiment neural network for document sentiment analysis. Data Sci. Eng. **5**(2), 180–192 (2020)
12. Joe, H., Ward, J.: Hierarchical grouping to optimize an objective function. J. Am. Stat. Assoc. **58**(301), 236–244 (1963)
13. Kang, D., et al.: A dataset of peer reviews (peerread): Collection, insights and NLP applications. In: NAACL. pp. 1647–1661 (2018)

14. Li, S., Zhao, W.X., Yin, E.J., Wen, J.: A neural citation count prediction model based on peer review text. In: EMNLP, pp. 4913–4923 (2019)
15. Maaten, L.V.D., Hinton, G.: Visualizing data using t-sne. J. Mach. Learn. Res. **9**, 2579–2605 (2008)
16. Manzoor, E., Shah, N.B.: Uncovering latent biases in text: Method and application to peer review. arXiv e-prints pp. arXiv-2010 (2020)
17. Price, S., Flach, P.A.: Computational support for academic peer review: a perspective from artificial intelligence. Commun. ACM **60**(3), 70–79 (2017)
18. Shah, N.B., Tabibian, B., Muandet, K., Guyon, I., Von Luxburg, U.: Design and analysis of the nips 2016 review process. J. Mach. Learn. Res. **19**, 1–34 (2018)
19. Stelmakh, I.: Experiments with the ICML 2020 peer-review process. https://blog.ml.cmu.edu/2020/12/01/icml2020exp/
20. Stelmakh, I., Shah, N.B., Singh, A.: On testing for biases in peer review. In: NeurIPS, pp. 5287–5297 (2019)
21. Tran, D., et al.: An open review of openreview: A critical analysis of the machine learning conference review process. arXiv preprint arXiv:2010.05137 (2020)
22. Wang, K., Wan, X.: Sentiment analysis of peer review texts for scholarly papers. SIGIR, pp. 175–184 (2018)

Unsafe Driving Behavior Prediction for Electric Vehicles

Jiaxiang Huang, Hao Lin, and Junjie Yao[✉]

East China Normal University, Shanghai, China
{51184501018,51205901039}@stu.ecnu.edu.cn,
junjie.yao@cs.ecnu.edu.cn

Abstract. There is an increasing availability of electric vehicles in recent years. With the revolutionary motors and electric modules within the electric vehicles, the instant reactions bring up not only improved driving experience but also the unexpected unsafe driving accidents. Unsafe driving behavior prediction is a challenging tasks, due to the complex spatial and temporal scenarios. However, the rich sensor data collected in the electric vehicles shed light on the possible driving behavior profiling.

In this paper, based on a recent electric vehicle dataset, we analyze and categorize the unsafe driving behaviors into several classes. We then design a deep learning based multi-feature fusion approach for the unsafe driving behavior prediction framework. The proposed approach is able to distinguish the unsafe behaviors from normal ones. Improved performance is also demonstrated in the different feature analysis of unsafe behaviors.

Keywords: Electric vehicles · Feature fusion · Unsafe behavior prediction

1 Introduction

Electric Vehicles (EVs) have developed rapidly in recent years, and taking over the market share of traditional internal combustion engine vehicles [4,20]. The increasing popularity of EVs brings about concerns for the driving safety. There have been many works [10,12,13,16,23] on driving patterns recognition and abnormal/unsafe driving behaviors detection. Here, the problem is to identify relationships between vehicle driving features. Most of the methods are based on the collected different kinds of sensors, indicating vehicle speed, three-axis accelerations, steering angle, etc. However, existing works [11,14,15] are limited in the low frequency and inadequate sensor data collection.

Thanks to the wide usage of sensor technologies within the EVs or smartphones, researchers can obtain plenty of vehicle data via different kinds of sensors, in a more real-time manner. In this paper, we conduct empirical studies

J. Yao—This work was supported by NSFC grant 61972151.

on several days' driving traces collected from some new types of electric taxis. There are more than 50 dimensions of features collected by sensor data and the frequency 1 Hz.

Figure 1 shows the comparison of a safe driving period and a danger driving period in two-axis accelerations, vehicle speed and trajectories feature dimensions. We can see that features of *safe period* are varying in a small margin and the trajectories don't have many sharp trends, while in the *danger period*, features fluctuate in a certain extent and there are often sharp turns in trajectories.

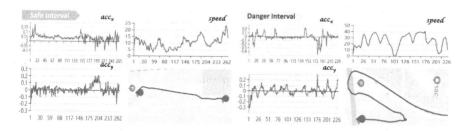

Fig. 1. Comparison of safe/unsafe driving behaviors

To predict the unsafe behavior earlier is a challenging task, due to the time constraint and the complex spatial-temporal scenarios. Following the abnormal/unsafe driving behavior classification [23], here we categorize the unsafe driving behavior into four classes, i.e., sharp left turn, sharp right turn, sudden acceleration and sudden deceleration. We label these as unsafe/risky types and while the others are normal/safe ones.

Unsafe Driving Behavior Prediction is a time series problem. Most of the time series classification approaches [8,18] have difficulties in dealing with the huge amounts of features but have promising performance even when the training set is small. In contrast, deep learning based methods [5,7] can learn low-dimensional features but suffer from a shortage of labeled data. Recently, there are some weak supervision/semi-supervised approaches, i.e., [26].

In this paper, based on the rich input features, we proposed to utilize the feature interactions for the unsafe behavior prediction. Specifically, we model the input features into the low dimensional embedded representation. We then fuse them with the help of attention mechanism. We later design multiple layers of deep learning model for the behavior prediction. We conduct extensive experiments to evaluate the feature importance of driving behaviors classification on our dataset.

To summarize, this paper has the following contributions:

- We conduct data mining and danger behavior identification on a real electric vehicle dataset.
- We study on the deep learning based approach for fine granularity driving behavior prediction.

– We analyze and compare the sensor feature importance for driving behavior prediction.

The rest of this paper is organized as follows: Sect. 2 discusses related work, Sect. 3 introduces preliminaries of the data and problem definition. Section 4 introduces the proposed method. The experimental results on electric taxis dataset are presented in Sect. 5, and the paper concludes with a summary of the research in Sect. 6.

2   Related Work

In this section, we briefly review the related literature of this work.

Electric Vehicles: There are many works on sensor data analysis from electric vehicles. [14–17,21,23] make use of smartphone sensing of vehicle dynamics for pattern recognition and driving behavior modeling, while [6,10–13] are based on sensors within the vehicles.

In the problem of safety risk estimation or driver identification, [23] introduced many patterns of abnormal driving behaviors such as weaving, swerving, slideslipping, fast U-turn, sudden braking, etc. The comparison of three low-pass filtering methods to deal with high frequency noises in raw sensor data.

This paper focuses on the electric vehicle data in a fine granularity and design effective pattern mining approaches.

Time Series Classification: In many cases, conventional machine learning algorithms such as SVM [3], Random Forest [1] and XGBOOST [2] can get fine performance in multivariate time series classification. However, as aforementioned, these methods may suffer from a lot of work handling raw time series manually, especially when the data is in multivariate format.

Recently, deep learning based methods [5,22,24–26] achieve promising performance in multivariate time series classification task. [7] proposed a model consisting of an LSTM layer and stacked CNN layer along with a Squeeze-and-Excitation block to generate latent features. [5] presented an encoding scheme to convert time series into sparse spatial temporal spike patterns along with a new training algorithm to classify the patterns. [26] takes advantage of attentional prototype learning. Different from the conventional approaches, deep learning based methods learn the latent features by training convolutional or recurrent networks with large-scale labeled data.

Feature Fusion: [10,12,13] notes that abnormal driving behaviors can be identified using threshold evaluation over sensor data. Specifically, [10] introduced that if the absolute value of acceleration on the y-axis is greater than 4 m/s^2, the vehicle may experience a sudden acceleration/braking. When there is a gyroscope, the sharp turn can be identified if the absolute value of angular speed on the z-axis is greater than 0.45 rad/s. [12] introduced that when the vehicle speed is between 60–100 km/h, the sudden acceleration/braking can be identified the same as [10], but the sharp turn can then be identified if the absolute value of acceleration on the x-axis is greater than 3 m/s^2 without the need of a gyroscope. However plenty of analysis on sensor data, most work scarcely used the deep learning methods to help model the data and improve the performance. [23] did a lot of work on extracting and selecting features manually and used SVM as the classifier for identifying abnormal driving behaviors. [11] made use of four basic machine learning algorithms including KNNs, RFs, MLP, Adaboost and a ensembled model based on them for driver identification but the overall performance isn't good enough.

In this work, we follow the prototype learning classification method to tackle the safety risk labeling problem for electric taxis run data with multi-dimensional features.

3 Preliminary

In this section, we first describe the used electric vehicle dataset and then illustrate the problem of driving behavior prediction.

3.1 Electric Vehicle Dataset

The raw data is collected from different sensors embedded in electric vehicles, i.e., speedometer, accelerometer, pressuremeter, gps, and turn-lights indicators. There are more than 50 collected feature dimensions including longitude, latitude, speed, 3-axis acceleration, accelerator pressure and brake pressure, and etc. The traces are in several days, and the sensor frequency 1 Hz.

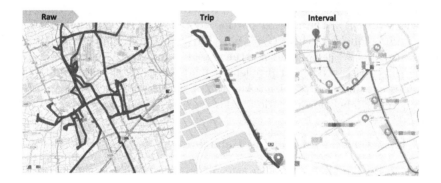

Fig. 2. Complete trajectory, trip and specific period in the electric vehicle.

While the trip starts from that a vehicle begins to run and ends with charging, the time span of a trip is too long for a specific driving behavior analysis because a danger behavior usually occurs in a sudden moment. Therefore, we further extract much shorter travel data from trip data, denoted as periods. We use the threshold method to do the extraction. The comparison of trajectories in raw, trip and period data is visualized in Fig. 2.

There are more than 50 dimensions of features collected by sensors, but most of them are not correlated with driving behaviors. Therefore, based on data characteristics and inspired by [10,12,16,23], the features we choose for further exploration and experiments include *vehicle speed, x&y -axis accelerations, accelerator pressure, brake pressure* and *turn lights indicators.*

Due to environmental dynamics, there are many high frequency noises in the collected raw data which has an impact on analyzing the dynamics of different driving behaviors. The period extraction process has not taken these noises into consideration, thus we conduct low-pass filtering to the extracted period data, first to remove the high frequency noise and yet capture the statistical features presented in the traces. In this paper, we experiment with three low-pass filters in our dataset, i.e., simple moving average filter (SMAF), dynamic exponential smoothing filter (DESF) and Gaussian filter (GF). We finally select DESF as the low-pass filter to remove high frequency noises for that DESF is able to not only return the nicely fitted curve but also preserve effective features of different driving behaviors.

3.2   Problem Formulation

Given a group of period set $G = \{\mathbf{Cn}_1, \mathbf{Cn}_2, \ldots, \mathbf{Cn}_p\} \in \mathcal{R}^{p \times n \times k}$, where p is the number of periods, n is the length of each period and k is feature dimension. There is a class label y associated with each period, denoted as $\boldsymbol{y} = \{y_1, y_2, \ldots, y_p\} \in \mathcal{R}^p$, and y_i has two values to represent the safety or risk type of an period respectively.

The training set for driving behavior prediction is a tuple of labeled examples, denoted as $((G, \boldsymbol{y}))$. The labeled portion contains tuples of period set G and corresponding labels $\boldsymbol{y}$, where $G = \{\mathbf{Cn}_1, \mathbf{Cn}_2, \ldots, \mathbf{Cn}_{\tilde{p}}\}$, and $\mathbf{Cn}_i$ denotes the input features of ith period and p is the size of samples.

The safety risk prediction problem is modeled as a two-class multivariate time series classification problem. And the objective is to construct a classifier to predict class labels for an period series.

3.3   Characteristics of Driving Behaviors

In most cases, the vehicle is on a safe mode, an example is shown in Fig. 3. From Fig. 3(a) we can see that the vehicle drives almost in a straight line, and Fig. 3(b) shows that the vehicle is running in a relatively low speed which we can recognize it as a safe period, with a safety label attached to it and saved as the experimental label.

Discussed in [10,12,16,23], danger behaviors often occur when vehicles are making sharp turns or sharp speed changes. Here we define four types of danger behaviors in this paper: *sharp left turn, sharp right turn, sudden acceleration* and *sudden deceleration.*

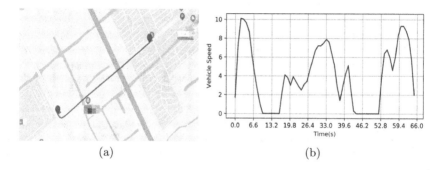

(a)   (b)

Fig. 3. (a) Visualized trajectory of a safe period. (b) Vehicle speed curve of a safe period

Sharp left turn is making an abrupt redirection towards the left side when driving along a generally straight course, while *sharp right turn* is an abrupt redirection towards the right side. *Sudden acceleration* is when the driver slams on the accelerator and the vehicle speed increases sharply in a sudden moment, while the *sudden deceleration* is when the driver slams on the brake and the vehicle speed slows down in a very short time.

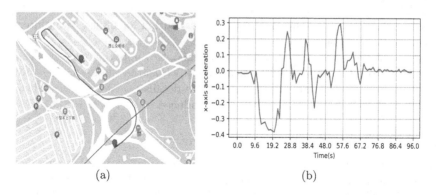

(a)   (b)

Fig. 4. (a) Visualized trajectory of a sharp turn period. (b) X-axis acceleration curve of a sharp turn period.

4   Methods

In this section, we begin by introducing the overall architecture of the proposed method, then we explain interval series representation and the prototype learning classification method separately.

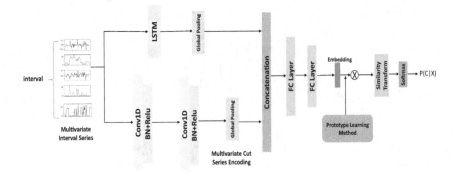

Fig. 5. Overall architecture of the unsafe driving behavior prediction task.

4.1   Overview of the Proposed Approach

Based on the reprocessing, we obtain a dataset for safety risk prediction task. Figure 5 shows the overall architecture of the classification model, denoted as **APT**. The input of the model is a set of multivariate interval series with multiple dimensions. For each dimension, the series shares the same length. A low-dimensional interval series embedding is learned in the encoding component. Specifically, we apply both the LSTM and 1 Dimensional Convolutional Layers to model the sequential information of the interval series and the relationships between different dimensions. The detailed description for multivariate interval series encoding will be introduced in Sect. 4.2.

After low-dimensional embeddings are learned, we apply the prototype learning method to implement the classification, which learns the each class prototype, and makes a notable improvement. The details of safety risk prediction using prototype learning method will be introduced in Sect. 4.3.

4.2   Driving Behavior Feature Representation

After obtaining interval series and associated labels, we use deep learning methods to conduct feature encoding. Specifically, we apply both a long-short term memory network (LSTM) [19] and a multi-layer convolutional network [9]. For LSTM, we first obtain the contextual embedding and then apply a global average pooling operation and get the output E_{lstm}. For the convolutional part, after each convolutional layer, we choose both Batch Normalization and Leaky Relu with a global average pooling applied for each convolutional layer, and the output is E_{cov}. Then we concatenate the results and get the output E_{combo}. Finally, we design two fully connected layers on E_{combo} to generate the low-dimensional feature representation (embedding) of the interval series.

4.3   Behavior Prediction Method

After low-dimensional embeddings are learned, we use the embeddings of training samples as the input to learn the prototype for each class. Here, the class prototype is a feature representation (embedding) of each class, which contains the same embedding size as the time series. Specifically, the class prototype is a weighted combination of the training samples in the same class, where the weights of the training samples are trained by an attention layer. The intuition behind this is to learn a class prototype for each class, which has smaller distances to the data samples in the same class, but larger distances to data samples in different classes. The architecture of prototype learning method is shown in Fig. 6, which learns each class prototype from training data.

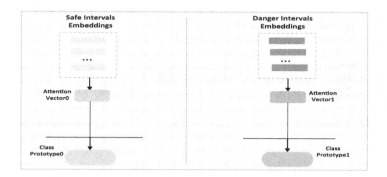

Fig. 6. Prototype learning framework

Let $H = [\mathbf{h}_1, \ldots, \mathbf{h}_{|S|}] \in \mathcal{R}^{|S| \times d}$ be a matrix of interval series embeddings of training data, where S is the set of indices for labeled data samples and $\mathbf{h}_i \in \mathcal{R}^{1 \times d}$ is the embedding vector for the ith data sample in the dataset. Then the prototype embedding of class k can be presented by a weighted sum of labeled and data as follows:

$$c_k = \sum_i A_{k,i} H_{k,i} \tag{1}$$

Here $A_{k,i}$ is the weight of the ith labeled data sample and $H_{k,i}$ is the corresponding embedding of the labeled data sample. The attentional vector A of class k for labeled data can be computed by Eq. (2) as follows:

$$A_k = softmax\left(\mathbf{w}_k^T tanh(V_k H_k^T)\right) \tag{2}$$

where $\mathbf{w} \in \mathcal{R}^{u \times 1}$ and $V_k \in \mathcal{R}^{u \times d}$ are trainable parameters for the attention method and u is the size of hidden dimension for both trainable parameters. The distribution over classes for a given time series $x \in \mathcal{R}^d$ can be represented as a softmax over distances to the prototypes in the embedding space as follows:

$$p_\Theta(y = k|x) = \frac{exp\left(-D\left(f_\Theta(x), c_k\right)\right)}{\sum_i exp\left(-D\left(f_\Theta(x), c_i\right)\right)} \tag{3}$$

where the function D is the distance function to measure the distances between two embedding vectors. We applied the squared euclidean distance function to measure the distance between the time series embeddings. The training of the model can proceed by minimizing the negative log probability $\mathcal{J}(\Theta) = -logp_\Theta(y = k|\mathbf{x})$ of the true class via the Adam algorithm. The learning and Prediction strategy is shown in Algorithm 1.

Algorithm 1. Prototype Learning & Prediction Algorithm

Input: Labeled interval series embeddings H_k & Interval series x to be predicted
Output: Classification accuracy
1: **for** c in class k **do**
2:      Calculate attention vector A_k according to H_k
3:      Calculate prototype embedding c_k by (1)
   end for
4: **for** x in test set **do**
5:      Calculate distance between x and each class prototype by (3)
6:      Minimizing the negative log probability fo the true class via Adam
   end for
7: **return**

4.4   Types of Unsafe Driving Behaviors

Besides the normal/unsafe category labels, we simplify criterions for judgements of the four types of danger behaviors. Specifically, the *sharp left turn* and *sharp right turn* are unified as **sharp turns**, the judegments are made mainly based on x-axis acceleration curve and vehicle trajectories.

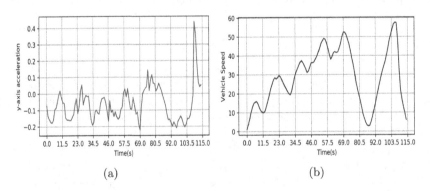

(a)   (b)

Fig. 7. (a) Y-axis acceleration curve of a sudden speed change period. (b) Vehicle speed curve of a sudden speed change period.

An example of a sharp turn period is shown in Fig. 4. From the observation of Fig. 4(a), there is a obvious fluctuation on x-axis acceleration between 19 s to 67 s, and from Fig. 4(b), we can see that the vehicle actually drives along a curve with a big radius and then takes a fast U-turn, which could be recognized as a danger behavior of *sharp turns*, then a risk label is got for this period and saved as the experimental label.

For *sudden acceleration* and *sudden deceleration*, they are unified as *sudden speed changes* which could not be judged from the vehicle trajectories, thus, the judgements are made mainly by y-axis acceleration and vehicle speed curves. An example of a sudden speed change period is shown in Fig. 7. From Fig. 7(a) we can observe that from 69 s to 115 s, the y-axis acceleration fluctuates drasticly from low to high, and Fig. 7(b) represents that the vehicle is driving at a high speed, and as the y-axis acceleration changes sharply, the vehicle speed also experiences sharp deceleration and acceleration, which could be recognized as a danger behavior of *sudden speed changes*, with a risk label got for this period and saved as the experimental label.

5   Experimental Study

In this section, we evaluate the proposed method in our real world dataset. First we introduce the evaluation settings. Then the performance of the proposed method is evaluated in two aspects: Classification Performance and Feature Importance Evaluation. All the experiments are conducted on a Centos Server with two 2080Ti GPUs, each with 16 GB memory.

5.1   Experimental Settings

Datasets. We evaluate the classification performance, feature importance evaluation on our real world dataset, denoted as **Electric vehicles**. Besides, we separate the total **Electric vehicles** dataset into four kinds of danger behaviors datasets, denoted as **Sharp Left Turn, Sharp Right Turn, Sudden Acceleration** and **Sudden Deceleration**, then conduct classification tasks on them using the proposed model.

The detailed descriptions of the dataset are as follows:

- *Electric vehicles:* It's the dataset we obtain after aforementioned distillation and labeling processes. The dataset contains 10 thousand run intervals labeled as safety or risk with 7-dimension features of length 180, and the safety/risk splits is about 5:1.

Metrics: We choose the classification accuracy and F1 score as the evaluation metric in the prediction tasks.

Baselines: We compare the proposed approach with two other approaches:

- **MLSTM-FCN** [7], the latest deep-learning framework for multivariate time series classification.

- **XGBOOST** [2], the traditional ensemble learning model which is deeply preferred in many competitions w.r.t time series. Additionally, for XGBOOST, we conduct feature extraction manually, i.e., calculating maximum, minimum, value range, mean, and standard deviation of acc_x, acc_y, etc. As well as feature selection using *feature_importance* method embedded in XGBOOST.

5.2 Evaluation of Classification Performance

The classification accuracy and f1 score of each method on Electric vehicles dataset are shown in Fig. 8. The best accuracy and f1 score are denoted with boldface. APT can outperform MLSTM-FCN and XGOOST due to prototype learning framework.

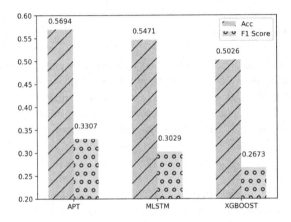

Fig. 8. Prediction performance comparisons on electric vehicles dataset

5.3 Behavior Type Prediction

The driving behavior dataset covers four kinds of danger behaviors including sharp left turn, sharp right turn, sudden acceleration and sudden deceleration.

- *Sharp Left Turn:* The dataset is a subset of Electric vehicles, which only contains the sharp left turn type of danger behaviors. There are about 483 intervals of this type, and the other settings are the same as Electric vehicles dataset.

- *Sharp Right Turn:* The dataset is similar as the Sharp Left Turn dataset, but it only contains the sharp right turn type of danger behaviors. There are about 236 intervals of this type.

- **Sudden Acceleration:** This dataset only contains the sudden acceleration type of danger behaviors and there are about 575 intervals of this type.

- **Sudden Deceleration:** The dataset is similar as the Sudden Acceleration dataset, but it only contains the sudden deceleration type of danger behaviors. There are about 391 intervals of this type.

Table 1. Unsafe driving behavior type detection

Datasets	Metrics	
	Accuracy	F1 score
Sharp left turn	0.7764	0.5035
Sharp right turn	0.7765	0.5225
Sudden acceleration	0.7565	0.5143
Sudden deceleration	0.6435	0.5137

Besides, we also conduct experiments on four types danger datasets using the proposed APT model, the classification accuracy and f1 score are shown in Table 1. The performance in total Electric vehicles dataset is much less than that in each seperate dataset, the reason may be that the mixture of four kinds danger behaviors features lead to confusions for the model to judge. Besides, comparing the performance in "Sudden Deceleration" to other 3 seperate datasets, classification accuracy decreases a lot while the f1 score stays at the same level, this represents that the model may have difficulty in identifying safe behaviors but it is still effective on finding danger behaviors which is more concerned by the industry.

5.4 Feature Importance Evaluation

We next study the influence of different features for the classification accuracy to find out what are the most important features that benefit to the safety or risk type of driving behaviors. The evaluation result is shown in Fig. 9. "w/o acc" represents the x-aixs and y-axis acceleration are exclusive in experiments, and the overall performance of each method decreases a lot; "w/o pedal" represents that the accelerator and brake pressure are exclusive, the overall performance decreases to some extents but is higher than "w/o acc"; the result of "w/o light" represents that when turn lights indicators are exclusive, performance would fall while the influence is slight. The results indicate that the variation of two axis accelerations have great influence on identification for danger behaviors when driving, which is in accord with former studies in the industry.

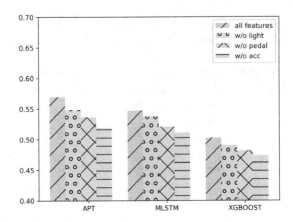

Fig. 9. Feature importance study

6   Conclusions

In this paper, we study features collected from various kinds of sensors within the electric vehicles and identify different unsafe driving behaviors.

We utilize multivaraite time series encoding to get the embeddings of driving behaviors and conduct deep learning based behavior prediction approach. The experimental results demonstrate that the proposed method could have great improvements in classification and recognizing unsafe behaviors than other baselines. In addition, we explore the feature importance on danger behaviors identification.

The future work will be focused on the integration of contextual information, such as traffic and weather conditions. And with the design of more elaborate prediction tasks, we can conduct fine-grained behaviors analysis and prediction.

References

1. Breiman, L.: Random forests. Mach. Learn. **45**(1), 5–32 (2001)
2. Chen, T., Guestrin, C.: Xgboost: a scalable tree boosting system. In: Proceedings of KDD, pp. 785–794 (2016)
3. Cortes, C., Vapnik, V.: Support-vector networks. Mach. Learn. **20**(3), 273–297 (1995)
4. Das, H., Rahman, M., Li, S., Tan, C.: Electric vehicles standards, charging infrastructure, and impact on grid integration: a technological review. Renew. Sustain. Energy Rev. **120**, 109618 (2020)
5. Fang, H., Shrestha, A., Qiu, Q.: Multivariate time series classification using spiking neural networks. In: Proceedings of IJCNN (2020)
6. Geng, Y., Du, J., Liang, M.: Abnormal event detection in tourism video based on salient spatio-temporal features and sparse combination learning. World Wide Web **22**(2), 689–715 (2019). https://doi.org/10.1007/s11280-018-0603-0
7. Karim, F., Majumdar, S., Darabi, H., Harford, S.: Multivariate LSTM-FCNs for time series classification. Neural Netw. **116**, 237–245 (2019)

8. Karlsson, I., Papapetrou, P., Boström, H.: Generalized random shapelet forests. Data Min. Knowl. Disc. **30**(5), 1053–1085 (2016)
9. Krizhevsky, A., Sutskever, I., Hinton, G.E.: ImageNet classification with deep convolutional neural networks. Commun. ACM **60**(6), 84–90 (2017)
10. Krumm, J., Horvitz, E.: Predestination: Inferring destinations from partial trajectories. In: Proceedings of UbiComp, pp. 243–260 (2006)
11. Li, Z., Zhang, K., Chen, B., Dong, Y., Zhang, L.: Driver identification in intelligent vehicle systems using machine learning algorithms. IET Intel. Transport Syst. **13**(1), 40–47 (2018)
12. Liu, J., Priyantha, B., Hart, T., Ramos, H.S., Loureiro, A.A.F., Wang, Q.: Energy efficient GPS sensing with cloud offloading. In: Proceedings of SenSys, pp. 85–98 (2012)
13. Liu, J., Zhong, L., Wickramasuriya, J., Vasudevan, : V.: uWave: accelerometer-based personalized gesture recognition and its applications. In: Proceedings of IEEE Pervasive and Mobile Computing, pp. 1–9 (2009)
14. Nawaz, S., Mascolo, C.: Mining users' significant driving routes with low-power sensors. In: Proceedings of SenSys, pp. 236–250 (2014)
15. NHTSA: The visual detection of DWI motorists (2011). http://www.shippd.org/Alcohol/dwibooklet.pdf
16. Ouyang, Z., Niu, J., Guizani, M.: Improved vehicle steering pattern recognition by using selected sensor data. IEEE Trans. Mob. Comput. **17**(6), 1383–1396 (2017)
17. Peng, Z., Gao, S., Li, Z., Xiao, B., Qian, Y.: Vehicle safety improvement through deep learning and mobile sensing. IEEE Network **32**(4), 28–33 (2018)
18. Schafer, P., Leser, U.: Multivariate time series classification with WEASEL+ muse (2017)
19. Sundermeyer, M., Schlüter, R., Ney, H.: LSTM neural networks for language modeling. In: Proceedings of InterSpeech (2012)
20. Ulm, G., Smith, S., Nilsson, A., Gustavsson, E., Jirstrand, M.: OODIDA: onboard/off-board distributed real-time data analytics for connected vehicles. Data Sci. Eng. **6**(1), 102–117 (2021)
21. Wang, Y., Yang, J., Liu, H., Chen, Y., Gruteser, M., Martin, R.P.: Sensing vehicle dynamics for determining driver phone use. In: Proceedings of MobiSys, pp. 41–54 (2013)
22. Yeh, Y.C., Hsu, C.Y.: Application of auto-encoder for time series classification with class imbalance. In: EasyChair Preprint (2019)
23. Yu, J., Chen, Z., Zhu, Y., Chen, Y., Kong, L., Li, M.: Fine-grained abnormal driving behaviors detection and identification with smartphones. IEEE Trans. Mob. Comput. **16**(8), 2198–2212 (2016)
24. Yuan, H., Li, G.: A survey of traffic prediction: from spatio-temporal data to intelligent transportation. Data Sci. Eng. **6**(1), 63–85 (2021)
25. Zhang, T., Gao, Y., Qiu, L., Chen, L., Linghu, Q., Pu, S.: Distributed time-respecting flow graph pattern matching on temporal graphs. World Wide Web **23**(1), 609–630 (2020). https://doi.org/10.1007/s11280-019-00674-0
26. Zhang, X., Gao, Y., Lin, J., Lu, C.T.: TapNet: multivariate time series classification with attentional prototypical network. In: Proceedings of AAAI, pp. 6845–6852 (2020)

Resource Trading with Hierarchical Game for Computing-Power Network Market

Qingzhong Bao, Xiaoxu Ren, Chunfeng Liu$^{(\boxtimes)}$, Xin Wang, Xiaofei Wang, and Chao Qiu

College of Intelligence and Computing, Tianjin University, Tianjin, China
{qingzhongbao,xiaoxuren,cfliu,wangx,xiaofeiwang,chao.qiu}@tju.edu.cn

Abstract. As the internet of things (IoT) and artificial intelligence (AI) continue to evolve, it has spawned a proliferation of heterogeneous data volumes and model complexity. The centralized cloud computing can no longer meet the computing needs of an intelligent society. Currently, the development of edge computing and next-generation network technologies has enabled people to gradually utilize the computing-power on the edge of the network to address the above challenges. As a novel resource-integration scheme, the computing-power network emerges, using high-efficiency network to integrate computing resources from the end, edge, and cloud to provide unified services to the outside world. However, most of the current researches focus on end-edge-cloud collaborative computing framework, and there is a lack of in-depth discussion on the market models and resource trading of the computing-power network. In this paper, we propose a computing-power market framework and formulate resource trading as a three-stage Stackelberg game. We prove the existence of Stackelberg equilibrium (SE) in game. Then the dynamic-game reinforcement learning (DG-RL) algorithm is designed to solve the optimization problem. The experimental results verify the feasibility of the framework and the excellent performance of the proposed algorithm.

Keywords: Cloud computing · Computing power network · Resource trading · Stackelberg game · Stackelberg equilibrium

1 Introduction

With the unprecedented booming of enabling technologies such as internet of things (IoT) and artificial intelligence (AI), the intelligent society where everything is sensed and connected is arriving. However, the analysis and processing of massive heterogeneous data have put forward higher demands on bandwidth, latency and security, while the algorithm models on a series of intelligent applications such as voice assistants and driverless applications are inseparable from the support of high-performance computing [17]. With the explosive growth of data and model complexity, the traditional centralized cloud computing has been unable to meet the computing-power demand for the intelligent society. The computing is gradually evolving towards distributed and networked.

© Springer Nature Switzerland AG 2021
L. H. U et al. (Eds.): APWeb-WAIM 2021, LNCS 12858, pp. 94–109, 2021.
https://doi.org/10.1007/978-3-030-85896-4_8

On the one hand, there are a large number of idle resource islands at the edge of the network due to geographical constraints. Some new computing paradigms, such as fog computing [23] and edge computing [13], start to sink some of the computing closer to the users. On the other hand, some AI services are more concerned about metrics such as latency. The users are willing to pay for more high-quality resources. The capacity and speed of the network have been greatly improved by the emerging communication technologies such as fifth-generation (5G). There are the business demand and the motivation for resource rental from the market. With the development of in-network computing [12], compute first network (CFN) [5] and compute-less networking [11], the integration of computing and network is becoming possible, forming the computing-power network [14]. The computing-power network establishes a platform for owners and users of the computing. The cloud, edge, and end are connected to the network, which effectively integrates the resources and unifies them as a pool of primary resources to provide services for users. It provides optimal resources and network connections to diverse demands of the users in the trading market, and optimizes the utilization of computing resources.

However, the resource trading market is always multi-player, where the users purchase the required resources from the providers, including network [16], computing [7], storage [6], etc. Since the total amount of resources is limited, the users compete with each other to purchase resources in the market and develop their own response strategies based on the behavior of other traders, constituting a dynamic market. The demand of users and the price of resources may change at any time. It is a challenge to optimize the resource trading model so that the utility of multi-player can be balanced.

To address the above challenges, game theory is widely used to model the trading process, such as non-cooperative games and Stackelberg games adopted in this paper. In [4], the authors formulate the multiple resource allocation problem between mobile edge-clouds and end-users as a two-stage Stackelberg game and show the existence of sub-game Stackelberg equilibrium. In [8], the remote cloud server is also considered, and the Stackelberg game is extended to three-stage. Nevertheless, the pricing approach in the trading model remains single. In [1], the authors study the games under three dynamic pricing mechanisms, such as bid-proportional allocation mechanism, uniform pricing mechanism and fairness-seeking differentiated pricing mechanism. Moreover, the impact of congestion effect and network effect on revenues in the trading model are further considered in [21].

In addition, most of the current works is focused on end-edge-cloud collaboration. In [14], the computing-power network is mentioned to meet the needs for multi-level deployment and flexible scheduling between collaborations. Similarly, a multi-cluster hierarchical resource scheduling scheme is discussed to allocate computing resources among clouds, edge devices and networks in [9]. In [18], Net-in-AI, a unified computing-power networking framework for AI, is proposed. However, there is still a lack of research on the trading model in the computing-power market.

In this paper, we formulate the computing-power trading problem as a three-stage Stackelberg game and propose the algorithm to solve the optimization problem. The key contributions of this paper are summarized as follows.

- We consider three players in the computing-power trading, i.e., users, computing-power provider (CPP) and computing network service provider (CNSP), and further establish computing-power market framework.
- We formulate the trading market as a hierarchical Stackelberg game and prove the existence of Stackelberg equilibrium (SE) in brief.
- To solve the optimization problems, we design the DG-RL algorithm with dynamic learning rate. The simulation results demonstrate the effectiveness of the framework and the satisfactory performance of the proposed algorithm.

The rest of this paper is structured as follows. The computing-power trading framework is described in Sect. 2. In Sect. 3, the three-stage Stackelberg game is formulated for the computing-power trading market. Next, Sect. 4 shows the detail of the DG-RL algorithm. Then we expand the experiments and discuss the simulation results. Finally, the conclusions and future work are shown in Sect. 6.

2   The Proposed Framework Description

As shown in Fig. 1, a computing-power market framework is proposed in this section. This framework consists of the following parts.

2.1   Users Layer

In the trading market framework, the users act as computing-power consumers. Based on the task requirements, they purchase resources from the market according to the task requirements to obtain good application services.

With the popularization of more and more intelligent applications such as automatic driving and virtual reality, the users are increasingly sensitive to the conditions such as latency. The users, whose resources are usually limited, are willing to pay more for a better business experience and constitute the consumers of the computing-power market. The users rent certain computing-power to complete the computational tasks of application services without caring about the hardware and software configuration, which reduces the threshold. Meanwhile, it is possible to pay on demand and adapt to the diversified needs of intelligent applications in different scenarios. It avoids equipping the expensive hardware for occasional peaks of computing and effectively reduces operating costs.

2.2   Computing-Power Provider Layer

Similar to power plants in the power industry, the CPP plays the role of maintaining and selling the computing-power for payment.

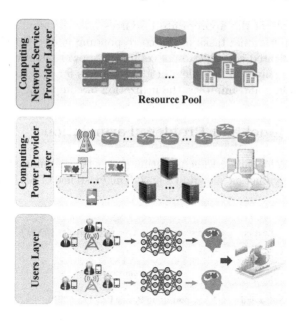

Fig. 1. Computing network market framework

Due to the development of new technologies like edge computing [13], the idle resources on the edge of the network are gradually developed and utilized. Different computing-power resources have different characteristics. Edge nodes may be closer to users with little network latency, while cloud platforms are more powerful and can perform high-performance computing. The users can select the appropriate computing-power resources to meet the task requirements. These resource owners constitute potential computing-power providers, together forming a pool of computing-power. The cloud computing nodes, edge computing nodes, and even individuals can sell the idle computing-power in the market to get some economic payoff instead of wasting it.

2.3   Computing Network Service Provider Layer

The CNSP is a bridge connecting users and computing-power providers in the trading framework, providing a transmission channel to deliver information and data. Through the efficient network, the CNSP integrates the computing-power resources of ends, edges and clouds, further provides the service in the form of resource pools. It makes the trading market more flexible and expandable, and breaks down the isolated island of computing resources due to geographical restrictions.

The CNSP is mainly responsible for embedding computing-power resources into the network, i.e. sensing, collecting and distributing computing-power resources of the whole network. When the user puts forward demand, the service provider will give the information about the current availability of resources.

Then, the user selects the appropriate resources and the service provider distributes the computational tasks to the corresponding nodes. On the one hand, it avoids the duplicated construction of computing-power facilities for users. On the other hand, it solves the problem of idle resources for providers. The CNSP optimizes scheduling and improves the utilization of computing resources.

3   System Model and Problem Formulation

In this section, we formulate the computing-power trading market as the three-stage Stackelberg game, as shown in Fig. 2. The existence of SE is analyzed.

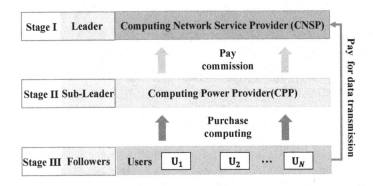

Fig. 2. Stackelberg game

3.1   System Model

The trading market of computing-power network consists of the user layer, the CPP layer and the CNSP layer. The CNSP determines how to price the data transferring service for the users and ensures the commission on the CPP. The CPP determines how to price the computing-power resources. And the users make sure the demand of the computing-power. Further, we consider the congestion effect on the utility of the players.

Users. The users need to purchase the computing-power from the CPP to complete the tasks. We define a set of users $\mathcal{N} = \{1, \ldots, N\}$. The computing-power demand for each user is denoted by x_i. The utility of user i is defined as

$$U_i = R(x_i) - p_c * x_i - p_d * D(x_i) - G(x). \tag{1}$$

The first term $R(x_i)$ is the reward function, which measures the utility that user i obtains when completing the task by purchasing the computing-power. It is defined as $R(x_i) = a * x_i - b * x_i{}^2$. The reward coefficients a, b are positive, and the decreasing marginal returns are captured by linear-quadratic function

[19]. The data size of each user $D(x_i)$ is $\frac{x_i}{K}$, where K represents the needed computing-power when the CPP computes 1 bit of data similar to [1]. Similarly, the congestion effect function $G(x)$ on the computing-power network is defined as $\lambda(\sum_{j \in \mathcal{N}} \frac{x_j}{K})^2$, where λ is the congestion coefficient. It represents that the user's utility is also affected by the total demand. In addition, the price of computing-power is represented by p_c and the price of data transferring service is denoted by p_d. Thus, the utility of user i is formulated as:

$$U_i = a * x_i - b * {x_i}^2 - p_c * x_i - p_d * \frac{x_j}{K} - \lambda(\sum_{j \in \mathcal{N}} \frac{x_j}{K})^2. \tag{2}$$

Computing-Power Provider. The CPP is responsible for providing computing-power to the users. The total amount that the users pay depends on the price of computing-power p_c. The cost of the CPP consists of two parts. One is the commission paid to the CNSP, and the other is the cost of operating computing-power such as the hardware costs and electricity consumption. Then, the profit of the CPP is expressed as:

$$P = \sum_{i \in \mathcal{N}} p_c * x_i - \sum_{i \in \mathcal{N}} \theta * x_i - \sum_{i \in \mathcal{N}} c_c * x_i, \tag{3}$$

where θ denotes the commission that the CPP paid the CNSP. And the cost per unit of computing-power of the CPP is denoted by c_c.

Computing Network Service Provider. The CNSP connects the CPP and the users, ensuring the entire computing network service. On the one hand, a variable percentage of the commission on the CPP is charged to the CNSP. On the other hand, the users pay the CNSP for transferring data. The CNSP determines the price of commission θ and the price of data transmission p_d. Therefore, the revenue of the CNSP is defined as:

$$S = \sum_{i \in \mathcal{N}} p_d * \frac{x_i}{K} + \sum_{i \in \mathcal{N}} \theta * x_i. \tag{4}$$

3.2   Problem Formulation

As mentioned above, the CNSP, CPP and users have different utility functions in the computing-power network market. The players are usually rational and independent individuals who maximize their own profits. The challenge is to balance their revenues. In our proposed model, we formulate the computing-power resource trading among the CNSP, CPP and users as a three-stage Stackelberg game, where the players make decisions sequentially.

In Stage I, the CNSP is the leader, who decides the data transmission price p_d of the users and the commission θ on the CPP to maximize its profit. We formulate the optimization problem of the CNSP as:

$$\max S(\theta, p_d)$$

$$\text{s.t.} \quad \begin{cases} \theta \geq 0, \\ p_d \geq 0. \end{cases}$$

In Stage II, the CPP, acting as the sub-leader, observes the commission and sets the price of computing-power to maximize the revenue. It is formulated as the optimization problem:

$$\max P(p_c)$$

$$\text{s.t.} \quad \begin{cases} p_c \geq 0, \\ p_c \geq \theta + c_c. \end{cases}$$

In Stage III, the users are the followers. The demand for the computing-power is determined to maximize the individual utility based on the CNSP and CPP decisions. The optimization problem of the users is defined as:

$$\max U_i(x_i)$$
$$\text{s.t.} \quad x_i \geq 0.$$

3.3   Game Analysis

As the above problems describe, the three-stage sequential game is formulated. The agents (i.e., CNSP, CPP and users) seek the best response strategies to realize its reward maximization. The SE is the object of this Stackelberg game.

Definition 1. *The SE point among the CNSP, CPP and users is a group of strategies (θ^*, p^*, x^*), meeting the following conditions:*

$$\begin{cases} S(\theta^*, x^*) \geq S(\theta, x^*), \\ P(\theta^*, p_c^*, x^*) \geq P(\theta^*, p_c, x^*), \\ U_i(p_c^*, x^*) \geq U_i(p_c^*, x). \end{cases} \tag{5}$$

In SE, no player can increase their revenue by unilaterally changing their strategy and there is no incentive to deviate from the equilibrium. Specifically, the SE is the stable solution with the largest probability, although it may not be the optimal solution to the system. Next, we verify the existence of SE in each stage of the Stackelberg game in brief.

We obtain the second partial derivative of 2 with respect to x_i, 3 with respect to p_c, and 4 with respect to θ. The derivation results are as follows:

$$\begin{cases} \frac{\partial^2 U_i}{\partial x_i^2} = -(2b + \frac{2\lambda}{K^2}) < 0, \\ \frac{\partial^2 P}{\partial p_c^2} = -\frac{N}{b + \frac{N\lambda}{K^2}} < 0, \\ \frac{\partial^2 S}{\partial \theta^2} = -\frac{N}{2b + \frac{2N\lambda}{K^2}} < 0. \end{cases} \tag{6}$$

It is obvious that $\frac{\partial^2 U_i}{\partial x_i^2}$, $\frac{\partial^2 P}{\partial p_c^2}$ and $\frac{\partial^2 S}{\partial \theta^2}$ are negative. Therefore, U_i, P and S are strictly concave and the NE exists in our Stackelberg game [22]. Accordingly, there are x^*, p_c^* and θ^* in the model, so that the users, CPP and CNSP can obtain optimal profit.

4 Multi-agent Reinforcement Learning Algorithm

In this section, the multi-agent system is introduced for the Stackelberg game in Sect. 3. We propose the DG-RL algorithm to search the SE of the CNSP, CPP and users.

4.1 Multi-agent Model

In the computing-power network system, the CNSP, CPP and users constitute a multi-agent model in the Stackelberg game. Considering that each player only seeks to maximize its reward, they are a non-cooperative relationship. Thus, it is almost impossible for them to know the strategies of other players, i.e. the information of the whole system environment for the agents is incomplete. It represents that the traditional algorithms based on complete information, such as backward induction [10,19,20], are no longer suitable for the proposed game model. Inspired by the excellent performance of agents such as AlphaStar [15] in the field of multi-player games, we search the agents' optimal strategies by the multi-agent reinforcement learning (MARL) and describe the problem as a Markov Decision Process (MDP).

In our multi-agent model, the players take actions in sequence. At first, the CNSP observes the environment and selects an action a_s. A new state s_s and a new reward r_s are generated. Then, the CPP takes an action a_p, and updates the state s_p and the reward r_p. Finally, the users decide the action a_u based on the current environment and the decisions of previous players. They receive a new state s_u and a new reward r_u. The players repeat the process until the algorithm converges.

4.2 Multi-agent Reinforcement Learning

Considering the problems such as the dynamic environment, orderly actions and inconsistent goals in our Stackelberg game, we design the DG-RL algorithm, extending from Q-learning. In order to adapt to the complex multi-agent environment, the algorithm adopts the dynamical learning parameters δ, inspired from the "Win or Learn Fast" principle of WoLF [3]. The combination allows agents to adjust quickly when losing, and learn cautiously when winning.

In the case of CNSP, the DG-RL algorithm tracks the average policy $\bar{\pi}(s_s, a_s)$ as a benchmark for the current policy $\pi(s_s, a_s)$ to evaluate the parameters. Therefore, the expected average reward with the average policy is $\sum_{a_s \in A_s} \bar{\pi}(s_s, a_s) Q((s_s, a_s))$, while the average reward with the current policy is

$\sum\limits_{a_s \in A_s} \pi(s_s, a_s)Q((s_s, a_s)$. The two variable learning rate parameters $\delta_w, \delta_l(\delta_w < \delta_l)$ in WoLF are introduced. When the CNSP's average reward is better than the expected value (i.e., it wins), the larger learning rate δ_w is adopted to learn cautiously. Otherwise, the smaller learning rate δ_l is used to adjust quickly. It is described as follows:

$$\delta = \begin{cases} \delta_w & \Gamma, \\ \delta_l & otherwise, \end{cases} \tag{7}$$

where Γ means

$$\sum_{a_s \in A_s} \bar{\pi}(s_s, a_s)Q((s_s, a_s) > \sum_{a_s \in A_s} \pi(s_s, a_s)Q((s_s, a_s). \tag{8}$$

Based on the fact that the algorithm tends to converge as the number of iterations increases, it tends to destroy the steady state if the initial learning rate is large, while a small initial learning rate causes the algorithm to converge slowly. Therefore, the learning rate parameters δ_w, δ_l are dynamically calculated, which is inversely proportional to the number of iterations k and directly proportional to the learning rate α. It is denoted as follows:

$$\begin{cases} \delta_w = \frac{\alpha}{100 + \frac{k}{200}}, \\ \delta_l = 2\delta_w. \end{cases} \tag{9}$$

The algorithm gradually increases the probability of the action which maximizes cumulative expectation. Otherwise, the probability of the action is decreased. In addition, the action probability $\pi(s_s, a_s) \in [0, 1]$ should be normalized to satisfy $\sum \pi(s_s, a_s) = 1$. In the algorithm, the current policy is updated as

$$\pi(s_s, a_s) \leftarrow \pi(s_s, a_s) + \Delta_{s_s, a_s}, \tag{10}$$

where

$$\Delta_{s_s, a_s} = \begin{cases} -\delta_{s_s, a_s} & a \neq \arg\max\limits_{a'_s \in A_s} Q(s_s, a'_s), \\ \sum\limits_{a'_s \neq a_s} \delta_{s_s, a'_s} & otherwise, \end{cases} \tag{11}$$

and

$$\delta_{s_s, a_s} = \min(\pi(s_s, a_s), \frac{\delta}{|A_s| - 1}). \tag{12}$$

Algorithm 1 shows the detail of DG-RL algorithm for the CNSP's price strategy. The solution of the optimal price strategy for the CPP and demand for users is similar.

5   Simulation Results and Discussions

In this section, some extensive experiments are conducted to evaluate the performance of the DG-RL algorithm. We verify the feasibility of the proposed trading framework and evaluate the performance of DG-RL algorithm.

Algorithm 1. DG-RL algorithm for the CNSP's price strategy

1: Initialize the learning rates α, the state counter $C(s_s) = 0$, $Q(s_s, a_s) = 0$, $\pi(s_s, a_s) = \frac{1}{|A_s|}$
2: **repeat**
3:    Update two learning rate parameters δ_w, δ_l as (9)
4:    Take an action a_s based on the current state s_s
5:    Receive the reward r_s and next state s'_s
6:    Update the $Q(s_s, a_s)$:
   $Q(s_s, a_s) \leftarrow Q(s_s, a_s)+$
$$\alpha[r_s + \gamma \max_{a_s \in A_s} Q(s'_s, a_s) - Q(s_s, a_s)]$$
7:    Update estimate of average policy $\bar{\pi}(s_s, a_s), \forall a_s \in A_s$:
   $C(s_s) \leftarrow C(s_s) + 1$
   $\bar{\pi}(s_s, a_s) \leftarrow \bar{\pi}(s_s, a_s) + \frac{1}{C(s_s)}(\pi(s_s, a_s) - \bar{\pi}(s_s, a_s))$
8:    Update and constrain the policy $\pi(s_s, a_s), \forall a_s \in A_s$:
   $\pi(s_s, a_s) \leftarrow \pi(s_s, a_s) + \Delta_{s_s, a_s}$
9: **until**

5.1 Experimental Setting and Algorithm Convergence

Firstly, the basic parameters are set for the players in the computing-power trading framework. In the simulation, we set the reward coefficient as $a = 10, b = 1$, and the congestion coefficient is $\lambda = 0.5$ for the users. We assume the needed computing-power per 1 bit is $K = 10$. The cost of unit computing-power for the CPP is set as $c_c = 10$. To simplify the problem, we fix the price charged by the CNSP for transmitting 1 bit to be $p_d = 20$. For the reinforcement learning algorithm parameters, the learning rate is $\alpha = 0.4$, and the discount factor

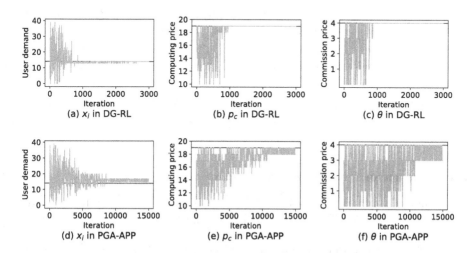

Fig. 3. Algorithm convergence compared with PGA-APP (Color figure online)

defining the importance of future rewards is $\gamma = 0.4$. Two variable learning parameters δ_w, δ_l are calculated as the Eq. (9).

Then, we verify the convergence of DG-RL algorithm and compare it with PGA-APP [24] algorithm. We set one CNSP, one CPP and four users in the trading market. In the subplots of Fig. 3, the green line represents the optimal solution of theoretical equilibrium. From Fig. 3(e), Fig. 3(e) and Fig. 3(f), it can be observed that PGA-APP algorithm performs poorly and converges slowly, which is due to multi-agent competition in the dynamic environment. In contrast, the introduction of the dynamic learning rate of DG-RL algorithm accelerates the convergence speed, as shown in Fig. 3(a), Fig. 3(b) and Fig. 3(c). The demand of the users, the computing-power price of the CPP and the commission of the CNSP converges to the vicinity of the SE point. It shows that the proposed algorithm is robust and is not sensitive to the selection of initial points.

To further verify the stability of DG-RL algorithm and the uniqueness of the equilibrium, we initialize the algorithm with different random values in Fig. 4: (a). $(\theta, p_c, x_i) = (3, 18, 18)$, (b). $(\theta, p_c, x_i) = (1, 18, 34)$, (c). $(\theta, p_c, x_i) = (3, 12, 3)$, (d). $(\theta, p_c, x_i) = (0, 18, 19)$. Regardless of the starting point, the algorithm eventually converges to the same equilibrium: $(\theta^*, p_c^*, x_i^*) = (4, 19, 14)$.

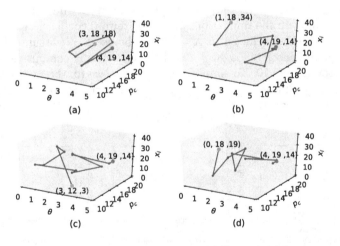

Fig. 4. Algorithm convergence with different initial value

5.2   Performance of DG-RL Algorithm

To evaluate the performance of DG-RL algorithm, we compare it with other algorithms (i.e., GIGA-WoLF [2], PGA-APP) and the theoretical optimal solutions. The simulations are performed in different user scenarios with weak congestion effect. The congestion factor is set to 0.05. From the subplots of Fig. 5, we can observe that the DG-RL algorithm denoted in the green line is closest to the optimal solution shown in the red line. Meanwhile, the GIGA-WoLF algorithm indicated by the blue line and PGA-APP algorithm represented by the purple line perform poorly. For example, the GIGA-WoLF algorithm achieves the larger profit for the CNSP in Fig. 5(a) and the smaller profit for individual user in Fig. 5(c) compared to the optimal solution. It represents that the benefits are not balanced, where the whole system is unstable. The above discussion shows the excellent performance of our proposed algorithm. It is because the learning rate parameters in DG-RL algorithm are computed dynamically. As the number of iterations increases, the learning rate decreases, which makes it easier to converge and stabilize.

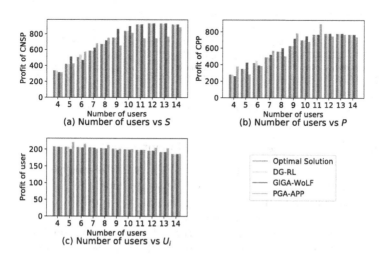

Fig. 5. Algorithm performance compared with different algorithms under different number of users (Color figure online)

5.3   Impacts of the Number of Users

Next, we evaluate the impact of the number of users on the profitability of all players in the market. As the number of users increases, the profit of individual user in Fig. 6(c) is decreasing, while the profits of the CPP in Fig. 6(b) and CNSP in Fig. 6(a) are gradually increasing. The reason is that the competition for computing-power resources is more intense with the increase in the number of users. On the one hand, the cost of individual user increases. On the other hand, the total number of computing-power resources rented by all users increases. In addition, we notice that the profits of the CPP in Fig. 6(b) and CNSP in Fig. 6(a) gradually saturate and reach an upper limit when the critical number of users is exceeded. It is because the computing-power resources of the CPP are limited. The dividend from the increase in the number of users disappears when all the resources in the market are rented out. Meanwhile, the profit of individual user decreases at a slower rate. Because the congestion cost function $G(x)$ in the Eq. (1) no longer increases and becomes a constant.

When the number of users is fixed, the profits of the CPP and users decrease as the price of data transmission increases. Especially, the more expensive the price, the larger the critical point of the number of users at which the profits tend to level off. As the excessive price makes the demand of users diminish, more people are needed to rent out the resources in the market.

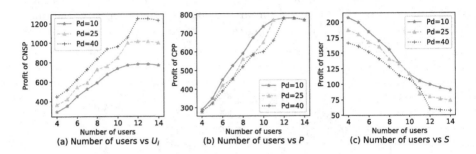

Fig. 6. Impact of the number of users with different data factor

5.4 Impacts of the Congestion Coefficient

Further, the impact of congestion effect λ on the utility is analyzed. First of all, we fix the number of users to 4. Figure 7 illustrates how the profits change as the congestion coefficient increases. As expected, the profit of individual user in Fig. 7(a) gradually decreases because of the increasing congestion cost. Especially, as the congestion factor increases, the difference in individual user's profit caused by the different p_d gradually decreases. It indicates that the congestion effect is becoming the dominant factor in the profit of users. In addition, the profit of CNSP in Fig. 7(b) also decreases. This is because the higher congestion coefficient makes users less willing to purchase, which reducing the total demand for computing resources.

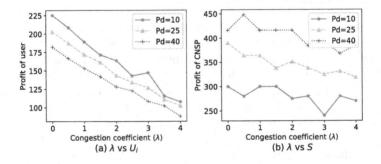

Fig. 7. Impact of the congestion effect with different data factor

Then, we fix the price of data transmission to 20 and observe the benefit of individual user and total demand of all users. As shown in Fig. 8(a), the greater the number of users, the greater the influence of congestion coefficient λ on the user's profit. It is due to the fact the computing-power network becomes congested as the number of users increases. Accordingly, the congestion cost increases. In addition, it can be observe that the higher congestion cost increases the number of users required to reach the upper limit of total demand in Fig. 8(b). It is because the congestion in the network makes the uses' experience worse, which leads to reduced demand.

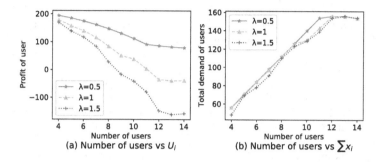

Fig. 8. Impact of the number of users with different congestion factor

6   Conclusions and Future Work

In this paper, we construct a three-stage Stackelberg game model for the computing-power network market. The payoff model is designed to stimulate players, such as the users, CPP and CNSP, to actively participate in computing-power trading, so as to maintain the smooth operation of the market. In particular, considering the impact of congestion effect on the users' experience, we also take it into account in the total cost function of users. We propose the DG-RL algorithm to learn the optimal strategy and solve the Stackelberg equilibrium. The simulation results demonstrate the excellent performance of the proposed algorithm. For future work, we may explore the impact of differential pricing on the trading model or study complex scenarios with multiple service providers, resource providers, and users.

References

1. Baek, B., Lee, J., Peng, Y., Park, S.: Three dynamic pricing schemes for resource allocation of edge computing for IoT environment. IEEE Internet of Things J. **7**(5), 4292–4303 (2020)
2. Bowling, M.: Convergence and no-regret in multiagent learning. In: Advances in Neural Information Processing Systems, vol. 17, pp. 209–216 (2005)
3. Bowling, M., Veloso, M.: Rational and convergent learning in stochastic games. In: International Joint Conference on Artificial Intelligence, vol. 17, pp. 1021–1026. Citeseer (2001)

4. Chen, Y., Li, Z., Yang, B., Nai, K., Li, K.: A Stackelberg game approach to multiple resources allocation and pricing in mobile edge computing. Future Gen. Comput. Syst. **108**, 273–287 (2020)
5. Król, M., Mastorakis, S., Oran, D., Kutscher, D.: Compute first networking: distributed computing meets ICN. In: Proceedings of the 6th ACM Conference on Information-Centric Networking, pp. 67–77 (2019) Distributed computing meets icn. In: Proceedings of the 6th ACM Conference on Information-Centric Networking. pp. 67–77 (2019)
6. Kuchuk, G., Nechausov, S., Kharchenko, V.: Two-stage optimization of resource allocation for hybrid cloud data store. In: 2015 International Conference on Information and Digital Technologies, pp. 266–271. IEEE (2015) allocation for hybrid cloud data store. In: 2015 International Conference on Information and Digital Technologies. pp. 266–271. IEEE (2015)
7. Mai, T., Yao, H., Li, F., Xu, X., Jing, Y., Ji, Z.: Computing resource allocation in LEO satellites system: a Stackelberg game approach. In: 2019 15th International Wireless Communications & Mobile omputing Conference (IWCMC), pp. 919–924. IEEE (2019) allocation in leo satellites system: A stackelberg game approach. In: 2019 15th International Wireless Communications & Mobile Computing Conference (IWCMC). pp. 919–924. IEEE (2019)
8. Meng, S., Wang, Y., Miao, Z., Sun, K.: Joint optimization of wireless bandwidth and computing resource in cloudlet-based mobile cloud computing environment. Peer-to-Peer Networking Appl. **11**(3), 462–472 (2018)
9. Mingxuan, L., Chang, C., Xiongyan, T., Tao, H., Jianfei, L., Qiuyan, L.: Research on edge resource scheduling solutions for computing power network. Front. Data Comput. **2**(4), 80–91 (2020)
10. Nie, J., Luo, J., Xiong, Z., Niyato, D., Wang, P.: A Stackelberg game approach toward socially-aware incentive mechanisms for mobile crowdsensing. IEEE Trans. Wireless Commun. **18**(1), 724–738 (2018)
11. Nour, B., Mastorakis, S., Mtibaa, A.: Compute-less networking: perspectives, challenges, and opportunities. IEEE Netw. **34**(6), 259–265 (2020)
12. Sapio, A., Abdelaziz, I., Aldilaijan, A., Canini, M., Kalnis, P.: In-network computation is a dumb idea whose time has come. In: Proceedings of the 16th ACM Workshop on Hot Topics in Networks, pp. 150–156 (2017)
13. Shi, W., Cao, J., Zhang, Q., Li, Y., Xu, L.: Edge computing: vision and challenges. IEEE Internet of Things J. **3**(5), 637–646 (2016)
14. Tang, X., et al.: Computing power network: the architecture of convergence of computing and networking towards 6G requirement. China Commun. **18**(2), 175–185 (2021)
15. Vinyals, O., et al.: Grandmaster level in starcraft ii using multi-agent reinforcement learning. Nature **575**(7782), 350–354 (2019)
16. Wang, G., Feng, G., Tan, W., Qin, S., Wen, R., Sun, S.: Resource allocation for network slices in 5G with network resource pricing. In: GLOBECOM 2017-2017 IEEE Global Communications Conference, pp. 1–6. IEEE (2017)
17. Wang, X., Han, Y., Leung, V.C., Niyato, D., Yan, X., Chen, X.: Convergence of edge computing and deep learning: a comprehensive survey. IEEE Commun. Surv. Tutorials **22**(2), 869–904 (2020)
18. Wang, X., Ren, X., Qiu, C., Cao, Y., Taleb, T., Leung, V.C.: Net-in-AI: a computing-power networking framework with adaptability, flexibility and profitability for ubiquitous AI. IEEE Network 35, 280–288 (2020)

19. Xiong, Z., Feng, S., Niyato, D., Wang, P., Zhang, Y.: In: Economic analysis of network effects on sponsored content: a hierarchical game theoretic approach. In: GLOBE-COM 2017-2017 IEEE Global Communications Conference, pp. 1–6. IEEE (2017)

20. Xiong, Z., Feng, S., Niyato, D., Wang, P., Zhang, Y., Lin, B.: A Stackelberg game approach for sponsored content management in mobile data market with network effects. IEEE Internet of Things J. **7**(6), 5184–5201 (2020)

21. Xiong, Z., Niyato, D., Wang, P., Han, Z., Zhang, Y.: Dynamic pricing for revenue maximization in mobile social data market with network effects. IEEE Trans. Wireless Commun. **19**(3), 1722–1737 (2019)

22. Yao, H., Mai, T., Wang, J., Ji, Z., Jiang, C., Qian, Y.: Resource trading in blockchain-based industrial Internet of Things. IEEE Trans. Industr. Inf. **15**(6), 3602–3609 (2019)

23. Yi, S., Li, C., Li, Q.: A survey of fog computing: concepts, applications and issues. In: Proceedings of the 2015 Workshop on Mobile Big Data, pp. 37–42 (2015)

24. Zhang, C., Lesser, V.: Multi-agent learning with policy prediction. In: Proceedings of the AAAI Conference on Artificial Intelligence, vol. 24 (2010)

Analyze and Evaluate Database-Backed Web Applications with WTool

Zhou Zhou🄳 and XuJia Yao(✉)

Shanghai Jiao Tong University, Shanghai, China
{clevelandalto,yaoxj}@sjtu.edu.cn

Abstract. Web applications demand low latency. In database-backed web applications, the latency is sensitive to the efficiency of database access. Hence, previous works have proposed various techniques to optimize the database access performance. However, the effectiveness of these techniques remains unverified when being applied to real-world applications. The reason is twofold. First, the benchmarks used to evaluate the methods in the literature differ from the real applications. Second, the diversity of applications makes it hard to predict whether a specific application will benefit from a certain technique.

To this end, this paper presents WTool, a tool that can automatically analyze and evaluate the database access in a specific web application. It first collects SQL queries in the application, then extracts the information about queries for analysis purposes. Furthermore, WTool is also able to generate configurable benchmark scripts based on collected queries. The user can use the scripts to simulate the database access of a specific application for performance evaluation. To demonstrate the usage WTool, we analyze 16 open-source web applications. We introduce several simple optimizations based on the analysis and evaluate them by the generated benchmark scripts. The result shows that the query throughput can be improved by up to 7×.

Keywords: Web application · Database

1 Introduction

Web applications desire low latency. When the latency is above 2 s, users become impatient, even abandon the web page [33,37]. For example, Amazon sales drop 1% when the latency increases by 100 ms [23]. As most web applications need to query data from the database to fulfill the user request (database-backed), its response latency depends on the database access efficiency. Hence, previous works have proposed various techniques to seek good performance. For instance, building secondary indexes or caching query results can save query processing time [29,34,38,42], while using a weak isolation level or controlling the transaction's execution based on its semantics [24,25,28,32,43,46] can provide better scalability under high contention scenarios.

© Springer Nature Switzerland AG 2021
L. H. U et al. (Eds.): APWeb-WAIM 2021, LNCS 12858, pp. 110–124, 2021.
https://doi.org/10.1007/978-3-030-85896-4_9

Unfortunately, the developers still face two challenges when leveraging these techniques to accelerate web applications. First, the effectiveness of the existing optimization techniques is seldom verified in real-world applications. Previous works commonly use standard benchmarks (e.g., OLTP-Bench [27]) to demonstrate their effectiveness and efficiency. However, these standard benchmarks cannot comprehensively represent the characteristics of a specific real-world application. A typical real-world application usually involves hundreds of transaction types deriving from complex business logic. In contrast, a standard benchmark may simulate less than ten transaction types abstracted from major functionality of a certain genre of applications.

Second, the diverse characteristics of database access lead to different performance requirements for DBMS among applications. Consequently, even if a DBMS or optimization technique is evaluated using a real application, the result might not stand for others. For example, Log-structured Merge Tree (LSM-Tree) is a write-optimal data structure. However, not all web applications are just at the "sweet spot." Therefore, it is hard to predict whether a specific application would benefit from a certain technique.

To this end, this paper presents WTool, a tool able to analyze and evaluate a specific web application automatically. We focus on web applications using Spring framework [18]. Through WTool, the user can easily collect, analyze, simulate and evaluate database access in a web application.

WTool consists of three major components: SQL collector, static analyzer, and benchmark generator. First, the SQL collector collects all possible SQL queries issued at runtime, leveraging a symbolic execution engine to achieve high coverage. Second, the static analyzer extracts basic information of collected queries. Moreover, it also exposes a programmatic interface for customized analysis. Finally, the benchmark generator generates a benchmark suite based on the gathered queries to evaluate the application. The user can configure parameters to simulate the desired workload.

To demonstrate the usage of WTool, we use it to analyze 16 open-source Spring web applications. We report several interesting findings during the analysis. Based on the result, we introduce a few simple optimizations and evaluate the effectiveness by the generated benchmark.

2   Background and Motivation

As a primary focus of WTool, we target the web applications using Spring framework [18]. This section provides a brief overview of Spring framework and discusses necessities that motivate our work.

2.1   Design of Spring Applications

Spring [18] is a popular application framework for Java. Spring has more than 42.1k stars on Github and is used by more than 309k open-source projects on

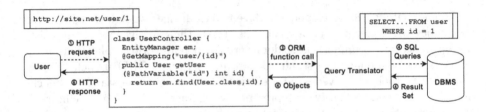

Fig. 1. Workflow of spring framework

Github. Spring supports the Model-View-Controller (MVC) [31] pattern and provides a RESTful Web Service feature [40].

Figure 1 shows an example of database-backed RESTful web application. A client request that targets an API endpoint such as `http://site.net/user/1`(1) triggers a corresponding *handler method*. The handler method executes the business logic and may manipulate the persistent data through an Object-Relation Mapping (e.g., Hibernate [35])(2). The ORM automatically synthesizes SQL queries accordingly(3) and issues them to the DBMS. It subsequently converts the received results back to objects(4) and returns to the caller(5). After the business logic finishes, the final response is returned to the client(6).

2.2   Challenges Faced by Developers

To understand the developer's challenges, we investigate three Spring applications [4,6,12] by manually analyzing their code and evaluating the performance.

Real-World Applications Differ from Standard Benchmarks. As a result, the effectiveness of optimization techniques remains uncertain in real-world applications even if verified on standard benchmarks. For instance, significant differences in the business logic and table schemas are revealed when comparing Poplar [12], a real-world social network application, and OLTP-bench [27], a benchmark abstracted from Twitter's workload.

For the business logic, the real application is much more complicated than the benchmark. Consider the case when a user tries to create a new post on the social network. OLTP-bench invokes an operation called "InsertTweet," which only involves a single insert statement. In contrast, Poplar invokes a handler method named "newFeed," which issues at least 10 SQL queries (some are conditionally issued). The complexity stems from Poplar's functionalities: a post may contain richer content such as photos and files; the user can assign tags to a post, which may further trigger the feed mechanism.

For the table schema, The benchmark usually adopts the third normal form (3NF) [26]. But applications can intentionally break it for performance. Both OLTP-bench and Poplar use a table named `user_profiles` to store the user information (e.g., `id` and `name`) and a table named `followers` to maintain the relationship between users. The `followers` table owns two columns, `user_id` and `follower_id`, both referencing the `user_profiles.id` column. As a result, retrieving a user's followers' names requires two queries on `followers` and `user_profiles` (or one query involving `JOIN`). On the other hand, Poplar replicates the `name` column in the `followers` table. Although violating the 3NF, a single query (without `JOIN`) is then sufficient for the same purpose.

```
// Halo - create comment
input: $article_id
INSERT INTO comments
   VALUES ($article_id,...);


// Halo - list articles
$article_ids =
SELECT $article_id,...
   FROM articles
   ORDER BY create_time
   LIMIT 10;
$comment_counts =
SELECT COUNT(*)
   FROM comment c
   WHERE c.article_id
      IN ($article_ids)
   GROUP BY c.article_id;
```

(a) Halo

```
// ForestBlog - create comment
input: $article_id
INSERT INTO comments
   VALUES ($article_id,...);
UPDATE articles
   SET comment_count =
   (SELECT COUNT(*) FROM comments c
   WHERE c.article_id = $article_id);

// ForestBlog - list articles
$article_ids,$comment_counts =
SELECT article_id,comment_count,...
FROM articles
ORDER BY create_time
LIMIT 10
```

(b) ForestBlog

Fig. 2. Example of two different blog web applications.

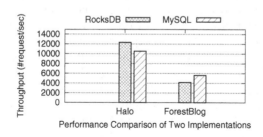

Fig. 3. Throughput (requests/sec) of two different implementations in Fig. 2.

The Requirements for Good Performance Vary Across Applications. The reason is that even for similar application functionality, the implementations across applications can be quite different. Accordingly, even though a DBMS or optimization technique has been tested on a real application, the result still does not stand for others. Figure 2 shows how two blog applications, Halo [6] and ForestBlog [4], handle `PostComment` and `ListArticle` requests. The major difference is the way counting the comments for a given article. Halo simply inserts a new comment and uses a range query to calculate the comment count on demand. ForestBlog instead maintains a column (`comment_count`) in the `articles` table and updates its value after inserting into the `comments` table.

We run these two applications on MySQL and RocksDB (MyRock) [11,15], with the `articles` and `comments` table populated by 10k and 100k records, respectively. 10 clients concurrently issue `PostComment` or `ListArticle` evenly. Figure 3 illustrates the result. RocksDB outperforms MySQL for Halo because it favors the append-only operation in Halo's `PostComment`. In contrast, for ForestBlog, the inefficient range query in RocksDB leads to less throughput than MySQL.

3   Design

This section describes the design of WTool. The system takes as input the source code of a Spring application. First, it collects the SQL queries by invoking test cases and may utilize the symbolic execution to increase the coverage. Then, it analyzes the collected queries, extracts basic information from each query (e.g., the query type and accessed tables) and builds a static conflict graph among multiple queries. This knowledge is exposed to users by programmatic interface for customized analysis. Finally, WTool generates configurable benchmark suites based on the queries.

3.1   SQL Collector

We observed that applications often involve database access during testing. Hence, the SQL collector takes advantage of developed test cases in the first place. It invokes all the test cases and captures the issued queries.

Unfortunately, test cases sometimes do not achieve satisfying coverage. In this case, the SQL collector generates supplementary test cases by symbolic execution. Specifically, the collector first identifies all handler methods by special annotations (e.g., `@GetMapping`) associated with the method. Second, the collector leverages Symbolic PathFinder [36,39], an open-source symbolic execution engine for Java programs, to symbolically execute each handler method and generate test cases correspondingly. Finally, additional queries are collected by invoking generated test cases.

During the process, upon each SQL query being issued, the collector also scans the program stack to locate the handler method that initiates this database access. Later, WTool can group the queries by their provenance to simulate the database access behavior at the handler method level.

3.2   Semantic Analyzer

The semantic analyzer extracts information from collected queries and exposes a programmatic interface for customized analysis. WTool provides four core abstraction: `Model`, `Query`, `Table` and `Column`. `Model` includes the database schema and all SQL queries. `Query` represents a single query and basic attributes extracted by WTool, e.g., the accessed tables. `Table` and `Column` abstract the schema of a table or a column. Figure 4 shows an example of a user-defined analysis task that counts read and write operations in each query.

```
1  Model model = WTool.analyze(<query_log_path>);
2  for (Query q : model.getQueries()) {
3    int nread = q.numOfKeywords(SELECT);
4    int nwrite = q.numOfKeywords(UPDATE,INSERT,DELETE);
5    record(q.getQueryId(), nread, nwrite);
6  }
```

Fig. 4. A simple analyzer.

Static Conflict Graph. Besides the attributes of a single query, the analyzer builds a static conflict graph (SC-graph) [41], to model the conflicts among queries. In an SC-graph, each vertex represents a SQL query. The edge is of two types: S(ibling)-edge and C(onflict)-edge. S-edge connects two consecutive queries in the same transaction. C-edge connects two queries if they potentially conflict at runtime, i.e., two queries access the same table, and at least one of them is a write operation.

The semantic analyzer constructs the SC-graph by three steps. First, it identifies transactions by finding queries enclosed by paired START and COMMIT commands in the query log. Each query not scoped by such pairs forms an implicit transaction by itself. All the queries and transactions are added as vertices in the SC-graph. Next, edges are added according to the definition. The analyzer examines each possible pair of to detect conflicts. Last, the graph is accessible to the user through two interfaces: Query.SNeighbors() and Query.CNeighbors().

```
function load_users(table_size)
  conn:query("CREATE TABLE users(id INT PRIMARY KEY, age INT)")
  for i = 1, table_size do
    conn:query("INSERT INTO users VALUES (%d, %d)",
      rand_unique_int(), rand_int())
  done
end

function user_handler_1(id)
  conn:query("SELECT * FROM users WHERE id=%d", id)
end
...
function user_handler_2(name, id)
  conn:query("UPDATE users SET name=%s WHERE id=%d", name, id)
end
...
config = {
  "table_size" = {"users": 10000},
  "data_distribution": {"users.age": "uniform"},
  "handler_frequency" = {"user_handler_1": 0.9}
}
```

Fig. 5. Example of synthesized benchmark scripts

3.3 Benchmark Script Generator

WTool can generate benchmark scripts from the gathered SQL queries. Particularly, it synthesizes Sysbench [20] scripts. Figure 5 shows a simple example of the synthesized script. On the top is the procedure that initializes and populates the database. As follows are the procedures that simulate the database access in method handlers. At the bottom, the `config` allows the user to controls parameters concerning the workload's characteristics. For example, the table size, the data distribution and the frequency of a handler being invoked at runtime.

4 Analyze the Web Applications

This section illustrates how to use WTool to analyze real-world applications. We selected 16 open-source Spring projects from GitHub based on their popularity, which covers various categories, like e-commerce, blogging, social network, etc. Table 1 shows the detail. We performed the analysis at the granularity of single query, transactions and database tables. As follows lists interesting findings and implications.

Table 1. The basic statistics of 16 applications. Read% is the proportion of SELECT queries out of all queries. Tbls and Txns stand for Tables and Transactions, respectively. #SQL is the total number of SQL queries appeared in the log. Some applications do not have coverage due to complex configuration problems.

Application	LOC	#Stars	#Handlers	Read%	#Tbls	#Txns	#SQL	Coverage
eladmin [2]	7.8k	4.7k	218	86.84%	28	1757	3041	72.5%
publicCMS [13]	32k	1.3k	559	85.45%	43	4398	30668	76.2%
febs [3]	6.5k	3.6k	70	58.33%	25	107	324	81.7%
guns [3]	7.2k	2.4k	71	72.61%	11	232	462	55.0%
jeesite [9]	20k	7.1k	231	46.49%	51	621	2469	70.9%
hsweb [8]	49k	6.8k	113	65.74%	79	266	1203	53.8%
halo [6]	16k	9.4k	291	83.22%	16	1268	4359	87.9%
forestblog [4]	3.0k	1.3k	86	94.93%	12	1421	1421	–
sagan [16]	12k	2.1k	35	60.75%	10	65	224	52.7%
springblog [19]	6.4k	1.5k	27	54.00%	5	59	271	20.3%
shopizer [17]	74k	1.4k	154	90.69%	78	622	4083	55.8%
broadleaf [1]	186k	1.3k	451	94.14%	187	7061	13256	52.7%
xmall [21]	23k	4.3k	152	62.98%	20	385	745	–
litemall [10]	55k	9.9k	364	86.45%	32	2926	3163	78.5%
pybbs [14]	9.4k	892	212	95.07%	16	6335	8063	82.8%
fanchaoo [5]	1.6k	314	26	66.10%	8	59	60	–

4.1 Single Query

Read Operation is More than Write in Web Applications. We first study the basic information, such as the total number of queries and the read-write ratio, as shown in Table 1. Though each handler method has 16.4 SQL queries on average, some handlers have as many as 54.9 queries and as few as only 2.3 queries. The ratio of read-only queries varies from 95.07% to 46.49%, and 9 out of 16 applications have a read ratio greater than 70%.

It Takes Cost to Use OFFSET. Almost all applications (15/16) use OFFSET operator, because *pagination* is a regular functionality in the web applications and is usually implemented by OFFSET. For example, consider litemall, an e-commerce application. The API ListProducts lists the products on sale, sorted by creation time with pagination. The corresponding SQL query is SELECT...FROM goods ORDER BY add_time LIMIT N OFFSET M. The result contains the M-th to (M+N)-th rows in the goods table, ordered by the add_time column.

Table 2. Performance of the ListProducts query with varying offset. The number of rows in the goods table is 100k.

Offset (M)	P50 latency (ms)	P90 latency (ms)	P99 latency (ms)
0	59.99	62.21	63.32
100	62.27	62.83	66.1
1,000	64.9	65.26	68.92
10,000	89.7	93.58	95.34

Unfortunately, OFFSET causes significant overhead when M increases. We evaluate the ListProducts query with the goods table populated by 100k rows. Table 2 shows the result. The DBMS must skip the first M rows before retrieving the next N rows. Obviously, this incurs considerable useless computation when M is far greater than N.

Implication: Pagination is a common requirement in web application. However, simply using OFFSET harms the performance. The developers should consider an alternative approach for pagination.

4.2   Transaction

Most Transactions is of Small Size. Table 3 shows the transaction size of different percentiles. It is noticed that 90% of transactions contain no more than 6 queries in all applications. However, the maximum size indicates the existence of large transactions.

Implication: Most transactions only contain a few queries. Thus, the DBMS should avoid the situation where a rare long-running transaction blocks plenty of short ones.

Table 3. Transactions statistics. *P50 s*, *P90 s*, *P99 s* are 50-, 90- and 99-percentile transaction size. *max* is the maximum of transaction size. *p* is the ratio of single-query explicit transactions out of all explicit transactions. *q* is the ratio of transactions that can be chopped out of all multi-query transactions. '/' indicates there is no explicit transaction in the application.

app	ela	pub	feb	gun	jee	hsw	hal	for	sag	spr	sho	bro	xma	lit	pyb	fan
P50 s	1	1	1	1	1	1	1	1	1	1	1	1	1	1	1	1
P90 s	1	2	4	1	2	5	1	1	2	3	2	1	1	1	1	1
P99 s	5	9	15	3	10	37	8	1	9	4	5	6	4	1	4	1
max	15	211	21	60	70	39	59	1	15	5	7	42	119	18	29	1
p	72.8%	66.6%	43.8%	33.3%	60.2%	38.5%	84.5%	/	67.6%	53.6%	61.3%	21.1%	64.5%	4.8%	58.2%	/
q	3.2%	0.8%	16.7%	12.5%	1.9%	24.0%	0.0%	/	0.0%	0.0%	59.8%	31.3%	0.0%	5.0%	0.0%	/

The Transactions are Overused. First, substantial explicit transactions are redundant. In 9 applications, more than 50% of *explicit* transactions contain only a single query. Since DBMS executes a single SQL as if there was an implicit transaction, the BEGIN and COMMIT is meaningless. As a result, the extra round-trips increase the overall latency.

Second, some transactions contain queries that are unnecessarily protected. Consider the example of Fig. 6, the first query of T_1 does not participate in any conflict. Thus, it is unnecessary to place it into a transaction.

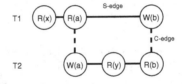

Fig. 6. Example of a overprotection.

We implement a simple algorithm to determine whether a query is overprotected based on transaction chopping [41]. In short, a query is overprotected if no C-edge connects to it, and, in that transaction, it is not between queries that are connected with C-edge. The last row of Table 3 shows that, for 5 out of 16 applications, more than 10% of multi-query transactions are candidates of chopping.

Implication: Developers tend to overuse transactions. A hypothetical explanation is that the complexity of the application hinders developers from determining an optimal transaction scope. Thus, static analysis tools such as WTool would be helpful.

4.3   Database Tables

More Than 70% SQL Queries Access only the 20% Tables. Some tables are much "hotter" than others. These tables usually correspond to the core business entity in the application. For instance, the orders table in an e-commerce application and the articles table in a blogging application.

Implication: Table access in web applications skews. Most of the access focus on few hot tables, which may become a potential performance bottleneck.

The Secondary Index is Not Configured Properly. The secondary index is a practical technique that accelerates look-up operation at the expense of write operation performance due to added maintenance cost. Thus, secondary indexes are suitable for columns that are intensively queried but rarely updated.

Table 4. Index access statistics. *Read Ratio* is the average read ratio of the columns where the index is missing.

app	ela	pub	feb	gun	jee	hsw	hal	for	sag	spr	sho	bro	xma	lit	pyb	fan
#Missing	2	26	3	1	3	5	6	5	0	0	15	42	1	33	2	0
Read ratio	0.91	0.96	0.96	1.0	0.95	0.98	0.92	0.93	/	/	0.95	0.97	0.97	0.92	0.96	/

In our experiment, a column is recognized suitable for indexing if the read access to it is E times more than updates, where E is a configurable threshold. A suitable but not-indexed column indicates a missing index. Table 4 then shows the number of missing indexes, with E set to 5. In 12 out of 15 applications, around 1 to 42 index ought to be added.

Implication: Developers may miss the indexing chance due to the quick evolution of the database schema. Some profiling tools that monitor the read-write ratio of columns can guide the index configuration.

5 Evaluation with WTool

We further introduce two simple optimizations and evaluate their effectiveness. We target two performance issues mentioned in the previous section: pagination with OFFSET and overused transactions.

5.1 Optimize Pagination

We remove the OFFSET clause from a paginated query. Instead, we add a predicate that matches the first row right after the last row in the previous result set. For example, the query SELECT...FROM goods ORDER BY add_time LIMIT N OFFSET M mentioned in Sect. 4.1, is rewritten to SELECT...FROM goods WHERE add_time > T ORDER BY add_time LIMIT N, where T is the max add_time ever seen. The value of T is maintained by the application code.

We apply and evaluate this optimization on litemall. We simulate a scenario where the user browses products page by page. The goods table is populated with 10k rows initially. 90% access goes to the handler method ListProducts.

Table 5. The effectiveness of the pagination optimization. "thpt." stands for throughput. "lat." stands for latency.

	Thpt. (#req/s)	P50 lat. (ms)	P90 lat. (ms)	P99 lat. (ms)
Original	488.21	12.53	19.40	23.29
Optimized	3452.66	5.12	5.37	7.70

The rest is evenly distributed among other handler methods (161 in total). We measure the overall peak throughput and single thread latency. As shown in Table 5, the throughput increase by 7×.

This optimization has a minor consistency issue when facing concurrent insertion. Provided we got the max T = 2019-01-01 from the previous query. Then, a new row with add_time <= 2019-01-01 is inserted. Consequently, the new row exists in neither the current nor the following pages. Nevertheless, we argue that the optimization is still generally applicable since such inconsistency does not affect user experience in most cases.

5.2   Eliminate Redundant Explicit Transaction

We configure Spring to skip the unnecessary BEGIN and COMMIT command and measure the performance improvement.

Table 6. The effectiveness of eliminating redundant BEGIN/COMMIT. "thpt." stands for throughput. "lat." stands for latency.

	Thpt. (#req/s)	P50 lat. (ms)	P90 lat. (ms)	P99 lat. (ms)
Original	9005.95	1.48	1.67	6.80
Optimized	13742.74	1.07	1.13	4.69

We apply and evaluate this optimization on PublicCMS. We simulate a scenario where most users are browsing the site information managed by the application. The sys_site table is populated with 50k rows. 90% of access goes to the handler method ListSites. The rest is evenly distributed among other handler methods (263 handlers in total). As shown in Table 6, the overall throughput increase by 1.52×, and the latency decreases by 30%.

6   Related Work

Static Analysis on Web Applications. A couple of works analyze web applications on the aspects of correctness [44] and performance [47–49].

ACIDRain [44] verifies the correctness of database-backed applications. It detects isolation anomalies on the static conflict graph based on given transactions and invariants. Although this work can find bugs, it may have a coverage issue since the user manually specifies the transactions. With the high-coverage SQL log collected by WTool, ACIDRain can achieve better precision and automation.

Yan [47] analyzes the performance behavior for database-backed applications. They first manually evaluate the application on different workloads and observe their behaviors. Then, they perform static analysis on the Ruby source code to check the impact of the observed behaviors. Next, they detect performance anti-patterns caused by ORM [48]. Compared with them, WTool is more than a piece of analysis work. It provides a tool for both analysis and evaluation. We believe WTool can take over the evaluation step and make the entire process more convenient. Furthermore, both works make some common observations, such as pagination, while we propose new findings such as transaction overprotection.

Benchmarks. Most works [29,43,45,46] use standard benchmarks or a specific web application to prove their efficiency. The TPC Benchmarks [22] and OLTP-Bench [27] are the most widely used ones. Each represents a category of applications. For instance, TPC-C represents the e-commerce applications. However, our analysis shows each individual benchmark cannot represent a broad range of real-world applications.

Some real-world applications are also used for evaluation, such as HotCRP [7]. The user can then configure the workload according to the statistics published online [30]. However, such public data is not always available or suitable for an arbitrary application. Simultaneously, an application cannot speak for others even if they are of the same genre. Instead, WTool works for any web application and generates a benchmark suite specific to the application, as long as its source code is available for the user.

7   Limitation

First, WTool currently focuses on Java applications. The restriction arises from its symbolic execution engine specific for Java byte code.

Second, WTool depends on static analysis. Thus, the analysis result may not reflect the runtime behavior.

8   Conclusion

We propose a tool (WTool) that can automatically analyze and evaluate a web application. It collects and analyzes the SQL queries. It is also able to generate benchmark scripts for performance evaluation automatically. To demonstrate how to use WTool, we analyze 16 Spring web applications. With the analysis result, we introduce several optimizations and evaluate their effectiveness with the benchmark generated by WTool. The evaluation result shows that these optimizations can improve performance by up to 7×.

References

1. Broadleaf. https://github.com/BroadleafCommerce/BroadleafCommerce. Accessed 18 Jun 2021
2. eladmin. https://github.com/elunez/eladmin. Accessed 18 Jun 2021
3. Febs-shiro. https://github.com/wuyouzhuguli/FEBS-Shiro. Accessed 18 Jun 2021
4. Forestblog. https://github.com/saysky/ForestBlog. Accessed 18 Jun 2021
5. forum. https://github.com/fanchaoo/forum. Accessed 18 Jun 2021
6. halo. https://github.com/halo-dev/halo. Accessed 18 Jun 2021
7. Hotcrp. https://hotcrp.com/. Accessed 18 Jun 2021
8. hsweb-framework. https://github.com/hs-web/hsweb-framework. Accessed 18 Jun 2021
9. jeesite. https://github.com/thinkgem/jeesite. Accessed 18 Jun 2021
10. litemall. https://github.com/linlinjava/litemall. Accessed 18 Jun 2021
11. Myrocks. https://myrocks.io/. Accessed 18 Jun 2021
12. Poplar. https://github.com/lvwangbeta/Poplar. Accessed 18 Jun 2021
13. Publiccms. https://github.com/sanluan/PublicCMS. Accessed 18 Jun 2021
14. pybbs. https://github.com/tomoya92/pybbs. Accessed 18 Jun 2021
15. Rocksdb. https://rocksdb.org/. Accessed 18 Jun 2021
16. sagan. https://github.com/spring-io/sagan. Accessed 18 Jun 2021
17. shopizer. https://github.com/shopizer-ecommerce/shopizer. Accessed 18 Jun 2021
18. spring-framework. https://github.com/spring-projects/spring-framework. Accessed 18 Jun 2021
19. Springblog. https://github.com/Raysmond/SpringBlog. Accessed 18 Jun 2021
20. sysbench. https://github.com/akopytov/sysbench. Accessed 18 Jun 2021
21. xmall. https://github.com/Exrick/xmall. Accessed 18 Jun 2021
22. Tpc benchmarks. http://www.tpc.org/information/benchmarks.asp (2001–2019). Accessed 18 Jun 2021
23. Forrester Consulting on behalf of Akamai Technologies, I.: ecommerce web site performance today: an updated look at consumer reaction to a poor online shopping experience. White paper (2009)
24. Bailis, P., Fekete, A., Franklin, M.J., Ghodsi, A., Hellerstein, J.M., Stoica, I.: Feral concurrency control: an empirical investigation of modern application integrity. In: Proceedings of the 2015 ACM SIGMOD International Conference on Management of Data, pp. 1327–1342. SIGMOD 2015, Association for Computing Machinery, New York (2015). https://doi.org/10.1145/2723372.2737784
25. Berenson, H., Bernstein, P., Gray, J., Melton, J., O'Neil, E., O'Neil, P.: A critique of ANSI SQL isolation levels. SIGMOD Rec. 24(2), 1–10 (1995). https://doi.org/10.1145/568271.223785
26. Codd, E.F.: Further normalization of the data base relational model. Research Report/RJ/IBM/San Jose, California RJ909 (1971)
27. Difallah, D.E., Pavlo, A., Curino, C., Cudre-Mauroux, P.: Oltp-bench: an extensible testbed for benchmarking relational databases. Proc. VLDB Endow. 7(4), 277–288 (2013). https://doi.org/10.14778/2732240.2732246
28. Faleiro, J.M., Abadi, D.J., Hellerstein, J.M.: High performance transactions via early write visibility. Proc. VLDB Endow. 10(5), 613–624 (2017). https://doi.org/10.14778/3055540.3055553
29. Gjengset, J., et al.: Noria: dynamic, partially-stateful data-flow for high-performance web applications. In: Proceedings of the 13th USENIX Conference on Operating Systems Design and Implementation, OSDI 2018, pp. 213–231. USENIX Association, USA (2018)

30. Harkins, P.B.: Lobste.rs access pattern statistics for research purposes. (2021). https://lobste.rs/s/cqnzl5/lobste_rs_access_pattern_statistics_for#c_hj0r1b Accessed 18 Jun 2021

31. Leff, A., Rayfield, J.: Web-application development using the model/view/controller design pattern. In: Proceedings Fifth IEEE International Enterprise Distributed Object Computing Conference, pp. 118–127 (2001). https://doi.org/10.1109/EDOC.2001.950428

32. Mu, S., Cui, Y., Zhang, Y., Lloyd, W., Li, J.: In: Extracting more concurrency from distributed transactions. In: Proceedings of the 11th USENIX Conference on Operating Systems Design and Implementation, OSDI 2014, pp. 479–494. USENIX Association, USA (2014)

33. Nah, F.F.H.: A study on tolerable waiting time: how long are web users willing to wait? Behav. Inf. Technol. **23**(3), 153–163 (2004). https://doi.org/10.1080/01449290410001669914

34. Nishtala, R., et al.: Scaling memcache at Facebook. In: 10th USENIX Symposium on Networked Systems Design and Implementation (NSDI 2013), pp. 385–398. USENIX Association, Lombard (2013)

35. O'Neil, E.J.: Object/relational mapping 2008: hibernate and the entity data model (edm). In: Proceedings of the 2008 ACM SIGMOD International Conference on Management of Data, pp. 1351–1356. Association for Computing Machinery, New York (2008). https://doi.org/10.1145/1376616.1376773

36. Pasareanu, C., Visser, W., Bushnell, D.H., Geldenhuys, J., Mehlitz, P., Rungta, N.: Symbolic pathfinder: integrating symbolic execution with model checking for java bytecode analysis. Autom. Softw. Eng. **20**, 391–425 (2013). https://doi.org/10.1007/s10515-013-0122-2

37. Patel, N.: Speed is a killer - why decreasing page load time can drastically increase conversions. https://neilpatel.com/blog/speed-is-a-killer/. Accessed 18 Jun 2021

38. Ports, D.R.K., Clements, A.T., Zhang, I., Madden, S., Liskov, B.: Transactional consistency and automatic management in an application data cache. In: Proceedings of the 9th USENIX Conference on Operating Systems Design and Implementation, pp. 279–292. OSDI 2010, USENIX Association, USA (2010)

39. Pǎsǎreanu, C.S., Rungta, N.: Symbolic pathfinder: symbolic execution of java bytecode. In: Proceedings of the IEEE/ACM International Conference on Automated Software Engineering, ASE 2010, pp. 179–180. Association for Computing Machinery, New York (2010). https://doi.org/10.1145/1858996.1859035

40. Richardson, L., Ruby, S.: RESTful Web Services. O'Reilly Media, Inc (2008)

41. Shasha, D., Llirbat, F., Simon, E., Valduriez, P.: Transaction chopping: algorithms and performance studies. ACM Trans. Database Syst. **20**(3), 325–363 (1995). https://doi.org/10.1145/211414.211427

42. Sidirourgos, L., Kersten, M.: Column imprints: A secondary index structure. In: Proceedings of the 2013 ACM SIGMOD International Conference on Management of Data, SIGMOD 2013, pp. 893–904. Association for Computing Machinery, New York (2013). https://doi.org/10.1145/2463676.2465306

43. Wang, Z., Mu, S., Cui, Y., Yi, H., Chen, H., Li, J.: Scaling multicore databases via constrained parallel execution. In: Proceedings of the 2016 International Conference on Management of Data, SIGMOD 2016, pp. 1643–1658. Association for Computing Machinery, New York (2016). https://doi.org/10.1145/2882903.2882934

44. Warszawski, T., Bailis, P.: Acidrain: concurrency-related attacks on database-backed web applications. In: Proceedings of the 2017 ACM International Conference on Management of Data, SIGMOD 2017, pp. 5–20. Association for Computing Machinery, New York (2017). https://doi.org/10.1145/3035918.3064037

45. Xie, C., et al.: Salt: combining acid and base in a distributed database. In: Proceedings of the 11th USENIX Conference on Operating Systems Design and Implementation, OSDI 2014, pp. 495–509. USENIX Association, USA (2014)

46. Xie, C., Su, C., Littley, C., Alvisi, L., Kapritsos, M., Wang, Y.: High-Performance ACID via Modular Concurrency Control, p. 279–294. Association for Computing Machinery, New York (2015). https://doi.org/10.1145/2815400.2815430

47. Yan, C., Cheung, A., Yang, J., Lu, S.: Understanding Database Performance Inefficiencies in Real-World Web Applications, pp. 1299–1308. Association for Computing Machinery, New York (2017). https://doi.org/10.1145/3132847.3132954

48. Yang, J., Yan, C., Subramaniam, P., Lu, S., Cheung, A.: Powerstation: Automatically detecting and fixing inefficiencies of database-backed web applications in ide. In: Proceedings of the 2018 26th ACM Joint Meeting on European Software Engineering Conference and Symposium on the Foundations of Software Engineering, ESEC/FSE 2018, pp. 884–887. Association for Computing Machinery, New York (2018). https://doi.org/10.1145/3236024.3264589

49. Yang, J., Yan, C., Wan, C., Lu, S., Cheung, A.: View-centric performance optimization for database-backed web applications. In: Proceedings of the 41st International Conference on Software Engineering, ICSE 2019, pp. 994–1004. IEEE Press (2019). https://doi.org/10.1109/ICSE.2019.00104

Semi-supervised Variational Multi-view Anomaly Detection

Shaoshen Wang$^{(\boxtimes)}$ (iD), Ling Chen, Farookh Hussain, and Chengqi Zhang

University of Technology Sydney, Sydney, Australia
{ling.chen,farookh.hussain,Chengqi.Zhang}@uts.edu.au

Abstract. Multi-view anomaly detection (Multi-view AD) is a challenging problem due to the inconsistent behaviors across multiple views. Meanwhile, learning useful representations with little or no supervision has attracted much attention in machine learning. There are a large amount of recent advances in representation learning focusing on deep generative models, such as Variational Auto Encoder (VAE). In this study, by utilizing the representation learning ability of VAE and manipulating the latent variables properly, we propose a novel Bayesian generative model as a semi-supervised multi-view anomaly detector, called MultiVAE. We conduct experiments to evaluate the performance of MultiVAE on multi-view data. The experimental results demonstrate that MultiVAE outperforms the state-of-the-art competitors across popular datasets for semi-supervised multi-view AD. As far as we know, this is the first work that applies VAE-based deep models on multi-view AD.

Keywords: Multi-view anomaly detection · VAE · Semi-supervised

1 Introduction

Anomaly Detection (AD) algorithms [3] aim to identify data points that are significantly different from the remaining data. While the traditional problem setting focuses on data of single-view, we have to deal with data of multiple views in many practical scenarios. For example, social media content usually contains texts, images and user behavior features that provide complementary information of the same items from different perspectives. Consequently, multi-view anomaly detection emerges as a crucial research problem that finds many real-world applications such as purchase behavior analysis [5], malicious insider detection [10], and disparity management [4].

Following the terminology proposed in [14] and [9], multi-view anomalies can be grouped into three categories: 1) *Attribute anomalies*, which refer to instances that exhibit abnormal behaviours in each view. For example, given the data of two views in Fig. 1, the yellow triangles represent an attribute anomaly because it behaves differently from other instances in each view. 2) *Class anomalies*, which refer to instances that exhibit inconsistent characteristics across different views. Such instances behave normally in each view. However, if multiple views are

© Springer Nature Switzerland AG 2021
L. H. U et al. (Eds.): APWeb-WAIM 2021, LNCS 12858, pp. 125–133, 2021.
https://doi.org/10.1007/978-3-030-85896-4_10

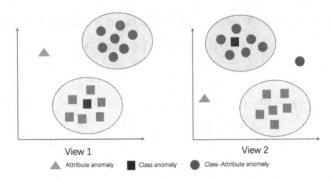

Fig. 1. Three classes of multi-view anomaly. (Color figure online)

considered collectively, the instances show inconsistent properties. For example, the red squares in Fig. 1 represent a class anomaly. Even though it appears to be normal by falling into a cluster in each view, it is similar to different sets of instances in different views. 3) *Class-attribute anomalies*, which are instances having characteristics of attribute anomalies in some views and properties of class anomalies in the other views. The purple circles in Fig. 1 correspond to a class-attribute anomaly.

Existing multi-view AD algorithms have their respective limitations in detecting the three types of anomalies simultaneously. For example, clustering-based algorithms, such as HOrizontal Anomaly Detection (HOAD) [5] and Affinity Propagation (AP) [11], become less effective when there is no clear tendency of clusters in the data; while other modals, such as Probabilistic Latent Variable Model (PLVM) [6], Latent Discriminant Subspace Representation (LDSR) and the recent Hierarchical Bayesian Model (HBM) [13], assume there exists a linear transformation between instances and a common latent variable shared by all views. However, it fails to capture the nonlinearities and impairs the detecting capability for complex data distributions. Moreover, it is risky to assume all the views share a same latent variable, especially for complicated data distribution. Therefore, more advanced algorithms are desired for multi-view AD.

Most existing anomaly detection methods are unsupervised, having access to unlabelled data including both normal and anomalous instances. In real practices, however, it is easy to obtain labeled normal samples because anomalies are defined to be rare [13]. Therefore, it is practically meaningful to develop semi-supervised anomaly detection algorithms trained on labeled normal data, which is supposed to have better performance as the trained model can capture characteristics of normal data better than those trained on polluted data.

In this paper, we propose a Bayesian generative model for semi-supervised multi-view anomaly detection, called MultiVAE. In order to learn the correlation between views directly and detect the inconsistency existing in aforementioned three types of anomalies, we leverage the representation learning ability of VAE to learn a latent distribution for each view, which is then used to reconstruct other views of the same instance. Three types of multi-view anomalies are detected by an anomaly score based on cross-view reconstruction losses. Further, we propose an importance weighted version of reconstruction loss to achieve higher accuracy and stability. Noticing that many real applications of multi-view AD involve data of discrete values, we introduce a Categorical distribution as the likelihood in the decoder of MultiVAE. To enable gradient-based optimization of the model, the Gumbel-softmax [7] technique is utilized to approximate the Categorical distribution.

2   Preliminaries

As a directed probabilistic graphical model (DPGM), a Variational Auto-encoder (VAE) [8] aims to learn a Bayesian latent variable model by maximizing the log-likelihood of the training data $\{x^{(i)}\}_{i=1}^{N}$ via variational inference. It introduces a distribution $q_\phi(z|x)$ to approximate the intractable true posterior $p(z|x)$. Mean and variance vectors μ_v and σ_v are estimated by the encoder, and the latent variable z_v is sampled via reparameterization trick [8]. Then, the decoder takes z_v as input to generate X_v' as a reconstruction for X_v. VAE is trained by maximizing the following Evidence Lower Bound (ELBO):

$$\mathcal{L} = \mathbb{E}_{z \sim q_\phi(z|x^{(i)})}[\log p_\theta(x^{(i)}|z)] - D_{\text{KL}}(q_\phi(z|x^{(i)})||p(z))$$

The importance weighted autoencoder (IWAE) [2] is an important variant of the vanilla VAE. IWAE computes a tighter lower bound through appropriate weighting of a multi-sample estimator, as

$$\mathcal{L}_{IWAE} = \mathbb{E}_{z^{1:K} \sim q_\phi(z|x)}[\log \Sigma_{k=1}^{K} \frac{1}{K} p_\theta(x|z^k)] - D_{\text{KL}}(q_\phi(z|x)||p_\theta(z))$$

3   Methodology

3.1   Problem Setting and Proposed Framework

Suppose that we are given N instances $\{X_1, ..., X_n\}$ with D views. $X_n = (x^{(1)}, ..., x^{(D)})$ is a set of multi-view observation vectors for the n-th instance, and $x^{(d)} \in \mathbb{R}^{M_d}$ is the observation vector of the d-th view where M_d is the corresponding dimensionality. The objective of semi-supervised multi-view AD is to find anomalous instances that have inconsistent characteristics or behaviors across multiple views (i.e., the three types of anomalies discussed in Sect. 1). The training set includes only normal instances while the testing set contains both normal and anomalous instances. For simplicity, we focus on the situation when $D = 2$. However, as will be discussed, our model can be extended to handle more views straightforwardly.

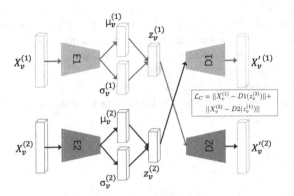

Fig. 2. Architecture of MultiVAE. The model aims to learn cross-view dependency by cross reconstruction.

As mentioned above, multi-view anomalies show inconsistencies between views. That is, if a data point is anomalous, it is likely that its cross-view dependency is lower than that of normal data points. Given a data instance X of two views, we model the cross-view dependency using the conditional distribution between two views, $p(X^{(2)}|X^{(1)})$ and $p(X^{(1)}|X^{(2)})$. Then, given a normal instance $X_i = [X_i^{(1)}, X_i^{(2)}]$ and an anomalous instance $X_j = [X_j^{(1)}, X_j^{(2)}]$ (being a class anomaly, an attribute anomaly, or a class-attribute anomaly), we have the following assumption:

$$p(X_i^{(2)}|X_i^{(1)}) + p(X_i^{(1)}|X_i^{(2)}) > p(X_j^{(2)}|X_j^{(1)}) + p(X_j^{(1)}|X_j^{(2)})$$

Based on the cross-view dependency assumption, we propose MultiVAE which generates one view from the other. For example, as shown in Fig. 2, the model utilizes the input of view_1 to estimate the latent variable $z_v^{(1)}$ and generate output for view_2. In the same time, view_2 is used to generate view_1. The model can be expressed as follows:

$$\mu^{(1)} = f_{\phi_1^1}(X^{(1)}), \sigma^{(1)} = f_{\phi_2^1}(X^{(1)}); \mu^{(2)} = f_{\phi_1^2}(X^{(2)}), \sigma^{(2)} = f_{\phi_2^2}(X^{(2)})$$

$$z_v^{(1)} \sim Gaussian(\mu^{(1)}, \sigma^{(1)}), z_v^{(2)} \sim Gaussian(\mu^{(2)}, \sigma^{(2)})$$

$$X_v^{'(2)} \sim p_{\theta_2}(X|z_v^{(1)}), X_v^{'(1)} \sim p_{\theta_1}(X|z_v^{(2)})$$

The parameters of model is set $\{\phi_1^1, \phi_2^1, \phi_1^2, \phi_2^2, \theta_1, \theta_2\}$. f is a function parameterized by NN serving as the encoder, p is a predefined distribution serving as the decoder. Note that, similar to VAE, we can seek help from amortized variational inference to estimate the parameters of the model.

Our framework can be extended straightforwardly to handle more views with linear time complexity with respect to the number of views. Suppose there are n views where $n > 2$, we can concatenate all the $n - 1$ views except view i to generate view i. Regarding the time complexity, suppose each encoder or decoder is implemented by Multilayer perceptron that has time consumption $O(1)$ for feed forward of one instance. Given n training instances, D encoders and D decoders, the overall time complexity is $O(nD)$ for training phase, $O(D)$ for detecting a single instance in testing phase.

3.2   Loss Function Deduction

For simplification, we denote $X_v^{(1)} = X_1$, $X_v^{(2)} = X_2$. Under the maximum likelihood estimation (MLE) framework, it would be complicated to directly maximize $p(X_1, X_2)$. Hence, we infer the parameters of the model in the way similar to the variational inference used in VAE. We derive an Evidence Lower Bound (ELBO) to approximate the log likelihood of $p(X_1, X_2)$, which can be formulated as follows:

$$\log p(X_1, X_2)$$
$$\geq \mathbb{E}_{q(z_1, z_2)} \left[\log \frac{p(X_1, X_2, z_1, z_2)}{q(z_1, z_2)} \right] \ (Jensen's\ inequality)$$
$$\approx \mathbb{E}_{q(z_1|X_1)q(z_2|X_2)} \left[\log \frac{p(X_2|z_1)p(X_1|z_2)p(z_1)p(z_2)}{q(z_1|X_1)q(z_2|X_2)} \right]$$
$$(mean\text{-}field\ approximation)$$
$$= -\mathcal{L}_C - D_{\text{KL}}(q_\phi(z_1|X_1)||p(z_1)) - D_{\text{KL}}(q_\phi(z_2|X_2)||p(z_2))$$

where $\mathcal{L}_C$ represents the reconstruction error, D_{KL} represents Kullback-Leibler divergence between two distributions, $p(z_1)$ and $p(z_2)$ can be isotropic multivariate Gaussian. In practice, we adopt the importance weighted ELBO as the training objective to obtain tighter lower bound and less variance:

$$\mathcal{L}_{MultiVAE} = \mathbb{E}_{z_1^{1:K} \sim q_\phi(z_1|X_1)} [\log \Sigma_{k=1}^K \frac{1}{K} p_\theta(X_2|z_1^k)] - D_{\text{KL}}(q_\phi(z_1|X_1)||p_\theta(z_1))$$
$$+ \mathbb{E}_{z_2^{1:K} \sim q_\phi(z_2|X_2)} [\log \Sigma_{k=1}^K \frac{1}{K} p_\theta(X_1|z_2^k)] - D_{\text{KL}}(q_\phi(z_2|X_2)||p_\theta(z_2))$$

3.3   Categorical Distribution for Discrete Data

Discrete data (e.g., categorical data) frequently appears in many real AD applications. VAE-based models usually use Gaussian or Bernoulli distribution as $p(x|z)$ for generating instances, which performs poorly on discrete data. In order to alleviate this issue, we assume that discrete data are generated from categorical distribution. We introduce a K dimensional categorical distribution $Cat(\pi_1, \pi_2...\pi_k)$ as $p(x|z)$ and assume K dimensional one-hot instance vector x sampled from the generative process: $x \sim p(x|z) = Cat(\pi_1, \pi_2...\pi_k)$ where $Cat(x = i|\pi_1, \pi_2...\pi_k) = \pi_i$ and $\sum_{i=1}^K \pi_i = 1$. However, this sampling process is not differentiable and the model cannot be optimized by gradient-based methods. We thus apply the Gumbel-Softmax re-parameterization trick [7] to approximate the sampling process and make it to be differentiated. The element i of vector x can be approximated as:

$$x_i = \frac{exp((\log(\pi_i) + g_i)/\tau)}{\Sigma_{j=1}^{K} exp((\log(\pi_j) + g_j)/\tau)} \; for \, i = 1, 2...K$$

where π_i is estimated by neural network in decoder, $\tau > 0$ is an adjustable hyper-parameter which controls how closely the samples approximate discrete values. A smaller τ means a closer approximation. $g \sim Gumbel(0, 1)$ are i.i.d. samples from standard Gumbel distribution.

3.4   Semi-supervised Multi-view Anomaly Detection Score Design

To detect the three types of multi-view anomalies, we compute an anomaly score for each instance. We analyze the behaviour of normal and abnormal data during the testing phase as follows:

For *normal instances*, since the correlation between views accords with normal training data, it's easy to reconstruct one view from another view. This gives rise to a smaller cross reconstruction error $\mathcal{L}_C$. For *Class anomalies*, since different view belongs to different class, it is inconsistent cross multiple views, making it difficult to reconstruct one view from another. The cross reconstruction error $\mathcal{L}_C$ should be high. For *Attribute anomalies*, since views belong to distribution different from that of the training data, the correlation between views is different from what the model has learned during training, which also leads to a high $\mathcal{L}_C$. For *Class-Attribute anomalies*, the situation is similar to *attribute anomalies* so that this type of anomalies can be detected by high $\mathcal{L}_C$ as well.

Overall, it is expected that the cross-view reconstruction error $\mathcal{L}_C$ for a normal instance is less than that of an anomalous instance, including *Class anomaly*, *Attribute anomaly* and *Class-attribute anomaly*. Therefore, we use $\mathcal{L}_C$ as the anomaly score for an instance x_i as follows (K is the number of importance weighted sampling):

$$S_{\text{MultiVAE}}(x_i) = \mathcal{L}_C = -(\mathbb{E}_{z_1^{1:K} \sim q_\phi(z_1|x_i^{(1)})}[\log \Sigma_{k=1}^{K} \frac{1}{K} p(x_i^{(2)}|z_1^k)]$$

$$+ \, \mathbb{E}_{z_2^{1:K} \sim q_\phi(z_2|x_i^{(2)})}[\log \Sigma_{k=1}^{K} \frac{1}{K} p(x_i^{(1)}|z_2^k)]) \tag{1}$$

As S_{MultiVAE} measures the reconstruction error, a higher score indicates a larger probability of an instance being anomalous.

4   Experiments

We compare our method with the HOrizontal Anomaly Detection (HOAD) [5], Affinity Propagation (AP) [11], the Probabilistic Latent Variable Model (PLVM) [6], the Latent Discriminant Subspace Representation (LDSR) [9] and the state-of-the-art Hierarchical Bayesian Model (HBM) [13] to evaluate performance of

MultiVAE. Seven datasets, including Thyroid, Annthyroid, Forestcover, Vowels, Pima, Wine and Glass, from the ODDS library [12] are used. We follow the same experimental setting in [13] for fair comparison. Three types of multi-view anomalies are generated in the same way described in previous works [9,13]. We use the area under the ROC curve (AUC) as the evaluation measure. The higher the AUC is, the better the approach performs.

Table 1 shows the average AUCs achieved by the comparing models on the 7 datsets of the training data (Some results of the baselines are from [13]). It demonstrates the advantage of our proposed approach for multi-view AD clearly, where MultiVAE consistently outperforms the other models on most datasets. This can be explained by the capability of capturing the correlation among multiple views via multiple latent vectors, supported by the non-linear learning ability of neural networks together with cross-view reconstruction.

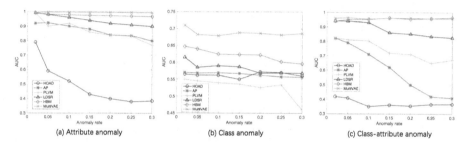

(a) Attribute anomaly   (b) Class anomaly   (c) Class-attribute anomaly

Fig. 3. The curves of AUC W.R.T anomaly rate in Pima dataset.

To investigate how the anomaly rate affects the performance of different models, we experiment on data polluted by an increasing percentage of outliers. Figure 3 shows the variation of AUCs on data set *pima* with outlier ratio of 2%, 5%, 10%, 15%, 20%, 25% and 30% for three types of outliers. We see that, in general, as the anomaly rate increases, the performance decreases. And the proposed method is comparatively robust compared with the other methods.

To evaluate the situation when there are more than two views of the data (i.e., $n > 2$), we run the comparative methods on the WebKB dataset [1], which has been widely used for evaluating multi-view learning algorithms. We use its Cornell subset in our experiment, which contains 195 webpages over 5 labels. Each webpage is described by four views: content, inbound link, outbound link and cites. Table 2 shows the AUC values of all compared methods on the dataset with outlier ratio of 5% and 10%. It can be observed that MultiVAE again achieves higher AUC than its competitors, which demonstrates the strength of our Bayesian detector.

Table 1. AUC values (mean±std) of semi-supervised multi-view AD on seven datasets with anomaly rate = 0.05. (A:Attribute anomaly; C:Class anomaly; C-A:Class-Attribute anomaly)

	Model	Thyroid	Annthyroid	ForestCover	Vowels	Pima	Wine	Glass
A	HOAD	.5202±.0864	.5078±.0724	.6801±.0866	.8540±.0691	.5921±.0768	.6503±.1574	.7083±.1410
	AP	.6737±.1164	.5747±.0669	.6774±.0739	.7062±.1125	.9376±.0293	.6947±.1078	.7497±.1117
	PLVM	.8989±.0091	.8904±.0363	.4870±.0126	.5481±.0067	.9086±.0083	.4058±.0481	.4087±.0246
	LDSR	.9751±.0074	.9876±.0022	.9983±.0005	.9181±.0153	.9858±.0057	**.9932±.0009**	**.9940±.0040**
	HBM	.9877±.0056	.9979±.001	.9995±.0027	.9875±.0071	.9877±.0044	.9417±.0450	.9530±.0292
	MultiVAE	**.9991±.0005**	**.9996±.0001**	**.9998±.0001**	**.9988±.0010**	**.9964±.0030**	.9658±.0316	.9824±.0165
C	HOAD	.5393±.0303	.5849±.0348	.6872±.0337	.3818±.0384	.5557±.0310	.7124±.0638	.4277±.0932
	AP	.5847±.0227	.5265±.0350	.7906±.0332	.7520±.0513	.5659±.0365	.5629±.0933	.5576±.0518
	PLVM	.5676±.0090	.4087±.0176	.6035±.0044	.5479±.0282	.5425±.0138	.4860±.0040	.5433±.0104
	LDSR	.8631±.0217	.7128±.0418	.7551±.0293	.9245±.0173	.5924±.0543	.5889±.0916	.7098±.0498
	HBM	.8744±.0205	.7383±.0450	.8672±.0197	.9360±.0158	.6354±.0400	.8373±.0424	.7613±.0570
	MultiVAE	**.9678±.0144**	**.7891±.0819**	**.9814±.0118**	**.9711±.0132**	**.6562±.0670**	**.9068±.0794**	**.7698±.1490**
C-A	HOAD	.4934±.0270	.4976±.0311	.4342±.0468	.5994±.1342	.4181±.0260	.5798±.0615	.5598±.0652
	AP	.6380±.0723	.5647±.0819	.8054±.0373	.8511±.0713	.7916±.0555	.5481±.1173	.7308±.0676
	PLVM	.7122±.0191	.8933±.0134	.8184±.0087	.6390±.0223	.8249±.0063	.7094±.0145	.9555±.0092
	LDSR	.9344±.0179	.9122±.0220	.9845±.0049	.9642±.0064	.9315±.0146	1±0	.9900±.0026
	HBM	.9863±.0075	.9842±.0076	.9857±.0095	.9757±.0082	.9510±.0169	.9201±.0470	**.9984±.0023**
	MultiVAE	**.9930±.0057**	**.9943±.0054**	**.9989±.0012**	**.9937±.0045**	**.9571±.0232**	.9018±.0872	.9456±.0300

Table 2. AUC values of competitors on 4-view WebKB dataset.

	HOAD	AP	LDSR	HBM	MultiVAE
5% anomalies	0.811	0.755	0.672	0.930	**0.942**
10% anomalies	0.769	0.715	0.647	0.922	**0.934**

5   Conclusion

We propose a VAE-based deep framework for multi-view AD. Under the framework, MultiVAE is developed to model the dependency between views for semi-supervised AD. Our experimental results on benchmark data and real-world data demonstrate the effectiveness of MultiVAE as the first effort that leverages variational auto-encoder in multi-view anomaly detection, by exploiting the cross-view reconstruction loss.

Acknowledgement. This work has been partially supported by ARC DP180100966.

References

1. Blum, A., Mitchell, T.: Combining labeled and unlabeled data with co-training. In: Proceedings of the Eleventh Annual Conference on Computational Learning Theory, pp. 92–100 (1998)
2. Burda, Y., Grosse, R., Salakhutdinov, R.: Importance weighted autoencoders. arXiv preprint arXiv:1509.00519 (2015)
3. Chandola, V., Banerjee, A., Kumar, V.: Anomaly detection: a survey. ACM Comput. Surv. **41**, 15:1–15:58 (2009)

4. Duh, K., Yeung, C.M.A., Iwata, T., Nagata, M.: Managing information disparity in multilingual document collections. ACM Trans. Speech Lang. Process. **10**, 1:1–1:28 (2013)
5. Gao, J., Fan, W., Turaga, D., Parthasarathy, S., Han, J.: A spectral framework for detecting inconsistency across multi-source object relationships. In: 2011 IEEE 11th International Conference on Data Mining, pp. 1050–1055. IEEE (2011)
6. Iwata, T., Yamada, M.: Multi-view anomaly detection via robust probabilistic latent variable models. In: Advances in Neural Information Processing Systems, pp. 1136–1144 (2016)
7. Jang, E., Gu, S., Poole, B.: Categorical reparameterization with Gumbel-Softmax. arXiv preprint arXiv:1611.01144 (2016)
8. Kingma, D.P., Welling, M.: Auto-encoding variational Bayes. arXiv preprint arXiv:1312.6114 (2013)
9. Li, K., Li, S., Ding, Z., Zhang, W., Fu, Y.: Latent discriminant subspace representations for multi-view outlier detection. In: Thirty-Second AAAI Conference on Artificial Intelligence (2018)
10. Liu, A.Y., Lam, D.N.: Using consensus clustering for multi-view anomaly detection. In: 2012 IEEE Symposium on Security and Privacy Workshops, pp. 117–124. IEEE (2012)
11. Marcos Alvarez, A., Yamada, M., Kimura, A., Iwata, T.: Clustering-based anomaly detection in multi-view data. In: Proceedings of the 22nd ACM International Conference on Information & Knowledge Management, pp. 1545–1548. ACM (2013)
12. Rayana, S.: Odds library (2016)
13. Wang, Z., Lan, C.: Towards a hierarchical Bayesian model of multi-view anomaly detection. In: Proceedings of the Twenty-Ninth International Joint Conference on Artificial Intelligence (2020)
14. Zhao, H., Fu, Y.: Dual-regularized multi-view outlier detection. In: Twenty-Fourth International Joint Conference on Artificial Intelligence (2015)

A Graph Attention Network Model for GMV Forecast on Online Shopping Festival

Qianyu Yu$^{(\boxtimes)}$, Shuo Yang, Zhiqiang Zhang, Ya-Lin Zhang, Binbin Hu,
Ziqi Liu, Kai Huang, Xingyu Zhong, Jun Zhou, and Yanming Fang

Ant Group, Hangzhou, China
{qianyu.yqy,kexi.ys,lingyao.zzq,lyn.zyl,bin.hbb,ziqiliu,
kevin.hk,xingyu.zxy,jun.zhoujun,yanming.fym}@antgroup.com

Abstract. In this paper, we present a novel Graph Attention Network based framework for GMV (Gross Merchandise Volume) forecast on online festival, called GAT-GF. Based on the well-designed retailer-customer graph and retailer-retailer graph, we employ a graph neural network based encoder cooperated with multi-head attention and self attention mechanism to comprehensively capture complicated structure between consumers and retailers, followed by a two-way regression decoder for effective predition. Extensive experiments on real promotion datasets demonstrate the superiority of GAT-GF.

Keywords: GMV forecast · GAT · e-commerce sales promotion

1 Introduction

GMV (Gross Merchandise Volume) forecast is an essential problem for shopping festivals (e.g., Double 11[1] and Double 12) on e-commerce platforms, since accurate GMV estimation can help platforms assess the sales ability of retailers and then provide better services. However, its materialization is non-trivial, with two major challenges based on the analysis on real data in Taobao.com[2]. **1). Abnormal sales in shopping festivals.** Figure 1 shows the average daily GMV of each month and shopping festivals for all the online retailers. We can find that the GMV distributions are indeed very skew, where the sales of Double 11 (Double 12) is extremely larger than usual days. Due to the lack of trend and seasonal patterns, classical statistical and time series based methods [1,2] are not suitable. **2). Different contributions derived from neighbors.** Through the intuitive analysis for the consumption behaviours of customers in the shopping festival from the perspective of gender in Fig. 2, we conclude that the consumption behaviours of different consumers vary greatly. Thus it is impressing to develop an ingenious module to capture structural impact derived from related

---

[1] https://en.wikipedia.org/wiki/Singles%27_Day.
[2] https://en.wikipedia.org/wiki/Taobao.

L. H. U et al. (Eds.): APWeb-WAIM 2021, LNCS 12858, pp. 134–139, 2021.
https://doi.org/10.1007/978-3-030-85896-4_11

retailers and customers in two main aspects: i) Different relationships between
retailers have different impacts. ii) Distinct consumption preferences of consumers in shopping festivals need to be carefully considered.

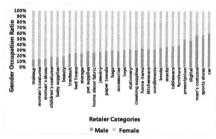

Fig. 1. GMV comparison of usual days
and sales promotion.

Fig. 2. Customers gender analysis of different retailer categories.

In this paper, we design an end-to-end graph neural network based model to
tackle the aforementioned challenges. Firstly, an R-C graph (short for **R**etailer-
Customer graph) consisting of the transactions between retailers and their consumers and an R-R graph (short for **R**etailer-**R**etailer graph) consisting of various relationships between retailers (e.g., supply chain [3] and warehouse sharing) are conducted to comprehensively explore complicated structure between
consumers and retailers. Following [4], we proposed GAT-GF, a novel **G**raph
ATtention network for **G**MV **F**orecast, consisting of a graph neural network
based encoder cooperated with multi-head attention and self attention mechanism and an effective two-way regression decoder. Extensive experiments on
large-scale real shopping festival datasets prove the effectiveness of our proposal.

2   The Proposed Model

Before the elaboration of the proposed GAT-GF, we briefly describe the input
of GAT-GF, which aims at fully exploring complicated structure between consumers and retailers for facilitating GMV forecast. Specifically, it contains an
R-C graph, where retailers and consumers are connected with transaction relationship and an R-R graph, where retailers are connected based on some domain
knowledge (e.g., house sharing or supply chain). Now, as shown in Fig. 3, we are
ready to zoom into each well-designed part of the proposed GAT-GF, i.e., a
graph neural network based encoder and a two-regression decoder.

2.1   Graph Neural Network Based Encoder

Information Extraction with Multi-head Attention. To fully consider
the different contributions derived from neighbors, we employ the multi-head

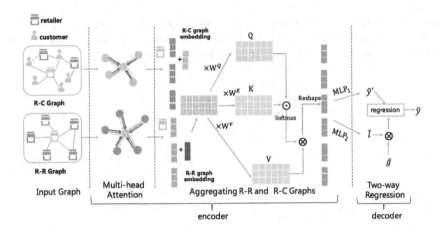

Fig. 3. The overall framework of GAT-GF.

attention mechanism [7] to adaptively learn the representation for each retailer, where each head may extract one aspect of customers' or retailers' influence, and different heads pay attention to different aspects. Therefore, the customers' and retailers' contribution can be divided without any manual defined strategy.

For each graph $\Phi \in (RR, RC)$, at the t-th aggregation (we suppose neighbour in T hops), we design our graph attention network layer using multi-head attention mechanism in [5], and we get the initial node representation $e_{i,\Phi}^{(t+1)}$:

$$e_{i,\Phi}^{(t+1)} = \overset{K}{\underset{k=1}{\|}} \sigma(\sum_{j \in \mathcal{N}_{i,\Phi}} \alpha_{ij,\Phi}^{k,(t)} W_\Phi^{k,(t)} h_{j,\Phi}^{(t)}), \tag{1}$$

where $\mathcal{N}_{i,\Phi}$ denotes node i's one-hop neighbour set in R-C or R-R graph. $h_{i,\Phi}^{(t)} \in \mathbb{R}^F$ represents node i's intermediate embedding at the t-th aggregation in graph Φ and $h_i^{(0)}$ is the original feature vector of node i, $\|$ represents concatenation, K is the number of attention heads, σ represents the activation function, and W is input linear transformation weight matrix. Here we define attention coefficients α_{ij}^k with a learnable parameter H as

$$\alpha_{ij}^k = \frac{\exp(H_{ij}^k(h_i \| h_j))}{\sum_{j' \in \mathcal{N}_j} \exp(H_{ij'}^k(h_i \| h_{j'}))}, \tag{2}$$

Information Aggregation with Self-attention. In macroscopic view, we adopt a self-attention mechanism to aggregate representations generated from R-R and R-C graph. In particular, inspired by the idea of positional encoding in [6], we also generate two learnable network type embedding $p_{i,\Phi} \in \mathbb{R}^{K \times F}$ for the R-R and R-C graph and obtain:

$$e_i^{(t)} = (e_{i,RR}^{(t)} + p_{i,RR}^{(t)}) \|(e_{i,RC}^{(t)} + p_{i,RC}^{(t)}). \tag{3}$$

Self-attention mechanism operates on the input encoding $e_i^{(t)} \in \mathbb{R}^{2K \times F}$, and computes the representation $h_i^{(t)}$ as:

$$h_i^{(t)} = \text{softmax} \frac{(e_i^{(t)} W^{Q,(t)})(e_i^{(t)} W^{K,(t)})^{\mathrm{T}}}{\sqrt{d_z}} (e_i^{(t)} W^{V,(t)}). \qquad (4)$$

W^Q, W^K and $W^V \in \mathbb{R}^{F \times d_z}$ are parameter matrices to learn. Once we obtain $h_i^{(t)}$, we can take it back to Eq. (1) to compute embeddings of the next hop hierarchically or compute the loss function in the next section.

2.2   Two-Way Regression Decoder

Given the embedding of each retailer based on our proposed encoder, we design a two-way decoder for final prediction. Beforehand, with the real data from Taobao.com, we give an intuitive analysis about the abnormal sales in shopping festivals, as shown in Fig. 4a and Fig. 4b. We observe that retailers do not change much between two adjacent months (Fig. 4a), while retailers whose lift in the shopping festival exceeds five times over the usual days occupy the overall retailers about 35%, and sales of these retailers compromise 96% sales volume of shopping festival (Fig. 4b). We take the inspiration that large share of sales in the shopping festival is dominated by a small number of retailers, and propose an effective two-way decoder with the consideration of the GMV lift prediction.

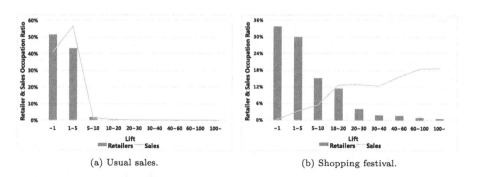

(a) Usual sales.   (b) Shopping festival.

Fig. 4. Lift comparison on usual sales and shopping festival sales.

In particular, the estimated GMV lift is multiplied by the average daily GMV, and we get the other prediction through this auxiliary task. Next, we combine the two predictions, and learn the parameters to balance them to get the final prediction result. Thus, final prediction is calculated as:

$$\tilde{y}_i = \underbrace{\alpha \mathbf{v}_G^{(T)} h_i^{(T)}}_{\text{GMV estimation}} + \beta \underbrace{(\mathbf{v}_l^{(T)} h_i^{(T)} + b_1)}_{\text{lift estimation}} \cdot \overline{g}_i + b_2, \qquad (5)$$

where $\tilde{y}_i$ denotes the final estimation of the GMV of retailer i, $\overline{g}_i$ is the average daily GMV of retailer i, $\mathbf{v}_G \in \mathbb{R}^{d_z}$ and $\mathbf{v}_l \in \mathbb{R}^{d_z}$ are parameters to transform the retailer embeddings to GMV and lift estimation, α and β are the parameters adjusting the two estimations to the final regression prediction, and b_1 and b_2 are the constant offsets. Then we employ a mean square error loss on the final node prediction.

3   Experiment

3.1   Experimental Setup

Samples. We choose the labeled samples (retailers) of Double 11 and Double 12 on the Taobao.com. In practice, online shopping platform predicts sales volume using data of months ahead of the shopping festival to provide services in advance accordingly. Therefore we employ retailers' attributes of June to Sep., which can be represented as Double 11-June (Double 11 using data of June) to Double 11-Sep.. As a result, our model is evaluated on 8 datasets (4 for each shopping festival respectively). Sales volume of shopping festival in 2018 year is considered as the training set, and 2019 as the testing set.

Comparison Methods. We take Gradient Boosting Decision Tree (**GBDT**), Neural Network (**NN**) and Graph Attention Network (GAT)-based models [5] (i.e., **GAT-RC** and **GAT-RR** with R-C and R-R graph, respectively) as baseline models. For fair comparison, we train all models with batch size of 64 and utilize Adam optimizer with learning rate of 1e–4 and regularization term of 2e–4. Moreover, we set the number of layer as 2 for NN and GAT based model and use 200 trees for the training of GBDT. We repeat the experiments for 3 times and the averaged results are reported.

3.2   Result Analysis

In order to reduce the prediction error, we take the logarithmic transformation of origin GMV as the regression goal. Besides, all the results reported in this section is on the testing set and the metric we used to measure the performance is the mean squared error (MSE).

Table 1 is the comparison result of the above methods (left) and ablation experiment (right). We can find that GAT-GF outperforms other models, which demonstrates the superiority of the proposed model. GAT-RR and GAT-RC outperforms GBDT and NN. It proves the effectiveness of R-R relations and R-C relations. However, the performance of GAT-RR is better than GAT-RC. It demonstrates the relation between retailers works better, and one reason is that leveraging related retailers' information is more direct to our goal. The performance of GAT-GF is better than GAT-RR and GAT-RC. It shows that fusing the R-R graph and R-C graph is positive. As the days approach the shopping festival, result is more accurate. It is because the feature and the graph are closer

Table 1. Performance comparison on 8 datasets. "-SA", "-TR", "-MH", "-NT" is short for GAT-GF by removing the self-attention, two-way regression, multi-head and network type embedding module, respectively.

Data	GBDT	NN	GAT-RR	GAT-RC	GAT-(RR,RC)	-SA	-TR	-MH	-NT	GAT-GF
Double 11-June	9.01	7.51	7.34	7.35	7.27	7.49	7.32	7.22	7.35	**7.19**
Double 11-July	6.50	6.47	6.33	6.44	6.31	6.33	6.29	6.32	6.26	**6.24**
Double 11-Aug.	5.75	6.18	5.65	5.61	5.57	5.57	5.58	5.53	5.57	**5.51**
Double 11-Sep.	4.68	4.70	4.60	4.61	4.57	4.61	4.54	4.60	4.57	**4.52**
Double 12-June	9.21	7.91	7.77	7.86	7.74	7.83	7.64	7.71	7.64	**7.56**
Double 12-July	7.19	7.27	7.05	7.06	6.99	6.98	6.99	7.05	7.04	**6.94**
Double 12-Aug.	6.63	6.59	6.43	6.51	6.41	6.42	6.44	6.39	6.44	**6.37**
Double 12-Sep.	5.82	5.80	5.68	5.76	5.66	5.73	5.74	5.68	5.64	**5.61**

to the day of shopping festival, and the same reason is that the results of the same month in Double 11 are better than that in Double 12. In the ablation experiment, we remove the modules we design and get four models – directly concatenates results from R-R and R-C graphs without self-attention, predicts GMV without auxiliary lift prediction, outputs embedding without multi-head mechanism, and removes network type embedding for input. The result shows that GAT-GF performs better than other models, which demonstrates the effectiveness of each module.

4   Conclusion

In this paper, we study the GMV forecast problem of the online shopping festival, which to the best of our knowledge is the first work. Experiments on the Taobao.com in the Double 11 and Double 12 show the validation our model and the ablation experiments show the effectiveness of each module we design.

References

1. Alon, I., Qi, M., Sadowski, R.J.: Forecasting aggregate retail sales: a comparison of artificial neural networks and traditional methods. J. Retail. Consum. Serv. **8**(3), 147–156 (2001)
2. Box, G.E., Jenkins, G.M., Reinsel, G.C., Ljung, G.M.: Time Series Analysis: Forecasting and Control. Wiley, Hoboken (2015)
3. Yang, S., Zhang, Z., Zhou, J., Wang, Y., Sun, W., Zhong, X., et al.: Financial risk analysis for SMEs with graph-based supply chain mining. In: IJCAI, pp. 4661–4667 (2020)
4. Hamilton, W.L., Ying, R., Leskovec, J.: Representation learning on graphs: methods and applications. arXiv preprint arXiv:1709.05584 (2017)
5. Veličković, P., Cucurull, G., Casanova, A., Romero, A., Lio, P., Bengio, Y.: Graph attention networks. arXiv preprint arXiv:1710.10903 (2017)
6. Vaswani, A., Shazeer, N., Parmar, N., Uszkoreit, J., Jones, L., Gomez, A.N., et al.: Attention is all you need. In: NIPS, pp. 5998–6008 (2017)
7. Li, J., Tu, Z., Yang, B., Lyu, M.R., Zhang, T.: Multi-head attention with disagreement regularization. arXiv preprint arXiv:1810.10183 (2018)

Suicide Ideation Detection on Social Media During COVID-19 via Adversarial and Multi-task Learning

Jun Li[1], Zhihan Yan[2], Zehang Lin[1(✉)], Xingyun Liu[3], Hong Va Leong[1],
Nancy Xiaonan Yu[4,5], and Qing Li[1]

[1] Department of Computing, The Hong Kong Polytechnic University,
Hong Kong, People's Republic of China
zehang.lin@connect.polyu.hk
[2] Department of Electronic and Electrical Engineering,
University College London, London, UK
[3] School of Psychology, Central China Normal University,
Wuhan, People's Republic of China
[4] Department of Social and Behavioural Sciences, City University of Hong Kong,
Hong Kong, People's Republic of China
[5] Shenzhen Research Institute of City University of Hong Kong,
Shenzhen, People's Republic of China

Abstract. Suicide ideation detection on social media is a challenging problem due to its implicitness. In this paper, we present an approach to detect suicide ideation on social media based on a BERT-LSTM model with Adversarial and Multi-task learning (BLAM). More specifically, BLAM combines BERT model with Bi-LSTM model to extract deeper and richer features. Furthermore, emotion classification is utilized as an auxiliary task to perform multi-task learning, which enriches the extracted features with emotion information that enhances the identification of suicide. In addition, BLAM generates adversarial noise by adversarial learning improving the generalization ability of the model. Extensive experiments conducted on our collected Suicide Ideation Detection (SID) dataset demonstrate the competitive superiority of BLAM compared with the state-of-the-art methods.

Keywords: Suicide ideation detection · Adversarial learning · Multi-task learning

1 Introduction

Globally, one person loses his/her life to suicide every 40 s. With the impact of the COVID-19 pandemic, this figure could be undervalued. With the development of online social media, the anonymity of some online communities allows people who are suffering from a deep wound to talk about their suicidal ideas freely, which may not be revealed in the real world. Therefore, many studies begin to focus on

© Springer Nature Switzerland AG 2021
L. H. U et al. (Eds.): APWeb-WAIM 2021, LNCS 12858, pp. 140–145, 2021.
https://doi.org/10.1007/978-3-030-85896-4_12

suicide ideation detection on social media. However, there are some inevitable challenges existing in suicide ideation detection on social media. First, the data relevant to suicide ideation on social media tend to be implicit [2]. Second, most of the data on social media are unstructured and full of noise, which makes data collection and processing difficult. Even though some researchers [2] try to utilize effective characteristics to explore the implicitness of suicide ideation from social media posts, they have not considered noisy words which could disturb the model's ability in learning implicitness.

In this paper, we utilize a **BERT-LSTM** model with **A**dversarial and **M**ulti-task learning (BLAM) to detect suicide ideation on social media. BLAM consists of feature extraction, adversarial learning and multi-task learning which can extract features related to user emotions and have better generalization ability.

2 Related Work

There is a body of work analyzing a wealth of information and users' language preferences from users' posts. On one hand, some works utilize dictionary-based methods like linguistic inquiry and word count (LIWC) to study suicidal posts on social media. For example, Gunn et al. [3] analyze the tweets from suicidal attempters within 24 h before they died. However, this kind of works mainly focuses on suicidal posts analysis instead of suicide prediction. On the other hand, more and more works turn to use machine learning to predict suicide ideation on social media via online posts. For example, Ambalavan et al. [1] extract a set of Trigrams, NLTK POS Tags and Customised POS Tags as features that improve classification performance on the dataset with 16-labels including methods and behaviors of suicide and it shows that the support vector machine (SVM) model yields the best performance. However, these methods tend to perform well with complex feature engineering, which is labor intensive [5]. Currently, deep learning model has been the most effective method because it can learn the representation of text automatically without much sophisticated feature engineering. Sinha et al. [9] and Sawhney et al. [7,8] predict the suicide ideation from the perspective of the order of the posts, social network structure and temporal information respectively. However, these works have not considered noisy words in social media and heavily rely on the data from a specific scenario.

3 Methodology

The proposed framework for suicide ideation detection is shown in Fig. 1. Given a post from social media, the feature extraction model (i.e., BERT, Bi-LSTM and $fc1$) first extracts the text feature f. Then, $fc2$ can use the feature to classify whether the post is *normal* or *suicidal* via two loss components (i.e., suicidal loss and adversarial loss). At the same time, emotion classification as an auxiliary task is performed by $fc2'$ for multi-task learning with emotion loss, which incorporates the information of the emotion into the extracted features. In particular, outputs from $fc1$ (i.e., f) are vectors, but outputs from $fc2$ and $fc2'$ are class labels (i.e., *normal* and *suicide* vs *anger, fear ...* and *joy*).

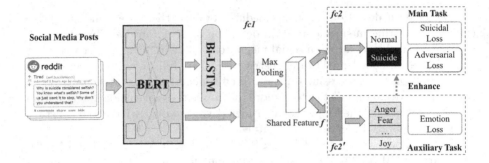

Fig. 1. The BLAM framework, which includes a BERT model, a Bi-LSTM model and three fully connected layers (i.e., $fc1$, $fc2$ and $fc2'$). In particular, '**Enhance**' means that the auxiliary task helps the main task improve its performance, which makes changes to weights of BERT, Bi-LSTM and $fc1$ to generate the shared feature f containing the information captured by emotion.

To summarize the previous discussions, we obtain the overall objective function as:

$$\mathcal{L} = \mathcal{L}_{suicide} + \mathcal{L}_{adv} + \mathcal{L}_{emotion} \tag{1}$$

$$\mathcal{L}_{suicide} = \frac{1}{N} \sum_{i=1}^{N} L_{ce} \left(\text{softmax} \left(W^{(2)} f_i + C^{(2)} \right), y_i^{suicide} \right) \tag{2}$$

$$\mathcal{L}_{adv} = \frac{1}{N} \sum_{i=1}^{N} L_{ce} \left(\text{softmax} \left(W^{(2)} f_i^* + C^{(2)} \right), y_i^{suicide} \right) \tag{3}$$

$$\mathcal{L}_{emotion} = \frac{1}{N} \sum_{i=1}^{N} L_{ce} \left(\text{softmax} \left(W^{(2')} f_i + C^{(2')} \right), y_i^{emotion} \right) \tag{4}$$

where $\mathcal{L}_{suicide}$, $\mathcal{L}_{adv}$ and $\mathcal{L}_{emotion}$ are the loss of the suicide ideation detection, adversarial and emotion respectively. N is the number of posts. L_{ce} is the cross-entropy loss function. f^* equals adversarial perturbations r_{adv} plus the feature embedding f [6]. $W^{(2)}$ and $C^{(2)}$, $W^{(2')}$ and $C^{(2')}$ are the weight and bias of $fc2$ and $fc2'$ respectively.

4   Experiments

4.1   Dataset

The dataset denoted as SID consists of online posts from Reddit[1] which is a forum for anonymous discussion [11]. SID dataset includes 5,000 posts collected from one subreddit named *SuicideWatch* in which people are considering to commit suicide and 5,000 posts collected from other popular subreddits, e.g.,

---

[1] www.reddit.com.

movies, books, etc. We label all posts from *SuicideWatch* as *Suicide* and other subreddits as *Normal.* For experiments, we randomly divide the collected SID dataset into a training set (7,500 posts) and a test set (2,500 posts) and ensure that the classes of each part are balanced.

4.2 Performance on the SID Dataset

Table 1. Performance of competing models on SID dataset.

Model	Accuracy	Recall	Precision	F1-score
TextCNN [4]	0.918	0.902	0.933	0.917
Bi-LSTM	0.916	0.906	0.925	0.915
CharCNN [10]	0.867	0.854	0.875	0.865
BERT	0.954	0.945	**0.964**	0.954
Our model BLAM	**0.964**	**0.971**	0.956	**0.963**

Table 1 summarizes the performances of BLAM and the methods on the SID dataset. From the table, we can highlight some observations as follows:

- The performance of the BERT-based methods, i.e., BERT and our model, are higher than other models, demonstrating the superiority of the BERT-based methods.
- Compared with other methods, CharCNN suffers from a worst performance. The reason is that it is difficult for CharCNN to abstract the concept of suicidal thoughts via character alone, while some implicit knowledge of pretrained word embedding could help with this task for other methods.
- Our BLAM model outperforms all models in most metrics, which demonstrates the effectiveness of BLAM.

4.3 Ablation Study

Table 2. Ablation of our proposed model on SID dataset.

Model	Accuracy	Recall	Precision	F1-score
BERT	0.954	0.945	**0.964**	0.954
BERT+Bi-LSTM	0.956	0.951	0.962	0.956
BERT+Bi-LSTM+Adversarial loss	0.958	0.956	0.960	0.958
BERT+Bi-LSTM+Emotion loss	0.963	0.967	0.958	0.962
Our model BLAM	**0.964**	**0.971**	0.956	**0.963**

To isolate the contributions of our work, we perform ablation study by evaluating several variants of our model, as shown in Table 2. From the table, we have some observations as follows:

- Bi-LSTM is limited for the performance improvement, possibly because BERT already has a strong feature extraction capability.
- When adding the adversarial loss, the performance of F1-score is improved because adversarial learning enhances the generalization of the model, which in turn enhances performance.
- The performance of F1-score is greatly improved by adding the emotion loss, which proves the effectiveness of multi-task learning.
- Although our proposed model on the metric of precision is a little lower than the base model (i.e., BERT), the improvement for our model in terms of the other metrics (i.e., accuracy, recall and F1-score) is much higher.

4.4   Importance of Emotion Feature

To explore which emotions help with feature learning in the suicide ideation detection task, we utilize the feature importance in random forest model for visualization. Specifically, we remove $fc2$ and replace $fc2'$ with a random forest model, and change the label to *Normal* or *Suicide* to train the random forest model. As shown in Fig. 2, some emotions, such as 'sadness', 'grief', and 'disappointment', contribute significantly to the suicide ideation detection task because they are some of the more negative emotions, which also indirectly demonstrate the effectiveness of our proposed multi-task learning approach.

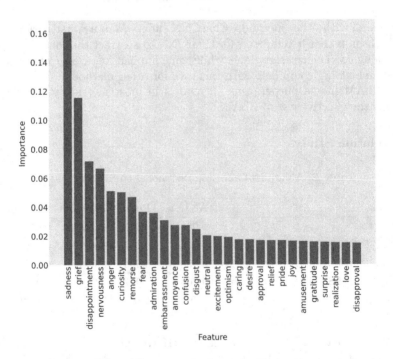

Fig. 2. Importance of emotion feature.

5 Conclusion

In this paper, we propose BLAM to detect suicide ideation on social media (i.e., Reddit). BLAM consists of feature extraction, adversarial learning and multi-task learning which can extract features related to user emotions and have better generalization ability. In addition, we collect a real-world dataset, upon which extensive experiments are conducted. The experimental results have demonstrated the effectiveness of our proposed model.

Acknowledgements. The research described in this paper has been supported by the Hong Kong Research Grants Council through a Collaborative Research Fund (project no. C1031-18G) and Shenzhen Philosophy and Social Sciences Fund in the 13th Five-year Plan (project no. SZ2018B020), P. R. China.

References

1. Ambalavan, A.K., Moulahi, B., Azé, J., Bringay, S.: Unveiling online suicide behavior: what can we learn about mental health from suicide survivors of reddit? In: MedInfo, pp. 50–54 (2019)
2. Cao, L., Zhang, H., Feng, L.: Building and using personal knowledge graph to improve suicidal ideation detection on social media. IEEE Trans. Multimedia (2020)
3. Gunn, J.F., Lester, D.: Twitter postings and suicide: an analysis of the postings of a fatal suicide in the 24 h prior to death. Suicidologi **17**(3), 28–30 (2012)
4. Kim, Y.: Convolutional neural networks for sentence classification. In: Moschitti, A., Pang, B., Daelemans, W. (eds.) EMNLP 2014, pp. 1746–1751. Association for Computational Linguistics (2014)
5. Liang, Y., Guo, B., Yu, Z., Zheng, X., Wang, Z., Tang, L.: A multi-view attention-based deep learning system for online deviant content detection. World Wide Web **24**(1), 205–228 (2021). https://doi.org/10.1007/s11280-020-00840-9
6. Miyato, T., Dai, A.M., Goodfellow, I.J.: Adversarial training methods for semi-supervised text classification. In: ICLR 2017 (2017). OpenReview.net
7. Sawhney, R., Joshi, H., Gandhi, S., Shah, R.: A time-aware transformer based model for suicide ideation detection on social media. In: Proceedings of the 2020 Conference on Empirical Methods in Natural Language Processing (EMNLP), pp. 7685–7697 (2020)
8. Sawhney, R., Joshi, H., Gandhi, S., Shah, R.R.: Towards ordinal suicide ideation detection on social media. In: Proceedings of the 14th ACM International Conference on Web Search and Data Mining, pp. 22–30 (2021)
9. Sinha, P.P., Mishra, R., Sawhney, R., Mahata, D., Shah, R.R., Liu, H.: Suicidal-a multipronged approach to identify and explore suicidal ideation in twitter. In: CIKM 2019, pp. 941–950 (2019)
10. Zhang, X., Zhao, J.J., LeCun, Y.: Character-level convolutional networks for text classification. In: Cortes, C., Lawrence, N.D., Lee, D.D., Sugiyama, M., Garnett, R. (eds.) NIPS 2015, pp. 649–657 (2015)
11. Zhang, Y., Wang, L., Zhu, J.J., Wang, X.: Conspiracy vs science: a large-scale analysis of online discussion cascades. World Wide Web **24**(2), 585–606 (2021). https://doi.org/10.1007/s11280-021-00862-x

Data Management

An Efficient Bucket Logging for Persistent Memory

Xiyan Xu and Jiwu Shu[(✉)]

Department of Computer Science and Technology, Tsinghua University, Beijing, China
shujw@tsinghua.edu.cn

Abstract. Logging is widely used to provide atomicity and durability for trans-actions in database management systems (DBMSs). For decades, the traditional logging protocol for disk-oriented database storage engines focuses on making a trade-off between data persistence and performance loss due to the large per-formance gap and access granularity mismatch between dynamic random-access memory (DRAM) and disks. With the development of persistent memory (PM) especially the release of the commercial Optane DC Persistent Memory Mod-ule (Optane DCPMM), a new class of storage engine which employs PM as its primary storage has emerged. The disk-based logging protocol is not suitable for these PM-aware storage engines, since PM provides data persistence and has low-latency comparable to DRAM. In this paper, we design and implement an efficient logging protocol for PM-aware storage engines: Bucket Logging (BKL). BKL uses the per-transaction log structure (i.e., bucket) to store logs internally and ensures efficient writing of metadata and logs. Benefit from multi version concurrency control, BKL only records small fixed-size log entries to implement fast logging and crash recovery. Moreover, we optimize our design based on our basic performance evaluation of Optane DCPMM. We implement a micro storage engine in MariaDB and using YCSB to evaluate BKL's performance on Optane DCPMM. The results show that the storage engine with BKL has $1.5 \times -7.1 \times$ higher throughput compared to InnoDB under write-heavy workloads. Compared with other logging protocol, BKL achieves higher throughput and better scalability and reduces the system performance recovery time by $1.4 \times -11.8 \times$.

Keywords: Logging and recovery · Persistent memory · Database · Multi version concurrency control

1 Introduction

Logging is widely used to provide atomicity and durability for transactions in database management systems (DBMSs). Currently, mature commercial DBMSs can be classified into disk-based and in-memory DBMSs based on the primary storage location of the database. Disk-oriented DBMSs maintain a buffer pool in memory to store copies of

---

The original version of this chapter was revised: errors in figures 1 and 3 were corrected. The correction to this chapter is available at https://doi.org/10.1007/978-3-030-85896-4_39

L. H. U et al. (Eds.): APWeb-WAIM 2021, LNCS 12858, pp. 149–163, 2021.
https://doi.org/10.1007/978-3-030-85896-4_13

pages retrieved from the database's primary storage (i.e., HDD or SSD). The performance of these DBMSs is constrained by the speed at which they persist changes to the log stored on these devices [1]. This is due to the large performance gap and access granularity mismatch between dynamic random-access memory (DRAM) and disks. In other words, the latency of block-addressable HDD/SSD is several orders of magnitude higher than byte-addressable DRAM. In-memory DBMSs with persistence assume that all data fits in the main memory and employ a limited logging mechanism and atomic operations in case of failure. These DBMSs sacrifice transactional support in pursuit of access speed thus they are not suitable for high consistency scenarios.

Persistent memory (PM) technologies, such as PCM [2], ReRAM [3], and the recently released Optane DC Persistent Memory Module (Optane DCPMM) [4], provide data persistence and affordable large capacity. Besides, PM can be plugged into DIMM slots to deliver low latency read and write access at cache line granularity. However, the performance of commercial PM (i.e., Optane DCPMM) is much more strongly dependent on access size, access type, pattern, and degree of concurrency than that of DRAM [5]. Therefore PM-oriented applications require more efficient software designs and modifications to reap significant performance benefits [4].

With the emergence of PM, several high-performance persistent memory databases which employ PM as primary storage [6–12] have recently been proposed. Persistent memory database eschews the page abstraction in storage engines since PM is byte-addressable, and uses raw pointers that map to data's location in PM. It can achieve a high level of transaction execution rate and system throughput. Previous work [13, 14] shows that both disk-based and in-memory database systems are not ideally suited for PM. Instead, specialized and efficient logging and recovery designs for native persistent memory databases are required.

In this work, we propose a logging and recovery design called **Bucket Logging** (BKL) that is well suited for PM-aware storage engines. Inspired by the scalable logging scheme proposed by Wang and Johnson [15], BKL stores log records in the individual log bucket for each transaction to eliminate the centralized lock contention. Benefit from multi version concurrency control (MVCC), it uses small fixed-size log entries and metadata to achieve efficient logging. Besides, BKL has made several optimizations for Optane DCPMM environments, such as providing bucket-binding buffer, flush instruction optimization, bucket-level and log-level pointer. BKL achieves good performance in our benchmark. The contributions of this work are as follows:

- We design and implement logging structures directly built on PM and the corresponding commit and recovery protocol, which provides persistent memory databases with high-performance logging and recovery abilities.
- Based on our basic performance evaluation of Optane DCPMM, we optimize the design of BKL and verify it on our PM-aware storage engine.
- We evaluate BKL in our PM-aware storage engine prototype on Optane DCPMM, the results show that BKL scales well with concurrent transactions and can quickly recover to the full throughput performance after crash.

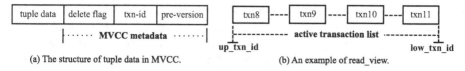

(a) The structure of tuple data in MVCC.   (b) An example of read_view.

Fig. 1. MVCC implementation.

2 Background

2.1 Transactions for Database Systems

In DBMS, the transaction mechanism guarantees ACID (Atomicity, Consistency, Isolation, Durability) properties through logging and concurrency control. Logging provides persistence consistency, which guarantees that the data is updated atomically and durably [16]. Concurrency control provides execution consistency, concurrent transactions are isolated and executed individually. MVCC [17] is widely used to increase the parallelism for DBMS. Our discussion in this paper is based on DBMSs which adopt MVCC for scheduling transactions. InnoDB is a typical MVCC-based storage engine, in which *read-committed* and *repeatable-read* isolation levels are supported by consistent *read view*.

Figure 1(a) shows the structure of tuple data in MVCC. *txn-id* holds the identifier of the transaction who modifies the tuple most recently. *pre-version* points to the previous version of the tuple. Figure 1(b) gives an example of *read view* which is used to define a consistent data version for other concurrent transactions. At *read-committed* isolation level, a transaction creates *read view* each time the transaction reads. DBMS generates a *read view* based on the current active transaction list. *up_txn_id* in *read view* holds the minimum *txn-id* in active (uncommitted) transactions, and *low_txn_id* holds the maximum *txn-id* in active transactions. If *txn-id* is smaller than *up_txn_id*, the transaction is visible to the *read view*. If *txn-id* is larger than *low_txn_id*, the transaction is invisible to the *read view*. In the middle of the two depends on the transaction isolation level. Otherwise (i.e., the *txn-id* is between *up_txn_id* and *low_txn_id*), the transaction is visible to the *read view* only when it is committed.

2.2 Log-Based Recovery Algorithms

Write-Ahead Logging (WAL) is widely used in database systems, it persists all changes in the log before applying them to the durable storage device. ARIES [18] is the most well-known recovery algorithm based on WAL, it takes *steal* and *no-force* strategies for recovery consistency. *Steal* strategy allows flushing uncommitted data into the durable storage device, *no-force* strategy allows deferring the data flush even if the transaction is already committed. To restore to a consistent state, the recovery process may take a long time to analysis, redo and undo.

Write-Behind Logging (WBL) [1, 14] is designed for MVCC-based persistent memory database systems, it records the changes in the log after flushing the data to PM. Moreover, WBL only logs what parts of the database have changed rather than how it was changed. At the runtime stage, all the modifications are stored in *Dirty Tuple Table* (DTT) in DRAM. At the commit stage, it first persists the modified tuple data in a batch of transactions. Then it writes a log record only containing a pair of local timestamps to identify uncommitted tuple without the before-images and after-images of tuples, which reduces the storage footprint of logging. Also, it adopts *steal* and *force* strategies and only needs an asynchronous undo process using a background thread when recover. However, the design of WBL presents some major limitations. First, it makes frequent updates in its centralized structure like DTT which increases the latency of each worker thread. Second, the background garbage collection thread needs to perform full table scans to find all uncommitted tuples which limit the system runtime performance until all rollback is completed. By contrast, BKL can avoid these two shortcomings. First, it uses distributed log buckets for different transactions avoiding contention for the centralized structure. Second, benefit from its well-designed commit protocol, BKL can recover to a consistent state within in a reasonable time.

3   Experimental Study on Optane DCPMM

In BKL, the small log entries are written sequentially to each separate area, but the traffic at the DIMM level may exhibit as stride accesses for concurrency transactions. Therefore, we evaluate the performance of small access of sequential and stride access patterns on Optane DCPMM. We use libpmem library [19] (with AVX-512 enabled) to evaluate two different instruction sequences: *ntstore* and store + *clwb*, followed by a *sfence*. See Sect. 5.1 for the experimental setup.

We use a single thread to execute the instructions 8 million times and get the average time as the latency. For sequential access, we store data to consecutive addresses. For stride access, we set the stride size to 4 KB. The results are shown in Fig. 2(a), where the solid line represents the latency of sequential access, and the dotted line represents the latency of stride access. Access smaller than 64 B shows high latency between 567 ns and 746 ns. For access larger than 64 B, the latency of sequential write is much lower than that of stride access. More specifically, the latency gap between sequential access and stride access is 2.6 × −2.9 × for *ntstore* and 3.4 × −4.5 × for *clwb*.

During the above experiments, we use ipmctl utility [19] to measure the actual write size to Optane DCPMM's hardware media. The results show that instruction type has little effect on hardware write size. Figure 2(b) plots the hardware write size (i.e., WS of Y-axis on the left) of sequential/stride access pattern and its corresponding write amplification value (i.e., WA of Y-axis on the right, it is the quotient of WS and access size). The hardware write size of sequential access is close to the access size and the WA value is between 1.0 and 2.3. While the hardware writes size of stride access is stable at about 256 B (the specific value is 260.1 B, there is a small deviation because ipmctl counts the write size of hardware media at 64 B granularity), which matches the access granularity (XPLine) of Optane DCPMM. With the increase of access size, the WA value decreases from 32.4 to 1.0. As a consequence, Optane DCPMM can efficiently handle and merge small stores, if they exhibit sufficient locality. In contrast, small writes with poor locality are inefficient since they require the hardware to perform an internal *read-modify-write* operation causing write amplification.

Figure 2(c) shows the bandwidth achieved at different access sizes for sequential access. Our bandwidth test uses 4 threads as it gives good results for all instructions. The data shows that the bandwidth of *ntstore* is 1.1 × −1.4 × that of *clwb*. Moreover, the bandwidth increases with the increase of access size and tends to be stable at 256 B. *ntstore* performs better in our test scenario. Because it can bypass the cache hierarchy, which is more suitable for writing large data.

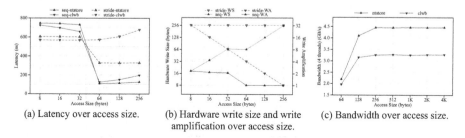

(a) Latency over access size.   (b) Hardware write size and write amplification over access size.   (c) Bandwidth over access size.

Fig. 2. Performance of small access on Optane DCPMM.

We conclude as follows: ①Avoid access smaller than cache line-granularity (i.e., 64 B), especially when the access exhibits poor locality. ②Access to Optane DCPMM displays optimal performance at XPLine-granularity (i.e., 256 B). According to the above test results, we get the idea of how to design and optimize BKL and verify it in Sect. 5.2: ①We set a log buffer for each bucket in DRAM to buffer and combine log entries for enhancing access locality and optimize IO granularity ②We set the default log buffer size of each bucket to 256 B and align the log flush size with 64 B, avoiding the impact of write amplification on performance.

4 Bucket Logging

4.1 System Overview

BKL maps a space (i.e., bucket zone) in PM with DAX (direct access) mode to hold log records from different transactions. The bucket zone is divided into a fixed number of buckets, and each bucket can only be assigned to one transaction at a time. Thus, when transactions write logs, they do not contend with a single global lock. Furthermore, to avoid buffer contention, BKL uses distributed log buffer, each bucket has its own log buffer (i.e., bucket buffer) in DRAM. The number of buckets represents the upper bound of concurrent transactions in BKL. The design of the per-transaction bucket will not become the bottleneck of transaction execution, because the number of buckets is far greater than the number of cores.

To achieve wear-leveling of log area, the round-robin allocation is used between buckets and inside buckets. For coarse-grained wear-leveling between buckets, the bucket-pointer is used to point to the location of the next free bucket. An active transaction gets a free bucket according to the bucket-pointer, then the bucket-pointer increases atomically and moves to the next bucket location. For fine-grained wear-leveling inside a bucket, log-pointer is used to point to the offset address of the next log entry. The round-robin mechanism separates the writes across a bucket to avoid the wear-out of the start position. Both bucket-pointer and log-pointers reside in DRAM, they can be recovered easily through the analysis of the log (see Sect. 4.4). Macroscopically, since each bucket has the same assignment probability, the assignment and access to the log area is approximately sequential, also the performance degradation caused by single-point access is avoided (Fig. 3).

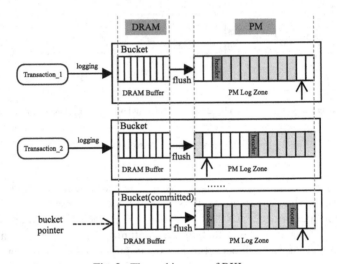

Fig. 3. The architecture of BKL.

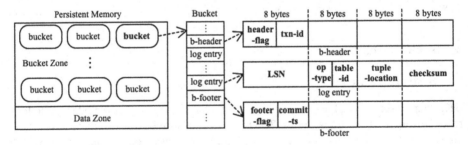

Fig. 4. The data structure of log bucket in BKL.

4.2 Data Structure of Log Bucket

A transaction requests a bucket only when begins to update the tuple data. Once the transaction gets a bucket, it needs to persist the metadata entries of the transaction and log entries during regular transaction processing. The data structure of the bucket is as shown in Fig. 4, the log entry is fixed size (i.e., 32 bytes), the metadata entry occupies 8 bytes and is aligned to 32 bytes. The first 2 bits of a log entry are used as entry type. There are two types of metadata entries of the bucket:

- *b-header*: records the identifier of the current active transaction (i.e., *txn-id*). It is persisted before the first log entry of the transaction.
- *b-footer*: records the commit or abort timestamp of the current transaction (i.e., *commit-ts*). It is persisted after the last log entry of the transaction.

Both *txn-id* and *commit-ts* are generated by a globally atomic monotonically increasing counter. After the crash, the initial value of the counter will be set to the id of the last transaction before crash, ensuring self-increment during the entire database life cycle. Moreover, both *b-header* and *b-footer* use 8-byte atomic write instructions to ensure integrity. BKL creates a log record in log area whenever the transaction makes a change to DBMS. Each log entry only records the type of operation and the location of the modified data. The *before-image* and *after-image* of the tuple data can be acquired through the version information in MVCC during recovery. A log entry contains:

- *LSN*: the log sequence number. It is generated by the local counter within the transaction and increased monotonically from *txn-id*.
- *op-type*: the type of operation (e.g., INSERT, UPDATE or DELETE).
- *table-id*: the identifier of the modified table. It shares 8 bytes with operation-type.
- *tuple-location*: records the location of tuple modified by the operation which can be used to locate the uncommitted tuple quickly in recovery.
- *checksum*: used to check the integrity of the log during recovery after the crash.

4.3 Commit Protocol

Figure 5 shows the runtime process and commit protocol in BKL. When a transaction is assigned to a worker thread, it first selects a free bucket to hold its transaction information and log records (①). Generally, applying one bucket is enough to store all the logs of a transaction (e.g., a 4 KB bucket can hold 128 log entries). In addition, BKL allows large transactions to apply for multiple buckets. In this situation, *b-header* and *b-footer* of this transaction must be persisted in each bucket, and the LSN is still incremented locally within the transaction. In the runtime phase, BKL first persists *b-header* containing the *txn-id* of the current transaction atomically (②). The current hardware architecture guarantees the 8-bytes atomic write operation, so we can make an atomic update for the bucket state change. Meanwhile, the transaction constructs the log entries in the log buffer and caches the new tuple version in the data buffer (③). During this period, the unstable tuple version is visible to the active transaction modified by the index tree.

BKL persists all the tuple data before transaction commit and ensures that the log entry persists before the tuple data. When the log buffer is full, the worker thread flushes all the log entries temporarily stored in the buffer to PM. Therefore, the buffer size of each bucket affects the flush frequency of the log. First, a batch of tuple data request space from the PM-aware allocator and add the applied address to the tuple-location in the corresponding log entries (④). Next the worker thread flushes the log entries to PM and follows by a fence instruction (⑤). Later the work thread flushes the tuple data to PM (⑥). Repeat steps ③ to ⑥ until all the logs and data are persisted. When the transaction to commit or rollback, BKL persists *b-footer* atomically containing the *commit-ts* of the current transaction (⑦).

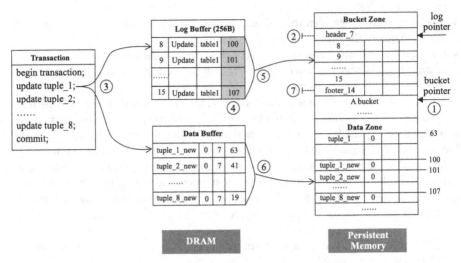

Fig. 5. Runtime process and commit protocol in BKL.

With BKL, the database does not need to periodically construct ARIES-style physical checkpoint to speed up recovery. This is because each log bucket contains the information needed for recovery: the logs and metadata of the latest transaction. The database only needs to retrieve this information during the analysis phase of the recovery process. Also, the database does not need to use checkpoint to truncate log records. With round-robin allocation inside the bucket, the log records of the latest transactions will override that of previously committed transactions.

4.4 Recovery Protocol

Recovery in BKL includes two phases: analysis and undo. There is no need for a redo phase because all the modifications of committed transactions are already present in the database. In analysis phase, recovery threads scan the whole bucket zone in parallel to identify the commit status of the transaction in each bucket after crash. For each bucket, the recovery thread locates the latest *b-header* with the largest *txn-id* (i.e., *max_txn-id*) and the latest *b-footer* with the largest *commit-ts* (i.e., *max_commit-ts*). A complete transaction commit process requires recording both *b-header* and the corresponding *b-footer* in the bucket. Since *txn-id* and *commit-ts* are globally increasing, the commit status of the transaction can be determined by the relationship between *max_commit-ts* and *max_txn-id*. There are two possible stages for log buckets.

Free Bucket. The transaction in the bucket is committed at the time of failure if *max_commit-ts* > *max_txn-id*. Since the tuple data is already persisted before the transaction commit, there is no need to redo the transaction in this type of bucket.

Bucket with Uncommitted Transaction. The transaction in the bucket is uncommitted if $max\_commit\text{-}ts < max\_txn\text{-}id$ or $b\text{-}footer$ is not found. Since LSN is locally increasing from txn_id, log entries with consecutive LSN starting from $max\_txn\text{-}id$ belong to the uncommitted transaction. To get all the log entries of an uncommitted transaction, the recovery thread scans the log records from $b\text{-}header$ (if it scans to the end address of the bucket, it continues from the start address) until the LSN is discontinuous. Then the database rolls back the operations in uncommitted transactions. For log entries with wrong checksum, the database needs to do nothing, and the PM-aware allocator will reclaim memory space of tuple data that has not been persisted. For log entries with correct checksum, the database marks the tuple data in tuple-location invisible to all transactions and the garbage collector will reclaim the PM space to avoid space leak.

After finishing recovery, BKL resets the bucket-pointer for bucket selection to the free bucket with the minimum $max\_txn\text{-}id$. Then BKL rebuild the log-pointer of each bucket. for free bucket, log-pointer is reset to the $b\text{-}footer$ with $max\_commit\text{-}ts$. The largest $txn\text{-}id$ before the crash will be used to initialize the generator of the transaction identifier.

5 Evaluation

5.1 Experimental Platform

All experiments are run on a system with an Intel Xeon Gold 6248R CPU (3.0 GHz), which has 24 physical cores, each core has 1.5 MB L1 cache and 24 MB L2 cache, and a shared 35.75 MB L3 cache. The system is equipped with 192 GB DRAM (6 channel × 32 GB/DIMM) and 512 GB Optane DCPMM (2 channel × 256 GB/DIMM) with address space interleaving (4 KB). Our machine runs Fedora 27 with a Linux v4.13.9 kernel.

We implemented a persistent memory storage engine prototype (Optane Storage Engine, OSE) in MariaDB (version 10.3.9) and evaluated our BKL on it. OSE implements a simplified version of the MVCC, and read-view-based data management architecture inspired by InnoDB. OSE implements the *read-committed* transaction isolation level. OSE supports hash indexes built on DRAM and uses row-based read-write locks to avoid data conflicts. Besides, we developed the PM-aware fail-safe space allocator using libpmem library. Transactions request space for tuple data from allocator in batches and confirm to allocator after data persistence. After a system failure, the allocator reclaims memory that has not been persisted and restores its internal metadata to a consistent state. We use 8 thousand buckets, and the size of each bucket is 8 KB. Although OSE is far from a complete storage engine, it is enough for us to perform various BKL-related tests on it.

We use YCSB benchmark tools in our evaluation. The database structure we use is composed of 10 *char(100)* columns, the primary key uses a hash-based index, and each tuple's size is approximately 1 KB. We set parameter *autocommit* to *false* and use parameter *batchsize* to control the number of operations performed by each transaction (16, unless specified), use parameter *threadcount* in each workload to control the number of client threads. The parameter *recordcount* and parameter *operationcount* in each workload are both 4 million (~4 GB). We mainly focus on the logging performance. Since read-only operations will not generate logs in our system, so we mainly use the following workload types (Table 1).

Table 1. Workload configurations of YCSB benchmark in our experimental evaluation.

Workload	Configuration
Load	insertportation = 1
Write-heavy	readportation = 0.05, updateportation = 0.95
Balanced	readportation = 0.5, updateportation = 0.5
Read-heavy	readportation = 0.95, updateportation = 0.05

5.2 Sensitivity Analysis

We explore the impact of different configurations on BKL's performance. We run the benchmark with 6 threads in the following sensitivity analysis. In order to improve the efficiency of log write to PM, BKL uses a DRAM-based buffer inside each bucket for log and data buffering, avoiding the performance degradation caused by excessive small write accesses to PM. As shown in Fig. 6(a), we run write-heavy workload and balanced workload under different log buffer size and guarantee that the data in each transaction is enough to trigger multiple flush buffer operations. We illustrate the performance loss of different log buffer size compared to the optimal setting (i.e., 256 B) in Fig. 6(b). As the write ratio decreases, the performance gap between different log buffer configuration size decreases. However, for different workloads, the database achieves best performance when the log buffer size is set to 256 B. For log buffer smaller than 256 B and *no-buffer* configuration, the log flush exhibits small random access which causes write amplification. For log buffer larger than 256 B, Low write frequency wastes high bandwidth and low latency of PM. When there are a large number of small transactions (such as single sentence commit transactions), log buffer improvement is limited.

We next measure the impact of PM-related instruction set extensions on the BKL's performance. Figure 6(c) presents the throughput of the DBMS for different workloads while using *clwb* or *ntstore* instructions in its sync primitive. Meanwhile, we evaluate the default configuration of libpmem library which uses *clwb* for access smaller than the threshold (default threshold = 256 B) and use *ntstore* for access larger than the threshold. The throughput under default configuration is slightly higher than that obtained with *ntstore* instruction. The throughput with *ntstore* is higher than that of *clwb*. As the write ratio decreases, the performance gap between *ntstore* and *clwb* decreases from 2.49 × to 1.03 ×. We conclude that for write-heavy workload and large size access, *ntstore* should be preferred. The Cascade Lake CPUs implement *clwb* as *clflushopt* for now. We look forward to the performance of *clwb* instruction on future processors, which retain the flushed cache-lines in the CPU's cache. In short, an efficient cache flushing primitive is critical for a high-performance PM-aware database.

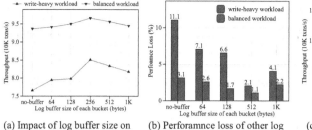
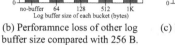
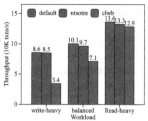

(a) Impact of log buffer size on the performance of BKL.

(b) Performance loss of other log buffer size compared with 256 B.

(c) Impact of flush instruction on the performance of BKL.

Fig. 6. The sensitivity evaluation of BKL.

5.3 Runtime Performance

We compare the performance of BKL against WBL since only WBL is the logging system designed for MVCC-based persistent memory databases except for BKL. We migrate the source code of WBL [20] to the OSE storage engine. Besides, we run InnoDB storage engine on PM (fs-dax mode, xfs-dax file system, but still use the traditional file system api) as the baseline.

As shown in Fig. 7, InnoDB achieves extremely low performance because its heavy-weight component is not suitable for PM. We first consider the read-heavy workload results shown in Fig. 7(a). These results provide an approximate upper bound on the DBMS's performance because 95% of the transactions do not modify the database and therefore the system does not have to construct many log records and write locks. The benefits of BKL are more prominent for the balanced and write-heavy workloads presented in Fig. 7(b) and Fig. 7(c). We observe that the BKL configuration delivers 1.2 × − 1.3 × higher throughput than the WBL configuration because of its lower logging overhead. Compared to WBL, BKL eliminates most of the structures that require concurrent access control. Each transaction only records logs in its own bucket with no centralized lock, neither no synchronization between threads. Since WBL relies on checkpoint thread to calculate and generate logs (i.e., Cp and Cd) periodically, the performance decreases heavily as threads increases.

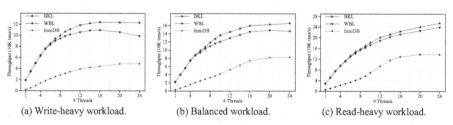

(a) Write-heavy workload.

(b) Balanced workload.

(c) Read-heavy workload.

Fig. 7. The throughput of the storage engine for the YCSB benchmark with different logging protocols on Optane DCPMM.

5.4 Recovery Performance

Quick recovery after system failures is one of the most important indicators for logging systems especially for the large amount of online data stored in the database. In order to measure the recovery capability of storage engines adopting different log systems, we first defined three throughput-related indicators to indicate the recovery status of the system.

- Service Available Time (SAT): the time taken from the application restart to the first transaction execution.
- Service Stable Time (SST): the time taken from the first transaction execution to producing the normal throughput (i.e., 90% of the throughput before the crash).
- Service Recovery Time (SRT): the system's complete recovery of stable throughput as a signal of the system's complete recovery, it is approximately the sum of SAT and SST.

To measure SRT, we implemented a micro-benchmark. First, we use YCSB's load workload to generate tons of data with different data scales and granularities to fill the database. To simulate crash, we use a timing script to kill the database process immediately when it is handling write-heavy workload at a specified time point. Then the script will start the database and perform the write-heavy workload again. We use 16 client threads in YCSB to process workload, and we will count the throughput changes of the database every 0.5 s.

In Fig. 8(a), We record the throughput fluctuations of the storage engines adopting BKL and WBL during recovery for 200 GB data. In order to facilitate analysis, we aligned the data by the crash time point. The first observation is that the SAT of the WBL (0.9 s) is smaller than BKL's (2.5 s), this is because WBL uses an asynchronous recovery process. After restarting, the system will immediately start working and start a clean-up thread to perform a full table scan. BKL uses a synchronous recovery process and does not start accepting requests until the recovery is complete. Since BKL only needs to scan the bucket zone to find the uncommitted bucket, by analyzing the log data in the bucket, it can quickly locate the dirty tuple data, and then perform the undo operation, so the recovery process can be completed in almost constant time. However, because the logs of WBL can only provide a dirty range, in order to find the dirty tuple data that needs to be restored, WBL starts a garbage thread to perform an asynchronous full table scan, which brings huge time overhead. Access to the tuple in the dirty range from other transactions will be blocked until the recovery is complete, which will greatly affect the system throughput. WBL used nearly 9.1 s of SST to complete the recovery compared to BKL which has almost no SST overhead. For SRT, BKL has increased by nearly 300% compared to WBL.

To illustrate the relationship between recovery time and data scale, we conducted synchronous recovery tests for different data volumes and data granularities. As shown in Fig. 8(b), total data ranges from 10 GB to 400 GB and two granularities of tuple data (1 KB and 100 B). As total data increases, the recovery time of WBL increases linearly, while BKL maintains almost constant and recovery time. Compared to WBL, BKL reduces the system performance recovery time by $1.4 \times -11.8 \times$. Besides, BKL is not sensitive to data of different granularities compared to WBL. This is particularly important for the recovery process of modern large-scale data systems.

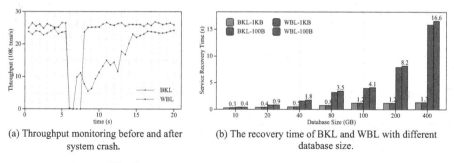

(a) Throughput monitoring before and after system crash.

(b) The recovery time of BKL and WBL with different database size.

Fig. 8. Recovery performance of BKL and WBL.

6 Related Work

Previous work on leveraging PM for DBMS design can be divided into two categories: (1) leveraging PM as an intermediate layer for accelerating logging [15, 21–23] or data access [24, 25] between DRAM and disk. Wang and Johnson [15] propose a scalable distributed logging on multicore and multi-socket hardware. PM is used as persistent log buffer for page-level or transaction-level log partitioning. Transactions commit immediately after buffering their commit records, and log records are only de-staged to disk when the log buffer is full. NV-Logging [21] and NVWAL [22] employ PM for logging subsystem and consume page-level I/O for data and log updates. Haubenschild M et al. [23] propose a two-stage per-thread logging. The first stage consists of a small number of log chunks organized in PM. A dedicated WAL writer thread picks up the full chunks and flush them into the second stage (i.e., SSD). These approaches are more cost-effective, but they only leverage the low-latency sequential writes of PM and does not exploit its ability to efficiently support random writes and fine-grained data access.

Andrei M et al. [24] present the early adoption of PM within the SAP HANA database, from the architectural and technical angles. They keep the disk-based persistency and place only a sub-set of the data (i.e., Main Column Fragment data structures) in PM. van Renen A et al. [25] propose a lightweight storage manager that simultaneously supports DRAM, PM, and SSD. Their design utilizes the byte addressability of PM and uses it as an additional caching layer that improves performance without losing the benefits from the even faster DRAM and the large capacities of SSDs.

(2) employing PM as primary storage of the whole database (i.e., persistent memory database). SOFORT [6] is a log-less columnar transactional storage engine, it speeds up the recovery by updating the persisted data in place in small increments based on dictionary encoding. Naveed Mustafa N U et al. [7] explore the implications of replacing the data storage subsystem with PM-based subsystem in PostgreSQL. Arulraj J et al. [14] present the design and implementation of DBMS architectures that are explicitly tailored

for PM, including logging and recovery (i.e., WBL) [1], storage and buffer management, and indexing. REWIND [8] is a user-space library for efficiently managing in-memory persistent data structures on PM using WAL to ensure recoverability. Some persistent memory storage engine prototypes, such as pmem-mariadb [9] and pmse (PM-aware MongoDB) [10], use the libpmemobj library from the PMDK [11] for ensuring fail-safe atomicity and consistency. pmem-redis [12] provides DCPMM Copy-On-Write Switch and Pointer Based Aof Switch for persistence.

7   Conclusion and Future Work

In this paper, we design and implement logging structures directly built on PM and the corresponding commit and recovery protocol, which provides PM-aware databases with high-performance logging and recovery abilities. BKL has made several optimizations for Optane DCPMM, such as lightweight log structures, bucket-binding buffers, write pointers for log and bucket levels. We evaluate BKL on our storage engine prototype. Experimental results show that BKL has higher throughput and better scalability and can recover to a consistent state rapidly after the crash.

In future work, we plan to expand the BKL scene, such as implement data replication, improve the scalability of BKL in multiple cores. Also, we will continue to optimize the design of our persistent memory storage engine prototype (OSE) and release it someday.

Acknowledgements. This material is supported by the National Key Research & Development Program of China (Grant No. 2018YFB1003301), the National Natural Science Foundation of China (Grant No. 61832011) and sponsored by Zhejiang Lab (NO. 2020KC0AB03).

References

1. Arulraj, J., Perron, M., Pavlo, A.: Write-behind logging. Proc. VLDB Endowment **10**(4), 337–348 (2016)
2. Wong, H., et al.: Phase Change Memory. Proc. IEEE **98**(12), 2201–2227 (2010)
3. Akinaga, H., Shima, H.: Resistive random access memory (ReRAM) based on metal oxides. Proc. IEEE **98**(12), 2237–2251 (2010)
4. Izraelevitz, J., Yang, J., Zhang, L., et al.: Basic performance measurements of the intel optane DC persistent memory module. arXiv preprint arXiv:1903.05714 (2019)
5. Yang, J., Kim, J., Hoseinzadeh, M., Izraelevitz, J., Swanson, S.: An empirical guide to the behavior and use of scalable persistent memory. In: 18th USENIX Conference on File and Storage Technologies (FAST 20), pp. 169–182 (2020).
6. Oukid, I., Booss, D., Lehner, W., Bumbulis, P., Willhalm, T.: SOFORT: A hybrid SCM-DRAM storage engine for fast data recovery. In: Proceedings of the Tenth International Workshop on Data Management on New Hardware, pp. 1–7 (2014)
7. Mustafa, N.U., Armejach, A., Ozturk, O., Cristal, A., Unsal, O.S.: Implications of non-volatile memory as primary storage for database management systems. In: 2016 International Conference on Embedded Computer Systems: Architectures, Modeling and Simulation (SAMOS), pp. 164–171 (2016)
8. Chatzistergiou, A., Cintra, M., Viglas, S.D.: Rewind: recovery write-ahead system for in-memory non-volatile data-structures. Proc. VLDB Endowment **8**(5), 497–508 (2015)

9. pmem-MariaDB.   https://github.com/pmem/pmdk-examples/tree/master/pmem-mariadb. Accessed 11 Aug 2020

10. pmse. https://github.com/pmem/pmse. Accessed 2 March 2021

11. PMDK. https://pmem.io/pmdk

12. pmem-redis. https://github.com/pmem/pmem-redis. Accessed 19 Apr 2019

13. DeBrabant, J., Arulraj, J., Pavlo, A., Stonebraker, M., Zdonik, S., Dulloor, S.: A prolegomenon on OLTP database systems for non-volatile memory. ADMS@ VLDB, (2014)

14. Arulraj, J., Pavlo, A.: Non-volatile memory database management systems. Synth. Lect. Data Manage **11**(1), 1–191 (2019)

15. Wang, T., Johnson, R: Scalable logging through emerging non-volatile memory. Proc. VLDB Endowment 7(10), 865–876 (2014).

16. Lu, Y., Shu, J., Sun, L.: Blurred persistence in transactional persistent memory. In: 31st Symposium on Mass Storage Systems and Technologies, pp. 1–13 (2015)

17. Wu, Y., Arulraj, J., Lin, J., Xian, R., Pavlo, A.: An empirical evaluation of in-memory multi-version concurrency control. Proc. VLDB Endowment **10**(7), 781–792 (2017)

18. Mohan, C., Haderle, D., Lindsay, B., Pirahesh, H., Schwarz, P.: ARIES: a transaction recovery method supporting fine-granularity locking and partial rollbacks using write-ahead logging. ACM Trans. Database Syst. **17**(1), 94–162 (1992)

19. ipmctl. https://github.com/intel/ipmctl. Accessed 1 April 2021

20. wbl. https://github.com/jarulraj/wbl. Accessed 1 April 2021

21. Huang, J., Schwan, K., Qureshi, M.K.: NVRAM-aware logging in transaction systems. Proc. VLDB Endowment **8**(4), 389–400 (2014)

22. Kim, W.H., Kim, J., Baek, W., Nam, B., Won, Y.: NVWAL: exploiting NVRAM in write-ahead logging. ACM SIGPLAN Notices **51**(4), 385–398 (2016)

23. Haubenschild, M., Sauer, C., Neumann, T., Leis, V.: Rethinking logging, checkpoints, and recovery for high-performance storage engines. In: Proceedings of the 2020 ACM SIGMOD International Conference on Management of Data, pp. 877–892 (2020)

24. Andrei, M., Lemke, C., Radestock, G., et al.: SAP HANA adoption of non-volatile memory. Proc. VLDB Endowment **10**(12), 1754–1765 (2017)

25. van Renen, A., Leis, V., Kemper, A., et al.: Managing non-volatile memory in database systems. In: Proceedings of the 2018 International Conference on Management of Data, pp. 1541–1555 (2018)

Data Poisoning Attacks
on Crowdsourcing Learning

Pengpeng Chen[1,3], Hailong Sun[2,3(✉)], and Zhijun Chen[1,3]

[1] SKLSDE Lab, School of Computer Science and Engineering,
Beihang University, Beijing, China
{chenpp,zhijunchen}@buaa.edu.cn
[2] School of Software, Beihang University, Beijing, China
sunhl@buaa.edu.cn
[3] Beijing Advanced Innovation Center for Big Data and Brain Computing,
Beihang University, Beijing, China

Abstract. Understanding and assessing the vulnerability of crowd-sourcing learning against data poisoning attacks is the key to ensure the quality of classifiers trained from crowdsourced labeled data. Existing studies on data poisoning attacks only focus on exploring the vulnerability of crowdsourced label collection. In fact, instead of the quality of labels themselves, the performance of the trained classifier is a main concern in crowdsourcing learning. Nonetheless, the impact of data poisoning attacks on the final classifiers remains underexplored to date. We aim to bridge this gap. First, we formalize the problem of poisoning attacks, where the objective is to sabotage the trained classifier maximally. Second, we transform the problem into a bilevel min-max optimization problem for the typical learning-from-crowds model and design an efficient adversarial strategy. Extensive validation on real-world datasets demonstrates that our attack can significantly decrease the test accuracy of trained classifiers. We verified that the labels generated with our strategy can be transferred to attack a broad family of crowdsourcing learning models in a black-box setting, indicating its applicability and potential of being extended to the physical world.

Keywords: Crowdsourcing · Adversarial machine learning · Data poisoning attack

1 Introduction

Crowdsourcing is a popular paradigm of outsourcing work to individuals in the form of an open call, and its success has been witnessed in various domains [19,24]. In the machine learning community, crowdsourcing is embraced as a tool for cost-effectively and efficiently collecting labels for training data [20]. Specifically, learning from crowdsourced labeled data (aka *crowdsourcing learning* [20]) involves two stages: aggregating multiple noisy labels of the same instance to be

© Springer Nature Switzerland AG 2021
L. H. U et al. (Eds.): APWeb-WAIM 2021, LNCS 12858, pp. 164–179, 2021.
https://doi.org/10.1007/978-3-030-85896-4_14

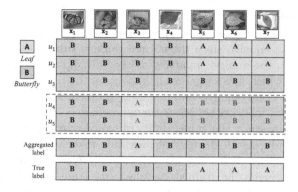

Fig. 1. The motivating example. Each worker is asked to select a label from the candidate ones {A : *Leaf, B* : *Butterfly*}. The normal workers are {u_1, u_2, u_3} and the malicious workers are {u_4, u_5}. The malicious workers adopt the TIA strategy and provide *carefully crafted* labels only based on the normal labels. Weighted majority voting [6] is applied to aggregate the noisy crowd labels to be accurate ones for instances used to train a classifier.

more reliable one (the *label aggregation* step) and training a classifier from the instances with aggregated labels (the *learning* step).

Despite the benefits of crowdsourcing, its openness brings opportunities for malicious parties to launch poisoning attacks for data sabotage [7,21], which can compromise the machine learning models. Therefore, understanding and assessing the vulnerability of crowdsourcing learning against the data poisoning attacks is an essential step to ensure the quality of classifier trained from crowdsourced labeled data [18].

Recent studies generally [7,8,21] focus on investigating the negative effect of malicious workers on *label aggregation* step of crowdsourcing learning and assume simple attack strategies such as submitting random labels or incorrect labels [8]. More recently, to exert the influence of data poisoning attacks on aggregated labels of Dawid Skene model [24], Miao et al. [13] introduce an intelligent data poisoning strategy (TIA) which enables the attacker to provide *carefully crafted* labels based on the normal ones. Although the variants [5,18] of TIA have been developed, these strategies also target to attack specific models (e.g., Gaussian truth model [22]) for *label aggregation* step. In fact, instead of the quality of aggregated labels, the performance of the classifier learned with labeled data is a main concern in crowdsourcing learning [20]. In *learning* step, the instances exhibit a distinctive influence on the final performance and the influential instances (e.g., *ambiguous* ones) are effective points to attack [12,14]. Regardless of this distinction of training instances, existing strategies [5,13,18] are ineffective in attacking crowdsourcing learning. For example[1], instance $\mathbf{x}_4$ in Fig. 1 contains a *kallima inachus* that embraces the characteristics of *Leaf*

---

[1] Label aggregation process of the *motivating example* is detailed in the supplementary file which is available at https://reurl.cc/Gme65d.

and *Butterfly*, which is highly ambiguous and influential. The malicious workers provide *carefully crafted* labels only based on the normal labels and treat x_1, x_2, x_3, and x_4 equally, since the normal workers submit the same labels to them. As a result, the malicious parties successfully flip the aggregated label of x_3 instead of x_4 which has a significant impact on the final performance of the trained classifier. Consequently, an interesting problem arises, *i.e. to maximally sabotage the victim model, what labels should malicious workers provide*.

In this work, we study the vulnerability of crowdsourcing learning by designing the efficient adversarial strategy of providing malicious workers' labels. We formalize the problem of finding the adversarial strategy whose objective is to maximally sabotage the trained classifier and transform the problem into a bilevel *min-max* optimization problem for the typical learning-from-crowds (LFC) model [15]. To the best of our knowledge, we are the first to investigate the impact of data poisoning attacks on the classifiers trained from crowdsourced labeled data. In our bi-level formulation, the inner maximization problem is highly *non-linear* and *non-convex*, which serves as a constraint of the outer minimization problem. To overcome this computational hurdle, we first solve the outer minimization problem with the dual transformation and derive the gradient of objective which is closely related to *the influence* of training instances. We further propose a poisoning attack algorithm (PATOC), which solves the outer minimization problem via reparameterization trick-based gradient descent method and the inner maximization problem by expectation-maximization (EM) algorithm. With PATOC, malicious workers can intelligently select instances to attack, that is, if this instance has *low influence on the trained classifier* and its aggregated label is difficult to be subverted, a malicious worker tries to hide her behavior by providing the label that most normal workers agree with; otherwise she instigates an effective attack by flipping the label.

The contributions of this work are summarized as follows.

- We identify the potential pitfalls in attacking crowdsourcing learning and formalize the problem of poisoning attacks whose objective is to maximally sabotage the classifier trained from crowdsourced labeled data.
- We transform the problem of finding the best adversarial strategy into a bilevel *min-max* optimization for typical LFC model and design an efficient poisoning mechanism that intelligently selects effective instances to attack.
- We conduct extensive evaluations on two real-world datasets and show that our strategy *substantially* improves the state-of-the-art attack strategies.

2   Problem Setting

The security threats are induced by the malicious clique in the step 2 of the framework as shown in Fig. 2. The attacker dominates the labels of the malicious parties to sabotage the classifier trained in the step 4. To some degree, the prediction results of the classifier trained from labeled instances have been tampered with in the step 5.

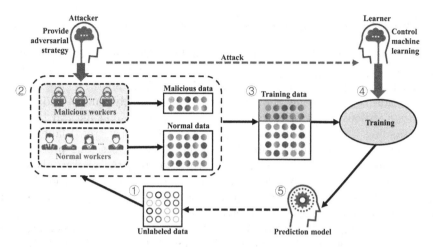

Fig. 2. Framework of crowdsourcing learning under data poisoning attacks. (1) The unlabeled data is published to the public crowdsourcing platform (e.g., Mechanical Turk) which assigns the same instance to *multiple* workers. (2) Besides the benign parties, there may exist malicious ones who usually form a clique and provide the labels manipulated by an attacker. (3) The labels are collected from all participating workers. (4) Some crowdsourcing learning approaches, such as the LFC model are used to infer accurate labels and learn the classifier from instances with inferred labels. (5) The classifier is utilized to *predict* the labels of new data.

Formally, let $X = \{\mathbf{x}_i\}_{i=1}^N$ denote the set of i.i.d. instances. The i-th instance $\mathbf{x}_i$'s true label is denoted by z_i which takes on two possible values, i.e., $z_i \in \{-1, 1\}$. We use $Z = \{z_i\}_{i=1}^N$ to denote the set of ground-truth labels of X. Let $\mathcal{U} = \{u_j\}_{j=1}^M$ be the normal worker set. The normal workers' labels are represented as a matrix $\mathbf{Y} = (y_{ij})_{N \times M}$, in which y_{ij} is the label from the normal worker u_j to instance $\mathbf{x}_i$. We assume there are M' malicious workers $\tilde{\mathcal{U}} = \{\tilde{u}_{j'}\}_{j'=1}^{M'}$ whose labels $\tilde{\mathbf{Y}} = (\tilde{y}_{ij'})_{N \times M'}$ are manipulated by the attacker, where $\tilde{u}_{j'}$ denotes the j'-th malicious worker and $\tilde{y}_{ij'}$ denotes the crowd label from $\tilde{u}_{j'}$ to $\mathbf{x}_i$. Let $\mathbf{Y}_{i*} = (y_{i1}, y_{i2}, \cdots, y_{iM})$ and $\tilde{\mathbf{Y}}_{i*} = (\tilde{y}_{i1}, \tilde{y}_{i2}, \cdots, \tilde{y}_{iM'})$ respectively denote the crowd labels from $\mathcal{U}$ and $\tilde{\mathcal{U}}$ to the i-th instance. Then, $f_{\mathbf{w}'} : \mathbb{R}^d \to \{-1, 1\}$ represents the victim model trained from the contaminated data $\mathcal{D}' = \{(\mathbf{x}_i, \mathbf{Y}'_{i*})\}_{i=1}^N$, where $\mathbf{Y}'_{i*} = (\mathbf{Y}_{i*}, \tilde{\mathbf{Y}}_{i*})$ denotes the label vector from all the participating workers $\{\mathcal{U}, \tilde{\mathcal{U}}\}$ to the i-th instance. The problem is to determine *what labels from malicious parties (i.e. $\tilde{\mathbf{Y}}$) are provided such that the victim model $f_{\mathbf{w}'}$ is sabotaged maximally.*

Similar to [5,13], we assume the attacker possesses some knowledge of normal labels to access the vulnerability of crowdsourcing learning in the worst case. This setting is reasonable as in several public crowdsourcing systems (such as Yelp) the ratings/labels are public [9]. *We relax this assumption by verifying the performance of proposed attack when malicious workers can access a small number of normal labels in experiments.*

3 Data Poisoning Attack Method

In this section, we first transform the problem formalized in Sect. 2 into a bilevel *min-max* problem in Sect. 3.1. Second, we discuss how to address this problem and introduce our adversarial algorithm PATOC in Sect. 3.2.

We begin by introducing the LFC model that is widely studied and applied to process various kinds of tasks, e.g., medical imaging and natural language understanding [15]. It simultaneously aggregates the noisy crowd labels to be more accurate labels while training the model, allowing these two processes to benefit from each other. To enhance the *learning* step, the workers' labels to the same instance are aggregated to be a more reliable one by considering the workers' abilities. Given a worker u_j, it models her performance with a confusion matrix, in which the principal diagonal elements $\mu_j = p\{y_{ij} = 1|z_i = 1\}$ and $\nu_j = p\{y_{ij} = -1|z_i = -1\}$ are treated as the ability parameters. To enforce the step of *label aggregation*, the learned model provides the prior of true labels. Let $\mathcal{H} = \{f_{\mathbf{w}}\}$ denote the family of linear discriminant functions, where $f_{\mathbf{w}}(\mathbf{x}) = \mathbf{w}^{\mathrm{T}}\mathbf{x}$ for any $\mathbf{x}, \mathbf{w} \in \mathbb{R}^d$. The probability for the class 1 can be modeled as a *logistic sigmoid* that acts on $f_{\mathbf{w}}$.

$$p\{z_i = 1|\mathbf{x}; \mathbf{w}\} = \sigma(\mathbf{w}^{\mathrm{T}}\mathbf{x}), \tag{1}$$

where $\sigma(\mathbf{w}^{\mathrm{T}}\mathbf{x}) = \frac{1}{1+e^{-x}}$ is the logistic sigmoid function. With the final classifier, the predicted label of instance $\mathbf{x}$ is $\mathrm{sgn}(\mathbf{w}^{\mathrm{T}}\mathbf{x} - 1/2)$, where $\mathrm{sgn}(x) = 1$ if $x \geq 0$, and -1, if $x < 0$. After learning the weight vector $\mathbf{w}$, Eq. 1 is used to provide the prior that 1 is the true label for instance.

Let $\Theta = \{\mathbf{w}, \{\mu_j, \nu_j\}_{j=1}^M\}$ be the parameters of LFC model. To estimate Θ, it adopts a maximum likelihood estimator as follows.

$$\Theta = \underset{\Theta}{\mathrm{argmax}} \ \mathrm{log} p(\mathcal{D}, Z; \Theta), \tag{2}$$

$\mathcal{D} = \{(\mathbf{x}_i, \mathbf{Y}_{i*})\}_{i=1}^N$ denotes the training set whose labels are normal.

3.1 Our Adversarial Strategy

To design the attack strategy, we transform the studied problem in Sect. 2 into a bilevel *min-max* optimization problem.

To make the victim model close to the attackers' target model, previous work [10,23] usually takes the Euclidean distance [10] or cosine similarity [23] between the weight vectors of the victim model and target model as the optimization objective. With these straightforward objectives, the generated adversarial examples always enjoy the strong attacking ability. Due to the heterogeneous characteristics of crowdsourcing data, these attacks cannot be applied to assess the vulnerability of crowdsourcing learning. A distinct point in our setting is that the victim model $f_{\mathbf{w}'}$ is trained from crowd labels. We reduce the victim model $f_{\mathbf{w}'} : \mathbb{R}^d \rightarrow \{-1, 1\}$ to weight vector $\mathbf{w}' \in \mathbb{R}^d$. Let $f_{\mathbf{w}^*} : \mathbb{R}^d \rightarrow \{-1, 1\}$ be the target model trained with $\mathcal{D}^* = \{(\mathbf{x}_i, -z_i)\}_{i=1}^N$ whose labels are totally flipped. Similarly, we reduce the model $f_{\mathbf{w}^*}$ to weight vector $\mathbf{w}^* \in \mathbb{R}^d$. To fulfill the adversarial aim, the attacker aims to make $\mathbf{w}'$ as close to $\mathbf{w}^*$ as possible. To this end, we define the objective function as the negative cosine similarity between $\mathbf{w}'$ and $\mathbf{w}^*$.

$$U(\mathbf{w}', \mathbf{w}^*) = -\mathbf{w}'^{\mathrm{T}} \mathbf{w}^* / \|\mathbf{w}'\| \|\mathbf{w}^*\|. \tag{3}$$

Minimizing the optimization objective entails understanding the LFC model with malicious workers. So, we formulate the problem studied of the LFC model under the adversarial environment as follows.

$$\Theta' = \operatorname*{argmax}_{\Theta'} \log p(\mathcal{D}', Z; \Theta'), \tag{4}$$

where $\Theta' = \{\mathbf{w}', \{\mu_j, \nu_j\}_{j=1}^M, \{\tilde{\mu}_{j'}, \tilde{\nu}_{j'}\}_{j'=1}^{M'}\}$ denotes the model parameters. Specifically, $\tilde{\mu}_{j'} = p\{\tilde{y}_{ij'} = 1|z_i = 1\}$ and $\tilde{\nu}_{j'} = p\{\tilde{y}_{ij'} = -1|z_i = -1\}$ denote the ability parameters of malicious worker $\tilde{u}_{j'}$.

With Eq. 3 and 4, the studied problem in Sect. 2 can be transformed into the following bilevel *min-max* optimization problem.

$$\min_{\tilde{\mathbf{Y}}} U(\mathbf{w}', \mathbf{w}^*).$$

$$s.t. \quad \Theta' = \operatorname*{argmax}_{\Theta'} \log p(\mathcal{D}', Z; \Theta')$$

$$\tilde{\mathbf{Y}} \in \{-1, 1\}^{N \times M'}. \tag{5}$$

In our bilevel formalization, the outer minimization problem optimizes the attackers' ultimate goal of sabotaging the learned model by finding the proper strategy $\tilde{\mathbf{Y}}$ while the inner maximization problem is to find the maximum likelihood estimator of the model's parameters Θ'.

3.2   Computing Our Attack Strategy

We provide the solution to the bilevel *min-max* problem formalized in Eq. 5. Based on Theorem 1, We develop our adversarial method PATOC, which solves the outer minimization problem via the reparameterization trick-based gradient descent method and the inner maximization problem by expectation-maximization (EM) algorithm.

Solving the Inner Maximization Problem. The inner maximization problem is resolved with the Expectation-Maximization (EM) algorithm.

E-step. It targets to infer the true label of each instance by computing the posterior probability $\rho_i = p\{z_i = 1|\mathcal{D}'; \Theta'\}$. On the basis of current estimate Θ', ρ_i is computed with Bayes' theorem.

$$\rho_i \propto p\{\mathbf{Y}'|z_i = 1\} p\{z_i = 1|\mathbf{x}; \mathbf{w}'\}$$

$$= \frac{a_i \tilde{a}_i \pi}{a_i \tilde{a}_i \pi + b_i \tilde{b}_i (1 - \pi)}, \tag{6}$$

where $\pi = \sigma(\mathbf{w}'^{\mathrm{T}}\mathbf{x})$,

$$a_i = \prod_j \mu_j^{\mathbf{I}(y_{ij}=1)}(1-\mu_j)^{\mathbf{I}(y_{ij}=-1)}, \quad \tilde{a}_i = \prod_{j'} \tilde{\mu}_{j'}^{\mathbf{I}(\tilde{y}_{ij'}=1)}(1-\tilde{\mu}_{j'})^{\mathbf{I}(\tilde{y}_{ij'}=-1)},$$

$$b_i = \prod_j \nu_j^{\mathbf{I}(y_{ij}=-1)}(1-\nu_j)^{\mathbf{I}(y_{ij}=1)}, \quad \tilde{b}_i = \prod_{j'} \tilde{\nu}_{j'}^{\mathbf{I}(\tilde{y}_{ij'}=-1)}(1-\tilde{\nu}_{j'})^{\mathbf{I}(\tilde{y}_{ij'}=1)}.$$

Here, $\mathbf{Y}' = \{(\mathbf{Y}_{i*}, \tilde{\mathbf{Y}}_{i*})\}_{i=1}^{N}$ denotes the label matrix from all the participating workers (i.e., $\mathcal{U}$ and $\tilde{\mathcal{U}}$) to X.

With computed $\{\rho_i\}_{i=1}^{N}$, we express the expectation of the log-likelihood in Eq. 5 as follows.

$$\mathbb{E}\{\log p(\mathcal{D}', Z; \Theta')\} = \sum_i \{\rho_i \log a_i \tilde{a}_i \pi + (1-\rho_i)\log b_i \tilde{b}_i (1-\pi)\}. \tag{7}$$

M-step. Fixing $\{\rho_i\}_{i=1}^{N}$, Θ' is computed by maximizing the expectation of the log-likelihood in Eq. 7 as follows.

$$\mu_j = \frac{\sum_i \rho_i \mathbf{I}(y_{ij}=1)}{\sum_i \rho_i}, \nu_j = \frac{\sum_i (1-\rho_i)\mathbf{I}(y_{ij}=-1)}{\sum_i (1-\rho_i)},$$

$$\tilde{\mu}_{j'} = \frac{\sum_i \rho_i \mathbf{I}(\tilde{y}_{ij'}=1)}{\sum_i \rho_i}, \tilde{\nu}_{j'} = \frac{\sum_i (1-\rho_i)\mathbf{I}(\tilde{y}_{ij'}=-1)}{\sum_i (1-\rho_i)}. \tag{8}$$

With probabilistic labels $\{\rho_i\}_{i=1}^{N}$, $\mathbf{w}'$ is derived by solving the following minimization problem.

$$\min_{f_{\mathbf{w}'} \in \mathcal{H}'} \sum_i \log(1 - \exp(-\rho'_i \cdot f_{\mathbf{w}'}(\mathbf{x}_i))) + \frac{1}{2}\|\mathbf{w}'\|^2, \tag{9}$$

where $\|\mathbf{w}'\|$ denotes 2-norm of $\mathbf{w}'$, $\mathcal{H}'$ denotes the space of possible hypotheses, and $\rho'_i = \mathrm{sgn}(\rho_i - 1/2)$. With Eq. 6 and 9, we can learn that the malicious worker can affect trained model $f_{\mathbf{w}'}$ by changing the probabilistic labels (i.e., $\{\rho_i\}_{i=1}^{N}$). Fixing the normal labels $\mathbf{Y}$, properly setting the malicious labels $\tilde{\mathbf{Y}}$ can affect or even dominate the trained model.

Solving the Outer Minimization Problem. We solve the outer minimization problem with the dual transformation and derive the gradient of objective w.r.t. the malicious labels (i.e., $\nabla_{\tilde{y}_{i,j'}} U$) which is closely related to *the influence* of training instances.

At first, the gradient $\nabla_{\tilde{y}_{i,j'}} U$ can be expressed with chain rule.

$$\nabla_{\tilde{y}_{i,j'}} U = \nabla_{w'_k} U \cdot \nabla_{\rho'_i} w'_k \cdot \nabla_{\rho_i} \rho'_i \cdot \nabla_{\tilde{y}_{i,j'}} \rho_i, \tag{10}$$

where w'_k denotes the k-th element of $\mathbf{w}'$, which is the weight associated with the k-th feature. It is *non-trivial* to compute the gradient $\nabla_{\rho'_i} w'_k$ due to the optimization process in Eq. 9, whose *closed-form* solution is hard to be derived.

To this end, we represent problem (9) as its *dual form* as follows.

$$\max_{\delta} \frac{1}{2}\delta^{\mathrm{T}}Q\delta + \sum_{i:\delta_i>0} \delta_i \log\delta_i + \sum_{i:\delta_i<1} (1-\delta_i)\log(1-\delta_i),$$

$$\delta_i \in [0,1], \forall i \in [N], \tag{11}$$

where $Q = \rho_i'\rho_{i'}'\mathbf{x}_i^{\mathrm{T}}\mathbf{x}_{i'}$, and the optimal $\mathbf{w}'$ is formulated as follows.

$$\mathbf{w}' = \sum_i \delta_i \rho_i' \mathbf{x}_i. \tag{12}$$

Note: Eq. 12 indicates that the larger δ_i of instance $\mathbf{x}_i$, the stronger its *influence* on the learned model parameterized by $\mathbf{w}'$. Thus, δ_i can be viewed as an indicator of $\mathbf{x}_i$'s influence on the learned model $f_{\mathbf{w}'}$. Then, taking the derivatives of both sides of Eq. 12, we have $\frac{\partial w_k'}{\partial \rho_i'} = \delta_i x_{ik}$. After computing $\nabla_{\rho_i'} w_k'$, we give Theorem 1 to derive $\nabla_{\tilde{y}_{i,j'}} U$.

Theorem 1. *Given a malicious worker $\tilde{u}_{j'}$ and a constant θ, the gradient of objective U w.r.t. malicious label $\tilde{y}_{i,j'}$ is computed as follows.*

$$\nabla_{\tilde{y}_{i,j'}} U = \delta_i x_{ik} \cdot \nabla_{w_k'} U \cdot \nabla_{\rho_i}\rho_i' \cdot \nabla_{\tilde{y}_{i,j'}}\rho_i, \tag{13}$$

where $\frac{\partial U}{\partial w_k'} = \frac{\mathbf{w}'^{\mathrm{T}}\mathbf{w}^*w_k' - ||\mathbf{w}'||^2 w_k^*}{||\mathbf{w}'||^3||\mathbf{w}^*||}$, $\frac{\partial \rho_i}{\partial \tilde{y}_{ij'}} = \frac{a_i b_i \tilde{a}_i \tilde{b}_i \pi(1-\pi)\log((\tilde{\mu}_{j'}\tilde{\nu}_{j'})/((1-\tilde{\mu}_{j'})(1-\tilde{\nu}_{j'})))}{(a_i\tilde{a}_i\pi+b_i\tilde{b}_i(1-\pi))^2}$, *and* $\frac{\partial \rho_i'}{\partial \rho_i} = \frac{4\theta \cdot e^{2\theta\rho_i}}{(e^{2\theta\rho_i}+1)^2}$.

Proof. Taking the derivatives of both sides of Eq. 3, we directly derive $\nabla_{w_k'} U$. To derive the $\nabla_{\tilde{y}_{i,j'}}\rho_i$, we treat $\tilde{y}_{ij'}$ as the probability that worker $\tilde{u}_{j'}$ provides label 1 to instance $\mathbf{x}_i$. Then, we calculate the $\nabla_{\tilde{y}_{i,j'}}\rho_i$ with Eq. 6. and obtain that $\frac{\partial \tilde{a}_i}{\partial \tilde{y}_{ij'}} = \tilde{a}_i \log(\frac{\tilde{\mu}_{j'}}{1-\tilde{\mu}_{j'}})$ and $\frac{\partial \tilde{b}_i}{\partial \tilde{y}_{ij'}} = \tilde{b}_i \log(\frac{1-\tilde{\nu}_{j'}}{\tilde{\nu}_{j'}})$. Then, we can obtain $\nabla_{\tilde{y}_{i,j'}}\rho_i$. As the function $h_1(x) = \mathrm{sgn}(x)$ is not continuous, we approximate $h_1(x) = \mathrm{sgn}(x)$ by $h_2(x) = \tanh(\theta x)$. Then we can compute $\frac{\partial \rho_i'}{\partial \rho_i} = \frac{4\theta \cdot e^{2\theta\rho_i}}{(e^{2\theta\rho_i}+1)^2}$. As we have $\frac{\partial w_k}{\partial \rho_i'} = \delta_i x_{ik}$, $\nabla_{\tilde{y}_{i,j'}} U$ can be computed with Eq. 10. Finally, we have Eq. 13. $\square$

Remarks: With Theorem 1, we can derive the gradient $\nabla_{\tilde{y}_{i,j'}} U$ which is closely related to δ_i that serves as the indicator of the $\mathbf{x}_i$'s influence on trained model $f_{\mathbf{w}'}$. But we cannot directly adopt the gradient descent due to the constraints of malicious labels, i.e., $\hat{\mathbf{Y}} = (\tilde{y}_{ij'})_{N \times M'} \in [0,1]^{N \times M'}$. To break this optimization dilemma, we resort to the reparameterization trick in the next section.

Our Poisoning Attack Algorithm PATOC. Based on Theorem 1, we develop the our method PATOC, which includes a two-step iteration process. The former serves to resolve the inner maximization problem while the latter tackles the outer minimization problem.

Step 1. On the basis of current estimate $\tilde{\mathbf{Y}}$, namely the optimal adversarial strategy, it applies the EM algorithm described in Sect. 3.2 to find the optimal parameters Θ' and $\{\delta_i\}_{i=1}^{N}$ that maximizes the log-likelihood in Eq. 5.

Algorithm 1: Poisoning ATtacks On CL (PATOC)

Input: Training set $\mathcal{D}$, weight vector $\mathbf{w}^*$, the number of malicious workers M'
Output: Adversarial strategy $\tilde{\mathbf{Y}}$
1 Initialize $\hat{\mathbf{Y}}$ and $\tilde{\mathbf{Y}}'$;
2 **while** *the change of* $\tilde{\mathbf{Y}}' >$ *tolerance* **do**
3   Update the parameters Θ' and $\{\delta_i\}_{i=1}^N$ with EM algorithm of Section 3.2;
4   **for** *each* $\tilde{y}'_{ij'}$ **do**
5   Update $\tilde{y}'_{ij'}$ with Equation 16;
6   Update $\tilde{y}_{ij'}$ with Equation 14;
7          $\tilde{y}_{ij'} = \text{sgn}(\tilde{y}_{ij'} - 1/2)$;

8 **return** *Adversarial strategy* $\tilde{\mathbf{Y}}$;

Step 2. On the basis of current estimate optimal parameters Θ' and $\{\delta_i\}_{i=1}^N$, it applies the *reparameterization trick-based* gradient descent method to derive the optimal $\tilde{\mathbf{Y}}$. We posit that $\tilde{\mathbf{Y}}$ is derived from its *ancestral matrix* $\tilde{\mathbf{Y}}'$.

$$\tilde{\mathbf{Y}} = \text{sigmoid}(\tilde{\mathbf{Y}}'), \tag{14}$$

where $\tilde{\mathbf{Y}}' = (\tilde{y}'_{ij'})_{N \times M'} \in \mathbb{R}^{N \times M'}$. Correspondingly, the gradient $\nabla_{\tilde{y}'_{i,j'}} U$ is calculated as follows.

$$\nabla_{\tilde{y}_{i,j'}} U = \nabla_{\tilde{y}'_{i,j'}} U \cdot \nabla_{\tilde{y}'_{i,j'}} \tilde{y}_{i,j'}, \tag{15}$$

where $\nabla_{\tilde{y}'_{i,j'}} \tilde{y}_{i,j'} = \text{sigmoid}(\tilde{y}'_{i,j'}) \cdot (1 - \text{sigmoid}(\tilde{y}'_{i,j'}))$. Then, the gradient descent algorithm is applied to update $\tilde{y}'_{ij'}$.

$$\tilde{y}'^{(t+1)}_{i,j'} \leftarrow \tilde{y}'^{(t)}_{i,j'} - \eta \nabla_{\tilde{y}'_{i,j'}} U, \tag{16}$$

where t denotes the index of iteration in gradient descent and η denotes the learning rate. In line 2, the change of $\tilde{\mathbf{Y}}'$ in two consecutive iterations is defined as $\sum_i^N \sum_{j'}^{M'} |\tilde{y}'^{(t+1)}_{ij'} - \tilde{y}'^{(t)}_{ij'}|$. With Eq. 16, we can obtain that $\sum_i^N \sum_{j'}^{M'} |\tilde{y}'^{(t+1)}_{ij'} - \tilde{y}'^{(t)}_{ij'}| = \sum_i^N \sum_{j'}^{M'} |\eta \nabla_{\tilde{y}'_{i,j'}} U|$. When $\sum_i^N \sum_{j'}^{M'} |\nabla_{\tilde{y}'_{i,j'}} U| >$ *tolerance*$/\eta$, the two-step iteration continues. In the experiments, we set *tolerance*$/\eta$ as 10^{-8} with the method of trial and error.

4 Experiments

4.1 Datasets and Baselines

The experiments are implemented on two real-world datasets labeled by the workers from Mechanical Turk, i.e., Music Genre Classification[2] [17] and

---

[2] Dataset is available at: http://amilab.dei.uc.pt/fmpr/mturk-datasets.tar.gz.

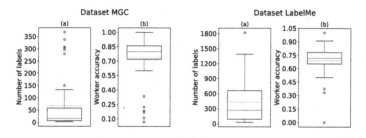

Fig. 3. Boxplots w.r.t. the number of labels from workers and their accuracies

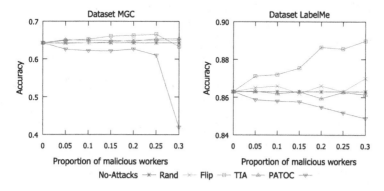

Fig. 4. Test accuracy w.r.t. the proportion of malicious workers

LabelMe[3] [16]. The Music Genre Classification dataset (MGC) contains one thousand samples concerning songs with 30 s in length, while Dataset LabelMe is an image classification dataset and contains 2,688 instances. In the dataset MGC (LabelMe), 700 (1,000) samples are labeled by 44 (59) web workers and 2,946 (2,547) crowd labels are obtained. For MGC, the feature of each instance is extracted to 124 dimensions with deep learning representation methods [17], while for LabelMe [16], the feature of each instance is extracted to 120 dimensions. Figure 3 shows the distributions of the number of labels per worker and their accuracies. We merged classes in order to end up with binary classification problems in the same way as [11] did.

We compare *our algorithm* PATOC with **TIA** [13]: it targets to subvert the labels aggregated by a representative model, Dawid and Skene [24] and only focus on the *label aggregation step* of crowdsourcing learning; **Rand**: the attacker lets the malicious workers provide the random label on each given item; **Flip** [8]: the malicious workers indiscriminately provide incorrect labels. We set $\theta = 10$ in PATOC, which makes the curve of $h_2(x)$ steeper and rather close to that of $h_1(x)$. Implementations on the two datasets are based on Python 3.5.6 and Keras 2.2.2. All experiments were performed on NVIDIA Tesla V100 GPUs.

---

[3] Dataset is available at: http://fprodrigues.com//publications/deep-crowds/.

4.2   Results and Analysis

Exp-1: With Varying the Proportion of Malicious Workers. We focus on the case that the number of malicious parties is a minority compared with the normal ones and vary the proportion of malicious workers from 0 to 0.30. For the sake of fairness, we set the proportion of instances annotated by per malicious worker to the average proportion of instances labeled by normal ones in the experiments. Figure 4 plots the test accuracy under different attack strategies. Note that *the attacker's goal is leading to* worse *values of test accuracy.* First, the test accuracy of the model under PATOC is the lowest among all the attack strategies. Second, we can observe that Flip increases the test accuracy. The reason is that the LFC model gives malicious labels negative weights, which help filter out potential incorrect labels.

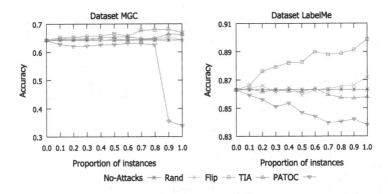

Fig. 5. Test accuracy w.r.t. the proportion of instances labeled by malicious workers

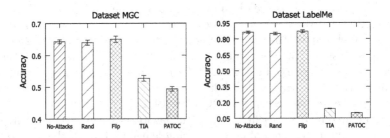

Fig. 6. Test accuracy w.r.t. limited knowledge of labels from normal parties

Exp-2: With Varying the Proportion of Instances. We assess the performance of PATOC with varying the proportion of instances annotated by per malicious worker. We set there are only 2 malicious workers. First, PATOC still launches the most effective attacks, despite each malicious worker labels partial instances as shown in Fig. 5. Second, under PATOC, sometimes the test accuracy slightly increases on the LabelMe dataset. This is because our formulation aims at degrading the model performance on the training data. We can observe that the distribution discrepancy between training data and test data has little effect on PATOC.

Exp-3: Performance with Limited Knowledge. We assume that an attacker can only observe the normal labels to 0.3 of the instances. Since PATOC and TIA entail analyzing the normal labels, in these two strategies, the malicious parties only annotate the instances whose normal labels they can observe. We set there exist only 3 malicious workers. As shown in Fig. 6, PATOC instigates the most effective attacks, though the malicious parties have limited knowledge.

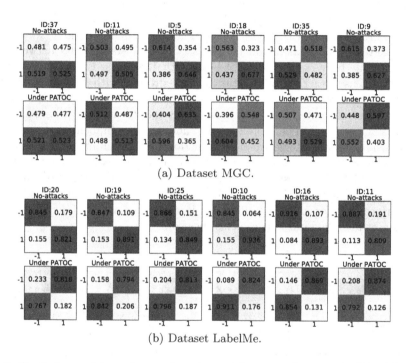

(a) Dataset MGC.

(b) Dataset LabelMe.

Fig. 7. Confusion matrices of *normal workers* with no attacks or under PATOC. The principal diagonal elements of a confusion matrix denote the ability parameters. The color intensity of the cells increases with the relative magnitude of value.

Exp-4: Confusion Matrices of Workers. Besides the trained classifier, the LFC model also estimates the confusion matrices of workers. The number of malicious workers is set to 3 and their knowledge of normal labels is also set to 0.3 of the instances. Figure 7 shows the confusion matrices of normal participants before and after being attacked. Similar to [4,16], we select six normal workers who provide the most labels. Under the PATOC, honest workers are mistaken for low-ability ones by the LFC model. For example, as for the LabelMe, the ability parameters of normal workers with ID 20 are 0.845 and 0.821 with no attacks; while they are only 0.233 and 0.182 under PATOC. In contrast, as shown in

Fig. 8, malicious workers were assigned with high-ability parameters which are higher than 0.850 in LableMe. The experimental results reveal the parameters of worker ability also significantly shift as an incidental effect of the attack.

Exp-5: Black-Box Attacks. As for the *black-box* attack, we apply the proposed attack method to generate malicious labels based on the LFC model, then use them to attack other different crowdsourcing learning models, i.e., MV+NN [20]: the labels are estimated by majority voting, and then a neural network classifier was trained with the aggregated labels; DS+NN: similar to MV+NN, except that the label aggregation algorithm is the Dawid Skene model [24]; AggNet [1]: the generalized LFC model, in which the classifier is based on a neural network. MW version of Crowd Layer [16]: the deep neural network is trained directly from the crowd labels with back-propagation. For LabelMe dataset, we use the pre-trained convolutional neural networks (CNN) layers of VGG network [16] and apply one fully connected (FC) layer with 128 units. For all datasets, we choose ReLU as the activation function and use dropout with *parameter* 0.5. The number of malicious workers is set to 2 (3) for MGC (LabelMe). As illustrated in Table 1, our generated malicious labels enjoy the strongest attacking abilities. The reason is that PATOC intelligently chooses more influential examples to attack, while other strategies treat each instance equally in model training. The result of Crowd Layer is resilient to many attacks, while vulnerable to PATOC in dataset MGC. This result supports the insights from previous research [16] which suggests that the MW approach of Crowd Layer is the one that gives the best performance for image classification datasets such as LabelMe, while MGC is a dataset involving music genre classification.

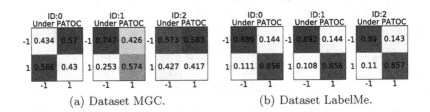

(a) Dataset MGC.   (b) Dataset LabelMe.

Fig. 8. Confusion matrices of *malicious workers* under PATOC.

Table 1. Black-box attack on different CL models. Our method generates malicious labels with strong transferability among different models

CL*	Attacks									
	Dataset MGC					Dataset LabelMe				
	No-Attacks	Rand	Flip	TIA	PATOC	No-Attacks	Rand	Flip	TIA	PATOC
MV+NN	0.682	0.680	0.502	0.578	**0.488**	0.862	0.851	0.297	0.329	**0.280**
DS+NN	0.708	0.710	0.530	0.569	**0.506**	0.863	0.848	0.300	0.335	**0.285**
AggNet	0.721	0.714	0.536	0.591	**0.503**	0.865	0.861	0.266	0.279	**0.215**
Crowd Layer	0.743	0.727	0.770	0.726	**0.280**	0.856	0.855	0.886	0.852	**0.841**

* "CL" row indicates different approaches to crowdsourcing learning.

5   Related Work

Data Poisoning Attacks on Machine Learning. As a class of adversarial machine learning, data poisoning [10,23] is generalized to analyze the vulnerabilities of many popular machine learning technologies, e.g., SVMs [2], regression learning [10]. In a data poisoning attack, the attacker attempts to affect or even dominate the final trained model by manipulating *the feature values or annotations* of training instances. Due to the heterogeneous characteristics of crowdsourcing data, most of the existing approaches [2,10,23] cannot be applied to attack crowdsourcing learning.

Crowdsourcing Learning. One conventional method of crowdsourcing learning is to aggregate the crowd labels to be more reliable ones using majority voting and then apply the supervised learning methods with the aggregated labels [20]. Here, the steps of *label aggregation* and *learning* are isolated processes. After the *label aggregation* step, several types of additional information about each instance in the training data, e.g., the features of it, are lost. However, this information may be good for further improving the quality of aggregated labels as well as re-training a more robust model. So the LFC model [15] jointly estimates the true labels and trains the classifier. Although different variants have been developed for the LFC model [1,16,17], they mainly develop the models specific to different scenarios. However, the impact of poisoning attacks on crowdsourcing learning has not been considered in these works. Thus, the proposed adversarial strategy also can be used to attack most of the existing variants of the LFC.

Data Poisoning Attacks on Crowdsourcing Learning. Although the importance of poisoning attacks has been recently recognized in crowdsourcing learning [7,8,17,21], existing efforts [3,7,8] only focus on investigating the effect of malicious behaviors on the *label aggregated step* of crowdsourcing learning. They concern the attackers who utilize simple strategies, e.g., submitting random labels or incorrect ones. In these attacks, the attacker wants to obtain rewards with fewer effort. More sophisticated attack strategies [5,7,13,18,21] entail a collection of colluders to trick quality control mechanisms based on the label aggregation models. No matter simple or sophisticated, these strategies ignore the existence of the instances which have more impacts on the performance in *learning* step [12,14]. Different from them, we consider the whole process of crowdsourcing learning (i.e., both *label aggregation* and *learning* steps) and select more influential instances when performing data poisoning attacks.

6   Conclusions

In this work, we identify the potential new paths for understanding the vulnerabilities of crowdsourcing learning. We transform the problem of optimal poisoning attacks into a bilevel program. To solve this problem, we propose PATOC, an effective approach to launching the attacks on the vulnerable instances in the training set which makes more difference to the trained model. Experimental results demonstrate that PATOC significantly outperforms the baselines *even with limited knowledge of normal labels*. In future work, we will develop strategies to defend against the data poisoning attacks on crowdsourcing learning.

Acknowledgment. This work was supported partly by National Key Research and Development Program of China under Grant No. 2019YFB1705902, and partly by National Natural Science Foundation under Grant No. (61932007, 61972013). We thank Shujie Wu and Huimin Wang for the help with the implementation of the proposed approach.

References

1. Albarqouni, S., Baur, C.: AggNet: deep learning from crowds for mitosis detection in breast cancer histology images. T-MI **35**(5), 1313–1321 (2016)
2. Biggio, B., Nelson, B., Laskov, P.: Poisoning attacks against support vector machines. In: Proceedings of ICML, pp. 1807–1814 (2012)
3. Chen, P., Sun, H., Fang, Y., Liu, X.: CONAN: a framework for detecting and handling collusion in crowdsourcing. Inf. Sci. **515**, 44–63 (2020)
4. Chen, Z., et al.: Structured probabilistic end-to-end learning from crowds. In: IJCAI, pp. 1512–1518 (2020)
5. Fang, M., Sun, M., Li, Q., Gong, N.Z., Tian, J., Liu, J.: Data poisoning attacks and defenses to crowdsourcing systems. arXiv preprint arXiv:2102.09171 (2021)
6. Fang, Y., Sun, H., Chen, P., Huai, J.: On the cost complexity of crowdsourcing. In: IJCAI, pp. 1531–1537 (2018)
7. Gadiraju, U., Kawase, R., Dietze, S.: Understanding malicious behavior in crowdsourcing platforms: the case of online surveys. In: CHI, pp. 1631–1640 (2015)
8. Ipeirotis, P.G., Provost, F., Wang, J.: Quality management on amazon mechanical turk. In: SIGKDD, pp. 64–67 (2010)
9. Jagabathula, S., Subramanian, L., Venkataraman, A.: Identifying unreliable and adversarial workers in crowdsourced labeling tasks. J. Mach. Learn. Res. **18**(1), 3233–3299 (2017)
10. Jagielski, M., Oprea, A., Biggio, B.: Manipulating machine learning: Poisoning attacks and countermeasures for regression learning. In: SP, pp. 19–35 (2018)
11. Kleindessner, M., Awasthi, P.: Crowdsourcing with arbitrary adversaries. In: ICML, pp. 2713–2722 (2018)
12. Koh, P.W., Liang, P.: Understanding black-box predictions via influence functions. In: ICML, pp. 1885–1894 (2017)
13. Miao, C., Li, Q., Su, L., Huai, M., Jiang, W.: Attack under disguise: an intelligent data poisoning attack mechanism in crowdsourcing. In: WWW, pp. 13–22 (2018)
14. Molnar, C.: Interpretable Machine Learning. Lulu.com (2019)
15. Raykar, V.C., et al.: Learning from crowds. JMLR **11**, 1297–1322 (2010)
16. Rodrigues, F.: Deep learning from crowds. In: AAAI, pp. 1611–1618 (2018)
17. Rodrigues, F., Pereira, F., Ribeiro, B.: Learning from multiple annotators: distinguishing good from random labelers. PRL **34**(12), 1428–1436 (2013)
18. Tahmasebian, F., Xiong, L., Sotoodeh, M., Sunderam, V.: Crowdsourcing under data poisoning attacks: a comparative study. In: Singhal, A., Vaidya, J. (eds.) DBSec 2020. LNCS, vol. 12122, pp. 310–332. Springer, Cham (2020). https://doi.org/10.1007/978-3-030-49669-2_18

19. Tong, Y., Zhou, Z., Zeng, Y., Chen, L., Shahabi, C.: Spatial crowdsourcing: a survey. VLDB J. **29**(1), 217–250 (2020)
20. Wang, L., Zhou, Z.H.: Cost-saving effect of crowdsourcing learning. In: IJCAI, pp. 2111–2117 (2016)
21. Yuan, D., Li, G., Li, Q., Zheng, Y.: Sybil defense in crowdsourcing platforms. In: CIKM, pp. 1529–1538 (2017)
22. Zhao, B., Han, J.: A probabilistic model for estimating real-valued truth from conflicting sources. In: Proceedings of the QDB, vol. 1817 (2012)
23. Zhao, M., An, B., Gao, W., Zhang, T.: Efficient label contamination attacks against black-box learning models. In: IJCAI, pp. 3945–3951 (2017)
24. Zheng, Y., Li, G., Li, Y., Shan, C., Cheng, R.: Truth inference in crowdsourcing: is the problem solved. PVLDB **10**(5), 541–552 (2017)

Dynamic Environment Simulation for Database Performance Evaluation

Chunxi Zhang[1], Rong Zhang[1(✉)], Qian Su[2], and Aoying Zhou[1]

[1] East China Normal University, Shanghai 200000, China
cxzhang@stu.ecnu.edu.cn, {rzhang,ayzhou}@dase.ecnu.edu.cn
[2] China Industrial Control Systems Cyber Emergency Response Team,
Beijing 100040, China
suqian@cics-cert.org.cn

Abstract. The wide popularity and the maturity of cloud platform promote the development of Cloud Native database systems. On-demand resource configuration is an attractive feature of cloud platforms, but its complexity in resource management challenges the benchmarking of database performance, which is no longer in a stand-alone test environment. Sharing or contending of resources aggravates the dynamics of environment, which can influence database performance much. In order to expose the real performance in production environment, environment simulation is prerequisite for benchmarking databases. Although Docker Containers have been promoted to isolate resources, we still cannot achieve the true resource isolation. In this paper, we first define four kinds of workload generators corresponding to the key environmental dimensions, then builds a multi-order polynomial linear regression model to calculate the correlation among workloads, and simulates the dynamical changes of environment. It is the first work to provide a complete and dynamic simulation to environment. We conduct comprehensive experiments on the open-source DBMS by running the standard benchmarks to verify the effectiveness of our work.

Keywords: Simulation · Environment · Evaluation

1 Introduction

The wide popularity and the maturity of cloud platforms promote the development of Cloud Native software systems, since cloud has the advantages of manageability, scalability and elasticity. In the latest work [3,6], it has been mentioned that there are more and more businesses migrating from the private environment to the public cloud. Though it is an attractive feature to service providers, it brings new challenges for software evaluations, because of its sharing or contending of resources among different softwares. Additionally, in order to make full use of the cloud resources, resource providers usually sell more quotients for larger profits. It then aggravates resource snatch and generates performance vibration.

© Springer Nature Switzerland AG 2021
L. H. U et al. (Eds.): APWeb-WAIM 2021, LNCS 12858, pp. 180–189, 2021.
https://doi.org/10.1007/978-3-030-85896-4_15

In such a case, resource isolation is prerequisite to guarantee stable service quality, which is usually achieved by Virtual Machines (abbr. VMs) and Docker Containers (abbr. DCs). For each VM, resources are assigned in advance, while DCs compete for shared resources at runtime. DCs can only provide the ability of packaging and running an application in a loose isolated environment, which is not a through solution due to the following reasons:

- Public resources, e.g., memory, processing unit or page cache, are shared among all DCs. Contention for resources and interference of actions become severer when using DCs by different applications.
- DCs are usually deployed on distributed nodes. Besides the resource consumed by each DC itself, distributed communication costs much more sharing bandwidth.

In this paper, we propose a workload generator for dynamic environment simulation. Firstly, we analyze and define four kinds of workload generators for four dimensions of resources, i.e., CPU, Memory, Disk IO and Network. Secondly, consider of resource consumption by each workload generator itself, we define a multi-order polynomial linear regression model to quantify the input of each workload. After all, we model the bi-impact between workloads.

The paper is organized as followings. In Sect. 2, we summarize the related work. In Sect. 3, we define four workload generators for environment. In Sect. 4, we design the workload association model. In Sect. 5, we demonstrate the validity of our design through experiments and conclusions are made in Sect. 6.

2   Related Work

Migrating production environments from corporate-owned data centers to cloud-based services is becoming popular [3]. Traditional performance engineering methods of the development and delivery of software systems are challenged by the non-deterministic characteristics of cloud platform. Additionally, the black box nature of public clouds and the cloud usage costs has become a barricade along the way of performance evaluation for cloud application [4,6], which also leads to expensive parameter optimization [1]. Specifically, in the domain of database performance debugging, slow queries are sensitive to the fluctuation of production environment [11]. It is obvious that simulation of production environment is critical to promote software systems to the cloud platform.

Environment simulation is to run a set of generated workloads to replicate the environment status, which is necessary for performance evaluation [9,10,12, 13]. There are two ways to generate workloads [2]. One is defining an analytic approach. The other one is collecting the running traces and generate workloads according to the running status. Considering the real workload characteristics, file access behaviours are modeled based on a user-oriented synthetic workload generator [8]. In [7], though it proposes to evaluate a DBMS by simulating its running environment, it does not consider the network resource or the bi-impact between resources. The simulation method cannot simulate the dynamicity of environment. So in this paper, we provide an effective workload generator for dynamic resource status simulation.

3   Workload Generator Definition

First of all, we define four types of fundamental workload generators corresponding to CPU, Memory, Disk IO and Bandwidth. These defined generators have the property of parameter sensitivity, and we can easily construct adaptive workload composition model for simulating environment status.

3.1   Workload Generator Definition

CPU-bound Workload: We define a computation intensive workload for CPU, i.e., Π *calculation* in Eq. 1. The intensity is controlled by Gregory–Leibniz series based on n and the number of threads tn in calculation. The larger n or the bigger tn consumes more CPU resource. It is implemented in *Java*, which will consume memory to launch *Java* program.

$$\frac{\Pi}{4} = \sum_{n=0}^{\infty} \frac{(-1)^n}{2 \cdot n + 1} \tag{1}$$

Memory-Bound Workload: We define a multi-thread array space applying function by $new()$ in $C++$ program to control memory consumption. Considering the expect memory consumption m for a time period s, threads T communicate with Linux signal function *Sigaction* to coordinate the execution time period set by *Setitimer*. Since this kind of software-based resource occupation also consumes CPU resource, each thread applies $m/\|T\|$ memory initially, which will be adjusted according to the global resource status considering the interaction among workloads.

IO-Bound Workload: We take Linux disk operation command dd for multi-thread disk IO operation, and the amount of IO, i.e., $io = \|T\| \cdot bs \cdot k$, is controlled by the number of threads $\|T\|$, the quantity $bs = size$ of each write and the total round of writing $count = k$ of each thread. At the end of test, we erase the file $file_i$ by writing $/dev/urandom$. Even though we call the kernel function for IO consumption, it has a positive impact to CPU for the calculation operation.

Network-Bound Workload: Netty[1] is programmed to generate network-bound workload. We first set the percentage of bandwidth usage, i.e., $size$; then we pack a string for each *TaskQueue* in Task Manager considering about the capacity ($iops = Input/Output\ Operations\ Per\ Second$) of each queue, and stream it to *Channel* continuously. Java code is implemented to call Netty and calculate the size of data for transferring, so network-bound workload has impact on both CPU and Memory.

---

[1] Netty: https://netty.io/.

4   Environment Simulation

Even though we define workloads Ψ on four semantic dimensions, i.e., environment space E, we cannot easily produce the resource status isolatedly because they have interactive impacts on each other. It may produce an environment deviation defined in **Definition 1** between the expected value and the generated value considering the mutual influence among simulation functions. Our purpose is to minimize the $devs$ along all dimensions.

Definition 1. For an environment variable $e_i \in E$, given the expected value x_i and the generated value y_i by the generation function $\Psi_i \in \Psi$, **Environment Deviation** dev_i is defined as the deviation between x_i and y_i, i.e., $dev_i = \frac{\|x_i - y_i\|}{x_i}$ with $y_i = \Psi_i(x_i)$.

4.1   Workload Modeling on Each Individual Dimension

For a single dimension $e_i \in E$, considering its generation function Ψ_i, we formalize the environment status simulation as a multi-order polynomial linear regression problem defined by Eq. 2, with x_i, y_i as the observed and generated value for e_i, and α_j as the model parameter.

$$\begin{cases} \hat{y}_i & = \Psi_i(x_i) = \alpha_0 + \sum_{j=1}^{n} \alpha_j x_i^j \\ y_i & = \hat{y}_i + \epsilon_i \end{cases} \tag{2}$$

The generation problem can be achieved by minimizing ϵ_i, that is

$$\arg\min_{\alpha} dev_i(x_i) = \arg\min_{\alpha} \|y_i - \hat{y}_i\|$$

For each environment dimension, we have its own multi-order regression function formulated by α, which does not care about the mutual influence among generators.

4.2   Modeling Environment by Learning Workload Interaction Among Dimensions

Bi-impact Modeling Between Dimensions. In Eq. 2, it aims to simulate the resource consumption on an individual dimension. As we have explained that the four dimensions of environment status may have impacts on each other, represented by z. Then we formulate this kind of impact from dimension e_i to the other one e_j by $\hbar_j(y_i)$ and the total impact for e_j is z_j defined in Eq. 3 with n as the order which is usually small and set by experiment.

$$\hat{z}_j(i) = \hbar_j(y_i) = \beta_0 + \sum_{k=1}^{n} \beta_k \cdot y_i^k; \quad \hat{z}_j = \sum_{i=1 \wedge i \neq j}^{4} (z_j(i)); \tag{3}$$

Considering the impact between the simulation workloads, we can learn all β parameter by solving $\arg\min_{\beta} dev_i(x) = \arg\min_{\beta} \|\hat{z}_j(i) - z_j(i)\|$.

Environment Status Generation Model. For simulating resource consumption status x_i on dimension e_i by our generator, considering the mutual influence of generators, i.e., Ψ, we get the expect input, i.e., y_i', usually $y_i' < x_i$. We can formalize the impact from dimensions other than e_i by:

$$\tilde{\Psi}_i(x_i) = \Psi_i(x_i - z_i) = y_i', \tag{4}$$

where z_i is the impact function from other dimensions. Given the resource status x_i on dimension e_i, we can calculate the corresponding input requirement y_i' by Eq. 4.

4.3 Dynamic Environment Simulation

Environment may keep changing along the time. Inputs X, Y and Z are four dimensional arrays with each dimension corresponding to one type of resource, e.g., e_d. A and B are metrices sized $4 \times (n+1)$ with n as the size of parameters, and each row, e.g., A_d, corresponds to the model parameters for e_d, i.e., α_d and β_d. Supposing we have a list of environment changing time points in $\hat{T}$, between which are the stable time periods for the environment status, we have the simulation targets O. For each time period, according to the target resource consumption $o_d \in O$, i.e., x in Eq. 4, it simulates the input y_d, i.e., y' in Eq. 4, for our generator, which is put into $\hat{Y}_d$. Our final generator inputs are stored in $\hat{Y}$.

5 Experiment Results

Experimental Setting: Our experiments are conducted on 4 nodes configured in RAID-5 on CentOS v.6.5. Each node is equipped with 2 Intel Xeon E5-2620 @ 2.13 GHz CPUs, 130 GB memory and 3 TB HDD disk. Nodes are connected using 1 Gigabit Ethernet. We deploy a centralized DB, i.e., MySQL ($v.5.6.28$) on different environment status which are simulated by different workloads to verify the effectiveness of our work.

Baseline: We take *Jeong* [7] as the comparison baseline. It simulates CPU, Memory, and Disk I/O consumptions without Network. *Jeong* defines a computation intensive task to simulate CPU usage define as *the number of CPU × CPU Clock Speed (MHz) × System Clock Speed (MHz) × Correction Factor*. It occupies memory by using a multithread data reading from disk into memory with the number of threads set to 5. For Disk IO simulation, it assigns a branch of threads to write the queued small files to disk parallely.

Workloads: In different environment, we run YCSB on MySQL and collect the real performance.

5.1 Environment Workload Demonstration

We first demonstrate the effectiveness of workload generators for environment simulation on each dimension. For each dimension e_i, we randomly generated

$1K$ groups of workloads, i.e., y_i, and executed to get the real workload, i.e., x_i, and the impact on other dimension z_i, which are used to learn the parameters α and β.

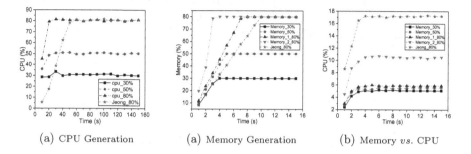

(a) CPU Generation   (a) Memory Generation   (b) Memory *vs.* CPU

Fig. 1. CPU consumption   **Fig. 2.** Memory consumption

Cpu-Bound Workload. Supposing we have the target CPU consumption set to 30%, 50% and 80%, by controlling the complexity, i.e., n, Π calculation can reach to our targets by 20 s shown in Fig. 1. The deviations between the simulations and the targets are small, among which the biggest is less than 1%. Though *Jeong* can have the similar result as we do by taking almost 2× more time, its generation is adjusted by *Correction Factor* which has lower adjustion efficiency than our model.

Memory-Bound Workload. We keep applying space for an array to consume Memory. Supposing we have the target memory consumption set to 30%, 50% and 80%. For 80% memory consumption, we take both the two-thread generation mode. It is easy to see that the small memory required, the faster to reach the target Fig. 2(a). For 80% memory consumption, though *Memory_2_80%* is 2× faster than *Memory_1_80%* to occupy memory, its CPU consumption is 2× higher as shown in Fig. 2(b). *Jeong* reads data from disk is slower than our method to generate the same size of memory consumption and also costs much more CPU resources shown in Fig. 2.

IO-bound Workload. We keep writing data to Disk by using a Linux disk operation command dd in a multi-thread mode. Supposing IO consumptions are set to 30%, 50% and 80%. As shown in Fig. 3(a), we can see that both our method and *Jeong* can reach the target setting very soon, around 1 s, but the CPU consumption by our generator is much smaller than that by *Jeong*. *Jeong* then has 2× higher CPU usages than our multi-thread generation mode. Our additional CPU consumption is bound by 10% in a single-thread mode as shown in Fig. 3(b).

Network-Bound Workload. Bandwidth consumption is simulated by Netty. We control the bandwidth consumption by adjusting the number of transmission per second, i.e., *iops* and the data size for transmission. Supposing we have the bandwidth occupation set to 30%, 50% and 80% as shown in Fig. 4, it is easy to reach our target environment by around 1s as shown in Fig. 4(a). Since it has high uncertainty on cluster network, the adjustment calculation costs more CPU than the other workloads, which is between 7%–15% as shown in Fig. 4(b).

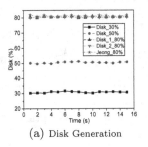
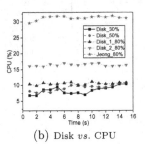

(a) Disk Generation   (b) Disk *vs.* CPU

Fig. 3. Disk IO consumption

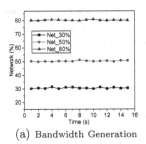
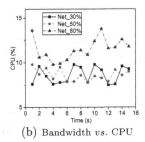

(a) Bandwidth Generation   (b) Bandwidth *vs.* CPU

Fig. 4. Bandwidth consumption

Summarization. According to these experiments, we can see that 1) workload generator usually has an interaction with each other; 2) our simulation method is more efficient than *Jeong* which does not provide simulation to Network.

5.2   Environment Simulation

Based on the bi-impact between workloads, we build the final simulation model in Eq. 4. We compare the simulated environment, i.e., *GeneValue* with the real environment, i.e., *RealValue*, by *deviation* defined in Eq. 5 on the four dimensions with 100 groups of test data. The deviations for CPU, Memory, Disk IO and Network are 3.78%, 1.46%, 3.73% and 2.96%, respectively. It means that our model is effective in environment simulation.

$$deviation = \frac{|RealValue - GeneValue|}{RealValue} \tag{5}$$

Dynamic Simulation of Environment. We generate 5 groups of resource consumption requirements randomly, and each group of resource status will last for 60 s as shown in Table 1. Our model can simulate each group of resource consumption very well bound by 5% deviation.

5.3   Environment Simulation Based on Real Applications

We launch YCSB workloads generated by OLTP-Bench [5] on MySQL by varying access thread sizes (60 and 120) and collect four groups of resource consumption status by nmon[2]. Since environment is not stable along with the running of benchmark workloads, we monitor and collect its resource consumption every 2 s, and calculate the average resource status for simulation. The simulation *deviation* is shown in Table 2, among which the *deviation* between *GeneValue* and *RealValue* is bound by 5%.

Table 1. Deviation for dynamic environment simulation

Period(s)		CPU	Memory	Disk IO	Network
0–60	Target	5.35%	58.91%	64.34%	45.69%
	SimulatedValue	5.41%	59.56%	65.17%	46.64%
	Deviation	1.1%	1.1%	1.3%	2.1%
60–120	Target	22.74%	30.69%	55.07%	8.94%
	SimulatedValue	23.02%	31.08%	55.63%	9.18%
	Deviation	1.24%	1.27%	1.1%	2.72%
120–180	Target	34.44%	74.68%	24.15%	6.15%
	SimulatedValue	34.87%	75.6%	24.95%	6.31%
	Deviation	1.27%	1.22%	3.3%	2.5%
180–240	Target	17.85%	59.7%	13.65%	19.55%
	SimulatedValue	17.37%	60.32%	13.81%	19.93%
	Deviation	−2.6%	1.03%	1.18%	1.98%
240–300	Target	67.62%	26.3%	22.21%	24.64%
	SimulatedValue	68.41%	26.62%	22.69%	25.13%
	Deviation	1.16%	1.22%	2.17%	2.01%

---
[2] nmon: http://nmon.sourceforge.net/pmwiki.php?n=Main.HomePage.

Table 2. Environment simulation on real applications

No.	Workload		CPU	Memory	Disk IO	Network
G1	$YCSB^{60}$	Target	62.51%	4.16%	19.68%	5.4%
		SimulatedValue	63.92%	4.21%	20.35%	5.51%
		Deviation	2.25%	1.2%	3.4%	5.51%
G2	$YCSB^{120}$	Target	71.65%	4.34%	18.98%	9.6%
		SimulatedValue	72.92%	4.38%	19.53%	9.15%
		Deviation	1.7%	1%	2.89%	−4.6%

6 Conclusion

In our work, we present a workload generator for environment simulation. We define a multi-order polynomial linear regression model for each resource, and consider the influence of individual resource workload among all. We launch a comprehensive set of experiments to verify the effectiveness of the model based on micro and macro evaluations.

Acknowledgment. This work is partially supported by National Science Foundation of China (No. 62072179) and 2020 the Key Software Adaptation and Verification Project (Database).

References

1. Bao, L., Liu, X., Wang, F., Fang, B.: ACTGAN: automatic configuration tuning for software systems with generative adversarial networks. In: Proceedings of the ASE, pp. 465–476. IEEE (2019)
2. Barford, P., Crovella, M.: Generating representative web workloads for network and server performance evaluation. In: Proceedings of the ACM SIGMETRICS, pp. 151–160 (1998)
3. Bondi, A.B.: Challenges with applying performance testing methods for systems deployed on shared environments with indeterminate competing workloads: position paper. In: Proceedings of the ACM/SPEC, pp. 41–44 (2016)
4. Diamantopoulos, D., Hagleitner, C.: HelmGemm: managing GPUs and FPGAs for transprecision GEMM workloads in containerized environments. In: Proceedings of the ASAP, vol. 2160, pp. 71–74. IEEE (2019)
5. Difallah, D.E., Pavlo, A., Curino, C.: OLTP-bench: an extensible testbed for benchmarking relational databases. Proc. VLDB Endow. **7**(4), 277–288 (2013)
6. He, S., Manns, G., Saunders, J., Wang, W., Pollock, L., Soffa, M.L.: A statistics-based performance testing methodology for cloud applications. In: Proceedings of the ESEC and SFSE, pp. 188–199 (2019)
7. Jeong, H.J., Lee, S.H.: A workload generator for database system benchmarks. In: Proceedings of the IIWAS, pp. 813–822. Citeseer (2005)
8. Kao, W.-I., Iyer, R.K.: A user-oriented synthetic workload generator. In: Proceedings of the ICDCS, pp. 270–271. IEEE Computer Society (1992)

9. Kerr, J., Reddy, P., Kosti, S., Izzetoglu, K.: UAS operator workload assessment during search and surveillance tasks through simulated fluctuations in environmental visibility. In: Schmorrow, D.D., Fidopiastis, C.M. (eds.) HCII 2019. LNCS (LNAI), vol. 11580, pp. 394–406. Springer, Cham (2019). https://doi.org/10.1007/978-3-030-22419-6_28

10. Li, Y., Zhang, R., Yang, X., Zhang, Z., Zhou, A.: Touchstone: generating enormous query-aware test databases. In: Proceedings of the USENIX ATC, pp. 575–586 (2018)

11. Ma, M., et al.: Diagnosing root causes of intermittent slow queries in cloud databases. Proc. VLDB Endow. **13**(8), 1176–1189 (2020)

12. Schäfer, D., Edinger, J., Breitbach, M., Becker, C.: Workload partitioning and task migration to reduce response times in heterogeneous computing environments. In: Proceedings of the ICCCN, pp. 1–11. IEEE (2018)

13. Tabebordbar, A., Beheshti, A., Benatallah, B., Barukh, M.C.: Feature-based and adaptive rule adaptation in dynamic environments. Data Sci. Eng. **5**(3), 207–223 (2020). https://doi.org/10.1007/s41019-020-00130-4

LinKV: An RDMA-Enabled KVS for High Performance and Strict Consistency Under Skew

Xing Wei, Huiqi Hu$^{(\boxtimes)}$, Xuan Zhou, and Aoying Zhou

School of Data Science and Engineering, East China Normal University,
Shanghai, China
simba_wei@stu.ecnu.edu.cn, {hqhu,xzhou,ayzhou}@dase.ecnu.edu.cn

Abstract. We present LinKV, a novel distributed key-value store that can leverage RDMA network to simultaneously provide high performance and strict consistency (i.e., per-key linearizability) for skewed workloads. To avoid the potential performance loss caused by load imbalance under skew, existing solutions will replicate popular items into different nodes' caches to support quick and even accesses. But for those writes hitting cache, there will be multiple consistency actions to guarantee linearizability, which degrade the overall performance. In this paper, we present a batch method to make multiple writes amortize those overheads caused by a round of consistency actions. While for reads, we introduce a lease-based scheme to make them quickly return the most recently completed batches of writes. Comparing to the state-of-the-art solutions, LinKV with above strategies can improve the throughput by $1.5-3\times$ and reduce the latency to about 10% with different write ratios under skew.

Keywords: Key-value store · Linearizability · Caching · RDMA

1 Introduction

Today's online services, such as e-commerce and social network, critically depend on the cache or storage provided by key-value stores (KVSs). So, as services scale to billions of users, the KVSs must provide adequate performance requirements. To this end, prevailing KVSs try to maintain items in the memory environment, and make all items partitioned across multiple machine nodes [1].

Although the item shards among multiple nodes can promote the parallelism for accesses, this design may suffer from the skewed workload, because the nodes containing popular items may receive far more access requests than other nodes, typically the following power-law distribution [2]. In practice, the skewed workload could lead to severe load imbalance among multiple nodes so that overall performance degrades quickly. Fortunately, the emergence of RDMA (Remote Direct Memory Access) network brings the opportunity to make in-memory KVS nodes organized under the non-uniform memory access (NUMA) abstraction, which allows requests to be uniformly distributed over different nodes. To avoid

© Springer Nature Switzerland AG 2021
L. H. U et al. (Eds.): APWeb-WAIM 2021, LNCS 12858, pp. 190–198, 2021.
https://doi.org/10.1007/978-3-030-85896-4_16

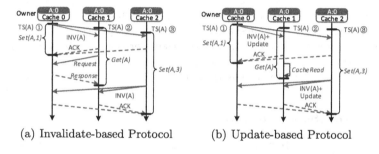

(a) Invalidate-based Protocol   (b) Update-based Protocol

Fig. 1. Consistency guarantee for per-key linearizability.

the frequent cross-node accesses, the KVSs under NUMA abstraction make each node augmented with a cache, thereby providing the typical ccNUMA (i.e., cache coherence NUMA) abstraction.

When popular items are replicated into multiple nodes' caches, a consistency model must be enforced under writes. To achieve that, existing ccNUMA KVSs try to adopt the update-based or invalidate-based protocol [3] to guarantee the strict consistency, which makes all operations linearizable. In the protocols, there are several cross-node actions (e.g., update or invalidation) during the procedure of each write hitting cache, in order to make distributed writes take effect orderly and reads witness the latest completed writes [8]. As the ccNUMA KVS serves millions of requests per second, even a small fraction of writes can cause massive cross-node actions, especially under the skew.

To reduce the overheads caused by cross-node actions, the intuitive solution is to handle multiple writes in a batch so that they could share the same round of cross-node actions. But under linearizability, such a solution poses new challenges to (*i*) make distributed batches of writes take effect orderly and (*ii*) enable each read to see the most recently completed batches of writes. In this paper, to meet these challenges, ❶ we first identify the mismatches between existing consistency guarantees and desirable performance requirements in ccNUMA KVSs. ❷ For the writes hitting cache, we then try to process writes in a batch and coordinate them to take effect orderly. ❸ Next, for the reads hitting cache, we introduce a lease-based strategy to force them to see the latest batches of writes that have taken effect globally. ❹ At last, we integrate above designs into the prototype called LinKV, and conduct the empirical evaluation to reveal the superiority.

2   Background and Related Work

2.1   Skew Mitigation Under ccNUMA Abstraction

Based on the modern RDMA network, all in-memory KVS nodes can be accommodated under the NUMA-like abstraction [6], wherein items are partitioned into different nodes and requests are evenly distributed across all nodes. By adopting RDMA primitives (i.e., read and write), all requests could bypass CPU to directly access the in-memory items on remote nodes, thereby mitigating the load imbalance caused by skew. However, the key limitation of this approach is that the vast majority of requests need to use the long-latency RDMA accesses to retrieve the popular items on remote nodes under skew [7]. To solve this issue, the symmetric cache as a mainstream component is introduced into each NUMA node to form the ccNUMA abstraction [4,7].

2.2 Enforcing Strict Consistency

Consistency Model. In terms of prevailing KVSs, their concern on consistency is to provide the guarantee on per-key basis [5], and there are no valid guarantees for the operations on different keys. As illustrated in [8], to avoid the anomalies, linearizability must maintain a total order over per-key operations, which should mandate: (i) writes must take effect in the sequential order consistent with real time (i.e., write serialization); (ii) reads must return the most recently completed writes (i.e., read consistency).

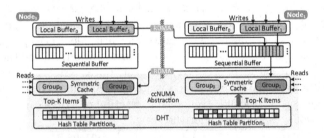

Fig. 2. The design overview of LinKV (two nodes) under ccNUMA abstraction.

Consistency Guarantee. Let us suppose a set of cache nodes initially containing the popular item $[A : 0]$, as shown in Fig. 1. To preserve linearizability for those operations on this cached item, the prevailing guarantees usually adopt the invalidate-based or update-based protocol [3] to enforce reads and writes to be linearizable. To satisfy the total order, each cached item binds a lamport clock to assign unique logical timestamps (TSs) to order the cache-hit operations. Thus, Get(A) has to wait for Set(A,1) to be done, and Set(A,3) has to wait for Get(A) to complete. In addition, for those write operations (e.g., Set(A,1) and Set(A,3)) under the invalidate-based protocol, they need to propagate an invalidate action to all nodes in case that follow-up reads see the older version of cached items, as shown in Fig. 1(a). When seeing the invalid cached item, the read operation (e.g., Get(A)) will update the latest write into the local cache. But under the update-based protocol, each write operation must propagate an additional update action to all nodes so that the cached item is updated into the latest version for following read operations, as shown in Fig. 1(b). For the write operations under any protocol, once all caches finish their received actions and reply acks, the writes will take effect instantly.

Obviously, there are many cross-node consistency actions in the existing guarantees, which can aggravate the burden of network and consuming massive computing resources. In addition, under the total order constraint, the long-latency execution of cross-node actions could severely block the execution of follow-up operations, which can leave the computing resources idle.

3 LinKV Design

Based on the analyses presented earlier, the primary goal of LinKV is to alleviate the overheads caused by the cross-node actions under linearizability so that each request processing can have abundant network and computing resources. Aiming at this goal, LinKV proposes a delicate workflow for the cache hit scenario[1], as shown in Fig. 2.

Batching Writes to Amortize the Overheads. From the perspective of the writes that are distributed across all nodes, their processing can be run in a batch rather than isolation. To do so, we introduce two innovative structures (i.e., local buffer and sequential buffer) to construct a delicate write workflow that makes multiple writes take effect in a batch to amortize the overheads caused by the cross-node actions (recall Sect. 2.2). Each LinKV node has multiple local buffers serving the writes on different node partitions. For those local buffers on different nodes, if they correspond to the same node partition, their writes will finally flush into the matched node's sequential buffer in a batch. Obviously, these batches of writes from different nodes can easily reach a unified order according to the sequences of sequential buffer slots, which do not take any cross-node action. Next, for the writes that just arrived, the sequential buffer then builds an "early-bird" message, and asynchronously broadcasts it into all nodes so that they are aware that there are new writes happened (like the invalidation action). Lastly, the sequential buffer commits received writes to make them take effect.

Enabling Reads to Quickly Return the Latest and Completed Writes. For those reads that are issued at different nodes, the cache is always regard as the optimal option to quickly provide the requested items. Meanwhile, by heralding what writes will take effect, the early-bird message can make the reads issued in any node quickly see these new writes instead of older cached items without any waiting interval. But, the reads could also see the writes that have not been committed through received messages, which obviously violate read consistency (recall Sect. 2.2). To this end, we will design a lease-based strategy to help reads quickly see the latest and completed writes.

4 Write

Within a LinKV node, to avoid each write directly taking effect via the cross-node actions (e.g., TS acquisition and update), the local buffers try to make the processing of concurrent writes coalesced and batched to amortize the overheads.

---

[1] The following discussion about reads and writes refers to the cache-hit cases.

4.1 Sequential Buffer Coordination

For the continuous arrivals of distributed batches of writes, the sequential buffer will periodically commit these writes to make them take effect according to those sequences of buffer slots and thus to preserve write serialization. In addition, to make later reads quickly see the writes to be committed, we set up a preparation point $\mathcal{P}_i$ to issue several tasks to pick up proper writes and make them prepared well for reads before they take effect at next commit point $\mathcal{E}_i$, as shown in Fig. 3.

Preparation Point. After the commit point $\mathcal{E}_{i-1}$, the sequential buffer will set a preparation point $\mathcal{P}_i$ instantly and run three preparatory tasks for the writes that will take effect at the commit point $\mathcal{E}_i$.

① Selection Task: Firstly, the sequential buffer needs to run a selection task to determine which writes will take effect and become visible at the next commit point $\mathcal{E}_i$. Intuitively, the selection task takes the preparation point $\mathcal{P}_i$ as a proper cut-off point, and selects those writes that arrived before this point $\mathcal{P}_i$ and have not taken effect.

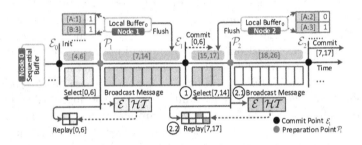

Fig. 3. Batch workflow coordinates fully distributed writes.

②.₁ Broadcast Task: The sequential buffer then will run a broadcast task to build an early-bird message for selected writes and propagate it to all nodes so that distributed reads can instantly see these writes when they take effect at the commit point $\mathcal{E}_i$. Essentially, the message should wrap the commit point (e.g., $\mathcal{E}_2$, 4B) for selected writes, and the memory address (e.g., $\mathcal{HT}_2$, 8B) of a small array-based hash table that will cover the selected writes through following replay task. After building a message, the broadcast task will use an RDMA-based MPI_Bcast operation to propagate it into all nodes.

②.₂ Replay Task: Meanwhile, the sequential buffer will also run a replay task to pick up the newer distinct ones from the selected writes, and insert them into the array-based hash table (mentioned above) to benefit the reads. More specifically, the replay task firstly duplicates the hash table with the latest writes, and then visits selected writes to insert the newer distinct ones into duplication, e.g., the writes within $[7, 17]$ are replayed into the duplication (i.e., $\mathcal{HT}_2$) based on hash table $\mathcal{HT}_1$.

Commit Point. Under the periodical setting, if the preparation has not been done at the commit point $\mathcal{E}_i$, the sequential buffer will ignore this point, and wait for the next point $\mathcal{E}_{i+1}$ to commit selected writes to make them take effect.

5 Read

5.1 Read Consistency Challenge

Under the write workflow presented in Sect. 4, the asynchronous early-bird message not only makes nodes aware of the writes to be committed, but also changes the behavior of reads, thereby bringing a challenge on the read consistency. We use Fig. 4 as an example to illustrate the problem. Suppose that $node_0$ has prepared the message $[\mathcal{E}_1, \mathcal{HT}_1]$ for a group of selected writes between commit points $\mathcal{E}_0$ and $\mathcal{E}_1$, and successfully broadcasted it to all nodes. Normally, the message arrives at all nodes before selected writes take effect at the commit point $\mathcal{E}_1$. Therefore, if a read is issued before the commit point $\mathcal{E}_1$, it can not be allowed to read the hash table $\mathcal{HT}_1$ according to this message. Otherwise, if the read returns a value from $\mathcal{HT}_1$, its behavior will violate read consistency due to see the write that is not completed. However, for the read issued after the point $\mathcal{E}_1$, if it ignores the message and directly accesses the cache, its behavior will also violate read consistency since it misses the latest write value. Because the reads on different nodes are not aware of the commit point $\mathcal{E}_1$ on $node_0$, a mechanism needs to be designed to guide reads to see the latest and completed writes with the help of a properly early-bird message.

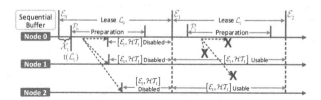

Fig. 4. Consistency analysis and lease strategy. The red cross means broadcast failure. (Color figure online)

5.2 Lease Strategy

Under the periodical setting, there is no new write committed between a commit interval from the point $\mathcal{E}_i$ to the point $\mathcal{E}_{i+1}$. Thus, for the message $[\mathcal{E}_i, \mathcal{HT}_i]$ that usually arrived at all nodes before point $\mathcal{E}_i$, it can keep serving the reads issued between the points $\mathcal{E}_i$ and $\mathcal{E}_{i+1}$ because there are the latest and completed writes in the hash table $\mathcal{HT}_i$. By leveraging the serving period of each message, we can design a lease-based strategy to guarantee the read consistency by providing the proper message for serving the reads during a specific period.

Basic Idea. In essence, a lease $\mathcal{L}_i$ is a contract given by a sequential buffer, and held by all nodes. It contains a message $[\mathcal{E}_i, \mathcal{HT}_i]$ and an expiration time $t(\mathcal{E}_{i+1})$ which indicate the message $[\mathcal{E}_i, \mathcal{HT}_i]$ can only serve reads before the time $t(\mathcal{E}_{i+1})$ of point $\mathcal{E}_{i+1}$ is reached, as analyzed above. Meanwhile, considering the message $[\mathcal{E}_{i+1}, \mathcal{HT}_{i+1}]$ starts to serve reads at the expiration time $t(\mathcal{E}_{i+1})$ of lease $\mathcal{L}_i$, the effective time of lease $\mathcal{L}_{i+1}$ should be the expiration time of lease $\mathcal{L}_i$. Thus, there is no time interval between two consecutive leases $\mathcal{L}_i$ and $\mathcal{L}_{i+1}$. Thus, by broadcasting the message with a lease, the reads issued at any time points can always acquire the requested items from proper messages.

5.3 Lease-Based Read

In this subsection, we will introduce how to integrate above lease design into the read workflow to provide high performance while preserving the read consistency.

(①) **Lease Check:** Firstly, the read request obtains its issuing time, and attempts to acquire a matched lease according to its issuing time. If the unstable network makes the lease broadcast fail (e.g., the lease $\mathcal{L}_2$ in Fig. 4), the read request will not find the matched lease in local node, and will proactively request this lease from the generation node.

(②) **Cache Update:** Next, the read request picks up the proper partition from the symmetric cache by hashing requested key. For those read requests that acquire the same lease $\mathcal{L}_i$ and correspond to the same partition, if the partition has not been updated to contain the hash table $\mathcal{HT}_i$ according to lease $\mathcal{L}_i$, these writes will contend for the opportunity to update the cache partition.

(③) **Item Access:** Once the cache partition update completes, the reads belonging to lease $\mathcal{L}_i$ can directly access the requested items from the $\mathcal{HT}_i$ in the partition while preserving read consistency.

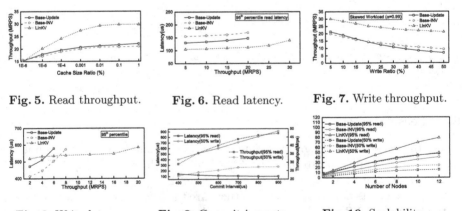

Fig. 5. Read throughput.   **Fig. 6.** Read latency.   **Fig. 7.** Write throughput.

Fig. 8. Write latency.   **Fig. 9.** Commit impacts.   **Fig. 10.** Scalability.

6   Experiment

The experiments run on 4 nodes connected by an InfiniBand switcher (56 Gbps Mellanox) and equipped with 128 GB memory, two CPUs (Intel(R) Xeon(R) Sliver 4110). The dataset is a total of 256 million distinct key-value pairs, which are hash-partitioned across all nodes. We evaluate our LinKV under the skewed workloads with the skew exponent $\alpha = 0.99$. For the comparison, we also implement two baselines, i.e., Base-INV and Base-Update, which respectively take the invalidate-based and update-based protocols to preserve linearizability.

Read-Intensive Performance. Figure 5 reveal how the cache size ratio affects the throughput under the 95% read ratio. Obviously, LinKV can have the better throughput improvement than other two systems with the increase of cache size ratio. It is because the batch of writes can avoid the frequent read blocking even under the 5% write ratio. But when increasing the cache size ratio into 0.01%, the throughput will not increase due to the limitation of system's resources. So we pick up 0.01% as the default cache size ratio. Moreover, we compare the 95th percentile latency of evaluated systems, as shown in Fig. 6. Note that the LinKV can always achieve the lowest latency under different throughputs. The reason is that the majority of read requests can directly fall in the cache, which will not be affected by writes during a lease period.

Write Performance. Figure 7 plots the throughput changes of all systems under the different write ratios. When varying the write ratio from 10% to 50%, LinKV can only decrease about 8 Mrps, which is obviously superior to Base-INV and Base-Update. It is because the cache-hit writes in LinKV can concurrently run in a batch to amortize the network and computing overheads. Meanwhile, we further compare the 95th percentile write latency of different systems under the write-heavy workloads (50% write ratio), as shown in Fig. 8. LinKV can always achieve the stable latency (516 μs) less than other two systems (596 μs and 592 μs) under the high throughput. This is because that LinKV adopts the periodical commit setting so that writes have the steady latency.

Commit Interval. Figure 9 studies the impact of commit interval on throughput and latency in LinKV. With the increase of commit interval, the period of lease becomes bigger so that the frequency of cache update decreases. Thus, the read-intensive workload can achieve the better throughput and latency. But, for the write-intensive workload, the writes will suffer from the increase of interval and have to wait for more time to be committed.

Scalability. We invest more nodes into evaluated systems to study the changes of throughput, as shown in Fig. 10. As we expect, the throughput of Base-Update and Base-INV increase slowly than LinKV. This is because the more nodes in the Base-INV and Base-Update could aggravate the execution blocking and increase traffic under the skewed workload.

7   Conclusion

In this paper, we introduce LinKV, an RDMA-enabled ccNUMA KVS providing both high performance and strict consistency under skew. By batching the writes and designing a lease-based strategy, the overheads of consistency actions can be amortized over multiple writes, and the reads can quickly see the latest writes. The key of this work is to pave the way on enforcing strict consistency of KVSs with fewer performance penalties.

Acknowledgements. This work was supported by National Science Foundation of China under grant number 61772202, also sponsored by CCF-Huawei Database System Innovation Research Plan.

References

1. Atikoglu, B., Xu, Y., Frachtenberg, E., Jiang, S., Paleczny, M.: Workload analysis of a large-scale key-value store. In: SIGMETRICS 2012, London, UK, pp. 53–64 (2012)
2. Bodík, P., Fox, A., Franklin, M.J., Jordan, M.I.: Characterizing, modeling, and generating workload spikes for stateful services. In: SoCC 2010, USA, pp. 241–252 (2010)
3. Burckhardt, S.: Principles of eventual consistency. Found. Trends Program. Lang. 1(1–2), 1–150 (2014)
4. Cai, Q., et al.: Efficient distributed memory management with RDMA and caching. PVLDB 11(11), 1604–1617 (2018)
5. DeCandia, G., et al.: Dynamo: Amazon's highly available key-value store. In: SOSP 2007, Stevenson, Washington, USA, pp. 205–220 (2007)
6. Dragojevic, A., Narayanan, D., Castro, M., Hodson, O.: Farm: fast remote memory. In: NSDI 2014, Seattle, WA, USA, pp. 401–414 (2014)
7. Gavrielatos, V., Katsarakis, A., Joshi, A., Oswald, N., Grot, B., Nagarajan, V.: Scale-out ccNUMA: exploiting skew with strongly consistent caching. In: EuroSys 2018, Porto, Portugal, pp. 21:1–21:15 (2018)
8. Lu, H., et al.: Existential consistency: measuring and understanding consistency at Facebook. In: SOSP 2015, Monterey, CA, USA, pp. 295–310 (2015)

Cheetah: An Adaptive User-Space Cache for Non-volatile Main Memory File Systems

Tian Yan[1], Linpeng Huang[1(✉)], and Shengan Zheng[2]

[1] Department of Computer Science and Engineering, Shanghai Jiao Tong University, Shanghai, China
{officialyan,lphuang}@sjtu.edu.cn
[2] Department of Computer Science and Technology, Tsinghua University, Beijing, China
venero@tsinghua.edu.cn

Abstract. Over the past decade, most NVMM file systems have been designed without detailed knowledge of real NVDIMMs. With the release of Intel Optane DC Persistent Memory, researchers find that the performance characteristics of real NVMM differ a lot from their expectations. The design decisions they made lead to limited scalability, significant software overhead, and severe write amplification.

We present Cheetah, a user-level cache designed for existing NVMM file systems to improve overall performance. Cheetah leverages the unique characteristics of Intel Optane DC persistent memory to design a fine-grained data block allocation policy in order to reduce write amplification. To minimize the impact of the long write latency of NVMM, Cheetah absorbs asynchronous writes in DRAM rather than NVMM. Our experimental results show that Cheetah provides up to 3.5× throughput improvement compared to the state-of-the-art NVMM file systems in write-intensive workloads.

Keywords: Non-volatile main memory · File system · Cache scheme

1 Introduction

Emerging fast, byte-addressable non-volatile main memory (NVMM), such as PCM [6] and Intel Optane DC persistent memory (Optane DCPMM [5]), is expected to revolutionize the memory and storage hierarchy of existing computer systems. NVMM can be directly placed on the memory bus, thereby allowing applications to access data via processor `load/store` instructions. Compared with traditional disks (HDDs and SSDs), NVMM offers lower latency and higher bandwidth while providing direct access.

Over the past decade, several state-of-the-art NVMM-aware file systems, such as BPFS [7], PMFS [8], and NOVA [16], have been proposed. These file systems leverage the Direct Access (DAX) feature of NVMM to avoid unnecessary copy.

© Springer Nature Switzerland AG 2021
L. H. U et al. (Eds.): APWeb-WAIM 2021, LNCS 12858, pp. 199–207, 2021.
https://doi.org/10.1007/978-3-030-85896-4_17

Since NVMMs are directly attached to the main memory bus, NVMM-aware file systems allow users to access file data directly without the OS page cache. Unfortunately, existing NVMM file systems have two major drawbacks. First, researchers find that the real NVDIMMs' performance is far from their expectations, especially its concurrency and write performance. The experimental results revealed in a recent report [17] exhibit NVMM has only about one-sixth write bandwidth than DRAM. Second, for different applications with various access patterns, the conventional fixed-size block allocation scheme is inefficient. Recent studies [15,17] show that Optane DCPMM utilizes 256-byte internal blocks to access data and has several storage mechanisms different from DRAM. Uniformed block allocation in file systems is not suitable for small writes since it causes severe write amplification.

To address the drawbacks, we propose Cheetah, a user-level cache for NVMM file systems. Cheetah combines the benefits of DRAM and NVMM to improve overall performance. To hide the long write latency of NVMM, Cheetah utilizes a small DRAM cache to absorb asynchronous writes. Cheetah offers an adaptive data block allocation policy for different writes to minimize write amplification. Cheetah is compatible with most kernel NVMM-aware file systems, such as NOVA [16], EXT4-DAX [2], XFS-DAX [4], etc.

Cheetah distinguishes itself from traditional DRAM cache schemes in several aspects. First, Cheetah adopts a more accurate profiler for caching the most suitable data in DRAM. Second, Cheetah adopts an adaptive cache replacement strategy, which dynamically adjusts the impact of different access patterns on data replacement. The contributions of this paper include:

- We design a profiler that accurately profiles I/O frequency of file data.
- We design a hybrid memory management module to manage file metadata and data on NVMM and DRAM effectively.
- We implement Cheetah and evaluate it by using a collection of micro-benchmarks and real applications. We find that Cheetah exhibits higher performance than the state-of-the-art file systems on a range of workloads.

2   Background

2.1   Non-volatile Main Memory

Non-volatile main memory (NVMM) is an emerging memory technology that provides byte-addressability and durability. NVMM also allows direct data access via processor load and store instructions. However, the past researches for NVMM have been made without detailed knowledge of real NVMM. Recent works [13–15,17] demonstrate that real Optane DCPMMs [5] have more complex performance characteristics than DRAM. Optane DCPMM utilizes 256-byte internal blocks to access data instead of completely byte-addressable access. It has up to about $2.1\times$ higher latency for sequential reads and $3.8\times$ higher latency for random reads compared to DRAM. Moreover, Optane DCPMM has limited scalability compared with DRAM.

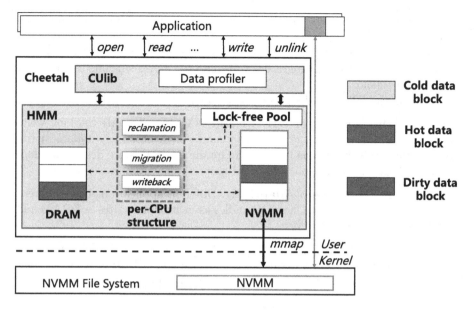

Fig. 1. Cheetah overview.

2.2 Direct Access and Memory Mapping

The Direct Access (DAX) feature of NVMM allows applications to use the CPU Load/Store instructions to directly access data in NVMM, bypassing the DRAM page cache. DAX eliminates all operating and file system code from the access path, providing the fastest way to access NVMM. Most NVMM-aware file systems [2,4,7,8,12,16] leverages DAX to shorten the critical path of file I/O. They also support mmap() mechanism that directly maps file data in NVMM into user address space. Upon a mmap() call, these file systems set up a mapping between file data pages and a range of addresses within an application's address space, reducing context switching and internal addressing overhead.

3 Design

Cheetah is a user-level cache that takes advantage of the benefits of DRAM and NVMM to accelerate file I/O for NVMM file systems. Figure 1 shows the architecture of Cheetah. Cheetah consists of a user-space library and a hybrid memory management module, namely *CUlib* and *HMM*.

CUlib is a user-space library linked to applications. *CUlib* provides common POSIX APIs and contains a *data profiler*. *Data profiler* is a process that profiles the access frequency of file data in order to cache data efficiently. *HMM* is a hybrid memory management module for managing metadata and data both in DRAM and NVMM. To achieve high scalability, HMM manages the hybrid memory space with three groups of threads: *writeback threads*, *reclamation threads*, and *migration threads*. The function of *writeback threads* is to periodically flush dirty data to NVMM for persistence. When the remaining space of the cache is almost used up, the *reclamation* threads evict blocks from cold data. By contrast, the *migration* threads migrate hot file data to DRAM when its temperature reaches a threshold.

We make the following design decisions in Cheetah:

Combined the Benefits of DRAM and NVMM. To hide the long write latency of NVMM, we leverage DRAM to handle asynchronously-updated write requests. Based on the unique features of Optane DCPMMs, we design an adaptive data block allocation policy to avoid write amplification.

Assign Write Destination Adaptively. Different applications have different synchronicity requirements. Cheetah handles asynchronous writes in DRAM and strives other writes to NVMM.

DRAM-Aware Cache Replacement. To obtain high DRAM utilization, Cheetah combines the access frequency of file data and DRAM usage to dynamically adjust the threshold for reclaiming cold data and migrating hot data.

3.1   CUlib

Cheetah provides a user-level library linked to applications called *CUlib* that is fully compatible with existing applications. When the file is opened, Cheetah calls the `mmap()` to map the file data. All interactions between Cheetah and the underlying file systems are based on the mapping regions. We design a module called *data profiler* that identifies what kind of data should be cached in DRAM.

Profiler. Cheetah not only caches hot data in DRAM but also migrates hot data from NVMM to DRAM. *Data profiler* considers both the current free space of DRAM and the access frequency of file data to set the dynamic threshold for identifying hot data. We denote the migration temperature as $T_{migration}$. Once a file's temperature reaches the $T_{migration}$, the migration threads begin to migrate file data to DRAM. T_{total} indicates the total temperature of all data in Cheetah and P_{used} shows the percentage of DRAM space used. The threshold is shown in the following equation:

$$T_{migration} = \begin{cases} T_{total} * 50\% & P_{used} < 50\% \\ T_{total} * P_{used} & 50\% \leq P_{used} < 80\% \\ \infty & 80\% \leq P_{used} < 100\% \end{cases}$$

Writes. *Data profiler* splits file writes into two types: asynchronously-updated writes and synchronously-updated writes. The reason is two-fold. First, persisting all data in NVMM immediately for applications is unnecessary and inefficient. Second, the long write latency of NVMM is always exposed to the critical path, leading to severe system performance degradation. *CUlib* utilizes *DRAM* to absorb asynchronous writes and reduce the high write latency on the critical path, increasing the lifetime of NVMM and improving scalability. For synchronously-updated writes, Cheetah strives it to NVMM directly.

Reads. For read operations with cache misses, the traditional approach has to go through the DRAM cache to fetch file data from disks. However, this approach is not suitable for hybrid DRAM/NVMM architecture. As NVMM and DRAM have similar read performance, Cheetah reads data directly from both DRAM and NVMM to avoid unnecessary data copies in the read path.

3.2 Hybrid Memory Management

HMM is an efficient management module in Cheetah for managing data and metadata on NVMM and DRAM.

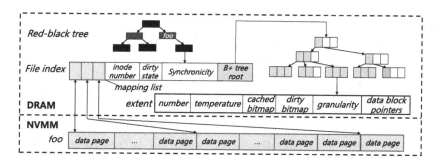

Fig. 2. Data management.

Metadata Management. *HMM* splits the data structures used for managing metadata into per-CPU and lock-free structures to avoid global locking and provide high scalability. Cheetah maintains LRU lists at each CPU to reclaim cold data blocks parallel. Cheetah uses lock-free queues [9] to manage the allocation and deallocation of metadata since it improves the overall throughput by preventing resource contention and context switching.

Fine-Grained Data Block Allocation Policy. Fixed-size data blocks in most file systems are allocated for all writes regardless of its size, which may cause high write amplification. To address the issue, we propose an adaptive data block allocation policy. Cheetah allocates data blocks by the write size. The data block sizes can be set to 256 B, 1 KB, 4 KB, all the way to 1 MB. The minimum block size is 256 B, which is equal to the internal buffer size of Intel Optane DCPMM [17]. Our policy dynamically allocates the most suitable block size according to the I/O size, minimizing write amplification.

Data Management. We utilize a structure called *extent* to manage data blocks. As shown in Fig. 2, each extent contains six fields and manages up to 1 MB data. When the application posts a write request, Cheetah searches the corresponding extents in the B+ tree. If the extents do not exist, new extents are allocated to the file. Reclamation and migration are performed at the granularity of the extent. The advantage of our approach is to make the best of data locality.

File Index. When a file is opened in Cheetah for the first time, Cheetah allocates a unique *index* for the file. Each index records the file metadata (Fig. 2). We build a set of red-black trees to index the files opened in Cheetah, which use the file inode numbers as the key to store the corresponding indexes.

4   Cache Replacement

Cheetah provides an efficient replacement policy to improve space utilization. We next describe the cache replacement policy in detail.

Temperature Profiling. When a data block is accessed, Cheetah increases the temperature of its corresponding extent according to the weight of the access type. The read and write weights are dynamically adjusted when dealing with different types of applications. Cheetah calculates the weight of reads and writes every two seconds, according to the real-time read-write ratio.

Cache Reclamation. Cheetah utilizes background threads to reclaim cold data blocks from the infrequently accessed files. The background threads reclaim the data blocks of different sizes. Once the number of allocated data blocks of any size reaches a threshold (e.g., 90% in our experiments), the reclamation threads wake up and begin to reclaim data blocks from cold *extents*, starting from the tail of LRU lists. We use $T_{threshold}$ (described in Sect. 3.1) as the threshold temperature for cache reclamation. Background threads reclaim all cached data blocks in the extent with temperature lower than $T_{threshold}$ until 20% of the data blocks in the cache are reclaimed.

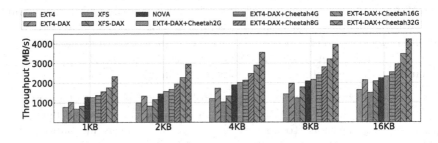

Fig. 3. Fio performance.

Migration. The purpose of migration is to cache more hot data for accelerating the future file I/O. Cheetah sets migration threads at per-CPU and utilizes a lock-free queue as a message buffer to communicate with migration threads. When the *data profiler* identifies an extent with hot temperature, Cheetah pops its index into a lock-free queue, and the migration thread wakes up and migrates its uncached data contained to DRAM.

5   Evaluation

In this section, we evaluate the performance of Cheetah by using a collection of benchmarks and real-world application workload.

5.1   Experimental Setup

Our experimental testbed machine consists of 2× Intel Xeon Gold 6240M CPUs, six 32 GB DDR4 DRAM, and six 256 GB Intel Optane DCPMMs. All the experiments are performed on Ubuntu 18.04 LTS with Linux kernel 4.13.

We use Cheetah-equipped EXT4-DAX (abbreviated as EXT4-DC) as the only Cheetah-equipped file system to compare with other file systems, such as XFS-DAX [4] and NOVA [16], in the FIO (Sect. 5.2) and Redis (Sect. 5.3) workloads. We vary the DRAM cache size available to Cheetah to show how performance changes with different Cheetah configurations. E.g. EXT4-DC (2 GB) means that the DRAM cache size of Cheetah is only 2 GB.

5.2   Microbenchmarks

We use Fio [3] to evaluate the performance of file operations. Fio is a flexible I/O test tool that provides different types of microbenchmarks. We vary the I/O size from 1 KB to 16 KB, and run the workload in single-thread. All I/O operations in this experiment are synchronous.

Figure 3 shows the performance improvement of Cheetah for write operations. EXT4-DC achieves nearly 2.1× higher performance than EXT4 and XFS and outperforms NOVA by 91% and XFS-DAX by 1.5× when the cache capacity is 32 GB. Non-DAX file systems perform poorly on synchronous write operations. Cheetah only absorbs asynchronous writes in DRAM, thus reducing the number of unnecessary double-copies. NOVA utilizes 4 KB pages to manage data. For small writes, this policy causes significant write amplification. Cheetah adopts a fine-grained data allocation policy to minimize write amplification, which allocates the most suitable data blocks instead of fix-sized data blocks.

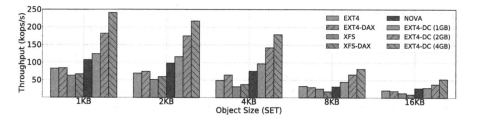

Fig. 4. Redis performance.

5.3 Redis

We use Redis [1] to evaluate the performance of the file systems with Cheetah. We run Redis in the AOF mode, which logs every write operation and persists data synchronously. We vary the object size from 1 KB to 16 KB.

Figure 4 shows the throughput of SET operations of different file systems. EXT4-DC outperforms EXT4-DAX by 51%, 1.2×, and 1.8× on average for the 1 GB, 2 GB, and 4 GB cache capacity, respectively. When the cache capacity is 4 GB, EXT4-DC improves the performance over NOVA by 1.3×, outperforms XFS-DAX, XFS and EXT4 by 3.5×, 3.2×, and 1.9×, respectively.

Compared with EXT4 and XFS, the performance advantage stems primarily from the design of adaptive write services. Compared with the NVMM-aware file systems, the per-CPU and lock-free structures adopted by Cheetah ensure that writing data into DRAM and migrating cold data to NVMM can be performed concurrently to achieve high bandwidth. Also, Cheetah provides direct access without the overhead of context switching and software stack.

6 Related Work

Existing NVMM-aware file systems can be classified into two categories: kernel-space and user-space.

1) *Kernel-space.* EXT4-DAX [2] and XFS-DAX [4] provide direct access capabilities to the native Linux file system. NOVA [16] is designed for hybrid DRAM/NVMM architecture. NOVA guarantees consistency and supports atomic operations through its log-structured design. It stores indexes in DRAM to accelerate lookup and utilizes the logs of each file to achieve high concurrency.

2) *User-Space.* Strata [11] and SplitFS [10] both utilize a split architecture to improve performance. Strata adopts the log digestion scheme to improve file access performance. SplitFS provides flexible guarantees for different applications.

7 Conclusion

We present Cheetah, a user-space cache for NVMM file systems to accelerate file I/O. Cheetah leverages the unique characteristics of Intel Optane DC persistent memory to reduce write amplification. Cheetah absorbs asynchronously-updated writes in DRAM to minimize the impact of long write latency of NVMM. Experimental results show that Cheetah enables applications to exploit the benefits from native file systems while providing significant performance improvements.

Acknowledgments. This work is supported by National Key Research & Development Program of China (Grant No. 2018YFB1003302), and SJTU-Huawei Innovation Research Lab Funding (Grant No. FA2018091021-202004). Shengan Zheng is supported by China Postdoctoral Science Foundation (Grant No. 2020M680570).

References

1. Redis (2010). https://github.com/redis/redis
2. Add support for NV-DIMMs to ext4 (2011). https://lwn.net/Articles/613384/
3. Flexible I/O tester (2011). https://github.com/axboe/fio
4. xfs:DAX support (2015). https://lwn.net/Articles/635514/
5. Intel Optane DC pesistent memory (2019). https://www.intel.com/content/www/us/en/architecture-and-technology/optane-dc-persistent-memory.html
6. Akel, A., Caulfield, A.M., Mollov, T.I., Gupta, R.K., Swanson, S.: Onyx: a prototype phase change memory storage array. In: HotStorage (2011)
7. Condit, J., et al.: Better I/O through byte-addressable, persistent memory. In: SOSP (2009)
8. Dulloor, S.R., et al.: System software for persistent memory (2014)
9. Frechilla, F.: Yet another implementation of a lock-free circular array queue (2011). https://www.codeproject.com/Articles/153898
10. Kadekodi, R., Lee, S.K., Kashyap, S., Kim, T., Kolli, A., Chidambaram, V.: SplitFS: reducing software overhead in file systems for persistent memory. In: SOSP (2019)
11. Kwon, Y., et al.: Strata: a cross media file system. In: SOSP (2017)
12. Ou, J., Shu, J., Lu, Y.: A high performance file system for non-volatile main memory. In: EuroSys (2016)
13. Patil, O., Ionkov, L., Lee, J., Mueller, F., Lang, M.: Performance characterization of a DRAM-NVM hybrid memory architecture for HPC applications using intel Optane DC persistent memory modules. In: Proceedings of the International Symposium on Memory Systems (2019)
14. Waddington, D., Kunitomi, M., Dickey, C., Rao, S., Abboud, A., Tran, J.: Evaluation of intel 3D-xpoint NVDIMM technology for memory-intensive genomic workloads. In: Proceedings of the International Symposium on Memory Systems (2019)
15. Wang, Z., Liu, X., Yang, J., Michailidis, T., Swanson, S., Zhao, J.: Characterizing and modeling non-volatile memory systems. In: MICRO (2020)
16. Xu, J., Swanson, S.: NOVA: a log-structured file system for hybrid volatile/nonvolatile main memories. In: FAST (2016)
17. Yang, J., Kim, J., Hoseinzadeh, M., Izraelevitz, J., Swanson, S.: An empirical guide to the behavior and use of scalable persistent memory. In: FAST (2020)

Topic Model and Language Model Learning

Chinese Word Embedding Learning with Limited Data

Shurui Chen[1], Yufu Chen[1], Yuyin Lu[1], Yanghui Rao[1(✉)], Haoran Xie[2],
and Qing Li[3]

[1] School of Computer Science and Engineering, Sun Yat-sen University,
Guangzhou, China
raoyangh@mail.sysu.edu.cn
[2] Department of Computing and Decision Sciences, Lingnan University Tuen Mun,
New Territories, Hong Kong
[3] Department of Computing, The Hong Kong Polytechnic University, Hung Hom,
Kowloon, Hong Kong

Abstract. With the increasing demands of high-quality Chinese word
embeddings for natural language processing, Chinese word embedding
learning has attracted wide attention in recent years. Most of the existing
research focused on capturing word semantics on large-scaled datasets.
However, these methods are difficult to obtain effective word embeddings with limited data used for some specific fields. Observing the rich
semantic information of Chinese fine-grained structures, we develop a
model to fully fuse Chinese fine-grained structures as auxiliary information for word embedding learning. The proposed model views the word
context information as a combination of word, character, pronunciation,
and component. Besides, it adds the semantic relationship between pronunciations and components as a constraint to exploit auxiliary information comprehensively. Based on the decomposition of shifted positive
pointwise mutual information matrix, our model could effectively generate Chinese word embeddings on small-scaled data. The results of word
analogy, word similarity, and name entity recognition conducted on two
public datasets show the effectiveness of our proposed model for capturing Chinese word semantics with limited data.

Keywords: Chinese word embedding · Matrix factorization · Chinese
fine-grained information

1 Introduction

Word embedding learning serves as a key to many tasks in natural language
processing, which can capture the semantic information of words by mapping
each word to a vector in a low-dimensional space. Currently, most of the existing
models require large-scaled corpora for training. However, the word embedding
trained from a general large-scaled corpus could be inconsistent to the actual
semantics, or even worse, may lack the results of some important vocabularies

© Springer Nature Switzerland AG 2021
L. H. U et al. (Eds.): APWeb-WAIM 2021, LNCS 12858, pp. 211–226, 2021.
https://doi.org/10.1007/978-3-030-85896-4_18

when applied to a specific small-scaled dataset [17,24]. In addition, the existing word embedding methods may suffer from the problem of data sparsity on a tiny corpus. Therefore, how to obtain accurate word embeddings with limited data is an important issue. For the two main methods of word embedding learning, i.e., matrix factorization (MF) and neural network (NN), Altszyler et al. [2] found that the MF based model (i.e., latent semantic analysis) performed much better than the NN based model (i.e., word2vec) when the training data is limited. In this vein, Levy and Goldberg [12] proposed the factorization of shifted positive pointwise mutual information (SPPMI) matrix for generating word embeddings, where the SPPMI matrix is pointwise mutual information of word-context pairs shifted by a given value and set to be positive. More recently, Xun et al. [26] addressed the problem of data sparsity by applying the matrix factorization on the global document-word information matrix as well as the local SPPMI matrix to improve word embedding learning. However, the aforementioned methods can not fully capture the semantic information for Chinese corpora.

Chinese is one of the most popular Asian languages, with 1.2 billion native speakers around the world. The popularity of Chinese and its unique linguistic characteristics determine the importance of in-depth research of Chinese word embedding. Some existing models viewed Chinese words as atomic units and studied the semantic relationship between words [15,16,18]. Several other research efforts stated that words should be divided into smaller units to obtain some information about the structure of words [3,5,6,14,22,28,29], e.g., the pronunciation and the component structure of Chinese characters are more fine-grained information and can be used as auxiliary information to capture word semantics. As an illustration, the pronunciation and the component structure of word "你好" (Hello) are shown in Fig. 1.

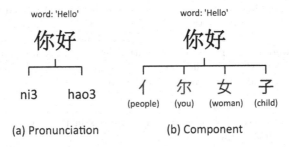

Fig. 1. The component and the pronunciation of word "你好" (Hello).

After investigating the benefit of those fine-grained information, we observe that there exist certain important roles of both the pronunciation and the component of Chinese characters, which is confirmed by the concept of pictophonetic characters. For example, the pictophonetic character "湖" (Lake) is composed of the semantic component " 氵 " (Water) and the phonetic component "胡" (Hu). It has the similar semantic as the semantic component " 氵 " (Water) and the same pronunciation as "胡" (Hu). Moreover, the pronunciation could be used to help the model distinguish words which have almost the same components. For example, the word "尖" (Sharp) and word "大小" (Size) have the same components but contain totally different semantics. Besides, we observe that there exist certain correlations between the pronunciation and the component of a Chinese character. It is intuitive to link some components with pronunciations because some components have specific pronunciations for them. For example, "糸" has a pronunciation of "si1". Moreover, we observe that the Chinese fine-grained structure has a strong relationship with specific fields, for example, "疒" (Illness) is connected with medical care and "辶" (Walk) is connected with traffic.

Inspired by aforementioned studies and observations, in this paper we propose a pronunciation and component guided Chinese word embedding (PCCWE) learning method[1] for limited data by factorizing the SPPMI matrix. The main contributions of this work are as follows: (i) We exploit pronunciations and components of Chinese characters as auxiliary information for Chinese word embedding learning. By utilizing the above distinguished characteristics of the Chinese language system, the proposed method could effectively capture the semantic relationship between Chinese words. (ii) We study the influence of correlations between pronunciations and components on Chinese word embedding learning. Such a correlation makes the captured semantic elements from components and pronunciations be closer to the optimal solution.

To the best of our knowledge, this is the first effective method of learning high-quality Chinese word embeddings using small-scaled datasets, e.g., the electronic medical texts which are often quite hard to achieve.

2 Related Work

The NN language models are classic and effective for word embedding learning. In a preliminary study, Bengio et al. [4] proposed a neural probabilistic language model to obtain word embeddings. Later, Mikolov et al. [15] introduced two three-layered neural network architectures, i.e., skip-gram (SG) and continuous bag-of-words (CBOW). They also accelerated SG and CBOW by negative sampling [16]. With the development of deep learning, the deep neural network architectures have shown good abilities of context semantic mining. ELMo proposed by Peters et al. [19] generated deep contextualized word representations by a bidirectional LSTM architecture. Devlin et al. [8] reported the problem of ELMo in the insufficient use of context information and proposed BERT which employed bidirectional encoder representations from transformer to deeply exploit the semantic information at the sentence level. Yu et al. [23] introduced a model named ERNIE by adding a continual framework with constant multi-task learning to the generative pre-training word representation learning method.

To improve word embedding learning over specific languages, some researchers noticed the effect of fine-grained information such as morphology. For Chinese word embedding learning, most of the existing methods are NN

---

[1] https://github.com/hostnlp/PCCWE.

based. Chen et al. [6] proposed the CWE model by combining words and Chinese characters on the basis of CBOW. Inspired by CWE [6], Xu et al. [25] modelled the similarity between words to disambiguate the meanings of characters in Chinese words. The other model named JWE [28] can be viewed as an extension of CWE, which exploits the component of Chinese characters. Su et al. [22] concentrated on glyphs of Chinese characters and extracted them from images. Cao et al. [5] divided Chinese characters into ordered stroke sequences and exploited the stroke n-gram information for word embedding learning. Zhang et al. [29] found the relationship between the semantic and the pronunciation in some Chinese characters, and viewed stroke, structure and pronunciation of Chinese characters as features for an n-gram language model. To improve Chinese word embedding learning, Yang [27] studied the latent semantic information of Chinese characters, including phonology, morphology, and semantics.

Unfortunately, the above NN based methods could suffer from the difficulty on training huge amount of parameters under some circumstances. In light of this consideration, there are other research efforts on the application of MF models to extract the word semantic information from count-based statistics. The latent semantic analysis (LSA) proposed by Scott et al. [7] would be the earliest relevant example of word embedding learning based on MF. LSA applied singular value decomposition (SVD) on the term-document matrix to generate word embeddings, and achieved better performance than the NN based model word2vec when applied to small-scaled datasets [2]. Then, Hofmann et al. [10] introduced probabilistic latent semantic analysis (pLSA) under the maximum likelihood hypothesis. Ding et al. [9] proved the equivalence between MF on the term-document matrix and pLSA, which strengthened the links on both research fields. In addition, Levy and Goldberg [12] and Li et al. [13] have both suggested that MF on the SPPMI matrix is equivalent to the SG model with negative sampling (i.e., SGNS). These shed light on other MF based word embedding learning methods. For instance, Salle et al. [21] employed a weighting scheme to SPPMI matrix factorization by assigning higher weights to frequent pairs. Pennington et al. [18] effectively learned word embedding by encoding the actual word semantic information in the form of co-occurrence ratios. Xun et al. [26] proposed a word embedding and topic discovery multi-task model which jointly applied MF on document-word and word co-occurrence matrices. Similarly, Ailem et al. [1] and Salah et al. [20] considered to conduct word embedding learning and text classification tasks simultaneously to enhance the performance of each other. However, these existing MF based methods may not perform effectively on Chinese word embedding learning because they ignored the semantics of fine-grained information in Chinese characters.

3   Methodology

In this section, we describe our MF based Chinese word embedding learning method (i.e., PCCWE), which exploits both pronunciations and components of Chinese characters to capture word semantics. Table 1 lists the notations used in this paper. We use bold uppercase letters such as M to represent matrices, bold lowercase letters such as w to represent embeddings, regular uppercase letters such as N to represent scalar constants, and regular lowercase letters such as λ to represent scalar variables.

Table 1. Frequently used notations.

Notation	Description
N_{word}	The number of distinct words
N_{char}	The number of distinct characters
N_{pro}	The number of distinct word pronunciations
N_{comp}	The number of distinct word components
d	The dimension of word embeddings
$M \in \mathbb{R}^{N_{word} \times N_{word}}$	Word pointwise mutual information matrix
$R \in \mathbb{R}^{N_{comp} \times N_{pro}}$	Occurrence numbers of component-pronunciation pairs
$W \in \mathbb{R}^{N_{word} \times d}$	Word embedding matrix
$V \in \mathbb{R}^{N_{word} \times d}$	Context embedding matrix
$W_v \in \mathbb{R}^{N_{word} \times d}$	Word-context embedding matrix
$C_h \in \mathbb{R}^{N_{char} \times d}$	Character embedding matrix
$W_{ch} \in \mathbb{R}^{N_{word} \times d}$	Word-character embedding matrix
$C_o \in \mathbb{R}^{N_{comp} \times d}$	Component embedding matrix
$W_{co} \in \mathbb{R}^{N_{word} \times d}$	Word-component embedding matrix
$P_r \in \mathbb{R}^{N_{pro} \times d}$	Pronunciation embedding matrix
$W_{pr} \in \mathbb{R}^{N_{word} \times d}$	Word-pronunciation embedding matrix
k	The negative sampling rate
λ_{char}	The weight of characters to context
λ_{comp}	The weight of components to context
λ_{pro}	The weight of pronunciations to context
λ_r	The penalty term of constraint

For a given Chinese corpus, we first generate the SPPMI matrix M by following [12]. For each component-pronunciation pair, we count the times of occurrences that the pair appears in the same word and denote all the pair occurrence times as R. Our goal is to obtain a high-quality word embedding matrix W. In our model, the context information contains the auxiliary information of Chinese charterers, which means the context embedding matrix V is the combination of word-context embedding matrix W_v, character embedding matrix C_h, component embedding matrix C_o, and pronunciation embedding matrix P_r. In our modelling process, we study the semantic relationship at the word level and consider the contribution of auxiliary information to each word.

3.1   Optimization Objective

For a context word related to the target word, we assume that it consists of word, character, pronunciation, and component embeddings. However, in the Chinese language system, there is a general type of characters called pictophonetic character which consists of both semantic and phonetic components. We notice that the phonetic component and pronunciation of the pictophonetic characters are repetitive. Thus, we ignore the pronunciation of a character when it is a pictophonetic character.

As pointed out in Sect. 1, we adopt the word co-occurrence SPPMI matrix to generate word embeddings. According to [12], the factorization of SPPMI matrix M under certain conditions is equivalent to SGNS [16], in which, the shifted value of SPPMI matrix is the negative sampling rate k. Particularly, for a target word w and one of its context words c, the corresponding item in M is $M_{w,c} = max(log \frac{\#(w,c) \cdot |\mathbb{D}|}{\#(w) \cdot \#(c)} - log\ k, 0)$. In the above, $\#(w,c)$ denotes the number of times that the target word w and context word c co-occurred in a fixed window size. $\#(w) = \sum_c \#(w,c)$ and $\#(c) = \sum_w \#(w,c)$. $\mathbb{D}$ is the set of all observed words and context pairs such as (w,c). The SGNS method implicitly factorized the SPPMI matrix M to word embedding matrix W and context embedding matrix V. In our study, the context information includes fine-grained structures of Chinese characters to address the data sparsity problem. Thus, we define the context embedding matrix as $V = W_v + \lambda_{char}C_h + \lambda_{comp}C_o + \lambda_{pro}P_r$, where λ_{char}, λ_{comp}, and λ_{pro} respectively represent the weights of characters, components and pronunciations to the corresponding context words.

Since the size of word vocabulary is often larger than that of character vocabulary, the dimension of W_v is inconsistent with C_h. The same issue exists for the dimensions of P_r and C_o. To address this, we propose to expand the embedding matrices C_h, C_o, P_r to W_{ch}, W_{co}, W_{pr} with the same size as W_v. Generally, a Chinese word is composed of multiple characters, components, and pronunciations. Thus, for a specific word, we assign the average embedding of the characters belonging to this word as its final character embedding W_{ch}. The other two matrices W_{co} and matrix W_{pr} are generated in the same way. An example of expanding W_{pr} for word "你好" (Hello) is shown in Fig. 2.

Then, the context embedding matrix is estimated by $V = W_v + \lambda_{char}W_{ch} + \lambda_{comp}W_{co} + \lambda_{pro}W_{pr}$, and our objective function with fine-grained information is $L_{basic} = \|M - W(W_v + \lambda_{char}W_{ch} + \lambda_{comp}W_{co} + \lambda_{pro}W_{pr})^T\|_2^2$, where $\|\cdot\|_2$ denotes the l_2 norm. This function is the basic objective function of word embedding learning by jointly modeling Chinese characters, components, and pronunciations. Moreover, we build a bridge between components and pronunciations by constructing a R matrix. This matrix represents the correlation degree between pronunciations and components, which is obtained from the statistic of occurrence frequency of pronunciation and component in the same words. In other words, the entry R_{ij} of R is the number of times that component Co_i and pronunciation Pr_j appear in the same word. We aim at making the embedding of each component to be close to the embedding of its corresponding pronunciation. Therefore, in order to make the model utilize fine-grained information

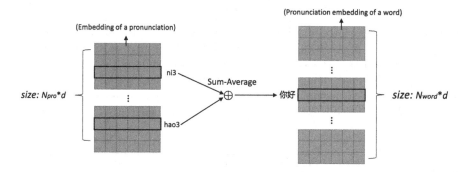

Fig. 2. An example of expanding $\boldsymbol{W}_{pr}$ for word "你好" (Hello).

more effectively, we use this rule of correlation through the following constraint: $L_{cons} = \| \boldsymbol{R} - \boldsymbol{C}_o \boldsymbol{P}_r^T \|_2^2$. Finally, our objective function is $L = L_{basic} + \lambda_r * L_{cons}$.

3.2 Parameter Inference

According to the above objective function, we use the alternating least squares (ALS) method to update $\boldsymbol{W}, \boldsymbol{W}_v, \boldsymbol{W}_{ch}, \boldsymbol{W}_{pr}$, and $\boldsymbol{W}_{co}$.

First, the partial derivation of each parameter is obtained by $\frac{\partial L}{\partial W} = 2\boldsymbol{W}\boldsymbol{V}^T\boldsymbol{V} - 2\boldsymbol{M}\boldsymbol{V}$, $\frac{\partial L}{\partial W_v} = -2\boldsymbol{M}^T\boldsymbol{W} + 2\boldsymbol{V}\boldsymbol{W}^T\boldsymbol{W}$, $\frac{\partial L}{\partial W_{ch}} = \lambda_{char} * (-2\boldsymbol{M}^T\boldsymbol{W} + 2\boldsymbol{V}\boldsymbol{W}^T\boldsymbol{W})$, $\frac{\partial L}{\partial W_{pr}} = \lambda_{comp} * (-2\boldsymbol{M}^T\boldsymbol{W} + 2\boldsymbol{V}\boldsymbol{W}^T\boldsymbol{W})$, $\frac{\partial L}{\partial W_{co}} = \lambda_{pro} * (-2\boldsymbol{M}^T\boldsymbol{W} + 2\boldsymbol{V}\boldsymbol{W}^T\boldsymbol{W})$, $\frac{\partial L}{\partial C_o} = \lambda_r * (2\boldsymbol{C}_o\boldsymbol{P}_r^T\boldsymbol{P}_r - 2\boldsymbol{R}\boldsymbol{P}_r)$, and $\frac{\partial L}{\partial P_r} = \lambda_r * (2\boldsymbol{P}_r\boldsymbol{C}_o^T\boldsymbol{C}_o - 2\boldsymbol{R}^T\boldsymbol{C}_o)$.

Second, these parameters are updated by alternatively setting the partial derivation to zero in each iterative process, as follows:

$$\boldsymbol{W}^T = (\boldsymbol{V}^T\boldsymbol{V})^{-1}(\boldsymbol{V}^T\boldsymbol{M}^T), \tag{1}$$

$$\boldsymbol{W}_v^T = (\boldsymbol{W}^T\boldsymbol{W})^{-1}\boldsymbol{W}^T\boldsymbol{M} - \lambda_{char}\boldsymbol{W}_{ch}^T - \lambda_{comp}\boldsymbol{W}_{pr}^T - \lambda_{pro}\boldsymbol{W}_{co}^T, \tag{2}$$

$$\boldsymbol{W}_{ch}^T = [(\boldsymbol{W}^T\boldsymbol{W})^{-1}\boldsymbol{W}^T\boldsymbol{M} - \boldsymbol{W}_v^T - \lambda_{comp}\boldsymbol{W}_{pr}^T - \lambda_{pro}\boldsymbol{W}_{co}^T] \,/\, \lambda_{char}, \tag{3}$$

$$\boldsymbol{W}_{pr}^T = [(\boldsymbol{W}^T\boldsymbol{W})^{-1}\boldsymbol{W}^T\boldsymbol{M} - \boldsymbol{W}_v^T - \lambda_{char}\boldsymbol{W}_{ch}^T - \lambda_{pro}\boldsymbol{W}_{co}^T] \,/\, \lambda_{comp}, \tag{4}$$

$$\boldsymbol{W}_{co}^T = [(\boldsymbol{W}^T\boldsymbol{W})^{-1}\boldsymbol{W}^T\boldsymbol{M} - \boldsymbol{W}_v^T - \lambda_{char}\boldsymbol{W}_{ch}^T - \lambda_{comp}\boldsymbol{W}_{pr}^T] \,/\, \lambda_{pro}, \tag{5}$$

$$\boldsymbol{C}_o^T = (\lambda_r * \boldsymbol{P}_r^T\boldsymbol{P}_r)^{-1}(\lambda_r * \boldsymbol{P}_r^T\boldsymbol{R}^T), \tag{6}$$

$$\boldsymbol{P}_r^T = (\lambda_r * \boldsymbol{C}_o^T\boldsymbol{C}_o)^{-1}(\lambda_r * \boldsymbol{C}_o^T\boldsymbol{R}). \tag{7}$$

In each iterative process, the character matrix C_h is updated according to W_{ch}. Specifically, for each character embedding, the changes of its related word-character embeddings are recorded, and the average value of all recorded changes are taken as the final change value of this character embedding. In the same way, component and pronunciation matrices C_o and P_r are updated according to W_{co} and W_{pr}. Algorithm 1 presents the parameter inference for our method.

Algorithm 1: Parameter inference for the proposed PCCWE.

Input: M;
Output: W, W_v, C_h, C_o, P_r.
1 Initialize W, W_v, C_h, C_o, P_r by random values;
2 **repeat**
3   Generate matrices W_{ch}, W_{co}, and W_{pr} according to C_h, C_o, and P_r;
4   Update W, W_v, W_{ch}, W_{co}, and W_{pr} by Equations (1)-(5);
5   Incorporate W_{ch}, W_{co}, and W_{pr} into C_h, C_o, and P_r respectively;
6   Update C_o and P_r by Equations (6) and (7);
7 **until** *termination criterion is met*;
8 return W, W_v, C_h, C_o, P_r.

3.3   Time and Space Complexity

Here, we analyze the time and space complexity of our method. For updating the word embedding matrix W, the time complexity is $O(2 * N_{word} * d^2 + d^3 + N_{word}^2 * d)$, including the costs of matrix multiplication and inversion. For updating matrices W_v, W_{ch}, W_{co}, and W_{pr}, the time complexity is $O(2*N_{word}* d^2 + d^3 + N_{word}^2 * d + 3 * N_{word} * d)$, which adds a matrix addition operation compared with the update of W. The time complexity of updating C_h, P_r, and C_o is $O(d * (N_{word} + N_{char}))$, $O(d * (N_{word} + N_{pro}) + N_{pro} * d^2 + N_{comp} * d^2 + d^3 + N_{pro} * N_{comp} * d)$, and $O(d * (N_{word} + N_{comp}) + N_{pro} * d^2 + N_{comp} * d^2 + d^3 + N_{pro} * N_{comp} * d)$, respectively.

The memory requirement of our method includes: the input matrix M and R, with a size of $O(N_{word}*N_{word})$ and $O(N_{comp}*N_{pro})$; the output matrices V, W_v, W_{ch}, W_{co}, W_{pr}, C_h, P_r, and C_o, with a size of $O(d*(5*N_{word}+N_{char}+ N_{pro}+N_{comp}))$; the temporary matrices $W^T W$, $V^T V$, $V^T M^T$, $W^T M$, $P_r^T P_r$, $P_r^T R^T$, $C_o^T C_o$, and $C_o^T R$, with a size of $O(4*d*d+2*d*N_{word}+d*N_{comp}+ d*N_{pro})$. Thus, the total space complexity of our method is $O(N_{word} * N_{word} + d * (7 * N_{word} + N_{char} + N_{pro} + N_{comp} + 2 * d))$.

4   Experiments

4.1   Datasets

The news dataset NLPIR[2] is constructed by collecting the news reports happened between October and December in 2009. The medical named entity recognition dataset Yidu[3] is a text set of Chinese electronic medical records provided by the 2019 CCKS Evaluation Task. We use the whole text set for training word embeddings after removing sentences with less than 5 words. The statistics of the used datasets are presented in Table 2, including the numbers of documents, non-repeated words, non-repeated characters, non-repeated pronunciations, and non-repeated components. We utilize opencc toolkit[4] to convert traditional Chinese to simplified Chinese and jieba toolkit[5] for word segmentation.

Table 2. Statistics of the datasets.

Dataset	#documents	#words	#characters	#pronunciations	#components
NLPIR	3637	30772	3347	1055	429
Yidu	3275	7573	1613	777	360

4.2   Baselines and Settings

We compare our PCCWE with both NN and MF based methods. The NN baselines include SGNS [15], CWE [6], JWE [28], cw2vec [5], ssp2vec [29], BERT [8], and ERNIE [23]. The MF baselines include Glove [18], SPPMI [12], and CLM [26]. To explore the role of different modules in the proposed method, we denote our model without the constraint term (i.e., $\lambda_r = 0$) as PCCWE w/o L_{cons}, our model without components (i.e., $\lambda_{comp} = 0$) as PCCWE w/o C_o, and our model without pronunciations (i.e., $\lambda_{pro} = 0$) as PCCWE w/o P_r.

Following [6], word analogy and word similarity tasks are used for evaluation. After filtering out-of-vocabulary words from NLPIR, the Analogy dataset remained 336 word pairs, and the Sim240 and Sim297 datasets remained 160 and 173 word pairs, respectively. The Yidu corpus is not used here because its words are mainly medical terms, and the remaining word pairs in the Analogy, Sim240, and Sim297 datasets are extremely limited. Moreover, one of the important applications of word embeddings is the usage in certain downstream tasks. Here, we evaluate word embeddings via named entity recognition (NER). The used dataset for NER is the Chinese electronic medical records (i.e., Yidu), which contains six types of labels: Disease and diagnosis, Anatomical site, Laboratory examination, Surgical operation, Medicine, and Imaging examination. We adopt

---

[2] http://www.nlpir.org/wordpress/download/NLPIR-news-corpus.rar.
[3] http://openkg.cn/dataset/yidu-s4k.
[4] https://github.com/BYVoid/OpenCC.
[5] https://github.com/fxsjy/jieba/.

the Bi-LSTM CRF model proposed by Huang et al. [11] to perform NER, where word embeddings trained from the Yidu corpus are fed into the input layer. We use sixty percent of the document set as the training set, and the other forty percent as the testing set. The precision, recall, and F1 score values on the testing set are reported. For all NN based methods, the context window size is set to 5, the negative sampling rate is 5, and the word embedding size is 300. Words with frequency less than 25 in the NIPIR dataset were ignored during training. For the Yidu dataset, the frequency threshold is 2. The hyper parameters of our method λ_{char}, λ_{comp}, λ_{pro}, and λ_r were selected by grid searching on the validation set produced by 10% of the task datasets, in which, the parameter values for grid searching were set to $[0.0, 1.0]$ with step size as 0.1.

The component and pronunciation information of Chinese characters are collected from an online Chinese dictionary[6]. In addition, the list of pictophonetic characters are obtained from online website[7]. All the experiments are conducted on a KVM Processor equipped with CPU @ 2.20 GHz, 8 cores and 16G memory.

4.3   Result Analysis

Quantitative Comparison. As shown in Table 3, our method achieves state-of-art results on the word analogy task and performs quite competitively on the word similarity task. Specifically, it is noteworthy that the performance of the MF based models is generally better than that of the NN based models. Because the NN based models suffer from their complicated network parameter adjustment when applied onto limited data. By contrary, the MF based models could approach the optimal solution more quickly in a small dataset. Moreover, the fine-grained models including CWE, JWE, cw2vec, and ssp2vec could achieve much better performance than the general SGNS, for the reason that the auxiliary information might abundantly enrich semantic information and alleviate the problem of data sparsity. The incorporation of auxiliary information could lead our model to gather relevant word pairs closer and separate irrelevant word pairs. It means that our model could capture more precise semantics and find proper words for word analogy task. On the other hand, our model enlarges the gap between irrelevant words and gets different results of semantic similarity compared to manually annotated relevance scores for word similarity task. Thus, our PCCWE could obtain the best result on the word analogy task and slightly decrease on the word similarity task when compared with PCCWE w/o C_o. Conclusively, the experimental results reveal that integrating auxiliary information with an MF based method enables the model to learn Chinese word embeddings effectively on a small corpus.

Table 4 presents the results on the NER task, which indicates that the proposed PCCWE achieves the best performance in all metrics. Our PCCWE w/o C_o and PCCWE w/o P_r come to the second ranked results in three metrics,

---

[6] http://www.zdic.net/.

[7] http://xh.5156edu.com/page/z9907m3552j18976.html.

Table 3. Results of word analogy and word similarity tasks trained on NLPIR, where the best results are bolded, and the second ranked results are underlined.

Models		$Analogy$ 336 Pairs	Sim240 160 Pairs	Sim297 173 Pairs
NN based	SGNS	0.1264	0.3192	0.4144
	CWE	0.1868	0.4511	0.4512
	JWE	0.1593	0.4480	0.4916
	cw2vec	0.1538	0.2785	0.3952
	ssp2vec	0.1566	0.3552	0.4699
	BERT	0.0385	0.2767	0.4144
	ERNIE	0.0220	0.3411	0.3870
MF based	GLOVE	0.1676	0.3760	0.4561
	SPPMI	0.3599	<u>0.5308</u>	0.4814
	CLM	0.3511	0.5298	0.4908
	PCCWE w/o C_o	0.3846	**0.5360**	**0.4985**
	PCCWE w/o P_r	0.3736	0.5141	0.4811
	PCCWE w/o L_{cons}	<u>0.3984</u>	0.5219	<u>0.4942</u>
	PCCWE	**0.4396**	0.5179	0.4753

which seems to provide evidence of the effectiveness by introducing the contribution of components and pronunciations respectively. The results of our PCCWE w/o L_{cons} show that adding both components and pronunciations may cause some semantic confusion problems. Thus, the constraint proposed by PCCWE on the semantics of components and pronunciations is necessary when introducing both of them. For baseline models, JWE achieves a good result on precision when compared to other NN based methods. The cw2vec model and the ssp2vec model have similar results on the three metrics, validating that the pronunciation information may have little effect on the n-gram mechanism. Surprisingly, the CLM model performs worse than SPPMI. The reason may be that the trained topics used in CLM are not applicable to NER tasks.

We also list the average running time (seconds) of different models on NLPIR per epoch in Table 5, where the results of BERT, ERNIE, and CLM are not presented since they contain other learning tasks. Note that the average time costs of PCCWE w/o C_o, PCCWE w/o P_r, PCCWE w/o L_{cons}, and PCCWE are nearly the same. Besides, MF-based and NN-based models can reach convergence within 20 and 50 epochs on this dataset, respectively. The results indicate that the efficiency of our PCCWE is quite competitive as compared with baselines.

Case Study. To intuitively present the semantic relationship of the component and the pronunciation embeddings trained by our model, we take 6 components as examples and find 10 pronunciations according to the nearest pronunciation embeddings for each component. After dimension reduction, we illustrate the locations of components and pronunciations in Fig. 3. Each sample component is marked in violet and by circle, and its corresponding pronunciation is marked in yellow and by rectangle. We observe that the actual pronunciation of each component are semantically close to the corresponding component. We may

Table 4. Results of the NER task trained on Yidu, where the best results are bolded, and the second ranked results are underlined. Note that we eliminate feature engineering and heuristic rules on this task to evaluate the effectiveness of word embeddings.

Models		Precision	Recall	F1-score
NN Based	SGNS	0.2698	0.1518	19.43
	CWE	0.3460	0.2321	27.79
	JWE	0.3737	0.1514	21.55
	cw2vec	0.3083	0.1844	23.08
	ssp2vec	0.3021	0.2077	24.62
	BERT	0.3409	0.2340	27.75
	ERNIE	0.3349	0.2181	26.42
MF Based	GLOVE	0.3595	0.2250	27.68
	SPPMI	0.4548	0.2613	33.19
	CLM	0.4380	0.2522	32.01
	PCCWE w/o C_o	<u>0.4971</u>	0.3365	40.13
	PCCWE w/o P_r	0.4898	<u>0.3460</u>	<u>40.55</u>
	PCCWE w/o L_{cons}	0.4917	0.3443	40.50
	PCCWE	**0.4995**	**0.3595**	**41.45**

Table 5. The average running time (seconds) of different models on NLPIR per epoch.

Model	SGNS	CWE	JWE	cw2vec	ssp2vec	Glove	SPPMI	**PCCWE**
Time	36	42	72	120	204	54	24	30

draw a conclusion that the semantics of both components and pronunciations have been learnt effectively through our model training.

In this part, we make some case studies to qualitatively evaluate the ability of our model in effectively capturing the word semantics. We select two target words " 腹胀 (Abdominal distention)" and " 感冒药 (Cold medicine)" in the Yidu dataset as examples. According to the results presented in Table 4, we choose three baseline methods which achieved good performance (i.e., CWE, JWE, and SPPMI) for comparison.

As we can see in Table 6, for word " 腹胀 (Abdominal distention)", there are more irrelevant terms for baseline models. For example, the words " 未见 (Hidden)" and " 同时 (Meanwhile)" are selected as similar words to " 腹胀 (Abdominal distention)" by JWE. Our models can capture more relevant words, such as " 恶心 (Nausea)", " 腹痛 (Bellyache)", and " 腹泻 (Diarrhea)" which are related to "Belly illness". Moreover, we observe that both baseline models and our proposed models found more relevant neighbor words of " 腹胀 (Abdominal distention)" than those of " 感冒药 (Cold medicine)". Intuitively, this is probably because the word " 腹胀 (Abdominal distention)" appears 603 times while the word " 感冒药 (Cold medicine) only appears 13 times in the corpus. In spite of this, our model PCCWE w/o P_r could find " 阿莫西林 (Amoxicillin)" as the similar word for " 感冒药 (Cold medicine). From the above two target words and their five most similar words, it indicates that our proposed model can capture more accurate word semantic relations than baseline models on the small-scaled Yidu dataset.

5   Conclusion

In this paper, we propose an MF based Chinese word embedding learning model using limited data. We exploit pronunciation and component as auxiliary information and study the inner relationship between them to effectively capture word semantic relations. We validate our proposed models by two representative tasks and comparative experiments, which indicates that the proposed model has achieved large improvements on Chinese word embedding learning with limited data. In the future, we plan to explore the effectiveness of Chinese auxiliary information in other areas. For instance, Chinese auxiliary information may have positive impacts on some downstream tasks such as emotion detection.

Acknowledgment. We are grateful to the reviewers for their valuable comments. This work has been supported by the National Natural Science Foundation of China (61972426) and Guangdong Basic and Applied Basic Research Foundation (2020A1515010536).

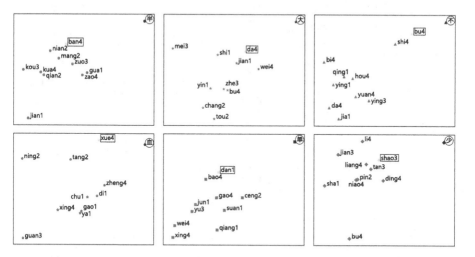

Fig. 3. The 2-D illustration of the sample component vectors and their nearest 10 pronunciation vectors. The components are marked in violet and by circle. The corresponding pronunciations of these components are marked in yellow and by rectangle.

Table 6. Given each target word, we list the top 5 similar words from different models.

Target word 1	腹胀 Abdominal distention				
CWE	解次 Solution	带 Belt	瑞舒伐 Rosuvar	无肩 Shoulderless	核仁 Nucleolus
JWE	肝胆胰 Hepatobiliary pancreas	可见 Visible	同时 Meanwhile	右肺 Right lung	癌行 Cancer Deal
SPPMI	恶心 Nausea	呕吐 Vomit	纳差 Poor appetite	嗳气 Belch	腹痛 Bellyache
PCCWE w/o C_o	恶心 Nausea	呕吐 Vomit	腹痛 Bellyache	嗳气 Belch	纳差 Poor appetite
PCCWE w/o P_r	恶心 Nausea	呕吐 Vomit	腹痛 Bellyache	纳差 Poor appetite	呕血 Haematemesis
PCCWE w/o L_{cons}	恶心 Nausea	呕吐 Vomit	腹痛 Bellyache	进食 Eat	纳差 Poor appetite
PCCWE	恶心 Nausea	呕吐 Vomit	腹泻 Diarrhea	腹痛 Bellyache	呕血 Haematemesis
Target word 2	感冒药 Cold medicine				
CWE	流涎 Salivation	紫绀 Cyanosis	破坏 Destroy	大于 Greater than	两眼 Two eyes
JWE	大于 Greater than	播散 Dissemination	处 Place	两眼 Two eyes	完善 Perfect
SPPMI	自服 Self-medication	早孕 Early pregnancy	自行 By oneself	孕 Pregnancy	孕早期 First trimester
PCCWE w/o C_o	自服 Self-medication	早孕 Early pregnancy	反应 Reaction	孕 Pregnancy	孕早期 First trimester
PCCWE w/o P_r	自服 Self-medication	孕 Pregnancy	自行 By oneself	早孕 Early pregnancy	阿莫西林 Amoxicillin
PCCWE w/o L_{cons}	自服 Self-medication	自行 By oneself	孕 Pregnancy	早孕 Early pregnancy	反应 Reaction
PCCWE	自服 Self-medication	早孕 Early pregnancy	自行 By oneself	孕早期 First trimeste	反应 Reaction

References

1. Ailem, M., Salah, A., Nadif, M.: Non-negative matrix factorization meets word embedding. In: SIGIR, pp. 1081–1084 (2017)
2. Altszyler, E., Sigman, M., Slezak, D.F.: Comparative study of LSA vs word2vec embeddings in small corpora: a case study in dreams database. CoRR abs/1610.01520 (2016)
3. Avraham, O., Goldberg, Y.: The interplay of semantics and morphology in word embeddings. In: EACL, pp. 422–426 (2017)

4. Bengio, Y., Ducharme, R., Vincent, P., Jauvin, C.: A neural probabilistic language model. J. Mach. Learn. Res. **3**, 1137–1155 (2003)
5. Cao, S., Lu, W., Zhou, J., Li, X.: cw2vec: learning Chinese word embeddings with stroke n-gram information. In: AAAI, pp. 5053–5061 (2018)
6. Chen, X., Xu, L., Liu, Z., Sun, M., Luan, H.: Joint learning of character and word embeddings. In: IJCAI, pp. 1236–1242 (2015)
7. Deerwester, S., Dumais, S.T., Furnas, G.W., Landauer, T.K., Harshman, R.: Indexing by latent semantic analysis. J. Am. Soc. Inf. Sci. **41**(6), 391–407 (1990)
8. Devlin, J., Chang, M., Lee, K., Toutanova, K.: BERT: pre-training of deep bidirectional transformers for language understanding. In: NAACL-HLT, pp. 4171–4186 (2019)
9. Ding, C., Li, T., Peng, W.: On the equivalence between non-negative matrix factorization and probabilistic latent semantic indexing. Comput. Stat. Data Anal. **52**(8), 3913–3927 (2008)
10. Hofmann, T.: Probabilistic latent semantic analysis. In: UAI, pp. 289–296 (1999)
11. Huang, Z., Xu, W., Yu, K.: Bidirectional LSTM-CRF models for sequence tagging. CoRR abs/1508.01991 (2015)
12. Levy, O., Goldberg, Y.: Neural word embedding as implicit matrix factorization. In: NIPS, pp. 2177–2185 (2014)
13. Li, Y., Xu, L., Tian, F., Jiang, L., Zhong, X., Chen, E.: Word embedding revisited: a new representation learning and explicit matrix factorization perspective. In: IJCAI, pp. 3650–3656 (2015)
14. Luong, M.T., Socher, R., Manning, C.D.: Better word representations with recursive neural networks for morphology. In: CoNLL, pp. 104–113 (2013)
15. Mikolov, T., Chen, K., Corrado, G., Dean, J.: Efficient estimation of word representations in vector space. In: ICLR Workshop (2013)
16. Mikolov, T., Sutskever, I., Chen, K., Corrado, G.S., Dean, J.: Distributed representations of words and phrases and their compositionality. In: NIPS, pp. 3111–3119 (2013)
17. Peng, Y., Jiang, H.: Leverage financial news to predict stock price movements using word embeddings and deep neural networks. In: NAACL-HLT, pp. 374–379 (2016)
18. Pennington, J., Socher, R., Manning, C.D.: Glove: global vectors for word representation. In: EMNLP, pp. 1532–1543 (2014)
19. Peters, M.E., et al.: Deep contextualized word representations. arXiv preprint arXiv:1802.05365 (2018)
20. Salah, A., Ailem, M., Nadif, M.: Word co-occurrence regularized non-negative matrix tri-factorization for text data co-clustering. In: AAAI, pp. 3992–3999 (2018)
21. Salle, A., Idiart, M., Villavicencio, A.: Matrix factorization using window sampling and negative sampling for improved word representations. arXiv preprint arXiv:1606.00819 (2016)
22. Su, T.R., Lee, H.Y.: Learning Chinese word representations from glyphs of characters. arXiv preprint arXiv:1708.04755 (2017)
23. Sun, Y., et al.: ERNIE 2.0: a continual pre-training framework for language understanding. In: AAAI, pp. 8968–8975 (2020)
24. Tang, D., Wei, F., Yang, N., Zhou, M., Liu, T., Qin, B.: Learning sentiment-specific word embedding for twitter sentiment classification. In: ACL, pp. 1555–1565 (2014)
25. Xu, J., Liu, J., Zhang, L., Li, Z., Chen, H.: Improve Chinese word embeddings by exploiting internal structure. In: NAACL-HLT, pp. 1041–1050 (2016)
26. Xun, G., Li, Y., Gao, J., Zhang, A.: Collaboratively improving topic discovery and word embeddings by coordinating global and local contexts. In: SIGKDD, pp. 535–543 (2017)

27. Yang, Q., Xie, H., Cheng, G., Wang, F.L., Rao, Y.: Pronunciation-enhanced Chinese word embedding. Cogn. Comput. **13**(3), 688–697 (2021)
28. Yu, J., Jian, X., Xin, H., Song, Y.: Joint embeddings of Chinese words, characters, and fine-grained subcharacter components. In: EMNLP, pp. 286–291 (2017)
29. Zhang, Y., et al.: Learning Chinese word embeddings from stroke, structure and pinyin of characters. In: CIKM, pp. 1011–1020 (2019)

Sparse Biterm Topic Model for Short Texts

Bingshan Zhu[1,2], Yi Cai[1,2(✉)], and Huakui Zhang[1,2]

[1] Key Laboratory of Big Data and Intelligent Robot, South China University
of Technology, Ministry of Education, Guangzhou, China
ycai@scut.edu.cn
[2] South China University of Technology, Guangzhou, China

Abstract. Extracting meaningful and coherent topics from short texts
is an important task for many real world applications. Biterm topic model
(BTM) is a popular topic model for short texts by explicitly model word
co-occurrence patterns in the corpus level. However, BTM ignores the
fact that a topic is usually described by a few words in a given corpus. In other words, the topic word distribution in topic model should
be highly sparse. Understanding the sparsity in topic word distribution
may get more coherent topics and improve the performance of BTM. In
this paper, we propose a sparse biterm topic model (SparseBTM) which
combines a spike and slab prior into BTM to explicitly model the topic
sparsity. Experiments on two short texts datasets show that our model
can get comparable topic coherent scores and higher classification and
clustering performance than BTM.

Keywords: Topic modeling · Short texts · Topic sparsity

1 Introduction

With the rapid development of the Internet, millions of data have been produced
on the Web with different forms, such as news articles, blogs, instant messages,
or social media posts. These data have the potential to offer value to people.
For example, we can know what people concern from social media posts because
people often share their opinions and experiences in daily life in the social media
platform. Understanding such data and extracting some useful information from
such data is a challenging work for humans. Hence, it is necessary to find a useful
tool to understand the latent semantic concept contained in those texts.

In text mining domain, topic model is a useful method to extract meaningful and semantic structures (topics) in texts. It can offer people the ability to
explore and search data well by summarizing the themes contained in texts.
Traditional topic model like Latent Dirichlet Allocation (LDA) [2] exploited
document level word co-occurrence patterns implicitly to discover topics in the
collection. In LDA, a document is considered as bag-of-words data and supposed to be described by a few number of topics. A topic is assumed to be a

© Springer Nature Switzerland AG 2021
L. H. U et al. (Eds.): APWeb-WAIM 2021, LNCS 12858, pp. 227–241, 2021.
https://doi.org/10.1007/978-3-030-85896-4_19

probabilistic distribution over the vocabulary (i.e. topic word distribution), and a document is assumed to be a probabilistic distribution over topics (i.e. document topic distribution). Because topic models can summarize documents in a high semantic level and their interpretability, they have been used in a lot of applications such as information retrieval [26], document summarization [30], hashtags recommendation [22], document classification [28,31] and so on.

Though traditional topic models has been successfully applied to normal texts such as academic papers and news articles, it fails to produce coherent and high quality topics when directly applied to short texts because the word co-occurrence patterns in short texts are usually sparse [29]. Specifically, the short texts such as tweets and Web page titles lack rich context for identifying the senses of ambiguous words in the documents.

To address this problem, Yan et al. [29] proposed biterm topic model (BTM) over short texts. This model explicitly captures the word co-occurrence patterns in the corpus level rather than in the document level as in LDA. The experiments in [29] showed that BTM can produce more coherent topics than LDA over short texts, and even in normal texts, BTM can obtain comparable performance than LDA. However, BTM ignores the property that a topic is usually correlated to a few words in the vocabulary. In real world, a topic is described by just a few words, not all the words in the vocabulary. We call this property as topic sparsity. It indicates that the topic word distribution produced by topic models should be highly sparse, that is the topic's word probabilities should focus on a small proportion of words in the vocabulary. Previous work solving this problem can be classified into two main categories: probabilistic topic models and non-probabilistic topic models. The methods in the first category introduce some specific sparse priors into probabilistic topic models to induce topic sparsity. For example, Wang and Blei [25] and Lin et al. [13] used a spike and slab prior to control the topic sparsity in probabilistic topic models. The second category relaxes the probability distribution constraint of the topic word representations. They control the topic sparsity directly by imposing regularizations over posterior distributions [17]. For example, the non-negative matrix factorization (NMF) [6] can achieve topic sparsity by using regularizers such as lasso, group lasso and so on. Moreover, the idea of sparse coding has also been introduced into the non-probabilistic topic models [16,17,33].

Though there are many works have been proposed to deal with the topic sparsity problem in topic models, it is not considered in BTM with the spike and slab prior. Like the first category, we introduce a spike and slab prior for the topic word distribution into biterm topic model to explicitly model the topic sparsity. Based on BTM, we propose a model called sparse biterm topic model (SparseBTM), aiming to obtain more sparse and coherent topics while modeling word co-occurrence patterns explicitly using BTM to solve the data sparsity problem in short texts. Overall, our contributions can be summarized as following:

- To address the topic sparsity problem in BTM, we use the spike and slab prior to explicitly model the topic sparsity in the topic word distribution.

- We conduct experiments on two short texts, WebSnippets and TMNtitle, along with topic coherence, document classification and document clustering tasks. Experimental results show that our model can achieve better or comparable performance than BTM, which validates the effectiveness of our method.

2 Related Work

2.1 Topic Models over Short Texts

There are two main categories of topic models applied on short texts. The first category uses some heuristic methods like aggregation strategy based on metadata of documents, such as users [3] and hashtags [15] to create longer pseudo documents and then apply standard topic models. Though they can improve the performance of topic models to some extent, these methods depend heavily on the data, because not all datasets contain corresponding metadata. Some works combine the aggregation strategy and topic learning into a unified model [12,19,34]. In this case, it is hard to determine the number of pseudo documents, which has great effect on the performance of their models.

While the second category changes the assumption of the model to fit into the situation in short texts. Dirichlet Multinomial Mixture model (DMM) [32] assumed that a document contains only one topic. In this setting, the word co-occurrence patterns are implicitly enriched for topic learning. Moreover, Yan et al. [29] proposed biterm topic model to model word co-occurrence patterns explicitly in the corpus level. They transformed the dataset into a biterm set, where a biterm is an unordered pair of words in the vocabulary. Using biterms instead of words, they can enrich the word co-occurrence patterns naturally. There are many other works published based on BTM [7,10,14] and DMM [9,11]. These methods take the relationship between words into consideration, either in the form of word embeddings or neural networks to improve the performance of BTM or DMM. However, all of models above don't take the topic sparsity into consideration.

2.2 Sparse Topic Model

There are two categories of topic models with sparsity enhanced: probabilistic topic models and non-probabilistic topic models. In the first category, an direct way to encode topic sparsity is to set the value approaching zero for the symmetric Dirichlet parameter of the topic word distributions. However, the topic word distributions obtained in this way may not be truly sparse and too small value for this parameter may reduces the smoothing effects, resulting in degradation of model performance. The spike and slab prior is widely used in variable selection [20], and has been introduced into topic modeling. Wang and Blei [25] first introduced a spike and slab prior to decouple the sparsity and smoothness in the topic word distribution of hierarchical Dirichlet process (HDP) [23], a nonparametric counterpart of LDA. Lin et al. [13] both addressed the sparsity of topics per document and terms per topic, the authors introduced spike and slab priors not only in topic word distribution but also in document topic distribution. Our model take a similar approach as their model. Doshi-Velez et al. [5] proposed to use a three-parameter Indian Buffet Process to model topic sparsity and document sparsity simultaneously.

For the non-probabilistic topic models, the topic word distribution is not necessarily a probabilistic distribution. Zhu and Xing [33] proposed sparse topical coding (STC) using Laplacian prior to directly control the sparsity of inferred representations. Moreover, Peng et al. [16] introduced sparse groups to encode sparsity of words and documents considering group sparse patterns. Peng et al. [17] imposed hierarchical sparse prior to leverage the prior information of relevance between sparse coefficients. Different from those works above, we introduce a spike and slab prior to model the sparsity of the topic word distribution based on BTM.

3   Our Method

3.1   A Brief Review of BTM

Topic Generation. The graphical representation of BTM is shown in Fig. 1(a) and the notations used in this paper is shown in Table 1. Given a short text collection, BTM transforms it into a biterm set $\mathbb{B}$ firstly. And the generative process is stated as follows:

- For each topic $k \in \{1, 2, \ldots, K\}$:
  1. sample $\phi_k \sim \text{Dirichlet}(\beta)$
- For the whole biterm set $\mathbb{B}$:
  1. sample the global topic distribution $\theta \sim \text{Dirichlet}(\alpha)$
- For each biterm b in the whole biterm set $\mathbb{B}$:
  1. sample a topic assignment $z_b \sim \text{Multinomial}(\theta)$
  2. sample two words $w_i, w_j \sim \text{Multinomial}(\phi_{z_b})$

The joint probability of $\mathbb{B}$, θ, ϕ and z is calculated by:

$$p(\mathbb{B}, \theta, \phi, z) = \left[\prod_{k=1}^{K} p(\phi_k; \beta) \right] \left[p(\theta; \alpha) \prod_{b=1}^{N_B} p(z_b; \theta) p(w_i; \phi_{z_b}) p(w_j; \phi_{z_b}) \right] \quad (1)$$

Parameter Inference. The model parameters is inferred using collapsed Gibbs sampling. The topic word distribution ϕ_k and the global topic distribution θ can be calculated by:

$$\phi_{k,w} = \frac{n_{k,w} + \beta}{\sum_w n_{k,w} + V\beta}$$

$$\theta_k = \frac{n_k + \alpha}{N_B + K\alpha} \quad (2)$$

Since we cannot obtain the document topic distribution directly, the probability of topic k given a document d is calculated as following:

$$p(z = k|d) = \sum_b p(z = k|b)p(b|d) \tag{3}$$

And we need to estimate $p(b|d)$ and $p(z = k|b)$ for each biterm b as following:

$$p(b|d) = \frac{n_b}{n_d} \tag{4}$$

$$p(z = k|b) = \theta_k \phi_{k,w_i} \phi_{k,w_j} \tag{5}$$

where n_b is the number of biterm b in document d, n_d is the total number of biterms in document d.

3.2   SparseBTM

The main idea to encode topic sparsity in BTM is to restrict the word simplex over Dirichlet distributions. We use auxiliary Bernoulli variables to achieve this goal. A Bernoulli variable is used to determine whether a term is selected by a topic. Specifically, let $\omega_{k,r}$ indicating whether a term r in the vocabulary is selected by the topic k. However, if we use $\boldsymbol{\omega}_k = (\omega_{k,1}, \ldots, \omega_{k,V})$ directly in the Dirichlet distribution, it can produce an ill-defined Dirichlet distribution. Dirichlet$(s\boldsymbol{\omega}_k)$ is not well-defined when $\boldsymbol{\omega}_k = \mathbf{0}$, because the parameters of Dirichlet distribution must be positive real numbers. To address this issue, a

Table 1. Notations.

K	Number of topics
V	Vocabulary
$\mathbb{B}$	Biterm set
N_B	Number of biterms in the corpus
θ	Global topic distribution
α	Dirichlet parameter of global topic distribution θ
η_k	Probability of a term r selected by topic k
$\omega_{k,r}$	Bernoulli variable indicating whether a term r is selected by topic k
β	Dirichlet parameter of topic word distribution in BTM
ϕ_k	Topic word distribution
x, y	Parameters of η_k
s	Smoothing prior
t	Weak smoothing prior
z	Topic assignment
$\mathbb{I}(\cdot)$	Indicator function

weak smoothing prior t (s is called smoothing prior) is introduced as in [13]. The $\boldsymbol{\omega}_k = (\omega_{k,1}, \ldots, \omega_{k,V})$ is referred to "spike", and the smoothing priors (s and t) are refered to "slab" in statistics. In this way, the topic word distribution is sampled from Dirichlet($s\boldsymbol{\omega}_k + t\mathbf{1}$).

The graphical representation of our model is shown in Fig. 1(b). In the graphical representation, the shaded nodes represent the parameters that can be configured ahead and observed data, while the unshaded nodes represent the latent variables or parameters that should be inferred.

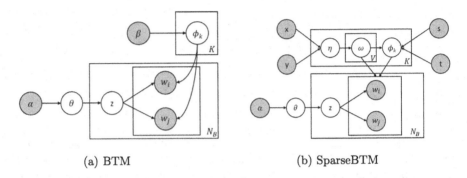

(a) BTM   (b) SparseBTM

Fig. 1. The graphical representations of (a) BTM and (b) SparseBTM.

Topic Generation. Given a short text collection, we first transform it into a biterm set $\mathbb{B}$ as in [4]. Suppose there are K topics in the corpus, using the graphical representation of SparseBTM, the generative process of SparseBTM is presented as following:

- For each topic $k \in \{1, 2, \ldots, K\}$:
  1. sample $\eta_k \sim \text{Beta}(x, y)$
  2. for each term $r \in \{1, 2, \ldots, V\}$:
     (a) sample $\omega_{k,r} \sim \text{Bernoulli}(\eta_k)$, $\boldsymbol{\omega}_k = (\omega_{k,1}, \ldots, \omega_{k,V})$
     (b) sample $\boldsymbol{\phi}_k \sim \text{Dirichlet}(s\boldsymbol{\omega}_k + t\mathbf{1})$
- For the whole biterm set $\mathbb{B}$:
  1. sample the global topic distribution $\boldsymbol{\theta} \sim \text{Dirichlet}(\alpha)$
- For each biterm b in the whole biterm set $\mathbb{B}$:
  1. sample a topic assignment $z_b \sim \text{Multinomial}(\boldsymbol{\theta})$
  2. sample two words $w_i, w_j \sim \text{Multinomial}(\boldsymbol{\phi}_{z_b})$

Actually, we generate different $\omega_{k,r}$ for each term r in the vocabulary. Before generating $\omega_{k,r}$, we first generate η_k from Beta(x, y), which determines the probability of a topic k choosing term r. After sampling $\omega_{k,r}$, we can sample the topic word distribution $\boldsymbol{\phi}_k$ from Dirichlet($s\boldsymbol{\omega}_k + t\mathbf{1}$). To generate each biterm b in the whole biterm set, we first sample the topic assignment z_b from Multinomial($\boldsymbol{\theta}$), and then sample two words from corresponding topic word distribution Multinomial($\boldsymbol{\phi}_{z_b}$). From the generation process above, we can obtain the joint probability of $\mathbb{B}$, $\boldsymbol{\eta}$, $\boldsymbol{\omega}$, $\boldsymbol{\phi}$, $\boldsymbol{\theta}$ and $\boldsymbol{z}$:

$$p(\mathbb{B}, \boldsymbol{\eta}, \boldsymbol{\omega}, \boldsymbol{\phi}, \boldsymbol{\theta}, \boldsymbol{z}; x, y, s, t, \alpha) = \left[\prod_{k=1}^{K} p(\eta_k; x, y) \prod_{r=1}^{V} p(\omega_{k,r}; \eta_k) p(\phi_k; s\boldsymbol{\omega}_k + t\mathbf{1}) \right] \cdot$$
$$\left[p(\boldsymbol{\theta}; \alpha) \prod_{b=1}^{N_B} p(z_b; \boldsymbol{\theta}) p(w_i; \boldsymbol{\phi}_{z_b}) p(w_j; \boldsymbol{\phi}_{z_b}) \right]$$

(6)

Parameter Inference. We use the zero-order collapsed variational bayes inference method (CVB0) [1] to estimate the parameters of our model. After collapsed out the model parameters $\boldsymbol{\theta}$, $\boldsymbol{\phi}_k (k = 1, 2, \ldots, K)$, and $\boldsymbol{\eta}$ in Eq. 6, we derivative the updated formula for the latent variables $\boldsymbol{z}$ and $\boldsymbol{\omega}$.

The variational Bernoulli parameters for $\boldsymbol{\omega}$:

$$\hat{\eta}_{k,r} = \hat{q}(\omega_{k,r} = 1) = \frac{\eta^1_{k,r}}{\eta^1_{k,r} + \eta^0_{k,r}}$$
$$\eta^1_{k,r} = (x + H_k^{-kr}) \Gamma(N_{k,r} + s + t)$$
$$\qquad B(s + Vt + sH_k^{-kr}, N_k + sH_k^{-kr} + Vt)$$
$$\eta^0_{k,r} = (y + V - 1 - H_k^{-kr}) \Gamma(s + t)$$
$$\qquad B(Vt + sH_k^{-kr}, N_k + s + sH_k^{-kr} + Vt)$$

(7)

The variational Multinomial parameters for $\boldsymbol{z}$:

$$\hat{\gamma}_{b,k} = \hat{q}(z_b = k)$$
$$\propto (N_k^{-b} + \alpha) \left(\frac{N_{k,w_i}^{-b} + s\hat{\eta}_{k,w_i} + t}{2N_k^{-b} + sH_k + Vt} \right) \cdot$$
$$\left(\frac{N_{k,w_j}^{-b} + s\hat{\eta}_{k,w_j} + t}{2N_k^{-b} + sH_k + Vt + 1} \right)$$

(8)

where $H_k = \sum_r \hat{\eta}_{k,r} (k = 1, 2, \ldots, K)$, $N_{k,r} = \sum_{b \in B_r} \hat{\gamma}_{b,k} (k = 1, 2, \ldots, K)$, $N_k = \sum_b \hat{\gamma}_{b,k} (k = 1, 2, \ldots, K)$, and B_r is the set of biterms containing word r. The superscript $-kr$ and $-b$ mean without considering $\omega_{k,r}$ and biterm b, respectively. $\Gamma(\cdot)$ and $B(\cdot)$ are gamma function and beta function, respectively. We obtain the topic word distribution $\boldsymbol{\phi}_k$ and the corpus's topic distribution $\boldsymbol{\theta}$ in the following way:

$$\phi_{k,w} = \frac{N_{k,w} + s\hat{\eta}_{k,w} + t}{N_k + sH_k + Vt}$$
$$\theta_k = \frac{N_k + \alpha}{\sum_k N_k + K\alpha}$$

(9)

The document's topic distribution is inferred as the same as BTM, which is shown in Eq. 3–5.

4 Experiments

To show the effectiveness of our method, we evaluate it in three different ways: (1) *topic coherence*, it evaluates the quality of topic word distribution by calculating the semantic coherence scores in each topic; (2) *document classification*, it evaluates the quality of the document topic distributions by performing a document classification task using the documents' topic representations; and (3) *document clustering*, it evaluates the topic model without depending on any extrinsic methods. In this setting, each topic is considered as a cluster, and the documents will be assigned the topic k with highest value of conditional probability $p(z = k|d)$.

4.1 Datasets

We use the following two short texts datasets to evaluate our method.

- **WebSnippets**[1]: This collection contains Google search snippets for 8 domains, which are Education-Science, Health, Engineering, Sports, Politics-Society, Business, Computers and Culture-Arts-Entertainment. We use the datasets provided by [18]. For preprocessing, we remove the symbol "-" in words ending with "-". We also remove the words whose document frequency is less than 3 and words with fewer than 3 characters. Finally, we remove duplicated documents and documents with words less than 3.
- **TMNtitle**[2]: This collection contains the titles of the Tag My News [24] dataset. It contains documents from 7 generic categories covering Sport, Business, U.S., Health, Sci&Tech, World and Entertainment. For preprocessing, we just remove duplicated documents in the collection.

The number of documents, the number of distinct words, the average number of words in documents, and the number of categories of the two datasets after preprocessing are listed in Table 2.

Table 2. Summary of two datasets.

Dataset	#doc	#vocabulary	#avglen	#categories
WebSnippets	12106	7359	15.2	8
TMNtitle	30845	6347	4.94	7

4.2 Evaluation Methods

In this section, we describe our evaluation methods in detail.

- **Topic coherence** Röder et al. [21] explored a lot of metrics to measure the semantic coherence in a topic. These metrics calculate the semantic coherence scores for topics by listing top N words (words with highest probabilities) in each topic. The authors splited the topic coherence pipeline into four stages and found that the method called C_V measure performs best in all metrics.

---

[1] http://jwebpro.sourceforge.net/data-web-snippets.tar.gz.
[2] Can be downloaded from https://github.com/pgcool/iDocNADEe/.

According to [27], given a topic z and its top N words with highest probabilities $\{w_1, \ldots, w_N\}$, C_V can be defined by:

$$C_V(z) = \frac{1}{N} \sum_{i=1}^{N} s_{cos}(\boldsymbol{v}_{\text{NPMI}}(w_i), \boldsymbol{v}_{\text{NPMI}}(w_{1:N}))$$

$$\boldsymbol{v}_{\text{NPMI}}(w_i) = \{\text{NPMI}(w_i, w_j)\}_{j=1,2,\ldots,N}$$

$$\boldsymbol{v}_{\text{NPMI}}(w_{1:N}) = \left\{ \sum_{i=1}^{N} \text{NPMI}(w_i, w_j) \right\}_{j=1,2,\ldots,N} \qquad (10)$$

$$\text{NPMI}(w_i, w_j) = \frac{\log \frac{p(w_i, w_j) + \epsilon}{p(w_i) p(w_j)}}{-\log(p(w_i, w_j) + \epsilon)}$$

where s_{cos} means the cosine similarity function, $p(w_i)$ is the probability of w_i, $p(w_i, w_j)$ is the co-occurrence probability of w_i and w_j within a window in the reference corpus and ϵ is used to avoid dividing by zero. We compute C_V using the implementation in gensim[3].

- **Classification performance** Topic models can produce a topic representation for each document in the corpus. That is each document d in the corpus can be represented as a vector $[p(z = 1|d), \ldots, p(z = K|d)]$. These representations can be seen as low-dimensional representations of documents which can be used in some text mining tasks such as text classification. We use the topic representations to perform a classification task to measure the quality of our model. We split the dataset into training set and testing set according to ratio 7:3. We choose the logistic regression classifier with one-vs-rest strategy, with the regularization parameter C taken in $\{0.001, 0.1, 1, 10, 100\}$. Five-fold cross-validation is used to train the classifier. Finally, the micro-F1 score is used to evaluate the classifier's performance.
- **Clustering performance** Topic models can be seen as a soft clustering algorithm, where topic is considered as cluster. We use two standard metrics to show the effectiveness of SparseBTM in clustering evaluation. The first one is Normalized Mutual Information (NMI). It measures the agreement of two label assignments, and is calculated using the mutual information between two assignments penalized by their entropy. Assume the two label assignments are U and V, where U is the class membership assignment and V is the cluster membership assignment. NMI can be defined by:

$$\begin{aligned} \text{NMI} &= \frac{\text{MI}(U, V)}{[\text{H}(U) + \text{H}(V)]/2} \\ &= \frac{\sum_{i,j} \frac{|U_i \cap V_j|}{N} \log(\frac{|U_i||V_j|}{N|U_i \cap V_j|})}{\left(\sum_i \frac{|U_i|}{N} \log \frac{|U_i|}{N} + \sum_j \frac{|V_j|}{N} \log \frac{|V_j|}{N} \right)/2} \end{aligned} \qquad (11)$$

where $\text{MI}(U, V)$ is the mutual information between U and V, $\text{H}(U)$ and $\text{H}(V)$ are the entropy of U and V, respectively. The second is Adjusted Rand

---

[3] https://radimrehurek.com/gensim/models/coherencemodel.html.

Index(ARI) [8]. It is the correct-for-chance version of Rand Index, which is a metric based on pairwise comparisons between two label assignments. If two documents have the same class and the same cluster, or they are in different classes and different clusters, then the assignments are considered as correct, else false. ARI can be defined by:

$$ARI = \frac{\sum_{i,j} \binom{|U_i \cap V_j|}{2} - \left[\sum_i \binom{|U_i|}{2} \sum_j \binom{|V_j|}{2}\right] / \binom{N}{2}}{\frac{1}{2}\left[\sum_i \binom{|U_i|}{2} + \sum_j \binom{|V_j|}{2}\right] - \left[\sum_i \binom{|U_i|}{2} \sum_j \binom{|V_j|}{2}\right] / \binom{N}{2}} \tag{12}$$

The score range for ARI is $[-1, 1]$.

4.3   Baseline and Parameter Settings

We compare our method with the following model:

- **BTM:** the biterm topic model proposed by [29]. It explicitly models the word co-occurrence patterns in the corpus level to deal with the problem of low-quality topics over short texts in traditional topic models. We use the code implemented by the authors[4].

For BTM, we run 1000 Gibbs sampling iterations and set $\alpha = 50/K$, $\beta = 0.01$. For SparseBTM, the maximum number of iterations is set to be 800, $\alpha = 50/K$, $x = y = 1$, $s = 0.01$, $t = 10^{-7}$. In WebSnippets dataset, we set the number of topics to be $\{20, 30, 40, 50, 60, 70\}$, while in TMNtitle dataset, we set the number of topics to be $\{20, 25, 30, 35, 40, 45\}$. We show the topic coherence scores with top N words in topics where N is taken in $\{10, 15, 20\}$. We run all of the models 5 times through different initializations, and report the average result in three evaluation methods finally.

4.4   Experimental Results

Topic Coherence. The topic coherence scores are presented in Table 3, 4, 5 and 6. From the results, we can make a conclusion as following: (1) SparseBTM achieves comparable topic coherence scores in WebSnippets though it doesn't outperform BTM in all settings; (2) In TMNtitle, however, our model obtain the highest topic coherence scores in all settings. It shows that introducing a spike and slab prior into BTM can actually help to improve the topic coherence scores.

Classification Performance. The classification performance of all methods are shown in Fig. 2. We can see that SparseBTM achieves highest micro-F1 score in all settings (except $K = 40$ in WebSnippets dataset) on both datasets. It shows that the topic representations of documents obtained from SparseBTM is more discriminative than BTM in the text classification task, which indicates that introducing the spike and slab prior into BTM can improve the performance of document classification.

---

[4] https://github.com/xiaohuiyan/BTM.

Table 3. Topic coherence scores on WebSnippets dataset, with K in $\{20, 30, 40\}$.

Model	$K = 20$			$K = 30$			$K = 40$		
	$N = 10$	$N = 15$	$N = 20$	$N = 10$	$N = 15$	$N = 20$	$N = 10$	$N = 15$	$N = 20$
BTM	**0.5021**	0.4251	0.3746	0.4994	**0.4203**	**0.3728**	**0.5118**	**0.4280**	**0.3772**
SparseBTM	0.5001	**0.4295**	**0.3847**	**0.5010**	0.4202	0.3718	0.5024	0.4179	0.3752

Table 4. Topic coherence scores on WebSnippets dataset, with K in $\{50, 60, 70\}$.

Model	$K = 50$			$K = 60$			$K = 70$		
	$N = 10$	$N = 15$	$N = 20$	$N = 10$	$N = 15$	$N = 20$	$N = 10$	$N = 15$	$N = 20$
BTM	0.4924	**0.4224**	0.3769	**0.4987**	**0.4240**	0.3750	**0.5030**	**0.4257**	0.3740
SparseBTM	**0.4930**	0.4149	**0.3770**	0.4965	0.4218	**0.3764**	0.4978	0.4198	**0.3747**

Table 5. Topic coherence scores on TMNtitle dataset, with K in $\{20, 25, 30\}$.

Model	$K = 20$			$K = 25$			$K = 30$		
	$N = 10$	$N = 15$	$N = 20$	$N = 10$	$N = 15$	$N = 20$	$N = 10$	$N = 15$	$N = 20$
BTM	0.3469	0.3246	0.3126	0.3597	0.3248	0.3217	0.3839	0.3419	0.3303
SparseBTM	**0.3640**	**0.3320**	**0.3252**	**0.3848**	**0.3378**	**0.3337**	**0.3874**	**0.3459**	**0.3350**

Table 6. Topic coherence scores on TMNtitle dataset, with K in $\{35, 40, 45\}$.

Model	$K = 35$			$K = 40$			$K = 45$		
	$N = 10$	$N = 15$	$N = 20$	$N = 10$	$N = 15$	$N = 20$	$N = 10$	$N = 15$	$N = 20$
BTM	0.3864	0.3396	0.3313	0.3928	0.3449	0.3376	0.4081	0.3514	0.3423
SparseBTM	**0.3914**	**0.3452**	**0.3407**	**0.4057**	**0.3519**	**0.3417**	**0.4097**	**0.3593**	**0.3493**

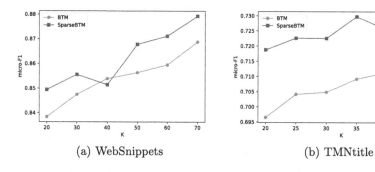

(a) WebSnippets   (b) TMNtitle

Fig. 2. The classification performance on two datasets.

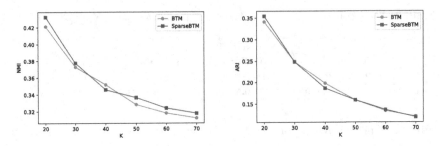

Fig. 3. The clustering performance on WebSnippets dataset.

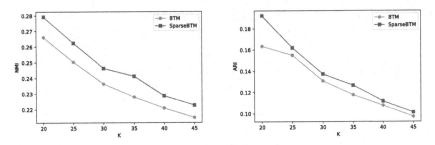

Fig. 4. The clustering performance on TMNtitle dataset.

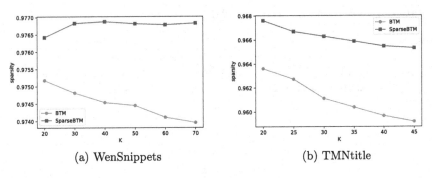

(a) WenSnippets   (b) TMNtitle

Fig. 5. Topic sparsity on two datasets.

Clustering Performance. The results on clustering evaluation can be seen in Fig. 3 and Fig. 4. The NMI and ARI scores decrease when topic number getting larger in two methods. In WebSnippets dataset, SparseBTM obtains comparable and even better performance than BTM in almost all settings except $K = 40$, while in TMNtitle dataset, it beats BTM in all settings. These results show that SparseBTM can achieve a better clustering performance than BTM, which shows that introducing spike and slab prior is helpful to improve the quality of BTM in terms of clustering performance.

Sparsity. Following [25], we define the topic's sparsity of two models as the ratio of zero entries over the total number of entries in $\phi = \{\phi_{k,r}\}$:

$$sparsity = \frac{\sum_{k=1}^{K}\sum_{r=1}^{V}\mathbb{I}(\phi_{k,r} < threshold)}{K \cdot V} \tag{13}$$

where $threshold$ is used to determine the zero entries in ϕ. In this paper, we set $threshold = 10^{-3}$. The results of topic sparsity are shown in Fig. 5. We can find that the topic sparsity of SparseBTM is higher than BTM, which indicates that SparseBTM can improve the model's topic sparsity by introducing the spike and slab prior into BTM. What's more, the topic sparsity of our model is more stable than BTM when topic number K getting larger.

5   Conclusion

In this paper, we propose a sparse biterm topic model, called SparseBTM, to explicitly model topic sparsity based on BTM. The main idea is to introduce a spike and slab prior to control the sparsity of the topic word distribution. Experiments on topic coherence, classification performance and clustering performance show that our method can achieve better or comparable scores with BTM in topic coherence and perform better in the document classification task and clustering evaluation task. Moreover, SparseBTM achieve higher topic sparsity than BTM, which shows that the spike and slab prior is effective in controlling the topic sparsity in BTM.

Acknowledgments. This work was supported by National Natural Science Foundation of China (No. 62076100), National Key Research and Development Program of China (Standard knowledge graph for epidemic prevention and production recovering intelligent service platform and its applications), the Fundamental Research Funds for the Central Universities, SCUT (No. D2201300, D2210010), the Science and Technology Programs of Guangzhou(201902010046), the Science and Technology Planning Project of Guangdong Province (No. 2020B0101100002).

References

1. Asuncion, A., Welling, M., Smyth, P., Teh, Y.W.: On smoothing and inference for topic models. In: Proceedings of the 25th Conference on Uncertainty in Artificial Intelligence, pp. 27–34 (2009)
2. Blei, D.M., Ng, A.Y., Jordan, M.I.: Latent dirichlet allocation. J. Mach. Learn. Res. **3**, 993–1022 (2003)
3. Chen, W., Wang, J., Zhang, Y., Yan, H., Li, X.: User based aggregation for biterm topic model. In: Proceedings of the 53rd Annual Meeting of the Association for Computational Linguistics and the 7th International Joint Conference on Natural Language Processing (Volume 2: Short Papers), pp. 489–494 (2015)
4. Cheng, X., Yan, X., Lan, Y., Guo, J.: BTM: topic modeling over short texts. IEEE Trans. Knowl. Data Eng. **26**(12), 2928–2941 (2014)

5. Doshi-Velez, F., Wallace, B.C., Adams, R.: Graph-sparse LDA: a topic model with structured sparsity. In: 29th AAAI Conference on Artificial Intelligence (2015)
6. Heiler, M., Schnörr, C.: Learning sparse representations by non-negative matrix factorization and sequential cone programming. J. Mach. Learn. Res. **7**, 1385–1407 (2006)
7. Huang, J., Peng, M., Li, P., Hu, Z., Xu, C.: Improving biterm topic model with word embeddings. World Wide Web **23**(6), 3099–3124 (2020). https://doi.org/10.1007/s11280-020-00823-w
8. Hubert, L., Arabie, P.: Comparing partitions. J. Classif. **2**(1), 193–218 (1985)
9. Li, C., Wang, H., Zhang, Z., Sun, A., Ma, Z.: Topic modeling for short texts with auxiliary word embeddings. In: Proceedings of the 39th International ACM SIGIR conference on Research and Development in Information Retrieval, pp. 165–174 (2016)
10. Li, X., Zhang, A., Li, C., Guo, L., Wang, W., Ouyang, J.: Relational biterm topic model: short-text topic modeling using word embeddings. Comput. J. **62**(3), 359–372 (2019)
11. Li, X., Zhang, J., Ouyang, J.: Dirichlet multinomial mixture with variational manifold regularization: topic modeling over short texts. Proc. AAAI Conf. Artif. Intell. **33**, 7884–7891 (2019)
12. Lin, H., Zuo, Y., Liu, G., Li, H., Wu, J., Wu, Z.: A pseudo-document-based topical n-grams model for short texts. World Wide Web **23**(6), 3001–3023 (2020)
13. Lin, T., Tian, W., Mei, Q., Cheng, H.: The dual-sparse topic model: mining focused topics and focused terms in short text. In: Proceedings of the 23rd International Conference on World Wide Web, pp. 539–550 (2014)
14. Lu, H.Y., Xie, L.Y., Kang, N., Wang, C.J., Xie, J.Y.: Don't forget the quantifiable relationship between words: using recurrent neural network for short text topic discovery. In: 31st AAAI Conference on Artificial Intelligence (2017)
15. Mehrotra, R., Sanner, S., Buntine, W., Xie, L.: Improving LDA topic models for microblogs via tweet pooling and automatic labeling. In: Proceedings of the 36th International ACM SIGIR Conference on Research and Development in Information Retrieval, pp. 889–892 (2013)
16. Peng, M., et al.: Sparse topical coding with sparse groups. In: Cui, B., Zhang, N., Xu, J., Lian, X., Liu, D. (eds.) WAIM 2016. LNCS, vol. 9658, pp. 415–426. Springer, Cham (2016). https://doi.org/10.1007/978-3-319-39937-9_32
17. Peng, M., Xie, Q., Wang, H., Zhang, Y., Tian, G.: Bayesian sparse topical coding. IEEE Trans. Knowl. Data Eng. **31**(6), 1080–1093 (2018)
18. Phan, X.H., Nguyen, L.M., Horiguchi, S.: Learning to classify short and sparse text & web with hidden topics from large-scale data collections. In: Proceedings of the 17th International Conference on World Wide Web, pp. 91–100 (2008)
19. Quan, X., Kit, C., Ge, Y., Pan, S.J.: Short and sparse text topic modeling via self-aggregation. In: 24th International Joint Conference on Artificial Intelligence (2015)
20. Ročková, V., George, E.I.: The spike-and-slab LASSO. J. Am. Stat. Assoc. **113**(521), 431–444 (2018)
21. Röder, M., Both, A., Hinneburg, A.: Exploring the space of topic coherence measures. In: Proceedings of the 8th ACM International Conference on Web Search and Data Mining, pp. 399–408 (2015)
22. She, J., Chen, L.: TOMOHA: topic model-based hashtag recommendation on Twitter. In: Proceedings of the 23rd International Conference on World Wide Web, pp. 371–372 (2014)

23. Teh, Y.W., Jordan, M.I., Beal, M.J., Blei, D.M.: Sharing clusters among related groups: hierarchical dirichlet processes. In: Advances in Neural Information Processing Systems, pp. 1385–1392 (2005)
24. Vitale, D., Ferragina, P., Scaiella, U.: Classification of short texts by deploying topical annotations. In: Baeza-Yates, R., et al. (eds.) ECIR 2012. LNCS, vol. 7224, pp. 376–387. Springer, Heidelberg (2012). https://doi.org/10.1007/978-3-642-28997-2_32
25. Wang, C., Blei, D.M.: Decoupling sparsity and smoothness in the discrete hierarchical dirichlet process. In: Advances in Neural Information Processing Systems, pp. 1982–1989 (2009)
26. Wei, X., Croft, W.B.: LDA-based document models for ad-hoc retrieval. In: Proceedings of the 29th Annual International ACM SIGIR Conference on Research and Development in Information Retrieval, pp. 178–185 (2006)
27. Wu, X., Li, C., Zhu, Y., Miao, Y.: Short text topic modeling with topic distribution quantization and negative sampling decoder. In: Proceedings of the 2020 Conference on Empirical Methods in Natural Language Processing (EMNLP), pp. 1772–1782 (2020)
28. Wu, X., Cai, Y., Li, Q., Xu, J., Leung, H.: Combining weighted category-aware contextual information in convolutional neural networks for text classification. World Wide Web **23**(5), 2815–2834 (2020)
29. Yan, X., Guo, J., Lan, Y., Cheng, X.: A biterm topic model for short texts. In: Proceedings of the 22nd International Conference on World Wide Web, pp. 1445–1456 (2013)
30. Yang, G., Wen, D., Chen, N.S., Sutinen, E., et al.: A novel contextual topic model for multi-document summarization. Expert Syst. Appl. **42**(3), 1340–1352 (2015)
31. Yang, Y., et al.: Dataless short text classification based on biterm topic model and word embeddings. In: 29th International Joint Conference on Artificial Intelligence (2020)
32. Yin, J., Wang, J.: A dirichlet multinomial mixture model-based approach for short text clustering. In: Proceedings of the 20th ACM SIGKDD International Conference on Knowledge Discovery and Data Mining, pp. 233–242 (2014)
33. Zhu, J., Xing, E.P.: Sparse topical coding. In: Proceedings of the 27th Conference on Uncertainty in Artificial Intelligence, pp. 831–838 (2011)
34. Zuo, Y., et al.: Topic modeling of short texts: a pseudo-document view. In: Proceedings of the 22nd ACM SIGKDD International Conference on Knowledge Discovery and Data Mining, pp. 2105–2114 (2016)

EMBERT: A Pre-trained Language Model for Chinese Medical Text Mining

Zerui Cai[1], Taolin Zhang[2,3], Chengyu Wang[3], and Xiaofeng He[1(✉)]

[1] School of Computer Science and Technology, East China Normal University,
Shanghai, China
hexf@cs.ecnu.edu.cn
[2] School of Software Engineering, East China Normal University, Shanghai, China
[3] Alibaba Group, Hangzhou, China
chengyu.wcy@alibaba-inc.com

Abstract. Medical text mining aims to learn models to extract useful information from medical sources. A major challenge is obtaining large-scale labeled data in the medical domain for model training, which is highly expensive. Recent studies show that leveraging massive unlabeled corpora for pre-training language models alleviates this problem by self-supervised learning. In this paper, we propose EMBERT, an entity-level knowledge-enhanced pre-trained language model, which leverages several distinct self-supervised tasks for Chinese medical text mining. EMBERT captures fine-grained semantic relations among medical terms by three self-supervised tasks, including i) context-entity consistency prediction (whether entities are of equivalence in meanings given certain contexts), ii) entity segmentation (segmenting entities into fine-grained semantic parts) and iii) bidirectional entity masking (predicting the atomic or adjective terms of long entities). The experimental results demonstrate that our model achieves significant improvements over five strong baselines on six public Chinese medical text mining datasets.

Keywords: Pre-trained language model · Chinese medical text mining · Self-supervised learning · Deep context-aware neural network

1 Introduction

The outbreak of COVID-19 brings an urgent need for text mining techniques to discover valuable medical information automatically [14,30]. Although a lot of medical texts have been accumulated online, training models for medical text mining often require large-scale annotated data. A significant challenge arises in that labeling high-quality medical data is expensive since the data must be collected by experts with domain knowledge.

Pre-trained Language Models (PLMs) trained on unlabeled data ease the demand for annotated data by self-supervised learning [1,5]. Existing works on PLMs often focus on the general domain. For example, BERT [9], SpanBERT

Table 1. Characteristics of Chinese medical texts, including i) diversity of synonyms, ii) nestification of entities and iii) misunderstanding of long entities in different medical text mining tasks. The blue underscore contents corresponding to English translations in brackets are shown to explain why this example belongs to the underlying category.

Task	Example	Characteristics
Question Matching	• 我父亲07年8月查出患有结核病，请问用什么药好？ (My father was diagnosed with *tuberculosis* in August 2007. Which kind of medicine is suitable?) • 连续三周咳，怀疑是痨病，请问吃什么药？ (Coughing for three weeks may be a sign for *consumption*. What medicine should I take?)	Diversity of Synonyms
Named Entity Recognition	• 新型冠状病毒肺炎的症状一般有发热、干咳等。 (Symptoms of *COVID-19* generally include fever, dry coughing, etc.)	Nestification of Entities
Question Answering	• Question: 糖尿病酮酸中毒怎么办 (What to do with *diabetic ketoacidosis*?) • Answer (Correct): 按酸中毒程度不同采取相应治疗措施...(According to the degree of *acidosis*, take appropriate treatment measures...) • Answer (Incorrect): 糖尿病需要综合治疗... (*Diabetes* needs to be treated comprehensively...)	Misunderstanding of Long Entities

[18], XLNet [35] and SemBERT [39] outperform previous models in various downstream NLP tasks [4,16,33,34], which are pre-trained over large-scale unstructured corpora collected from Wikipedia or BookCorpus [9]. However, applying models for the general domain directly to the closed domain usually leads to unsatisfactory result due to the differences in text characteristics [24]. To the best of our knowledge, MC-BERT [36] is the only Chinese medical pre-trained model, which merely applies the whole-word level masking with domain-specific entities and phrases to Chinese medical corpus, neglecting the internal relations of medical entities. We hypothesis that the pre-training method of MC-BERT is sub-optimal, as we observe that there exist three unique characteristics in Chinese medical texts, illustrated in Table 1.

i) **Diversity of Synonyms:** Many terms with different surface forms actually refer to the same concept. Specially, the colloquial expressions and professional terminology of a medical concept may be seemingly irreverent. For example, although "肺结核" (tuberculosis in modern medicine) and "痨病" (consumption in traditional Chinese medicine) mean the same disease, it is difficult for models to learn without medical background knowledge.

ii) **Nestification of Entities:** In the Chinese medical knowledge graph, a lot of Chinese medical entities contain multiple sub-entities. For example, in the entity "新型冠状病毒肺炎" (COVID-19), both "肺炎" (pneumonia) and "新型冠状病毒" (novel coronavirus) are also entities in the KG. In previous works, MC-BERT [36] only masks the complete entity, neglecting the fine-grained information of the sub-entities.

iii) **Misunderstanding of Long Entities:** Besides the above characteristics, there are also strong semantic relations among those sub-entities. Existing open-domain PLMs [31,36] do not consider the semantic relations between the core entities (named atomic terms) [21] and the entities other than the atomic terms in the long entities (named adjective terms). Refer to the example w.r.t. "糖尿病" (diabetes) and "糖尿病酮酸" (diabetic ketoacidosis) in Table 1.

In this paper, we propose EMBERT, a pre-trained model for Chinese medical text mining[1]. EMBERT leverages three novel self-supervised tasks for pre-training that are utilized to model Chinese medical entities in fine grains:

- **Context-Entity Consistency Prediction**: In the medical knowledge graph[2], we leverage the relation *"SameAs"* to build a thesaurus and replace terms with their synonyms in the corpus to generate more training samples. For each sample, we promote our model to predict whether the entities for replacing are consistent with its context.
- **Entity Segmentation:** We segment long entities by our rule-based system and label the resulting sub-entities contained in the entity. Then, our model is trained to predict sub-entities with labels mentioned above as ground-truth.
- **Bidirectional Entity Masking:** For each long entity, we merge the sub-entities into an adjective term and an atomic term. Meanwhile, we propose a bidirectional masking strategy to capture internal semantic relations within the long entity. We mask the adjective term and predict it based on the representation of atomic terms and vice versa.

In the experiments, we choose BERT-base [9], BERT-wwm [6], RoBERTa [23], ERNIE [38], MC-BERT [36] as the baseline models and apply our model to six Chinese medical datasets to evaluate its performance. The results shows that EMBERT achieves significant improvement compared to strong baselines on all six datasets. In summary, our work contributions are as follows:

- We propose a novel Chinese medical PLM by modeling the distinct characteristics of medical terms, which is named EMBERT.
- Three self-supervised learning tasks are introduced to capture the semantic relations at the entity level, including context-entity consistency prediction, entity segmentation and bidirectional entity masking.
- Experimental results on six Chinese medical text mining datasets show that our model achieves significant improvement over strong baselines.

The rest of this paper is organized as follows. Section 2 summarizes the related work on PLMs. Details of our approach for Chinese medical text mining are

---

[1] "EMBERT" refers to Entity-rich Medical BERT.
[2] http://www.openkg.cn/.

described in Sect. 3. Implementation detailed and experimental results are presented in Sect. 4. Finally, We summarize our paper and discuss the future work in Sect. 5.

2 Related Work

We overview the related work on open-domain and domain-specific PLMs.

2.1 Pre-trained Language Models in the Open Domain

As discovered, the meaning of a word depends on the context [2,8,29]. Hence, several PLMs have been proposed to learn context-aware word distributed representations. ELMo [26] is proposed to extract context-sensitive features leveraging bidirectional long short-term memory networks (LSTMs) [13]. However, feature-based language models such as ELMo only produce token representations that serve as basic input features, rather than acting as a backbone encoder. Recently, a two-stage training paradigm, namely pre-training and fine-tuning, is proposed to train models on large-scale corpora to learn general syntactic and semantic knowledge. Next, the models are fine-tuned on downstream tasks. SA-LSTMs [7] is proposed to train auto-encoders by LSTM, achieving a more stable training process and generalizing better. OpenAI GPT [27] utilizes multiple transformer decoder layers [32], and learns contextualized token representations by unidirectional auto-regressive language model objective. BERT [9] (as well as its robustly optimized version RoBERTa [23]) is trained based on bidirectional transformer architecture by two novel self-supervised tasks, including mask language modeling (MLM) and next sentence prediction (NSP). Following BERT, a large number of PLMs have been proposed to further improve performance in various NLP tasks, leveraging the following three techniques, such as self-supervised pre-training (Baidu-ERNIE [31] and spanBERT [18]), encoder architectures (XLNet [35]) and multi-task learning (MT-DNN [22]).

2.2 Pre-trained Language Models in Medical Domain

Developing PLMs in the medical domain has been a hot topic recently. To the best of our knowledge, BioBERT [20] is the first work that preforms continuous pre-training on a biomedical domain corpora (PubMed abstracts and PMC full-text articles) based on BERT in English. BlueBERT [25] is pre-trained on PubMed abstracts and MIMIC-III clinical notes and evaluated on the Biomedical Language Understanding Evaluation (BLUE) benchmark. ClinicalBert [15] utilizes the clinical notes including lab values and medications instead of plaintext data based on BERT. Meanwhile, PubMedBERT [10] learns model weights from scratch by large-scale training corpus and argues that the key point of training domain-specific PLMs is learning from scratch, which can obtain an in-domain vocabulary, alleviating the out-of-vocabulary (OOV) problem. Yet there are very few works on Chinese medical PLM, mainly due to the limitations of data resources. The work MC-BERT [36] proposes the entity masking

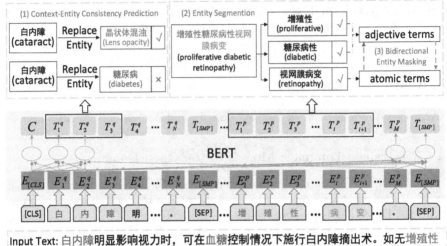

Fig. 1. Model overview. EMBERT incorporates three novel self-supervised pre-training tasks: context-entity consistency prediction, entity segmentation and bidirectional entity masking. Contents in brackets refer to English translations. (Best viewed in color.) (Color figure online)

and phrase masking mechanisms in a coarse-grained aspect to learn the medical word representations from a medical corpora while neglects the internal relations of medical entities. In this paper, we propose three novel self-supervised tasks in fine-grained entity-level aspects to further enhance the understanding of Chinese medical texts.

3   The EMBERT Model

In this section, we formally present EMBERT, a self-supervised PLM for Chinese medical text mining. We first introduce three novel pre-training tasks, namely context-entity consistency prediction, entity segmentation and entity bidirectional masking. Finally, we give the whole training loss of EMBERT. Figure 1 illustrates our model architecture.

3.1   Context-Entity Consistency Prediction

In Chinese medical knowledge graphs, there is a kind of relation "SameAs", meaning that two entities refer to the same concept, such as "白内障" (cataract) and "晶状体混浊" (phacoscotasmus). We build a thesaurus leveraging the relations mentioned above and replace a target entity with its synonym or a randomly selected entity, increasing the training samples simultaneously. In this task, we promote our model to predict whether the given entity is consistent with its context. If an entity is replaced with its synonym, the meaning would still be consistent. Formally, we denote the output token representations of the PLM by $\mathbf{x_1}, \cdots, \mathbf{x_n}$. The output tokens of the i-th replaced entity are $x_{s_i}, \cdots, x_{e_i}$, where (s_i, e_i) means the starting position and the ending position of the entity. Particularly, we predict the consistency of the entity with its context as c_i using the output context-aware encodings of its boundary token $\mathbf{x}_{s_i-1}$ and $\mathbf{x}_{e_i+1}$ as $\mathbf{y}_i$:

$$\mathbf{y}_i = f\left(\mathbf{x}_{s_i-1}, \mathbf{x}_{e_i+1}\right) \tag{1}$$

We implement the representation function $f_c(\cdot)$ as a 1-layer feed-forward network with the GeLU activate function [12] and layer normalization [3].

$$\mathbf{h}_i = [\mathbf{x}_{s_i-1}; \mathbf{x}_{e_i+1}]$$
$$\mathbf{y}_i = \mathrm{LayerNorm}\left(\mathrm{GeLU}\left(\mathbf{W}_1\mathbf{h}_i\right)\right) \tag{2}$$

where $\mathbf{W}_1$ is the trainable matrix. We then utilize the vector representation $\mathbf{y}_i$ to predict c_i. The loss function of this task (denoted as $\mathcal{L}_{eccp}$) is shown as follows:

$$\mathbf{p}_\theta(c_i \mid \mathbf{y_i}) = \mathrm{SoftMax}(\mathbf{W}_2\mathbf{y}_i)$$
$$\mathcal{L}_{eccp} = -\frac{\sum_{i=1}^N m_i \log \mathbf{p}_\theta\left(c_i \mid \mathbf{y_i}\right)}{N} \tag{3}$$

where $\mathbf{W}_2$ is the trainable matrix, m_i is the ground-truth label (consistent or inconsistent) and N is the total number of entities.

3.2 Entity Segmentation

As long entities usually have complicated semantic meanings, in this task, we promote the model to segment the entities into semantic parts. The ground-truth labels are given by our rule-based system depicted in the Appendix.

In practice, the model is asked whether the given position t is the end of a sub-entity or not, and the prediction from the model is marked as s_t. Formally, given the i-th nested entity $x_{s_i}, \cdots, x_{e_i}$, we further split it into j-th fine-grained sub-entities $x_{s_{ij}}, \cdots, x_{e_{ij}}$. As the last tokens of sub-entities are the split positions, we label $x_{e_{ij}}$ as positive, with the rest of the tokens in the entities labeled as negative. Tokens in the non-entity part of the sentence are ignored. We implement the token representation $\mathbf{y_t}$ and the loss of this task similar to token-level masked language modeling while we only have two categories for the model to predict:

$$\mathbf{y_t} = \tanh\left(\mathbf{W}_3\mathrm{LayerNorm}\left(\mathrm{GeLU}\left(\mathbf{W}_4\mathbf{x_t}\right)\right) + \mathbf{b}\right)$$
$$\mathbf{p}_\theta(s_t \mid \mathbf{y_i}) = \mathrm{SoftMax}(\mathbf{W}_5\mathbf{y_t}) \tag{4}$$

where the matrices $\mathbf{W}_3, \mathbf{W}_4$ and $\mathbf{W}_5$ are initialized randomly. The loss function of entity segmentation $\mathcal{L}_{est}$ is as follows:

$$\mathcal{L}_{est} = -\sum_{i=1}^N m_t \log \mathbf{p}_\theta\left(s_t \mid \mathbf{y_t}\right) \tag{5}$$

where m_t is the ground-truth label and N is the length of the sentence.

3.3   Bidirectional Entity Masking

We observe that long entities can be further divided into two parts: adjective terms and atomic terms. In this task, we mask one of the components and predict it based on the other and vice versa. Hence, the bidirectional masking strategy can model the relationship between semantic units in long entities.

Formally, we denote the adjective term as $x_{s_{adj_i}}, \cdots, x_{e_{adj_i}}$ and the atomic term as $x_{s_{ato_i}}, \cdots, x_{e_{ato_i}}$. We take the case of masking the atomic term as an example. We represent the token in the atomic term utilizing the output hidden state vector $\mathbf{x}_{s_{adj_i}}, \mathbf{x}_{e_{adj_i}}$, as well as the relative position embedding $\mathbf{p}_{j-s_{ato_i}}$ of the target token:

$$\mathbf{y}_j = f_b\left(\mathbf{x}_{s_{adj_i}}, \mathbf{x}_{e_{adj_i}}, \mathbf{p}_{j-s_{ato_i}}\right) \tag{6}$$

The representation function $f_b(\cdot)$ is 2-layer feed-forward network with GeLU and layer normalization similar to spanBERT [18]:

$$\begin{aligned}
\mathbf{h}_j^0 &= \left[\mathbf{x}_{s_{adj_i}}; \mathbf{x}_{e_{adj_i}}; \mathbf{p}_{j-s_{adj_i}}\right] \\
\mathbf{h}_j^1 &= \text{LayerNorm}\left(\text{GeLU}\left(\mathbf{W}_6\mathbf{h}_j^0\right)\right) \\
\mathbf{y}_j &= \text{LayerNorm}\left(\text{GeLU}\left(\mathbf{W}_7\mathbf{h}_j^1\right)\right)
\end{aligned} \tag{7}$$

We use the vector representation $\mathbf{y}_j$ to predict the token x_j and compute the cross-entropy loss $\mathcal{L}_{bem}^{ato_i}$ for the i-th entity similar to MLM:

$$\begin{aligned}
\mathbf{p}_\theta(x_j \mid \mathbf{y}_j) &= \frac{\exp(\mathbf{y}_j \cdot \mathbf{w}_j)}{\sum_{k=1}^K \exp(\mathbf{y}_j \cdot \mathbf{w}_k)} \\
\mathcal{L}_{bem}^{ato_i} &= -\sum_{j=s_{ato_i}}^{e_{ato_i}} m_j \log \mathbf{p}_\theta\left(x_j \mid \mathbf{y}_j\right)
\end{aligned} \tag{8}$$

where K is the size of the vocabulary and $\mathbf{w}_j$ is the representation of the embedding layer of the true token in the position j in the original sentence.

Those $\mathcal{L}_{bem}^{ato_i}$ sum to $\mathcal{L}_{bem}^{ato}$. Similarly, We acquire $\mathcal{L}_{bem}^{adj}$ for predicating the adjective term and the loss of this task $\mathcal{L}_{bem}$ is the sum of the two mentioned loss functions, i.e.,

$$\mathcal{L}_{bem} = \mathcal{L}_{bem}^{ato} + \mathcal{L}_{bem}^{adj} \tag{9}$$

3.4   Overll Loss Function

In summary, the total loss of EMBERT is the sum of four losses:

$$\mathcal{L}_{total} = \mathcal{L}_{ex} + \lambda_1\mathcal{L}_{cecp} + \lambda_2\mathcal{L}_{est} + \lambda_3\mathcal{L}_{bem} \tag{10}$$

where $\mathcal{L}_{ex}$ is the existing loss function used in BERT [9]. λ_1, λ_2 and λ_3 are the hyper-parameters in this model.

Table 2. The statistical data and metrics of the six datasets.

Dataset	Train	Dev	Test	Task	Metric
cNNER *	12000	3000	5000	Nested-NER	F1
cMedQANER [36]	1,673	175	215	NER	F1
cMedQQ [36]	16,071	1,793	1,935	PI	F1
cMedQNLI [36]	80,950	9,065	9,969	NLI	F1
cMedQA [37]	186,771	46,600	46,600	QA	ACC@1
WebMedQA [11]	252,850	31,605	31,655	QA	ACC@1

* cNNER is the Chinese Nested Named Entity Recognition task released in CHIP 2020. (http://cips-chip.org.cn/2020/eval1)

4 Experiments

In this section, we conduct extensive experiments to evaluate the performance of EMBERT over multiple datasets. We also compare EMBERT with strong baselines to show its superiority for Chinese medical text mining.

4.1 Experimental Settings

The pre-training data used in EMBERT is collected from the DXY community medical question answering data[3] and the DXY BBS data[4]. The total amount of data is 5 GB. The pre-processing of the pre-training corpus is similar to that of BERT [9]. For one document in the corpus, we use punctuation as the split symbol to generate text segments. We aggregate these text segments into raw training samples that are no longer than 512 tokens. Details on processing Chinese medical entities are further described in the Appendix.

The model configurations of all BERT-based models are the same as BERT-base[5]. We use a linear warmup schedule with a peak value of 5e-5 and the warmup proportion is 10% of the total training steps. The AdamW optimizer [19] is used with default parameters ($\beta_1 = 0.9, \beta_2 = 0.999, \epsilon = 1e-8$) and a decoupled weight decay of 0.01. Our implementation uses a batch size of 256 with a maximum length of 512. For the bidirectional entity masking task, we use 200-dimension positional embeddings. The hyper-parameters $\lambda_1, \lambda_2, \lambda_3$ of the pre-training loss are $2, 2, 0.5$[6] respectively. The pre-training process is run on a single RTX-Titan GPU and takes nearly ten days to complete.

---

[3] https://portal.dxy.cn/.
[4] https://www.dxy.cn/bbs/newweb/pc/home.
[5] https://huggingface.co/bert-base-chinese.
[6] In the experiment, we try several groups of hyper-parameters and find that the setting [2, 2, 0.5] performs well.

Table 3. Performance of the five baseline models and EMBERT on six datasets. ♣ and ♠ indicate EMBERT initialized by BERT-base and MC-BERT, respectively.

Model	Dataset					
	cMedQQ	cMedNLI	cMedQANER	cNNER	cMedQA	WebMedQA
MC-BERT	87.16	96.36	83.99	66.61	74.46	80.54
ERNIE-THU	87.03	96.04	84.43	66.87	74.13	79.96
BERT-wwm	86.82	96.08	83.12	66.59	72.96	79.68
RoBERTa	86.97	96.11	83.29	66.72	73.18	79.57
BERT-base	86.72	96.06	83.07	66.46	73.82	79.72
EMBERT♣	87.59	96.50	84.49	67.07	75.10	80.51
EMBERT♠	**88.06**	**96.59**	**85.02**	**67.22**	**75.32**	**80.63**

4.2 Baseline Models and Downstream Task Datasets

In our experiments, we choose five strong PLMs as our baselines. I) BERT-base [9] is the PLM trained by two self-supervised tasks, including MLM (Masked Language Model) and NSP (Next Sentence Prediction). II) BERT-wwm [6] explicitly forces the model to recover the whole word in pre-training tasks, which is much more challenging. III) RoBERTa [23] changes the model hyper-parameters, training strategies, and the corpus, with the BERT model re-trained. IV) MC-BERT [36] proposes the entity masking and phrase masking self-supervised tasks in the Chinese medical domain. V) ERNIE [36] infuses knowledge graph embedding generated by TransE algorithm into BERT layer, thus equipping BERT with structural knowledge of KG. Note that we generate TransE embedding with our KG and pre-train ERNIE with the same setting of EMBERT.

Our experimental datasets include the following six datasets, involving two Named Entity Recognition (NER) tasks, two Question Answering (QA) tasks, one Natural Language Inference (NLI) task and one Paraphrase Identification (PI) task. The dataset statistical results are shown in Table 2. Note that cMedQANER, cMedQQ, cMedQNLI and cMedQA are from ChineseBLUE[7]. The cMedQANER dataset is labeled from the Chinese community question answering dataset. Each cMedQQ sample contains a question pair with the task of predicting whether the two sentences are similar. Both cMedQNLI and cMedQA consist of question-answer pairs from BBS. The cNNER dataset is from the Chinese medical NER evaluation of CHIP 2020. WebMedQA is a real-world Chinese medical question answering dataset collected from online health consultancy websites [11].

---

[7] https://github.com/alibaba-research/ChineseBLUE. We do not include other datasets in our experiments due to their small sizes.

4.3   Overall Model Results

Table 3 shows the performance of EMBERT and the baselines on each dataset. Compared with general-domain PLMs, MC-BERT and EMBERT achieve much larger improvement, which demonstrates that it is essential to perform close-domain pre-training for obtaining promising results. Also, it can be seen that EMBERT achieves notable improvement pre-trained from both BERT-base and MC-BERT, demonstrating the effectiveness of our model and suggests EMBERT boosts performance in a different way from MC-BERT. Besides, although EMBERT uses a much smaller training corpus, our model outperforms MC-BERT significantly on most datasets. The only exception is WebMedQA (EMBERT 80.51% vs MC-BERT 80.54% on ACC@1). We suggest that is because the texts of the dataset are more similar to the corpus used by MC-BERT.

4.4   Ablation Studies

To evaluate the effects of three important components in our model, we remove them and test our model on four datasets, respectively. Since MC-BERT uses BERT-base as the starting point of pre-training, we also evaluate EMBERT from BERT-base rather than MC-BERT to avoid the influence of MC-BERT. The experimental results are summarized in Table 4.

As we can see, the performance of EMBERT drops greatly when we remove any components from our model. This phenomenon suggests that our pre-training methods are beneficial across a variety of tasks. On the two NER datasets, the effect of *Entity Segmentation* plays a major role in performance improvement, and we conjecture that it is because this mechanism injects entity boundary information into the model, which is critical for the NER task.

For cMedQQ, most of the performance degradation is caused by removing the *Context-Entity Consistent Prediction* task (–0.37% on F1). Note that the questions in this task are relatively short, and the contexts of words are relatively incomplete. Therefore, the ability to match keywords with possibly different surface forms between question pairs is highly important. On the other hand, since our model learns lots of synonyms with the aforementioned mechanism, it is reasonable to achieve a notable improvement.

The *Bidirectional Entity Masking* mechanism improves the performance of the cMedQA task performance significantly. We manually check 100 samples where EMBERT predicts the right answers and EMBERT without bidirectional entity masking does not. According to our observation, the EMBERT without the mechanism often makes mistakes because parts of the long entities are often treated as normal words, while the complete EMBERT does not as it can understand the long entities better as we expect.

4.5   Analysis of Attention Weight Distributions

In our EMBERT model, we propose three pre-training mechanisms to capture semantic relations between and inside Chinese medical entities. To further verify

Table 4. Ablation studies on four datasets.

Model	Dataset			
	cMedQQ	cMedQANER	cMedQA	cNNER
EMBERT♠	**88.06**	**85.02**	**75.32**	**67.22**
EMBERT♣	87.59	84.49	75.10	67.07
MC-BERT	87.16	83.99	74.46	66.61
w/o entity consistency	**87.22** | −0.37 ↓	84.22	74.68	66.84
w/o bidirectional mask	87.43	84.28	**74.25**| −0.85↓	67.03
w/o entity segmentation	87.54	**84.14**| −0.35↓	74.89	**66.71**| −0.36↓
w/o all above	87.02	83.76	74.03	66.48

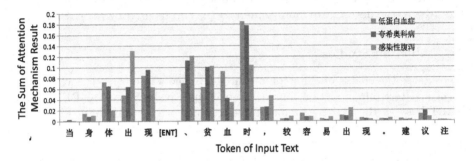

Fig. 2. The sum of attention weights of each token to "[ENT]" from the intermediate layer of EMBERT. "[ENT]" refers to three types of entity. "低蛋白血症" (hypoproteinemia) and "夸希奥科病" (kwashiorkor) are the synonymous entities. "感染性腹泻" (gastroenteritis) is an entity randomly selected from the Chinese medical knowledge graph. Due to the limitation of the page width, we only show 20 tokens in the sentence.

the effect of our mechanisms, we perform two additional intrinsic experiments as described below.

Attention Weight Similarity. We hypothesize that an entity should have a similar influence on the attention weight to the context with its synonym than that of a randomly selected entity. Therefore, we take a sentence from our pre-training corpus an entity "低蛋白血症" (hypoproteinemia), and then replace the entity with its synonymous term and a randomly selected entity respectively as an example in Fig. 2. The resulting three sentences are the same anywhere except on the position of the replaced entity. We feed the three sentences into EMBERT separately and take out the attention matrix at layer 11. The attention from the positions of the replaced entity to other positions in the sentences is summed for each sentence. We can easily tell that the attention weights of the entity "低蛋白血症" (hypoproteinemia) are much more similar to the attention weights of the synonym "夸希奥克病" (hypoproteinemia), which has a very different surface form than that of the randomly selected entity "感染性腹泻" (gastroenteritis).

Attention Weights Heat Map. In addition, we analyze the effect of mechanisms on long entities in our model. Figure 3 illustrates the self-attention token weights in BERT-base and EMBERT. Each row values are attention weights from the corresponding token to all tokens, which sum to one. The darker the colors of the squares in the figure, the greater the similarity between the tokens learned by the model. In this example, "再生障碍性贫血" (aplastic anemia) is a long entity and "丙肝" (HCV) is a short entity in Chinese. It can be seen from Fig. 3 that EMBERT pays the *most* attention to other tokens within the same entity while the attention weights of BERT are *scattered* over all tokens (see Fig. 3 blue line of dashes). Hence, EMBERT represents entities in sentences much better than BERT. Meanwhile, we also find that tokens in adjective terms attend to atomic terms in EMBERT much more than those in BERT, such as "贫血" (anemia) in "再生障碍性贫血" (aplastic anemia).

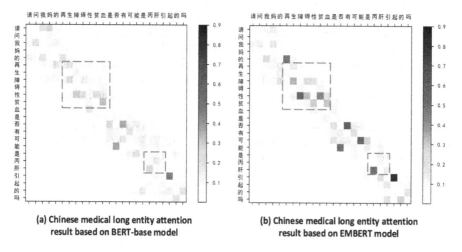

(a) Chinese medical long entity attention result based on BERT-base model

(b) Chinese medical long entity attention result based on EMBERT model

Fig. 3. Chinese long entity attention weights sum based on different pre-trained language models from all heads at layer 10. The blue line of dashes illustrate the self-attention weights of some important Chinese entities in the sentence. (Color figure online)

Table 5. Results on Chinese medical tasks with different corruption rates.

Corruption rate	cMedQQ	cMedQANER	cMedQA	cNNER
7.5%	87.49	84.80	74.89	66.93
15%	**88.06**	85.02	**75.32**	67.22
25%	87.80	**85.28**	75.11	**67.28**

4.6   Varying the Corruption Rate

In this section, we discuss the impact of different corruption rates. We pre-train EMBERT with different corruption rates and test them on four datasets across three tasks. The results are summarized in Table 5. In general, we find that the corruption rates have a limited effect, which is consistent with previous work [28]. The only exception is that NER tasks have maintained a steady improvement with the corruption rate increases, and we hypothesize that it is because the model has more chances to learn boundary information on a large-scale corpus. However, a larger corruption rate does degrade performances on other tasks. In order to keep a balance of the performances of EMBERT on a variety of tasks, we use a corruption rate of 15% as default.

5   Conclusion and Future Work

In this paper, we propose a large-scale PLM for Chinese medical text mining, namely EMBERT. Specifically, EMBERT captures internal and external entity-level semantic relations by three self-supervised tasks. As a result, our model achieves significant improvement over five strong baselines on six Chinese medical text mining datasets. Note that it is possible to further expand our method for other languages while overcoming the differences in language characteristics and the lack of resources. In the future, we will try to gather texts from different sources for evaluating the effect of EMBERT in more fine-grained domains.

Acknowledgements. This work is supported by the National Key Research and Development Program of China under Grant No. 2016YFB1000904. We thank the anonymous reviewers for their careful reading and insightful comments on our manuscript.

Appendix

Entity Segmentation. To segment long entities, we first build an entity vocabulary with a cut-point set. Similar to MC-BERT, we leverage AutoPhrase [17] to harvest a set of high-quality entities in the medical domain from the training corpus. Those entities combined with entities in the KG form the final entities vocabulary. Meanwhile, we utilize the segmentation model generated by AutoPhrase to create primitive segmentation results of entities. Next, we calculate the frequency of the characters at the start or the end of each segment. The characters with the top-100 frequency are manually checked and can be used as hints of segmentation, which are selected to form the cut-point set.

Long and Short Entity Detection. Initially, we choose entities in the vocabulary that are longer than three characters as long entity candidates. For the other entities, we regard them as short entities and use them as user-defined dictionary for Jieba[8], a popular Chinese word segmentation tool. For each long entity candidate, we first split at the positions of characters in the cut-point set, then feed each split part into Jieba, and combine all the return values to get intermediate segmentation results for the long entity candidate. Additionally, for long entities candidates being cut into too many single characters, we treat them as errors, and use the segmentation model from AutoPhrase to correct the segmentation results of those long entities candidates. Finally, if a long entities candidate can not be segmented into any smaller pieces, we regard it as a short entity. The remaining long entity candidates are treated as true long entities.

References

1. Alyafeai, Z., AlShaibani, M.S., Ahmad, I.: A survey on transfer learning in natural language processing. CoRR arXiv:2007.04239 (2020)
2. Apresjan, J.D.: Regular polysemy. Linguistics **12**(142), 5–32 (1974)
3. Ba, J.L., Kiros, J.R., Hinton, G.E.: Layer normalization. arXiv:1607.06450 (2016)
4. Baumann, A.: Multilingual language models for named entity recognition in German and English. In: RANLP, pp. 21–27 (2019)
5. Chronopoulou, A., Baziotis, C., Potamianos, A.: An embarrassingly simple approach for transfer learning from pretrained language models. In: NAACL, pp. 2089–2095 (2019)
6. Cui, Y., et al.: Pre-training with whole word masking for chinese BERT. CoRR arXiv:1906.08101 (2019)
7. Dai, A.M., Le, Q.V.: Semi-supervised sequence learning. In: NIPS, pp. 3079–3087 (2015)
8. Deane, P.D.: Polysemy and cognition. Lingua **75**(4), 325–361 (1988)
9. Devlin, J., Chang, M., Lee, K., Toutanova, K.: BERT: pre-training of deep bidirectional transformers for language understanding. In: NAACL-HLT, pp. 4171–4186 (2019)
10. Gu, Y., et al.: Domain-specific language model pretraining for biomedical natural language processing. CoRR arXiv:2007.15779 (2020)
11. He, J., Fu, M., Tu, M.: Applying deep matching networks to Chinese medical question answering: A study and a dataset. BMC Med. Inf. Decis. Making **19**(2), 91–100 (2019)
12. Hendrycks, D., Gimpel, K.: Gaussian error linear units (gelus). arXiv:1606.08415 (2016)
13. Hochreiter, S., Schmidhuber, J.: Long short-term memory. Neural Comput. **9**(8), 1735–1780 (1997)
14. Hosseini, P., Hosseini, P., Broniatowski, D.A.: Content analysis of Persian/Farsi tweets during COVID-19 pandemic in Iran using NLP. CoRR arXiv:2005.08400 (2020)
15. Huang, K., Altosaar, J., Ranganath, R.: Clinicalbert: modeling clinical notes and predicting hospital readmission. arXiv preprint arXiv:1904.05342 (2019)
16. Jiang, Z., El-Jaroudi, A., Hartmann, W., Karakos, D.G., Zhao, L.: Cross-lingual information retrieval with BERT. In: CLSSTS@LREC, pp. 26–31 (2020)

---

[8] https://github.com/fxsjy/jieba

17. Shang, J., Liu, J., Jiang, M., Ren, X., Voss, C.R., Han, J.: Automated phrase mining from massive text corpora. IEEE Trans. Knowl. Data Eng. **30**(10), 1825–1837 (2018)

18. Joshi, M., Chen, D., Liu, Y., Weld, D.S., Zettlemoyer, L., Levy, O.: Spanbert: improving pre-training by representing and predicting spans. Comput. Linguist. **8**, 64–77 (2020)

19. Kingma, D.P., Ba, J.: Adam: a method for stochastic optimization. arXiv:1412.6980 (2014)

20. Lee, J., et al.: Biobert: a pre-trained biomedical language representation model for biomedical text mining. Bioinformatics **36**(4), 1234–1240 (2020)

21. Liu, Q., Wu, L., Yang, Z., Liu, Y.: Domain phrase identification using atomic word formation in Chinese text. Knowl. Based Syst. **24**(8), 1254–1260 (2011)

22. Liu, X., He, P., Chen, W., Gao, J.: Multi-task deep neural networks for natural language understanding. In: ACL, pp. 4487–4496 (2019)

23. Liu, Y., et al.: Roberta: a robustly optimized BERT pretraining approach. CoRR arXiv:1907.11692 (2019)

24. Liu, Z., Huang, D., Huang, K., Li, Z., Zhao, J.: Finbert: a pre-trained financial language representation model for financial text mining. In: IJCAI, pp. 4513–4519 (2020)

25. Peng, Y., Yan, S., Lu, Z.: Transfer learning in biomedical natural language processing: an evaluation of BERT and ELMo on ten benchmarking datasets. arXiv:1906.05474 (2019)

26. Peters, M.E., et al.: Deep contextualized word representations. In: NAACL, pp. 2227–2237 (2018)

27. Radford, A., Wu, J., Child, R., Luan, D., Amodei, D., Sutskever, I.: Language models are unsupervised multitask learners. OpenAI Blog **1**(8), 9 (2019)

28. Raffel, C., et al.: Exploring the limits of transfer learning with a unified text-to-text transformer. CoRR arXiv:1910.10683 (2019)

29. Ravin, Y., Leacock, C.: Polysemy: An Overview. Polysemy: Theoretical and Computational Approaches, pp. 1–29 (2000)

30. Sarker, A., Lakamana, S., Hogg-Bremer, W., Xie, A., Al-Garadi, M.A., Yang, Y.: Self-reported COVID-19 symptoms on Twitter: an analysis and a research resource. J. Am. Med. Inf. Assoc. **27**(8), 1310–1315 (2020)

31. Sun, Y., et al.: ERNIE: enhanced representation through knowledge integration. CoRR arXiv:1904.09223 (2019)

32. Vaswani, A., et al.: Attention is all you need. In: NIPS, pp. 5998–6008 (2017)

33. Xu, H., Liu, B., Shu, L., Yu, P.S.: BERT post-training for review reading comprehension and aspect-based sentiment analysis. In: NAACL, pp. 2324–2335 (2019)

34. Xu, S., Shen, X., Fukumoto, F., Li, J., Suzuki, Y., Nishizaki, H.: Paraphrase identification with lexical, syntactic and sentential encodings. Appl. Sci. **10**(12), 4144 (2020)

35. Yang, Z., Dai, Z., Yang, Y., Carbonell, J.G., Salakhutdinov, R., Le, Q.V.: Xlnet: generalized autoregressive pretraining for language understanding. In: NeurIPS, pp. 5754–5764 (2019)

36. Zhang, N., Jia, Q., Yin, K., Dong, L., Gao, F., Hua, N.: Conceptualized representation learning for Chinese biomedical text mining. In: WSDM 2020 HealthDay (2020)

37. Zhang, S., Zhang, X., Wang, H., Cheng, J., Li, P., Ding, Z.: Chinese medical question answer matching using end-to-end character-level multi-scale CNNs. Appl. Sci. **7**(8), 767 (2017)
38. Zhang, Z., Han, X., Liu, Z., Jiang, X., Sun, M., Liu, Q.: ERNIE: enhanced language representation with informative entities. In: ACL, pp. 1441–1451 (2019)
39. Zhang, Z., et al.: Semantics-aware BERT for language understanding. In: AAAI, pp. 9628–9635 (2020)

Self-supervised Learning for Semantic Sentence Matching with Dense Transformer Inference Network

Fengying Yu, Jianzong Wang$^{(\boxtimes)}$, Dewei Tao, Ning Cheng, and Jing Xiao

Ping An Technology (Shenzhen) Co., Ltd., Shenzhen, China

Abstract. Semantic sentence matching concerns predicting the relationship between a pair of natural language sentences. Recently, many methods based on interaction structure have been proposed, usually involving encoder, matching, and aggregation parts. Although some of them obtain impressive results, the simple encoder training from scratch cannot extract the global features of sentences effectively, and the transmission of information in the stacked network will cause certain loss. In this paper, we propose a Densely-connected Inference-Attention network (DCIA) to maximize the use of the feature from each layer of the network by dense connection mechanism and to get robust encoder by self-supervised learning (SSL) based on contrastive method, which can maximize the mutual information between global features and local features of input data. We have conducted experiments on Quora, MRPC, and SICK dataset, the experimental results show that our method owns competitive results on these dataset where we drive 89.13%, 78.1% and 87.7% accuracies respectively. In addition, the accuracy of DCIA with SSL will surpass the one of DCIA without SSL by about 2%.

Keywords: Semantic sentence matching · Self-supervised learning · Dense connection mechanism · Mutual information

1 Introduction

Semantic sentence matching (SSM) is a fundamental problem in natural language understanding, which needs to judge the relationship between two sentences. In paraphrase identification (PI), semantic sentence matching is used to identify whether two sentences have identical meaning or not. In natural language inference (NLI), a sentence matching model receives two sentences, namely *premise* and *hypothesis*, and is asked to determine the relationship between them from a set *entailment*, *contradiction* and *neutral*. Recently, the prevailing pattern addresses this task by either using Siamese Networks [2] or depending on Matching-Aggregation framework [27]. The former maps two sentences to the same vector space by stacked CNN or RNN making a decision based on two vectors. The later interacts two sentences during the representation part by attention mechanisms and aggregates all information to predict the relationship

© Springer Nature Switzerland AG 2021
L. H. U et al. (Eds.): APWeb-WAIM 2021, LNCS 12858, pp. 258–272, 2021.
https://doi.org/10.1007/978-3-030-85896-4_21

of sentences. No matter the Siamese Network or Matching-Aggregation framework, they all have a feature encoder made of CNN, RNN or SAN to get a vector sentence representation. However, the encoder trained from scratch cannot extract the high-quality features of sentences that truly represent the sentence and pays more attention to the local information of the sentence according to the training objective.

In order to improve the performance of the encoder, we apply self-supervised learning based on the contrastive method. A good encoder should be able to extract the unique representation belonging to this sentence, so as to distinguish it from other sentences. INFOMAX [8] maximizes the average mutual information between the global representation and local regions of the input to improve the representation's quality for classification task in the computer vision field, we designed an SSL task to introduce this idea into the field of natural language processing field. The final output of the multi-layer encoder is a global feature while the result of the middle layer is a local feature, which keeps the same idea with [8]. We believe the global and local features from the same sentence should be similar and labeled True, the other is the opposite. By maximizing mutual information, the encoder has strong representation quality and the ability to find the unique features of each sentence to help the downstream tasks.

Most of the recent work uses stack mechanisms to connect each layer causing information vanishment when the network deepens, even if using highway network [22] or residual connection [7]. Densenet [9] applies densely connectivity patterns on CNN and Densely-connected Recurrent networks [11] realize them on RNN. They all prove that dense mechanisms can work well on different network structures. Our model densely connects each inference-attention block which makes sure to maximum information flow from the start layer to the end. Original Transformer has already used the residual connection to solve the gradient vanishing problem. However, DCIA not only maintains the original Transformer's residual connection in each block but also introduces dense connection between adjacent blocks. After that, we also use global average logits (GAL) to further maximize the use of information in each layer of the network.

Besides using densely-connected mechanisms to connect each adjacent block, we also introduce an inference-attention block to model the semantic inference information between two sentences at every single layer. Previous work often uses interaction mechanisms after stacking several neural network blocks. For instance, BiMPM [28] matches two sentences in multiple perspectives after stacked Bi-LSTM. Our contributions are two-fold as follow:

- We design a self-supervised learning task based on the contrastive method, which can maximize the mutual information between global information and local information to get a more effective encoder.
- For the first time, our model applies a dense connection pattern with global average logits on the Transformer decoder like layer, which makes sure to maximize the use of each layer of information.

2 Related Work

2.1 Self-supervised Learning

Self-supervised learning has been successfully applied in many fields, such as natural language processing and computer vision [15]. In the field of natural language processing, there are many large pre-training models of Bert series [4], which not only refresh the records of many tasks, but also solve insufficiency problem of data annotation. However this large-scale pre-training model needs lots of training data and computational power. Recently, there is some SSL work in the vertical field, such as using SSL to extract summary [26] and applying SSL on speech recognition [20] and multi-language translation [21]. At the same time, there are SSL based on contrastive methods, like [8] hoping to learn a better encoder to represent the input data and [13] attempting to achieve commonsense reasoning. On the one hand, our work applies self-supervised learning to the task of SSM. On the other hand, by maximizing the mutual information between two sentence pairs in the encoder input and output, we can get an encoder which can better represent the original data information through self-supervised learning.

2.2 Semantic Sentence Matching

There are two main frameworks for Sentence Matching [14]: sentence encoding model and sentence pair interaction models. Most of the recent outstanding work use the sentence pair interaction models. In this framework, the encoder often uses CNN, RNN or SAN to extract the sentence distribution, such as DIIN [6] and RE2 [29], while they all train from scratch to extract the representation of sentence. Some work uses supervised learning [3] or multi-task learning [10] to get the representation of sentence, but they need lots of labeled data from different data set.

RNN models, like BiMPM [28] and ESIM [18], can get the long range dependency, but it cannot compute in parallel, so it needs more time on training step. Our model updates the Transformer [25] decoder which achieves good performance on the mechanical translation task, while the original transformer uses residual connection stack each block, which may impede information flow from start to end. Densenet [9] use densely connection mechanism to make sure the information directly connected at each layer. Densely-connected Recurrent models [11] use densely connection on recurrent network, and achieved state of the art performance on sentence matching task. The key part of sentence matching task is to find the semantic relation between a sentence pair. Also, deep attention networks [30] use cross-attention and self-attention to do the multi-turn response selection task. Even though this transformer based model is recurrent and convolution free, each block in their architecture connects each layer by using stack mechanism.

3   Our Approach

In this section, we give the definition of task and describe our network architecture in 4 parts: Encoding Block, Inference-attention Block, Densely-connected inference Block and global average logits. The overview of DCIA with self-supervised learning is shown in Fig. 2, the detail of Inference block is at Fig. 3. Figure 1 illustrates the training steps of our work combining with SSL. First, we construct sentence pairs without relationship by randomly pairing the sentences and take the features from the same sentence as positive samples and the features from different sentences as negative samples. Then, we use self-supervised learning to pre-train the encoder blocks. At last, we train the whole model with specific downstream tasks. The details will be introduced in the following sections.

Step1: construct unlabeled sentence pair data

Three men are playing in lake	several man are enjoying the water
women are standing	two women wearing red are standing
the man is driving a car	the man isn't driving a car
what is good soul	why is confession good for soul

Randomly Pairing

Three men are playing in lake	why is confession good for soul
women are standing	several man are enjoying the water
the man is driving a car	two women wearing red are standing
what is good soul	the man isn't driving a car

Step2: pre-train encoder block

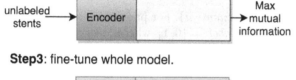

unlabeled stents → Encoder → Max mutual information

Step3: fine-tune whole model.

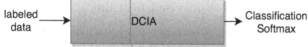

labeled data → DCIA → Classification Softmax

Fig. 1. Illustration of our proposed methods.

3.1   Task Definition

Semantic sentence matching can be represented as two parts: sentence pair and label. $P = (p_1, p_2, \ldots, p_{l_p})$ and $Q = (q_1, q_2, \ldots, q_{l_q})$ are used to denote the input sentence pair where p_i/q_j is the ith/j^{th} word of the sentence P/Q and l_p/l_q is the length of sentence P/Q. The *label* means the relationship of sentence pair which is task depended. Specifically, for a natural language inference task, P is a premise sentence, Q is a hypothesis sentence, and *label* =

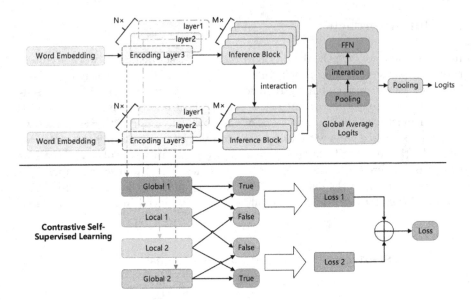

Fig. 2. The overview of Densely-connected Transformer. There are N layers of encoding part and M layers of Inference block. At SSL part, the output of last layer (layer 3 in figure) of encoder point to global feature, and the output of middle layer of encoder point to local features. While pre-training the Encoder, the global feature and the local feature from the same sentence are taken as positive sample and the global feature and the local feature from the different sentences are treated as negative sample.

$\{entailment, contradiction, neutral\}$. For paraphrase identification task, P and Q are two sentences, and $label = \{0, 1\}$ where $label = 0$ means P and Q are paraphrase, $label = 1$ otherwise.

3.2   Encoding with Self-supervised Learning

At Encoding Block, we stack N encoding blocks to capture the local and global feature of sentence. We consider that in the multi-layer stacked network, the local features are extracted from the low-level and the high-level extracts the global features. Encoding block is the same as the encoder of transformer, the output of multi-layer encoder is as follow:

$$\boldsymbol{y} = Multi\_layer(\boldsymbol{p}) \tag{1}$$

$\boldsymbol{p}$ is the input sentence, our goal is to maximize the mutual information between local feature and global feature of input sentence. The mutual information is represented as follow:

$$p(\boldsymbol{y}|\boldsymbol{x}) = max\ I(\boldsymbol{x};\ \boldsymbol{y}) \tag{2}$$

$\boldsymbol{y}$ represents the output of encoding block which is global feature of sentence $\boldsymbol{p}$, and $\boldsymbol{x}$ represents the output of middle layer which is local feature of sentence

p. The other sentence is the same. For a good encoder, it should be able to maximize the mutual information between global feature and the local feature. we use Jensen-Shannon divergence (JSD) to estimate the mutual information [8]:

$$max\ I(\boldsymbol{x};\ \boldsymbol{y}) = max(\mathbb{E}_{\boldsymbol{x}\sim p(\boldsymbol{y}|\boldsymbol{x})p(\boldsymbol{x})}[\log(\sigma(T(\boldsymbol{x},\boldsymbol{y})))]$$

$$+\mathbb{E}_{\boldsymbol{x}\sim p(\boldsymbol{y}|\boldsymbol{x})p(\boldsymbol{x}')}[\log\left(1 - \sigma(T(\boldsymbol{x}',\boldsymbol{y}))\right)]) \tag{3}$$

$$loss = -\ I(\boldsymbol{x};\ \boldsymbol{y}) \tag{4}$$

The function T in Eq. 3 represents a classifier, and $\boldsymbol{x}$, $\boldsymbol{y}$ are the local and global feature of same sentence, while the $\boldsymbol{x}'$ is the local feature of the other sentence. The input is a sentence pair, so there are two classifiers. As our goal is to maximize the mutual information, we let the loss be equal to the negative mutual information as Eq. 4. We derive two losses from the sentence pair and we add them up to get the final objective of this part. While pre-training the encoder, we take the global feature and local feature of a sentence as the positive sample and the global feature of a sentence and the local feature of the other sentence as the negative sample, which is shown in Fig. 2.

3.3   Inference-Attention Block

The inference-attention block is shown at Fig. 3.

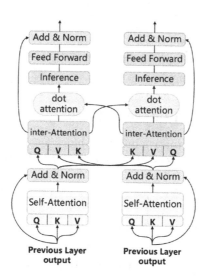

Fig. 3. Overview of inference block

Inference-attention block consists of 3 main sub-layers: multi-head self-attention layer, multi-head inter-attention layer and inference layer. The input of self-attention is from the same sentence, but one of the input is from another sentence for inter-attention. The function of self-attention function AF_{self} and inter-attention function AF_{inter} are at bellow.

$$AF_{self}(\boldsymbol{P}_q, \boldsymbol{P}_k, \boldsymbol{P}_v) = softmax(\frac{\boldsymbol{P}_q \boldsymbol{P}_k^T}{\sqrt{d_k}})\boldsymbol{P}_v \tag{5}$$

$$AF_{inter}(\boldsymbol{P}_q, \boldsymbol{Q}_k, \boldsymbol{Q}_v) = softmax(\frac{\boldsymbol{P}_q \boldsymbol{Q}_k^T}{\sqrt{d_k}})\boldsymbol{Q}_v \tag{6}$$

After a self-attention with residual add and layer normalization, an inter-attention layer is used to get the information of other sentence. The output of two inter-attention referred as $\boldsymbol{x}_i$ and $\boldsymbol{y}_j$ where i, j is the length of sentence, then the inference information $\boldsymbol{\alpha}_i$ and $\boldsymbol{\beta}_j$ are the weighted summation of $\boldsymbol{x}_i$ and $\boldsymbol{y}_j$. The attention weight a_{ij} is calculated by $\boldsymbol{x}_i$ and $\boldsymbol{y}_j$ with dot product attention. Then we get $\boldsymbol{enx}$ by concatenating $\boldsymbol{x}_i$, the difference and the element-wise product of $\boldsymbol{x}_i$ and $\boldsymbol{\alpha}_i$, which attempts to collect various semantic information from different aspects. After going through a feed forward network (FFN) with ReLU activation function to reduce the dimension, inference information is concatenated with the output of inter-attention. Finally we apply Layer Normalization (LN) to get the output of this block, the equation for $output_p$ is as follow, $output_q$ is same:

$$
\begin{aligned}
output_p &= LN([Relu(FFN_0(\boldsymbol{enx})); \boldsymbol{x}_i]) \\
FFN_0(\boldsymbol{x}) &= \boldsymbol{W}_0\boldsymbol{x} + \boldsymbol{b}_0 \\
\boldsymbol{enx} &= [\boldsymbol{x}_i; \boldsymbol{x}_i - \boldsymbol{\alpha}_i; \boldsymbol{x}_i \odot \boldsymbol{\alpha}_i] \\
\boldsymbol{\alpha}_i &= \sum_{j=1}^{l_q} \frac{exp(a_{ij})}{\sum_{k=1}^{l_q} exp(a_{ik})} \boldsymbol{y}_j \\
a_{ij} &= \boldsymbol{x}_i \boldsymbol{y}_j^T
\end{aligned}
\tag{7}
$$

3.4 Densely-Connected Inference Block

This part describes an alternative inference block leveraging a dense connection pattern. The connected pattern of encoder block of DCIA is stack mechanism which can be described as follow:

$$
\begin{aligned}
\boldsymbol{b}_t &= Block_t(\boldsymbol{x}_t) \\
\boldsymbol{x}_t &= \boldsymbol{b}_{t-1}.
\end{aligned}
\tag{8}
$$

where $\boldsymbol{b}_t$ represents the output of the t-th block and $\boldsymbol{x}_t$ is the input, this is the original stack connection mechanism. The stack connection pattern can build up higher level representation. However, deeper network may cause gradient vanishing or exploding during training. Also, stack mechanism only uses the last layer complex information which may cause the lose of information at previous layers. The residual connection [18] solves the gradient vanishing or exploding problem and makes the gradient transfer better in the backward pass.

$$\boldsymbol{b}_t = Block_t(\boldsymbol{x}_t)$$
$$\boldsymbol{x}_t = \boldsymbol{b}_{t-1} + \boldsymbol{x}_{t-1}. \tag{9}$$

Depend on Eq. 9, residual connection directly adds the input to the output of the block in order to avoid the impede of gradient transfer. Even though residual connection solves some disadvantages of stack pattern, the add operation prevents the block directly getting the information from previous block. Inspired by Densenet [9], our model uses concatenation operation directly connected to adjacent block and uses a project operation to maintain the dimension of output at each block.

$$\boldsymbol{b}_t = Block_t(Project_1(\boldsymbol{x}_t)),$$
$$\boldsymbol{x}_t = [\boldsymbol{b}_{t-1}; \boldsymbol{x}_{t-1}], \tag{10}$$
$$Project_2(\boldsymbol{x}) = \boldsymbol{W}_1\boldsymbol{x} + \boldsymbol{b}_1.$$

where $\boldsymbol{W}_1 \in R^{2d \times d}$, $\boldsymbol{b}_1 \in R^d$. This part is not fully the same as the Densenet. Our method only uses concatenation operation to connect each layer with it's previous layer causing the huge dimensional growth. Autoencoder (AE) has been tried in our model as bottleneck component [11], but it does not perform well on our model. So DCIA only concatenates adjacent layer and use project operation to prevent the growth of dimension.

3.5   Global Average Logits

The Global Average Logits (GAL) receives the output from each layer of inference block. The Densely-connected inference block represents each sentence P and Q as $\boldsymbol{x}_i^k, where k \in \{P, Q\}$ and i is in range of M which is the number of layer of inference block. This part interacts with the results of each layer from inference block and calculates logits. It is does not only rely on the final output of inference block to make prediction but also considers the results of the middle layer. For example, in $\boldsymbol{z}_i$, we attempt to find various latent relationships between two sentence in different aspects like element-wise product and difference. Each layer's logits are obtained as follows:

$$logits_i = Project_3(\boldsymbol{z}_i),$$
$$\boldsymbol{z}_i = [\boldsymbol{enc}_p; \boldsymbol{enc}_q; \boldsymbol{enc}_p \odot \boldsymbol{enc}_q; |\boldsymbol{enc}_p - \boldsymbol{enc}_q|],$$
$$\boldsymbol{enc}_k = mean(\boldsymbol{y}^k), \tag{11}$$
$$\boldsymbol{y}^k = Inference\_Layer_i(\boldsymbol{x}^k).$$

where $mean$ represents calculating the average. After getting the results of each layer, we can get the final logits through average pooling mechanism. Finally, a softmax function is used to obtain a probability of each class. Also, the objective function is to minimize the following cross entropy:

$$loss = -\sum_{i=1}^{N}[y_i \log prob_i + (1 - y_i)\log(1 - prob_i)] \tag{12}$$

where the y_i represents the ground truth label.

4   Experiments and Analysis

In this section, we verify each part of the model and analysis the effect of each component on Quora. The ablation experiments established on dense connection which shows that it is effective and performs much better than other connective pattern. Also, we compare the performance of concatenating all previous layers with adjacent one. On MRPC dataset, we compare the effect before and after adding self-supervised learning to DCIA and other baseline model. Second part is the evaluation of our model on two tasks including paraphrase identification and natural language inference. For paraphrase identification, we use MRPC dataset to indicate whether the question is duplicated or not. For natural language inference task, we use SICK [1] to prove the inference ability of our model.

4.1   Implementation Details

We use 300-dimensional pre-trained $GloVe$ word embeddings [17], and fix during training step. We use random initial vector for OOV problem, and try CNN/LSTM char embedding for OOV word, but the performance has not been significantly improved, also it brought the increase of training time and number of the parameters. The multi-head attention layer uses $H = 3$ heads, $d_{model} = 300$ no matter inter-attention or self-attention, and hidden size of feed forward network use $h_{ff} = 256$. Also, the dropout rate used at each sub-layer is 0.2. We use Tensorflow to implement our model, and train model on single Nvidia V100 GPU. The best single model consists of $N = 3$ encoding block, $M = 3$ Densely-connected inference block, the batch size is 128. Also, The model is optimized using Adam optimizer with initial learning rate of 0.0001.

4.2   Effectiveness of Densely Connect and GAL

This section presents the results of experiments which reveals the effectiveness of dense connections on the Quora dataset. We compare three different connection patterns: traditional stacking method, residual connection and densely-connected method on infer-attention block of our model.

As we can see from Table 1, DCIA has a higher accuracy no matter compare with stack connect model or residual connect model which indicates that our method is more effective on connecting each block at this task. The comparison experiment of different type of bottleneck component which applies to reduce the dimension of parameter shows that simple feed forward network without activation function is better than Autoencoder (AE). We believe if the model uses AE as bottle component, then there ought to be two loss functions on our model: one is the loss function for AE and the other is the softmax cross entropy for classification, which may add up to the strong demand in data and difficulty

Table 1. Ablation of densely-connected on Quora dev set

Model	ACC
Stack-connected model	87.37
Residual-connected model	88.10
Densely-connected with AE	87.12
Densely-connected concat all pre-layer	87.50
DCIA w/GAP	88.13
DCIA w/single FFN	87.43
DCIA (Ours)	88.34

of training. Also, DCIA only concatenates the information from previous block, our experiment also tries to concatenate the information from all previous block. The result shows that concatenating all previous blocks hugely increases the number of parameters, but it does not improve the performance.

Then for the final information fusion part, we tried various ways, such like Global Average Pooling which averages the feature map of each layer at inference block and uses simple FFN to make the final predict. The experiment result shows that global average logits (GAL) is better than others which makes sufficient use of the information of each layer.

This experiment shows that the effectiveness of densely-connected part of our model performs better than stack-connected or residual-connected. And the contrasting experiment between AE and FFN shows that FFN is more suitable for our model to be the bottleneck component. Also, according to the accuracy, increment with the number of densely-connected layer further proves the effectiveness of dense connect mechanism.

4.3 Effectiveness of Inference-Attention

The inference-attention block is an important part of our model. The effectiveness of this block is shown by comparing with traditional transformer encoder block and decoder block. We also try it without inference part to verify the

Table 2. Effectiveness of inference-attention on Quora dev set

Model	ACC (%)
DCIA w/ transformer encoder	87.22
DCIA w/ transformer decoder	87.76
Infer-attention w/o inference	87.21
Infer-attention w/o inter-attention	88.19
Infer-attention w/o self-attention	88.30
DCIA (Ours)	88.34

functionality of this sub-layer and set inference part at different positions of inference-attention block. Then, we evaluate the effectiveness of inter-attention and self-attention in inference-attention block. The result is shown at Table 2.

Depending on the experiment result, if our model changes inference-attention block to transformer encoder, the accuracy decreases more than 1% and decreases almost 1% with transformer decoder, which shows that our inference-attention block indeed improves the model performance and acts much better than transformer encoder and decoder. Also, the ablation test on inference-attention shows that each part of inference-attention has its own affect, no matter whichever is removed and it will have impact on model performance. Also, after putting inference part at different position of inference-attention, the bottom of the block is the best position of this part. Based on the result of the experiment, this block is not like vanilla transformer encoder or decoder. Instead, it can extract semantic information of sentence and can model the inference relationship between a sentence pair as well.

4.4   Effectiveness of Self-supervised Learning

In order to verify the effectiveness of our self-supervised learning task, we combine this SSL task with other popular network structures. We build classic Siamese Network structure based on popular network CNN, LSTM and Transformer, they all use same FFN at final part to make prediction. Experimental results at Table 3 show that the performance of training from scratch is worse than using self-supervised learning to pre-train the encoder part of the model.

Table 3. Comparison results (ACC) of using SSL and not using SSL on MRPC test set

Model	W/o SSL (%)	W/SSL (%)
CNN	67.3	68.9
LSTM	67.9	69.3
Transformer	64.6	66.3
ESIM	71.0	73.4
DCIA (Ours)	76.7	78.1

Table 4. Experiment on the influence of labeled data on Model at MRPC test set

Method	Acc (1k)	Acc (2k)	Acc (full)
DCIA w/o SSL	43.5	51.2	76.7
DCIA	70.3	71.7	78.1

At the same time, according to the accuracy curve at Fig. 4, we can see that the model will converge faster after using SSL for pre-training. After using self-supervised learning, the model will perform well at the beginning and achieve the best performance faster. The Transformer_ori started with a low accuracy, we think this is because transformer is hard to train and needs more data.

The experiment also verifies the reduction of the demand for labeled data by self-supervised learning, the detail is at Table 4. The performance keeps growing when the amount of labeled training data increases. While using the self-supervised learning only uses 2000 pieces of data, the result is similar to that of

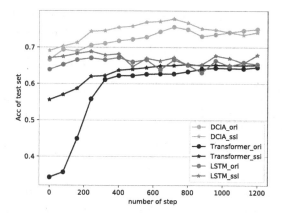

Fig. 4. The influence of self-supervised learning on the model convergence, ori indicates without SSL.

the model without SSL. The result shows that our self-supervised method are effective and reasonable, which can really capture more sentence information.

4.5 Experiments on Paraphrase Identification

For paraphrase identification task, we evaluate our model on "Quora Question Pairs" dataset with same split version of BiMPM [28]. Table 5 shows the result of our DCIA model on Quora dataset. The author of BiMPM reports the base line model L.D.C network, multi-perspective with LSTM (MP-LSTM), multi-perspective with CNN (MP-CNN). Also, we compare our model with the DIIN [6], RE2 [29] and self-attention network pt-DecAttchar.c on this task.

Table 5. Accuracy (%) on Quora dataset by single model without any external knowledge

Model	Test (%)
MP-CNN [28]	81.38
MP-LSTM [28]	83.21
L.D.C [28]	85.55
BiMPM [28]	88.17
pt-DecAttchar.c [24]	88.40
DIIN [6]	89.06
RE2 [29]	89.20
DCIA w/o SSL (Ours)	88.71
DCIA w/ SSL (Ours)	89.13

Table 6. Accuracy (%) on MRPC test set. * indicates replicated results with our reimplementation

Model	Test (%)
DiscSent [10]	72.5
InferSent [3]	76.2
Byte mLSTM [19]	75.0
GenSen [23]	78.6
ESIM* [18]	71.0
RE2* [29]	72.7
DCIA w/o SSL (Ours)	76.7
DCIA w/SSL (Ours)	78.1

The experimental results show the performance of DCIA with and without self supervised learning. Our model DCIA without SSL improves almost 7.5%

than MP-CNN and 5.5% than MP-LSTM, which illustrates DCIA performs better than traditional convolutional or recurrent network even without SSL. Also, we compare our model with pt-DecAttchar.c which is a self-attention network pretrained on a noisy dataset of automatically collected question paraphrases. The result shows that our original model has a higher accuracy on test set. On DINN and RE2, our original model has a little gap from them, but combined with SSL, the model outperforms DINN and is on the par with RE2. The experiment result on PI task with Quora dataset reveals the effectiveness of our original model and shows that SSL can further improve the performance for PI tasks.

Result on MRPC [5] is at Table 6. Compared to DiscSent, our model improves the performance by 4% in accuracy even without SSL. After the pre-training with SSL, there is only 0.5% gap between our results and GenSen. Gense and InferSent use data from multiple data sets to train sentence vectors, but our work does not use any external information. This dataset has fewer training data than Quora, so we decrease the number of block at each part of model on this dataset.

4.6   Experiments on Natural Language Inference

We evaluate our model on natural language inference task over SICK [16]. The experiment result shows that DCIA without SSL has performed better than many models training with external data. The accuracy report is at Table 7.

Table 7. Accuracy (%) on SICK test set by single model without any external knowledge. * indicates replicated results with our reimplementation

Model	Test (%)
Skipthought [12]	82.3
Illinois LH [10]	84.5
InferSent [3]	86.3
GenSen [23]	87.8
ESIM* [18]	83.2
RE2* [29]	85.5
BERT* [4]	87.7
DCIA w/o SSL (Ours)	85.3
DCIA w/ SSL (Ours)	87.7

GenSen [23] and InferSent [3] use multiple datasets to get sentence vectors by multi-task training, which has achieved good results in this task. Even though the original DCIA did not work as well as they did, there are 2.4% improvements through self-supervised learning on encoder part, which makes it exceed the previous model InferSent more than 1% and on the par of GenSen. Also, we reimplement ESIM [18] and RE2 [29] with Tensorflow and the accuracies of ESIM and RE2 are lower than DCIA with SSL. SICK dataset only has no more than 5000 training samples, so DCIA only needs a small amount of data to extract the information of sentence and avoid over fitting. In addition, we also attempt to implement BERT [4] on SICK dataset, which achieves the same accuracy as our model. However, BERT owns 110M parameters while our model only uses 4.3M ones and has fewer layers to encode and infer. Therefore, our model could use much less inference time than BERT. Besides, our model only depends on training dataset while BERT pre-trained with a large amount data, but we still derive a competitive result, which shows the strengths of our model.

5 Conclusion

In this paper, we propose DCIA network with self-supervised learning for semantic sentence matching task. By densely connecting each single block of inference attention for each layer in model, we get information without any changes from previous layers. Our work reveals that self-supervised learning is favorable in large-scale training data and can act well on small vertical fields. In the future, we hope to see more self-supervised learning applications in the vertical field.

Acknowledgements. This paper is supported by National Key Research and Development Program of China under grant No. 2018YFB0204403, No. 2017YFB1401202 and No. 2018YFB1003500. Corresponding author is Jianzong Wang from Ping An Technology (Shenzhen) Co., Ltd.

References

1. Bowman, S.R., Angeli, G., Potts, C., Manning, C.D.: A large annotated corpus for learning natural language inference. In: EMNLP (2015)
2. Bromley, J., Guyon, I., LeCun, Y., Säckinger, E., Shah, R.: Signature verification using a "Siamese" time delay neural network. In: NIPS (1993)
3. Conneau, A., Kiela, D., Schwenk, H., Barrault, L., Bordes, A.: Supervised learning of universal sentence representations from natural language inference data. In: EMNLP (2017)
4. Devlin, J., Chang, M.W., Lee, K., Toutanova, K.: BERT: pre-training of deep bidirectional transformers for language understanding. In: NAACL (2019)
5. Dolan, W., Brockett, C.: Automatically constructing a corpus of sentential paraphrases. In: IWP@IJCNLP (2005)
6. Gong, Y., Luo, H., Zhang, J.: Natural language inference over interaction space. In: ICLR (2017)
7. He, K., Zhang, X., Ren, S., Sun, J.: Deep residual learning for image recognition. In: CVPR (2016)
8. Hjelm, R.D., et al.: Learning deep representations by mutual information estimation and maximization. In: ICLR (2019)
9. Huang, G., Liu, Z., van der Maaten, L., Weinberger, K.Q.: Densely connected convolutional networks. In: CVPR (2017)

10. Jernite, Y., Bowman, S.R., Sontag, D.: Discourse-based objectives for fast unsupervised sentence representation learning. Computation and Language. arXiv:1705.00557 (2017)
11. Kim, S., Kang, I., Kwak, N.: Semantic sentence matching with densely-connected recurrent and co-attentive information. In: AAAI (2018)
12. Kiros, R., et al.: Skip-thought vectors. In: NIPS (2015)
13. Klein, T., Nabi, M.: Contrastive self-supervised learning for commonsense reasoning. In: ACL (2020)
14. Lan, W., Xu, W.: Neural network models for paraphrase identification, semantic textual similarity, natural language inference, and question answering. In: COLING (2018)
15. Liu, X., et al.: Self-supervised learning: Generative or contrastive. arXiv preprint arXiv:2006.08218 (2020)
16. Marelli, M., Menini, S., Baroni, M., Bentivogli, L., Bernardi, R., Zamparelli, R.: A sick cure for the evaluation of compositional distributional semantic models. In: LREC (2014)
17. Pennington, J., Socher, R., Manning, C.D.: Glove: Global vectors for word representation. In: EMNLP (2014)
18. Qian, C., Zhu, X., Ling, Z.H., Si, W., Inkpen, D.: Enhanced LSTM for natural language inference. In: ACL (2017)
19. Radford, A., Jozefowicz, R., Sutskever, I., A, B.: Learning to generate reviews and discovering sentiment. Machine Learning. arXiv:1704.01444 (2018)
20. Ravanelli, M., et al.: Multi-task self-supervised learning for robust speech recognition. In: ICASSP (2020)
21. Siddhant, A., et al.: Leveraging monolingual data with self-supervision for multilingual neural machine translation. In: ACL (2020)
22. Srivastava, R.K., Greff, K., Schmidhuber, J.: Training very deep networks. In: NIPS (2015)
23. Subramanian, S., Trischler, A., Bengio, Y., Pal, C.J.: Learning general purpose distributed sentence representations via large scale multi-task learning. In: ICLR (2018)
24. Tomar, G.S., Duque, T., Täckström, O., Uszkoreit, J., Das, D.: Neural paraphrase identification of questions with noisy pretraining. In: SWCN@EMNLP (2017)
25. Vaswani, A., et al.: Attention is all you need. In: NIPS (2017)
26. Wang, H., et al.: Self-supervised learning for contextualized extractive summarization. In: ACL (2019)
27. Wang, S., Jiang, J.: A compare-aggregate model for matching text sequences. In: ICLR (2016)
28. Wang, Z., Hamza, W., Florian, R.: Bilateral multi-perspective matching for natural language sentences. In: IJCAI (2017)
29. Yang, R., Zhang, J., Gao, X., Ji, F., Chen, H.: Simple and effective text matching with richer alignment features. In: ACL (2019)
30. Zhou, X., et al.: Multi-turn response selection for chatbots with deep attention matching network. In: ACL (2018)

An Explainable Evaluation of Unsupervised Transfer Learning for Parallel Sentences Mining

Shaolin Zhu[1], Chenggang Mi[2(✉)], and Xiayang Shi[1]

[1] Zhengzhou University of Light Industry, Zhengzhou 453000, China
[2] Northwestern Polytechnical University, Xi'an, China
michenggang@nwpu.edu.cn

Abstract. The parallel sentences are known as very important resources for training cross-lingual natural language process applications, such as machine translation (MT) systems. However, these resources are not available for many low-resource language pairs. Existing methods mined parallel sentences using transfer learning. Although several attempts can get a good performance, they are not able to explain why transfer learning can help mining parallel sentences for low-resource language pairs. In this paper, we propose an explainable evaluation to quantity why transfer learning is useful for parallel sentence mining. Besides, we propose a novel unsupervised transfer learning that can maintain the robustness of transfer learning. Experiments show that our proposed method improves the performance of mined parallel sentences compared with previous methods in a standard evaluation set. In particular, we achieve good results at two real-world low-resource language pairs.

Keywords: Natural language processing · Machine translation · Transfer learning · Parallel sentences · Low-resource language pairs

1 Introduction

Parallel corpus is known as a very important resource for many cross-lingual natural language processing (NLP), such as neural machine translation (NMT) [1], cross-lingual sentiment classification [2], information retrieval [3] et al. Especially, the parallel sentences heavily affect the performance of trained machine translation systems. However, these resources are only available for a few language pairs and domains while the others suffer from the scarcity problem [4]. Therefore, obtaining parallel sentences are very crucial to apply cross-lingual NLP tasks.

To obtain massive parallel sentences, many researchers used transfer learning to mine bilingual data for low-resource language pairs. [5] firstly used transfer learning to identify parallel sentences for low-resource language pairs. They brought evidence of transfer learning to mine parallel data for low-resource language pairs. They used the proposed LASER[1] to mine parallel sentences in 93

---

[1] https://github.com/facebookresearch/LASER

L. H. U et al. (Eds.): APWeb-WAIM 2021, LNCS 12858, pp. 273–281, 2021.
https://doi.org/10.1007/978-3-030-85896-4_22

languages. Although these approaches are effective in mining parallel sentences, they only explained that the language-invariant can make transfer learning effective. They don't quantity and demonstrate the language-invariant between different languages is constant. In fact, several researchers question those language representations are not entirely language-internal agnostic [6]. [7] pointed that language-invariant only exits in closely-related[2] language pairs and there is an obvious semantic gap in distant language pairs. We also test several methods on more realistic scenarios, we find the results are not always promising. For instance, when we use existed methods to mine parallel sentences on distant language pairs, we find the accuracies are at least below 10% than closely-related language pairs (see Sect. 5). This means that selecting suitable source languages is very important for transfer learning. Therefore, we need to give an explainable evaluation to quantify different languages for transfer learning.

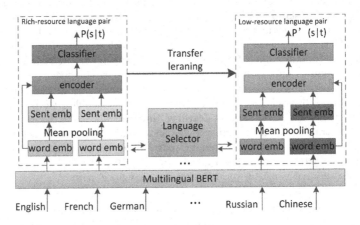

Fig. 1. Our proposed method that based on transfer training for parallel sentences detection on a non-parallel language pair.

In this paper, we firstly propose the Gromov-Hausdorff (GH) distance to check the extent of language-invariant between languages. The Gromov Hausdorff (GH) distance to check how well two language embedding spaces can be aligned. [7] pointed out that if two languages satisfy the language-invariant, the distribution of word representations are similar. It means if two languages satisfy the language-invariant, the Gromov Hausdorff (GH) distance is very small or close to zero. Then, we design a language selector to maintain the robustness of transfer learning in different languages. As illustrated in Fig. 1, we firstly employ an unsupervised multi-lingual word embeddings (MulBERT) model [8] to train a shared word representations vector space on monolingual corpora. Then, we

---

[2] We mean that the etymologically close languages are closely-related languages such as English-French. The distant languages are etymologically different such as English-Chinese.

obtain sentence embeddings by mean-pooling the outputs of multilingual BERT [8], which is trained on monolingual corpora. In parallel, we treat detecting parallel sentences as a classifying task and encode multi-view semantic representations for the classifier in rich-resources language pairs. In our model, we use two views for the classifier: (i) word representations; (ii) sentence representations. In particular, we use a language selector to select suitable rich-resource languages when we transfer them into low-resource language pairs. In addition to achieving good results on BUCC shared task, we demonstrate the effectiveness of our model using an example of low-resource language pairs where parallel corpora are not available.

2 Evaluation for Transfer Learning

Transfer learning is based on the assumption that similar distribution of word representations between languages in many natural language processing applications [9]. A similar assumption means that there is an orthogonal mapping matrix to map one embedding space to another [10]. The orthogonal mapping matrix can be formally defined as follows:

$$||I - W^T W||^2 = 0 \tag{1}$$

where W is a matrix that maps the source embedding X into the target Y as $WX = Y$. In other words, the above equation means the embedding spaces are similar and the multilingual word embeddings are language-invariant [7]. [5] used transfer learning that is based on the language-invariant of multilingual word representations to obtain parallel sentences. However, they don't quantify the language-invariant between languages. At the same time, they don't demonstrate the language-invariant of different language how affects transfer learning. In this paper, we propose the Gromov Hausdorff (GH) distance to check how well two language embedding spaces can be aligned. The GH distance between two metric spaces is a measure of the worst-case or diametric distance between the spaces. Intuitively, if any two languages satisfy the language-invariant, the GH distance of word representations of different languages is close to 0 value. Concretely, given two word embeddings X, and Y with a Euclidean distance function $D(.,.)$, the Hausdorff distance is defined as:

$$H(X,Y) = max\{\sup_{x \epsilon X} \inf_{y \epsilon Y} D(x,y), \sup_{y \epsilon Y} \inf_{x \epsilon X} D(y,x)\} \tag{2}$$

The GH distance minimizes the Hausdorff distance overall mappings between X and Y, thereby providing a quantitative estimate of the two word embedding spaces. The GH distance is defined as:

$$H(X,Y) = \inf_{f,g}(f(X), g(Y)) \tag{3}$$

where f, g belongs to a set of mappings. In experiments as Sect. 5, we can find the values of $||I - W^T W||$ and GH distances are bigger for distant language pairs than closely-relative language pairs.

3 Unsupervised Transfer Learning for Mining Parallel Sentences

The overview of our unsupervised model architecture is as shown in Fig. 1. Our proposed approach based on transfer learning to mine parallel data is composed of three components: an unsupervised multilingual BERT, a language selector, and a multi-view classifier.

3.1 Language Selector

Previous works [11] indicate that cross-lingual transfer learning work well when their representations are language-invariant. We use the unsupervised multilingual BERT to map the word representations into a shared space. Although we can generate shared word representations for different languages by using the unsupervised multilingual BERT, there is still a semantic gap between languages [12]. In this paper, we propose a language selector to evaluate the semantic gap and select high language-invariant source languages. In detail, the language selector is trained to quantify the language-invariant between the mapped source and target embeddings. Then, we select a source language pair that has a minimum GH distance to implement transfer learning. The objective of a selector is to minimize its ability to identify the source and target embeddings. The selector can be written as follows:

$$P(S_i|T) = min\{H(S_1, T), ..., H(S_n, T)\} \tag{4}$$

where $P(S_i|T)$ denotes that we select the ith source language pair to implement transfer learning, (S, T) corresponds to source and target language. Through the quantifiable process, we can effectively analyze transfer learning how to work well in mining parallel sentences and select suitable source language pairs.

3.2 Transfer Learning for Mining Parallel Data

In this paper, we propose unsupervised transfer learning to mine parallel data of low-resource scenarios. In this paper, we use a feed-forward neural network based on LSTM with two hidden layers as an encoder to implement the classifier. Then, we train a classifier to match predicted labels with ground truth from the parallel sentences in rich-resource language pairs as follows:

$$P(s|t) = \frac{e^{enc(\theta)}}{1 + e^{enc(\theta)}} \epsilon(0, 1) \tag{5}$$

where θ denotes parameters of the encoder $enc(.)$. Then, we transfer the trained model into mining parallel data for low-resource language pairs. The detail process is as follows: We firstly train a classifier model on rich-resource language pairs (such as English-Chinese or English-French). In parallel, we use the language selector to quantify the language-invariant of different language representations and select a suitable language to keep language-invariant between different languages. After that, we transfer the pre-trained classifier model to detect parallel sentences for low-resource language pairs. Finally, we use detected parallel data to train the classifier again in low-resource language pairs for better performance. When we transfer the model into a new language pair, we need to share the hyper-parameters of the classifier model and encoder the first detecting parallel sentences in low-resource language pairs. Therefore, we consider the difference between the two models by evaluating the embeddings:

$$L_c(low) = enc[\Theta] + \underbrace{H_{GH}(X||Y)}_{min} \qquad (6)$$

where X is the representations in rich-resource language pairs, Y is the representations in low-resource language pairs. $H_{GH}(.||.)$ is measure the difference between two distributions by using the proposed language selector. By this, we can hold the performance of the model when performing transfer learning.

4 Experimental Setting

For evaluating the language-invariant for the later transfer learning, we the MUSE and the VecMap dataset. The MUSE used by [10] consists of word representations trained on Wikipedia[3]. The VecMap introduced by [13] consists of the CBOW word representations trained on the WacKy crawling corpora[4]. Then, we test our proposed method on a shared evaluation task (so-called BUCC[5]) that contains four language pairs(English-French, English-German, English-Russian, English-Chinese). The shared task provides a gold standard to assess retrieval systems for precision, recall, and F_1-score. We applied our approach to all language pairs of the BUCC18 shared task. In our experiments, we compare our method with several baselines [5,14–17], with the goal of evaluating performance on BUCC.

Table 1. The results of quantify language difference.

		en-fr	fr-de	de-ru	en-it	en-tr	fr-zh	zh-ja
MUSE	GH	0.15	0.21	0.47	0.46	0.81	0.98	0.21
	$\|I - W^T W\|$	0.14	0.17	5.57	5.61	8.93	15.68	0.08
	$V - GH$	4.52	6.13	14.95	14.38	17.63	19.32	5.76
VecMap	GH	0.13	0.18	0.44	0.41	0.78	0.91	0.23
	$\|I - W^T W\|$	0.1	0.15	5.02	4.89	18.04	20.65	5.26
	$V - GH$	4.46	6.08	14.36	14.21	17.47	19.58	5.43

---

[3] https://github.com/facebookresearch/MUSE.
[4] https://github.com/artetxem/vecmap.
[5] https://comparable.limsi.fr/bucc2018/bucc2018-task.html.

5   Results and Discussions

5.1   Empirical Evaluation of GH Distance

Table 1 summarizes the GH distances obtained for different language pairs. We find that etymologically closely-relative language pairs such as en-fr and en-it have a very low GH distance and can be aligned well using an orthogonal matrix. In contrast, we find that distant language pairs such as en-tr and en-zh have a high GH distance. To further corroborate this, we compute the GH distance in all words of different languages as $V - GH$. We find that the $V - GH$ distance exhibits similar results. It implies that as the GH distance increases, it becomes increasingly difficult to keep the language-invariant. Furthermore, we also compute correlations against an empirical measure of the orthogonality of two embedding spaces by computing $||I - W^T W||$, where W is a mapping from one language to the other obtained from an unsupervised method [10]. Note that an advantage of this metric is that it can be computed even when supervised dictionaries are not available. We obtain a strong correlation with this metric as well.

5.2   Results on BUCC

Noted that, our method doesn't rely on any bilingual data of low-resource language pairs. Therefore, we can call that our method is unsupervised for low-resource language pairs. This is a fair comparison to other unsupervised methods. From Table 3, we achieve an increase of F_1 compared with unsupervised baselines for all language pairs. It also can be seen that the precision and recall of the proposed method is significantly increased for all language pair than unsupervised methods. [5] also used transfer learning to mine parallel sentences. However, their method needs strong supervision which is not available in low-resource language pairs. In our experiments, we delete the supervision for real-world low-resource settings. We directly use English-French to implement transfer learning without

Table 2. Results of our proposed systems on the BUCC shared task's training set for the 4 language-pairs. We also report the results of baselines as described in their paper. "-" represents the result are not reported in ther paper, respectively.

	En-Fr			En-De			En-Ru			En-Zh		
	P	R	F_1	P	R	F_1	P	R	F_1	P	R	F_1
[5]	87.5	85.8	86.6	82.5	81.5	82.9	63.6	63.4	62.5	63.1	61.8	62
[15]	50.5	38.1	43.4	48.5	39.1	43.3	37.4	18.7	24.9	–	–	–
[16]	–	–	73.0	–	–	74.9	–	–	69.6	–	–	60.1
[14]	39.0	52.6	44.8	23.7	44.5	30.9	17.3	24.9	20.4	–	–	–
[17]	–	–	78.7	–	–	80.1	–	–	77.1	–	–	67.0
Proposed method+(en-fr)	87.5	85.8	86.6	–	–	–	–	–	–	–	–	–
Proposed method+(de-ru)	–	–	–	–	–	–	74.1	74.2	74.2	–	–	–
Proposed method+(zh-ja)	–	–	–	–	–	–	–	–	–	80.7	78.6	79.6
Proposed method+(en-fr)	–	–	–	82.5	81.5	82.9	–	–	–	–	–	–

encoding the language-invariant by simultaneous training French-German parallel data. We also test whether the performance is various or not only using transfer learning without considering the language-invariant.

5.3 Results on Low-Resource Language Pair

In the above section, we simulate the low-resource scenario to justify our method on the BUCC dataset. In this section, we evaluate our mined parallel sentences on real-world low-resource language pairs. We apply our method to the English-Esperanto(En-Es) and Chinese-Kazakh(Zh-Kz) language pairs. As there is no gold standard to evaluate mining parallel sentences, we use mined parallel sentences to train machine translation systems which can reflect the quality of mined parallel sentences.

We use openNMT[6] to train the machine translation system. The results are as in Table 4. Note that for English-Esperanto, we use English-French parallel sentences as rich-resource language pairs to transfer to English-Esperanto. We use the language selector to calculate the GH value of French-Esperanto is 0.2. Therefore, French and Esperanto have relatively high similarities. At the same time, we use the Chinese-Uyghur language pair to transfer to Chinese-Kazakh. The language selector shows Uyghur-Kazakh is a closely-relative language pair. Based on the scores in Table 4 it can be seen that we achieve a significant performance increase compared to the unsupervised baseline. It is well-known that the quality and quantity heavily affect the performance of the machine translation. The results of Table 4 demonstrate that the proposed method actually is effective, especially for low-resource language pairs.

6 Conclusion

In this paper, we propose an explainable evaluation to quantity why transfer learning is useful for parallel sentence mining. Moreover, we proposed an app-

Table 3. Results of our proposed systems on the BUCC shared task's training set for the 4 language-pairs. We also report the results of baselines as described in their paper. "-" represents the result are not reported in ther paper, respectively.

	En-Fr			En-De			En-Ru			En-Zh		
	P	R	F_1	P	R	F_1	P	R	F_1	P	R	F_1
[5]	87.5	85.8	86.6	82.5	81.5	82.9	63.6	63.4	62.5	63.1	61.8	62
[15]	50.5	38.1	43.4	48.5	39.1	43.3	37.4	18.7	24.9	–	–	–
[16]	–	–	73.0	–	–	74.9	–	–	69.6	–	–	60.1
[14]	39.0	52.6	44.8	23.7	44.5	30.9	17.3	24.9	20.4	–	–	–
[17]	–	–	78.7	–	–	80.1	–	–	77.1	–	–	67.0
Proposed method+(en-fr)	87.5	85.8	86.6	–	–	–	–	–	–	–	–	–
Proposed method+(de-ru)	–	–	–	–	–	–	74.1	74.2	74.2	–	–	–
Proposed method+(zh-ja)	–	–	–	–	–	–	–	–	–	80.7	78.6	79.6
Proposed method+(en-fr)	–	–	–	82.5	81.5	82.9	–	–	–	–	–	–

---

[6] https://opennmt.net/.

Table 4. BLEU scores on different language pairs.

Methods	en-fr	en-de	en-ru	en-zh	en-es	zh-kz
[15]	23.8	25.6	24.3	22.1	18.5	21.6
[16]	26.6	27.6	25.9	23.6	20.2	22.8
[14]	21.2	23.8	22.9	19.6	16.3	19.3
[17]	25.2	26.7	27.2	23.5	23.6	22.7
Proposed method	29.4	28.8	27.3	25.6	24.3	25.8

roach based on unsupervised transfer learning to mine parallel sentences. Our method can effectively use the bilingual data of rich-resource language pairs. We transfer the model of rich-resource language pairs into a low-resource situation without any supervision of low-resource language pairs. In particular, we propose a language selector to quantify language-invariant to explain why can benefit transfer learning. Experiments show that an explainable evaluation can do explain why transfer learning is effective by the performance of mined parallel sentences compared with previous methods in a standard evaluation set. In particular, we achieve excellent results at two real-world low-resource language pairs.

References

1. Belinkov, Y., Bisk, Y.: Synthetic and natural noise both break neural machine translation. In: International Conference on Learning Representations (2018)
2. Chen, Z., Shen, S., Hu, Z., Lu, X., Mei, Q., Liu, X.: Emoji-powered representation learning for cross-lingual sentiment classification. In: The World Wide Web Conference, pp. 251–262 (2019)
3. Sun, S., Duh, K.: Clirmatrix: a massively large collection of bilingual and multilingual datasets for cross-lingual information retrieval. In: Proceedings of the 2020 Conference on Empirical Methods in Natural Language Processing (EMNLP), pp. 4160–4170 (2020)
4. Bouamor, H., Sajjad, H.: H2@ bucc18: Parallel sentence extraction from comparable corpora using multilingual sentence embeddings. In: Proceedings of Workshop on Building and Using Comparable Corpora (2018)
5. Artetxe, M., Schwenk, H.: Massively multilingual sentence embeddings for zero-shot cross-lingual transfer and beyond. Trans. Assoc. Comput. Linguist. 7, 597–610 (2019)
6. Karthikeyan, K., Wang, Z., Mayhew, S., Roth, D.: Cross-lingual ability of multilingual bert: An empirical study. In: International Conference on Learning Representations (2019)
7. Patra, B., Moniz, J.R.A., Garg, S., Gormley, M.R., Neubig, G.: Bilingual lexicon induction with semi-supervision in non-isometric embedding spaces. In: Proceedings of the 57th Annual Meeting of the Association for Computational Linguistics, pp. 184–193 (2019)
8. Lample, G., Conneau, A.: Cross-lingual language model pretraining. arXiv preprint arXiv:1901.07291 (2019)

9. Ziser, Y., Reichart, R.: Deep pivot-based modeling for cross-language cross-domain transfer with minimal guidance. In: Proceedings of the 2018 Conference on Empirical Methods in Natural Language Processing, pp. 238–249 (2018)
10. Lample, G., Conneau, A., Ranzato, M., Denoyer, L., Jégou, H.: Word translation without parallel data. In: International Conference on Learning Representations (2018)
11. Fei, H., Li, P.: Cross-lingual unsupervised sentiment classification with multi-view transfer learning. In: Proceedings of the 58th Annual Meeting of the Association for Computational Linguistics, pp. 5759–5771 (2020)
12. Pires, T., Schlinger, E., Garrette, D.: How multilingual is multilingual bert?" In: Proceedings of the 57th Annual Meeting of the Association for Computational Linguistics, pp. 4996–5001 (2019)
13. Dinu, G., Lazaridou, A., Baroni, M.: Improving zero-shot learning by mitigating the hubness problem. arXiv preprint arXiv:1412.6568 (2014)
14. Hangya, V., Braune, F., Kalasouskaya, Y., Fraser, A.: Unsupervised parallel sentence extraction from comparable corpora. In: Proceedings of IWSLT (2018)
15. Hangya, V., Fraser, A.: Unsupervised parallel sentence extraction with parallel segment detection helps machine translation. In: Proceedings of the 57th Annual Meeting of the Association for Computational Linguistics, pp. 1224–1234 (2019)
16. Keung, P., Salazar, J., Lu, Y., Smith, N.A.: Unsupervised bitext mining and translation via self-trained contextual embeddings. arXiv preprint arXiv:2010.07761 (2020)
17. Kvapilíková, I., Artetxe, M., Labaka, G., Agirre, E., Bojar, O.: Unsupervised multilingual sentence embeddings for parallel corpus mining. In: Proceedings of the 58th Annual Meeting of the Association for Computational Linguistics: Student Research Workshop, pp. 255–262 (2020)

Text Analysis

Leveraging Syntactic Dependency and Lexical Similarity for Neural Relation Extraction

Yashen Wang[✉]

National Engineering Laboratory for Risk Perception and Prevention (RPP),
China Academy of Electronics and Information Technology of CETC, Beijing, China
yswang@bit.edu.cn

Abstract. Relation extraction is an important task in knowledge graph completion, information extraction and retrieval task. Recent neural models (especially with attention mechanism) have been shown to perform reasonably well. However, they sometimes fail to: (i) understand the semantic similarity of words with the given entities; and (ii) capture the long-distance dependencies among the words and entities such as co-reference. Moreover, this paper proposes a novel relation extraction model, which leverages syntactic dependency and lexical similarity for enhancing attention mechanism, to get rid of dependence for rich labeled training data. We conduct experiments on widely-used real-world datasets and the experimental results demonstrate the efficiency of the proposed model, even compared with latest state-of-the-art Transformer-based models.

Keywords: Neural relation extraction · Leveraging syntactic dependency · Lexical similarity

1 Introduction

Relation extraction aims at detecting the semantic relationship between two entities in a sentence. For example, given the sentence: "··· *Isaacs marriage to Rebecca, by whom he has two sons, Esau and jacob*···", the goal is to recognize the "has_child" relation held between entity "*Isaac*" and entity "*Esau*". Traditional feature-based and kernel-based approaches require extensive feature engineering [14]. Deep neural networks such as Convolutional Neural Networks (CNNs) and Recurrent Neural Networks (RNNs) have the ability of exploring more complex semantics and extracting features automatically from raw texts for relation extraction tasks [2,4]. Recently, attention mechanisms have been introduced to deep neural networks to improve their performance [11]. Especially, the Transformer-based models [7,26] are based *solely* on self-attention and have demonstrated better performance than traditional RNNs [1,25].

Though these models have been shown to perform reasonably well on distantly supervised data, they sometimes fail to: (i) understand the *semantic*

L. H. U et al. (Eds.): APWeb-WAIM 2021, LNCS 12858, pp. 285–299, 2021.
https://doi.org/10.1007/978-3-030-85896-4_23

similarity of words with the given entities; and (ii) capture the *long-distance dependencies* among the words and entities such as co-reference. Moreover, deep neural networks normally require sufficient *labeled* data to train their numerous model parameters. The scarcity or low quality of training data will limit the model's ability to recognize complex relations and also cause over-fitting issue. Recent studies have shown that incorporating prior knowledge from external lexical resources or syntactic dependency into deep neural network [6] can reduce the reliance on training data and improve relation extraction performance.

To solve these problems, we propose a novel attention mechanism, which (i) leverages extra lexical knowledge graph to measure semantic similarity; and (ii) utilizes both the semantic meaning of the words and their dependency distance from the two entities together. Moreover, we combine *global* sentence-level information and *local* entity-level information, for capturing hierarchical and multi-granularity pieces of evidence for identifying the relation Finally, the experimental results show that it achieves state-of-the-art results for relation extraction task. In summary, the main contributions of the paper are:

(i) We propose a novel attention mechanism which incorporates *global* information from sentence with *local* information from entities, to effectively capture the informative linguistic clues for relation extraction and find the relation when sentences are long and entities are located far from each other.

(ii) The proposed attention mechanism is used to measure the *semantic similarity* of words with the given entities and combine it with the *dependency distance* of words from the given entities to measure their influence in identifying the relation. The semantic signals from semantic similarity and dependency distance could be fully interacted with each other in the proposed model.

2 Preliminary

2.1 Problem Definition

Following [12], given a sentence s and two entities e_1 and e_2 marked in the sentence, find the relation $r(e_1, e_2)$ between these two entities in s from a pre-defined set of relation-types R. Note that, the relation between the entities is argument order-specific, i.e., $r(e_1, e_2)$ and $r(e_2, e_1)$ are *not* the same in our point of view, so that it's more difficult and challenging. Overall, the input to the system is a sentence s and two entities e_1 and e_2, and the output is the relation $r(e_1, e_2) \in R$.

2.2 Definition 1: Concept

Following [6,17], we define a "concept" as a set or class/category of "entities" or "things" within a domain, such that words belonging to similar classes get similar representations. E.g., "microsoft" and "amazon" could be represented by concept COMPANY. Probase [22] is used in our study as knowledge graph.

2.3   Definition 1: Instance Conceptualization

Given a word w_i in a specific context s, instance conceptualization algorithm enables to select the open-domain concepts $C_{w_i} = \{< c_j, p_j > | j = 1, \cdots, |C_{w_i}|\}$ from the knowledge graph Probase which own the optimal ability for discriminatively representing the given word w_i in the current context s. The numerical value p_j represents the probability numerical value of the concept c_j for word w_i in the given text s. E.g., given a text as input (e.g., "microsoft unveils office for apple's ipad"), we generate the concepts for word "apple" C_{apple} = {<COMPANY,0.7467>, <BRAND,0.6557>, <PRODUCT,0.5412>, $\cdots$ } from Probase in this text context. Note that, concept plays an important role in the proposed model, the semantic similarity of words with the given entities mentioned above is utilized in the following Sect. 3.4, and then the concept-based semantic similarity will be fully interacted with syntactic dependency later in Sect. 3.5. In this paper, we utilize the state-of-the-art text conceptualization algorithm proposed in [6][1], which co-ranks the concepts and words simultaneously in an iterative procedure.

3   Methodology

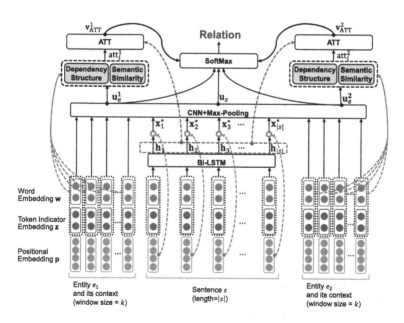

Fig. 1. The illustration of the proposed relation extraction model, which leverages syntactic dependency and lexical similarity for enhancing attention mechanism.

---

[1] Note that, although many text conceptualization algorithms could be adopted here, we choose the state-of-the-art one [6], because it is not central to this study.

Figure 1 sketches the overall architecture of the proposed relation extraction model, denoted as **DS-ATT**, leveraging syntactic dependency and lexical similarity for enhancing attention mechanism.

3.1   Input Generation

The proposed model utilizes six types of embedding vectors: (i) word embedding vector $\mathbf{w} \in \mathbb{R}^{d_w}$ (this paper denotes word as notation $w \in V$ and V indicates vocabulary); (ii) entity token indicator embedding vector $\mathbf{z} \in \mathbb{R}^{d_z}$, which indicates if a word belongs to entity e_1, entity e_2, or does not belong to any entity; (iii) position embedding vector $\mathbf{p}^1 \in \mathbb{R}^{d_p}$ representing the distance of a word from the start token of entity e_1; (iv) position embedding vector $\mathbf{p}^2$ representing the distance of a word from the end token of entity e_1; (v) position embedding vector $\mathbf{p}^3$ representing the distance of a word from the start token of entity e_2; (vi) position embedding vector $\mathbf{p}^4$ representing the distance of a word from the end token of entity e_2. Wherein, $\{d_w, d_z, d_p\}$ indicates the dimensionality of word embedding vector $\mathbf{w}$, entity token indicator embedding vector $\mathbf{z}$, positional embedding vector ($\{\mathbf{p}^1, \mathbf{p}^2, vp^3, \mathbf{p}^4\}$), respectively.

Conventionally, a bi-directional Long Short-Term Memory (Bi-LSTM) layer is introduced here to capture the interaction among words in a sentence $s = (w_1, \cdots, w_{|s|})$, wherein $|s|$ indicates the sentence length. Overall, the input to this layer is the concatenated vector $\mathbf{x}_t \in \mathbb{R}^{d_w+d_z}$ of word embedding vector $\mathbf{w}_t$ and entity token indicator embedding vector $\mathbf{z}_t$, as follows: $\mathbf{x}_t = [\mathbf{w}_t; \mathbf{z}_t]$. Then, we define $\overrightarrow{\mathbf{h}_t} \in \mathbb{R}^{d_w+d_z}$ and $\overleftarrow{\mathbf{h}_t} \in \mathbb{R}^{d_w+d_z}$ as the output at the t-th step of the forward LSTM ($\overrightarrow{\text{LSTM}}(\cdot)$) and backward LSTM ($\overleftarrow{\text{LSTM}}(\cdot)$), respectively. Hence,

$$\overrightarrow{\mathbf{h}_t} = \overrightarrow{\text{LSTM}}(\mathbf{x}_t, \mathbf{h}_{t-1}) \tag{1}$$

$$\overleftarrow{\mathbf{h}_t} = \overleftarrow{\text{LSTM}}(\mathbf{x}_t, \mathbf{h}_{t+1}) \tag{2}$$

Finally, we concatenate them to generate the t-th Bi-LSTM output $\mathbf{h}_t \in \mathbb{R}^{2(d_w+d_z)}$, as follows: $\mathbf{h}_t = [\overrightarrow{\mathbf{h}_t}; \overleftarrow{\mathbf{h}_t}]$.

3.2   Sentence-Level Semantic Vector Generation

The Convolutional Neural Network (CNN) is leveraged for extracting the sentence-level *global* semantics for relation extraction task, which is widely used in previous relation extraction models [23]. We concatenate the positional embedding vectors $\{\mathbf{p}_t^1, \mathbf{p}_t^2, vp_t^3, \mathbf{p}_t^4\}$ of w_t with the corresponding hidden representation of the Bi-LSTM layer (i.e., $\mathbf{h}_t$ defined in Sect. 3.1), as follows: $\mathbf{x}_t^* = [\mathbf{h}_t; \mathbf{p}_t^1; \mathbf{p}_t^2; \mathbf{p}_t^3; vp_t^4]$ Wherein, $\mathbf{x}_t^* \in \mathbb{R}^{2(d_w+d_z+2d_p)}$ indicates the concatenated vector for the t-th word. Moreover, we define the sentence-level convolutional filter vector as $\mathbf{f}_s \in \mathbb{R}^{2k \times (d_w+d_z+2d_p)}$, wherein k indicates the window size (i.e., the filter width). Then, the index i moves from 1 to $|s|$ and produces a set of values $\{u_i | i \in [1, \cdots, |s|]\}$, as follows:

$$u_i = \mathbf{f}_s^{\top}([\mathbf{x}_{i-\frac{k-1}{2}}^*; \cdots; \mathbf{x}_i^*; \cdots; \mathbf{x}_{i+\frac{k-1}{2}}^*]) \tag{3}$$

With efforts above, the max-pooling operation (i.e., max_pooling($\cdot$)) chooses the maximum $\hat{u}$ from these values $\{u_i | i \in [1, \cdots, |s|]\}$ as a feature:

$$\hat{u} = \text{max\_pooling}(u_1, \cdots, u_{|s|}) \tag{4}$$

We define $\#f_s$ as the number of sentence-level filters, and we get a sentence-level semantic vector $\mathbf{u}_s \in \mathbb{R}^{\#f_s}$, as follows:

$$\mathbf{u}_s = [\hat{u}_1, \cdots, \hat{u}_{\#f_s}] \tag{5}$$

3.3 Entity-Level Semantic Vector Generation

Inspired by [12,20], the nearby (i.e., *context*) words of an entity can give significant information about the entity. Thus we use the tokens of an entity and its nearby tokens to generate its vector representation, and this vector representation is very important for our model, which is demonstrated in the following experimental section.

Similar to the procedure of sentence-level semantic vector generation discussed in Sect. 3.2, we also utilize the convolution operation with max-pooling (i.e., max_pooling($\cdot$)) in the context of an entity to obtain its vector representation $\mathbf{v}_e$, described as follows. We define the entity-level convolutional filter vector as $\mathbf{f}_e \in \mathbb{R}^{k(d_w+d_z)}$, wherein k indicates the context window size. Besides, $\mathbf{x}$ is also the concatenated vector of word embedding vector ($\mathbf{w}$) and entity token indicator embedding vector ($\mathbf{z}$), as defined in Sect. 3.1. We define i_b and i_e as the begin index and end index of the sequence of words comprising an entity and its neighboring context in the sentence, where $1 \leq i_b \leq i_e \leq |s|$. Then the index i moves from i_b to i_e, and produces a set of values $\{u_{i_b}, u_{i_b+1}, \cdots, u_{i_e}\}$. Therefore, u_i in Eq. (3) is reformed as follows:

$$u_i = \mathbf{f}_e^{\top}([\mathbf{x}_{i-\frac{k-1}{2}}; \cdots; \mathbf{x}_i; \cdots; \mathbf{x}_{i+\frac{k-1}{2}}]) \tag{6}$$

Similar to the mechanism discussed in Sect. 3.2, the max-pooling operation chooses the maximum u_{max} from these values as a feature. With $\#f_e$ number of entity-level filters, we get the entity representation vector $\mathbf{u}_e \in \mathbb{R}^{\#f_e}$, as follows:

$$\mathbf{u}_e = [\hat{u}_1, \cdots, \hat{u}_{\#f_e}] \tag{7}$$

With efforts above, we do this for both entities (e_1 and e_2) and get $\mathbf{u}_e^1 \in \mathbb{R}^{\#f_e}$ and $\mathbf{u}_e^2 \in \mathbb{R}^{\#f_e}$ as their vector representation, respectively.

3.4   Lexical Semantic Similarity Based on Concept

We measure the *semantic similarity* of words with the given entities, as follows. This measurement fully utilizes the entity *concept* information [21] which represents the domains or categories of entities in lexical KG Probase. Probase is widely used in research about short-text understanding [15,16,22] and text representation [6].

Given i-th word w_i, we denote its concept set as $C_{w_i} = \{c_1, c_2, \cdots, c_{|C_{w_i}|}\}$, consisting the corresponding concepts deriving from Probase by leveraging single instance conceptualization algorithm [15,16,19]. Wherein, we use $|C_{w_i}|$ to denote the size of this set and c_j to denote the feature of the j-th concept in this set. In the same vein, C_{e_1} and C_{e_2} indicates the concept set for entity e_1 and entity e_2, respectively, with help of aforementioned lexical knowledge graph. If the entity mention of entity e contains multiple words, we could generate concept set of entity e as follows: $C_e = C_{w_1} \bigcup C_{w_2} \bigcup C_{w_{|e|}}$ wherein, $|e|$ indicates the number of the words segmented from entity e after max-matching [6,15] by using Probase. With efforts above, we measure the semantic similarity of word w_i with entity e_1, as follows:

$$\text{sim}(w_i, e_1) = \frac{|C_{w_i}| \cup |C_{e_1}|}{|C_{e_1}|} \tag{8}$$

Generally speaking, $\text{sim}(w_i, e_1)$ could also be regarded as the concept-level attention score for the i-th word w_i from entity e_1. Similarly, the semantic similarity between the word w_i and the entity e_2 is:

$$\text{sim}(w_i, e_2) = \frac{|C_{w_i}| \cup |C_{e_2}|}{|C_{e_2}|} \tag{9}$$

3.5   DS-ATT: Attention Based on Syntactic Dependency and Lexical Similarity

This section proposes a novel attention mechanism based on *syntactic* structure of a sentence, which is derived from the sentence's dependency parse tree. In the proposed model, we define the dependency distance to every word from the head token (last token) of an entity as the number of edges along the dependency path. For entity e_1 in the given sentence s,

$$\sigma_i^1 = \begin{cases} \dfrac{\exp[\text{sim}(w_i, e_1)]}{2^{l_i^1} - 1} & l_i^1 \in [1, m] \\[2ex] \dfrac{\exp[\text{sim}(w_i, e_1)]}{2^m} & \text{otherwise} \end{cases} \tag{10}$$

Wherein, l_i^1 indicates the dependency distances of the i-th word w_i from entity e_1. $\text{sim}(w_i, e_1)$ is defined as the semantic similarity of word w_i with the given entity e_1 (Eq. (8) in Sect. 3.4). Besides, notation m indicates the distance window size. With efforts above, the normalized attention scores for the i-th word w_i in given sentence s with respect to entity e_1, i.e., att_i^1, is defined as follows:

$$\text{att}_i^1 = \frac{\sigma_i^1}{\sum_j \sigma_j^1} \tag{11}$$

Similarly, for entity e_2, the normalized attention scores for the i-th word with respect to e_2 is computed as follows:

$$\sigma_i^2 = \begin{cases} \dfrac{\exp[\text{sim}(w_i, e_2)]}{2^{l_i^2} - 1} & l_i^2 \in [1, m] \\[2ex] \dfrac{\exp[\text{sim}(w_i, e_2)]}{2^m} & \text{otherwise} \end{cases} \tag{12}$$

$$\text{att}_i^2 = \frac{\sigma_i^2}{\sum_j \sigma_j^2} \tag{13}$$

Wherein, l_i^2 indicates the dependency distances of the i-th word from entity e_2. From Eqs. (10) and (12), we could observe that, we utilize both the *semantic meaning* of the words (i.e., concept information) and their *dependency distance* from the two entities together in our attention mechanism. Finally, the attention vectors $\mathbf{v}_{\text{ATT}}^1$ and $\mathbf{v}_{\text{ATT}}^2$ according to the two entities (e_1 and e_2) respectively, are determined as follows, respectively:

$$\mathbf{v}_{\text{ATT}}^1 = \sum_{i=1}^{|s|} \text{att}_i^1 \mathbf{h}_i \tag{14}$$

$$\mathbf{v}_{\text{ATT}}^2 = \sum_{i=1}^{|s|} \text{att}_i^2 \mathbf{h}_i \tag{15}$$

3.6 Objective

In summary, we concatenate $\mathbf{u}_s$ (details in Sect. 3.2), $\mathbf{v}_{\text{ATT}}$ (details in Sect. 3.5), $\mathbf{u}_e^1$ and $\mathbf{u}_e^2$ (details in Sect. 3.3), and this concatenated feature vector is fed into a feed-forward layer with softmax activation to predict the normalized probabilities for the relation labels, as follows:

$$\mathbf{r} = \text{SoftMax}\{\mathbf{M}^\top [\mathbf{u}_s; \mathbf{v}_{\text{ATT}}^1; \mathbf{v}_{\text{ATT}}^2; \mathbf{u}_e^1; \mathbf{u}_e^2] + \mathbf{b}\} \tag{16}$$

Wherein, $\mathbf{M} \in \mathbb{R}^{(\#f_s + 2\#f_e + 4(d_w + d_z)) \times |R|}$ is the weight matrix, $\mathbf{b} \in \mathbb{R}^{|R|}$ is the bias vector, and $\mathbf{r} \in \mathbb{R}^{|R|}$ is the vector of normalized probabilities of relation labels, with each dimensionality representing the confidence for each relation type.

The objective function for relation extraction is defined as follows:

$$\mathcal{L} = -\frac{1}{B^*} \sum_{j=1}^{B^*} \log[\mathcal{P}(r_j|s_j, e_{j,1}, e_{j,2}, \Theta)] \tag{17}$$

Wherein, $\mathcal{P}(r_i|s_i, e_{i,1}, e_{i,2}, \Theta)$ is the conditional probability of the *true* relation r_j when the sentence s_j, two entities belonging to sentence s_j (i.e., $e_{j,1}$ and $e_{j,2}$), and the model parameters Θ are given. Besides, notation B^* represents the mini-batch of size.

4 Experiments

4.1 Datasets and Metric

We conduct our main experiments on dataset TACRED, a large-scale relation extraction dataset introduced by [25]. Concretely, TACRED contains over 106k sentences with hand-annotated subject and object entities, as well as the relations between them. It is a very complex relation extraction dataset with 41 relation-types and a no-relation class when no-relation is hold between entities. The dataset is widely-suited for real-word relation extraction since it is unbalanced with 79.5% no-relation samples, and multiple relations between different entity pairs can be exist in one sentence. Besides, the samples are normally long sentences with an average of 36.2 words. Since the dataset is already partitioned into train (68,124 samples), dev (22,631 samples) and test (15,509 samples) sets, comparative models could tune model hyper-parameters using dev set, and then evaluate model using test set. The evaluation metrics are micro-averaged precision, recall and F-1 score.

4.2 Comparative Models

The comparative models could be concluded into several classes: (i) CNN-based models; (ii) RNN-based models; (iii) CNN-RNN hybrid models; (iv) Self-attention-based models; and (v) Transformer-based models.

- **CNN**: The classical convolutional neural network for sentence classification [8].
- **CNN+PE**: CNN with position embeddings dedicated for relation classification [13].
- **GCN**: The graph convolutional network over the pruned dependency trees of the sentence [24].
- **AGGCN**: Attention Guided Graph Convolutional Networks, a soft-pruning model which directly takes full dependency trees as inputs [4].
- **LSTM**: The long short-term memory network to sequentially model the texts, and classification is based on the last hidden output [5].
- **LSTM+PA**: Similar position-aware attention mechanism is used to summarize the LSTM outputs [18].

- **LSTM+SA**: A segment attention based sequence model for relation extraction task, wherein a segment attention layer is employed on top of the LSTM [2].
- **C-GCN**: Contextualized GCN, wherein the input vectors are obtained using bi-directional LSTM network [24].
- **SELF**: Self-attention-based model, which utilizes self-attention encoder to model the input sentence [1].
- **SELF-KATT**: A knowledge-attention encoder which incorporates prior knowledge from external lexical resources into deep neural networks for relation extraction task [10].
- **BERT+SPAN**: A pre-training method that is designed to better represent and predict spans of text [7], on the basic of Transformer.
- **BERT+EPG**: [26] proposes a entity pair graph based neural network model, which combines sentence semantic features generated by pre-trained BERT model with graph topological features for relation classification.

4.3 Experimental Results

Table 1 shows the results of baseline as well as our proposed models on TACRED dataset. The superscript †, ‡ and § respectively denote statistically significant improvements over state-of-the-art **C-GCN** [24], **SELF-ATT** [1] and **BERT+SPAN** [7] ($p < 0.05$). It is observed that our proposed models (i.e., **DS-ATT** and **DS-ATT**) outperform all the comparative models by at least 2.42% in metric of Precision and at least 3.25% in metric of F-1 score. Meanwhile, it achieves comparable results with current Transformer-based models in metric of micro-averaged precision, while we defeats the self-attention encoders (i.e., **SELF-ATT** and **BERT+SPAN**) by 17.96% and 7.77%, in this metric, which are the current state-of-the-art single-model systems.

Compared with self-attention encoder [1,7], it is observed that the proposed attention model results in higher precision but lower recall. This is reasonable since the proposed attention mechanism focuses on capturing the significant linguistic clues of relations based on external knowledge (lexical knowledge from Probase emphasized here in Sect. 3.4), it will result in high precision. Moreover, compared with self-attention encoder (e.g., **BERT+SPAN** and **BERT+EPG**), the proposed **DS-ATT** is able to capture more long-distance dependency features by learning from data with fewer parameters, resulting in better recall, as shown in Table 1. While Transformer-based language models have been shown to be powerful in various NLP tasks, they often have significantly more parameters (although their lite variants have been proposed such as [9]), require much more training data, and take much longer to train than the proposed models. We think that, by integrating self-attention, and the dependency-attention and lexical knowledge used the proposed approaches, we could achieve a more balanced precision and recall, demonstrating the complementary effects of self-attention and dependency-attention mechanisms. From the perspective of performance, experimental results show that the precision F-1 score generated by our approach are higher and more robust, compared with state-of-the-art

Table 1. Micro-averaged precision (P), recall (R) and F-1 Score on TACRED dataset. The superscript †, ‡ and § respectively denote statistically significant improvements over state-of-the-art **C-GCN**, **SELF-ATT** and **BERT+SPAN** ($p < 0.05$).

Models	Precision	Recall	F-1 Score
CNN [8]	**72.1**	50.3	59.2
CNN+PE [13]	58.2	55.4	61.1
GCN [24]	69.8	59.0	64.0
C-GCN [24]	69.9‡	63.3	66.4
AGGCN [4]	73.1	64.2	68.2
LSTM [5]	61.4	61.7	61.5
LSTM+PA [18]	65.7	64.5	65.1
LSTM+SA [2]	69.0	66.2	67.6
SELF [1]	64.6	68.6†	66.5
SELF-KATT [10]	67.1	68.4	67.8
BERT [3]	69.1	63.9	66.4
BERT+EPG [26]	74.4	67.3	70.6
BERT+SPAN [7]	70.8†‡	**70.9†‡**	70.8†‡
DS-ATT (Ours)	**76.2†‡§**	70.2†‡	**73.1†‡§**

Transformer-based model. Even the ablative variant of the proposed model, i.e., **-Syntactic Dependency** runs neck-and-neck with **BERT+SPAN**, which will discussed later in Sect. 4.3. Besides, from a structural point-of-view, we consider the proposed **DS-ATT** as complementary to rather than competing with Transformer-based language models, and consider replacing encoder with Transformer to construct lexical similarity and syntactic dependency guided Transformer as a promising future extension.

We use the tokens of an entity and its nearby tokens (with window size of k) to obtain its vector representation. More interestingly, we found that the F-1 score can be controlled by adjusting the priority parameter k. Similarly, dependency-distance window size m also affects the overall performance. Figure 2 shows impact of k and m on F-1 score. Wherein, **DA-ATT-k** indicates the performance of the proposed model based on different context window size k when m is fixed. Note that, this experiment utilize the value of k from $\{3, 5, 7, 9, 11\}$. Similarly, **DA-ATT-m** indicates the performance on different dependency-distance window size m with fixed k. Figure shows that, as k and m increases, F-1 score increases. Larger value of k (or m) does not boot the result improvement, and conversely the performance decreases along with more additional computational effort. We argue that more noise is introduced with the increasing of each windows size mentioned above. F-1 score reaches the acceptable and highest value when performance and complexity are balanced ($k = 9$ and $m = 6$).

Table 2. Results of adding NER embeddings (denoted as NER) and entity categorical embeddings (denoted as CATEGORY) to the proposed **DS-ATT** model

Model	Precision	Recall	F-1 Score
DS-ATT	76.2	70.2	73.1
+NER	76.3	**70.6**	73.3
+CATEGORY	76.5	70.3	73.3
+BOTH	**76.8**	70.5	**73.5**

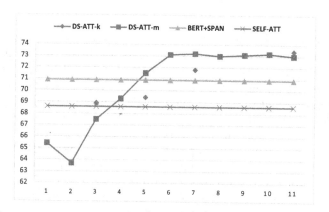

Fig. 2. Change of F1 score as the context window size k and dependency-distance window size m changes.

Besides, note that, it is more flexible for the proposed model for absorbing other kinds of features. For example, Table 2 shows the results of adding NER embeddings of each token to self-attention channel, and entity (subject and object) categorical embeddings to the proposed **DS-ATT** as additional feature vectors. We use dimensionality of 40 and 50 for NER and entity categorical embeddings respectively, and the two embedding matrixes are learned by the neural network. Results show that adding NER and entity categorical information to **DS-ATT** improves F-1 score by 0.2 respectively, and adding both improves precision significantly, resulting a new best F-1 score, improving F-1 score by 0.4.

Ablation Study. To study the contribution of each component in the proposed **DS-ATT** model, namely syntactic dependency and lexical similarity, we run an ablation study on the TACRED dev set (see also Table 3). We can observe that adding either syntactic dependency (details in Sect. 3.5) or concept-based semantic similarity (details in Sect. 3.4), improves the performance of the model.

Table 3. An ablation study of the best **DS-ATT** model on TACRED dataset.

Model	F-1 Score
DS-ATT	73.1
–Syntactic dependency	71.2
–Lexical similarity	69.4
–Entity vector	71.3
–Position vector	70.8

This suggests that both components can assist neural relation prediction task to learn better information from text and produce better representations for entities and sentences, where the lexical similarity seems to be playing a more significant role. Comparing the two ablation variant models, the lexical similarity has been demonstrated to achieves the best performance. As shown in Table 3, by leveraging lexical similarity (i.e., **-Syntactic Dependency**), the F-1 score is improved by 2.60%, compared with **-Lexical Similarity**. Moreover, the variant keeping lexical similarity has comparable performance with **BERT+SPAN**, while the variant removing lexical similarity regresses to basic Transformer-based **SELF** and **BERT**.

Moreover, when we remove the position embedding and only use word embedding as input, the score drops by 2.4%, which indicates that it is important to let the proposed attention aware of position information. Note that, the entity-level semantic vector representation (u_e^1 and u_e^2) are also fed into objective function (Eq. (16)). Through ablation study, we find that, removing the entity-level vector when predicting the normalized probabilities for the relation labels in Eq. (16), hurts the result by 3.1% F-1 score and degenerates to the performance **BERT+SPAN**.

Attention Visualization. For verifying the complementary effects of the proposed attention models and self-attention encoder, this section compares the attention weights assigned to tokens from the two encoders. Table 4 reports the attention visualization results on sample sentences. In Table 4, for each sample sentence, attention weights from the proposed attention models (i.e., **DS-ATT**) are visualized first, followed by self-attention encoder (e.g., **BERT+SPAN** and **SELF-ATT**). It is observed that the proposed neural relation extraction model leveraging syntactic dependency and lexical similarity **DS-ATT**, focuses more on the specific keywords or cue phrases of certain relations, such as "citizenship", "run" and "citoyen".

Table 4. Attention visualization for the proposed neural relation extraction model leveraging syntactic dependency and lexical similarity (**DS-ATT**) and self-attention encoder (**SELF-ATT** and **BERT+SPAN**). Wherein, tokens are highlighted based on the attention weights assigned to them. Best presented in color, and entities presented in bold font

Relation	Text	Result
president_of	[**Donald Trump**] was elected the 45th President of the [**United States**], after defeating Democratic candidate Hillary Clinton.	DS-ATT (ours):✓
	[**Donald Trump**] was elected the 45th President of the [**United States**], after defeating Democratic candidate Hillary Clinton.	BERT+SPAN:✓
	[**Donald Trump**] was elected the 45th President of the [**United States**], after defeating Democratic candidate Hillary Clinton.	SELF-ATT:✓
company	[**Lazard**], the investment bank run by [**Bruce Wsserstein**], said yesterday that strength in its merger advisory ⋯	DS-ATT (ours):✓
	[**Lazard**], the investment bank run by [**Bruce Wsserstein**], said yesterday that strength in its merger advisory ⋯	BERT+SPAN:✓
	[**Lazard**], the investment bank run by [**Bruce Wsserstein**], said yesterday that strength in its merger advisory ⋯	SELF-ATT:✗
nationality	Officially a citoyen [**Jonathan Littell**], the American author whose novel on the holocaust "the kindly one" was last year's literary hit in [**France**], has been granted french citizenship, agence france-presse reported yesterday.	DS-ATT (ours):✓
	Officially a citoyen [**Jonathan Littell**], the American author whose novel on the holocaust "the kindly one" was last year's literary hit in [**France**], has been granted french citizenship, agence france-presse reported yesterday.	BERT+SPAN:✗
	Officially a citoyen [**Jonathan Littell**], the American author whose novel on the holocaust "the kindly one" was last year's literary hit in [**France**], has been granted french citizenship, agence france-presse reported yesterday.	SELF-ATT:✗

5 Conclusion

We introduce a novel attention model which effectively incorporates global information with local information for relation extraction task, by leveraging syntactic dependency and lexical similarity. The proposed attention mechanism transforms texts from word space into relational semantic space and captures the informative linguistic clues of relations effectively.

Acknowledgements. We thank anonymous reviewers for valuable comments. This work is funded by: (i) the National Natural Science Foundation of China (No. U19B2026); (ii) the New Generation of Artificial Intelligence Special Action Project (No. AI20191125008); (iii) the National Integrated Big Data Center Pilot Project (No. 20500908, 17111001,17111002).

References

1. Bilan, I., Roth, B.: Position-aware self-attention with relative positional encodings for slot filling. arXiv abs/1807.03052 (2018)
2. Bowen, Y., Zhang, Z., Liu, T., Wang, B., Li, S., Li, Q.: Beyond word attention: using segment attention in neural relation extraction. In: IJCAI (2019)

3. Devlin, J., Chang, M.W., Lee, K., Toutanova, K.: BERT: pre-training of deep bidirectional transformers for language understanding. In: NAACL-HLT (2019)
4. Guo, Z., Zhang, Y., Lu, W.: Attention guided graph convolutional networks for relation extraction. arXiv abs/1906.07510 (2019)
5. Hochreiter, S., Schmidhuber, J.: Long short-term memory. Neural Comput. **9**, 1735–1780 (1997)
6. Huang, H., Wang, Y., Feng, C., Liu, Z., Zhou, Q.: Leveraging conceptualization for short-text embedding. IEEE Trans. Knowl. Data Eng. **30**(7), 1282–1295 (2018)
7. Joshi, M., Chen, D., Liu, Y., Weld, D.S., Zettlemoyer, L., Levy, O.: SpanBERT: improving pre-training by representing and predicting spans. Trans. Assoc. Comput. Linguist. **8**, 64–77 (2019)
8. Kim, Y.: Convolutional neural networks for sentence classification. In: EMNLP (2014)
9. Lan, Z., Chen, M., Goodman, S., Gimpel, K., Sharma, P., Soricut, R.: ALBERT: a lite BERT for self-supervised learning of language representations. arXiv abs/1909.11942 (2020)
10. Li, P., Mao, K., Yang, X., Li, Q.: Improving relation extraction with knowledge-attention. In: EMNLP/IJCNLP (2019)
11. Lin, Y., Shen, S., Liu, Z., Luan, H., Sun, M.: Neural relation extraction with selective attention over instances. In: ACL (2016)
12. Nayak, T.: Effective attention modeling for neural relation extraction. In: CoNLL 2019 (2019)
13. Nguyen, T.H., Grishman, R.: Relation extraction: perspective from convolutional neural networks. In: VS@HLT-NAACL (2015)
14. Rink, B., Harabagiu, S.M.: UTD: classifying semantic relations by combining lexical and semantic resources. In: SemEval@ACL (2010)
15. Song, Y., Wang, H., Wang, Z., Li, H., Chen, W.: Short text conceptualization using a probabilistic knowledgebase. In: Proceedings of the Twenty-Second International Joint Conference on Artificial Intelligence - Volume Volume Three, pp. 2330–2336 (2011)
16. Song, Y., Wang, S., Wang, H.: Open domain short text conceptualization: a generative + descriptive modeling approach. In: Proceedings of the 24th International Conference on Artificial Intelligence (2015)
17. Wang, F., Wang, Z., Li, Z., Wen, J.R.: Concept-based short text classification and ranking. In: The ACM International Conference, pp. 1069–1078 (2014)
18. Wang, J., Wang, Z., Zhang, D., Yan, J.: Combining knowledge with deep convolutional neural networks for short text classification. In: Twenty-Sixth International Joint Conference on Artificial Intelligence, pp. 2915–2921 (2017)
19. Wang, Y., Huang, H., Feng, C.: Query expansion based on a feedback concept model for microblog retrieval. In: International Conference on World Wide Web, pp. 559–568 (2017)
20. Wang, Y., Huang, H., Feng, C., Zhou, Q., Gu, J., Gao, X.: CSE: conceptual sentence embeddings based on attention model. In: 54th Annual Meeting of the Association for Computational Linguistics, pp. 505–515 (2016)
21. Wang, Y., Liu, Y., Zhang, H., Xie, H.: Leveraging lexical semantic information for learning concept-based multiple embedding representations for knowledge graph completion. In: APWeb/WAIM (2019)
22. Wu, W., Li, H., Wang, H., Zhu, K.Q.: Probase: a probabilistic taxonomy for text understanding. In: ACM SIGMOD International Conference on Management of Data, pp. 481–492 (2012)

23. Zeng, D., Liu, K., Lai, S., Zhou, G., Zhao, J.: Relation classification via convolutional deep neural network. In: COLING (2014)
24. Zhang, Y., Qi, P., Manning, C.D.: Graph convolution over pruned dependency trees improves relation extraction. In: EMNLP (2018)
25. Zhang, Y., Zhong, V., Chen, D., Angeli, G., Manning, C.D.: Position-aware attention and supervised data improve slot filling. In: EMNLP (2017)
26. Zhao, Y., Wan, H., Gao, J., Lin, Y.: Improving relation classification by entity pair graph. In: ACML (2019)

A Novel Capsule Aggregation Framework for Natural Language Inference

Chao Sun, Jianzong Wang[✉], Fengying Yu, Ning Cheng, and Jing Xiao

Ping An Technology (Shenzhen) Co., Ltd., Shenzhen, China

Abstract. Recent advances have advocated the use of complex attention mechanism to capture interactive information between *premise* and *hypothesis* in Natural Language Inference (NLI). However, few studies have focused on the further processing of matching feature, i.e. information aggregation. In this paper, we first investigate a novel capsule network for NLI, referred as Gcap. Gcap utilizes a gated enhanced fusion operation to obtain richer features between massive soft alignment information. Then the capsule aggregates those features through routing algorithms. Benefit from the routing mechanism of the capsule network, Gcap can dynamically generate feature vectors for subsequent classifier. Evaluation results demonstrate that our model achieves accuracy of 89.1%, 88.2% and 79.6% (79.3%) on SNLI, SciTail and MultiNLI datasets respectively, which outperforms the strong baseline with gains of 0.2%, 1.4% and 0.3% (0.6%). In particular, we compare the runtime inference efficiency of BERT and our model. Our model can attain up to 33.3× speedup in online inference time. Thanks to dynamic aggregation, Gcap shows a strong ability to distinguish those cases that are easily confused.

Keywords: Natural language inference · Information aggregation · Gated enhanced fusion · Capsule network · Dynamic aggregation

1 Introduction

Natural Language Inference (NLI) is a fundamental task in natural language understanding, while it is known as a challenging problem. In NLI task, we are given two sentences, namely *premise* and *hypothesis*, and the model judges their relationships from the candidates sets including *entailment*, *contradiction* and *neutral*, which is beneficial to other natural language processing problems, such as response selection and reading comprehension.

Neural models based on soft-attention alignments are proved to be effective nowadays. The key point is to establish an alignment between *premise* and *hypothesis*. Table 1 illustrates the soft alignment between sentence pairs. In first sentence pairs, words, "A man", "woman", "child" and "beach" in premise, should correspond to "dad", "mom", "A child" and "beach" in hypothesis respectively, which seems to be easy for traditional NLI models with pre-trained word

© Springer Nature Switzerland AG 2021
L. H. U et al. (Eds.): APWeb-WAIM 2021, LNCS 12858, pp. 300–315, 2021.
https://doi.org/10.1007/978-3-030-85896-4_24

Table 1. Example of SNLI datasets. The labels of the three examples are neutral, entailment and contradiction from top to bottom.

Premise: A man, woman, child enjoying themselves on a beach.
hypothesis: A child with mom and dad, on summer vacation at the beach.
Label: *neutral*
Premise: A man, woman, and child enjoying themselves on a beach.
hypothesis: A family of three is at the beach.
Label: *entailment*
Premise: A man, woman, and child enjoying themselves on a beach.
hypothesis: A family of three is at the mall shopping.
Label: *contradiction*

embeddings, e.g., GloVe embeddings [1]. The reason why sentence matching task is challenging is that there are also phrase-level and sentence-level alignments in addition to word-level. For example, *"A man, woman and child"* in second sentence pairs compare to *"A family of three"*, which shows the **multi-worlds** problem. Apparently, those problems need complicated semantic information matching and strong information aggregation capabilities.

The existing mainstream matching networks only focus on the richer alignment features and ignore the aggregation of alignment information, which causes insufficient ability to capture higher-order semantic information. For example, many studies enrich their alignment representation through introducing external knowledge [2,3], designing complex matching methods [4,5] and just fusing alignment features by fully connected layers or RNNs [6]. These simple aggregation layers will drown useful information in massive information, cannot reach an informative high-level semantic feature map and therefore lose phrase-level or sentence-level semantic information.

To address this problem, we introduce capsule networks, which decide the credit attribution between nodes from low-level capsules to high-level capsules and additionally improve the generalization capability through iteratively routing processes [7]. It has been proved to have potential for solving many NLP tasks [8–10]. On the other hand, gated mechanism is commonly used for information extraction from time series, showing powerful information fusion capability.

Most recently, BERT sets new state-of-the-art performance on various sentence classification and sentence-pair regression tasks and the BERT based models become the mainstream of NLP applications [11–13]. However, those pretraining based models like BERT make it difficult to be applied to online inference tasks because of its huge amount of parameters and resource consumption nature.

Given those problems, we improve the performance of NLI in two ways. Firstly, we design two kinds of fusion operations called Gated Enhanced Fusion (GEF) and Gated Fully Fusion (GFF) for richer matching features. This fusion method based on gating mechanism is used to fuse the alignment features and original features to ensure that valuable features are passed to the higher layers from massive useless information. Secondly, we introduce the capsule aggregation network, which acts as a clustering-like method to automatically learn part-whole relationships by dynamic routing processes.

In conclusion, the contributions of this paper are listed as follows:

- Paying attention to the fusion operation, we propose the Gated Enhanced Fusion (GEF) and Gated Fully Fusion Module (GFF) to obtain rich semantics.
- We first introduce capsule network as the aggregation layer to automatically increase or decrease the connection strength. Therefore our model obtains the most convincing interactive representation of sentences.
- Benefit from the novel capsule network, we can make fully use of different feature combinations as low-level capsules without falling into dimensional explosion.

2   Related Work

The development of the model is inseparable from the powerful data set, especially in Natural Language Processing. These models could be roughly divided into two types: the *Siamese architecture* and the *representation-matching-aggregation paradigm*.

The ESIM [14] learns soft-alignments between sentence pairs after BiLSTM encoding, then aggregates them with another BiLSTM layer. The BiMPM model [15] pays attention to matching layer and match sentence pairs from bilateral multi-perspective. Stochastic answer network (SAN) [16] explores the use of multi-step inference. Original semantics-oriented attention and deep fusion network (OSOA-DFN) [5] focus on the original semantic representations and attention information propagation cross-layer. DRr-Net [17] pays close attention to a small region of sentences at each step and re-read the important words. Neural graph matching networks are proposed to deal with multiple word segmentation for Chinese short text matching [18]. More recently, BERT-based models have become the mainstream of NLP applications [19–21].

On the one hand, the concept of "capsule" was firstly introduced to address the representational limitations of CNNs and RNNs for its ability to automatically learn part-whole relationships [22]. Subsequently, capsule networks are proposed to replace the scalar-output feature with vector-output capsules and max-pooling with routing-by-agreement [7]. To deal with overlapped features in aspect-level sentiment classification, capsule networks are utilized to construct vector-based feature representation and cluster features by an EM routing algorithm [23]. In document-level translation, the query-guided capsule networks are utilized to explore the relationship between context words, distinguishing the roles of context words [10]. Hyperbolic capsules are designed to capture fine-grained document information for Multi-Label Classification and significantly improved the performance of solving tail labels problem [24].

On the other hand, gates are commonly utilized to control information propagation in NLP. For example, different gates are used to handle long-term memory and dependencies in LSTM [25] and GRU [26]. The SeG [27] designs a selective gate to aggregate sentence-level representations into bag-level one and preventing noise representation being propagated. In computer vision, gates are used to learn the precise boundary information to encode edge features into final representation [28].

3   Proposed Method

Given $(\boldsymbol{p}, \boldsymbol{h}, y)$, where $\boldsymbol{p} = \{\boldsymbol{p}_1, \cdots, \boldsymbol{p}_i, \cdots, \boldsymbol{p}_{l_p}\}$ and $\boldsymbol{h} = \{\boldsymbol{h}_1, \cdots, \boldsymbol{h}_j, \cdots, \boldsymbol{h}_{l_h}\}$, $\boldsymbol{p}$ and $\boldsymbol{h}$ are a premise and hypothesis with a length l_p and l_h in NLI task, respectively. Our goal is to learn a matching model $g\,(\cdot)$ to predict a label y from a relationship set $\{entailment, contradiction, neural\}$.

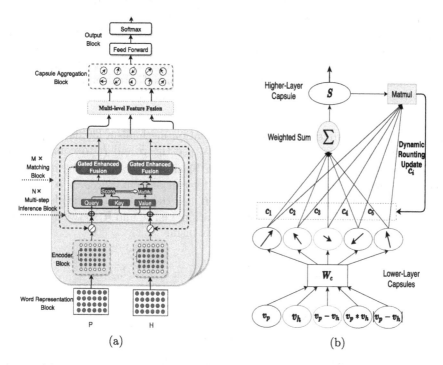

(a)   (b)

Fig. 1. (a) The overview of our proposed model architecture (*best viewed in color*). From bottom to top is word representation block, encoder block, multi-step inference block, aggregation block and output block. The encoder block, multi-step inference block constitute the matching network we designed and each layer of matching network includes an N-step inference block, whereas the whole model consists of an M-layer inference block, an aggregation block and an output block. Here we only draw three layers. (b) the proposed Capsule Aggregation Operation. $\boldsymbol{s}$ is the output capsule. $\boldsymbol{W}_c$ are projection matrices. c_i is the coupling coefficient.

Figure 1(a) illustrates a high-level overview of our model, which includes four components: word representation block, matching block, aggregation block and output block. Generally, we define the matching block as consisting of encoder block and multi-step inference block. In this work, we utilize the stacked matching blocks to obtain richer alignment features.

3.1 Word Representation

This layer represent each word in p and h with l-dimension vector, i.e. $p_i = \{p_{i,1}, p_{i,2}, \cdots, p_{i,l}\}$, $h_i = \{h_{i,1}, h_{i,2}, \cdots, h_{i,l}\}$. In our model, the word embedding is a fixed 300-dimension vector pre-trained with Glove [1].

3.2 Matching Block

The well-designed layer aims to obtain the matching information of the two sequence vectors, i.e., the richer alignment features, which is extremely important for subsequent aggregation operations.

From simple consideration, we use multi-layer convolution networks with same padding [29] as encoder block to capture N-gram information. The output of different window size of the filters, which are applied for various grams, are concatenated. We found that recurrent networks or self-attention based modules do not contribute to better results and slow down our model.

Multi-step Inference. Generally, the attention mechanism [30] is adopted to obtain the cross attention information. We use the p and h to compute the attention weights $e_{ij} = \bar{p}_i \bar{h}_j^T$ as shown in black solid frame in the middle of Fig. 1(a), then words in p are represented by dependent words in h through calculated attention scores where $\bar{p}$ and $\bar{h}$ are the output of encoder block. Finally, we obtain the interactive representation, i.e., $\tilde{p}_i$ and $\tilde{h}_i$ between *premise* and *hypothesis* via the cross-attention mechanism.

$$\tilde{p}_i = \sum_{j=1}^{l_h} \frac{exp(e_{ij})}{\sum_{k=1}^{l_h} exp(e_{ik})} \bar{h}_i, \forall i \in [1, ..., l_p]$$

$$\tilde{h}_j = \sum_{i=1}^{l_p} \frac{exp(e_{ij})}{\sum_{k=1}^{l_p} exp(e_{kj})} \bar{p}_i, \forall j \in [1, ..., l_h]$$

(1)

Complex connections cannot usually be obtained by one-step reasoning at once. In this work, we simply employ a stack of N interaction blocks to collect evidence of multi-step inference as the alignment features, i.e., attention over attention. Take p as an example, the whole multi-step inference block can be defined by

$$E_p^{I_i} = [O_p^{I_j-1}; O_{enc_p}^j]$$

(2)

$$C_p^{I_i} = CrossAttention\left(E_p^{I_i}, E_h^{I_i}\right)$$

(3)

$$C_p^{I_i} = \mathbf{GEF}\left(C_p^{I_i}, E_p^{I_i}\right) \tag{4}$$

$$O_p^{I_i} = LayerNorm\left(C_p^{I_i} \oplus E_p^{I_i}\right) \tag{5}$$

Where $i \in [1, ..., N], j \in [1, ..., M]$, $E_p^{I_i}$, $O_p^{I_i}$ is the input and output of the i-th inference layer respectively. For the j-th matching module, $O_{enc_p}^j$ is the encoder output and we perform N-step inference. In Eq. (2), we combine the encoder features $O_{enc_p}^j$ with the matching information of the previous layer $O_p^{I_{j-1}}$ by direct concatenation for the purpose of augmenting the matching information propagation. $O_p^{I_0}$ represent the original word representation. Equation (3) is the general form of cross attention. In Eq. (4), we use a gate mechanism to fuse the original information and alignment features. The details are described in the next section. At the same time, the residual connection makes the stack inference information propagate more effectively, as shown in Eq. (5). We do the same operations for h.

Gated Enhanced Fusion. The basic task in alignment feature fusion is to aggregate useful information together under the interference of massive useless information. ESIM [14] computes the difference and the element-wise product for the tuple $<\bar{p}, \tilde{p}>$ and $<\bar{h}, \tilde{h}>$ corresponding to $<C_p^{I_i}, E_p^{I_i}>$ and $<C_h^{I_i}, E_h^{I_i}>$ in our framework, to sharpen local inference information and model some high-order interaction. However, they just conducted the concatenation operation between vectors and found that feeding the tuples into feedforward neural networks does not further help the inference accuracy. We reasonably conclude that it suffers from mixing the useful information with a large amount of non-informative features. In this paper, we design the Gated Enhanced Fusion (GEF) based on gate mechanism to control information flow. Specifically, $X, \bar{X}$ represent the original feature and the alignment feature respectively. A one-layer feed forward network is applied to X to element-wisely produce gating value, which is formally denoted as

$$\bar{X} = Relu(\bar{X}W_1) \quad g = sigmoid(XW_2 + b_1)$$
$$\bar{X} = g * \bar{X} + (1-g) * X \tag{6}$$

where $W_1, W_2 \in \mathbb{R}^{l \times l}$, l is the dimension of the hidden state. The final fusion output is

$$\tilde{X} = Relu([Gate(X, \bar{X}); Gate(X, X - \bar{X}); Gate(X, X * \bar{X})]W_3 + b_2) \tag{7}$$

Multi-level Feature Fusion. In semantic segmentation, feature maps of higher levels are with lower resolution and combining the complementary strengths of multiple level feature maps would achieve the goal of both high resolution and rich semantics [31]. Inspired by this, we fuse M feature maps by Gated Fully Fusion Module (GFF) [31], where M feature maps $\{X_i \in \mathbb{R}^{l_x \times H}\}_{i=1}^M$ are extracted from the M stacked matching blocks. The GEF is formally defined as

$$\overline{X}_M = (1+G_M)*X_M + (1-G_M)*\sum_{i=1}^{M-1} G_i*X_i \tag{8}$$

where each gate map $G_i = sigmoid(f(w_i * X_i))$, f is convolutional operation parameterized with w_i.

3.3 Capsule Aggregation Block

Capsule network [7] was first proposed to address the representational limitations and exponential inefficiencies of CNN by extracting features in the form of vectors. It allows the networks to automatically learn the intrinsic spatial part-whole relationship constituting viewpoint invariant knowledge that automatically generalizes to novel viewpoints. On one hand, it can increase or decrease the connection strength to the lower level capsules by dynamic routing for each higher level capsule, which acts like clustering methods. On the other hand, it is a more efficient way for features encoder. In our paper, we explore its ability to learn hierarchical relationships between consecutive layers and using it to aggregate the final feature.

Specifically, to learn the high-level representation of each sentence, we conduct both average and max pooling to the GFF output $\dot{p}$ and $\dot{h}$, which is not sensitive to the sequence and shows stronger robustness. The final fixed length vector v_p and v_h is as follows.

$$v_p = [\dot{p}_{ave}; \dot{p}_{max}] \quad v_h = [\dot{h}_{ave}; \dot{h}_{max}] \tag{9}$$

Previous studies always concatenate the feature vector $[v_p; v_h]$ or its evolved form $[v_p; v_h; v_p \odot v_p; v_p - v_h]$ to the vanilla MLP classifier to predict the final label.

However, it suffers from the insufficient feature extraction capability or dimensional explosion for MLP. In our study, those feature vectors act as child capsules, i.e. $\{v_p, v_h, v_p \odot v_p, v_p - v_h, |v_p - v_h|\}$ in Fig. 1(b), and the parent capsule automatically extract the features from lower-level capsules based on routing algorithm without additional parameters.

Dynamic Routing. Between two neighbor layers l and $l+1$, there are two sets of capsules $\{u_1, ..., u_m\}$ and $\{v_1, ..., v_n\}$. Routing processes are introduced to route lower-layer capsules into the higher layer for capturing hierarchical relationships between two consecutive layers. First, we transform the capsules u_i into a collection of candidates $\{\hat{u}_{j|1}, ..., \hat{u}_{j|m}\}$ by multiplying a linear transformation matrix W_c. Then the high-level capsule v_j is generated by a weighted sum over projected low-level capsules $\{\hat{u}_{j|1}, ..., \hat{u}_{j|m}\}$, denoted as

$$\hat{u}_{i|j} = W_c u_i \quad v_j = \sum_{i=1}^{m} c_{ij}\hat{u}_{i|j} \tag{10}$$

where c_{ij} is a coupling coefficient iteratively updated by routing process on original logits b_{ij}, $c_{ij} = \frac{exp(b_{ij})}{\sum_j exp(b_{ij})}$. The sum of all the coefficients for capsule j is 1 for the softmax. The dynamic routing process is reflected in the initial digit of b_{ij} is updated with routing by agreement a scale product between two consecutive capsule layers.

$$b_{ij} \leftarrow \hat{u}_{j|i} \cdot b_j \quad v_j = \frac{||v_j||^2}{1 + ||v_j||} \frac{v_j}{||v_j||^2} \tag{11}$$

where v_j is limited in range $[0, 1]$ with a non-linear squashing function. In this work, n is equal to 1, which means there is only one higher-level capsule.

EM Routing. EM-based routing method [32] is another routing algorithm where the vector-based features get clustered in the high-level capsules by an EM based algorithm. the distribution parameters of input capsules and output capsules dynamically updates through E-step and M-step. Details are omitted in this paper.

4   Experiments and Analyses

In this section, we first introduce the training process of our model in detail, then we report our experimental results on SNLI, SciTail and MultiNLI dataset. Next, through a series of ablation experiments, we analyze the effectiveness of each part of the model.

4.1   Model Training

The whole experiments are implemented in Tensorflow [33] and trained on Nvidia V100 GPU. Word embeddings are pre-loaded with $300d$ GloVe embeddings [1] and fixed during training. For out-of-vocabulary (OOV) words, we initialize the embeddings to zeros. The window size of the filters vary from 3, 4, 5 for encoding trigrams, four-grams and five-grams information respectively. There are 50 filters for each window size and the parameters are not shared. The hidden size is slightly different on different datasets. On SNLI dataset, the hidden size is 150 whereas 200 on MultiNLI and SciTail dataset.

We use the Adam optimizer with the initial learning rate of 0.01, an exponentially decay ratio of 0.95 and a linear warmup. In each matching network, we apply the dropout rate with a keep probability of 0.8 after each fully-connected layer. The number of multi-step inference layer is turned among $\{1, 2, 3, 4\}$, and we stack different layers of matching block from candidate sets $\{1, 2, 3, 4\}$. In capsule aggregation layer, 5 child (lower-level) capsules are aggregated to 1 parent (higher-level) capsule with 150 dimensions for SNLI and 200 dimensions for Multinli and Scitail. Given gradient explosion, we set gradient clipping with a threshold of 5. Different activation functions, such as GeLU and ReLU, are applied at different stages of the network.

In our stacked structures, the number of Encoder layers(E), Matching layers(M) and Inference layers(N) varies with the data set, where E = 2 M = 3 N = 1 in SNLI, E = 3 M = 3 N = 2 in Scitail and E = 2 M = 3 N = 2 in MultiNLI.

4.2   Overall Performance

The number of iterations in the capsule network is an empirical parameter. Previous studies show 3 iterations convergences fast and performs best [34]. So we utilize 3 iterations in all our experiments. We only introduce the pre-trained Glove vectors. Therefore, we compare our results with the competitive baselines which are not pre-training based model like BERT [11] or ensemble model.

Table 2. Performance comparison of all published models on SNLI **test** set. The * represents the model with external information or it's an ensemble model and † represents our implement.

Model	Params	Test (%)
Handcrafted features [35]	–	78.2
BiMPM [15]	1.6M	87.5
600D ESIM + 300D Syntactic TreeLSTM* [14]	7.7M	88.6
Stochastic Answer Network [16]	3.5M	88.5
KIM* [3]	4.3M	88.6
CSRAN [36]	13.9M	88.7
300D DMAN* [2]	9.2M	88.8
DRCN [37]	6.7M	88.9
DIIN* [38]	17M	88.9
OSOA-DFN [5]	–	88.8
ADIN [39]	–	88.8
RE2 [40]	2.8M	88.9
BERT†[11]	109M	**90.2**
Gcap-DR	3.7M	**89.1**
Gcap-EM	3.7M	89.0

SNLI. [35] is a benchmark dataset for NLI. It contains 570K human annotated sentence pairs with labels "entailmen", "neutral" and "contradiction". Table 2 reports the results of different models. Top of the table shows a handcrafted features model reported by [35], which consider BLEU score, N-gram, and the length difference between *premise* and *hypothesis*.

In the middle part of the table are some methods based on deep neural networks, which are sorted by the accuracy of the test set. As we can see, the performance of our Gcap model outperforms all the single model and achieves new state-of-the-art performance with relatively few parameters. It can be seen that both the dynamic routing and EM routing method outperform the strong baselines.

Comparison of BERT. Benefits from sufficient external information, the BERT [11] obtains the accuracy of 90.2%. However, huge resource consumption is disastrous for online reasoning. In this section, we compare the runtime inference efficiency of BERT and our model in a single V100 GPU and CPU (Intel Xeon Gold-6130 @2.10 GHz) for batch inference (batch size = 1, 32) on 1000 queries of sequence length 128. We average the time taken for predicting labels for all the sentence pairs for each model aggregated over 100 runs and the results are reported in Fig. 2. In terms of parameters, the BERT is 29.5 times as large as our model, and it achieves 6.8 lower inference speed than the Gcap-DR. As for online inference (CPU, batch size 32), we observe our model has the

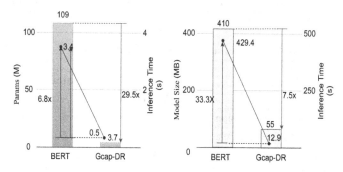

Fig. 2. The parameters, model size and inference time with BERT and Gcap-DR. The parameters and inference time (on GPU, batch size 32) are shown on the left, and the model size and online inference time (CPU, batch size 1) are shown on the right.

Table 3. Experimental result on SciTail

Model	Acc (%)
CAFE [41]	83.8
CSRNN [36]	86.7
HCRN [42]	80.0
ADIN [39]	84.6
RE2 [40]	86.0
OSOA-DFN [5]	86.8
Gcap-DR	88.0
Gcap-EM	**88.2**

Table 4. Experimental result on MultiNLI

Model	M-ma/M-mis
CAFE [41]	78.7/77.9
DIIN [38]	78.8/77.8
MwAN [43]	78.5/77.7
SAN [16]	79.3/78.7
AF-DMN [44]	76.9/76.3
ADIN [39]	78.8/77.9
Gcap-DR	79.6/**79.3**
Gcap-EM	**79.7**/79.1

speedup of 33.3× compared to BERT. Further, our Gcap-DR can achieve 7.8× model size compression, which leads to fewer resource consumption for online.

SciTail. [45] is an entailment dataset created from science questions and answers, which contains 27,026 examples with 10,101 examples are labeled as entails and 16,925 examples with neutral label. As shown in Table 3, OSOA-DFN [5] performs multiple attention layers for better matching through repeatedly reading the important information between two sentences, which builds a high score. Our model still achieves the best single model score, significantly outperforming these baselines such as OSOA-DFN (+1.4%) and CSRNN (+1.5%).

MultiNLI. corpus [46] contains 433k sentences pairs for NLI. Similar to SNLI, each pair is labeled with one of the following relationships: entailment, contradiction, or neutral. The Gcap again achieves the highest accuracy rate, outperforming the SAN (+0.3%/+0.6%) in Table 4, which incorporate a recurrent state and generate the output through multi-step inference, setting a strong baseline, especially on mismatched set.

Table 5. Ablation study on SNLI and SciTail **dev** set.

Ablation model	SNLI		Scitail	
	Param	Acc (%)	F1-score	Acc (%)
-w/o Gated Enhanced Fusion	2.1M	89.1	88.6	89.0
-w/o Multi-level Feature Fusion	3.6M	89.1	88.5	88.9
-w/o Dynamic Capsule Aggregation	3.9M	89.3	89.2	89.7
Gcap-DR (Base)	3.7M	**89.4**	89.4	90.0
Gcap-EM	3.7M	89.2	**90.5**	**91.0**

4.3   Ablation Experiments

As shown in Table 5, we conduct a full ablation experiment on SNLI and Scitail development dataset to find out which component makes our model effective. The Gcap-DR model is set as the benchmark model on both datasets, although Gcap-EM performs better on the SciTail dev sets.

Effects of Gated Enhanced Fusion. Getting rid of the gated enhanced fusion, we fusion the alignment features in feed-forward networks, which has proven to be very effective in RE2 [40]. The performance drops by 0.3% to 89.1% on SNLI dev set, at the same time, the amount of parameters drops by 1.6 million, which indicates its powerful ability to capture the useful features from massive information. Obviously, its cost is prominent, which brings large increase in the amount of parameters. On SciTail dev set, the accuracy drops to 89.0% and F1 score reduced by 1%.

Effects of Multi-level Feature Fusion. We modify the structure of Gcap by removing multi-level feature fusion. The result shows that the accuracy drops from 89.4% to 89.1% (90.0% to 88.9%) with a margin of 0.3% (1.1%) on SNLI (SciTail) set. This module reduces the fluctuation of the accuracy rate during our ablation experiments with few parameter increases.

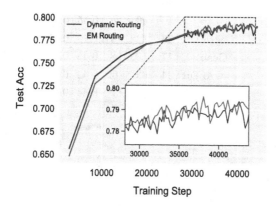

Fig. 3. Performance on the **matched** set of MultiNLI with different routing strategy.

Effects of Dynamic Capsule Aggregation. In order to explore the effects of dynamic aggregation, we replace the capsule network with a fully connected layer. More specifically, we concatenate those low-level capsules and feed the **long** vector into feedforward neural network i.e., $v = [v_p; v_h; v_p \odot v_p; v_p - v_h]W_4 + b_4, v \in \mathbb{R}^{5h}$, which causes the accuracy decreases by 0.1% and 0.3% and increase in parameters. Thanks to the dynamic aggregation mechanism, the number of our features could be a large value without a sharp increase in parameters.

Effects of DR and EM. Furthermore, we explore the performance of the aggregation layer routing algorithm. It should be noticed that Gcap-EM has slightly smaller parameters than Gcap-DR in our work although the principle of the algorithm is essentially different. Figure 3 shows that the DR routing aggregation model initially convergences faster than the EM aggregation model. After 20,000 steps, Gcap-EM surpassed Gcap-DR and achieved a higher value.

4.4 Case Study

In this section, we specifically analyzed the impact of capsules on sentence matching. In Table 6, we select samples with different prediction results for analysis, that is, each sample in Table 6 has different prediction results based on the real label.

Table 6. Class statistics results with different prediction results on SNLI **test** set by different models (0, 1, 2 represent entailment, neutral and contradict respectively). Ablation study on SNLI and SciTail **dev** set.

Actual	Model	Predict			Class statistics	
		0	1	2	F1	AUC
0	-w/o DR	56	103	25	0.37	0.58
	Gcap	109	49	26	0.55	0.66
1	-w/o DR	36	122	79	0.46	0.51
	Gcap	77	102	58	0.45	0.55
2	-w/o DR	24	63	69	0.42	0.60
	Gcap	28	61	67	0.44	0.61

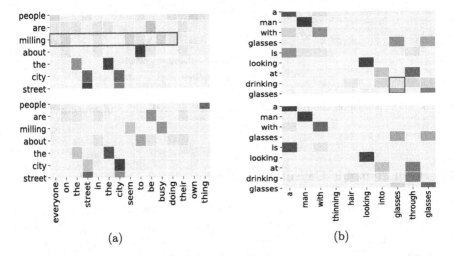

(a)   (b)

Fig. 4. (a) Final attention score on different models. The upper is the result of Gcap. The real label is entailment, and the prediction label of model without DR is neutral. The horizontal axis represents *premise*. (b) Final attention score on different models. The horizontal axis represents *hypothesis*.

From Table 6 we can find that the model without dynamic aggregation can not even distinguish between *neutral* and *entailment* (Among the 184 sentence pairs with real label 0, 103 are misidentified as label 1, and only 56 are correctly reasoned). The F1 score of class *entailment* is much smaller than Gcap (0.37 vs 0.55). Among 103 samples of reasoning errors, 95 are correctly reasoned by the soft-alignment affected by dynamic aggregation. As shown in Fig. 4(a), we call it the typical multi-worlds problem, that is, one word in a sentence needs to be aligned with several words in another sentence to make correct reasoning. The key word "milling" implies "people seem to be busy doing something" and obviously, dynamic aggregation aligns richer information. Another case is shown in Fig. 4(b), the meanings of the words "glasses" and "drinking glasses" are quite different. In the model without DR the incomplete alignment lead to model misjudgment. Thanks to the dynamic aggregation of Gcap, it capture the weakly phase-level alignment, which determines the relationship between the sentence pair.

5 Conclusion

In this paper, we pay attention to the process of feature aggregation in NLI task, proposing a dynamic capsule aggregation and gated enhanced fusion network, which achieve very competitive results on SNLI, SciTail and MultiNLI datasets. It should be noted that it is a general method and can be suitable for other tasks.

Acknowledgments. This paper is supported by National Key Research and Development Program of China under grant No.2018YFB0204403, No.2017YFB1401202 and No.2018YFB1003500. Corresponding author is Jianzong Wang from Ping An Technology (Shenzhen) Co., Ltd.

References

1. Pennington, J., Socher, R., Manning, C.D.: Glove: Global vectors for word representation. In: EMNLP (2014)
2. Pan, B., Yang, Y., Zhao, Z., Zhuang, Y., Cai, D., He, X.: Discourse marker augmented network with reinforcement learning for natural language inference. In: ACL (2018)
3. Chen, Q., Zhu, X., Ling, Z.H., Inkpen, D., Wei, S.: Neural natural language inference models enhanced with external knowledge. In: ACL (2018)
4. Wang, L., et al.: One vs. many qa matching with both word-level and sentence-level attention network. In: COLING (2018)
5. Liu, M., Zhang, Y., Xu, J., Chen, Y.: Original semantics-oriented attention and deep fusion network for sentence matching. In: IJCNLP 2019 (2019)
6. Ye, Z.-X., Ling, Z.-H.: Multi-level matching and aggregation network for few-shot relation classification. In: ACL (July 2019)
7. Sabour, S., Frosst, N., Hinton, G.E.: Dynamic routing between capsules. In: NIPS (2017)
8. Zhao, W., Ye, J., Yang, M., Lei, Z., Zhang, S., Zhao, Z.: Investigating capsule networks with dynamic routing for text classification. In: EMNLP (2018)
9. Srivastava, S., Khurana, P., Tewari, V.: Identifying aggression and toxicity in comments using capsule network. In: TRAC@COLING 2018 (2018)
10. Yang, Z., Zhang, J., Meng, F., Gu, S., Feng, Y., Zhou, J.: Enhancing context modeling with a query-guided capsule network for document-level translation. In: EMNLP/IJCNLP (November 2019)
11. Devlin, J., Chang, M.W., Lee, K., Toutanova, K.: Pre-training of deep bidirectional transformers for language understanding. In: NAACL-HLT, Bert (2019)
12. Zhang, S., Huang, H., Liu, J., Li, H.: Spelling error correction with soft-masked BERT. In: ACL (July 2020)

13. Jia, C., Shi, Y., Yang, Q., Zhang, Y.: Entity enhanced BERT pre-training for Chinese NER. In: EMNLP (November 2020)
14. Chen, Q., Zhu, X., Ling, Z., Wei, S., Jiang, H., Inkpen, D.: Enhanced LSTM for natural language inference. In: ACL (2017)
15. Wang, Z., Hamza, W., Florian, R.: Bilateral multi-perspective matching for natural language sentences. In: IJCAI (2017)
16. Liu, X., Duh, K., Gao, J.: Stochastic answer networks for natural language inference. CoRR, arXiv:1804.07888 (2018)
17. Zhang, K., et al.: Drr-net: Dynamic re-read network for sentence semantic matching. In: AAAI (2019)
18. Chen, L., et al.: Neural graph matching networks for chinese short text matching. In: ACL (2020)
19. Reimers, N., Gurevych, I.: Sentence-bert: Sentence embeddings using siamese bert-networks. In: EMNLP/IJCNLP (2019)
20. Zhang, Z., et al.: Semantics-aware BERT for language understanding. In: AAAI (2020)
21. Li, B., Zhou, H., He, J., Wang, M., Yang, Y., Li, L.: On the sentence embeddings from pre-trained language models. In: EMNLP (November 2020)
22. Hinton, G.E., Krizhevsky, A., Wang, S.D.: Transforming auto-encoders. In: Honkela, T., Duch, W., Girolami, M., Kaski, S. (eds.) ICANN 2011. LNCS, vol. 6791, pp. 44–51. Springer, Heidelberg (2011). https://doi.org/10.1007/978-3-642-21735-7_6
23. Du, C.: Capsule network with interactive attention for aspect-level sentiment classification. In: EMNLP/IJCNLP (2019)
24. Chen, B., Huang, X., Xiao, L., Jing, L.: Hyperbolic capsule networks for multi-label classification. In: ACL (2020)
25. Hochreiter, S., Schmidhuber, J.: Long short-term memory. Neural Comput. **9**, 1735–1780 (1997)
26. Cho, K., et al.: Learning phrase representations using RNN encoder-decoder for statistical machine translation. In: EMNLP (October 2014)
27. Li, Y., et al.: Self-attention enhanced selective gate with entity-aware embedding for distantly supervised relation extraction. In: EMNLP (2019)
28. Takikawa, T., Acuna, D., Jampani, V., Fidler, S.: Gated-scnn: Gated shape CNNs for semantic segmentation. In: ICCV, pp. 5228–5237 (2019)
29. Collobert, R., Weston, J., Bottou, L., Karlen, M., Kavukcuoglu, K., Kuksa, P.P.: Natural language processing (almost) from scratch. J. Mach. Learn. Res. **12**, 2493–2537 (2011)
30. Vaswani, A.: Attention is all you need. In: NIPS (2017)
31. Li, X., Zhao, H., Han, L., Tong, Y., Tan, S., Yang, K.: Gated fully fusion for semantic segmentation. In: AAAI (2020)
32. Hinton, G., Sabour, S., Frosst, N: Matrix capsules with EM routing. In: ICLR (2018)
33. Abadi, M., et al.: TensorFlow: Large-scale machine learning on heterogeneous systems (2015). Software available from tensorflow.org
34. Xiao, L., Zhang, H., Chen, W., Wang, Y., Jin, Y.: Mcapsnet: Capsule network for text with multi-task learning. In: EMNLP (2018)
35. Bowman, S.R., Angeli, G., Potts, C., Manning, C.D.: A large annotated corpus for learning natural language inference. In: EMNLP (2015)
36. Tay, Y., Luu, A.T., Hui, S.C.: Co-stack residual affinity networks with multi-level attention refinement for matching text sequences. In: EMNLP (2018)

37. Kim, S., Kang, I., Kwak, N.: Semantic sentence matching with densely-connected recurrent and co-attentive information. In: AAAI (2018)
38. Gong, Y., Luo, H., Zhang, J.: Natural language inference over interaction space. In: ICLR (2018)
39. Liang, D., Zhang, F., Zhang, Q., Huang, X.J.: Asynchronous deep interaction network for natural language inference. In: EMNLP/IJCNLP (2019)
40. Yang, R., Zhang, J., Gao, X., Ji, F., Chen, H.: Simple and effective text matching with richer alignment features. In: ACL (2019)
41. Tay, Y., Luu, A.T., Hui, S.C.: Compare, compress and propagate: Enhancing neural architectures with alignment factorization for natural language inference. In: EMNLP (2018)
42. Tay, Y., Luu, A.T., Hui, S.C.: Hermitian co-attention networks for text matching in asymmetrical domains. In: IJCAI (2018)
43. Tan, C., Wei, F., Wang, W., Lv, W., Zhou, M.: Multiway attention networks for modeling sentence pairs. In: IJCAI (2018)
44. Liu, M., Zhang, Y., Xu, J., Chen, Y.: Original semantics-oriented attention and deep fusion network for sentence matching. In: EMNLP/IJCNLP (2019)
45. Khot, T., Sabharwal, A., Clark, P.: A textual entailment dataset from science question answering. In: AAAI, SciTail (2018)
46. Williams, A., Nangia, N., Bowman, S.R.: A broad-coverage challenge corpus for sentence understanding through inference. In: NAACL-HLT (2017)

Learning Modality-Invariant Features by Cross-Modality Adversarial Network for Visual Question Answering

Ze Fu[1,2], Changmeng Zheng[1,2], Yi Cai[1,2(✉)], Qing Li[3], and Tao Wang[4]

[1] School of Software Engineering, South China University of Technology,
Guangzhou, China
{seorangefu,sethecharm}@mail.scut.edu.cn, ycai@scut.edu.cn
[2] Key Laboratory of Big Data and Intelligent Robot (SCUT), MOE of China,
Shanghai, China
[3] Department of Computing,
The Hong Kong Polytechnic University, Hong Kong SAR, China
qing-prof.li@polyu.edu.hk
[4] Department of Biostatistics and Health Informatics, Institute of Psychiatry,
Psychology and Neuroscience, King's College London, London, UK

Abstract. *Visual Question Answering* (VQA) is a typical multimodal task with significant development prospect on web application. In order to answer the question based on the corresponding image, a VQA model needs to utilize the information from different modality efficiently. Although the multimodal fusion methods such as attention mechanism make significant contribution for VQA, these methods try to co-learn the multimodal features directly, ignoring the large gap between different modality and thus poor aligning the semantic. In this paper, we propose a *Cross-Modality Adversarial Network* (CMAN) to address this limitation. Our method combines cross-modality adversarial learning with modality-invariant attention learning aiming to learn the modality-invariant features for better semantic alignment and higher answer prediction accuracy. The accuracy of model achieves 70.81% on the *test-dev* split on the VQA-v2 dataset. Our results also show that the model narrows the gap between different modalities effectively and improves the alignment performance of the multimodal information.

Keywords: Visual question answering · Domain adaptation · Modality-invariant co-learning

1 Introduction

Visual Question Answering (VQA) requires model to answer the question based on the corresponding image. With significant development prospect on the web application such as cross-modal retrieval [13,22] and assisting the visually impaired [12], VQA attracted many researchers' attention in recent years.

L. H. U et al. (Eds.): APWeb-WAIM 2021, LNCS 12858, pp. 316–331, 2021.
https://doi.org/10.1007/978-3-030-85896-4_25

As a challenging multimodal task, it is crucial to locate the key objects in both textual and visual modalities to answer the question. For instance, to answer the question *'What color is the apple?'* based on the image of a red apple, the model should align the semantic between the textual word *apple* and the visual object apple in this V-Q pair to seek the key information about the word *color*. In other words, the model should well align the semantic between image and question to understand the question in a fine-grained level. Recently, researchers focus on the better representation fusion [5] and co-learning methods [24] such as attention mechanism [21] to achieve well semantic alignment in VQA.

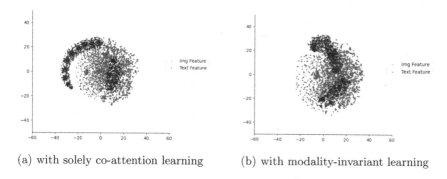

(a) with solely co-attention learning   (b) with modality-invariant learning

Fig. 1. Visualization of multimodal feature distribution by t-SNE [16]. The red and blue dots represent the text and image features respectively. (Color figure online)

However, these methods try to fuse the multimodal features directly, ignoring the large gap between different modalities. Suffering from this gap, the correlation between multimodal information is hard to capture, which causes the poor semantic alignment of multimodal information. As shown in the Fig. 1(a), under the attention-based method [24], the visual and textual feature distributions exist large gap between different modalities and fuse with barely satisfactory, which might cause the coarse alignment of the semantic and the decline of answer prediction accuracy. Thus, it is supposed to narrow the gap between different modalities for better alignment of multimodal semantic information.

Besides, some recent researches [1,2,17] show that there are language priors existing in the VQA dataset [9]. For instance, to answer the question *'What color is the banana?'*, the answers in the training set are *yellow* with high probability. Thus, the model tends to answer the question without understanding the image and still achieves high accuracy. This phenomenon causes the VQA model to learn superficial representation without image information to answer the question. In this case, if the banana images in the test data are all the green ones, the model suffering from the priors would also predict the wrong answer *yellow*.

To address the first limitation, we consider to obtain the modality-invariant features to narrow the gap between different modalities. Inspired by domain adaptation method [7] which reduces domain shift of source and target domains by adversarial learning, we consider it is a good choice to utilize adversarial learning to obtain modality-invariant features. As shown in Fig. 1(b), after bridging the modality gap by modality-invariant learning, the multimodal features learned by our model are in well fusion with narrow modality gap.

Moreover, to counter the language priors, some recent works [18,20] are proposed to discourage the VQA model from exploiting language biases in question encoding. As a comparison, we utilize the modality-invariant features belonging neither to the textual modality nor the visual modality to counter the modality priors as they are *modality-invariant*. The modality-invariant character urges the model to exploit information from both modalities without preferentially choosing their subordinate modality. Therefore, the priors of either modality can be avoided more effectively without the single modality regularization.

In this paper, we propose the structure named *Cross-Modality Adversarial Network* (CMAN) which obtains modality-invariant features to counter the modality gap and co-learns these features for fine-grained alignment. Firstly, exploit modality discriminator and gradient reverse layer to implement adversarial training during the optimization. After countering the modality gap, the modality-invariant features are obtained by the feature extractor and bring benefit to subsequent co-learning module. Furthermore, as the adversarial training solely aligns the distributions of different modalities, we need to align the modality-invariant features in a fine-grained level. Therefore, we propose modality-invariant attention learning to not only align the distributions but also the semantic between visual and textual modalities. With the well semantic alignment of multimodal information, the more accurate answer prediction can be obtained.

In conclusion, the main contribution of this paper are as follows:

(1) We propose the cross-modality adversarial learning module to obtain modality-invariant features for VQA task. The cross-modality adversarial learning maps the multimodal features into a shared representation space which provides a similar semantic distribution for multimodal semantic alignment.
(2) We utilize modality-invariant attention learning to capture the correlation of multimodal information in a fine-grained level. With shared-representing of the features, the correlation captured by co-attention mechanism can be obtained more easily and accurately. The effective modality-invariant learning achieves accurate semantic understanding and higher prediction accuracy.
(3) We evaluate our model on the well-known benchmark VQA-v2 and VQA-cp-v2 datasets. The ablation study and result analysis show that our model achieves better fusion performance and narrows the gap between different modalities effectively.

2   Related Work

In this section, we introduce several relevant works about our model proposed by previous researchers.

Visual Question Answering (VQA). VQA is a typical multimodal task proposed by Agrawal *et al.* [4]. It requires the model to answer the textual question based on the corresponding visual image. In many recent works [10,24], VQA is regarded as a multi-classification task that the model needs to predict the correct choice in a pre-extracted answer set. With significant achievement made in computer vision and natural language processing, researchers made great progress in VQA task. Anderson *et al.* [3] proposed bottom-up and top-down manners by using one of the classic object detection model Faster R-CNN [19] which brings high-quality regional features. Yu *et al.* [24] proposed modular co-attention network to make full use of attention mechanism for multimodal representation co-learning. Liu *et al.* [15] obtained effective answer-related presentation by adversarial learning. Besides, as the language priors existing in the datasets [9], there are some works which try to address this problem by reconstructing the data distribution in datasets [2].

However, the recent multimodal fusion methods ignore the large gap between different modalities. The discrepancy between different representation spaces make the model hard to be well aligned. As compared, our model narrows the modalities gap by using the cross-modality adversarial training to map the features to a shared representation space and achieving better semantic alignment.

Domain Adaptation. Domain adaptation is a series of approaches used to improve the model testing performance in the label lacking target domain while the model is trained solely on the labeled source domain. Ganin *et al.* [7] proposed unsupervised domain adaptation which can be implemented in the deep architecture easily. It is efficient that the model can be trained on the source domain with fully labeled data while achieves great test performance on the target domain lacking of labeled data by using unsupervised domain adaptation. Zhang *et al.* [25] used domain adaptation to train a personalized response generation models for conversational robots. Inspired by these methods, we exploit adversarial training to obtain modality-invariant features for VQA to counter the modality gap.

3 Methodology

In this section, we describe the *Cross-Modality Adversarial Network* (CMAN) in detail. As shown in Fig. 2, CMAN consists five processing modules. Features representation module represents raw multimodal data. Information integration and cross-modality adversarial learning modules obtain the modality-invariant features. The modality-invariant attention learning and feature fusion and answer prediction modules are set for fine-grained semantic alignment and fusion. The following description would follow the data flow during the propagation procedure.

3.1 Features Representation

Question Representation. The input questions I_x are tokened to words and cut into maximum of 14 words. Then, the tokens are represented into vectors by

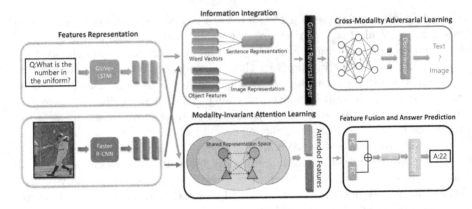

Fig. 2. The model flowchart of Cross-Modality Adversarial Network(CMAN). The arrows denote the direction of data-flow. For precise visualization, we divide our model into several modules, which are Features Representation, Information Integration, Cross-Modality Adversarial Learning, Modality-Invariant Attention Learning and Feature Fusion and Answer Prediction.

the pre-trained 300-D GloVe word embeddings. We pass the word embeddings through the simple LSTM network with the hidden size h_x and choose the output features for every word as the textual feature representation. As a result, a question is represented as $X \in \mathbb{R}^{m \times d_x}$.

Image Representation. The input images I_y are represented as a set of regional object features through the bottom-up manner [3]. These features can be easily obtained by extracting the bounding-box visual features from Faster R-CNN (with ResNet-101 as its backbone) pre-trained on Visual Genome Dataset. We follow [24] to set the confidence threshold to filter the detected object and control the number of objects $n \in [10, 100]$ per image. Finally, the image is represented as $Y \in \mathbb{R}^{n \times d_y}$.

In conclusion, the input data I_x, I_y have been projected to features extracted by a series of representation operation. Then, we regard all the representing operators above as a integrated feature extractor G_f with learnable parameters θ_f. Thus, the representation operation can be denoted as :

$$X, Y = G_f(I_x; I_y; \theta_f)$$

3.2   Information Integration

While the features are extracted in different modalities and grains, the quantities of question and image features exist large gap (about 1:8). Thus, as the textual/visual features act as the positive/negative samples for the following modality discriminator, the original input ratio of the multimodal features impacts the performance of adversarial learning. Thus, we integrate the information of single modality features into one representation to avoid the quantity difference.

To make full use of all the extracted features, we utilize averaging operation to integrate the semantic of whole sentence and image. Finally, the integration operation can be denoted as below:

$$S = \{S_x, S_y\} = \{\frac{1}{m} \sum_{i=1}^{m} x_i, \frac{1}{n} \sum_{j=1}^{n} y_j\}$$

where S denotes the representation set of the integrated textual and visual features S_x, S_y.

3.3 Cross-Modality Adversarial Learning

After the representation module and information integration, the integrated question and image features are obtained. However, suffering from the large gap between different modalities, these multimodal features are hard to align their semantic accurately. Therefore, we insert a modality discriminator into the model structure to narrow this gap by implementing the adversarial training as shown in Fig. 3.

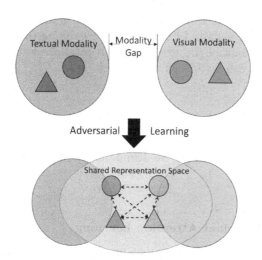

Fig. 3. The schematic diagram of cross-modality adversarial learning and modality-invariant attention learning. The adversarial learning maps the multimodal features into a shared representation space. The arrows with dashed lines represent the semantic alignment between modality-invariant features implementing by the modality-invariant attention learning.

In the implementation, we exploit the following module as the modality discriminator - Multi Layer Perception mapping the integrated multimodal features S_x and S_y into a shared representation space with the dimension d_g and a fully connected network working as the classifier to discriminate the features modality.

The modality discriminator G_d with learnable parameters θ_d takes question features S_x and image features S_y as input data S and predicts the probabilities of features subordinate modality s :

$$s = G_d(S; \theta_d)$$

and the adversarial loss of the modality discriminator is defined as following:

$$L_d = -\frac{1}{n+m} \sum_{i=1}^{n+m} t_i \log(G_d(S_i; \theta_d)) - (1 - t_i) \log(1 - (G_d(S_i; \theta_d)))$$

where t_i denotes the subordinate modality label of the i-th sample.

In the conventional training procedure, the discriminator attempts to classify the modality of features as accurately as possible. However, the modality-invariant features should be able to confuse the modality discriminator because they have been projected into a shared representation space. Thus, the classification loss of modality discriminator would decrease as the optimizer plays a role while the modality-invariant features preventing the converge of the discriminator's loss. Therefore, we implement the *Gradient Reverse Layer* (GRL) [7] to achieve this goal. GRL is an identity mapping in the feed-forward propagation. Without any extra learning parameter, the gradient multiplied by $-\lambda I$ (I denotes an identity matrix) let the loss increase during the back-propagating. λ is a trade-off constant of the adversarial loss ratio. As we denote GRL as R, the implementation can be defined as followed:

$$R(x) = x$$

$$\frac{\partial R(x)}{\partial x} = -\lambda I$$

After implementing the GRL, we define the final loss of adversarial learning as below:

$$L_{adv} = R(L_d)$$

3.4   Modality-Invariant Attention Learning

Although the gap between different modalities has been narrowed, it is also crucial to align the visual and textual information to predict the accurate answer. Based on the application of co-attention mechanism proposed in [8,24], we implement the co-learning of modality-invariant features based on the self-attention mechanism [21] to achieve well semantic alignment.

While the multimodal features are mapped into a shared representation space, we denote the modality-invariant features as $\hat{X}, \hat{Y}$. Firstly, we exploit the self-attention mechanism inside single modality to capture the core semantic of the representation. This operation can be denoted as:

$$\hat{X}_s = softmax(\frac{\hat{X} \cdot \hat{X}^T}{\sqrt{d_g}})\hat{X}$$

where $\sqrt{d_g}$ denotes the square root of the dimension of the shared representation space. Similarly, $\hat{Y}_s$ can also be obtained by the same operation.

Then, to learn the accurate visual representation of the image to answer the question, we consider to align the visual information by textual information. As we obtained the modality-invariant features, we regard $\hat{X}, \hat{Y}$ as a set of features in the shared representation space. Thus, without suffering from the modalities gap, the textual information can be fused into the visual feature by applying guided attention mechanism easily:

$$\hat{Y}_{sx} = softmax(\frac{\hat{X}_s \cdot \hat{Y}_s^T}{\sqrt{d_g}})\hat{Y}_s$$

The co-learning procedure above can be utilized with multi-level. In the experiments, we set the level at 6 in our model. Then, we obtain the attended modality-invariant features $\hat{X}_s, \hat{Y}_{sx}$ which contain well-aligned semantic information after the adversarial learning and the modality-invariant attention learning. Furthermore, taking $\hat{X}_s$ as an instance, the attended features $\hat{X}_s \in \mathbb{R}^{m \times d_g}$ represent rich information from many words, we need to integrate the information into a single sentence representation for further feature fusion and prediction. Therefore, we utilize the summation operation among the words to obtain the final attended modality-invariant representation. The same operation can be done on the $\hat{Y}_{sx} \in \mathbb{R}^{n \times d_g}$. As a result, we obtain the final representation $\hat{X}^* \in \mathbb{R}^{d_g}, \hat{Y}^* \in \mathbb{R}^{d_g}$ for further fusion.

3.5 Feature Fusion and Answer Prediction

After a series of modality-invariant learning modules, we obtain the well-aligned modality-invariant visual and textual representation. Then, We design the feature fusion module to aggregate the information into a representation for classification. The feature fusion is set as below:

$$Z = W_x \hat{X}^* + W_y \hat{Y}^*$$

where $W_x \in \mathbb{R}^{d_z \times d_g}$ and $W_y \in \mathbb{R}^{d_z \times d_g}$ denote the trainable weight matrix.

Finally, the representation Z will be projected into the answer space by using the linear projection. Then we implement a sigmoid operation on it and obtain the probabilities of classification $z \in \mathbb{R}^l$. Then, according to the operation above, we denote the final answer predictor as:

$$z = G_p(Z; \theta_p) = sigmoid(W_p Z + b_p)$$

where $W_p \in \mathbb{R}^{l \times d_p}$ is the learnable weight matrix. θ_p denotes the learnable parameters of predictor G_p.

3.6 Optimization

As our model combines the GRL to obtain modality-invariant features, the optimization would be a little different with the traditional propagation procedure. Firstly, the overall loss of our model is denoted as:

$$L = L_p(G_p(G_f(I_x; I_y; \theta_f); \theta_p))) + L_{adv}(G_d(G_f(I_x; I_y; \theta_f); \theta_d)))$$

where L_p denotes the loss of answer predictor.

During the optimization, the answer predictor G_p tries to classify the category as accurately as possible. Meanwhile, the modality discriminator G_d which is confused by the modality-invariant features results in the increase of its loss. The stochastic update of the parameters with the implementing of GRL during the back-propagating can be denoted as below:

$$\theta_f^* \leftarrow \theta_f - \mu(\frac{\partial L_p}{\partial \theta_f} - \lambda \frac{\partial L_d}{\partial \theta_f})$$
$$\theta_p^* \leftarrow \theta_p - \mu \frac{\partial L_p}{\partial \theta_p}$$
$$\theta_d^* \leftarrow \theta_d - \mu\lambda \frac{\partial L_d}{\partial \theta_d}$$

where μ denotes the learning rate of the optimizer.

4 Experiments

In this section, we evaluate the performance of CMAN in the benchmark VQA-v2 dataset and the VQA-CP-v2 dataset. To valid the effectiveness of the CMAN, we conduct several experiments including the ablation study, performance on different benchmarks, visualization of distribution and case study.

4.1 Datasets

VQA-v2 [9] is a dataset composed of 204K of images from COCO dataset and several corresponding question-answer pairs annotated by human beings. It is a commonly used benchmark in which the researchers evaluate their VQA model. The dataset is divided into three split: *train* (80k images and 444k QA pairs), *val* (40k images and 214k QA pairs) and *test* (80k images and 448k QA pairs). Besides, there are two additional subsets named *test-dev* and *test-standard* for the researchers to compare their model with others online.

VQA-CP-v2 [2] is a reconstruction of VQA-v2 dataset which avoids the language priors existing in the original dataset. As many researchers have found that the model tends to achieve great performance by exploiting the language priors and learning superficial representation, the VQA-CP-v2 dataset is a benchmark proposed to valid whether the model understand the semantic in visual and textual modality without language priors.

4.2   Implementation Details

The hyper-parameters setup in our experiment is set as followed. We choose the Adam Solver with the parameters $\beta_1 = 0.9$ and $\beta_2 = 0.98$ as the optimizer. We train the model with the max epoch 15 and the batchsize 128. The base learning rate μ is set to $1e^{-4}$ and decayed by 15% every 2 epochs after 10 epochs.

The dimension of the input textual and visual feature d_x, d_y is set to 512 and 2048. And the dimension d_g and d_p of the shared representation space and the fusion module is 512. To adjust the impact of different ratio of adversarial loss, we set the λ impacted by a constant η which is set to 10. Following the suggestion given by [7], we denote the λ as below to suppress the noisy signal from the modality discriminator at early training stage:

$$\lambda = \eta(\frac{2}{1 - e^{-10p}} - 1)$$

where $p \in [1, 15]$ denotes the current epoch during the training.

The ablation study and result analysis will be held in the *val* split of VQA-v2 and VQA-CP-v2 datasets. Meanwhile, we compare our model trained on *train+val+vg* split with other model using relevant methods in the *test-dev* split of VQA-v2 dataset.

4.3   Result Analysis

Results on VQA-v2 and VQA-CP-v2 Datasets. We show the quantitative results at first. As shown in Table 1, our model achieves the best performance compared to other adversarial learning based models and baseline models.

Up-Dn [3] is a classic model which firstly uses bottom-up and top-down manners to combine visual and textual information for VQA. SAN [23], BAN [11] are strong baseline models using attention mechanism for VQA. MuRel [6] designs multimodal relational cell to improve the reasoning ability of model and exploits bi-linear fusion to capture the correlation between multimodal features. ALARR [15] exploits adversarial learning to capture answer information into the representation. ALMA [14] is proposed to learn the joint representation to effectively reflect the answer-related information by adversarial learning and multimodal attention. DFAF [8] fuses multi-modal features with intra- and inter-modality information flow. However, the methods mentioned above do not notice the gap between modalities and thus still remain improvement potential. With the combination of cross-modal adversarial learning and modality-invariant attention learning, the model achieves the 70.81% overall accuracy compared to others using attention mechanism or adversarial learning.

Table 1. Comparison of models performance on *test − dev* VQA-v2 dataset

Models	Y/N	Num	Others	All
Up-Dn [3]	81.82	44.21	56.05	65.32
SAN [23]	82.98	46.88	58.99	67.50
MuRel [6]	84.77	49.84	57.85	68.03
ALAM [14]	84.62	47.08	58.14	68.12
ALARR [15]	85.08	41.12	59.64	68.61
BAN [11]	85.31	50.93	60.26	69.52
DFAF [8]	86.09	53.32	60.49	70.22
CMAN (ours)	**86.93**	**53.47**	**60.96**	**70.81**

Besides, we also evaluate our models on *val* split of VQA-CP-v2 dataset. As CMAN obtains modality-invariant features to align the semantic, it achieves significant performance by exploiting the textual and visual information more effectively with better semantic alignment. As depicted in Table 2, our model achieves the overall accuracy at 42.76% and beats all the comparing models, even the one with Q-Adv and DoE modules [18] proposed to counter language priors.

Table 2. Comparison of models performance on VQA-CP-v2 dataset

Models	All
SAN [23]	24.96
SAN + Q-Adv + DoE [18]	33.29
Up-Dn [3]	39.74
Up-Dn + Q-Adv + DoE [18]	41.17
BAN [11]	39.31
MuRel [6]	39.54
CMAN (ours)	**42.76**

Visualization by t-SNE. We analyze the effect of adversarial learning and modality-invariant attention learning in this part. First, we select 250 image and question pairs from *test* split of VQA-v2 dataset randomly and implement the t-SNE tools [16] to visualize the feature distribution with and without the adversarial learning. We set the perplexity of t-SNE at 60 and initialize it by PCA. As shown in Fig. 1(a), without obtaining the modality-invariant features, the visual and textual features distribution fuse barely satisfactory. After the adversarial learning which bridges the gap between modalities, the multimodal features are in well fusion as depicted in Fig. 1(b). The distinguish between distribution shows the effectiveness of adversarial learning.

Ablation Study. We perform the ablation study of our model as followed. All the results are obtained on the *val* split of VQA-v2 dataset. First, the input ratio of the visual/textual features affect the performance of modality discriminator as we illustrate in Sec 3.2. As shown in Table 3, the overall accuracy increases slightly with closer input ratio. To test the impact of different integrating operation, we also compare the results of summation with averaging operation.

Table 3. Accuracy with different modality discriminator input ratio on VQA-v2 *val*

Input ratio (Text:Vis)	1:8	1:4	1:2	1:1	Avg	Sum
Overall accuracy	66.76	66.80	66.82	66.89	**66.94**	66.90

Besides, we also evaluate the performance of our variant models. As shown in Table 4., with the increase of modality-invariant attention learning levels, the overall accuracy attends higher in an appropriate cascade. Besides, the result of our complete model achieves best score in ablation study as all the modules come into play. GA and MIAL in the table represent using solely guided-attention and modality-invariant attention learning to co-learn the representation respectively. M-Adv denotes the cross-modality adversarial learning module. Ig means the integration which we operate on the multimodal features before adversarial learning. The number after the hyphen denotes the cascade level of the module. As a results, the more modules are added into the model structure, the better performance model can achieve. Interestingly, after the information integration operation, the performance on counting problem are slightly dropped down than the one without it. We consider that the integration might ignore the quantity information between all objects as the objects are averaged to one representation.

Table 4. The ablation experiments in *val* split of VQA-v2 dataset.

Variant models	Y/N	Num	Others	All
GA-2	83.39	46.06	55.22	64.60
MIAL-2	83.97	47.48	57.79	66.27
M-Adv + MIAL-4	84.17	48.39	58.07	66.61
M-Adv + MIAL-6	84.36	**48.96**	58.08	66.76
M-Adv + Ig + MIAL-6 *(CMAN)*	**84.63**	48.51	**58.36**	**66.94**

Case Study. We show some cases to study the performance of our model in some specific samples.

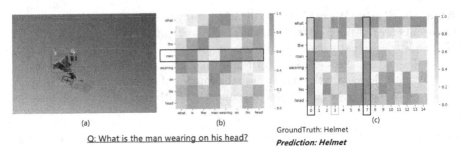

(a)   (b)   (c)

Q: What is the man wearing on his head?

GroundTruth: Helmet

Prediction: Helmet

Fig. 4. We provide a specific case to analysis the model ability. (a) The image provided in a VQA triplet. We highlight the detected bounding boxes for further analysis. (b) The attention map of textual question. The darker color of the grid means the corresponding words are more relevant. (c) The attention map of textual question and visual image. The Y-axis of the map represents the textual words of sentence. The X-axis represents the index of visual objects. The color represents the same meaning as (b).

In Fig. 4(b), our model regards the word *man* as the key object because it separates most of the attention on it. Besides, it considers the phrase *What is wearing on his head?* as the most relevant semantic about the key object. As shown in Fig. 4(c), our model focus more on the correlation between *0th*, *7th* objects with most important textual semantic phrase *man wearing on his head*. Besides, the *0th*, *7th* visual objects in Fig. 4(a) point to the helmet, which indicates that the model captures the correct correlation between the key multimodal objects. As a comparison, the *3rd* visual object which is detected as *coat* might also be strong related to the word *wearing*. However, as it does not match the key semantic objects of the question, our model solely separate little attention on it. With the co-learning between modality-invariant features, our

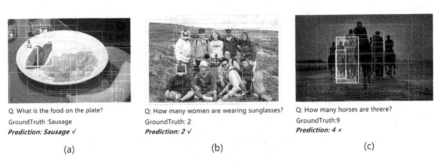

Q: What is the food on the plate?

GroundTruth :Sausage

Prediction: Sausage √

(a)

Q: How many women are wearing sunglasses?

GroundTruth: 2

Prediction: 2 √

(b)

Q: How many horses are threre?

GroundTruth:9

Prediction: 4 x

(c)

Fig. 5. We provide two more positive cases for validating the well alignment achieved by our model. Besides, we provide some negative samples to discuss the limitation as well.

model focus more on the correlation between key visual and textual semantic objects without suffering from the gap between modalities.

As shown in Fig. 5(a) and (b), we highlight the objects/words that our model concentrates on. With the correct concentration achieved by accurate semantic alignment, the model can achieve great prediction accuracy. However, there are still some limitation appeared in our method. Although the bottom-up features extracted from Faster R-CNN can represent important objects that should be focused on and bring large help to our alignment works, they might not be absolutely effective in some situations. As shown in Fig. 5(c), as the objects overlapped in the picture, the detector can not distinguish all the objects for the following representation learning. Although we try to align the information from different modalities by using modality-invariant features, it is still hard to well-align the semantic with the visual information which is of poor quality.

5   Conclusion

In this paper, we propose CMAN to explore the effectiveness of modality-invariant features to counter the modalities gap. With the implementation of cross-modal adversarial learning, the model achieves better semantic alignment without suffering from the modality gap. Furthermore, we utilize the modality-invariant attention learning to align the key visual objects and textual information. With the visualization and result analysis, we valid the effectiveness of modality-invariant features. In the further future, We will explore the potential of modality-invariant features by constructing more complex alignment mechanism and augmenting the reasoning ability of model.

Acknowledgments. This work was supported by National Natural Science Foundation of China (No. 62076100), National Key Research and Development Program of China (Standard knowledge graph for epidemic prevention and production recovering intelligent service platform and its applications), the Fundamental Research Funds for the Central Universities, SCUT (No. D2201300, D2210010), the Science and Technology Programs of Guangzhou (201902010046), the Science and Technology Planning Project of Guangdong Province (No. 2020B0101100002).

References

1. Agrawal, A., Batra, D., Parikh, D.: Analyzing the behavior of visual question answering models. In: Proceedings of the 2016 Conference on Empirical Methods in Natural Language Processing, pp. 1955–1960 (2016)
2. Agrawal, A., Batra, D., Parikh, D., Kembhavi, A.: Don't just assume; look and answer: Overcoming priors for visual question answering. In: Proceedings of the IEEE Conference on Computer Vision and Pattern Recognition, pp. 4971–4980 (2018)
3. Anderson, P., et al.: Bottom-up and top-down attention for image captioning and visual question answering. In: Proceedings of the IEEE Conference on Computer Vision and Pattern Recognition, pp. 6077–6086 (2018)

4. Antol, S., et al.: VQA: visual question answering. In: Proceedings of the IEEE International Conference on Computer Vision, pp. 2425–2433 (2015)

5. Ben-Younes, H., Cadene, R., Cord, M., Thome, N.: MUTAN: multimodal tucker fusion for visual question answering. In: Proceedings of the IEEE International Conference on Computer Vision, pp. 2612–2620 (2017)

6. Cadene, R., Ben-Younes, H., Cord, M., Thome, N.: MUREL: multimodal relational reasoning for visual question answering. In: Proceedings of the IEEE/CVF Conference on Computer Vision and Pattern Recognition, pp. 1989–1998 (2019)

7. Ganin, Y., Lempitsky, V.: Unsupervised domain adaptation by backpropagation. In: International Conference on Machine Learning, pp. 1180–1189. PMLR (2015)

8. Gao, P., et al.: Dynamic fusion with intra-and inter-modality attention flow for visual question answering. In: Proceedings of the IEEE/CVF Conference on Computer Vision and Pattern Recognition, pp. 6639–6648 (2019)

9. Goyal, Y., Khot, T., Summers-Stay, D., Batra, D., Parikh, D.: Making the V in VQA matter: elevating the role of image understanding in visual question answering. In: Proceedings of the IEEE Conference on Computer Vision and Pattern Recognition, pp. 6904–6913 (2017)

10. Jiang, H., Misra, I., Rohrbach, M., Learned-Miller, E., Chen, X.: In defense of grid features for visual question answering. In: Proceedings of the IEEE/CVF Conference on Computer Vision and Pattern Recognition, pp. 10267–10276 (2020)

11. Kim, J.H., Jun, J., Zhang, B.T.: Bilinear attention networks. In: Proceedings of the 32nd International Conference on Neural Information Processing Systems, pp. 1571–1581 (2018)

12. Lasecki, W.S., Zhong, Y., Bigham, J.P.: Increasing the bandwidth of crowdsourced visual question answering to better support blind users. In: Proceedings of the 16th International ACM SIGACCESS Conference on Computers and Accessibility, pp. 263–264 (2014)

13. Liu, Y., Peng, Y., Lim, K., Ling, N.: A novel image retrieval algorithm based on transfer learning and fusion features. World Wide Web **22**(3), 1313–1324 (2019)

14. Liu, Y., Zhang, X., Huang, F., Cheng, L., Li, Z.: Adversarial learning with multimodal attention for visual question answering. IEEE Trans. Neural Netw. Learn. Syst. (2020)

15. Liu, Y., Zhang, X., Huang, F., Li, Z.: Adversarial learning of answer-related representation for visual question answering. In: Proceedings of the 27th ACM International Conference on Information and Knowledge Management, pp. 1013–1022 (2018)

16. Van der Maaten, L., Hinton, G.: Visualizing data using t-SNE. J. Mach. Learn. Res. **9**(11), 2579–2605 (2008)

17. Manjunatha, V., Saini, N., Davis, L.S.: Explicit bias discovery in visual question answering models. In: Proceedings of the IEEE/CVF Conference on Computer Vision and Pattern Recognition, pp. 9562–9571 (2019)

18. Ramakrishnan, S., Agrawal, A., Lee, S.: Overcoming language priors in visual question answering with adversarial regularization. In: Proceedings of the 32nd International Conference on Neural Information Processing Systems, pp. 1548–1558 (2018)

19. Ren, S., He, K., Girshick, R., Sun, J.: Faster R-CNN: towards real-time object detection with region proposal networks. IEEE Trans. Pattern Anal. Mach. Intell. **39**(6), 1137–1149 (2016)

20. Rennie, S.J., Marcheret, E., Mroueh, Y., Ross, J., Goel, V.: Self-critical sequence training for image captioning. In: Proceedings of the IEEE Conference on Computer Vision and Pattern Recognition, pp. 7008–7024 (2017)

21. Vaswani, A., et al.: Attention is all you need. In: NIPS (2017)
22. Xu, X., He, L., Lu, H., Gao, L., Ji, Y.: Deep adversarial metric learning for cross-modal retrieval. World Wide Web **22**(2), 657–672 (2019)
23. Yang, Z., He, X., Gao, J., Deng, L., Smola, A.: Stacked attention networks for image question answering. In: Proceedings of the IEEE Conference on Computer Vision and Pattern Recognition, pp. 21–29 (2016)
24. Yu, Z., Yu, J., Cui, Y., Tao, D., Tian, Q.: Deep modular co-attention networks for visual question answering. In: Proceedings of the IEEE/CVF Conference on Computer Vision and Pattern Recognition, pp. 6281–6290 (2019)
25. Zhang, W.N., Zhu, Q., Wang, Y., Zhao, Y., Liu, T.: Neural personalized response generation as domain adaptation. World Wide Web **22**(4), 1427–1446 (2019)

Difficulty-Controllable Visual Question Generation

Feng Chen[1], Jiayuan Xie[1], Yi Cai[1(✉)], Tao Wang[2], and Qing Li[3]

[1] School of Software Engineering, South China University of Technology, Guangzhou
China and the Key Laboratory of Big Data and Intelligent Robot, Guangzhou, China
{sefengchen,sexiejiayuan}@mail.scut.edu.cn, ycai@scut.edu.cn
[2] Department of Computing, The Hong Kong Polytechnic University,
Hung Hom, Hong Kong
tao.wang@kcl.ac.uk
[3] Department of Biostatistics and Health Informatics, King's College London,
London, UK
qing-prof.li@polyu.edu.hk

Abstract. Visual Question Generation (VQG) aims to generate questions from images. Existing studies on this topic focus on generating questions solely based on images while neglecting the difficulty of questions. However, to engage users, an automated question generator should produce questions with a level of difficulty that are tailored to a user's capabilities and experience. In this paper, we propose a Difficulty-controllable Generation Network (DGN) to alleviate this limitation. We borrow difficulty index from education area to define a difficulty variable for representing the difficulty of questions, and fuse it into our model to guide the difficulty-controllable question generation. Experimental results demonstrate that our proposed model not only achieves significant improvements on several automatic evaluation metrics, but also can generate difficulty-controllable questions.

Keywords: Difficulty controllable · Visual question generation · Multimodal

1 Introduction

Recent years see the popularity of multi-modal research on vision, audio and language. Popular tasks include video classification [41], video captioning [24] and cross-modal retrieval [44]. Video captioning aims at generating captions for describing videos. Different from generating video-related captions, Visual Question Generation (VQG) aims to generate questions from images [30]. In recent years, VQG has obtained great attention from both the computer vision and the natural language processing communities. VQG has been widely used in education and dialogue systems, e.g., providing demonstrations in child education [21] or initializing the dialogue of human-computer conversation [13].

© Springer Nature Switzerland AG 2021
L. H. U et al. (Eds.): APWeb-WAIM 2021, LNCS 12858, pp. 332–347, 2021.
https://doi.org/10.1007/978-3-030-85896-4_26

Recent studies on VQG have largely focused on generating one [18,30] or more [7,14] questions from an image, none of them have taken the difficulty of questions into account. However, difficulty plays an important role in the evaluating quality of generated questions. For example, in the education area, it is a natural way for teachers to test students by questions of different difficulty levels, so that students of different levels can be well distinguished through this test [10]. If questions are too easy or too hard, each student answers rightly or wrongly, which makes it difficult to distinguish different students. Thus, it is necessary for us to control the difficulty of generated questions to balance the difficulty of a test.

Answer: away

Q1(Human): Is the bench facing toward or away from the viewer ? (Easy, DIF:82%)

Q2(Our model): Which direction is the bench facing ? (Hard, DIF:27%)

Fig. 1. A sample of generated questions from human and our model on the VQA v2.0 dataset.

In this paper, we introduce difficulty control for VQG, namely Difficulty-controllable Visual Question Generation (DVQG). Different from previous VQG tasks, DVQG needs to take the difficulty of questions into account additionally in order to generate questions with a specific level of difficulty. To tackle the DVQG task, the first step is to define the difficulty of questions. In the education area, Wajeeha et al. [43] propose difficulty index (DIF) to evaluate the difficulty of questions. DIF represents the percentage of students who correctly answer the questions. A high value of DIF indicates that most persons answer correctly and it indirectly suggests that questions are easy. By contrast, a low value of DIF shows that most people answer wrongly and it indirectly proves that questions are hard. As shown in Fig. 1, Q1 is considered as an easy question and Q2 is considered as a hard question according to the DIF value. This is because most people answer Q1 correctly by explicitly finding the answer from Q1. However, it's expensive and time-consuming to measure the difficulty of questions by answering questions manually. Thus, we design an automatic labeling strategy that uses VQA models to simulate humans to label the difficulty levels of questions.

Inspired by this study, we define a difficulty variable to represent the difficulty of questions and fuse it into our model to guide the difficulty-controllable question generation. Our model is built on text style transfer [4,26] which generates questions towards a specified style, i.e., easy or hard. Specifically, we propose a network that contains a difficulty control mechanism, namely Difficulty-controllable Generation Network (DGN), to control the difficulty of generated questions. The difficulty control mechanism combines difficulty variable into decoder initialization and input of each time step, so as to control the difficulty of generated questions.

To summarize, our contributions are as follows:

- We introduce a DVQG task that aims to generate quesitons with a specific level of difficulty, which can be useful in many applications, e.g., generating difficulty-appropriate questions to distinguish students of different levels in education.
- We propose a novel model that contains a difficulty control mechanism. The difficulty control mechanism combines difficulty variable into decoder initialization and input of each time step, so as to control the difficulty of generated questions.
- We build the first dataset that contains 327,887 easy questions and 133,691 hard questions for generation and evaluation. Comprehensive experiments show that our framework not only outperforms the baseline models on several automatic evaluation metrics, but also can generate difficulty-controllable questions.

2   Related Work

2.1   Text Question Generation

Question Generation (QG) from text has been investigated for many years in natural language processing. Early works on QG proposed rule-based approaches to tackle this task. Specifically, they designed hand-crafted templates or rules to generate interrogative sentences [12,22,28]. However, these approaches are time-consuming and labor-intensive and difficult to extend to other domains.

With the rise of deep learning, recent studies focus on using end-to-end neural networks to generate questions automatically [23,31,36,42,46,48]. Du et al. [5] firstly use an attention-based sequence-to-sequence model to generate questions from sentences, achieving better performance than rule-based systems in both automatic and human evaluations. However, since they do not consider the target answer, their model could not control which part of the sentences the generated questions are asking about. Therefore, existing studies mainly focus on the answer-related QG, which generates a question based on a given text and a target answer [16,29,47]. To generate answer-related questions, Zhou et al. [47] utilize answer positions to make the model aware of the target answer. Kim et al. [16] propose an answer-separated seq2seq model that treats the passage and the target answer separately for better utilization of the information from both sides. Ma et al. [29] propose a neural question generation model with sentence-level semantic matching and answer position inferring to consider the whole question semantics and answer position-aware features.

Additionally, some researchers recently investigate difficulty-controllable question generation. Gao et al. [8] define a difficulty-controllable question generation task and propose an end-to-end approach to learn the question generation with designated difficulty levels. Kumar et al. [20] investigate the problem of difficulty-controllable question generation from knowledge graphs, and present a transformer-based model that incorporates difficulty estimation based on named entity popularity to generate difficulty-controllable questions.

2.2   Visual Question Generation

VQG is a challenging task and has attracted the attention of the multimodal community in recent years. Recently, some methods try to use rule-based or deep learning methods to generate questions from images. Ren et al. [33] use WordNet and NLTK to identify a possible answer word and then convert a given sentence into a corresponding question through a rule-based algorithm. Mostafazadeh et al. [30] collect three VQG datasets and propose several generative and retrieval models to tackle the VQG task. In their experiment setting, only one question is generated from an image. In fact, different people might have different questions about the same image. Based on this intuition, some researchers focus on how to generate diverse questions [7,14,45]. Zhange et al. [45] propose a model that automatically generates visually grounded questions with diverse types for a single image. Mostafazadeh et al. [7] propose a question type driven framework to generate multiple questions for a given image with different focuses. Jain et al. [14] propose an algorithm for diverse question generation which combines the advantages of variational autoencoders with long short-term memory networks. Besides, there exist some works that combine VQG with other tasks. Li et al. [25] consider VQG as a dual task of VQA and build an end-to-end unified model to train together. Jain et al. [13] propose a discriminative method for the visual dialog task, which is a combination of two complementary tasks: predicting a contextual answer to a given question and predicting a contextual follow-up question to a given question-answer pair. However, most previous studies focus on generating questions solely based on images while neglecting the difficulty of questions. Inspired by Gao et al. [8] that propose to generate difficulty-controllable questions from text, this work explores difficulty-controllable visual question generation, which has to additionally consider the difficulty information in order to generate questions with specified difficulty levels.

3   Our Proposed Framework

3.1   Problem Definition

In this section, we define a Difficulty-controllable Visual Question Generation (DVQG) task, which aims to generate questions that satisfy the specified difficulty levels based on the images and target answers. Formally, given an image I, a target answer A and a specified difficulty level d, the DVQG task aims to find the best question $\bar{Q}$,

$$\bar{Q} = \arg\max_Q \mathrm{Prob}(Q|I, A, d; \theta) \tag{1}$$

where $\mathrm{Prob}(Q|I, A, d; \theta)$ is a conditional probability of generating the question Q, θ are model parameters.

In order to generate questions that satisfy the specified difficulty levels as much as possible, we proposed an end-to-end framework which contains a difficulty control mechanism. An overview of our proposed framework is shown in Fig. 2. Firstly, we use image encoder and answer encoder to encode images and answers respectively. And then a fusion module is introduced to extract answer-related image features from these encoder outputs. Finally, in order to generate questions with specified difficulty levels, we design a decoder with a difficulty control mechanism. Specifically, the difficulty control mechanism combines difficulty variable into decoder initialization and decoder input at each time step, so as to control the difficulty of generated questions.

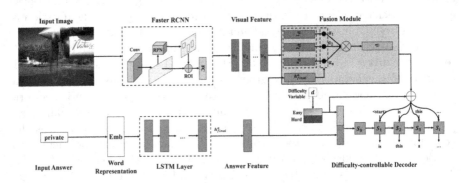

Fig. 2. Overview of difficulty-controllable visual question generation framework with image encoder, answer encoder, fusion module and difficulty-controllable decoder. Here we use faster RCNN as our image encoder and an uni-directional LSTM as our answer encoder.

3.2   Image Encoder

Several studies on VQA have verified that object-level features performs better than a grid of features [39,40]. This is because questions usually involve the attributes of objects or relationships between objects. Objects and other salient image regions are more worthy of attention for answering questions [6,35]. Therefore, different from the previous method using VGGNet [38] or ResNet [11] to extract a grid of features of the image, we extract object-level features from Up-Down model [1]. The object-level features are obtained from a Faster RCNN [34] model pretrained on Visual Genome dataset [19]. Formally, given an image I, we use Faster RCNN to extract a set of image features $V = \{v_1, v_2, ..., v_n\}$, $v_i \in \mathbb{R}^M$, where i is the number of objects, M is the dimension of image features and v_i is the feature representation of i-th object. Here we use 36 objects per image for the sake of efficiency. These image features are fixed during training.

The obtained visual object features V can be denoted as:

$$V = \text{RCNN}(I; \theta_{RCNN}) \tag{2}$$

3.3 Answer Encoder

The answer encoder is used to extract contextual features from the target answer A. The answer encoder takes word embeddings w of answers as input. We use a one-layer uni-directional LSTM to compute a contextualized representation for every word in the target answer A,

$$h_t^a = \text{LSTM}(w_t, h_{t-1}^a) \tag{3}$$

where w_t is the word embedding of t-th word and h_t^a is the hidden state of the LSTM at time t. The hidden state h_{final}^a at the last time step of the answer encoder represents the overall feature of the target answer.

3.4 Fusion Module

We design a fusion module to jointly attend the image representation and the answer representation. The fusion module takes the whole image features V and answer feature h_{final}^a as input, and outputs a context vector $\hat{v}$,

$$\alpha_i = w_a^T \text{relu}(W_v v_i + W_a h_{final}^a) \tag{4}$$

$$\alpha = \text{softmax}(\alpha) \tag{5}$$

$$\hat{v} = \sum_{i=1}^{n} \alpha_i v_i \tag{6}$$

where $w_a \in \mathbb{R}^H$, $W_v \in \mathbb{R}^{H \times M}$ and $W_a \in \mathbb{R}^H$ are trainable weight and H is the size of the middle layer. The context vector $\hat{v}$ usually focuses on an answer-related component of the image, which can reflect the key information of the image.

3.5 Difficulty-Controllable Decoder

DVQG can be regarded as text style transfer, which generates questions towards a specified style, i.e., easy or hard. Therefore, followed recent works on text style transfer [4,26], we design a decoder with a difficulty control mechanism. Specifically, we define a difficulty variable $d = \{0, 1\}$ (e.g., 0 means easy and 1 means hard). Then, the difficulty variable d is mapped to a fixed-dimensional vector d_e according to a randomly initialized matrix. We initialize the decoder with the answer representation h_{final}^a and difficulty embedding d_e to guide the generation process,

$$s_0 = [h_{final}^a; d_e] \tag{7}$$

Moreover, to fuse the difficulty information in every step of question generation, the decoder uses the difficulty embedding d_e as the input at each time step. Specifically, at time step t-th, we calculate the decoder hidden state as follow:

$$u_t = \text{LSTM}(u_{t-1}, [\hat{v}; w_t; d_e]) \tag{8}$$

u_t is fed into a fully-connected layer and a softmax activation to get the word probability distribution:

$$p(y_t) = \text{softmax}(W_y u_t + b_y) \tag{9}$$

where W_y and b_y are parameters to be learned.

3.6 Training and Inference

Given an image I, a target answer A, and a specified difficult level d, the training objective is to minimize the negative log-likelihood loss with regard to all parameters:

$$\mathcal{L} = - \sum_{(Q,I,A,d) \in \mathcal{D}} log\text{P}(Q \mid I, A, d; \theta) \tag{10}$$

where $\mathcal{D}$ is the training data and θ denotes model parameters.

During testing, our model generates a question Q by maximizing the log probability, and a question stops when the length of the sentence greater than maximum decoding length or meeting the end token "<end>". By taking different difficulty levels as input, our model can generate questions of different difficulty levels.

$$\bar{Q} = \arg\max_Q log\text{P}(Q \mid I, A, d; \theta) \tag{11}$$

4   Experimental Settings

In this section, we discuss (i) the dataset we use in our experiment, (ii) implementation details, (iii) evaluation metrics to measure the quality of generated questions and the models for comparison, (iv) results and analysis of our proposed framework.

4.1   Training Data Construction

VQA v2.0 dataset [9] is the most widely used dataset for the VQA task. The dataset is used as the basis of the 2017 VQA Challenge, whose train, validation, test, test-dev splits have the size of 443,757/214,354/447,793/107,394, respectively. Each sample includes one image, ten answers, and one question related to the image, while the test and test-dev split only contain images and questions. Therefore, we use the train split and validation split for our experiment.

In the area of education, the difficulty of questions is one of the indicators to measure the quality of test papers. Instructors often set questions of different difficulty levels for knowledge testing. However, the difficulty of questions is inherently subjective: perception of difficulty is influenced by factors such as age, reasoning and inferential skills, extent of conceptual knowledge, ability to perform an accurate and fluent reading, etc. [3]. Therefore, different people may have different difficulty levels for the same question. Moreover, it's expensive and time-consuming to label the difficulty of questions manually. In order to avoid the ambiguity of "question difficulty" and reduce labor costs, we design an automatic labeling strategy to label the difficulty levels of questions.

Firstly, for simplicity, we define two difficulty levels for questions, i.e., easy and hard. Regarding the definition of the difficulty of questions, questions that are more likely to answer correctly by most persons can be denoted as easy questions; by contrast, questions that are more likely to answer wrongly by most persons can be denoted as hard questions. Then we employ two VQA models, namely Up-Down [1] and BAN [15], to simulate humans to automatically label the difficulty levels of questions according to two criteria: (1) a question is easy if both two VQA models answer correctly; (2) a question is hard if both two VQA models answer wrongly. We remove the remaining questions to suppress ambiguity.

It's unreasonable to train the VQA models on the original data split of VQA v2.0 dataset and use the models to label the difficulty of all questions in the VQA v2.0 dataset. This is because the models will overfit the training data and label all questions in training data as easy. To avoid this problem, we use a 6-fold cross-validation strategy to label the difficulty of all questions in the VQA v2.0 dataset. In 6-fold cross-validation, the original data is randomly split into 6 subsets. Of the 6 subsets, 4 subsets are used as training data, 1 subset is used as validation data and the last subset is used as test data. The cross-validation process is then repeated 6 times, with each of the six subsets used exactly once as the test data. As a result, we obtain 327,887 easy questions and 133,691 hard questions. We re-divided easy questions and hard questions into train/validation/test splits, which contains 369,261/46,158/46,159 samples, and the proportion of easy questions in the three splits is about 71%. The data statistics are given in Table 1.

Table 1. The statistics of our dataset.

	Train	Validation	Test
Easy questions	262,309	32,789	32,789
Complex questions	106,952	13,369	13,370
Easy ratio	71.04%	71.04%	71.03%

4.2   Experimental Details

We implement our model in Pytorch and train the model with two GTX 2080 Ti. We use the image features extracted from the Up-Down model, 32 objects per image and the image features size is 2048. The image features are fixed during training. In the data preprocessing step, we convert words to lowercase and use space to split words. Since each question contains 10 answers annotated by 10 annotators, here we use the Highest frequency answer among the 10 in our framework. We use the randomly initialized word embeddings of dimension 1024, which are trainable during training. Both answer encoder and decoder share the same vocabulary and word embeddings. We randomly initialize a trainable 1024-dimensional difficulty embedding. We use a single layer in all LSTM and the number of hidden units in all LSTM is 1024. Dropout with a probability of 0.5 is applied for both the fusion module and the decoder.

We use AdaMax optimizer [17] with a learning rate of 0.002 and train our models with a mini-batches of size 512 for 50 epochs. During training, we use the teacher forcing strategy and early stopping strategy. We save the optimal model according to the performance of the validation set. For all the results we use beam search decoding with a beam size of 5.

4.3 Evaluation Metrics

In order to measure the quality of generated questions, we used the following commonly-used metrics in question generation: BLEU-1, BLEU-2, BLEU-3, BLEU-4 [32], METEOR [2] and ROUGE-L [27]. We use the evaluation package released by [37] to compute them.

- **BLEU-n** is a commonly-used metric in machine translation that measures the average n-gram precision on a set of reference sentences.
- **METEOR** is a recall-oriented metric that calculates the similarity between candidate and reference in terms of exact, stem, synonym, and paraphrase matches between words and phrases.
- **ROUGE-L** is used to calculate the longest common sub-sequence recall of candidates compared to references.

4.4 Baselines and Ablation Tests

To validate the effectiveness of our model, we compare our mode with existing studies on VQG task. Comparison models mainly concern two groups of models: the baseline models and the variants of our model.

Baseline Models: the definitions of the models under comparison are as follows:

- **GRNN:** GRNN [30] is a model that uses VGGNet [38] as image encoder and GRU as decoder to generate questions solely based on images while neglecting answers.
- **IMVQG:** IMVQG [18] is a model that generates goal-driven visual questions. It uses ResNet [11] as image encoder and maximizes the mutual information between the generated question with the image as well as the target answer. In their experiment setting, questions can be generated from the target answers or answer categories. For fairness, we use IMVQG w/o category here.

Ablation Tests: We also conduct ablation tests against some key modules to figure out the contribution of each module. For fair comparison, we use the same parameter settings for each model. Moreover, we conduct experiments on the influence or image encoder to verify that the image features extracted by Faster RCNN can better represent the information of the images than VGGNet and ResNet.

4.5   Results of Visual Question Generation

Comparison with Existing Models: We first compare our model with two baseline models on VQA v2.0 dataset. Table 2 shows the automatic metrics results obtained by different models in the VQA v2.0 dataset. Firstly, IMVQG outperforms GRNN by a great margin, showing that answer information plays an important role in VQG. The answer information can help models focus on the key part of images that generated questions are asked about. Secondly, even without difficulty control mechanism, DGN w/o DC still performs better than all previous VQG models. This results from the fact that object-level features extracted by Faster RCNN can better represent images than a grid of features produced by VGGNet or ResNet. Finally, with the help of difficulty control mechanism, DGN achieves significant improvements and this verifies that the difficulty of questions can be used as additional information to generate the point questions, i.e., more similar to the ground truth.

Ablation Study: The second part of Table 2 shows the performance of our variant models. The results demonstrate that each module of our model plays an important role in improving VQG performance. Compared with DGN w/o DC, we can find that there is a considerable decrease in all metrics after removing fusion module, showing that fusion module can improve the performance by capturing the answer-related image features. Moreover, the performance drops significantly after removing answer encoder. This results from the fact that answer

Table 2. Automatic metrics of generated questions. Higher score is better and the best performance for each evaluation metric is highlighted in **boldface**. DC for Difficulty Control. FM for Fusion Module. AE for Answer Encoder.

	BLEU-1	BLEU-2	BLEU-3	BLEU-4	METEOR	ROUGE-L
GRNN	29.17	18.28	12.32	8.97	11.75	32.11
IMVQG	39.67	29.54	22.89	18.37	18.32	44.14
DGN	**43.89**	**33.70**	**26.86**	**22.08**	**20.99**	**47.48**
DGN(VGGNet)	42.47	32.23	25.42	20.72	20.00	46.21
DGN(ResNet)	42.30	31.96	25.10	20.35	19.81	45.89
DGN w/o DC	43.11	33.17	26.53	21.93	20.74	47.14
DGN w/o DC,FM	43.00	32.84	26.07	21.38	20.49	46.76
DGN w/o DC,FM,AE	29.64	18.77	12.83	9.36	12.09	32.63

information can be used as additional information to guide the model to generate answer-related questions. After using VGGNet or ResNet instead of Faster RCNN, the performance drops significantly, indicating that object-level features extracted by Faster RCNN performs better than a grid of features extracted by VGGNet or ResNet.

4.6 Difficulty Control Results

We run VQA models to evaluate the difficulty of our generated easy and hard questions. VQA models are trained on the same train/validation splits of VQG models. We use the new evaluation metric, which is robust to inter-human variability in phrasing the answers, to evaluate VQA models.

$$\mathrm{Acc}(ans) = \min \left\{ \frac{\#\text{humans that said } ans}{3}, 1 \right\} \tag{12}$$

We just evaluate DGN model that can control the difficulty of questions. We first show the performance of VQA models on questions generated by DGN model using the easy labels, then we feed the reverse difficulty labels to demonstrate our model can control the difficulty of generated questions. Specifically, we construct three datasets to evaluate the difficulty of generated questions: 1) VQA v2.0 (original): questions in the test set generated by human; 2) VQA v2.0 (easy to hard): For the easy questions of the VQA v2.0 (original) dataset, we use hard difficulty labels instead of easy difficulty labels to generate questions; 3) VQA v2.0 (hard to easy): For the hard questions of the VQA v2.0 (original) dataset, we use easy difficulty labels instead of hard difficulty labels to generate questions.

Table 3 shows the performance of VQA models on the results of DGN model. Compared with the VQA performance on VQA v2.0 (original) dataset generated by human, we can see that VQA models perform worse on VQA v2.0 (easy to hard) dataset and perform better on VQA v2.0 (hard to easy) dataset. It shows that DGN model is able to generate easier or harder questions, validating the effectiveness of the difficulty-controllable decoder. In other words, DGN model can generate difficulty-controllable question by taking different difficulty labels as input.

Table 3. The results of controlling difficulty, measured with VQA models. The scores in brackets are performance gap between questions generated with original difficulty label and questions generated with reverse difficulty label.

	VQA v2.0 (original)	VQA v2.0 (easy to hard)	VQA v2.0 (hard to easy)
Up-Down	68.61	47.01	70.61(+23.60)
BAN	69.19	48.22	71.66(+23.44)

Table 4. Human evaluation on questions generated by the models. Fluency (F), difficulty (D) and Relevance (R) are rated on a 1–3 scale.

	Easy question set			Hard question set		
	F	D	R	F	D	R
IMVQG	2.89	1.76	1.84	2.74	1.95	1.61
DGN	2.91	1.54	2.04	2.76	2.17	1.81

Answer: forward
Human: Is the cow looking forward or backward? (Easy)
IMVQG: What direction is the man looking?
DGN: Is the cow looking forward or backward? (Easy)
DGN*: Which way is the cow looking? (Hard)

case 1

Answer: private
Human: What kind of plane is this? (Hard)
IMVQG: Is the plane taking off or landing?
DGN: What kind of plane is this? (Hard)
DGN*: Is this a public or private plane? (Easy)

case 2

Fig. 3. Sample output questions generated by human (ground truth questions), the baseline model and our models.

4.7 Human Evaluation

We conducted human evaluations to analyze the quality of the questions generated by baseline model IMVQG and our best model DGN. We randomly sample 100 easy questions and 100 complex questions generated by IMVQG and DGN. Each sample contains an image, a specified answer and the questions generated by IMVQG and DGN model, without showing the difficulty labels to annotators. We asked three annotators with rich educational experience to score the questions on a scale of 1 to 3 (3 for the best) in terms of Fluency (F), Difficulty (D) and Relevance (R). Fluency measures the grammatical correctness and fluency of the generated questions. Difficulty measures the syntactic divergence and the reasoning needed to answer the question. Relevance evaluates whether the generated questions are related to the images and specified answers.

Table 4 shows the results of human evaluation. All models achieve high scores on "Fluency", showing that neural models have powerful language modeling capabilities. For "Difficulty", we can find that DGN model is able to generate easier or more complex questions than IMVQG model, indicating the superiority of our proposed framework by utilizing the difficulty control mechanism. Finally, DGN model outperforms IMVQG model in terms of "Relevance" by a large gap, which proves that object-level features extracted by Faster RCNN and fusion module can help DGN model ask questions to the point.

4.8   Case Study

In order to show the effectiveness of our framework, we present some examples of generated questions in Fig. 3. In cases 1, IMVQG model generates a question which is not related to the image, while DGN model is able to generate to the point questions with the help of fusion module and object-level features extracted by Faster RCNN. Besides, DGN model can control the difficulty of generated questions. Specifically, by taking the easy difficulty label as input, DGN model generates an easy question that has more hints like "forward or backward" to answer the question more easily. When we input the hard difficulty label into the model, DGN model tends to generate a relatively hard question that has fewer hints to answer. In case 2, IMVQG model generates a question that is not about the target answer "private", while both DGN and DGN* are able to generate to the point questions. Specifically, by taking the easy difficulty label, DGN* tends to contain more hints like "public or private" in the generate question, while DGN contains less and its generated question is relatively difficult.

5   Conclusion

In this paper, we propose the Difficulty-controllable Visual Question Generation task, which has never been investigated before. We propose an end-to-end framework that contains a difficulty control mechanism to solve this task. Specifically, the difficulty control mechanism combines difficulty information into decoder initialization and input of each time step, so as to control the difficulty of generated questions. Experiments show that our proposed framework not only achieves the best performance on several automatic evaluation metrics, but also is able to generate difficulty-controllable questions.

For future work, there are some interesting dimensions to explore, such as jointly modeling question generation with other task [25], asking multiple questions simultaneously with different focuses [7] and visual dialog [13].

Acknowledgements. This work was supported by National Natural Science Foundation of China (No. 62076100), National Key Research and Development Program of China (Standard knowledge graph for epidemic prevention and production recovering intelligent service platform and its applications), the Fundamental Research Funds for the Central Universities, SCUT (No. D2201300, D2210010), the Science and Technology Programs of Guangzhou (201902010046), the Science and Technology Planning Project of Guangdong Province (No. 2020B0101100002).

References

1. Anderson, P., et al.: Bottom-up and top-down attention for image captioning and visual question answering. In: CVPR, pp. 6077–6086 (2018)
2. Denkowski, M.J., Lavie, A.: Meteor universal: language specific translation evaluation for any target language. In: WMT@ACL, pp. 376–380 (2014)
3. Desai, T., Moldovan, D.I.: Towards predicting difficulty of reading comprehension questions. In: FLAIRS Conference, pp. 8–13 (2019)
4. dos Santos, C.N., Melnyk, I., Padhi, I.: Fighting offensive language on social media with unsupervised text style transfer. In: ACL, pp. 189–194 (2018)
5. Du, X., Shao, J., Cardie, C.: Learning to ask: neural question generation for reading comprehension. In: ACL, pp. 1342–1352 (2017)
6. Egly, R., Driver, J., Rafal, R.D.: Shifting visual attention between objects and locations: evidence from normal and parietal lesion subjects. J. Exper. Psychol. Gen. 123(2), 161–77 (1994)
7. Fan, Z., Wei, Z., Li, P., Lan, Y., Huang, X.: A question type driven framework to diversify visual question generation. In: Lang, J. (ed.) IJCAI, pp. 4048–4054 (2018)
8. Gao, Y., Bing, L., Chen, W., Lyu, M.R., King, I.: Difficulty controllable generation of reading comprehension questions. In: IJCAI, pp. 4968–4974 (2019)
9. Goyal, Y., Khot, T., Summers-Stay, D., Batra, D., Parikh, D.: Making the V in VQA matter: elevating the role of image understanding in visual question answering. In: CVPR, pp. 6325–6334 (2017)
10. Ha, L.A., Yaneva, V., Baldwin, P., Mee, J.: Predicting the difficulty of multiple choice questions in a high-stakes medical exam. In: BEA@ACL, pp. 11–20 (2019)
11. He, K., Zhang, X., Ren, S., Sun, J.: Deep residual learning for image recognition. In: CVPR, pp. 770–778 (2016)
12. Heilman, M., Smith, N.A.: Good question! statistical ranking for question generation. In: HLT-NAACL, pp. 609–617 (2010)
13. Jain, U., Lazebnik, S., Schwing, A.G.: Two can play this game: visual dialog with discriminative question generation and answering. In: CVPR, pp. 5754–5763 (2018)
14. Jain, U., Zhang, Z., Schwing, A.G.: Creativity: generating diverse questions using variational autoencoders. In: CVPR, pp. 5415–5424 (2017)
15. Kim, J., Jun, J., Zhang, B.: Bilinear attention networks. In: NIPS, pp. 1571–1581 (2018)
16. Kim, Y., Lee, H., Shin, J., Jung, K.: Improving neural question generation using answer separation. AAAI 33, 6602–6609 (2019)
17. Kingma, D.P., Ba, J.: Adam: a method for stochastic optimization. In: ICLR (2015)
18. Krishna, R., Bernstein, M., Fei-Fei, L.: Information maximizing visual question generation. In: CVPR, pp. 2008–2018 (2019)
19. Krishna, R., et al.: Visual genome: connecting language and vision using crowd-sourced dense image annotations. Int. J. Comput. Vis. 123, 32–73 (2017)
20. Kumar, V., Hua, Y., Ramakrishnan, G., Qi, G., Gao, L., Li, Y.: Difficulty-controllable multi-hop question generation from knowledge graphs. ISWC 11778, 382–398 (2019)
21. Kunichika, H., Katayama, T., Hirashima, T., Takeuchi, A.: Automated question generation methods for intelligent English learning systems and its evaluation. In: Proceedings of ICCE (2004)
22. Labutov, I., Basu, S., Vanderwende, L.: Deep questions without deep understanding. In: ACL, pp. 889–898 (2015)

23. Li, J., Gao, Y., Bing, L., King, I., Lyu, M.R.: Improving question generation with to the point context. In: Inui, K., Jiang, J., Ng, V., Wan, X. (eds.) EMNLP-IJCNLP, pp. 3214–3224 (2019)

24. Li, X., Zhou, Z., Chen, L., Gao, L.: Residual attention-based LSTM for video captioning. World Wide Web **22**(2), 621–636 (2019)

25. Li, Y., et al.: Visual question generation as dual task of visual question answering. In: CVPR, pp. 6116–6124 (2018)

26. Liao, Y., Bing, L., Li, P., Shi, S., Lam, W., Zhang, T.: Quase: sequence editing under quantifiable guidance. In: EMNLP, pp. 3855–3864 (2018)

27. Lin, C.: ROUGE: a package for automatic evaluation of summaries, pp. 74–81 (2004)

28. Lindberg, D., Popowich, F., Nesbit, J.C., Winne, P.H.: Generating natural language questions to support learning on-line. In: ENLG, pp. 105–114 (2013)

29. Ma, X., Zhu, Q., Zhou, Y., Li, X.: Improving question generation with sentence-level semantic matching and answer position inferring. In: AAAI, pp. 8464–8471 (2020)

30. Mostafazadeh, N., Misra, I., Devlin, J., Mitchell, M., He, X., Vanderwende, L.: Generating natural questions about an image. In: ACL (2016)

31. Nema, P., Mohankumar, A.K., Khapra, M.M., Srinivasan, B.V., Ravindran, B.: Let's ask again: refine network for automatic question generation. In: Inui, K., Jiang, J., Ng, V., Wan, X. (eds.) EMNLP-IJCNLP, pp. 3312–3321 (2019)

32. Papineni, K., Roukos, S., Ward, T., Zhu, W.: Bleu: a method for automatic evaluation of machine translation. In: ACL, pp. 311–318 (2002)

33. Ren, M., Kiros, R., Zemel, R.: Exploring models and data for image question answering. In: NIPS, pp. 2953–2961 (2015)

34. Ren, S., He, K., Girshick, R.B., Sun, J.: Faster R-CNN: towards real-time object detection with region proposal networks. In: NIPS, pp. 91–99 (2015)

35. Scholl, B.J.: Objects and attention: the state of the art. Cognition **80**(1–2), 1–46 (2001)

36. Scialom, T., Piwowarski, B., Staiano, J.: Self-attention architectures for answer-agnostic neural question generation. In: Korhonen, A., Traum, D.R., Màrquez, L. (eds.) ACL, pp. 6027–6032 (2019)

37. Sharma, S., El Asri, L., Schulz, H., Zumer, J.: Relevance of unsupervised metrics in task-oriented dialogue for evaluating natural language generation. arXiv:1706.09799 (2017)

38. Simonyan, K., Zisserman, A.: Very deep convolutional networks for large-scale image recognition. In: ICLR (2015)

39. Teney, D., Anderson, P., He, X., van den Hengel, A.: Tips and tricks for visual question answering: learnings from the 2017 challenge. In: CVPR 2018, pp. 4223–4232 (2017)

40. Teney, D., Liu, L., van den Hengel, A.: Graph-structured representations for visual question answering. In: CVPR, pp. 3233–3241 (2017)

41. Tian, H., Tao, Y., Pouyanfar, S., Chen, S.-C., Shyu, M.-L.: Multimodal deep representation learning for video classification. World Wide Web **22**(3), 1325–1341 (2019)

42. Tuan, L.A., Shah, D.J., Barzilay, R.: Capturing greater context for question generation. In: AAAI, pp. 9065–9072 (2020)

43. Wajeeha, D., et al.: Difficulty index, discrimination index and distractor efficiency in multiple choice questions. Ann. PIMS **4** (2018). ISSN:1815–2287

44. Xu, X., He, L., Lu, H., Gao, L., Ji, Y.: Deep adversarial metric learning for cross-modal retrieval. World Wide Web **22**(2), 657–672 (2019)

45. Zhang, S., Qu, L., You, S., Yang, Z., Zhang, J.: Automatic generation of grounded visual questions. In: Sierra, C. (ed.) IJCAI, pp. 4235–4243 (2017)
46. Zhao, Y., Ni, X., Ding, Y., Ke, Q.: Paragraph-level neural question generation with maxout pointer and gated self-attention networks. In: Riloff, E., Chiang, D., Hockenmaier, J., Tsujii, J. (eds.) EMNLP, pp. 3901–3910 (2018)
47. Zhou, Q., Yang, N., Wei, F., Tan, C., Bao, H., Zhou, M.: Neural question generation from text: a preliminary study. NLPCC **10619**, 662–671 (2017)
48. Zhou, W., Zhang, M., Wu, Y.: Question-type driven question generation. In: Inui, K., Jiang, J., Ng, V., Wan, X. (eds.) EMNLP-IJCNLP, pp. 6031–6036 (2019)

Incorporating Typological Features into Language Selection for Multilingual Neural Machine Translation

Chenggang Mi[1(✉)], Shaolin Zhu[2], Yi Fan[3], and Lei Xie[1]

[1] School of Computer Science, Northwestern Polytechnical University, Xi'an, China
{michenggang,lxie}@nwpu.edu.cn
[2] School of Software, Zhengzhou University of Light Industry, Zhengzhou, China
zhushaolin003@163.com
[3] School of Aeronautics, Northwestern Polytechnical University, Xi'an, China
fan_yionline@163.com

Abstract. In this paper, we propose to use rich semantic and typological information of languages to improve the language selection method for multilingual NMT. In particular, we first use a graph-based model to output the most semantic similarity languages; then, a random forest model is built which integrates features such as data size, language family, word formation, morpheme overlap, word order, POS tag and syntax similarity together to predict the final target language(s). Experimental results on several datasets show that our method achieves consistent improvements over existing approaches both on language selection and multilingual NMT.

Keywords: Language selection · Neural machine translation · Typological feature

1 Introduction

Multilingual NMT has attracted more and more attentions due to its advantages that can: 1) translate many language pairs using only one model; 2) enhance the translation performance of low-resource language pairs by knowledge sharing and transferring among related languages. Therefore, how to define the "relatedness" between languages becomes a very important topic in multilingual NMT. For example, [18] develop a framework that clusters languages into different groups and trains one multilingual model for each cluster, which shows some improvements in low-resource NMT. However, there existing different kinds of taxonomies for language family in the world, using only one specific taxonomy (Ethnologue[1]) is not solid enough. [12] propose to select transfer languages for NLP task based on multiple distance features, however, their method has two drawbacks: first, features used in their model are queried from URIEL Typological Database [13] directly, which doesn't reflect the language similarity of

---

[1] https://www.ethnologue.com/.

© Springer Nature Switzerland AG 2021
L. H. U et al. (Eds.): APWeb-WAIM 2021, LNCS 12858, pp. 348–357, 2021.
https://doi.org/10.1007/978-3-030-85896-4_27

the true corpora; second, the method is designed for general NLP tasks, not the multilingual NMT, therefore, some situations are not fully considered.

In this paper, we propose to use typological and semantic features jointly to improve the performance of language selection for multilingual NMT. In particular, we first use multilingual word embeddings to build the semantic similarity model of languages; then, a semantic feature and several typological features (such as word formation, word order, POS, etc.) are integrated into a random decision forest to build the final language selection model. Instead of put efforts on one or two characteristics of language, our proposed language selection method covers several characteristics of language. Compared with previous studies, our proposed method has the following advantages:

First, we propose to use semantic similarity as the primary feature to measure the relatedness between two languages.

Second, besides the semantic information, several typological features are also introduced to further optimize the language selection model for multilingual NMT.

2   Methodology

2.1   Overall Architecture

In this study, we try to address the language selection problem for multilingual NMT from three points: 1) semantic similarity between languages; 2) typological features and 3) language selection model. Several studies on NMT show that semantic information is helpful for machine translation, as it can help in enforcing meaning preservation and handling data sparseness [2,17]. So, we propose to use semantic similarity to measure the relatedness between languages as the first principle. Typological information such as word formation, word order, POS tagging have also been proved very helpful in many cross-lingual NLP tasks. We use and extend this information as features in our language selection problem. To achieve a promising performance, we consider the language selection as a ranking problem and propose a random decision forest to combine these features together.

2.2   Features

Semantic Feature. As the bilingual alignments are trained separately, the performance of multilingual word embedding will become worse if word embeddings in many languages mapped into a single common vector space [1]. In this study, we extend the work of [4] and propose to use a multilingual word embedding model to represent the similarity between two languages.

Given $N + 1$ languages in our multilingual NMT task, we choose one of them l_{pivot} as a pivot language. Due to the main contribution of multilingual NMT model is transferring linguistic knowledge from high-resource language to low-resource language. We propose to select a resource-rich language as l_{pivot} according to prior knowledge such as language family.

In our language selection task for multilingual NMT, we compare the graphs $G_l^{(l_{pivot})}$ across all other languages l and a pivot language l_{pivot}. Each word in l_{pivot} can be defined as one node in graph as:

$$r_u^{(l_{pivot})} = (w_l^{(l_{pivot})}(u, v))_{v \in V^{(l_{pivot})}} \tag{1}$$

where $u \in V\left[G_l^{l_{pivot}}\right] = V^{(l_{pivot})}$. The distance between two graphs can be defined as:

$$d(G_l^{(l_{pivot})}, G_{l'}^{(l_{pivot})}) = \frac{1}{|V^{(l_{pivot})}|} \sum_{u \in V^{(l_{pivot})}} \left\| r_u^l - r_u^{l'} \right\| \tag{2}$$

Finally, we define the semantic distance between two language l and l' as the average graph distance:

$$D(l_{pivot}, l') = \frac{1}{N-1} d(G_l^{l_{pivot}}, G_{l'}^{l_{pivot}}) \tag{3}$$

Typological Features

Word Formation. As the word formation of a language plays a very important role in the syntax and semantic representation in NLP task. In previous study, word formation has been used as a key feature in NLP [9]. We collect word formation information from Wikipedia.

The definition of the word formation feature can be defined as:

$$f_{wf}(Lan_A, Lan_B) = \begin{cases} 0, & WF(Lan_A) = WF(Lan_B) \\ 1, & Otherwise \end{cases} \tag{4}$$

where Lan_A and Lan_B are two languages, $WF(.)$ is a function that output the word formation type of a given language. This function can be implemented as a search algorithm.

Word Order. [5] calculated numbers of languages and language families of word orders. We find that a specific word order may include languages belong to different language families. For example, there are 2275 languages with SVO word order, and they belong to 239 language families. This inspire us that although two languages belong to different families, they may share the same word order.

Word order can reflect the syntax structure of a language. For example, if language A has the SOV word order and language B also belongs to SOV, language C has the SVO, A and B should more relatedly compared with C. Although there existing some special instances, we only focus on the commonly used word order of a language.

POS Tagging. POS tagging is used to assign grammatical information of each word given a sentence. Previous study shown that if two languages are closely related, they may share the similar POS information [14]. Given a source sentence in language A as src_A and a target sentence in language B as tgt_B. These two sentences are translated of each other. If the POS sequence of src_A is similar with tgt_B, A and B should be closely related.

Syntax Similarity. To measure the syntax similarity between two languages, we first parse the syntax structure of bilingual sentences in training data, then, we use a tree edit distance algorithm to compute the similarity between two syntax trees.

Language Family. In this study, we consider the language family as a feature in language selection model for multilingual NMT, which can be defined as

$$f_lf(Lan_A, Lan_B, LF) = \begin{cases} 0, & LF(Lan_A) = LF(Lan_B) \\ 1, & Otherwise \end{cases} \tag{5}$$

where Lan_A and Lan_B are two languages in training data, $LF()$ indicates a function that output the language family according to a given language. It should be noted that there existing several standards to classify languages, we only consider the Ethnologue in this study.

Linguistic Independent Features

Data Size. The most important advantage of multilingual NMT model is that low-resource language pairs can learn translation knowledge from rich-resource language pairs, and the amount of datasets can reflect whether a given language pair is resource-poor or resource rich.

Different from the traditional definition of a high/low-resource language, we instead named a language is low-resource when the size of its datasets is smaller than one fiftieth of the most resource-rich language (s) in the multilingual NMT. For example, if the size of a language A is $s(A)$, and the size of most resource-rich language B is $s(B)$, and $s(A) < s(B) * 1/50$, the language A can be considered low-resource language in our proposed model. Therefore, the data size feature can be defined as:

$$f_{ds} = \begin{cases} 0, & s(A) < \frac{1}{50}s(B) \\ 1, & s(A) \geq \frac{1}{50}s(B) \end{cases} \tag{6}$$

where $s(X)$ means the size of X language datasets. A is the current language and B is the most resource-rich language. This feature means when the size of current language datasets is less than one in fifty of the most resource-rich language, we can consider the current language as a resource-poor language.

Morpheme Overlap. Word and subword overlap are proposed to measure the relatedness between two languages from word and subword level [12]. The disadvantage of word overlap is that the data sparseness affects the model training. Although the subword overlap can overcome the data sparseness problem to some extent, linguistic knowledge may missed. In this study, we propose to use morpheme as the basic unit to measure the language similarity. In particular, we first obtain morphemes of a word given a language by a pre-trained morphological analyzer. The morpheme overlap feature used in this paper can be defined as:

$$OL_{morph} = \frac{|M_{lan_A} \bigcap M_{lan_B}|}{|M_{lan_A}| + |M_{lan_B}|} \tag{7}$$

To better measure the relatedness between two languages from lexical level, we also propose to use word overlap as one part of the overlap feature:

$$OL_{word} = \frac{|W_{lan_A} \bigcap W_{lan_B}|}{|W_{lan_A}| + |W_{lan_B}|} \tag{8}$$

The morpheme overlap feature can be defined as:

$$f_{morph} = \alpha OL_{morph} + \beta OL_{word} \tag{9}$$

To balance the morpheme and word level overlap, we define the morpheme overlap as the weighted sum of morpheme and word overlap, α and β are weights of two parts, respectively.

2.3   Language Selection Model

To integrate above features into a model effectively, we build the language selection model based on a random decision forest (RDF), which consists of several decision trees in which their predictions are combined into a final prediction.

We use the GBDT [8] model with LambdaRank as our training method [3]. This method works by learning an ensemble of decision-tree-based learners using gradient boosting. One of our research goals is to understand what linguistic or statistical features of a dataset play important roles in multilingual NMT, especially in low-resource settings.

3   Experimental Setup

3.1   Data

We evaluate the effectiveness of our proposed method on IWSLT datasets[2], which include multiple languages from TED. This datasets contain data on 23 languages to English and English to 23 languages, which collected from IWSLT evaluation campaign from year 2011 to 2018. The details of these datasets can be found in [18].

3.2   Settings

Data Preprocessing. To perform the multilingual NMT experiments, we first preprocess datasets as follows: For all language pairs, we carry out tokenization using tokenizer defined in the open-source toolkits Moses[3]. For Japanese and Chinese, we perform word segmentation by KyTea[4] and Jieba[5], respectively. All the data has been segmented into sub-word symbols using Byte Pair Encoding

---

[2] https://iwslt.org/.

[3] https://github.com/moses-smt/mosesdecoder.

[4] https://github.com/neubig/kytea.

[5] https://github.com/fxsjy/jieba.

(BPE) [16]. We learn the BPE operations for all languages together, which results in a shared vocabulary of 90K BPE tokens.

We compute the syntax similarity of two languages with an open source tree edit distance tool. Other features such as word order, word formation can be collected from Wikipedia. We extract the morphemes according to a universal morphological analysis model [10]. Language family features of each language can be collected from Ethnologue.

Baseline Systems. We compare our model with four existing baselines GoogleMNMT [7], LangClusterMNMT [18], LangSenstiveMNMT [20] and LangRank [12].

Language Selection Model. We first extract all features according to Sect. 2.2; then, we define our language selection model based on a random decision forest (RDF). For the semantic similarity feature, we set the threshold as 0.6; For word formation, we assigned 0, 1, 2 to each word formation methods such as derivations, inflection and compounding, respectively; Similar to word formation, we also set 0, 1, 2, 3, 4, 5, 6 for each word order (SOV, SVO, VSO, VOS, OVS and OSV); Due to the overlap of languages is measured by the word and subword level, we define the overlap feature based on the mixed of these two parts; To syntax distance, we assign the tree edit distance as feature directly. We use Normalized Discounted Cumulative Gain (NDCG) [6] to evaluate the performance of the language selection model. This evaluation protocol was also used in language choosing for cross-lingual NLP tasks, which is very close related to our study [12].

Multilingual NMT Model. We follow the work of [7], and added an artificial token to the input sequence to indicate the required target language; all other parts of the model as described in [21]. For the multilingual model training, we up sample the data of each language to make all languages have the same size of data. The mini batch size is set to roughly 8192 tokens. We train the individual models with 4 NVIDIA Tesla V100 GPU cards and multilingual models with 8 of them. We follow the default parameters of Adam optimizer [11] and learning rate schedule in [19]. For the individual models, we use 0.2 dropout, while for multilingual models, we use 0.1 dropout according to the validation performance. During inference, we decode with beam search and set beam size to 4 and length penalty $\alpha = 1.0$ for all the languages. We evaluate the translation quality by tokenized case sensitive BLEU [15] with multi-bleu.pl.

3.3 Results and Analysis

Language Selection. In Table 1, we present the results of language selection. For **Langtyp (all)** we include all available features in our models, while for **Langtyp (dataset)** and **Langtyp (sem)** we include only the subsets of dataset-dependent and dataset-independent features, respectively. For **Langtyp(typ)** we include the subsets of typological features. The performance of predicting transfer languages for the multilingual NMT task using single-feature baselines,

Langrank and **Langtyp** are shown in Table 1. First, using **Langtyp** with either all features or a subset of the features leads to substantially higher NDCG than using single-feature heuristics. The predictions of **Langtyp** consistently surpass the baselines. For multilingual NMT, the ranking quality of the best **Langtyp** model is almost double that of the best single-feature baseline. Furthermore, using dataset-dependent features on top of the linguistic distance ones enhances the quality of the **Langtyp** predictions. The best results for MT is the one using typological features in **English→X** using all features in **X→English** translations. **Langtyp** with only dataset features outperforms the semantic-only **Langtyp**. In addition, it is important to note that **Langtyp** with only semantic-only features still outperforms all heuristic baselines. This means that our model is potentially useful even before any resources for the language and task of interest have been collected, and could inform the data creation process.

Table 1. Language selection results compare with several strong baseline models.

Feature type	Feature	English-> X	X-> English
Semantic	Semantic similarity	28.2	28.8
Typology	Word formation	3.4	3.6
	Word order	13.7	14.6
	Language family	25.8	26.0
	POS	12.5	12.9
	Syntax similarity	25.8	26.3
Linguistic independent	Overlap	29.6	30.2
	Data size	3.8	4.1
Langrank(all)		**50.3**	**50.9**
Langtyp(all)		**51.5**	**52.6**
Langtyp(sem)		**50.4**	**50.3**
Langtyp(data)		**51.6**	**51.9**
Langtyp(typ)		**51.8**	**52.2**

Multilingual NMT. We first show the results of **23 languages→English** translations in Tables 4 and 5 and **English→23 languages** translations in Tables 2 and 3. We have several observations.

One-to-many setting is usually considered as more difficult than many-to-one setting, as it contains different target languages which is hard to handle. Here we show how our method performs in one-to-many setting in Tables 2 and 3. It can be seen that our method can maintain the accuracy (even better on most languages) compared with other methods in all language pairs, both on low-resource and resource-rich settings. One important reason is that our proposed language selection model incorporating several features into a model,

Table 2. Multilingual NMT results on English to X compare with several strong baseline systems (Part 1)

En-> X	Ar	Bg	Cs	De	El	Es	Fa	Fr	He	Hu	It	Ja
[7]	23.94	31.08	29.25	30.21	32.58	27.70	18.52	23.34	28.91	20.72	26.04	10.48
[18]	25.27	32.22	30.47	31.33	33.67	28.81	19.64	24.63	30.03	21.89	27.10	11.57
[20]	25.59	32.63	30.68	31.64	33.85	29.20	19.93	24.99	30.56	22.12	27.38	12.83
[12]	25.83	32.97	30.98	31.95	34.28	29.53	20.28	25.20	30.79	22.38	27.65	13.12
Our	**26.15**	**33.30**	**31.32**	**32.26**	**34.50**	**29.98**	**20.55**	**25.62**	**31.14**	**22.66**	**27.91**	**13.40**

Table 3. Multilingual NMT results on English to X compare with several strong baseline systems (Part 2)

En-> X	Nl	Pl	Pt	Ro	Ru	Sk	Sl	Th	Tr	Vi	Zh
[7]	34.29	19.03	31.15	26.94	17.90	25.47	21.08	17.35	21.03	25.72	14.08
[18]	35.43	20.24	32.33	27.97	19.43	26.61	22.12	18.46	22.09	26.95	15.13
[20]	35.72	20.53	32.55	28.26	19.78	26.93	22.35	18.74	22.33	27.28	15.37
[12]	35.95	20.80	32.82	28.50	20.14	27.29	22.69	19.15	22.56	27.56	15.54
Our	**36.27**	**21.25**	**33.20**	**28.87**	**20.46**	**27.68**	**23.18**	**19.41**	**22.98**	**27.85**	**15.89**

which includes typological, semantic features. Due to the language clustering can put related languages together, some semantic knowledge can also be transferred during model training. So the language clustering model outperforms the baseline model significantly. The **LangClusterMNMT** consider the language clustering and language specific at the same time, so its performance achieves better results than **LangSenstiveMNMT**. The **LangRank** method employ several features in the language selection, so the results can reflect the relatedness among languages from different aspects. The results of **23 languages→English** translations on the IWSLT dataset are reported in Tables 4 and 5. It can be seen that the multi-baseline model performs worse than the other models, while in contrast, our method performs better on all the 23 languages. Particularly, our method improves the accuracy of some languages with more than 2 BLEU scores over multi-baseline models. Our proposed model incorporate several features into the language selection model, results in best performance than other systems. For many-to-one translations, the source-side language can be defined during translation, so the multilingual NMT model can learn more translation knowledge compare with one-to-many translation. Although the **LangClusterMNMT** method [18] can share the translation knowledge in the same cluster, there existing different kinds of taxonomies for language family in the world, using only one specific taxonomy (Ethnologue) is not solid enough. **LangRank** select transfer languages for NLP task based on multiple distance features, however, this method has two drawbacks: first, features used in their model are queried from URIEL Typological Database [13] directly, which doesn't reflect the language similarity of the true corpora; second, the method is designed for general NLP tasks, not the multilingual NMT, therefore, some situations are not fully considered.

Table 4. Multilingual NMT results on X to English compare with several strong baseline systems (Part 1)

X-> En	Ar	Bg	Cs	De	El	Es	Fa	Fr	He	Hu	It	Ja
[7]	11.15	27.40	19.52	24.08	25.70	27.46	12.50	21.72	17.94	14.29	25.70	12.09
[18]	12.37	28.85	20.81	25.27	27.11	28.93	13.79	22.85	19.23	15.47	26.81	13.33
[20]	12.65	29.10	21.14	25.50	27.48	29.32	14.15	22.98	19.45	15.69	27.03	13.50
[12]	12.86	29.32	21.33	25.75	27.73	29.64	14.42	23.45	19.58	15.80	27.26	13.67
Our	13.12	29.61	21.50	26.08	28.04	29.78	14.76	23.90	19.85	16.02	27.55	13.98

Table 5. Multilingual NMT results on X to English compare with several strong baseline systems (Part 2)

X-> En	Nl	Pl	Pt	Ro	Ru	Sk	Sl	Th	Tr	Vi	Zh
[7]	28.85	10.73	27.60	20.05	12.72	16.95	13.00	27.41	10.98	28.56	9.28
[18]	29.98	11.95	28.63	21.14	13.84	18.18	14.25	28.55	12.11	29.79	10.52
[20]	30.12	12.15	28.80	21.42	14.03	18.35	14.54	28.76	12.35	29.90	10.74
[12]	30.35	12.36	29.12	21.68	14.35	18.58	14.67	28.90	12.62	30.24	10.96
Our	30.67	12.59	29.40	22.80	14.55	18.79	14.84	29.20	12.89	30.59	11.23

4   Conclusion

We propose a typological information motivated language selection method for multilingual NMT. Our method includes three parts: 1) Semantic similarity calculation, which measures the semantic relationship between two languages based on bilingual word embeddings; 2) Typological information motivated features, which measures language similarity from different aspects, such as word formation, word order; 3) Features integration, which is proposed to combine language selection results into the multilingual NMT model. Experimental results on several datasets shown that our proposed approach can consistently improve the performance of multilingual NMT, especially on low-resource settings. In our future work, we plan to use typological information such as contact and genealogical relatedness between languages in the language selection task.

Acknowledgments. This research was funded by the National Natural Science Foundation of China (No. 61906158).

References

1. Alaux, J., Grave, E., Cuturi, M., Joulin, A.: Unsupervised hyperalignment for multilingual word embeddings. arXiv preprint arXiv:1811.01124 (2018)
2. Belinkov, Y., Màrquez, L., Sajjad, H., Durrani, N., Dalvi, F., Glass, J.: Evaluating layers of representation in neural machine translation on part-of-speech and semantic tagging tasks. arXiv preprint arXiv:1801.07772 (2018)
3. Burges, C.J.: From RankNet to LambdaRank to LambdaMart: an overview. Learning **11**(23–581), 81 (2010)

4. Eger, S., Hoenen, A., Mehler, A.: Language classification from bilingual word embedding graphs. arXiv preprint arXiv:1607.05014 (2016)
5. Hammarström, H.: Linguistic diversity and language evolution. J. Lang. Evol. **1**(1), 19–29 (2016)
6. Järvelin, K., Kekäläinen, J.: Cumulated gain-based evaluation of IR techniques. ACM Trans. Inf. Syst. (TOIS) **20**(4), 422–446 (2002)
7. Johnson, M., et al.: Google's multilingual neural machine translation system: enabling zero-shot translation. Trans. Assoc. Comput. Linguist. **5**, 339–351 (2017)
8. Ke, G., et al.: LightGBM: a highly efficient gradient boosting decision tree. Adv. Neural Inf. Process. Syst. **30**, 3146–3154 (2017)
9. Khurana, D., Koli, A., Khatter, K., Singh, S.: Natural language processing: state of the art, current trends and challenges. arXiv preprint arXiv:1708.05148 (2017)
10. Kim, Y.B.: Universal morphological analysis using structured nearest neighbor prediction (2011)
11. Kingma, D.P., Ba, J.: Adam: a method for stochastic optimization. arXiv preprint arXiv:1412.6980 (2014)
12. Lin, Y.H., et al.: Choosing transfer languages for cross-lingual learning. In: Proceedings of the 57th Annual Meeting of the Association for Computational Linguistics, pp. 3125–3135, July 2019
13. Littell, P., Mortensen, D.R., Lin, K., Kairis, K., Turner, C., Levin, L.: URIEL and lang2vec: representing languages as typological, geographical, and phylogenetic vectors. In: Proceedings of the 15th Conference of the European Chapter of the Association for Computational Linguistics, vol. 2, Short Papers, pp. 8–14 (2017)
14. Naseem, T., Snyder, B., Eisenstein, J., Barzilay, R.: Multilingual part-of-speech tagging: two unsupervised approaches. J. Artif. Intell. Res. **36**, 341–385 (2009)
15. Papineni, K., Roukos, S., Ward, T., Zhu, W.J.: BLEU: a method for automatic evaluation of machine translation. In: Proceedings of the 40th Annual Meeting of the Association for Computational Linguistics, pp. 311–318 (2002)
16. Sennrich, R., Haddow, B., Birch, A.: Improving neural machine translation models with monolingual data. arXiv preprint arXiv:1511.06709 (2015)
17. Song, L., Gildea, D., Zhang, Y., Wang, Z., Su, J.: Semantic neural machine translation using AMR. Trans. Assoc. Comput. Linguist. **7**, 19–31 (2019)
18. Tan, X., Chen, J., He, D., Xia, Y., Qin, T., Liu, T.Y.: Multilingual neural machine translation with language clustering. arXiv preprint arXiv:1908.09324 (2019)
19. Vaswani, A., et al.: Attention is all you need. arXiv preprint arXiv:1706.03762 (2017)
20. Wang, Y., Zhou, L., Zhang, J., Zhai, F., Xu, J., Zong, C.: A compact and language-sensitive multilingual translation method. In: Proceedings of the 57th Annual Meeting of the Association for Computational Linguistics, pp. 1213–1223 (2019)
21. Wu, Y., et al.: Google's neural machine translation system: bridging the gap between human and machine translation. arXiv preprint arXiv:1609.08144 (2016)

Removing Input Confounder for Translation Quality Estimation via a Causal Motivated Method

Xuewen Shi[1,2], Heyan Huang[1,2], Ping Jian[1,2(✉)], and Yi-Kun Tang[1,2]

[1] School of Computer Science and Technology, Beijing Institute of Technology, Beijing, China
{xwshi,hhy63,pjian,tangyk}@bit.edu.cn
[2] Beijing Engineering Research Center of High Volume Language Information Processing and Cloud Computing Applications, Beijing 100081, China

Abstract. Most state-of-the-art QE systems built upon neural networks have achieved promising performances on benchmark datasets. However, the performance of these methods can be easily influenced by the inherent features of the model input, such as the length of input sequence or the number of unseen tokens. In this paper, we introduce a causal inference based method to eliminate the negative impact caused by the characters of the input for a QE system. Specifically, we propose an iterative denoising framework for multiple confounding features. The confounder elimination operation at each iteration step is implemented by a Half-Sibling Regression based method. We conduct our experiments on the official datasets and submissions from WMT 2020 Quality Estimation Shared Task of Sentence-Level Direct Assessment. Experimental results show that the denoised QE results gain better Pearson's correlation scores with human assessments compared to the original submissions.

Keywords: Quality estimation · Causal inference · Machine translation

1 Introduction

Recently, with the renaissance of deep learning, neural machine translation (NMT) has gained remarkable performances [1]. Nevertheless, translation quality is not consistent across language pairs, domains and datasets [2], and the absence of guarantee of translation adequacy may be deceptive to NMT users in real-world applications. Therefore, it is imperative to introduce quality estimation (QE) mechanism [6] to inform users about the credibility of a given NMT output.

Generally, QE aims to automatically estimate the quality of NMT output at run-time without using human reference translations. Most state-of-the-art QE approaches that achieve promising performances are built upon neural networks and involve pre-trained representations [5]. However, the output of deep neural networks can be easily influenced by the inherent characters of the model inputs [3]. These confounder information from the inherent features of the model input can bring difficulties and unfairness to QE, making the results of QE systems less credible.

© Springer Nature Switzerland AG 2021
L. H. U et al. (Eds.): APWeb-WAIM 2021, LNCS 12858, pp. 358–364, 2021.
https://doi.org/10.1007/978-3-030-85896-4_28

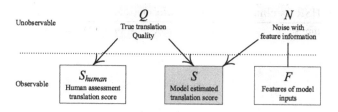

Fig. 1. Causal directed acyclic graph in our proposed method, which shows the relations among the true translation quality Q, model estimated score S and the inherent features of model inputs F. The undirected line between N and F means that N and F are correlative and do not require an explicit causality.

In this paper, we introduce a causal motivated approach to eliminate negative impacts caused by the inherent features of the inputs for QE systems. Figure 1 shows a causal directed acyclic graph (DAG) in our proposed method. Suppose that Q is an unobservable conceptual true translation quality, and the observed model estimated score S can be seen as the degraded version of Q with some noise N. For a QE system, a part of the noise is relevant to the inherent features of the model inputs, which can be regard as systemic error. Intuitively, the human assessment translation score S_{human} is approximate to Q, although it is also affected by some potential noises inevitably. This causal structure demonstrates that if we subtract the F-related information from S, then the noise which is correlative to F will be eliminated. Specifically, we utilize the Half-Sibling Regression (HSR) [4] method to perform the causal motivated denoising operation. Since there may be various possible features impacting S, we propose an iterative denoising framework for the multiple features. At each iteration step, we verify the independence assumption of HSR by an empirical condition, before performing our HSR based denoising operation. We also devise a self-adoptive denoising rate method to dynamically adjust the intensity of noise reduction.

We conduct experiments on the datasets and the submission results of WMT 2020 Quality Estimation Shared Task of Sentence-Level Direct Assessment (QEDA) [5]. The detailed technology used in the submission is black-box for this work, and we perform our denoising approach with just official public datasets and less assumptions. The experimental results indicate that our denoised scores gain an increase up to 58% on Pearson's correlation with human reference compared with the original submitted results.

2 Approach

2.1 Eliminating Confounder Information via Half-Sibling Regression

On the assumption of $F \perp\!\!\!\perp Q$, trying to predict S from F is a vehicle to selectively capture N's influence on S. If we subsequently remove the influence, we will obtain a more idealized estimation of Q referred as S^*. (F does not need to have an explicit causal effect on N and vice versa. The only thing confirmed is that they contain

---

Algorithm 1. HSR for eliminating feature information. See section 2.1 for more details.

Input: The feature set $F = \{f_1, ..., f_m\}$, the model estimated DA scores: $S = \{s_1, ..., s_m\}$, and a denoising rate $\beta \in [0, 1]$.

1: Compute the optimal weights $(a,^* b^*)$ for a linear regression $R(f) = af + b$:

$$(a^*, b^*) = \arg\min_{a,b} \frac{1}{m} \sum_{i=1}^{m} |R(f_i) - s_i|^2 \tag{2}$$

2: Subtract feature information from the model estimated score:

$$S^* \leftarrow S - \beta \times R(F) \tag{3}$$

Output: The feature eliminated score set S^*.

---

information of each other, i.e. $F \not\perp\!\!\!\perp N$.) We utilize the Half-Sibling Regression (HSR) [4] method to perform the causal noise elimination procedure.

$$S^* \leftarrow S - E[S|F], \tag{1}$$

where $E[S|F]$ means the F's effects on S. The value of $E[S|F]$ can be obtained by a regression model which is trained on the observed (S, F) pairs. Therefore, when we subtract $E[S|F]$ from S, the noise caused by F is eliminated. In this paper, we only consider the linear correlation among the variables, and apply a linear regression to perform $E[S|F]$ for Eq. (1). A sketch of the HSR procedure is described in Algorithm 1.

2.2 Finding and Eliminating Confounder Information

Since there is a strong assumption of $F \perp\!\!\!\perp Q$ for HSR, which strictly restricts the usage conditions of the algorithm. As an intrinsic property of Y, F cannot be completely independent of Q in theory. Schölkopf [4] points that it is also a sufficient condition that N is almost independent of Q in practice. Therefore, it is sufficient to verify the above relaxed condition approximately through the dataset before performing HSR algorithm.

For the specific QE task of sentence-level DA, we expect the model estimated score to be as approximate as possible to the human generated score S_{human} instead of the true translation quality Q. Therefore, we can perform HSR operations on S as long as S_{human} and F satisfy $S_{human} \perp\!\!\!\perp F$, without paying attention to the conceptual situation of Q. Specifically, suppose (F_t, S_t), (F_v, S_v) and (F, S) are $(features, scores)$ pairs of the training data, the validation data and the test data, respectively. Note that S_t and S_v are human generated score sets while S is model generated. We first compute the correlation of each $(features, scores)$ pair in turn to get c_t, c_v and c. Then, we execute the step function $\text{Condition}(c_t, c_v, c)$ in Eq. (5) and get the return value. If the value is true, then we perform HSR operation on S.

$$\text{Condition}(c_t, c_v, c) = \begin{cases} \text{true} & c > 0.05 \text{ and } \max(c_t, c_v) < 0 \\ \text{true} & |c| - \max(|c_t|, |c_v|) > |c|/2 \\ \text{false} & \text{otherwise} \end{cases} \tag{5}$$

In this paper, we suppose that there are $k = 5$ kinds of features: 1) SrcL, the length of the source sentence; 2) TransL, the length of the translation; 3) Median, the median

---

Algorithm 2. Eliminating noise information.

Input: A group of feature sets of the training data: $\mathcal{F}_t = \{F_t^1, \cdots, F_t^k\}$, DA scores of the training data: S_t; a group of feature sets of the validation data: $\mathcal{F}_v = \{F_v^1, \cdots, F_v^k\}$, DA scores of the validation data: S_v; a group of feature sets of the test data: $\mathcal{F} = \{F^1, \cdots, F^k\}$, the model estimated DA scores: S.

1: Initialize $S^* \leftarrow S$
2: **for** $i = 1; i \leftarrow i + 1; i < k$ **do**
3:    Compute the Pearson's correlation coefficient: (F_t^i, S_t), (F_v^i, S_v), and (F_i, S):

$$c_t \leftarrow \text{Pearson}(F_t^i, S_t), c_v \leftarrow \text{Pearson}(F_v^i, S_v), c \leftarrow \text{Pearson}(F_i, S)$$

4:    **if** Condition(c_{train}, c_{dev}, c) (see Eq. (5)) is true **then**
5:       Compute the self-adoptive denoising rate β by

$$\beta = \begin{cases} 1 - \max(|c_t|, |c_v|)/|c| & c \times c_t > 0, c \times c_v > 0 \\ 1 & \text{otherwise} \end{cases}, \tag{4}$$

6:       Execute HSR (see Algorithm 1) with the inputs of F_i, S^* and β, and get new S^*

$$S^* \leftarrow S^* - E[S^*|F_i]$$

7:    **end if**
8: **end for**
Output: The de-noised score set after z-mean normalization $S^* \leftarrow (S^* - \mu(S^*))/\sigma(S^*)$.

---

number of the word frequency of the translation; 4) Mode, the modal number of the word frequency of the translation; 5) Mean, the arithmetic mean value of the word frequency of the translation, and there is no limitation of independence between each kind of features, i.e. they may correlate with each other. We propose an iterative method that verify and eliminate the influence of these features in turn, and then the model estimated score S is updated at each iteration step. We also apply a self-adoptive denoising rate to avoid punish the noise too much. The whole noise elimination approach for multiple features is shown in Algorithm 2.

3 Experiments

We use the data from WMT 2020 Quality Estimation Shared Task 1[1]: Sentence-Level Direct Assessment [5]. The he experimental results are evaluated in term of the Pearson's correlation metric for the predictions against official provided human DA scores.

3.1 Main Results

Table 1 shows 18 disparate QE systems with 77 original submissions, of which 32 submissions meet the denoising conditions, involving 15 systems. We find that 5 systems meet the condition 3 times or more, which indicates that some systems themselves are

---

[1] http://www.statmt.org/wmt20/quality-estimation-task.html.

Table 1. Comparisons of Pearson's correlations between the original submissions (c) and the denoised submissions (c′) on the test data. "-" represents that the submitted result does not meet the denoising conditions and no denoising operation is performed.

#	Team	En-Zh		Ru-En		Ro-En		Et-En		Si-En		Ne-En	
		c	c' ↑	c	c' ↑	c	c' ↑	c	c' ↑	c	c' ↑	c	c' ↑
1	NiuTrans	.551	–	.816	–	.916	–	.833	–	.698	–	.830	–
2	TransQuest	.537	–	.808	–	.908	–	.824	–	.685	.687	.822	–
3	Bergamot-LATTE	.530	.536	.796	–	.906	–	.826	–	.682	.683	.814	–
4	IST and Unbabel	.494	.495	.767	–	.891	–	.770	–	.638	.642	.792	–
5	XC	.465	–	.783	–	.882	–	.764	–	.626	.627	.778	–
6	nc	.444	–	–	–	–	–	–	–	–	–	–	–
7	TMUOU	.438	.445	.781	–	.896	.	.792	.792	.668	.669	.785	–
8	Bergamot	.429	.430	–	–	.796	–	.681	.681	.560	–	.662	–
9	JXNU-CCLQ	.426	.427	–	–	–	–	–	–	–	–	–	–
10	IST and Unbabel	.346	–	.	–	.708	–	.690	–	.565	.565	.604	.604
11	Bergamot-LATTE	.321	.323	–	–	.693	.695	.642	.643	.513	.514	.600	.600
12	WL Research	.298	.300	.596	.601	.821	.822	.637	–	.577	–	.687	–
13	RTM	.259	.274	–	–	.703	.712	.614	–	.541	.542	–	–
14	**baseline**	.190	–	.548	.552	.685	–	.477	.477	.374	.374	.386	–
15	FVCRC	.085	–	.399	–	.650	.652	–	–	.388	.	.488	.491
16	Mak	.	–	.543	.542	–	–	–	–	–	–	–	–
17	nc	–	–	.411	.416	–	–	–	–	–	–	–	–
18	nc	–	–	–	–	.846	–	–	–	–	–	–	–

susceptible to the noise caused by input features. The overall results show that our proposed denoising approach achieves improvement of Pearson's correlations up to an increase of 58%. Among the 32 noise eliminated DA results, there are 28 systems gain the original submissions, and only 4 decline.

3.2 Distribution of the Eligible Features Under the Denoising Condition

Figure 2(a) shows the heatmap of the eligible features in different language pairs. We can see that the most selected features are the length of source sentence and the mode number of the word frequency in the target sentence. We also present the arithmetic mean of Pearson(F_t, S_t) and Pearson(F_v, S_v) in Fig. 2(b), and Fig. 2(c) shows the averaged Pearson(F, S) for all submitted QE results in the corresponding language pairs. Comparing Fig. 2(b) and Fig. 2(c), we can find that for the Pearson correlations between DA scores and the features of input, the human annotated data and the QE systems are basically consistent in most cases. Combining Fig. 2(a), we can find that the differences between Fig. 2(b) and Fig. 2(c) are the main features that meet the denoising condition.

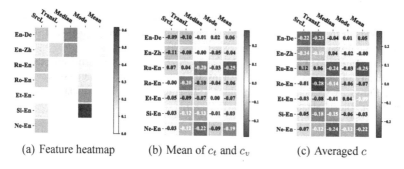

(a) Feature heatmap   (b) Mean of c_t and c_v (c) Averaged c

Fig. 2. The heatmap of the eligible features distribution (a) and the averaged feature-score Pearson correlations for the given datasets and the submission results (b and c) in different languages pairs.

4 Conclusion and Future Work

For a neural network based QEDA system, model outputs are easily interfered by the noise caused by the intrinsic characters of the model inputs. In this work, we propose a causal motivated HSR-based denoising method for the outputs of QEDA systems. The experimental results show that the denoised results gain higher Pearson's correlation scores with human assessments compared to the original submissions. In the future, we will apply the proposed noise elimination method to NMT models, and we expect the denoising mechanism to optimize the searching process during the NMT decoding step, in order to obtain better translation candidates.

Acknowledgments. This work is supported by the National Key Research and Development Program of China (Grant No. 2017YFB1002103) and the National Natural Science Foundation of China (No. 61732005).

References

1. Barrault, L., et al.: Findings of the 2020 conference on machine translation (WMT20). In: Proceedings of the Fifth Conference on Machine Translation, pp. 1–55. Association for Computational Linguistics, Online (November 2020)
2. Koehn, P., Knowles, R.: Six challenges for neural machine translation. In: Proceedings of the First Workshop on Neural Machine Translation, pp. 28–39. Association for Computational Linguistics, Vancouver (August 2017)
3. Ott, M., Auli, M., Grangier, D., Ranzato, M.: Analyzing uncertainty in neural machine translation. In: Dy, J.G., Krause, A. (eds.) Proceedings of the 35th International Conference on Machine Learning, ICML 2018, Stockholmsmässan, Stockholm, Sweden, July 10–15, 2018. Proceedings of Machine Learning Research, vol. 80, pp. 3953–3962. PMLR (2018)
4. Schölkopf, B., et al.: Modeling confounding by half-sibling regression. Proc. Natl. Acad. Sci. USA **113**(27), 7391–7398 (2016)

5. Specia, L., Blain, F., Fomicheva, M., Fonseca, E., Chaudhary, V., Guzmán, F., Martins, A.F.T.: In: Findings of the WMT 2020 shared task on quality estimation, pp. 743–764. Association for Computational Linguistics, Online (November 2020)
6. Specia, L., Turchi, M., Cancedda, N., Cristianini, N., Dymetman, M.: Estimating the sentence-level quality of machine translation systems. In: Proceedings of the 13th Annual conference of the European Association for Machine Translation. European Association for Machine Translation, Barcelona, Spain (May 14–15 2009)

Text Classification

Learning Refined Features for Open-World Text Classification

Zeting Li[1,2], Yi Cai[1,2(✉)], Xingwei Tan[3], Guoqiang Han[2], Haopeng Ren[1,2], Xin Wu[1,2], and Wen Li[4]

[1] Key Laboratory of Big Data and Intelligent Robot (South China University of Technology), Ministry of Education, Guangzhou, China
ycai@scut.edu.cn
[2] South China University of Technology, Guangzhou, China
[3] Department of Computer Science, University of Warwick, Coventry, England
[4] CNTC Guangdong Tobacco Corporation, Beijing, China

Abstract. Open-world classification requires a classifier not only to classify samples of the observed classes but also to detect samples which are not suitable to be classified as the known classes. State-of-the-art methods train a network to extract features for separating known classes firstly. Then some strategies, such as outlier detector, are used to reject samples from unknown classes based on the feature space. However, this network as a feature extractor cannot model comprehensive features of known classes in an open world scenario due to limited training data. This causes a problem that the strategies are unable to separate unknown classes from known classes accurately in this feature space. Motivated by the theory of psychology and cognitive science, we utilize class descriptions summarized by human to refine discriminant features and propose a regularization with class descriptions. The regularization is incorporated into DOC (one of state-of-the-art models) to improve the performance of open-world classification. The experiments on two text classification datasets demonstrate the effectiveness of the proposed method.

Keywords: Natural language processing · Open world classification · Prototype learning

1 Introduction

Closed-world assumption is widely made in traditional classification tasks [6,7,23], which assumes that all samples in future data belong to the classes which have been observed in previous data. However, this assumption cannot stand in real-world scenarios. For instance, when classifying user-generated text in social media, there always will be new topics in newly acquired data. It is not suitable to put these new samples, which probably belong to new classes, into any of the predefined topics. In text classification, Fei and Liu [5] first introduce the open-world setting, in which classifiers are required to classify samples into one of known classes, or an "unknown" class which represents all unobserved classes.

L. H. U et al. (Eds.): APWeb-WAIM 2021, LNCS 12858, pp. 367–381, 2021.
https://doi.org/10.1007/978-3-030-85896-4_29

Table 1. Documents in DBpedia dataset. The known classes are "Artist; Animal; Educational institution". Class "Written work" is one of the unknown classes.

Type	Class name	Document
Known	Artist	Vincenzo Barboni (1802–1859) was an Italian painter mainly depicting sacred subjects in a Neoclassical style.
	Artist	Ivan Matias is an American singer songwriter producer arranger hip hop ghostwriter and entrepreneur from Brooklyn NY.
	Animal	Eupithecia parcirufa is a moth in the Geometridae family. It is found in Bolivia.
	Educational Institution	Gore High School is one of two secondary schools in Gore New Zealand. It is located on Coutts Road in the west of Gore.
Unknown	Written Work	Pinball is an American literary magazine based in Chapel Hill North Carolina that publishes fiction essays visual art and comics online.

Table 2. Class descriptions of some classes in DBpedia dataset.

Class	Class description
Artist	An artist is a person engaged in an activity related to creating art, practicing the arts, or demonstrating an art. The common usage in both everyday speech and academic discourse refers to a practitioner in the visual arts only. However, the term is also often used in the entertainment business, especially in a business context, for musicians and other performers (although less often for actors)...

In recent years, deep neural networks have been applied on open-world text classification. Yang et al.[25] apply multiple loss functions to project samples onto a region near the prototype of the corresponding class in feature space. Then the samples belonging to unknown classes are rejected according to the distances between the samples and prototypes. However, the feature extractor in their methods is solely learnt from limited training data where there is no information about unknown classes. This causes a problem that the feature extractor cannot capture comprehensive features of known classes in an open world scenario. Thus the open-world classifiers are unable to detect samples of unknown classes accurately in this feature space. The reason is that the unknown classes are hardly distinguishable from the known classes by the features.

To demonstrate the limitation of previous works and our motivation intuitively, we give an example in DBpedia dataset, shown in Table 1. Assuming that the labelled documents of three classes "Artist; Animal; Educational Institution" are given, the model needs to reject the document of class "Written Work" in Table 1 when testing. Firstly, we determine Hot Training Phrases (HTPs) [11] of class "Artist", which make significant contribution to the classification of class "Artist". As shown in Table 5, phrase "be an italian" and phrase "be a singer songwriter" have strong distinguishing power to separate class "Artist" from the other known classes in one of state-of-the-art methods DOC [19], because these two phrases often appear in documents about "Artist" and seldom appear in documents of the other known classes. But phrase 'be an italian" isn't a strong indication that documents belong to class "Artist" in open-world scenario. Classifying documents that contain similar phrase "be an italian" into class "Artist" may result in misclassifying documents from unknown classes into class "Artist", such as one of unknown classes "Written Work". However, these two phrases "be an italian" and "be a singer songwriter" cannot be distinguished only using labeled documents of known classes. Additional information is needed to filter out irrelevant feature such as phrase "be an italian".

In psychology and cognitive science, it is found that humans use schemas (mental structures of preconceived ideas) to categorize objects [13] instead of learning characteristics of objects from scratch. Schemas contains knowledges about classes such as salient features of classes, which can be used additional information to filter out irrelevant features. Class descriptions summarized by humans can be seen as realization of schema. With the class description of "Artist" (shown in Table 2), we can learn phrase "be a singer songwriter" is more relevant to "Artist" class than phrase "be an italian" because the former is semantically similar with term "actor" and "writer" in the class description. By filtering out features such as phrase "be an italian" and retaining features such as phrase "be a singer songwriter", we can further improve unknown classes recognition while maintaining an excellent accuracy on known classes recognition.

Motivated by this intuition, we propose a model called Refined Features for Open Text Classification (RFOTC), which incorporates class descriptions into the process of feature learning to acquire a refined feature space. Class descriptions can be found in dictionaries or knowledge bases. In our experiments, we use the descriptions of class names which are extracted from Wikipedia. It can boost the recall scores of unknown classes through filtering out irrelevant features and retaining relevant features. This model consists of two key components: a classifier with multiple 1-vs-rest sigmoid layer, a feature regularization loss function which incorporates class descriptions [18]. The classifier calculates the membership of known classes and learns the importance of features for classification. During training, the feature regularization function can filter out irrelevant features by drawing samples close to the corresponding class description in feature space.

In summary, our contributions are listed as following:

– we propose a model called **R**efined **F**eatures for **O**pen **T**ext **C**lassfication (RFOTC) based on psychology and cognitive theory, which introduces class descriptions into the process of feature learning to obtain a refined feature space.
– We conduct extensive experiments on two datasets. The results demonstrate the effectiveness of the proposed method. We also conduct ablation tests to study the impacts of class descriptions in the proposed model.

2   Related Work

Open-world classification (also called open-set recognition in computer vision area) aims to build a classifier to classify new samples into one of known classes or reject samples belonging to unknown classes. Existing methods on open world classification can be classified into traditional machine learning methods and deep learning methods.

Traditional Machine Learning methods, such as Support Vector Machines (SVM) [4], Nearest Neighbor (NN) [21], Sparse Representation [22], etc. are modified with some constraints for open-world classification. Scheirer et al. [17] formalize open space risk as the relative measure of the open space (the positively labeled space far from the training positive samples) to the overall space. Scheirer et al. [17] reduce open space risk by using a slab instead of a half-space decision space. Scheirer et al. [16] propose Weibull-calibrated SVM (W-SVM) with non-linear kernel RBF to further reduce the open space risk by positively labelling only the sets with finite measure. Fei and Liu [5] incorporate center-based similarity learning with SVM to limit the open space risk by learning a score based on similarities, reducing the positively labeled space into a spherical area with a finite radius in original document space. Extreme value theory (EVT) [10] is used to calculate the membership of known classes and thresholds of class membership are used to limit open space risk [16]. Zhang and Patel [27] modify sparse representation-based classifier [22] for open-set assumption and model the matched and the non-matched reconstruction errors distributions via EVT which are used to determine test samples' identity. Bendale and Boult [1] extend Nearest Class Mean (NCM) into Nearest Non-Outlier (NNO) which rejects test samples based on their distances to the means of known classes.

However, these methods based on traditional machine learning heavily rely on feature engineering and are difficult to apply on large-scale data. Deep learning models have been successfully applied on closed-set classification without relying on feature engineering. There are some works that adapt classification layer in deep network for open-world classification. Bendale and Boult [2] adapt meta-recognition concept on activation vectors (the scores from the penultimate layer of deep network) to estimate the probabilities for deep networks failure. Bendale and Boult [2] replace the softmax layer with an OpenMax layer that calibrate softmax scores for enabling to reject samples from unknown classes. OpenMax rejects samples with equally likely logits, which may be samples that are difficult to classify. Instead of the softmax layer, Shu et al. [19] apply multiple 1-vs-rest sigmoid layers to form decision boundary that can separate one class from the other known classes accurately and further tighten the boundaries by Gaussian fitting. Besides the logits of classifiers, other information is also considered into rejecting samples from unknown classes, such as latent representation for reconstruction [26]. Xu et al. [24] propose a meta-classifier which can reject samples from unknown classes. Their model relies on a large-scale additional text dataset which contains a large meta-training class set and features of known classes and unknown classes. However, it is difficult to acquire such additional dataset in some scenarios.

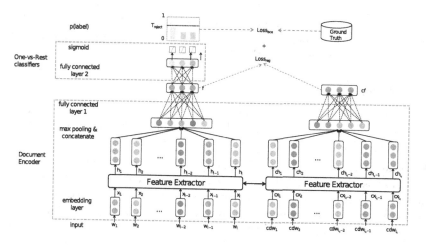

Fig. 1. The architecture of the proposed model

Another solution is to combine an unknown class detector with a closed world classifier. Various loss functions are introduced during training for learning feature space, where the inter-class variance and the intra-class compactness are maximized so that samples from unknown classes can be detected via distance-based outlier detector or density-based outlier detector [12]. Oza and Patel [15] provide another an unknown classes detector, which is based on the reconstruction errors conditioned on class identity.

3 Model

In order to create a feature space, where unknown classes can be separated from known classes more accurately, we propose a model called Refined Features for Open Text Classification (RFOTC). The whole framework is shown in Fig. 1. This model uses feature regularization via class descriptions to aid the feature extractor to extract features, which can avoid the inclusion of irrelevant features.

3.1 Problem Definition

Let C_K and C_U be two separate sets of known and unknown classes respectively. Given a set of documents with corresponding class labels

$$D = \{(d_1, y_1), (d_2, y_2), ..., (d_n, y_n)\} \tag{1}$$

where d_i is the i-th document, y_i is the class label of this document, the model can classify samples into corresponding known classes or reject samples which do not belong to any known classes in the test stage. The i-th document $d_i = \{w_1, w_2, ..., w_{l_i}\}$ consists of l_i words. All class labels y_i, which classifiers have access to during modeling, belong to known set C_K. The goal of open world text classification is to build a classifier which can assign correct known labels to documents that belong to the classes in C_K and a unique label indicating unknown classes to documents that belong to the classes in C_U.

3.2   Model Framework

The model consists of multiple One-vs-Rest classifiers and a feature regularization component. Specifically, One-vs-Rest classifiers contain a document encoder and a fully connected layer followed by sigmoid layer.

Document Encoder. Given a document d which contains l words, a document encoder aims to output a feature representation for the document. The document encoder is composed of a word embedding layer, 1 feature extractor, a Max-Pooling layer and a fully-connected layer activated by ReLU functions.

The embedding layer represented as a function f_0 converts words into embedding vectors:

$$\mathbf{x}_{1:l} = f_0(d) = f(w_{1:l}) \tag{2}$$

where $\mathbf{x}_t \in \mathbb{R}^n$. $\mathbf{x}_t$ denotes a n-dimension embedding vector corresponding to the t-th word w_t in a document.

Then, Convolutional Neural Networks (CNN) [8] encodes word embeddings into feature representations. Recurrent Neural Networks [3] and Transformers [20] can also be adopted as a feature extractor.

When CNN is used as a feature extractor, convolution is performed over word embeddings with different filters followed by activation function Rectified Linear Unit (ReLU) [14]. The output of the convolution layer for the t-th words is computed as:

$$\mathbf{h}_t = \text{ReLU}(\mathbf{W}_c \cdot \mathbf{x}_{t:t+s} + \mathbf{b}) \tag{3}$$

where $\mathbf{x}_{t:t+s}$ is the concatenation of s word embeddings for the t-th sliding window, $\mathbf{W}_c \in \mathbb{R}^{k \times (s \times n)}$ denotes the convolutions matrix and $\mathbf{b} \in \mathrm{R}^k$ is the bias (k is the total number of filters).

For better capturing the interaction among words, we use a representative Bi-directional long short-term memory (BiLSTM) instead of CNN. The BiLSTM layer reads the document from both directions and compute the hidden states for each word:

$$\overrightarrow{\boldsymbol{h}}_t = \overrightarrow{\text{LSTM}}\left(\overrightarrow{\boldsymbol{h}}_{t-1}, \boldsymbol{x}_t\right), \overleftarrow{\boldsymbol{h}}_t = \overleftarrow{\text{LSTM}}\left(\overleftarrow{\boldsymbol{h}}_{t-1}, \boldsymbol{x}_t\right) \tag{4}$$

where $\overrightarrow{\boldsymbol{h}}_t, \overleftarrow{\boldsymbol{h}}_t \in \mathrm{R}^m$ denotes the t-th hidden state of the forward and backward LSTM respectively (m is the dimension of hidden states).

We concatenate the hidden states from both directions to produce word representation:

$$h_t = [\overrightarrow{\boldsymbol{h}}_t; \overleftarrow{\boldsymbol{h}}_t] \tag{5}$$

Afterwards, max-over-time pooling is performed over word representations to select significant features $\mathbf{h}$. Given $\mathbf{h}$ as the input, the fully connected layer activated by activation function ReLU produces document representation $\mathbf{f}$:

$$\mathbf{f} = \text{ReLU}(\mathbf{W}_d \cdot \text{Max-Pooling}(\mathbf{h}_{1:l}) + \mathbf{b}_c) \tag{6}$$

where $\mathbf{W}_d \in \mathbb{R}^{r \times o}$ and $\mathbf{b}$ denote the parameters of the fully connected layer (o and r indicate the output dimension of the Max-Pooling layer and the fully connected layer respectively).

One-vs-Rest Classifiers. Inspired by Shu et al. [19], the proposed model utilizes $m = |C_K|$ sigmoid layers as the final output layers of the 1-vs-rest classifiers to determine whether a sample belongs to a certain known class. If a sample does not belong to any known class, it will be rejected as a sample from unknown classes. Each sigmoid layer contains a decision boundary which separates positive samples (belong to this class) from negative samples (do not belong to this class). The j-th sigmoid function predicts the probability of a document of belonging to the j-th class:

$$p(y = c_j) = sigmoid(\mathbf{v}_j'^{\top} \cdot \mathbf{h} + b_j') \tag{7}$$

where $v_j' \in \mathbb{R}^r$, $b_j' \in \mathbb{R}$ are parameters of the j-th 1-vs-rest classifier layer.

The m 1-vs-rest classifier layers are trained through binary cross entropy loss $Loss_{bce}$:

$$Loss_{bce} = \sum_{i=1}^{N} \sum_{j=1}^{m} (-\mathbb{I}(y_i = c_j) \log p(y_i = c_j)$$
$$- \mathbb{I}(y_i \neq c_j) \log(1 - p(y_i = c_j))) \tag{8}$$

where $\mathbb{I}$ is the indicator function.

For a test sample, if the predicted probabilities of all 1-vs-rest sigmoid layers are lower than the corresponding thresholds, the example will be classified as unknown classes. Otherwise, it will be classified as one of the known classes, which has the highest predicted probability:

$$\hat{y} = \begin{cases} \text{reject, if } p(y = c_j) < t_j, \forall c_j \in C_K \\ \text{argmax}_{c_j \in C_K} p(y = c_j), \text{ otherwise.} \end{cases} \tag{9}$$

3.3 Feature Regularization via Class Descriptions

In existing models, feature extractor can only access the information in training data, where there is no information about unknown classes. This will lead to the inclusion of irrelevant features, because model may wrongly conclude that these features are helpful to separate known classes from each other. However, these features will have a negative effect on rejecting unknown classes. Thus, we propose to inject the knowledge of class descriptions, because class descriptions are summarized by humans who have a deeper understanding of the world. They have seen a large number of things, and can summarize discriminative features in the descriptions, which can help our model select more relevant features and filter out irrelevant features.

Our model utilizes class descriptions to regularize the training of feature extractor. Inspired by [25], we design a loss function $Loss_{reg}$:

$$Loss_{reg} = \sum_{i=1}^{N} \| \mathbf{f} - \mathbf{cf} \|_2^2 \tag{10}$$

where f denotes the feature representation of the sample and cf is the feature representation of the corresponding class description. $\|\|_2^2$ represents Euclidean distance.

Instead of training prototypes for known classes in [25], we treat the feature representations of known classes descriptions as class prototypes. It is based on the intuition that all samples from the same class are supposed to be close to the corresponding class description in feature space.

To update the parameters of our model, we minimize the overall training loss function $Loss$ which consists of binary cross entropy loss $Loss_{bce}$ and feature regularization loss $Loss_{reg}$:

$$Loss = Loss_{bce} + \alpha * Loss_{reg} \tag{11}$$

where α refers to the weights of $Loss_{reg}$.

4   Experiments

Extensive experiments are conducted to answer the following three questions. Question Q1: Do our method and variants perform better than the base model DOC? Question Q2: Can the introduction of class descriptions improve the performance of our proposed model on open world classification task? Question Q3: Can our method outperform the state-of-the-art model(i.e., $GCPL$ [25])? The details of the experiments are described in Sect. 4.1, 4.2, 4.3 and 4.4. In Sect. 4.5, we answer the above three questions by analyzing the results of the experiments.

4.1   Compared Methods

We compare our method to two existing start-of-the-art open world text methods and conduct the ablation experiments by deleting class description from the inputs of RFOTC. CNN and BiLSTM are both used as feature extractor in these three models. The cored of these models are introduced as follows: **DOC.** In this work [19], multiple 1-vs-rest sigmoid layers are used to offer a decision boundary for each known classes instead of applying a softmax function as the final output layer. Instead of using individual reject threshold for each One-vs-Rest classifier, we use the same rejection threshold among all One-vs-Rest classifiers for fair comparison with our model. **GCPL.** combines the prototype based classifiers with convolutional neural networks and classifies samples taking account of the distance to class prototypes [25]. **RFOTC (w/o descriptions).** is a variant of RFOTC for analyzing the effectiveness of class descriptions. We drop the class descriptions from the inputs of RFOTC and replace **cf** in feature regularization loss with learnable parameters that have the sample shape.

4.2   Datasets

In our experiment, two datasets are used for evaluating our method. The detail descriptions of them are listed as follows:

Table 3. The experiment results on 20Newsgroup dataset. $RFOTC^\dagger$, $RFOTC^\ddagger$, $RFOTC^\S$ and $RFOTC^\P$ represents RFOTC (w/o description) +BiLSTM, RFOTC (w/o description) +CNN, RFOTC+BiLSTM and RFOTC+CNN respectively.

% Of known classes	Methods	Overall			Known			Unknown		
		F1	P	R	F1	P	R	F1	P	R
25%	DOC+BiLSTM	73.80	72.91	77.47	70.90	69.18	75.88	88.29	91.54	85.40
	DOC+CNN	77.11	77.96	77.64	74.29	75.20	75.02	91.21	91.76	90.71
	GCPL+BiLSTM	77.53	78.17	80.40	75.10	75.25	**79.08**	89.66	**92.75**	87.04
	GCPL+CNN	73.70	77.70	71.09	70.30	75.36	66.88	90.71	89.39	**92.13**
	$RFOTC^\dagger$	75.10	76.52	75.96	72.16	73.61	73.41	89.80	91.03	88.73
	$RFOTC^\ddagger$	78.00	78.38	78.68	75.35	**75.65**	76.30	91.28	92.04	90.59
	$RFOTC^\S$	75.74	76.95	76.73	72.87	74.07	74.31	90.05	91.38	88.87
	$RFOTC^\P$	**78.40**	**78.38**	79.51	**75.81**	75.58	77.34	**91.35**	92.39	90.38
50%	DOC+BiLSTM	77.68	80.43	77.11	77.77	80.69	77.24	76.77	77.85	75.86
	DOC+CNN	78.62	79.99	78.68	78.53	79.95	78.68	79.54	80.44	78.74
	GCPL+BiLSTM	80.30	81.66	80.82	80.31	81.67	**81.00**	80.28	81.62	79.05
	GCPL+CNN	77.36	81.79	74.28	76.99	82.23	73.16	81.12	77.33	**85.46**
	$RFOTC^\dagger$	79.26	80.53	79.09	79.15	80.53	78.97	80.35	80.54	80.23
	$RFOTC^\ddagger$	80.49	81.62	80.43	80.44	81.64	80.41	80.95	81.41	80.58
	$RFOTC^\S$	78.85	80.56	78.70	78.82	80.63	78.71	79.15	79.89	78.60
	$RFOTC^\P$	**80.96**	**82.26**	80.63	**80.87**	**82.29**	80.50	**81.89**	**81.93**	81.93

20Newsgroups.[1] is an English news dataset which contains 20 different topics. Each topic consists of approximately 1000 documents. We use words that appear more than 2 times, and the max sequence length of a document is limited to 2000 words.

DBpedia. [28] is an ontology classification dataset that includes 14 non-overlapping classes. Each class contains 45,000 textual data collected from Wikipedia, including 40,000 samples for training and 5,000 samples for testing. We select 20,000 words that appears most frequently. The max sequence length of a document is limited to 200 words.

4.3   Class Descriptions

We use the explanations of class names in Wikipedia[2] as class descriptions. It contains not only the definitions of class names but also additional knowledge, such as the development of Mac OS in the class description of class "comp.sys.mac.hardware". Note that classes in 20Newsgroups are organized into a hierarchy. We take the smallest granularity semantic to select appropriate class descriptions as the class descriptions are supposed to contain the most discriminating feature.

---

[1] http://qwone.com/~jason/20Newsgroups/.
[2] https://en.wikipedia.org/wiki/.

Table 4. The experiment results on DBpedia dataset. $RFOTC^\dagger$, $RFOTC^\ddagger$, $RFOTC^\S$ and $RFOTC^\P$ represents RFOTC (w/o description)+BiLSTM, RFOTC (w/o description)+CNN, RFOTC+BiLSTM and RFOTC+CNN respectively.

% Of known classes	Methods	Overall			Known			Unknown		
		F1	P	R	F1	P	R	F1	P	R
25%	DOC+BiLSTM	77.76	76.22	84.59	75.72	71.95	85.70	85.92	93.30	80.14
	DOC+CNN	81.62	80.02	86.56	79.70	76.47	86.91	89.29	94.21	85.14
	GCPL+BiLSTM	67.18	65.59	87.20	68.02	57.53	**96.13**	63.79	**97.84**	51.49
	GCPL+CNN	83.10	81.56	**87.78**	81.27	78.26	88.07	90.42	94.79	86.61
	$RFOTC^\dagger$	79.22	77.95	84.95	77.12	74.09	85.49	87.61	93.46	82.76
	$RFOTC^\ddagger$	83.39	82.45	87.22	81.59	79.46	87.20	90.61	94.42	87.32
	$RFOTC^\S$	81.02	80.56	85.36	79.05	77.31	85.46	88.91	93.56	84.96
	$RFOTC^\P$	**84.11**	**83.67**	86.70	**82.26**	**81.07**	86.06	**91.53**	94.11	**89.24**
50%	DOC+BiLSTM	84.00	83.40	87.59	84.64	82.78	89.58	79.57	87.74	73.67
	DOC+CNN	86.42	86.72	88.44	86.90	86.44	89.82	83.04	88.64	78.85
	GCPL+BiLSTM	82.69	81.11	**90.51**	84.31	79.48	**94.84**	71.33	**92.52**	60.21
	GCPL+CNN	87.51	87.28	89.89	87.89	86.86	91.27	84.82	90.25	80.21
	$RFOTC^\dagger$	86.27	85.96	88.94	86.69	85.49	90.43	83.31	89.24	78.48
	$RFOTC^\ddagger$	87.85	88.11	89.53	88.18	87.87	90.61	85.51	89.77	81.98
	$RFOTC^\S$	84.97	84.91	87.90	85.54	84.46	89.65	81.02	88.04	75.62
	$RFOTC^\P$	**88.18**	**88.68**	89.57	**88.51**	**88.52**	90.54	**85.86**	89.82	**82.77**

4.4   Experimental Settings

Documents in 20 Newsgroups dataset are randomly split into three parts: 60% of documents for training, 10% for validation, 30% for testing. In DBpedia, we use standard training/test split and pick 5000 documents from each class in training set as validation set and the others as training set. Then, we alter the number of known classes in the range of 25%, 50% of all classes and use all classes for testing. For each proportion, we randomly select the proportion of all classes as known classes, then repeat the experiment 10 times. For evaluation, we treat all of the unknown classes as one class, because we are not supposed to know the difference between them. We report performance as the average of ten runs with different known/unknown classes, including F1, precision and recall score. Besides the macro measure of overall (m+1) classes, we calculate the average measure of the models on known classes and unknown class.

We use CNN or RNN as feature extractor in DOC, GCPL and our methods. For CNN, the filter sizes are $3, 4, 5$ and the number of filters for each filter size is 150. For RNN, the dimension of hidden layer is 250. The dimension of document representations is set to 250. We use dropout on the embedding layer and the hidden layer with a rate of 0.2. Adam optimizer [9] is used to optimize the overall loss 11 and the learning rate is 1e–3 in all experiments. The results in all experiments are produced by selecting the best reject threshold from 0 to 1.

Table 5. Top Ten HTPs of *Artist* class in one of state-of-the-art methods DOC and our method RFOTC.

Rank	DOC		RFOTC	
	HTP	Freq	HTP	Freq
1	⟨unk⟩) was an italian	119	is an american singer songwriter	120
2	is an american country music	94	) was an italian painter	79
3	) was an italian painter	85	an italian painter of the	50
4	) is an american singer	76	an american singer songwriter and	46
5	is an american comic book	69	was an italian painter of	45
6	) is an american musician	50	) is an american singer	44
7	) is a japanese voice	48	is a japanese voice actress	37
8	is an american r b	31	was an italian painter mainly	33
9	was an italian painter of	28	is an american comic book	33
10	) is a norwegian jazz	28	is an english singer songwriter	33

4.5 Results and Analysis

Q1: Do our Method and Variants Perform Better than the Base Model DOC? The performances of DOC and our models are shown in Table 3 and Table 4. The results demonstrate that our model and variants achieve remarkable improvements in macro F1 score (about $0.9 \sim 3.3\%$) over DOC. Compared to DOC, experiments using RFOTC (w/o descriptions) show a improvement $0.9 \sim 1.9\%$ in macro F1 score. Our fully model combined with CNN outperforms DOC by $+1.3 \sim +2.5$ macro F1 score. RFOTC (w/o descriptions) obtains stable improvements (about $1.3 \sim 2.3\%$) and RFOTC achieves improvements varying from 1.0% to 3.3% in macro F1 score over DOC when we employ RNN as feature extractor. Experiments confirm that unknown classes and known classes can be distinguished easier in the refined feature space learned by RFOTC. In our model, we employ prototype loss to increase the intra-class compactness in the feature representation and make the feature representation more robust by introducing class descriptions. Experiments show that open world text classification can benefit from the robustness of feature extractor.

Q2: Can the Introduction of Class Descriptions Improve the Performance on open World Classification Task? As shown in Table 3 and Table 4, our fully model RFOTC+CNN increases the macro F1 score by 0.5% under 50% setting on 20Newsgroup dataset and by 0.3% under 50% setting on DBpedia dataset compared to RFOTC (w/o descriptions)+CNN, while RFOTC+BiLSTM decreases the macro F1 score by 0.4% under 50% setting on 20Newsgroup dataset and by 1.3% under 50% setting on DBpedia dataset compared to RFOTC (w/o descriptions)+BiLSTM. These two comparisons may lead to two opposite conclusions. However, we believe that class descriptions can improve the performance in open world classification. The reason why the introduction of class description causes a drop is that there are distinct long-distance semantics between the class description of a class and documents related to this

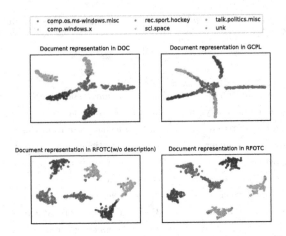

Fig. 2. Document representation obtained by using different models. We select one run under 25% setting in 20Newsgroups dataset.

class. In details, class description provides definition of a class and additional knowledge about the class, while documents describe instances of the class. In the example of the introduction, the class description of class "Artist" illustrates the use of the term "Artist" and the document describes a painter "Vincenzo Barboni". It follows that it would degrade the classification performance if we force the documents to be close to the corresponding class descriptions in the long-distance semantic space. RNN aims to model long-distance semantic correlations in a document. This is why our fully model RFOTC combined with BiLSTM perform worse than our ablated model. On the other hand, there are semantically related term between documents and corresponding class descriptions, such as "painter" and "actors" in Table 1. These terms are closely related to the classes. When RFOTC employs CNN as feature extractor, it can filter out irrelevant features by drawing samples close to the corresponding class description in feature space. To make a conclusion, the introduction of class descriptions can improve the performance in open world classification task when CNN is used as the feature extractor.

Q3: Can our Method Surpass the State-of-the-Art Model? Our model RFOTC + CNN obtains the best macro F1 performance under all the settings on both 20Newsgroups and DBpedia datasets. The reason is that GCPL aims to learn discriminative features to distinguish known classes and may include irrelevant features in feature space. In this way, samples of unknown classes cannot be separated from those of known classes. By introducing class descriptions, our proposed model can filter out irrelevant features and acquire a refined feature space that contains robust features. On the other hand, the performance of our model is more stable than GCPL on different datasets. We believe that robust features contribute to the model stability. To intuitively understand the performances of different models, we provide visualizations of document representation

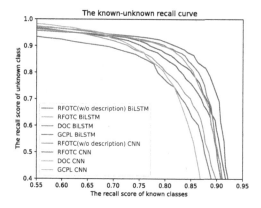

Fig. 3. The known-unknown recall score curve in 20Newsgroups. We evaluate the models by varying the rejection threshold from 0 to 1.

in the compared models and our models. As shown in Fig. 2, our model is easier to separate documents of different categories. This confirms that class descriptions can help to refine discriminative features and improve the performance in the open world classification task. The increase of the rejection threshold leads to the decrease of the recall of known classes and the increase of the recall of unknown class. Since the rejection threshold is valid to the performance of the threshold-based models, varying rejection thresholds are used in all models. We plot curves describing the relationship between mean recall of known classes and recall of unknown class. As observed in Fig. 3, RFOTC+CNN obtains better recall score of unknown class when keeping the same recall score of known classes than other models. In other words, it is more appropriate to use feature representation obtained by our model on open world classification task.

5   Discussion and Conclusion

The experiments show that class description can provide better-quality features. However, it is obvious that class descriptions are not available when the classes in a task are not nominal. For example, models need to recognize different digits in MINIST database, which hardly have semantic meaning. That is why we choose text classification as our testing ground, because text classification task usually has classes which have abundant semantic meaning.

To conclude, we propose a model which injects external knowledge from class description into feature encoder. It excludes some irrelevant features which have negative influence on separating known classes and unknown classes. The experiments demonstrate that the proposed method can improve the F1 merit on both datasets. When we apply RFOTC on a new dataset, it may need to adjust the hyperparameters manually to trade off the performances of unknown classes and the performances of known classes. For future work, we are interested in designing a loss incorporating class description without hyperparameter or with general feasible hyperparameter.

Acknowledgement. This work was supported by National Natural Science Foundation of China (No. 62076100), National Key Research and Development Program of China (Standard knowledge graph for epidemic prevention and production recovering intelligent service platform and its applications), the Fundamental Research Funds for the Central Universities, SCUT (No. D2201300, D2210010), the Science and Technology Programs of Guangzhou(201902010046), the Science and Technology Planning Project of Guangdong Province (No. 2020B0101100002), the Guangdong Provincial Tobacco Monopoly Bureau (company) funded scientific and technological project (No. 2020440000240054).

References

1. Bendale, A., Boult, T.: Towards open world recognition. In: Proceedings of the IEEE Conference on Computer Vision and Pattern Recognition, pp. 1893–1902 (2015)
2. Bendale, A., Boult, T.E.: Towards open set deep networks. In: Proceedings of the IEEE Conference on Computer Vision and Pattern Recognition, pp. 1563–1572 (2016)
3. Chung, J., Gülçehre, Ç., Cho, K., Bengio, Y.: Empirical evaluation of gated recurrent neural networks on sequence modeling. CoRR arXiv:1412.3555 (2014)
4. Cortes, C., Vapnik, V.: Support-vector networks. Mach. Learn. **20**(3), 273–297 (1995)
5. Fei, G., Liu, B.: Breaking the closed world assumption in text classification. In: Proceedings of the 2016 Conference of the North American Chapter of the Association for Computational Linguistics: Human Language Technologies, pp. 506–514 (2016)
6. Feng, S., Wang, Y., Liu, L., Wang, D., Yu, G.: Attention based hierarchical lstm network for context-aware microblog sentiment classification. World Wide Web **22**(1), 59–81 (2019)
7. Hu, R., Zhu, X., Zhu, Y., Gan, J.: Robust SVM with adaptive graph learning. World Wide Web **23**(3), 1945–1968 (2020)
8. Kim, Y.: Convolutional neural networks for sentence classification. In: Proceedings of the 2014 Conference on Empirical Methods in Natural Language Processing (EMNLP), pp. 1746–1751 (2014)
9. Kingma, D.P., Ba, J.: Adam: A method for stochastic optimization. arXiv preprint arXiv:1412.6980 (2014)
10. Kotz, S., Nadarajah, S.: Extreme Value Distributions: Theory and Applications. World Scientific, Singapore (2000)
11. Liang, B., Li, H., Su, M., Bian, P., Li, X., Shi, W.: Deep text classification can be fooled. In: IJCAI (2018)
12. Lin, T., Xu, H.: Deep unknown intent detection with margin loss. In: Proceedings of the 57th Conference of the Association for Computational Linguistics, ACL 2019, pp. 5491–5496 (2019)
13. Markus, H.: Self-schemata and processing information about the self. J. Pers. Soc. Psychol. **35**(2), 63 (1977)

14. Nair, V., Hinton, G.E.: Rectified linear units improve restricted boltzmann machines. In: ICML (2010)
15. Oza, P., Patel, V.M.: C2ae: Class conditioned auto-encoder for open-set recognition. In: Proceedings of the IEEE Conference on Computer Vision and Pattern Recognition, pp. 2307–2316 (2019)
16. Scheirer, W.J., Jain, L.P., Boult, T.E.: Probability models for open set recognition. IEEE Trans. Pattern Anal. Mach. Intell. **36**(11), 2317–2324 (2014)
17. Scheirer, W.J., de Rezende Rocha, A., Sapkota, A., Boult, T.E.: Toward open set recognition. IEEE Trans. Pattern Anal. Mach. Intell. **35**(7), 1757–1772 (2012)
18. Schro, F., Kalenichenko, D., Philbin, J.: Facenet: A unified embedding for face recognition and clustering. In: Proceedings of the IEEE conference on computer vision and pattern recognition, pp. 815–823 (2015)
19. Shu, L., Xu, H., Liu, B.: Doc: Deep open classification of text documents. In: Proceedings of the 2017 Conference on Empirical Methods in Natural Language Processing, pp. 2911–2916 (2017)
20. Vaswani, A., et al.: Attention is all you need. In: Advances in neural information processing systems, pp. 5998–6008 (2017)
21. Veenman, C.J., Reinders, M.J.: The nearest subclass classifier: a compromise between the nearest mean and nearest neighbor classifier. IEEE Trans. Pattern Anal. Mach. Intell. **27**(9), 1417–1429 (2005)
22. Wright, J., Yang, A.Y., Ganesh, A., Sastry, S.S., Ma, Y.: Robust face recognition via sparse representation. IEEE Trans. Pattern Anal. Mach. Intell. **31**(2), 210–227 (2008)
23. Wu, X., Cai, Y., Li, Q., Xu, J., Leung, H.: Combining weighted category-aware contextual information in convolutional neural networks for text classification. World Wide Web **23**(5), 2815–2834 (2020). https://doi.org/10.1007/s11280-019-00757-y
24. Xu, H., Liu, B., Shu, L., Yu, P.S.: Open-world learning and application to product classification. World Wide Web Conf. WWW **2019**, 3413–3419 (2019)
25. Yang, H.M., Zhang, X.Y., Yin, F., Liu, C.L.: Robust classification with convolutional prototype learning. In: Proceedings of the IEEE Conference on Computer Vision and Pattern Recognition, pp. 3474–3482 (2018)
26. Yoshihashi, R., Shao, W., Kawakami, R., You, S., Iida, M., Naemura, T.: Classification-reconstruction learning for open-set recognition. In: Proceedings of the IEEE Conference on Computer Vision and Pattern Recognition, pp. 4016–4025 (2019)
27. Zhang, H., Patel, V.M.: Sparse representation-based open set recognition. IEEE Trans. Pattern Anal. Mach. Intell. **39**(8), 1690–1696 (2016)
28. Zhang, X., Zhao, J., LeCun, Y.: Character-level convolutional networks for text classification. In: Advances in neural information processing systems, pp. 649–657 (2015)

Emotion Classification of Text Based on BERT and Broad Learning System

Sancheng Peng[1], Rong Zeng[2], Hongzhan Liu[2(✉)], Guanghao Chen[1],
Ruihuan Wu[2], Aimin Yang[3], and Shui Yu[4]

[1] Laboratory of Language Engineering and Computing, Guangdong University
of Foreign Studies, Guangzhou 510006, China
psc346@aliyun.com
[2] Guangdong Provincial Key Laboratory of Nanophotonic Functional Materials
and Devices, South China Normal University, Guangzhou 510006, China
wurh@scnu.edu.cn
[3] College of Computer, Guangdong University of Technology,
Guangzhou 510006, China
[4] School of Computer Science and Cyber Engineering, Guangzhou University,
Guangzhou 510006, China
Shui.yu@gzhu.edu.cn

Abstract. Emotion classification is one of the most important tasks of natural language processing (NLP). It focuses on identifying each kind of emotion expressed in text. However, most of the existing models are based on deep learning methods, which often suffer from long training time, difficulties in convergence and theoretical analysis. To solve the above problems, we propose a method for emotion classification of text based on bidirectional encoder representation from transformers (BERT) and broad learning system (BLS) in this paper. The texts are input into BERT pre-trained model to obtain context-related word embeddings and all word vectors are averaged to obtain sentence embedding. The feature nodes and enhancement nodes of BLS are used to extract the linear and nonlinear features of text, and three cascading structures of BLS are designed to transform input data to improve the ability of text feature extraction. The two groups of features are fused and input into the output layer to obtain the probability distribution of each kind of emotion, so as to achieve emotion classification. Extensive experiments are conducted on datasets from SemEval-2019 Task 3 and SMP2020-EWECT, and the experimental results show that our proposed method can better reduce the training time and improve the classification performance than that of the baseline methods.

Keywords: Text · Emotion classification · BERT · Broad learning system · Cascading structure

1 Introduction

With the rapid development and popularization of technologies, such as mobile Internet, social networks, and online applications, people have gradually changed

L. H. U et al. (Eds.): APWeb-WAIM 2021, LNCS 12858, pp. 382–396, 2021.
https://doi.org/10.1007/978-3-030-85896-4_30

from network information acquirers to producers. Social networks have become an essential medium for people to exchange their information and express their feelings. People can use mobile phones, computers and other terminal devices to share their information on various network platforms, and further to express their opinions anytime and anywhere, such as product reviews, news reviews, and movie reviews. Therefore, a large account of texts have emerged on Internet, and most of which contain emotional information. Emotion analysis on these text can help to understand the views and positions of users, and also can help enterprises, research institutions, and decision-making department of government to grasp emotional trend of society [2,14].

There are two main tasks for emotion analysis [1]: emotion recognition and emotion classification. Emotion recognition aims at determining whether the text carries emotions. Emotion classification aims at identifying which emotion expressed in text (such as happy, sad, angry, etc.). Some examples for emotion classification are listed as follows.

E1. My puppy **unfortunately** passed away yesterday. (sad)
E2. It is not going well! I am **outraged** in class every day! (angry)
E3. I especially **like** the weather today! (happy)

Thus, emotion classification is more granular and specific than emotion recognition. In this paper, we focus on classifying emotion of text. Emotion classification methods of text are divided into three types: i) method based on emotion dictionary; ii) method based on traditional machine learning; iii) method based on deep learning.

As to classification method based on emotion dictionary, it uses predefined emotion dictionary [15] to count the number of emotional words in text and calculates the emotional intensity to evaluate emotional tendency of text. This method primarily relies on the quality and coverage of emotion dictionary. Due to the complex vocabulary, sentence patterns, and expressions of online text (including multiple combinations of letters, symbols, icons, and words, such as T.T crying,O_O surprised, etc.) and continuous emergence of new online words, there are difficulty in constructing, maintaining, and expanding high quality emotion dictionary.

As to classification method based on traditional machine learning, it employs traditional machine learning model to learn the underlying laws in text, and then uses the trained model to classify emotions of new text. However, it usually requires complex feature engineering [19]: mainly including text data preprocessing (such as text segmentation, stop word removal, word frequency statistics, etc.) and feature selection (such as n-gram features, TF-IDF features, syntactic features, etc.). Besides, the vector representation of traditional machine learning is highly sparse, and the feature expression capability is weak.

As to classification method based on deep learning, it adopts a deep neural network containing multiple hidden layers to automatically extract features of text, which solves the weak capability of feature representation and learning large-scale data and high cost of feature engineering. Thus, this method has become popular for emotion classification of text. Although the learning ability of deep neural network is very powerful, its training time is long and convergence speed is pretty low, due to its complex structure and too many parameters. BLS [4] is a flat network based on the random vector function-link network (RVFLN) [17], which has the advantages of simple structure, incremental modelling, convenient theoretical analysis and strong generalization ability. Thus, we propose a method for emotion classification based on BERT and BLS. The contributions of this work are listed as follows:

- We introduce BERT pre-trained model to generate sentence embedding. The texts are input into BERT to obtain context-related word embeddings, and all word vectors are averaged mathematically to obtain sentence embedding.
- We design three cascading structures for BLS to improve feature extraction capability of BLS, which include the cascading of feature nodes BLS (CFBLS), the cascading of enhancement nodes BLS (CEBLS), and the cascading of feature nodes and enhancement nodes (CFEBLS).
- We conduct extensive experiments on datasets from SemEval-2019 Task 3 and SMP2020-EWECT, the experimental results show that our proposed method can effectively reduce training time and improve emotion classification performance than that of baseline methods.

The remainder of this paper is organized as follows: In Sect. 2, we provide an overview for related work of emotion classification, and design a method for emotion classification by introducing BERT and BLS in Sect. 3. In Sect. 4, we conduct many experiments by comparing our proposed model with baseline methods, and conclude this paper and discuss our future research in Sect. 5.

2   Related Work

As a high-quality emotional dictionary is difficult to build based on massive text data, it is difficult to apply dictionary-based methods. Thus, many researchers have begun to use traditional machine learning methods. Pang et al. [16] used traditional machine learning methods to solve emotion classification problem. Majeed et al. [13] used KNN, decision tree, SVM and random forest to classify emotions in the Roman Urdu corpus containing 18k sentences. Xu et al. [21] used tree structure-based event representation method and Multi-Kernel SVMs text feature extraction method to solve the emotion cause extraction problem.

In recent years, many researchers have begun to apply deep learning techniques to classify emotion of text. Cao et al. [3] summarized and compared various emotion classification methods based on deep learning (including DAN, CNN, BiLSTM, Attention, etc.), and enumerated challenges and research trends of emotion classification. Li et al. [10] proposed a multi-channel BiLSTM model to obtain emotional information by combining emotional words and grammatical knowledge with BiLSTM. Yuan et al. [22] used the improved TextCNN to build an emotion analysis network and applied it to emotion analysis of financial texts.

Although the deep network model has strong learning capability, due to a large number of parameters and complex network structure, it leads to long training time, large amounts of computing resources, and difficulty in theoretical analysis. In addition, deep network models such as RNN and LSTM are prone to gradient explosion and gradient vanishing during training [18]. As a flat network, BLS has many advantages, such as simple structure, short training time, and good generalization performance, which has become an alternative for deep learning. At present, many researchers have theoretically optimized and expanded BLS [11,23] according to practical applications [8,20]. However, few researchers have used BLS for emotion classification of text. Thus, we attempt to use BLS and its three cascading structures to extract text features for realizing emotion classification in this paper.

3 Modeling on Emotion Classification Based on BERT and BLS

In this section, we will introduce how to model emotion classification of text based on BERT and BLS, including the overall structure of proposed model, introduction of BERT pre-trained model for sentence embedding, BLS for emotion classification,incremental learning of BLS, and design of cascading structures based on BLS.

3.1 Overview of Model Structure

The structure of our proposed model is designed by combining BERT pre-trained model with BLS. The specific structure is shown in Fig. 1.

The texts are input into BERT pre-trained model to obtain context-related word vectors $v_i, i = 1, 2, ..., n$, and all word vectors are averaged to obtain sentence embedding v. v is input into feature nodes and enhancement nodes of BLS to obtain linear and nonlinear features of text. Two groups of features are fused and input into the output layer Y and softmax layer to obtain the probability distribution of each kind of emotions. BLS in Fig. 1 is replaced with CFBLS, CEBLS, and CFEBLS in our extensive experiments, respectively.

3.2 BERT Pre-trained Model for Sentence Embedding

BERT [6] is composed of multiple transformer blocks. The encoder of transformer consists of a multi-head attention layer and a feed-forward layer, which performs layer normalization for each layer. Multi-head attention layer contains multiple self-attention layers that can obtain current word information and semantic information. Multi-head attention layer expands the capacity by obtaining different aspects of attention information from multiple self-attention layers.

The input of BERT consists of three parts: i) Token embedding: it uses a specific number to represent the corresponding word in sentence according to the relationship between word and its number in vocabulary; ii) Segment embedding:

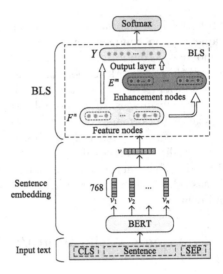

Fig. 1. Model structure

it uses 0 and 1 to distinguish any two sentences; iii) Position embedding: it uses a sequence number to indicate the position of word in text.

Usually, last hidden layer of BERT is used as word vector and all word vectors are averaged mathematically to obtain sentence embedding, the specific is shown as follows:

$$v = \frac{1}{n} \sum_{i=1}^{n} v_i \tag{1}$$

where v_i denotes word vector of the i th word in a sentence for the total number of words n. v denotes the sentence embedding with dimension of 768.

3.3   BLS for Emotion Classification of Text

The basic concept of BLS is that sentence embedding X is linearly transformed into feature nodes, which are nonlinearly transformed into enhancement nodes, and feature nodes and enhancement nodes are input into output layer to obtain the results of system. Its structure is shown in Fig. 2.

Given the training data $\{X, Y\} \in \mathbb{R}^{N \times (M+C)}$, where N denotes the number of samples, M denotes the dimension of feature, and C denotes the number of emotion classes. Sentence embedding X is linearly transformed into n groups of feature nodes, then, feature nodes F_i is described as follows:

$$F_i = g\left(XW_{fi} + \beta_{fi}\right), i = 1, 2, ..., n \tag{2}$$

where g denotes a linear activation function, and W_{fi} and β_{fi} denote weight matrix and bias matrix generated randomly, respectively. We assume $F^n \triangleq [F_1, F_2, ..., F_n]$ as the n groups of features nodes. F^n are nonlinearly transformed

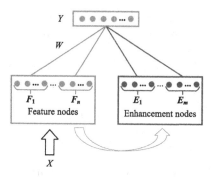

Fig. 2. Broad learning system (BLS)

into m groups of enhancement nodes, then, enhancement nodes E_j is described as follows:

$$E_j = \varphi \left(F^n W_{ej} + \beta_{ej} \right), j = 1, 2, ..., m \tag{3}$$

where φ denotes a nonlinear activation function, and W_{ej} and β_{ej} denote weight matrix and bias matrix generated randomly, respectively. We assume $E^m \triangleq [E_1, E_2, ..., E_m]$ as the m groups of enhancement nodes. Thus, output Y of BLS can be represented as follows:

$$Y = [F^n, E^m] W = AW \tag{4}$$

where W denotes output weights and $A = [F^n, E^m]$ denotes input matrix.

We assume A^+ is a pseudo-inverse matrix of A, then $W = A^+ Y$. To effectively reduce the calculation time and to prevent overfitting, the ridge regression is used to calculate A^+, the specific is listed as follows:

$$A^+ = \lim_{\lambda \to 0} \left(\lambda I + A A^T \right)^{-1} A^T \tag{5}$$

3.4 Incremental Learning of BLS

Generally, as the dataset of emotion classification contains lots of training data, if all the data are input into the system at once will allocate a lot of memory space. Thus, we present a model to update output weight when training data are input in batches. In addition, the updated output weights should contain information of previous and current training data.

Given the first batch of training data $\{X_1, Y_1\} \in \mathbb{R}^{N \times (M+C)}$ and current input matrix A_1, the current output weights W_1 can be represented as follows:

$$W_1 = \lim_{\lambda \to 0} \left(\lambda I + A_1^{\mathrm{T}} A_1 \right)^{-1} A_1^{\mathrm{T}} Y_1 \tag{6}$$

We assume $S_1 = \lim_{\lambda \to 0} \left(\lambda I + A_1^{T} A_1 \right)$ as the memory matrix when the first batch of training data are input. Thus, W_1 can be represented as follows:

$$W_1 = S_1^{-1} A_1^{\mathrm{T}} Y_1 \tag{7}$$

Given the second batch of training data $\{X_2, Y_2\} \in \mathbb{R}^{N \times (M+C)}$ and current input matrix A_2, the current output weight W_2 can be represented as follows:

$$
\begin{aligned}
W_2 &= \lim_{\lambda \to 0} \left(\lambda I + \begin{bmatrix} A_1 \\ A_2 \end{bmatrix}^{\mathrm{T}} \begin{bmatrix} A_1 \\ A_2 \end{bmatrix} \right)^{-1} \begin{bmatrix} A_1 \\ A_2 \end{bmatrix}^{\mathrm{T}} \begin{bmatrix} Y_1 \\ Y_2 \end{bmatrix} \\
&= \lim_{\lambda \to 0} \left(\lambda I + A_1^{\mathrm{T}} A_1 + A_2^{\mathrm{T}} A_2 \right)^{-1} \left(A_1^{T} Y_1 + A_2^{T} Y_2 \right) \\
&= \left(S_1 + A_2^{\mathrm{T}} A_2 \right)^{-1} \left(A_1^{\mathrm{T}} Y_1 + A_2^{\mathrm{T}} Y_2 \right)
\end{aligned}
\tag{8}
$$

We assume $S_2 = S_1 + A_2^{\mathrm{T}} A_2$ as the memory matrix when the second batch of training data are input. Thus, W_2 can be represented as follows:

$$
\begin{aligned}
W_2 &= S_2^{-1} S_1 S_1^{-1} A_1^{\mathrm{T}} Y_1 + S_2^{-1} A_2^{\mathrm{T}} Y_2 \\
&= S_2^{-1} \left(S_2 - A_2^{T} A_2 \right) W_1 + S_2^{-1} A_2^{\mathrm{T}} Y_2 \\
&= W_1 + S_2^{-1} A_2^{\mathrm{T}} \left(Y_2 - A_2 W_1 \right)
\end{aligned}
\tag{9}
$$

When the k th batch of training data are input, the output weight W_k can be represented as follows:

$$
W_k = W_{k-1} + S_k^{-1} A_k^{T} \left(Y_k - A_k W_{k-1} \right)
\tag{10}
$$

where $S_k = S_{k-1} + A_k^{T} A_k$ saves the information of the first k batches of training data.

3.5   Three Cascading Structures of BLS

As a flexible flat network, BLS can be expanded according to many real-world applications. To extract deep-level emotion features of text, it is necessary to cascade each group of nodes to enhance the capability of feature extraction. Thus, we design three cascading structures by expanding BLS [5], including CFBLS, CEBLS, and CFEBLS.

In CFBLS, n groups of feature nodes $F_1, F_2, ..., F_n$ are connected in a cascading manner, and the specific structure is shown in Fig. 3.

Given the training data $\{X, Y\} \in \mathbb{R}^{N \times (M+C)}$, the first group of feature nodes F_1 can be represented as follows:

$$
F_1 = g \left(X W_{f1} + \beta_{f1} \right) \triangleq g \left(X; \{W_{f1}, \beta_{f1}\} \right)
\tag{11}
$$

where W_{f1} and β_{f1} denote weight matrix and bias matrix generated randomly, respectively. F_1 is linearly transformed into the second groups of feature nodes F_2, which can be represented as follows:

$$
\begin{aligned}
F_2 &= g \left(F_1 W_{f2} + \beta_{f2} \right) \\
&= g \left(g \left(X W_{f1} + \beta_{f1} \right) W_{f2} + \beta_{f2} \right) \\
&\triangleq g^2 \left(X; \{W_{fi}, \beta_{fi}\}_{i=1,2} \right)
\end{aligned}
\tag{12}
$$

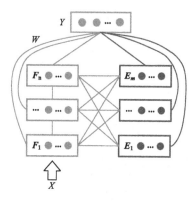

Fig. 3. Cascading of feature nodes BLS (CFBLS)

Thus, we can deduce that feature nodes F_k are represented as follows:

$$F_k = g\left(F_{k-1}W_{fk} + \beta_{fk}\right)$$
$$\overset{\Delta}{=} g^k\left(X; \{W_{fi}, \beta_{fi}\}_{i=1}^k\right), k = 1, 2, ..., n \qquad (13)$$

where W_{fk} and β_{fk} denote weight matrix and bias matrix generated randomly, respectively. According to Eq. (3), n groups of feature nodes are nonlinearly transformed into m groups of enhancement nodes. Finally, Eq. (5) is used to solve the pseudo-inverse matrix A^+, and then output weight $W = A^+Y$.

CEBLS connects m groups of feature nodes $E_1, E_2, ..., E_m$ in a cascading manner, and the specific structure is shown in Fig. 4.

Given the training data $\{X, Y\} \in \mathbb{R}^{N \times (M+C)}$, feature nodes E_i are same as Eq. (2). The n groups of feature nodes F^n are nonlinearly transformed into the first group of enhancement nodes E_1, which can be represented as follows:

$$E_1 = \varphi\left(F^n W_{e1} + \beta_{e1}\right) \overset{\Delta}{=} \varphi\left(F^n; \{W_{e1}, \beta_{e1}\}\right) \qquad (14)$$

where W_{e1} and β_{e1} denote weight matrix and bias matrix generated randomly, respectively. Then, E_1 is nonlinearly transformed into the second groups of enhancement nodes E_2, which can be represented as follows:

$$E_2 = \varphi\left(E_1 W_{e2} + \beta_{e2}\right)$$
$$= \varphi\left(\varphi\left(F^n W_{e1} + \beta_{e1}\right) W_{e2} + \beta_{e2}\right) \qquad (15)$$
$$\overset{\Delta}{=} \varphi^2\left(F^n; \{W_{ei}, \beta_{ei}\}_{i=1,2}\right)$$

Thus, we can deduce that the u th enhancement nodes are represented as follows:

$$E_u \overset{\Delta}{=} \varphi^u\left(F^n; \{W_{ei}, \beta_{ei}\}_{i=1}^u\right), u = 1, 2, ..., m \qquad (16)$$

where W_{ei} and β_{ei} denote weight matrix and bias matrix generated randomly, respectively. Finally, Eq. (5) is used to solve the pseudo-inverse matrix A^+, and then output weight $W = A^+Y$.

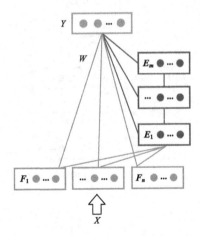

Fig. 4. Cascading of enhancement nodes BLS (CEBLS)

CFEBLS connects n groups of feature nodes and m groups of enhancement nodes in a cascading manner and the specific structure is shown in Fig. 5.

Given the training data $\{X, Y\} \in \mathbb{R}^{N \times (M+C)}$, the k th feature nodes F_k are the same as Eq. (10), and the u th enhancement nodes E_u are the same as Eq. (13). Eq. (5) is used to solve the pseudo-inverse matrix A^+, and then output weight $W = A^+ Y$.

4   Experiment

We conduct comparative experiments on datasets like SemEval-2019 Task 3[1] and SMP-2020 EWECT[2] to verify the effectiveness of our proposed method. We compare the performance of our proposed method with baseline methods under the same evaluation metrics. The experimental device is a laptop with Intel-i5-9400 2.9 GHz CPU, Nvidia 1660Ti GPU, and 16 GB memory.

4.1   Dataset

SemEval-2019 Task 3 is a short text of three rounds of English dialogue, including four emotions (i.e., happy, sad, angry, other). The specific is shown in Table 1.

The dataset involves a lot of irregular syntax, emotions, abbreviations, etc., which will adverse to emotion classification. Thus, Scikit-learn and Ekphrasis toolkit are adopted to process the datas as follows: i) Multiple consecutive punctuation are simplified as a single one (e.g., "!!!!" is simplified as "!"); ii) Informal words are simplified as the corresponding correct words (e.g., "goooooooood" is simplified as "good"); iii) Emojis are converted to the corresponding paraphrase (e.g., ":-(" is converted to "Unhappy face").

---

[1] https://www.humanizing-ai.com/emocontext.html.
[2] https://smp2020ewect.github.io/.

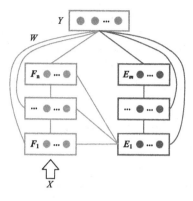

Fig. 5. Cascading of feature nodes and enhancement nodes (CFEBLS)

Table 1. SemEval-2019 Task 3 emotion distribution

Class	Train	Dev	Test
Happy	5191	180	369
Sad	6357	151	308
Angry	6027	182	324
Other	12585	2242	4508

SMP2020-EWECT consists of two types datasets usual Weibo and virus Weibo, including six classes of emotions (i.e., happy, angry, sad, fear, surprise, neutral). The statistic of emotion distribution is shown in Table 2.

Table 2. SMP2020-EWECT emotion distribution

Class	Usual			Virus		
	Train	Dev	Test	Train	Dev	Test
Happy	5379	391	1018	4423	923	1540
Angry	8344	586	1508	1322	314	463
Sad	4990	346	900	649	165	219
Fear	1220	87	210	555	75	190
Surprise	2086	170	373	197	17	68
Neutral	5749	420	990	1460	476	520

4.2   Baseline Methods

We compare the model proposed in this paper with the following baseline models.

- **SVM** [12]: It is a baseline model for most NLP tasks, which uses a traditional support vector machine as a classifier.

- **TextCNN** [9]: It is the first convolutional neural network model applied for text classification.
- **RCNN** [7]: It combines a recurrent neural network with a convolutional neural network to capture sequential and local features of text.
- **BiLSTM** [3]: It views sentence as a sequence of words, and uses bidirectional LSTM to extract features of text.
- **BiLSTM-ATTN** [3]: It adds an attention layer over the BiLSTM layer. Attention layer can help model focus on more attention put into the area to obtain more detailed information of text.

4.3 Parameter Setting

The kernel size of TextCNN is set to 3/4/5. The number of hidden units of RCNN is set to 200, and the kernel size is set to 2. The number of layers of BiLSTM is set to 2, and the number of hidden units in each layer is set to 400. BiLSTM- ATTN uses a BiLSTM layer with 400 hidden units. To ensure the length of input text is consistent, the length of input text of deep network is set to 100. In addition, BERT pre-trained model is adopted to generate word embeddings for these baseline methods.

The parameters of BERT+BLS, BERT+CEBLS, BERT+CFBLS, and BERT+CFEBLS are set as follows: In SemEval-2019 Task3, the number of feature nodes and enhancement nodes are set to 2000 and 1000, respectively; and sentence embedding of the three rounds of dialogue are spliced to get sample embedding with dimension of 2304. In usual Weibo and virus Weibo of Smp2020-EWECT, the number of feature nodes are set to 2000 and 600, respectively; and the number of enhancement nodes are set to 500 and 200, respectively.

4.4 Results and Analysis

In this paper, *Accuracy* and $Macro-F1$ are used to compare the performance of each methods. Table 3 and Table 4 show the accuracy and Macro-$F1$ of each method, respectively.

Table 3. The results of each model on SemEval-2019 Task 3 dataset

Model	Accuracy	Macro-$F1$
SVM	0.831	0.617
TextCNN	0.895	0.726
RCNN	0.893	0.621
BiLSTM	0.846	0.657
BiLSTM-ATTN	0.842	0.661
BERT+BLS	0.882	0.725
BERT+CFBLS	0.884	0.726
BERT+CEBLS	0.885	0.729
BERT+CFEBLS	0.887	0.732

Table 4. The results of each model on SMP2020-EWECT dataset

Model	Usual		Virus	
	Accuracy	Macro-$F1$	Accuracy	Macro-$F1$
SVM	0.691	0.636	0.683	0.529
TextCNN	0.759	0.722	0.761	0.601
RCNN	0.734	0.683	0.71	0.553
BiLSTM	0.751	0.713	0.76	0.584
BiLSTM-ATTN	0.756	0.714	0.765	0.591
BERT+BLS	0.761	0.72	0.761	0.581
BERT+CFBLS	0.762	0.721	0.761	0.583
BERT+CEBLS	0.765	0.723	0.763	0.584
BERT+CFEBLS	0.763	0.724	0.764	0.587

From Table 3 and Table 4, we can observe that SVM has the worst performance because SVM has weak capability of text feature extraction and sparse feature representation. As a deep learning-based approaches, RCNN and BiLSTM perform better than SVM, since BiLSTM can extract series information of text. As an extension to BiLSTM, BiLSTM-ATTN shows a slight improvement. This may be because that attention mechanism can learn informative stance-aware sentence representation. TextCNN, which is a text classification model based on CNN, achieves the best performance among all the baseline methods. It is worth noting that the accuracy of RCNN and TextCNN in SemEval-2019 Task3 is higher than other methods. The main reason is that the class distribution of test set is highly imbalanced (other account for 82%). The proposed methods yield better performance than baseline models in most of tasks.

The advantages of our proposed method mainly include two aspects: i) Feature nodes and enhancement nodes effectively extract text feature. ii) BLS can solve effectively pseudo-inverse matrix by using ridge regression to prevents overfitting. In addition, BERT+CFBLS, BERT+CEBLS and BERT+CFEBLS perform better than BERT+BLS (BERT+CFEBLS performs best), which shows that cascading structures of BLS can effectively enhance the capability of text feature extraction.

Table 5 and Table 6 show the training time of each method.

Table 5. The training time of each model on SemEval-2019 Task 3 dataset

Model	Training time(s)
SVM	460.7
TextCNN	2002.8
RCNN	6487.6
BiLSTM	4950
BiLSTM-ATTN	5725.6
BERT + BLS	21.9
BERT + CFBLS	43.5
BERT + CEBLS	17.8
BERT + CFEBLS	41.6

Table 6. The training time of each model on SMP2020-EWECT dataset

Model	Training time (s)	
	Usual	Virus
SVM	152.1	16.7
TextCNN	3041.7	1816.6
RCNN	3020.8	2004.2
BiLSTM	11952.8	3483.7
BiLSTM-ATTN	12214.2	5599.3
BERT+BLS	11.6	0.9
BERT+CFBLS	29.5	1.4
BERT+CEBLS	10.6	0.8
BERT+CFEBLS	26.2	1.2

From Table 5 and Table 6, we can observe that the training time of SVM is shorter than that of other baseline models. However, the training time for these baseline methods based on deep learning is very long. The reason is that gradient descent based on back-propagation is adopted to update a large number of parameters for them. Due to the uncertainty of convergence process, these methods need to consume a lot of computing source. The training time of our proposed model is significantly less than that of all the baseline models. The reason is that our proposed model only need to calculate output weights by Eq. (5).

5   Conclusion and Future Research

In this paper, we explored the current research status of emotion classification, and proposed an emotion classification method to solve the problems, such as long training time, and difficulty in theoretical analysis of deep learning methods, based on BERT and BLS. In our proposed model, BERT was used to generate sentence embedding, and BLS was used to extract text features and realize emotion classification. The experimental results show that our model can reduce the training time and improve the performance of system. As to our future work, we will plan to optimize the network structure of BLS to improve the performance of text emotion classification, and further verify the effectiveness of our proposed method with more kinds of data sets. We will also plan to study emotion classification of multi-language and cross-domain.

Acknowledgments. This work is partially supported by the National Natural Science Foundation of China under Grant No. 61876205, the Ministry of education of Humanities and Social Science project under Grant No. 20YJAZH118, and the Bidding Project of Laboratory of Language Engineering and Computing under Grant No. LEC2017ZBKT001

References

1. Aman, S., Szpakowicz, S.: Identifying expressions of emotion in text. In: Matoušek, V., Mautner, P. (eds.) TSD 2007. LNCS (LNAI), vol. 4629, pp. 196–205. Springer, Heidelberg (2007). https://doi.org/10.1007/978-3-540-74628-7_27
2. Bouazizi, M., Ohtsuki, T.: Multi-class sentiment analysis on twitter: classification performance and challenges. Big Data Min. Analytics **2**(3), 181–194 (2019)
3. Cao, L., Peng, S., Yin, P., Zhou, Y., Yang, A., Li, X.: A survey of emotion analysis in text based on deep learning. In: 2020 IEEE 8th International Conference on Smart City and Informatization (iSCI), pp. 81–88 (2020)
4. Chen, C.L.P., Liu, Z.: Broad learning system: an effective and efficient incremental learning system without the need for deep architecture. IEEE Trans. Neural Netw. Learn. Syst. **29**(1), 10–24 (2018)
5. Chen, C.L.P., Liu, Z., Feng, S.: Universal approximation capability of broad learning system and its structural variations. IEEE Trans. Neural Netw. Learn. Syst. **30**(4), 1191–1204 (2019)
6. Devlin, J., Chang, M.W., Lee, K., Toutanova, K.: Bert: Pre-training of deep bidirectional transformers for language understanding. In: Proceedings of the 2019 Conference of the North American Chapter of the Association for Computational Linguistics: Human Language Technologies (NAACL-HLT), pp. 4171–4186. Minneapolis, Minnesota (2019)
7. Girshick, R., Donahue, J., Darrell, T., Malik, J.: Rich feature hierarchies for accurate object detection and semantic segmentation. In: Proceedings of the IEEE Conference on Computer Vision and Pattern Recognition (CVPR), pp. 580–587. Columbus, Ohio (2014)
8. Han, M., Feng, S., Chen, C.L.P., Xu, M., Qiu, T.: Structured manifold broad learning system: a manifold perspective for large-scale chaotic time series analysis and prediction. IEEE Trans. Knowl. Data Eng. **31**(9), 1809–1821 (2019)
9. Kim, Y.: Convolutional neural networks for sentence classification. In: Proceedings of the 2014 Conference on Empirical Methods in Natural Language Processing (EMNLP), pp. 1746–1751. Doha, Qatar (2014)

10. Li, W., Qi, F., Tang, M., Yu, Z.: Bidirectional lstm with self-attention mechanism and multi-channel features for sentiment classification. Neurocomputing **387**, 63–77 (2020)

11. Liu, Z., Zhou, J., Chen, C.L.P.: Broad learning system: feature extraction based on k-means clustering algorithm. In: 2017 4th International Conference on Information, Cybernetics and Computational Social Systems (ICCSS), pp. 683–687. Dalian, China (2017)

12. Lv, Y., et al.: Aspect-level sentiment analysis using context and aspect memory network. Neurocomputing **428**, 195–205 (2021)

13. Majeed, A., Mujtaba, H., Beg, M.O.: Emotion detection in roman Urdu text using machine learning. In: Proceedings of the 35th IEEE/ACM International Conference on Automated Software Engineering Workshops (ASE), pp. 125–130. New York (2020)

14. Mäntylä, M.V., Graziotin, D., Kuutila, M.: The evolution of sentiment analysis–a review of research topics, venues, and top cited papers. Comput. Sci. Rev. **27**, 16–32 (2018)

15. Nasukawa, T., Yi, J.: Sentiment analysis: Capturing favorability using natural language processing. In: Proceedings of the 2nd International Conference on Knowledge Capture (K-CAP), pp. 70–77. New York (2003)

16. Pang, B., Lee, L., Vaithyanathan, S.: Thumbs up? sentiment classification using machine learning techniques. In: Proceedings of the 2002 Conference on Empirical Methods in Natural Language Processing (EMNLP), pp. 79–86. PA, USA (2002)

17. Pao, Y.H., Park, G.H., Sobajic, D.J.: Learning and generalization characteristics of the random vector functional-link net. Neurocomputing **6**(2), 163–180 (1994)

18. Pascanu, R., Mikolov, T., Bengio, Y.: On the difficulty of training recurrent neural networks. In: Proceedings of the 30th International Conference on Machine Learning (ICML), vol. 28, pp. 1310–1318. Atlanta, Georgia, USA (2013)

19. Scott, S., Matwin, S.: Feature engineering for text classification. In: Proceedings of the 16th International Conference on Machine Learning (ICML), vol. 99, pp. 379–388. Bled, Slovenia (1999)

20. Xu, M., Han, M., Chen, C.L.P., Qiu, T.: Recurrent broad learning systems for time series prediction. IEEE Trans. Cybern. **50**(4), 1405–1417 (2020)

21. Xu, R., Hu, J., Lu, Q., Wu, D., Gui, L.: An ensemble approach for emotion cause detection with event extraction and multi-kernel svms. Tsinghua Sci. Technol. **22**(6), 646–659 (2017)

22. Yuan, X., Li, Y., Xue, Z., Kou, F.: Financial sentiment analysis based on pretraining and TextCNN. In: Jia, Y., Zhang, W., Fu, Y. (eds.) CISC 2020. LNEE, vol. 706, pp. 48–56. Springer, Singapore (2021). https://doi.org/10.1007/978-981-15-8458-9_6

23. Zou, W., Xia, Y., Cao, W.: Dense broad learning system based on conjugate gradient. In: 2020 International Joint Conference on Neural Networks (IJCNN), pp. 1–6. Glasgow, United Kingdom (2020)

Improving Document-Level Sentiment Classification with User-Product Gated Network

Bing Tian[1], Yong Zhang[2(✉)], and Chunxiao Xing[2]

[1] DCST, BNRist, RIIT, Institute of Internet Industry, Tsinghua University, Beijing, China
`tb17@mails.tsinghua.edu.cn`
[2] BNRist, Department of Computer Science and Technology, RIIT, Institute of Internet Industry, Tsinghua University, Beijing, China
{`zhangyong05,xingcx`}`@tsinghua.edu.cn`

Abstract. Document-level sentiment classification is a fundamental task in Natural Language Processing (NLP). Previous studies have demonstrated the importance of personalized sentiment classification by taking user preference and product characteristics on the sentiment ratings into consideration. The state-of-the-art approaches incorporate such information via attention mechanism, where the attention weights are calculated after the texts are encoded into the low-dimensional vectors with LSTM-based models. However, user and product information may be discarded in the process of generating the semantic representations. In this paper, we propose a novel User-Product gated LSTM network (UP-LSTM), which incorporates user and product information into LSTM cells at the same time of generating text representations. Therefore, UP-LSTM can dynamically produce user- and product-aware contextual representations of texts. Moreover, we devise another version of it to improve the training efficiency. We conduct a comprehensive evaluation with three real world datasets. Experimental results show that our model outperforms previous approaches by an obvious margin.

1 Introduction

Document-level sentiment classification is a fundamental task in Natural Language Processing (NLP). It aims to predict the sentiment polarity or intensity (e.g. 1–5 stars on review sites) of a document. It has been widely applied in many real world applications, such as opinion mining [5], financial analysis [13],text search [24,25,29,37] and product analysis [22]. Early studies train classifiers with extensive hand-crafted features from texts [5,17]. Recently deep neural networks have been widely exploited for this problem [34,36,38]. They take the text as input and generate the semantic representations in the format of low-dimensional vectors.

It has been a common sense that the user's preference and product's characteristics have a significant influence on the sentiment ratings. To enable personalized sentiment classification, many previous studies [3,21,22] incorporate

© Springer Nature Switzerland AG 2021
L. H. U et al. (Eds.): APWeb-WAIM 2021, LNCS 12858, pp. 397–412, 2021.
https://doi.org/10.1007/978-3-030-85896-4_31

user and product information into deep neural networks. The UPNN model [22] first tackles this problem by bringing in a text preference matrix for each user and product at the word level and uses it as an operator to modify the semantic meaning of a word on the input layer. However, such method suffers from data sparsity. Besides, the interaction between texts and user and product information is insufficient as this approach simply concatenates user and product preference vectors with document representation. In order to better combine user and product information with text representation at the semantic level, recent studies [30,35] incorporate user and product information via attention mechanism along with Long Short-Term Memory (LSTM) based models. They first learn the text representation with LSTM models and then utilize the user and product information to compute the context's attention vector to help generate the personalized document representations.

Case 1: The movie is **good** .<sssss> ..... .<sssss>
But the environment of the cinema is very **poor** and **shabby**....<sssss>

Case 2: When i moved from tempe to downtown phoenix , i was a little devastated ...<sssss>
But it was ok because... Before I left for work at 6pm. <sssss>
So whatever my boyfriend...i would drink before i went to work . <sssss>
But then, i got a job ... <sssss>
Where was i to go to get my iced mocha so early that was n't starbucks and was not 15 minutes away ?? <sssss>
I had been to conspire before , but the hours were different .
Then i learned they were open nice and early , and within a quick 1 minute drive from my home . <sssss>
The coffee is good .

Fig. 1. Two typical examples

Though the effectiveness of attention based models, they still have the following limitations: since the weights in attention mechanism are applied after the text is encoded in the form of contextual vectors, the user- and product-related information could be already discarded and user- and product-irrelevant information may be retained in traditional LSTM cells in the encoding process.

This problem causes two issues. On the one hand, some of the semantic information is useless for a specific user or product. These user- or product-irrelevant information would adversely harm the final sentiment representation. This is because when the LSTM cell encounters an important token for the sequence semantics, this token's information is retained in every follow-up hidden state. Consequently, even if a good attention vector is produced via the user and product information, these hidden state vectors would contain useless information which is magnified to some extent. On the other hand, the correlation between words and the specific user or product may not be sufficiently kept in hidden states since the user and product information are not introduced in the process of context modeling.

We take two typical examples from real world datasets to illustrate these two issues in Fig. 1. Case 1 and case 2 are reviews about products: *Movie* and *Cafe* respectively. For the positive *movie* review '*The movie is good.* ⋯ . *But the environment of the cinema is very poor and shabby.* ' in case 1, the words '*poor*' and '*shabby*' are product irrelevant information and should not be taken into account. However, since these words are also informative words and important to semantics of the text, these information will be preserved in the hidden state vectors during the text encoding process in attention-based models. Even if '*good*' is assigned a large weight in the attention vector later, the information of '*poor*' and '*shabby*' will still be integrated into the final context representation and augmented. For the *Cafe* review in case 2, obviously, this comment is mainly about the user's new home, job, boyfriend or something. In this case, classic LSTM will retain a lot of information about these things and the information of '*Cafe*' in the last sentence will be not valued enough in hidden state vectors.

Therefore, we argue that the process of text encoding itself should be personalized for the task of document-level sentiment analysis. Specifically, it should be user- and product-aware and capture the following information:

- For different users, same word might express different emotional intensity. For example, a strict user might use "good" to express an excellent attitude, but a lenient user may use "good" to evaluate an ordinary product.
- Similarly, a product also has a collection of product-specific words suited to evaluate it. For example, people prefer using "sleek" and "stable" to evaluate a smartphone, while use "wireless" and "mechanical" to evaluate a keyboard.

To resolve these issues, we propose a novel User-Product gated LSTM network (UP-LSTM), which integrates personalized information in the early stage of text representation rather than leave it to the attention mechanism in the later stage. This is realized by incorporating user and product information into LSTM cells. As a result, UP-LSTM would be able to dynamically produce user- and product-aware contextual representations. Specifically, we design a user/product gate to control the influence of user/product specificity on text representation, and help to reflect user/product information to model personalized sentiment preference. In every time step, the user and product gates can select key information in the context according to the current input and user/product vectors and filter useless information for the given user and product. Meanwhile, the vectors of user and product information can influence the process of context modeling and keep the important information in the context words' hidden states. Let's go back to the example in Fig. 1. For the '*Movie*' review in case 1, our UP-LSTM introduces user and product information in the context modeling process, which means it can obtain the current product information '*movie*' when encoding the texts. As a result, it can smartly filter informative but product-irreverent words '*poor*' and '*shabby*' utilizing product gates, as these descriptions are not used to describe a movie. Similarly in case 2, most of this review is commenting on other things and says very little about '*Cafe*'. Nevertheless, our UP-LSTM can correctly preserve enough information about the true product '*Cafe*' in the context with the help of the current product vector of '*Cafe*'.

Moreover, to further reduce the number of parameters and improve efficiency, we propose an improved version of UP-LSTM, i.e. UP-CLSTM, which couples input and forget gates instead of separately deciding what to forget and what new information to be added. Experimental results on 3 real world datasets show that our model outperforms previous approaches by an obvious margin.

The contributions of this paper are summarized as following:

- We propose a novel LSTM variant to introduce the user and product information into the process of context modeling with user and product gates.
- To reduce the number of parameters and improve efficiency, we propose an improved version, named UP-CLSTM, which couples input and forget gates.
- We conduct extensive experiments on three real world datasets. The results demonstrate the effectiveness of our proposed methods.

2 Related Work

Text classification has been extensively studied in the field of NLP. Many recent studies are based on deep neural networks and have achieved promising performance [4,12,20,23]. Sentiment Classification is the automated process of identifying opinions in text. There are three levels of granularity for the sentiment classification problem [36]: aspect-level, sentence-level and document-level sentiment classification. The aspect-level sentiment classification targets at predicting fine-grained sentiments of comments with respect to the given aspect terms or categories [18,27,31]. The sentence-level sentiment classification aims to determine the sentiment expressed in each single given sentence [9,10,14,16]. While the document-level sentiment classification is to assign an overall sentiment rating to an opinion document. In this paper, we aim at the document-level problem.

Traditional approaches utilized rich features to improve the performance of sentiment classification such as bag of opinion [17] and sentiment lexicon [11,40]. Recently neural network models have been introduced into document-level sentiment classification due to its ability of automatically learning the text representation, such as applications based on CNN [26,32] and RNN variants [21,33,39]. These methods just focused on learning better text representation and ignored other information.

Personalized sentiment classification has become a popular topic recently. To this end, Tang et al. [22] proposed UPNN to utilize the user and product information to improve sentiment classification by introducing a text preference matrix and a representation vector for each user and product. Wu et al. [28] proposed a personalized approach for microblog sentiment classification where each user has a personalized sentiment classifier. Recent approaches incorporate user and product information via attention mechanism [3,6,30,35]. The UPA [3] and HUAPA [30] models devised word and sentence level attentions respectively to take account of the global user preference and product characteristics. Yuan et al. [35] further considered the inherent correlation between users and products with external memory and constructed user and product specific document representations via attention mechanism. However user- and product-related information could be already discarded in the process of generating the semantic representations before attentions in these models. To address this kind of problem , in the field of aspect-level sentiment classification, Xing et al. [31] introduced aspect information into the process of modeling context before attention mechanism via incorporating the aspect information into the input gate, forget gate and output gate in classic LSTM, which are proved to enable generate more effective contextual vectors than attention mechanism. Different from this model, in this paper, to fully exploit the potential of user and product information in personalized sentiment classification, we directly add two new gates: user and product gates to obtain user- and product-aware contextual representations of texts.

3   Methodology

In this section, we first describe how to integrate the user and product gates into LSTM cells so as to enhance text semantic representation. Then, we introduce the overall architecture of the model and details of training. Finally, we improve UP-LSTM by coupling the input and output gates for efficiency.

3.1   The UP-LSTM Cell

LSTM [8] is a variant of RNN that is designed to learn long term dependencies. In each time step t, it uses the embedding vector x_t of the context word corresponding to current time step as input. The basic update equations of LSTM are as follows:

$$\begin{pmatrix} i_t \\ f_t \\ \tilde{c}_t \end{pmatrix} = \begin{pmatrix} \sigma \\ \sigma \\ \tanh \end{pmatrix} (W[h_{t-1}, x_t] + b), \tag{1}$$

$$c_t = f_t \odot c_{t-1} + i_t \odot \tilde{c}_t, \tag{2}$$

$$o_t = \sigma(W_o[h_{t-1}, x_t] + b_o), \tag{3}$$

$$h_t = o_t \odot \tanh(c_t) \tag{4}$$

where h_t and c_t are the cell states. In this paper, we use the original LSTM model as the cornerstone of our work, while it is easy to extend our proposed techniques to other RNN variants.

Based on above update operations of LSTM, we add the user and product gates to each LSTM cell to produce user- and product-aware contextual representations. The gates are added in the manner shown in Fig. 2. The user gate is computed by x_t and the user vector U. It controls the influence of user specificity on text semantic representation for the current input x_t. Similarly, the product

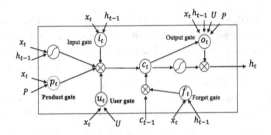

Fig. 2. The structure of UP-LSTM cell

gate is computed by x_t and the product vector P. It controls the influence of product specificity on text semantic representation for the current input x_t. It can be formalized as follows:

$$u_t = \sigma(W_{xu}x_t + \sigma(W_u U) + b_u), \tag{5}$$

$$p_t = \sigma(W_{xp}x_t + \sigma(W_p P) + b_p), \tag{6}$$

where $U \in R^{du}$ and $P \in R^{dp}$ are user and product vectors, respectively. $W_{xu} \in R^{d \times dx}, W_u \in R^{d \times du}, W_{xp} \in R^{d \times dx}, W_p \in R^{d \times dp}$ are the weighted matrices. $b_u, b_p \in R^d$ are biases. Parameters du and dp stand for the dimensions of user and product vectors, respectively. dx is the dimension of word vector and d is the number of hidden cells.

Correspondingly, we replace Eq. 2 and Eq. 3 with Eq. 7 and Eq. 8 in a cell of UP-LSTM.

$$c_t = f_t \odot c_{t-1} + i_t \odot u_t \odot p_t \odot \tilde{c}_t, \tag{7}$$

$$o_t = \sigma(W_o[h_{t-1}, x_t] + W_{uo}U + W_{po}P + b_o). \tag{8}$$

The benefits of UP-LSTM are two-fold: (1) The output gate o_t, which controls the extent of information flow from the current cell state to the hidden state vector of this time step, is influenced by the user vector U and the product vector P as shown in Eq. 8. Thus we can obtain the personalized text representation with such information. (2) As the user vector U and the product vector P are initially stored in u_t and p_t, they are firstly transferred to c_t through Eq. 7 and then to c_{t+1}, c_{t+2} and every follow-up state. In this process, the user gate u_t and the product gate p_t can model user and product sentiment preference by additional user and product information in each time step.

3.2 Overall Architecture

Based on above discussion of the UP-LSTM model, we then come up with the overall architecture for the task of sentiment classification. The details are shown in Fig. 3. It consists of three layers: an embedding layer, an encoding layer (with UP-LSTM as encoder) and an output layer. Next we will introduce them separately.

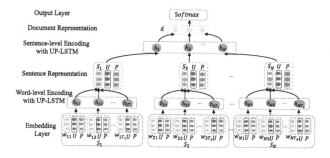

Fig. 3. Overall model architecture for training

Embedding Layer. The embedding layer maintains a look-up table to generate the word representation associated with the user and product information. Given a sentence with words w_{it}, $t \in [0, T]$ and the corresponding user id u and the product id p, it embeds the words, user and product to vectors through the word embedding matrix $\boldsymbol{W}_e$, $\boldsymbol{x}_{it} = \boldsymbol{W}_e w_{it}$, the user embedding matrix $\boldsymbol{W}_u$, $\boldsymbol{U} = \boldsymbol{W}_u u$, and the product embedding matrix $\boldsymbol{W}_p$, $\boldsymbol{P} = \boldsymbol{W}_p p$ respectively.

Encoding Layer. On the encoding layer, we project the raw document into a vector representation and then build a classifier on it to perform sentiment classification. To this end, we take document structure into consideration via a hierarchical framework. Specifically, assume that a document has N sentences and each sentence s_i contains T_i words. w_{it} with $t \in [1, T]$ represents the words in the ith sentence. The hierarchical UP-LSTM encoder is conducted in both word and sentence levels as following.

In the word level encoder, we use the output of embedding layer as input and adopt UP-LSTM as the basic building block for sequence encoder. At each time step t, given input $\boldsymbol{x}_t$, user vector $\boldsymbol{U}$, product vector $\boldsymbol{P}$ and previous hidden state $\boldsymbol{h}_{t-1}$, the current hidden state $\boldsymbol{h}_t$ is updated by:

$$\boldsymbol{h}_t = \text{UP-LSTM}(\boldsymbol{h}_{t-1}, \boldsymbol{x}_t, \boldsymbol{U}, \boldsymbol{P}, \theta) \tag{9}$$

We use UP-LSTM$(\cdot, \cdot, \cdot)$ as a shorthand for the computing process defined in Eq. 1 to Eq. 8. θ refers to all parameters of UP-LSTM. In each time step, we feed the word $\boldsymbol{x}_{it}$ into the UP-LSTM cell to obtain the hidden state. The final representation of sentence s_i is the hidden state $\boldsymbol{h}_{T_i}$ of the last time step.

Similarly, at the sentence level, we feed the output of word level encoders $[\boldsymbol{s}_1, \boldsymbol{s}_2, ..., \boldsymbol{s}_N]$ into the UP-LSTM and take the hidden state of the last time state as the document representation $\boldsymbol{d}$. As we incorporate the user and product vectors into LSTM cells, such information can be utilized in the process of generating hidden states at each time step rather than on top of the output of LSTM as attention based methods [3, 30, 35] did.

Output Layer. Since the document vector d is the high level personalized representation of the document, it can be then fed into a softmax layer for classification in Eq. 10

$$\hat{y} = softmax(\boldsymbol{W}_y\boldsymbol{d} + \boldsymbol{b}_y) \tag{10}$$

We adopt cross-entropy to compute the training loss $L(\hat{y}, y)$ shown in Eq. 11:

$$L(\hat{y}, y) = -\Sigma_{i=1}^{N_k}\Sigma_{j=1}^{C}y_{ij}log(\hat{y}_{ij}) \tag{11}$$

where N_k refers to the number of training samples and C is the class number. y_{ij} is the ground truth label and $\hat{y}_{ij}$ is the predicted probability.

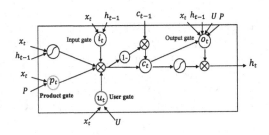

Fig. 4. UP-CLSTM: a variant of UP-LSTM with coupled input and forget gates

3.3 Coupling Input and Forget Gates

Inspired by [7], we propose an improved version of UP-LSTM, namely UP-CLSTM, to reduce the number of parameters and improve efficiency. The basic idea of UP-CLSTM is shown in Fig. 4. UP-CLSTM uses coupled input and forget gates instead of separately deciding what to forget and what new information to add. Specifically, we remove the forget gate in Eq. 7, as shown in Eq. 12.

$$\boldsymbol{c}_t = (1 - \boldsymbol{i}_t \odot \boldsymbol{u}_t \odot \boldsymbol{p}_t) \odot \boldsymbol{c}_{t-1} + \boldsymbol{i}_t \odot \boldsymbol{u}_t \odot \boldsymbol{p}_t \odot \tilde{\boldsymbol{c}}_t \tag{12}$$

Since the user gate $\boldsymbol{u}_t$ and product gate $\boldsymbol{p}_t$ can be regarded as input filters, we replace the forget gate $\boldsymbol{f}_t$ with $1 - \boldsymbol{i}_t \odot \boldsymbol{u}_t \odot \boldsymbol{p}_t$ in Eq. 12.

4   Evaluation

In this section, we introduce the empirical results of our UP-LSTM on document-level sentiment classification and discuss the effectiveness of user and product gates.

4.1 Experiment Setup

Datasets. We evaluate the effectiveness of our model on three document-level datasets with user and product information: IMDB, Yelp 2013 and Yelp 2014, which are from IMDB and Yelp Dataset Challenge in 2013 and 2014 following [22]. We randomly split these datasets into training sets, development sets and testing sets with the proportion of 80%, 10% and 10% as previous studies [3,30,35] did. Detailed statistics about these datasets are displayed in Table 1. Following previous studies, we use two evaluation metrics: *Accuracy* measures the overall sentiment classification performance; while *RMSE* measures the divergences between predicted sentiment label and ground truth label.

Table 1. Statistics of datasets

Datasets	#Classes	#Docs	#Users	#Products	#Docs/ User	#Docs/ Product	#Sens/ Doc	#Words/ Sen
IMDB	10	84919	1310	1635	64.82	51.94	16.08	24.54
Yelp 2013	5	78966	1631	1633	48.42	48.36	10.89	17.38
Yelp 2014	5	231163	4818	4194	47.97	55.11	11.41	17.26

Baseline Methods

- NSC uses a hierarchical LSTM network to encode review text for sentiment classification.
- HAN is an attention-based NSC for document classification with both word-level and sentence-level attentions [34].
- BERT$_{base}$ and BERT$_{large}$ is a BERT model designed for document classification [1].
- UPNN introduces a text preference matrix and a representation vector for each user and product into CNN sentiment classifier [22].
- UPA incorporates the global user preference and product characteristics into document sentiment classifier via word and sentence level attentions [3].
- DUPMN proposes a dual memory network model with two separate memory networks for user context and product context built at the document level through a hierarchical learning model [19].
- HCSC contextualizes words to contain both short and long range word dependency features and constructs shared vectors from similar users and products by word usages to improve their representations [2].
- HUAPA applys two individual hierarchical neural networks to generate two representations with user attention or with product attention, and then designs a combined strategy to make use of the two representations for sentiment prediction [30].
- RRP-UPM incorporates user and product information with external memory by extracting information from representative users and products for review rating prediction [35].

Hyper-Parameter Settings. We pre-train the 200-dimensional word embeddings on each dataset with SkipGram [15]. We set the user and product embeddings' dimension to be 200, and randomly initialize them from a uniform distribution $U(-0.01, 0.01)$ and trained along with the model. To speed up the training process, we limit the maximum number of sentences within a review document to be 30. Similarly, each sentence has no more than 30 words. We truncate the exceeded part and exclude them from training. The dimensions of hidden states in LSTM cell are set to 200. The models are trained using Adam optimizer with mini-batch size 16 and we empirically set initial learning rate to be 0.0001. Finally, we select the best parameters based on the performance on the development set, and evaluate the effectiveness on the test set.

4.2   Results and Analysis

End-to-end Performance. The overall experimental results are shown in Table 2. N/A means that the original paper did not report experimental results on the corresponding dataset. As we mentioned before, there are two categories of methods: the methods only focusing on the text content; and those incorporating the text content, the user and the product information. From the results, we have the following observations. Firstly, the overall performance of the

Table 2. Comparisons of all models on three datasets

Models	IMDB		Yelp2013		Yelp2014	
	Acc.	RMSE	Acc.	RMSE	Acc.	RMSE
Models without User and Product Information						
UPNN(CNN and no UP)	0.405	1.629	0.577	0.812	0.585	0.808
NSC	0.443	1.465	0.627	0.701	0.637	0.686
HAN	0.490	1.325	0.638	0.691	0.646	0.678
Models with User and Product Information						
TextFeature+UPF	0.402	1.774	0.561	1.822	0.579	0.791
UPNN(CNN)	0.435	1.602	0.596	0.784	0.608	0.764
UPNN(NSC)	0.471	1.443	0.631	0.702	N/A	N/A
NSC + UPA	0.533	1.281	0.650	0.692	0.667	0.654
NSC + UPA(BiLSTM)	0.529	1.247	0.655	0.672	0.669	0.654
DUPMN	0.539	1.279	0.662	0.667	0.676	0.639
HCSC	0.542	1.213	0.657	0.66	N/A	N/A
HUAPA	0.550	1.185	0.683	0.628	0.686	0.626
RRP-UPM	0.562	1.174	0.69	0.629	0.691	0.621
UP-LSTM (ours)	0.572	1.157	0.691	0.658	0.7	0.629
UP-CLSTM (ours)	**0.581**	**1.132**	**0.698**	**0.624**	0.71	0.612
Models pre-trained on large corpus						
BERT$_{base}$	0.540	1.203	0.687	0.655	0.717	0.613
BERT$_{large}$	0.563	1.162	0.690	0.626	**0.721**	**0.599**

models incorporating user and product information is much better than those only with text content. This result is consistent with previous studies [3,16,30] and demonstrates the importance of the user preference and the product characteristics on the sentiment classification. Secondly, our model achieves a competitive performance on all datasets even compared with BERT models which have been pre-trained on large corpus, demonstrating the advantage of introducing user and product gates into LSTM cells.

Next, we make a detailed analysis on the results. For methods in the first category, we see that most models achieve poor performance since they only use the text content. Among them, HAN performs best since it takes the hierarchical structure of documents into consideration, indicating the effectiveness of capturing the hierarchical structure of documents for document representations. However, when modeling contexts, HAN only focuses on the semantics of texts and ignores the crucial characteristics of users and products. As our UP-LSTM takes both document structure and user/product information into consideration, it obtains an average of 6.3% improvement of accuracy on three datasets over HAN.

For the methods in the second category, we observe that all methods considering user and product information achieve improvements compared to the corresponding methods in the first category. For example, NSC+UPA obtains an average of 4.8% improvement on three datasets in accuracy compared with NSC. It indicates that the user and product information is essential for sentiment classification. Our model outperforms all baselines on the three datasets. Specifically, our UP-LSTM and UP-CLSTM show averages of 0.7% and 1.5% improvement of accuracy respectively to RRP-UPM, the state-of-the-art method that encodes user and product information via two different attention mechanisms. The significant improvement of our model indicates that it can better model user and product information via incorporating them into LSTM cells in the context modeling stage instead of using attention mechanism, where user and product information may be already discarded. Moreover, UP-CLSTM that uses coupled input and forget gates not only reduces the number of parameters, but also improves the performance to some extent compared with UP-LSTM.

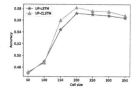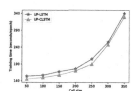

Fig. 5. (a) and (b) show how accuracy and the training time change when we vary the cell size in IMDB

Impact of Parameters and Efficiency. In the standard RNN, different cell sizes may lead to different performances. We investigate the impact of this parameter as well as the training efficiency for UP-LSTM and UP-CLSTM by varying the cell size of LSTM to observe how the performance and training time change. The training time is evaluated on a GeForce GTX 2080Ti GPU. Due to space limitation, we only show the results of accuracy and the training time on IMDB dataset. As shown in Fig. 5(a), increasing cell size can improve accuracy, but the improvement slows down or it even deteriorates when cell size is larger than 200. On the other hand, as shown in Fig. 5(b), the training time is continually increasing when cell size varies, and it is expensive to move from 250 to 350. In addition, UP-CLSTM always has a less training time than UP-LSTM when cell size varies. The reason is that the coupled input and forget gates in UP-CLSTM reduce the number of parameters and speed up the training process.

Table 3. Effectiveness of user and product gates

Models	IMDB		Yelp2013		Yelp2014	
	Acc	RMSE	Acc	RMSE	Acc	RMSE
LSTM	0.487	1.381	0.631	0.706	0.630	0.715
P-LSTM	0.509	1.326	0.653	0.695	0.640	0.713
U-LSTM	0.528	1.320	0.669	0.680	0.669	0.673
UP-LSTM	0.572	1.157	0.691	0.658	0.700	0.629

Ablation Tests. Next we conduct ablation analysis to validate the effectiveness of the user and product gates. We conduct experiments to investigate the effectiveness of these two gates on three datasets for sentiment classification respectively. We close the user gate and only consider the product gate to control the influence of product specificity by setting $u_t = 1$ in Eq. 5. Similarly, we then consider the user gate only by setting $p_t = 1$ in Eq. 6. Lastly, we close both gates and set $u_t = 1$ and $p_t = 1$, which means considering no user and product information for comparison. Table 3 shows the performances of different models on the three datasets. Here P-LSTM and U-LSTM represent the models with only the product gate and the user gate respectively. LSTM is the basic hierarchical LSTM network without the user or product gates. From this table, we observe that both gates are critical for improving the sentiment classification performances compared with the models with only one gate or no gate. This result illustrates that our UP-LSTM model better utilizes the user and product information with the help of such gates. Moreover, compared with the P-LSTM method, the U-LSTM method achieves better performance. It indicates the importance of user's preference for sentiment classification.

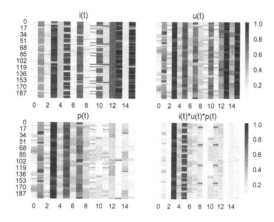

Fig. 6. Movie Review: "The movie is good, but the environment of the cinema is very poor and shabby". (Color figure online)

4.3 Visualization

To better understand how the user and product gates in our UP-LSTM help improve the sequence encoding, we visualize the input gate, user gate, product gate and their element wise product $i_t \odot u_t \odot p_t$ to analyze the semantic vectors generated by UP-LSTM. We use the sentence of 'Movie' review: "The movie is good, but the environment of the cinema is very poor and shabby" as the example for visualization. Activations of input gate, user gate, product gate and their element wise product for this sentence are shown in Fig. 6. The vertical axis is the dimension index from 0 to 199. The horizontal axis is the word index from 0 to 15 numbered from left to right. The color codes show activation values. From this figure, we can see that the input gate detects the important information from the input sentence. Most of its values corresponding to the informative words have large values, including word 3: 'good' as well as the product irrelevant word 13: 'poor' and word 15: 'shabby'. For general LSTM models without user and product gates, all these informative words are preserved in the cell state. As our product gate can make use of the product information, it can help filter the product irrelevant information and assign very small values for the words 'poor' and 'noisy'. Therefore, the state candidate filter $i_t \odot u_t \odot p_t$ in Eq. 12 has small values for the words 'poor' and 'shabby', which means the information of these words would not be preserved in the new state of UP-LSTM. Hence, our UP-LSTM can filter out the product irrelevant information and finally get the right prediction.

5   Conclusion

In this paper, we propose a novel variant of LSTM, termed as UP-LSTM for document level sentiment classification. We incorporate user and product information into LSTM cells by designing a user gate and a product gate in the context modeling stage to dynamically obtain user- and product-aware contextual representations. We then construct an end-to-end framework with UP-LSTM as the building block. Experimental results on three real world datasets show that our proposed model outperforms state-of-the-art methods by a substantial margin.

Acknowledgment. This work was supported by National Key R&D Program of China: 2018YFB1404401, 2018YFB1402701 and 2020AAA0109603; State Key Laboratory of Computer Architecture (ICT,CAS) under Grant No. CARCHA202008 and Institute of Precision Medicine, Tsinghua University.

References

1. Adhikari, A., Ram, A., Tang, R., Lin, J.: Docbert: BERT for document classification. CoRR arXiv:1904.08398 (2019)
2. Amplayo, R.K., Kim, J., Sung, S., Hwang, S.: Cold-start aware user and product attention for sentiment classification. In: ACL, pp. 2535–2544 (2018)
3. Chen, H., Sun, M., Tu, C., Lin, Y., Liu, Z.: Neural sentiment classification with user and product attention. In: EMNLP, pp. 1650–1659 (2016)
4. Devlin, J., Chang, M., Lee, K., Toutanova, K.: BERT: pre-training of deep bidirectional transformers for language understanding. In: NAACL-HLT, pp. 4171–4186 (2019)
5. Ding, X., Liu, B., Yu, P.S.: A holistic lexicon-based approach to opinion mining. In: WSDM, pp. 231–240 (2008)
6. Feng, S., Wang, Y., Liu, L., Wang, D., Yu, G.: Attention based hierarchical LSTM network for context-aware microblog sentiment classification. World Wide Web **22**(1), 59–81 (2018). https://doi.org/10.1007/s11280-018-0529-6
7. Greff, K., Srivastava, R.K., Koutník, J., Steunebrink, B.R., Schmidhuber, J.: LSTM: A search space odyssey. IEEE Trans. Neural Netw. Learning Syst. **28**(10), 2222–2232 (2017)
8. Hochreiter, S., Schmidhuber, J.: Long short-term memory. Neural Comput. **9**(8), 1735–1780 (1997)
9. Hsu, W.-Y., Hsu, H.-H., Tseng, V.S.: Discovering negative comments by sentiment analysis on web forum. World Wide Web **22**(3), 1297–1311 (2018). https://doi.org/10.1007/s11280-018-0561-6
10. Kim, Y.: Convolutional neural networks for sentence classification. In: EMNLP, pp. 1746–1751 (2014)
11. Lei, Z., Yang, Y., Yang, M.: Sentiment lexicon enhanced attention-based LSTM for sentiment classification. In: AAAI, pp. 8105–8106 (2018)
12. Liu, P., Qiu, X., Chen, X., Wu, S., Huang, X.: Multi-timescale long short-term memory neural network for modelling sentences and documents. In: EMNLP, pp. 2326–2335 (2015)
13. Luo, L., Ao, X., Pan, F., Wang, J., Zhao, T., Yu, N., He, Q.: Beyond polarity: Interpretable financial sentiment analysis with hierarchical query-driven attention. In: IJCAI, pp. 4244–4250 (2018)
14. Ma, Y., Li, Q.: A weakly-supervised extractive framework for sentiment-preserving document summarization. World Wide Web **22**(4), 1401–1425 (2018). https://doi.org/10.1007/s11280-018-0591-0

15. Mikolov, T., Sutskever, I., Chen, K., Corrado, G.S., Dean, J.: Distributed representations of words and phrases and their compositionality. In: NIPS, pp. 3111–3119 (2013)
16. Qian, Q., Huang, M., Lei, J., Zhu, X.: Linguistically regularized LSTM for sentiment classification. In: ACL, pp. 1679–1689 (2017)
17. Qu, L., Ifrim, G., Weikum, G.: The bag-of-opinions method for review rating prediction from sparse text patterns. In: COLING, pp. 913–921 (2010)
18. Schouten, K., Frasincar, F.: Survey on aspect-level sentiment analysis. IEEE Trans. Knowl. Data Eng. **28**(3), 813–830 (2016)
19. Shen, J., et al.: Dual memory network model for sentiment analysis of review text. Knowl. Based Syst. **188**, 105004 (2020)
20. Sutskever, I., Vinyals, O., Le, Q.V.: Sequence to sequence learning with neural networks. In: NIPS, pp. 3104–3112 (2014)
21. Tang, D., Qin, B., Liu, T.: Document modeling with gated recurrent neural network for sentiment classification. In: EMNLP, pp. 1422–1432 (2015)
22. Tang, D., Qin, B., Liu, T.: Learning semantic representations of users and products for document level sentiment classification. In: ACL, pp. 1014–1023 (2015)
23. Tian, B., Zhang, Y., Wang, J., Xing, C.: Hierarchical inter-attention network for document classification with multi-task learning. In: IJCAI, pp. 3569–3575 (2019)
24. Wang, J., Lin, C., Li, M., Zaniolo, C.: Boosting approximate dictionary-based entity extraction with synonyms. Inf. Sci. **530**, 1–21 (2020)
25. Wang, J., Lin, C., Zaniolo, C.: Mf-join: Efficient fuzzy string similarity join with multi-level filtering. In: ICDE, pp. 386–397 (2019)
26. Wang, J., Wang, Z., Zhang, D., Yan, J.: Combining knowledge with deep convolutional neural networks for short text classification. In: IJCAI, pp. 2915–2921 (2017)
27. Wang, Y., Huang, M., Zhu, X., Zhao, L.: Attention-based LSTM for aspect-level sentiment classification. In: EMNLP, pp. 606–615 (2016)
28. Wu, F., Huang, Y.: Personalized microblog sentiment classification via multi-task learning. In: AAAI, pp. 3059–3065 (2016)
29. Wu, J., Zhang, Y., Wang, J., Lin, C., Fu, Y., Xing, C.: Scalable metric similarity join using mapreduce. In: ICDE, pp. 1662–1665 (2019)
30. Wu, Z., Dai, X., Yin, C., Huang, S., Chen, J.: Improving review representations with user attention and product attention for sentiment classification. In: AAAI, pp. 5989–5996 (2018)
31. Xing, B., Liao, L., Song, D., Wang, J., Zhang, F., Wang, Z., Huang, H.: Earlier attention? aspect-aware LSTM for aspect-based sentiment analysis. In: IJCAI, pp. 5313–5319 (2019)
32. Xue, W., Li, T.: Aspect based sentiment analysis with gated convolutional networks. In: ACL, pp. 2514–2523 (2018)
33. Yang, M., Tu, W., Wang, J., Xu, F., Chen, X.: Attention based LSTM for target dependent sentiment classification. In: AAAI, pp. 5013–5014 (2017)
34. Yang, Z., Yang, D., Dyer, C., He, X., Smola, A.J., Hovy, E.H.: Hierarchical attention networks for document classification. In: NAACL HLT, pp. 1480–1489 (2016)
35. Yuan, Z., Wu, F., Liu, J., Wu, C., Huang, Y., Xie, X.: Neural review rating prediction with user and product memory. In: CIKM, pp. 2341–2344 (2019)
36. Zhang, L., Wang, S., Liu, B.: Deep learning for sentiment analysis: A survey. Wiley Interdiscip. Rev. Data Min. Knowl. Discov. **8**(4), e1253 (2018)
37. Zhang, Y., Wu, J., Wang, J., Xing, C.: A transformation-based framework for KNN set similarity search. IEEE Trans. Knowl. Data Eng. **32**(3), 409–423 (2020)

38. Zhao, K., et al.: Modeling patient visit using electronic medical records for cost profile estimation. In: DASFAA, pp. 20–36 (2018)

39. Zhao, K., et al.: Discovering subsequence patterns for next POI recommendation. In: IJCAI, pp. 3216–3222 (2020)

40. Zou, Y., Gui, T., Zhang, Q., Huang, X.: A lexicon-based supervised attention model for neural sentiment analysis. In: COLING, pp. 868–877 (2018)

Integrating RoBERTa Fine-Tuning and User Writing Styles for Authorship Attribution of Short Texts

Xiangyu Wang and Mizuho Iwaihara[✉]

Graduate School of Information, Production and Systems, Waseda University, 2-7 Hibikino, Wakamatsu-ku, Kitakyushu-shi, Fukuoka 808-0135, Japan
wangxiangyu@fuji.waseda.jp, iwaihara@waseda.jp

Abstract. Authorship Attribution (AA) is a fundamental branch of text classi-fication, aiming at identifying the authors of given texts. However, authorship attribution of short texts faces many challenges like short text, feature sparsity and non-standardization of casual words. Recent studies have shown that deep learning methods can greatly improve the accuracy of AA tasks, however they still represent user posts using a set of predefined features (e.g., word n-grams and character n-grams) and adopt text classification methods to solve this task. In this paper, we propose a hybrid model to solve author attribution of short texts. The first part is a pretrained language model based on RoBERTa to produce post representations that are aware of tweet-related stylistic features and their contex-tualities. The second part is a CNN model built on a number of feature embeddings to represent users' writing styles. Finally, we assemble these representations for final AA classification. Our experimental results show that our model on tweets shows the state-of-the-art result on a known tweet AA dataset .

Keywords: Authorship attribution · Short text classification · Social network contents · Pre-trained language model · RoBERTa · Salient writing styles

1 Introduction

Author Attribution (AA) is a field of natural language processing, which characterizes texts and identifies the author of a given text. With the widespread of social media, the role and effect of AA on short texts is increasingly becoming obvious. AA systems on social media posts can be used to avoid identity fraud [14], filter spams [9] and detect multiple IDs under one identical user. Compared with long texts, authorship attribution on short texts is more difficult and challenging, mainly due to the characteristics such as sparsity of short text features, non-standardization of casual or trending words, and massiveness of short text data.

Author attribution needs to integrate features on personal writing styles and text classification. Machine learning and neural network models for AA have been proposed, such as SVM [9], CNN [6, 8], and RNN [1]. These methods utilize stylistic features, such as word and character n-grams, syntactic, and semantic information [4, 14] for AA in

© Springer Nature Switzerland AG 2021
L. H. U et al. (Eds.): APWeb-WAIM 2021, LNCS 12858, pp. 413–421, 2021.
https://doi.org/10.1007/978-3-030-85896-4_32

tweets. Word and character n-grams can capture stylistic features on consecutive tokens, but incapable of capturing features that appear in longer contexts, such as a sentence.

In this paper, we propose a method for AA that exploits finetuning of the pretrained language model RoBERTa [8], to which we integrate a neural network model (CNN) for user writing styles. We introduce special encodings for constructs of tweets, such as mentions, URLs, and dates, so that RoBERTa can be aware of occurrences of these constructs along with their contexts, and reflect into embeddings of posts. The second contribution of this paper is to introduce user writing-style representations. We use a deep neural network to learn multi-view representations of user posts through different types of features. In contrast to existing AA methods which utilizes cross-entropy loss in training post embedding, we utilize triplet loss [3], so that the posts belonging to the same user should be close to each other in the post embedding space, and the posts from other users will be further pushed away. Finally, the learned writing-style embeddings are concatenated with the post embeddings to perform the AA task.

In our experiments, we compare our models with baseline models that are based on text classification by logistic-regression over TF-IDF scores, and deep neural network models (CNN or RNN) trained over character-level and word-level n-grams, and word embeddings. Also, we compare with the experimental results of [6] which adopts latent posting styles. Our results show superiority of our proposed model, which adopts the combination of finetuning of the pretrained language model and user-style embeddings, achieving the state-of-the-art on the AA dataset [14].

2   Related Work

In order to extract useful information from short texts for AA, a variety of features are investigated. Representative neural classifiers such as CNN, RNN, SVM, and the variant LSTM of RNN [3, 11, 13, 14], are applied to this field. Generally, in order to train these models, embeddings based on specific word n-grams and character n-grams [9, 14] are utilized to capture the syntactic features of the texts. Shrestha et al. [11] attempt to use character n-grams as the input to CNN to perform AA. Ruder et al. [12] investigate the use of CNN with various types of word and character n-grams, while Boenningoff et al. [2] propose a hybrid CNN-LSTM on word-level features to perform AA. Huang et al. [6] propose character embeddings with mixed word and character n-grams, to be used as the input of CNN and LSTM, showing remarkable performance. With the emergence of pretrained language models which show outstanding performance in the field of natural language processing, the application of pretrained models to AA is a natural direction. BertAA [10] is an early attempt, based on finetuning of the pre-trained language model BERT. BertAA has an additional dense layer and a softmax activation to perform authorship attribution.

Another aspect of authorship attribution can be characterized by stylometric features, for capturing authors' writing styles. Guthrie et al. [5] propose 166 features on texts for authorship attribution, including commonly used stylistic features. Their final experimental results showed that 15 features including punctuation marks, pronouns, fog index and average sentence length are the most effective. Huang et al. [6] introduce an additional feature set with 10 elements and apply these features to the CNN model to improve the AA accuracy.

In this paper, we propose a method to apply the pretrained language model RoBERTa [8] for sentence embeddings, where special encoding is introduced to capture tweet features. Also, we introduce user writing styles to be added into the prediction model. Post embeddings on style-related features are trained by a triplet-loss objective function to separate different users' post embeddings.

3 Methodology

In this section, we describe our proposed model. The model consists of two main parts. In the first part, the input text is passed through the 12 layers of RoBERTa, to obtain contextualized vector representations, and then a CNN classifier is applied. The second part is a novel embedding-based framework to learn users' writing styles.

3.1 Text Representation Module

RoBERTa Tokenizer. Yinhan Liu et al. [8] proposed a new pretrained model RoBERTa, which is built on BERT. Tweets are often including intentionally prolonged or truncated spellings, such as "cooool!" and "thks". We expect that the tokenizer of RoBERTa based on Byte Pair Encoding can properly decompose such out-of-vocabulary words into frequent subwords. We also expect that usage of particular subwords are corelated with writing styles of authors, as evidenced by the effective AA methods that utilize character-level n-grams [11, 12].

Improved Tokenizer. For encoding tweets, we need to add special tokens to RoBERTa. We observe that certain users frequently use mentions @ <username> and hashtags # <topic> [6]. In this paper, we deliberately add the token "< @ >" to notify RoBERTa about a mention, and the special token "<#>" to notify topics, which replaces the special identifiers in the dataset. For special text fragments that appear in tweets, such as URL, number, date and time, we use the letters "U", "N", "D" and "T" to replace them in the text preprocessing stage.

Sentence Embedding. RoBERTa consists of 12 transformer blocks and 12 self-focusing heads [8]. The maximum length of input tokens is 512, and the hidden layer size is 768. After setting the maximum sequence length of each text sample (tweet) to 128 tokens, the text is entered to RoBERTa. We extract feature vectors of the text data, namely the embedding vectors of words and sentences, which are used as high-quality feature input for our downstream neural network model (CNN).

For each sentence input, 12 separate vectors of length 768 are generated from the 12 layers. In order to obtain a single vector, we need to combine vectors from several layers. Note that different layers of RoBERTa encode quite different information, so the appropriate pooling strategy will vary depending on the application. In this paper, we propose three different vector combinations, as shown in Fig. 1, to obtain the final sentence embeddings. The combinations consist of 1) the last hidden layer, 2) the sum of last four hidden layer and 3) the concatenation of the last four hidden layers.

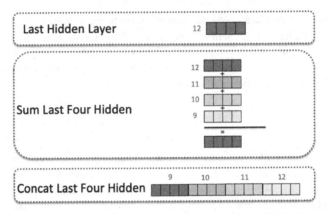

Fig. 1. Extracting contextualized vectors from multiple hidden layers

Neural Network Models. We enter sentence embeddings extracted from the multiple layers of the RoBERTa model as input for CNN. Here, we use the CNN model to automatically extract latent features of the input sequences and obtain a compact feature vector representation. Finally, we use a fully connected module with the softmax function to do authorship attribution on the representations.

Figure 2 illustrates the fusion part and the roles of the RoBERTa and CNN models for generating sentence representations. As shown in Fig. 2, we use a convolutional layer with different widths, allowing us to capture language features of diverse levels from morphemes to sentences. Yellow, red and green represent three filters of different sizes 768*3, 768*4 and 768*5, respectively. The CNN model receives multiple sentence embeddings from the top-four layers of RoBERTa, as input of the convolutional layer, where three types of filters with sizes w and n are applied. Then, we use the max-pooling function in the pooling layer to process the convolution results. Finally, we apply the softmax function after the fully connected module to execute author classification.

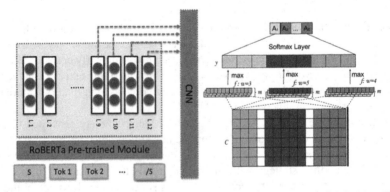

Fig. 2. Finetuning RoBERTa and CNN models for author attribution (Color figure online)

3.2 User Writing Style Module

Figure 3 illustrates the overall architecture of the User Writing Style Module. The module learns post representations using a triplet loss function [7], which is formed by first randomly sampling an anchor post $p_{u,i}$ and a positive post $p_{u,j}$ that belongs to the same user u. Then we also sample a negative post $p_{v,k}$, which is a post belonging to user v who is different from user u.

$$Triplet\ Loss = \max(D(A, P) - D(A, N) + margin, 0) \qquad (1)$$

Here, $D(x, y)$ is the cosine distance between the learned vector representations of x and y. The objective of this function is to keep the distance between the anchor and positive smaller than the distance between the anchor and negative.

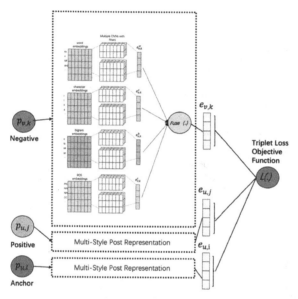

Fig. 3. Generating user-style embedding.

Feature Embeddings Extraction. As shown in Fig. 3, each anchor post $p_{u,i}$, positive post $p_{u,j}$ and negative post $p_{v,k}$ are entered to four CNN models, for respectively generating post embeddings on words, characters, bigrams and POS (part of speech) tags. For example, from $p_{v,k}$, word embedding $x_{v,k}^w$, character embedding $x_{v,k}^c$, bigram embedding $x_{v,k}^b$ and POS embedding $x_{v,k}^t$ are generated.

Fusion Function for Aggregating Post Features per User. We use a fusion function to combine all the four post embeddings:

$$e_{v,k} = Fuse\left(x_{v,k}^w, x_{v,k}^c, x_{v,k}^b, x_{v,k}^t\right) \qquad (2)$$

Here, Fuse(·) is a typical fusion kernel, such as Mean, Max and Capsule. The combined post embeddings of the posts by a user are aggregated into his/her final user-style embedding representation S_v, again by a common aggregator Mean, Max or Capsule. Finally, we compute for each user the cosine similarity between the query post and S_v.

3.3 Combination of Two Modules

Finally, we combine User Writing Styles Module and Text Representation Module, and the output probabilities of two modules are concatenated and classified using an additional logistic regression classifer. Figure 4 shows the overall architecture of our proposed model.

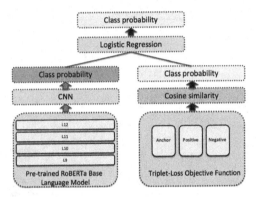

Fig. 4. Overall architecture of our proposed model.

4 Experiments

4.1 Experiment Setup

Datasets. We evaluate our AA methods on the dataset of Schwartz et al. [14], which is a corpus containing a group of approximately 9,000 Twitter users, and 1,000 posts attributed to each user, totaling 9 million posts.

4.2 Authorship Attribution Results

We randomly select 10 groups from the dataset, where each group contains 50 users, and each user has 1000 tweets. We evaluate the average accuracy of each model. Table 1 shows the experimental results.

It can be seen from the results that the traditional machine learning method of TF-IDF+Logistic Regression can achieve a good accuracy of 0.674, while the results obtained by the deep learning methods are significantly better than the machine learning method. For the CNN-based deep learning methods, CNN-WC2+LPS [6] shows the best performance with an accuracy of 0.836 within the baseline models.

For sentence embeddings extracted from RoBERTa, we discussed the three combination methods. Among them, concatenating the last four hidden layers as the input for CNN, combined with UWS (user writing style) shows the best performance, with an accuracy of 0.882, which is 4.6% higher than the existing best record by CNN-WC2+LPS [6]. We can surmise that the concatenation of the last four hidden layers encodes more information than just the last hidden layer and the sum of the last four hidden layers. Also, in all the RoBERTa-based models, the accuracy is improved by adding user writing styles.

Table 1. Overall methods' descriptions and results. WC: mixed words and character n-grams. LPS: latent posting styles. UWS: user writing styles

Methods		Descriptions	Accuracy
Baselines	TF-IDF+LR	Machine learning-based, calculating TF-IDF scores, then train a logistic regression classifier	0.674
	CNN-WC1 (1-gram)	Dense vectors of mixed words and character n-grams trained by Skip-Gram are supplied to the input layer of CNN	0.815
	CNN-WC2 (2-gram)		0.828
	CNN-WC3 (3-gram)		0.798
	CNN-WC1+LPS	Combinations of latent posting styles (LPS) with CNN-WC1, CNN-WC2, and CNN-WC3	0.824
	CNN-WC2+LPS		0.836
	CNN-WC3+LPS		0.806
RoBERTa & CNN models	RoBERTa+CNN (last hidden layer)	Extracting multiple hidden layers from RoBERTa and use different vector combinations as input features into CNN for classification task	0.868
	RoBERTa+CNN (sum last four hidden layers)		0.867
	RoBERTa+CNN (concat last four hidden layers)		0.871
RoBERTa & CNN+UWS models	RoBERTa+CNN (last hidden layer)+UWS	Combinations of User Writing Styles (UWS) and Text Representation (RoBERTa-CNN)	0.875
	RoBERTa+CNN (sum last four hidden layers)+UWS		0.879
	RoBERTa+CNN (concat last four hidden layers)+UWS		**0.882**

5   Conclusion and Future Work

In this paper, we proposed a new method for authorship attribution. Our model consists of a module for sentence embeddings and a module for user writing styles. Our model generates sentence representations by the concatenation of the last four hidden layers of RoBERTa, as the high-quality feature input for CNN. Furthermore, we introduced latent representations of user writing styles, which are per-user vectors learned from semantic and syntactic features of users' tweets. The concatenations of sentence embeddings and writing-style embeddings are used for final authorship attribution. Our model combing the two modules was evaluated on a publicly available AA dataset. The final experimental results show that our best model achieves an accuracy of 88.2%, which is 4.6% improvement over the state-of-the-art.

For future work, we will evaluate the models when the number of authors increases or the number of texts by the same author decreases. We also wish to explore other pretrained language models and consider improvements of user writing styles by modeling temporal factors of user posts.

References

1. Bagnall, D.: Author identification using multi-headed recurrent neural network. In: Working Notes Papers of the CLEF Evaluation Laboratories, vol. 1391 (2015)
2. Boenninghoff, B., Hessler, S., Kolossa, D., Nickel, R.: Explainable authorship verification in social media via attention-based similarity learning. In: IEEE International Conference on Big Data (Big data), pp. 36–45 (2019)
3. Cheng, D., Gong, Y., Zhou, S., Wang, J., Zheng, N.: Person re-identification by multi-channel parts-based CNN with improved triplet loss function. In: IEEE Conference on Computer Vision and Pattern Recognition, pp. 1335–1344 (2016)
4. Ding, S.H., Fung, B.C., Iqbal, F., Cheung, W.K.: Learning stylometric representations for authorship analysis. IEEE Trans. Cybern. **49**(1), 107–121 (2017)
5. Guthrie, D.: Unsupervised Detection of Anomalous Text. Ph.D. thesis, University of Sheffield (2008)
6. Huang, W., Su, R., Iwaihara, M.: Contribution of Improved Character Embedding and Latent Posting Styles to Authorship Attribution of Short Texts. In: Wang, X., Zhang, R., Lee, Y.-K., Sun, Le., Moon, Y.-S. (eds.) APWeb-WAIM 2020. LNCS, vol. 12318, pp. 261–269. Springer, Cham (2020). https://doi.org/10.1007/978-3-030-60290-1_20
7. Hu, Z., Lee, R.-W., Wang, L., Lim, E.-P., Dai, B.: DeepStyle: User Style Embedding for Authorship Attribution of Short Texts. In: Wang, X., Zhang, R., Lee, Y.-K., Sun, Le., Moon, Y.-S. (eds.) APWeb-WAIM 2020. LNCS, vol. 12318, pp. 221–229. Springer, Cham (2020). https://doi.org/10.1007/978-3-030-60290-1_17
8. Liu, Y., Ott, M., Goyal, N., Du, J., Joshi, M., Chen, D.: RoBERTa: A Robustly Optimized BERT Pretraining Approach. eprint arXiv:1907.11692 (2019)
9. Leepaisomboon, P., Iwaihara, M.: Utilizing latent posting style for authorship attribution on short texts. In: 2019 IEEE Fukuoka, Japan, pp. 1015–1022 (2019)
10. Fabien, M., Villatoro-Tello, E., Motlicek, P., Parida, S.: BertAA: BERT fine-tuning for authorship attribution. In: 17th International Conference on Natural Language Processing (2020)

11. Shrestha, P., Sierra, S., Gonzalez, F., Posso, P., Montes-y-Gomex, M., Solorio, T.: Convolutional neural networks for authorship attribution of short texts. In: Proceedings of 15th Conference European Chapter of the Association Computational Linguistics, Valencia, vol. 2, pp. 669–674 (2017)
12. Ruder, S., Ghaffari, P., Breslin, J.G.: Character-level and multi-channel convolutional neural networks for large-scale authorship attribution. National University of Ireland Galway, Technical Report, Insight Centre for Data Analytics (2016)
13. Stamatatos, E.: A survey of modern authorship attribution methods. J. Am. Soc. Inform. Sci. Technol. **60**(3), 538–556 (2009)
14. Schwartz, R., Tsur, O., Rappoport, A. Koppel, M.: Authorship attribution of micro-messages. In: Proceedings 2013 Conference Empirical Methods in Natural Language Processing, Seattle, pp. 1880–1891 (2013)

Dependency Graph Convolution and POS Tagging Transferring for Aspect-Based Sentiment Classification

Zexin Li$^{(\boxtimes)}$, Linjun Chen, Tiancheng Huang, and Jiagang Song

Guangxi Key Lab of Multi-Source Information Mining and Security,
College of Computer Science and Information Engineering,
Guangxi Normal University, Guilin, Guangxi, China
{chenlj,huangtcjohn,songjg}@stu.gxnu.edu.cn

Abstract. Aspect-based sentiment classification (ABSC) task is a fine-grained task in natural language processing, which mainly recognizes the sentiment polarity of various aspects in a sentence. Most of the existing work ignores the syntactic constraints of the local context, and few studies use feature enhancement when dealing with ABSC problems. To solve these problems, this paper proposes a new transfer learning model based on aspect sentiment analysis, namely LCF-TDGCN. It is based on local context focus mechanism and self-attention mechanism, and uses Part-Of-Speech (POS) tagging as an auxiliary task to enhance sentiment polarity. Secondly, this method utilizes the dependency graph convolution (DGC) to analyze the syntactic constraints of local context and capture long-term word dependencies. In addition, this paper integrates the pre-trained BERT model, and improves the performance of ABSC tasks by using syntactic information and word dependence. The experimental results on five different datasets show that the LCF-TDGCN produces good results.

Keywords: Aspect-based sentiment classification · Dependency graph convolution · Pos tagging transferring · Pretrained BERT

1 Introduction

Aspect-based sentiment analysis (ABSA) aims to identify fine-grained opinion polarity towards a specific aspect [6–8]. It requires that the model can automatically extract polarities of all aspects. Aspect-based sentiment classification (ABSC) is one of the most important subtasks of ABSA. ABSC aims to identify the sentiment polarity of aspects clearly given in sentences rather than to analyze the overall sentiment polarity at the sentence level or document level. In the task of ABSC, polarity is usually divided into three categories: positive, negative and neutral. For example, "this pen works very well, but the color is ugly.", the sentiment polarity of "work" and "color" are not consistent, with positive and negative sentiment polarity, respectively.

© Springer Nature Switzerland AG 2021
L. H. U et al. (Eds.): APWeb-WAIM 2021, LNCS 12858, pp. 422–432, 2021.
https://doi.org/10.1007/978-3-030-85896-4_33

ABSC task is a classification problem, and a large of models based on deep learning has been proposed to solve the ABSC problem, such as the early models [2,12] based on neural network methods and long short-term memory (LSTM). In the middle stage, Recurrent Neural Networks (RNNs) [10] was combined with an attention mechanism to solve the challenge of modelling semantic relatedness between context words and aspects. A fine-grained attention mechanism [3] was proposed, and it can capture the word-level interaction between aspect and context. Although attention-based models are very effective, they are not powerful enough to capture the syntactic dependency between the context word and the aspect in the sentence. To solve this problem, an Aspect-specific Graph Convolutional Networks (ASGCN) [14] was proposed, and it is the first ABSC model based on GCN. Although ASGCN captures the syntactic dependency, it does not consider that the words far from the aspect in the local context may hurt accurately predicting the polarity of a particular subject. In LCF-BERT [13], considering that the sentiment polarity is more related to its own nearby context words, the semantic relative distance (SRD) is added to focus on the characteristics of the local context, but they ignore the syntactic dependency in context and sentence.

To address the above limitations, this paper proposes a local context focus (LCF) attention mechanism dependency graph convolution model with transfer POS tagging, namely LCF-TDGCN. As far as we know, it is the first Graph Convolution Network attention model based on aspect-based sentiment classification using transfer learning. The LCF-TDGCN is an aspect-oriented graph convolution network transfer model based on the combination of multi-head self-attention (MHSA), LCF attention mechanism and the dependency graph convolution network (DGCN). It can correctly capture syntactic information and long-distance words, and solve the problem of long-distance multi-word dependence. Additionally, this model learns features from the global context at the sequence level and learns features from local context words related to specific aspects. The local context part calculates local context features according to SRD. In addition to its own features, the auxiliary tasks of Part-Of-Speech (POS) tagging are also used to enhance features and improve accuracy by transfer learning.

Experimental results on five benchmark datasets show that the LCF-TDGCN effectively solves the local problem of contextual syntactic dependence. Using transfer learning can effectively enhance features to improve performance, and it is superior to the most advanced sentiment classification models. We list the main advantages of our proposed method as follows:

- The transfer learning model of the ABSC task with dependency graph convolution is studied for the first time, which provides a new way of thinking for the polarity classification of research direction.
- By combining self-attention and local context focusing technology with graph convolution network, the syntactic constraints of local context are extracted effectively, and their potential is fully explored.
- The LCF-TDGCN model integrates the pre-trained model Bert and fine-tunes it. Experimental results show that the LCF-TDGCN model can significantly

improve the performance of the ABSC task on five datasets (especially the restaurant data set), producing good results.

2   Methodology

Model Architecture. Figure 1 shows the network structure of the LCF-TDGCN. The local context feature box (LCFB) unit is on the left, and the global context feature box (GCFB) unit is on the right. LCFB models the local context using an independent pre-trained $BERT^l$ layer and a transfer POS tagging model. Meanwhile, GCFB models the global context with another independent pre-trained $BERT^g$ layer. Different from the input sequence format of LCFB, which is formed in "[CLS] + text sequence + [SEP]" form BERT-BASE, the GCFB's input is formed in "[CLS] + text sequence + [SEP] + aspect + [SEP]". This kind of input format can improve the LCF-TDGCN model's performance.

The LCF-TDGCN starts from a $BERT^l$ layer and then feeds the context feature dynamic weighting (CDW) layer with the inputs, which is a weighted sum of outputs of BERT-shared later and features extracted by the auxiliary task POS tagging model so that the model can capture local contextual information of the text. Secondly, to obtain aspect-specific features, a multi-layer graph convolution structure is implemented after the CDW layer, and then the context feature dynamic mask (CDM) layer is used to filter out non-aspect words, making sure that only high-level specific features are retained. Finally, to predict aspect-based sentiments, the high-level specific features are concatenated with global context features obtained by the $BERT^g$ layer and then fed to the feature interactive learning (FIL) layer and output layer successively. In the FIL layer, local context features and global context features are learned interactively by the MHSA mechanism to enhance the model's ability to learn the profound correlation between context and aspects.

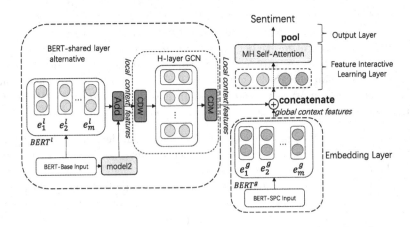

Fig. 1. Model architecture

BERT-Shared Layer. The BERT-shared layer is a Pre-trained Seq2Seq model for language understanding, and it can be regarded as the embedding layer. In order to achieve better performance, the fine-tuning learning process is necessary and indispensable. For pre-trained BERT, fine-tuning learning can improve the performance of most NLP tasks. LCF-TDGCN deployed two independent BERT shared layers to extract local and global context features. The symbolic inputs of LCFB and GCFB are represented by X_l and X_g, respectively, to get a preliminary output of local and global context features.

$$O^l_{BERT} = BERT^l\left(X^l\right) \tag{1}$$
$$O^g_{BERT} = BERT^g\left(X^g\right) \tag{2}$$

$BERT^l$ and $BERT^g$ are the corresponding BERT-shared layer modelling for the LCFB and the GCFB, respectively. O^l_{BERT} and O^g_{BERT} are the output representations of the LCFB and the GCFB processor, respectively.

Transfering POS Tagging. In our system, we first train the POS tagging model and then transfer the trained model as an auxiliary task to improve the effectiveness of the main task. In the main task, the data set is input into the frozen auxiliary task model to extract features, and the corresponding sentence coding vector O_2 can be obtained. Then according to different weights adding O_2 to the vector O_1, which comes from the BERT layer of the main task model. The result obtained finally is taken as the feature extracted from the main task. The formula of this part is as follows:

$$I = a * O_1 + b * O_2 \tag{3}$$
$$a + b = 1 \tag{4}$$

Both tasks are based on the input of BERT-BASE. O_1 comes from the local context feature behind the $BERT^l$ layer, and O_2 is the local context sentence vector encoded by the frozen POS tagging transfer model. a and b are the corresponding weights of O_1 and O_2, and the sum of a and b is 1. I is the enhanced feature as the input for the next step.

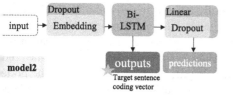

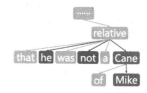

Fig. 2. POStagging's model architecture.   **Fig. 3.** Dependency tree

In the auxiliary task, we implement a multi-layer bi-directional LSTM (Bi-LSTM) to predict PoS tags using the Universal Dependencies English Web Treebank (UDPOS) dataset. The training model of the auxiliary task is shown in

Fig. 2, the output of the yellow star is the feature we want to extract, that is, the sentence coding vector. Our system needs to train the auxiliary task model firstly and then freeze this model for use in the main task process. In the LCF-TDGCN system, the accuracy of POS tagging is 89.32%, which is not high. We can consider using a more accurate POS tagging model in future work. In this paper, only to verify the effectiveness of POS tagging as an auxiliary task, so no more accurate model is used.

Graph Convolution Network (GCN) can be used to encode local information of unstructured data. The graph with K nodes is transformed into a adjacency matrix $\mathbf{M} \in \mathbb{R}^{k \times k}$. For convenience, we express the output of the f-th of node i as $\mathbf{f}_i^h$, where $\mathbf{f}_i^0$ is the initial state of node i. For H-layer GCN, $h \in [1, 2, \cdots, H]$ and $\mathbf{f}_i^h$ are the final states of node i. $\mathbf{W}^h$ is a linear transformation weight, $\mathbf{b}^h$ is a bias term, and σ is a nonlinear function, e.g. ReLU. The graph convolution of node representation can be written as follows:

$$\mathbf{f}_i^h = \sigma \left(\sum_{j=1}^{k} \mathbf{M}_{ij} \mathbf{W}^h \mathbf{f}_j^{h-1} + \mathbf{b}^h \right) \tag{5}$$

We use graph convolution network in the sentence dependency tree as the Fig. 3, which has two primary considerations. One is to use efficient graph convolution to encode the dependency structure on the input sentence. Because the convolution process only encodes the neighbour information, one node in the graph can only be affected by the adjacent nodes in F-step. In this way, the graph convolution in the sentence dependency tree provides a syntactic constraint for one aspect of the sentence to identify descriptive words according to syntactic distance. The other is that GCN on the dependency tree can aggregate discontinuous words into a small range and appropriately aggregate their features through graph convolution. Thus, GCN can deal with the situation that discontinuous words describe the polarity of an aspect.

Dependency Graph Convolution is GCN over dependency graph. How to use graph convolution on the dependency graph of a sentence? After constructing the dependency tree of a given sentence, we first obtain the adjacency matrix $\mathbf{M} \in \mathbb{R}^{k \times k}$ according to the words in the sentence. Then, according to the self circulation idea [4], each word is manually set to be adjacent to it. That is, the diagonal value of M is 1. GCN usually does not consider the direction, but the dependency tree is a directed graph, so we adjust the application of GCN for direct perception. The GCN variant is implemented in a multi-layered manner based on the BERT-shared layer output, i.e. $\mathbf{F}^0 = \mathbf{F}^c$ to make the node understand the context [15]. Then, the representation factor [4] of each node is updated by a normalized graph convolution operation as follows:

$$\tilde{\mathbf{f}}_i^h = \sum_{j=1}^n \mathbf{M}_{ij} \mathbf{W}^h \mathbf{g}_j^{h-1} \tag{6}$$

$$\mathbf{f}_i^h = \text{ReLU}\left(\tilde{\mathbf{f}}_i^h / (d_i + 1) + \mathbf{b}^h\right) \tag{7}$$

where $\mathbf{g}_j^{h-1} \in \mathbb{R}^{2d_h}$ is the j-th token's representation evolved from the preceding GCN layer while $\mathbf{f}_i^h \in \mathbb{R}^{2d_h}$ is the product of current GCN layer, and $d_i = \sum_{j=1}^n \mathbf{M}_{ij}$ is degree of the i-th token in the tree. The weights $\mathbf{W}^h$ and bias $\mathbf{b}^h$ are trainable parameters.

Semantic-Relative Distance. Through SRD, we can determine whether the context word belongs to the local context of the target, and its purpose is to assist the model to capture the local context. This article focuses on mining the local contextual information of the target. SRD is based on the concept of token-aspect pair, describing the distance between token and aspect. It counts the number of tokens facing the target side between each specific token as the SRD for all tokens. The SRD's formula as:

$$SRD_i = |i - P_a| - \left\lfloor \frac{m}{2} \right\rfloor \tag{8}$$

Among them, P_a and i the central position of the aspect and the context word, respectively. m is the length of the targeted aspect, and SRD_i is the SRD between the i-th token and the targeted aspect.

Dynamic Weighting. The context features a dynamic weighting (CDW) layer that focuses on the local context. In this layer, the context features' weight with less-semantic-relative will be decay, and the features of context word far away from the target will be reduced according to their SRD. Note that the features of semantically related context words are absolutely preserved. CDW weights feature by constructing a weighted vector V_i^w for each context word with relatively less semantics. The following is a formula for the weight matrix M of the input sequence:

$$V_i = \begin{cases} E & SRD_i \leq \alpha \\ \frac{SRD_i - \alpha}{n} \cdot E & SRD_i > \alpha \end{cases} \tag{9}$$

$$W = [V_0^w, V_1^w, \dots V_n^w] \tag{10}$$

$$O_{CDW}^l = I \cdot W \tag{11}$$

where SRD_i is the SRD between the i-th contextual token and a specific aspect. n is the length of the input sequence. α is the SRD threshold. O_{CDW}^l is the output of the CDW layer. "." denotes the vector dot product operation.

The output representation of local context can be attained based on the output of CDW. O_{CDW}^l needs to pass through a 2-layer graph neural convolution layer. D is the adjacency matrix generated by the syntax dependency tree. For CDW layers:

$$O^l = GCN(O_{CDW}^l, D) \tag{12}$$

$$O^l = GCN(O^l, D) \tag{13}$$

Dynamic Mask. In addition to local context features, the CDM layer will also mask the non-local context features learned by the GCN layer. When the CDM layer is deployed, relative representations of context words and aspects with relatively little semantics remain in the corresponding output locations, only a relatively small amount of semantic text body will be blocked. In the CDM, the features of all positions of non-local context words will be set to zero vectors, then we get the local context feature output as follows:

$$V_i = \begin{cases} E \ SRD_i \leq \alpha \\ O \ SRD_i > \alpha \end{cases} \quad (14)$$

$$M = [V_1^m, V_2^m, \cdots V_n^m] \quad (15)$$

$$O_{CDM}^l = O_l \cdot M \quad (16)$$

In order to cover the features of the non-local context, we define a feature masking matrix M, and V_i^m is the masking vector of each marker in the input sequence. α is the SRD threshold, and n is the input sequence length, including the aspect ratio. A token whose SRD related to the target aspect is less than the threshold is the local context. $E \in \mathbb{R}^{d_h}$ represents a vector, and $O \in \mathbb{R}^{d_h}$ represents a zero vector. "." represents the dot product operation of vectors. Finally, the local context function learned by the CDM layer delivered as O'.

3   Experiments

3.1   Datasets and Experimental Settings

In order to comprehensively evaluate the performance of the proposed model, our experiments are conducted on five datasets. One Twitter social dataset is originally built [2] containing Twitter posts, and the Laptops (LAP14) and Restaurant (REST14) datasets of SemEval-2014 Task4 subtask2 [8], the Restaurant (REST15) datasets from SemEval 2015 task 12 [7], the Restaurant (REST16) datasets from SemEval 2016 task 5 [6]. The polarity of each aspect on these datasets can be positive, neutral, and negative, regardless of polarity conflict labels. After the previous work [10], we delete the samples with four conflicting polarity or no explicit aspects in rest15 and rest16 sentences. Statistics for the dataset are reported in Table 1.

In task 2, the auxiliary task, we use the Universal Dependencies English Web Treebank (UDPOS) dataset to predict PoS tags. This dataset actually has two different sets of tags, universal dependency (UD) tags and Penn Treebank (PTB) tags. We'll only train our model on the UD tags. The samples' distribution of those datasets is not balanced. For example, most samples in the restaurant datasets are positive, while the neutral samples in the Twitter dataset account for the majority. The LAP14, REST15, and REST16 datasets are not sensitive to syntax information.

Table 1. The ABSA datasets

Datasets	Positive		Neural		Negative	
	Train	Test	Train	Test	Train	Test
Twitter	1561	173	3127	346	1560	173
Laptop	994	341	464	169	870	128
Restaurant14	2164	728	637	196	807	196
Restaurant15	912	326	36	34	256	182
Restaurant16	1240	469	69	30	439	117

Table 2. The hyperparameters settings

Task	H	Setting
Main taks	Learning rate	2×10^{-5}
	l2reg	0.00001
	SRD	5
Task2	Embedding_dim	384
	Dropout	0.25
	Batch_size	32

In addition to referring to some previous hyperparameters settings, we also conducted a control experiment and analyzed the experimental results to optimize the hyperparameters settings. Table 2 lists the superior parameters about the main task and task 2. Moreover, the number of GCN layers is set to 2, which is the best-performing depth in pilot studies. The default SRD setting for all experiments is 5, and additional instructions are provided for experiments using different SRDs. For our task 2 experiments, 300-dimensional pre-trained GloVe vectors are used to initialize word embeddings. All model weights are initialized with uniform distribution.

The experimental results are obtained by averaging three runs with the random initialization, where Accuracy and Macro-Averaged F1 are adopted as the evaluation metrics. We also carry out a paired t-test on both Accuracy and Macro-Averaged F1 to verify whether the improvements achieved by our models over the baselines are significant. This model uses the optimizer Adam, the cross-entropy loss and L2-regularization to train. We also adopt dropout and early stopping to ease overfitting.

3.2   Experimental Analysis

In this experiment, we compare the results provided by the proposed LCF-TDGCN model with those obtained by TD-LSTM [10], RAM [1], MemNet [11], IAN [5], ASGCN-DG [14], BERT-SPC [9], LCF-BERT [13]. Table 3 shows that the performance of the LCF-TDGCN on the five datasets beats all compared baselines. Further, the performance improvement of rest15 and rest16 is the largest, followed by lap14 and rest14. There are some improvements in Twitter, but the improvement effect is not obvious on other datasets. The possible reasons are as follows. First, the improvement on Twitter is unlikely to be due to the uneven distribution of samples in these datasets. For example, most of the samples in the restaurant dataset are positive, while the neutral sample in the Twitter dataset is the majority. Our auxiliary task is to transfer the trained POS tagging model, which can effectively obtain POS feature information through the sentence vector encoded by the POS tagging model. Then, Lap14, rest15 and rest16 datasets are not sensitive to syntactic information.

Table 3. Model comparison results (%) when a = 0.5, b = 0.5 in the formula Eq. (3). Average precision and Macro-F1 scores are more than 3 runs randomly initialized and their corresponding variances. The best result with each dataset is in bold.

Model	TWITTER		LAP14		REST14		REST15		REST16	
	Acc. (%)	F1 (%)	Acc. (%)	F1 (%)	Acc. (%)	F1 (%)	Acc. (%)	F1 (%)	Acc. (%)	F1 (%)
TD-LSTM	67.34±1.09	65.49±0.85	69.64±1.88	63.71±1.97	77.05±0.86	64.18±4.02	74.48±1.36	51.15±0.92	85.39±0.74	62.24±2.48
RAM	67.82±0.87	65.00±0.86	62.02±5.34	48.15±11.40	75.30±0.67	60.37±2.35	65.81±3.65	37.02±7.71	82.14±2.40	48.64±4.28
Memnet	65.37±8.81	62.00±8.96	66.72±6.38	61.50±5.33	77.02±3.07	63.56±8.44	73.19±2.69	51.11±4.33	83.66±1.63	59.24±5.97
IAN	69.94±0.66	67.27±0.78	64.79±3.35	55.21±6.80	75.68±0.68	60.90±2.25	70.30±2.10	43.97±2.52	78.19±8.13	47.76±4.58
ASGCN-DG	72.54±0.63	70.81±1.17	75.24±0.27	70.81±0.46	81.46±0.42	73.04±0.44	79.15±0.32	60.51±1.69	88.04±0.25	66.93±0.72
BERT-SPC	73.75±0.98	71.98±1.48	78.74±0.74	74.14±0.94	84.85±0.68	77.04±1.07	83.89±0.75	67.49±5.22	90.48±0.19	74.05±2.57
LCF-BERT	74.52±1.52	73.07±1.37	78.84±0.41	74.18±1.12	85.39±0.22	78.20±1.06	84.13±0.32	62.12±4.93	91.23±0.99	75.30±0.54
GCN^-	73.70±0.76	72.43±0.90	80.36±0.09	76.72±0.26	85.77±0.52	79.37±0.74	84.75±0.28	72.20±0.47	91.77±0.34	78.25±0.65
$task2^-$	74.28±1.16	72.93±0.97	80.36±0.63	76.98±0.70	85.48±0.81	79.21±1.38	83.76±0.18	70.43±1.31	91.50±0.09	78.13±0.28
LCF-TDGCN	**75.82±0.36**	**74.40±0.68**	**80.25±0.27**	**76.99±0.26**	**86.67±0.27**	**80.85±0.43**	**85.18±0.28**	**73.70±1.27**	**92.15±0.19**	**78.49±0.75**

Run Time. The Time for training the model an epoch, TWITTER is 00:06:24, LAP14 is 00.01.90, REST14 is 00:05:06, REST15 is 00.00:98, REST15 is 00:01:68.

In order to test the influence of the components of the LCF-TDGCN on the performance, we compare the performance of the LCF-TDGCN with its ablations. The results are shown in Table 3. GCN^- is an ablation of the LCF-TDGCN and remove the GCN module. $task2^-$ is an ablation of the LCF-TDGCN and remove Auxiliary task modules.

Contribution of DGC. Comparing the LCF-TDGCN with the GCN^-, and it is 1%–2% higher than the GCN^- on average in five datasets from Table 3. Especially on the TWITTER dataset, its effect is improved by about 2%. This result can prove the effectiveness of our dependency tree to build the GCN module.

Contribution of Auxiliary Task. Comparing the LCF-TDGCN with the $task2^-$, There is almost no improvement on the Twitter and lap14 datasets, and the improvement effect is about 1% - 2% on the rest14, rest15 and rest16 datasets. The LCF-TDGCN performs better in most cases, suggesting the superiority of our Transfer Learning mechanism. This is because our model can better capture the POS information, and from Table 3 when the sentence coding of our auxiliary task is greater than that of the main task, the promotion effect is better.

Impact of the Weight Ratio of the Main Experiment and the Auxiliary. From Fig. 4, first of all, the different ratios of primary and secondary tasks will affect the effect to varying degrees. Among them, the lap14, rest15 and rest16 datasets have the largest fluctuations in the proportion of primary and secondary tasks. From a comprehensive perspective of the five datasets, when the weight ratio of the primary and secondary tasks is 0.5 : 0.5, that is, a = 0.5, b = 0.5 in Eq. 3, and its performance is generally higher. At the same time, this can prove that our transfer learning POS tagging task to enhance features is effective. From the Fig. 4(f), we show the results when a = 80 and b = 20. Compared with the performance when a/b = 0.8/0.2, the performance is greatly reduced. Other levels of comparison are also made, but the results are not ideal. So when doing the weight ratio of a and b, use a + b = 1.

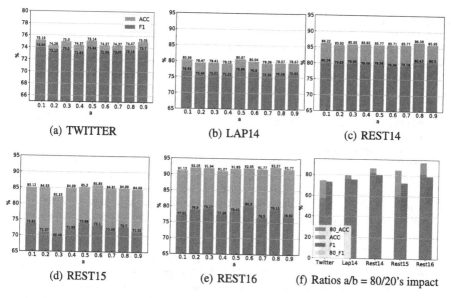

Fig. 4. 5 datasets' impact of ratios about a/b. In the five subgraphs (a) - (e), the abscissa represents the value of a in the formula Eq. (3), and $a + b = 1$ in the formula Eq. (4). In sub-figure (f) as a control group under the condition of $a + b = 1$, 80_ACC and 80_F1 use $a = 80$, $b = 20$, ACC and F1 use $a = 0.8$, $b = 0.2$.

4   Conclusions and Future Work

In this paper, a new aspect-based sentiment analysis model, which focuses on solving the problem of syntactic constraints in the local context and effectively captures the context information of the local context, is proposed. The DGC is introduced to process the constructed parsing tree, extract the syntactic information of sentence structure, correctly capture the syntactic information and long-distance words, and solve the long-range dependency problem. At the same time, the sentence vector is encoded by POS tagging assisted by transfer learning, and the weighted sum of the vector and the main task vector is carried out. In addition, this paper integrates the pre-trained BERT model, uses the local context attention mechanism and self-attention mechanism to significantly improve the performance of ABSC tasks and produces good results. In the future, we will optimize the combination function of the main task and the auxiliary task, not just the sum of weights. Moreover, in the graph dependency convolution network, a more reasonable relation graph, namely adjacency matrix, will be considered.

Acknowledgments. This work is partially supported by the Research Fund of Guangxi Key Lab of Multi-source Information Mining & Security (No. 20-A-01-01, No. 20-A-01-02), and the Innovation Project of Guangxi Graduate Education(No. JXXYYJSCXXM-2021-010, No. YCSW2021095).

References

1. Chen, P., Sun, Z., Bing, L., Yang, W.: Recurrent attention network on memory for aspect sentiment analysis. In: Proceedings of the 2017 Conference on Empirical Methods in Natural Language Processing, pp. 452–461. Association for Computational Linguistics, Copenhagen, Denmark (Sep 2017)
2. Dong, L., Wei, F., Tan, C., Tang, D., Zhou, M., Xu, K.: Adaptive recursive neural network for target-dependent twitter sentiment classification. In: Proceedings of the 52nd Annual Meeting of the Association for Computational Linguistics (volume 2: Short papers), pp. 49–54 (2014)
3. Fan, F., Feng, Y., Zhao, D.: Multi-grained attention network for aspect-level sentiment classification. In: Proceedings of the 2018 Conference on Empirical Methods in Natural Language Processing, pp. 3433–3442 (2018)
4. Kipf, T.N., Welling, M.: Semi-supervised classification with graph convolutional networks. In: Proceedings of the 5th International Conference on Learning Representations, ICLR 2017 (2017)
5. Ma, D., Li, S., Zhang, X., Wang, H.: Interactive attention networks for aspect-level sentiment classification. In: Sierra, C. (ed.) IJCAI, pp. 4068–4074. ijcai.org (2017)
6. Pontiki, M., et al.: SemEval-2016 task 5: Aspect based sentiment analysis. In: Proceedings of the 10th International Workshop on Semantic Evaluation (SemEval-2016), pp. 19–30. Association for Computational Linguistics, San Diego, California, June 2016
7. Pontiki, M., Galanis, D., Papageorgiou, H., Manandhar, S., Androutsopoulos, I.: SemEval-2015 task 12: Aspect based sentiment analysis. In: Proceedings of the 9th International Workshop on Semantic Evaluation (SemEval 2015), pp. 486–495. Association for Computational Linguistics, Denver, Colorado, June 2015
8. Pontiki, M., Galanis, D., Pavlopoulos, J., Papageorgiou, H., Androutsopoulos, I., Manandhar, S.: SemEval-2014 task 4: Aspect based sentiment analysis. In: Proceedings of the 8th International Workshop on Semantic Evaluation (SemEval 2014), pp. 27–35. Association for Computational Linguistics, Dublin, Ireland, August 2014
9. Song, Y., Wang, J., Jiang, T., Liu, Z., Rao, Y.: Attentional encoder network for targeted sentiment classification. CoRR abs/1902.09314 (2019)
10. Tang, D., Qin, B., Feng, X., Liu, T.: Effective lstms for target-dependent sentiment classification. In: Calzolari, N., Matsumoto, Y., Prasad, R. (eds.) COLING, pp. 3298–3307. ACL (2016)
11. Tang, D., Qin, B., Liu, T.: Aspect level sentiment classification with deep memory network. In: Su, J., Carreras, X., Duh, K. (eds.) EMNLP, pp. 214–224. The Association for Computational Linguistics (2016)
12. Vo, D.T., Zhang, Y.: Target-dependent twitter sentiment classification with rich automatic features. In: Twenty-Fourth International Joint Conference on Artificial Intelligence (2015)
13. Zeng, B., Yang, H., Xu, R., Zhou, W., Han, X.: LCF: a local context focus mechanism for aspect-based sentiment classification. Appl. Sci. 9(16), 3389 (2019)
14. Zhang, C., Li, Q., Song, D.: Aspect-based sentiment classification with aspect-specific graph convolutional networks. In: Inui, K., Jiang, J., Ng, V., Wan, X. (eds.) EMNLP/IJCNLP (1), pp. 4567–4577. Association for Computational Linguistics (2019)
15. Zhang, Y., Qi, P., Manning, C.D.: Graph convolution over pruned dependency trees improves relation extraction. In: Riloff, E., Chiang, D., Hockenmaier, J., Tsujii, J. (eds.) EMNLP, pp. 2205–2215. Association for Computational Linguistics (2018)

Machine Learning 1

DTWSSE: Data Augmentation with a Siamese Encoder for Time Series

Xinyu Yang[ORCID], Xinlan Zhang, Zhenguo Zhang[✉], Yahui Zhao, and Rongyi Cui

Department of Computer Science and Technology, Yanbian University,
977 Gongyuan Road, Yanji 133002, People's Republic of China
{2020050049,2019050390,zgzhang,yhzhao,cuirongyi}@ybu.edu.cn

Abstract. Access to labeled time series data is often limited in the real world, which constrains the performance of deep learning models in the field of time series analysis. Data augmentation is an effective way to solve the problem of small sample size and imbalance in time series datasets. The two key factors of data augmentation are the distance metric and the choice of interpolation method. SMOTE does not perform well on time series data because it uses a Euclidean distance metric and interpolates directly on the object. Therefore, we propose a DTW-based synthetic minority oversampling technique using siamese encoder for interpolation named DTWSSE. In order to reasonably measure the distance of the time series, DTW, which has been verified to be an effective method forts, is employed as the distance metric. To adapt the DTW metric, we use an autoencoder trained in an unsupervised self-training manner for interpolation. The encoder is a Siamese Neural Network for mapping the time series data from the DTW hidden space to the Euclidean deep feature space, and the decoder is used to map the deep feature space back to the DTW hidden space. We validate the proposed methods on a number of different balanced or unbalanced time series datasets. Experimental results show that the proposed method can lead to better performance of the downstream deep learning model.

Keywords: Data augmentation · Time series · Siamese encoder · Dynamic time warping

1 Introduction

Time series analysis is an important task in the field of data mining [10]. Deep learning is now widely used in time series analysis and has achieved significant success [8,11]. Since in many cases the cost of acquiring labeled time series data is large and the sample size of different classes of time series data is very imbalanced [12,18], deep learning models are likely to overfit or ignore the minority classes during training. The most effective way to solve these problems is to perform data augmentation by oversampling synthetic samples. Due to the high dimensionality of time series [19], the dimensions are time-correlated and it is

© Springer Nature Switzerland AG 2021
J. H. U et al. (Eds.): APWeb-WAIM 2021, LNCS 12858, pp. 435–449, 2021.
https://doi.org/10.1007/978-3-030-85896-4_34

difficult to compare the similarity between different time series [1], which makes data augmentation of time series data challenging.

SMOTE is one of the classical data augmentation methods [2,9]. However, the Euclidean distance used in this method does not represent the similarity between time series well, and direct interpolation of two time series may impair the temporal correlation between dimensions within the data.

In this work, we propose a novel method called **DTW**-based **S**ynthetic minority oversampling technique using **S**iamese **E**ncoder for interpolation (DTWSSE). Based on the classical SMOTE method for possible phase shifts and amplitude changes of the time series, we use the DTW [14] metric to measure the distance between time series. The encoder and decoder are trained in an unsupervised self-training manner. The encoder will learn the mapping relationship from DTW hidden space to Euclidean deep feature space, and the decoder will learn the mapping relationship from Euclidean deep feature space back to DTW hidden space. The process of interpolation on the Euclidean deep feature space and decoder mapping to the DTW hidden space is adapted to the DTW metric and better preserves the temporal properties of the time series. We validate our proposed method and its components on a number of time series datasets from different domains. The experimental results show that the components of our proposed method coordinate with each other to produce significant performance improvements in downstream deep learning models.

2   Related Work

Data augmentation aims to improve the performance of downstream models by synthesizing data [7]. SMOTE is a widely used data augmentation method for imbalanced data, which randomly selects some "center" samples from the minority of classes and interpolates between the "center" and its K-nearest neighbors to synthesize new data [2,9]. This method is based on Euclidean distance and direct interpolation of samples, which is contradictory to time series characteristics when dealing with time series data. Smart augmentation is a way to augment the data by adding a generator before the downstream model, which will intelligently synthesize new samples for training based on the downstream model [13]. The generators of this method are trained with supervised learning and downstream models together. However, this approach causes higher costs when training downstream models.

Dynamic time warping (DTW) is widely used for time series distance metric [14], which is aimed at the possible phase shift and amplitude change of time series, and it uses dynamic programming to align data at different time points to achieve a reasonable comparison of time series similarity. Autowarp is an end-to-end approach to learning better metric [1]. This method learns better metric from an unlabeled time series dataset by unsupervised learning. However, the model of this method needs to be pre-trained for each dataset.

Several studies have shown that interpolation in the deep feature space is feasible. *Upchur et al.* [15] shows that interpolation in deep feature space enables image semantic changes. *DeVries et al.* [5] shows that interpolation in feature space is superior to direct interpolation of objects. The feature spaces used by these methods are randomly generated by the model corresponding to the method.

The original design of Siamese neural network is to calculate the similarity of two inputs by mapping the two inputs to a new feature space through a neural network [3]. When using Contrastive loss, the model will make objects of the same class as close as possible in the feature space and objects of different classes as far as possible. The method proposed by *Utkin et al.* is to interpolate the output deep feature space of the siamese network [16]. However, the autoencoder used in this approach requires supervised learning using labeled data and cannot be used in cases where the amount of data is small.

3   The Proposed DTWSSE Method

The general architecture of DTWSSE is based on the classical SMOTE technology. The core idea of DTWSSE is to use the DTW metric, which has been verified as a valid metric for time series distance. Moreover, DTWSSE uses an autoencoder that has undergone a special unsupervised training process in order to adapt the DTW metric for the interpolation operation.

3.1   Make the Dataset Balanced

In this paper, each time series sample is denoted as $X_i = [x^1, x^2, ..., x^L]$ $(i = 1, 2..., N)$, where $x^i \in \mathbb{R}^M$ $(i = 1, 2, ..., L)$ and N is the sample size of the dataset. That is, each sample is an ordered collection of M-dimensional values of the length L, thus $X_i \in \mathbb{R}^{L \times M}$. Each sample in the dataset has a unique label C^i $(i = 1, 2, ..., N)$.

Suppose there are c classes in the dataset, and the dataset is needs to be augmented by a multiplier of T. We consider how to handle the data belonging to a class, firstly. To ensure the balance of classes in the augmented dataset, if the sample size of the class $\mathcal{A}$ is a, then the number of samples to be added by oversampling for this class is $onum_\mathcal{A}$.

$$onum_\mathcal{A} = \left\lfloor \frac{N \cdot T}{c} \right\rfloor - a \tag{1}$$

Next, we randomly select some "centers" within the class and use the KNN algorithm based on the DTW to obtain the k nearest neighbors of each "center". The number of "centers" selected in the class $\mathcal{A}$ is shown below. Note that the process of finding nearest neighbors is only done within the class.

$$cnum_\mathcal{A} = \left\lceil \frac{onum_\mathcal{A}}{k} \right\rceil \tag{2}$$

3.2 Use DTW to Select Instances for New Data Generation

We let a "center" be $\boldsymbol{X}_q = [x_q^1, x_q^2, ..., x_q^L]$, and another sample belonging to the class $\mathcal{A}$ is $\boldsymbol{X}_s = [x_s^1, x_s^2, ..., x_s^L]$. To calculate the DTW distance between $\boldsymbol{X}_q$ and $\boldsymbol{X}_s$, we first construct an $L \times L$ matrix D, where D_{ij} denotes the cost of aligning X_q^i to X_s^j.

$$D_{ij} = \left\| x_q^i - x_s^j \right\|_2^2 \tag{3}$$

The warping path $W = [w_1, w_2, ..., w_p, ..., w_P]$ $(L \le p < 2L)$ is the sequence of grid points, where each $w_p = (i_p, j_p)$ corresponds to an element D_{ij} of the matrix D. In addition, any warping path needs to satisfy the following three constraints:

(1) Boundary conditions: $w_1 = (1, 1)$, and $w_p = (L, L)$
(2) Monotonicity condition: $1 = i_1 \le i_2 \le ... \le i_P = L$ and $1 = j_1 \le j_2 \le ... \le j_P = L$
(3) Valid step: $w_p = (i_p, j_p) \implies$
    $w_{p+1} \in \{(i_p + 1, j_p), (i_p, j_p + 1), (i_p + 1, j_p + 1)\}$

The warping distance d is a function that maps a warping path to a non-negative real number.

$$d(\boldsymbol{X}_q, \boldsymbol{X}_s) = \sum_{t=1}^{P} D_{i_t j_t} \tag{4}$$

The DTW is the minimum value of the warping distance corresponding to all feasible warping paths.

$$DTW(\boldsymbol{X}_q, \boldsymbol{X}_s) = min_W \left\{ \sum_{t=1}^{P} D_{i_t j_t} \right\} \tag{5}$$

We define $dp(i, j)$ as the cumulative distance when moving to the element D_{ij} according to the warping path corresponding to DTW, so that the DTW can be calculated by the following dynamic programming formulation.

$$dp(i, j) = D_{ij} + min\{dp(i - 1, j), dp(i, j - 1), dp(i - 1, j - 1)\} \tag{6}$$

After calculating the DTW of $\boldsymbol{X}_q$ with other samples in class $\mathcal{A}$, the k nearest neighboring samples with the DTW distance to $\boldsymbol{X}_q$ are obtained. We assume that one of these k nearest neighbors is $\boldsymbol{X}_e$. Since we use the DTW to measure the distance between $\boldsymbol{X}_q$ and $\boldsymbol{X}_e$, we need to oversampling using the appropriate interpolation method corresponding to the DTW metric.

3.3 Interpolation Adapted to the DTW Metric

In this work, we use an autoencoder to achieve oversampling by interpolating on the Euclidean deep feature space. The encoder is a siamese neural network designed to learn to map data from the DTW hidden space to the Euclidean feature space, so that the DTW metric between time series is equivalent to the

Euclidean metric between latent vectors output by encoder. The decoder is a neural network that maps data from the Euclidean deep feature space back to the DTW hidden space.

We use a special unsupervised learning approach to train the autoencoder. The dataset for training the autoencoder is $\mathcal{D} = \left\{ \left[\left(S_i^1, S_i^2 \right), y_i \right] \right\}$, where S_i^1 and S_i^2 are randomly generated sequences and $S_i^1, S_i^2 \in \mathbb{R}^{L \times M}$. y_i is a label that is automatically generated after generating S_i^1 and S_i^2, which represents the DTW between S_i^1 and S_i^2.

As shown in Fig. 1, the sequences S_i^1 and S_i^2 will be input to encoder and generate the corresponding latent vectors h_i^1 and h_i^2.

$$h_i^1, h_i^2 = encoder \left(S_i^1, S_i^2 \right) \tag{7}$$

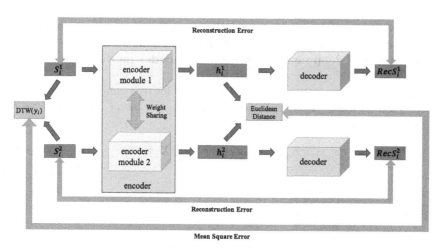

Fig. 1. An overview of the training process. The encoder is a siamese neural network that inputs two vectors at a time and generates two latent vectors. The decoder inputs one latent vector at a time and produces a reconstructed input vector. When training the encoder, the goal is to minimize the mean square error of the DTW distance between the input vectors and the Euclidean distance between the output vectors. When training the decoder, the goal is to minimize the reconstruction error of autoencoder.

When training the encoder, our goal is to minimize the mean square error between the Euclidean distance of h_i^1 and h_i^2 and the DTW of S_i^1 and S_i^2. Therefore, the loss function when we train the encoder can be expressed in the following form.

$$L_E = \frac{1}{|\mathcal{D}|} \sum_i \left(\left\| h_i^1 - h_i^2 \right\|_2 - y_i \right)^2 \tag{8}$$

It is important to emphasize that during the training process, the two modules of inside the encoder have the same structure and share weights, in other words, the encoder is a **Siamese neural network**. From another point of view, one of the encoder modules acts as a discriminator to the output of the other module.

The decoder will input two latent vectors h_i^1 and h_i^2, respectively, and output the reconstructed sequences $RecS_i^1$ and $RecS_i^2$.

$$RecS_i^1 = decoder\left(h_i^1\right)$$
$$RecS_i^2 = decoder\left(h_i^2\right)$$
(9)

Our goal in training the decoder is to minimize the reconstruction error between the output of the decoder and the input of the encoder. Thus, the loss function when training the decoder can be expressed in the following form. It is important to note that when training the decoder we need to fix the parameters of the encoder.

$$L_D = \frac{1}{2\,|\mathcal{D}|}\sum_i\left(\left\|S_i^1 - RecS_i^1\right\|_2\right)^2 + \frac{1}{2\,|\mathcal{D}|}\sum_i\left(\left\|S_i^2 - RecS_i^2\right\|_2\right)^2 \quad (10)$$

In practice, we first train the encoder until L_E converges, then train the decoder to learn to undo the mapping relationship. In addition, **we can use different architectures of deep neural networks as encoder module and decoder**, such as CNN, Fully-connected Neural Network.

After training, we use the above autoencoder for oversampling. As shown in Fig. 2, when we input X_q and X_e to the encoder, two latent vectors h_q and h_e will be generated correspondingly.

$$h_q, h_e = encoder\left(X_q, X_e\right) \quad (11)$$

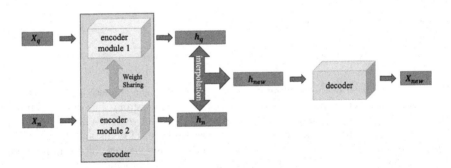

Fig. 2. An overview of the interpolation process. Each time the encoder inputs two time series and generates the corresponding latent vectors, we interpolate the two latent vectors and the decoder decodes them to form the new time series synthetic data.

Since the latent vector is in the Euclidean deep feature space, it is reasonable to perform interpolation between the latent vectors. The new sample X_{new} generated by oversampling and its corresponding latent vector h_{new} can be derived from the following equations.

$$h_{new} = h_q + rand\left(0, 1\right)\cdot\left(h_e - h_q\right) \quad (12)$$

$$X_{new} = decoder\left(h_{new}\right) \quad (13)$$

Since the decoder maps the latent vector from the Euclidean deep feature space back to the DTW hidden space, we implement an interpolation procedure that matches the DTW metric.

After interpolating once between all the "centers" selected in class $\mathcal{A}$ and their c nearest neighbors, we have completed the data augmentation of class $\mathcal{A}$. After the above process is done for all classes, we get the augmented time series dataset.

4 Experiment

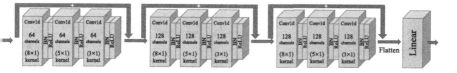

Fig. 3. The schematic diagram of the ResNet classifier architecture.

In this section, we validate the proposed method on several datasets for classification tasks. For all datasets, we use the same ResNet classifier [17], whose architecture is shown in Fig. 3. The only difference is that the data for training the classifier was obtained by different data augmentation methods.

In each experiment, to ensure the consistency of the experimental variables, the classifier is trained with 100 epochs using a mini-batch stochastic gradient descent method with a batch size of 32 for each experiment. We trained the classifier using the *Adam* optimizer with the hyper parameter lr set to $1e-3$, the loss function is the cross entropy between the output of the classifier and the corresponding label. In our previous work we found that larger expansion multipliers are more likely to yield good results, so when preprocessing dataset we set the expansion multiplier T to 10. In addition, we only consider the closest sample to the "center" in our experiments.

The specific architecture of the autoencoder used in the experiments is related to the dimension of the time series in the dataset. In some previous work, we found that the convergence of the loss function of autoencoder in the proposed method is easier when the dimension of the latent vector is 10 times the number of variables of the time series. So if the time series data $X_i \in \mathbb{R}^{L \times M}$, we set the dimension of the latent vector to $10 \cdot L \cdot M$, i.e. $h_i \in \mathbb{R}^{(10 \cdot L \cdot M) \times 1}$. In addition, encoder can be replaced with different architectures of neural networks, while the architecture of decoder should be symmetric with encoder. In our experiments we used CNN and Fully-connected Neural Network respectively for comparison, their architectures are shown in Fig. 4 and Fig. 5.

We performed each independent experiment 10 times and recorded 3 assessment metrics, the classifier was trained from scratch for each experiment. The **Top-1 accuracy** represents the best result the model can obtain, the **worst accuracy** represents the worst result the model can obtain, and the **average accuracy** with the best and worst accuracy removed represents the result the model can obtain in most cases. All results are obtained with a single NVIDIA® Tesla® V100 GPU.

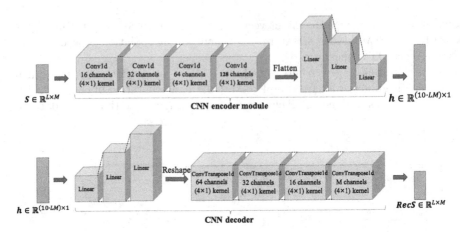

Fig. 4. The schematic diagram of autoencoder for CNN architecture. There are two encoder modules with the same structure and shared weights in one encoder. Decoder architecture is completely symmetric with encoder module.

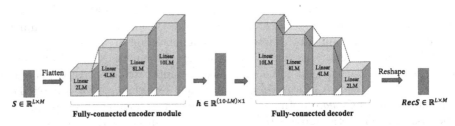

Fig. 5. The schematic diagram of autoencoder for Fully-connected Neural Network architecture. There are two encoder modules with the same structure and shared weights in one encoder. Decoder architecture is completely symmetric with encoder module.

4.1   Basic Results

We used 10 time series datasets to conduct experiments comparing the proposed method with the classical SMOTE method. These datasets are derived from images of hand bones and extracted by *Cao et al.* [4]. The feature numbers of the data in the above datasets are all 80, and the details are shown in Table 1. It is clear that these datasets are imbalanced.

In our experiments, we compared the results generated by the classifier trained on the original dataset, the dataset augmented by the classical SMOTE method, and the dataset augmented by the DTWSSE, respectively. We also documented the results of using autoencoder with different architectures. Since the dimension of all the data in the above datasets is 80×1, we set the dimension of the latent vector generated by encoder to 800×1. The experimental results are shown in Table 2.

Table 1. Summary of the time series datasets used in the experiments. The "#" in the table is short for "quantity".

Datasets	Train size	Test size	# of classes	# of minority class	# of majority class
DistalPhalanxTW	400	139	6	28	82
DistalPhalanxOutlineAgeGroup	400	139	3	30	257
DistalPhalanxOutlineCorrect	600	276	2	222	378
MiddlePhalanxTW	399	154	6	30	84
MiddlePhalanxOutlineAgeGroup	400	154	3	55	237
MiddlePhalanxOutlineCorrect	600	291	2	212	338
ProximalPhalanxTW	400	205	6	16	109
ProximalPhalanxOutlineAgeGroup	400	205	3	72	189
ProximalPhalanxOutlineCorrect	600	291	2	194	406
PhalangesOutlinesCorrect	1800	858	2	628	1172

Table 2. The performance results obtained by training the classifier with the dataset augmented by different methods. The "original" column indicates the result of training the downstream classifier using the original dataset without any data augmentation methods.

Metrics	Datasets	Original	SMOTE	DTWSSE (CNN)	DTWSSE (Fully-connected)
Top-1 Accuracy (%)	Dis.TW	64.75	69.06	69.06	**74.10**
	Dis.A.G	74.82	75.54	**76.98**	76.26
	Dis.C	79.71	79.71	**80.07**	77.90
	Mid.TW	53.90	52.60	56.49	**57.14**
	Mid.A.G	**64.94**	56.49	62.34	62.99
	Mid.C	**84.19**	83.85	**84.19**	83.16
	Pro.TW	**80.98**	79.02	**80.98**	80.49
	Pro.A.G	87.32	87.80	**88.29**	87.32
	Pro.C	91.41	91.07	**91.75**	**91.75**
	Pha	83.10	83.45	**83.68**	82.98
Worst accuracy (%)	Dis.TW	51.80	**63.31**	60.43	**63.31**
	Dis.A.G	47.48	**67.63**	**67.63**	66.91
	Dis.C	63.41	72.83	**73.55**	71.01
	Mid.TW	28.57	45.45	46.75	**50.00**
	Mid.A.G	42.86	46.10	**50.65**	46.10
	Mid.C	52.58	59.11	74.57	**74.91**
	Pro.TW	48.29	74.15	**74.63**	72.68
	Pro.A.G	73.66	80.98	**82.44**	80.00
	Pro.C	68.73	81.10	82.82	**85.22**
	Pha	55.13	**79.60**	**79.60**	78.67
Average accuracy (%)	Dis.TW	59.44	65.20	66.19	**67.72**
	Dis.A.G	66.64	71.04	**73.29**	72.57
	Dis.C	72.51	76.18	**76.95**	75.27
	Mid.TW	46.35	49.11	52.60	**52.84**
	Mid.A.G	54.46	51.22	**57.63**	56.25
	Mid.C	77.41	79.38	**79.98**	79.73
	Pro.TW	77.38	76.89	**78.90**	76.95
	Pro.A.G	83.78	**85.55**	85.06	85.18
	Pro.C	83.93	87.41	**88.92**	87.46
	Pha	73.86	81.15	**81.22**	80.36

It is observed that our proposed data augmentation method DTWSSE can significantly improve the classifier performance in most cases. Compared with the classical SMOTE method, DTWSSE leads to a significant improvement in the performance of the classifier. For example, on the *DistalPhalanxTW* dataset, the DTWSSE method using the DNN architecture autoencoder improved the Top-1 accuracy by 9.35% (74.10% v.s. 64.75%), the worst accuracy by 11.51% (63.31% v.s. 51.80%), and the average accuracy by 8.28% (67.72% v.s. 59.44%), respectively, compared to the case of no data augmentation. Compared with the classical SMOTE method, the Top-1 accuracy is improved by 5.04% (74.10% v.s. 69.06%), and the average accuracy is improved by 2.52% (67.72% v.s. 65.20%). Although the worst accuracy is equal between the two methods (63.31% v.s. 63.31%), DTWSSE is more likely to produce better results.

Another thing that can be observed is that the optimal autoencoder architecture is different for different datasets. While our proposed approach leads to a general improvement in data augmentation, switching to a suitable autoencoder architecture can lead to a further improvement. This also inspired us to use the deep learning model that best fits the characteristics of the time series data in a practical task.

4.2   Ablation Studies

In order to better understand the effectiveness of each component of DTWSSE, we conducted the following two ablation studies. We still used the above 10 datasets for our experiments.

First we considered the case of using the DTW metric and interpolating directly between time series. The experimental results are shown in the Table 3. We can clearly observe that most of the experimental results are degraded compared to DTWSSE because the autoencoder interpolation method adapted to DTW metric is not used. Compared to the classical SMOTE method, we cannot clearly distinguish which of the two methods is superior. For Top-1 Accuracy, the classical SMOTE method wins 5 times and the SMOTE method using the DTW metric wins 3 times; for Worst Accuracy, the ratio is 6:3; and for Average Accuracy, the ratio is 5:5. This may indicate that after finding the nearest neighbor of the "center" using the DTW distance, interpolation between the nearest neighbor and the "center" on the DTW feature space is necessary.

We also considered the case of using naive autoencoder to replace the autoencoder used in DTWSSE. The only difference with DTWSSE is the unsupervised training process of the autoencoder. For this experiment, we did not train encoder to learn how to map the DTW hidden space to the Euclidean deep feature space. Instead of designing the encoder as a siamese network and fixing the parameters of a certain part, we trained the encoder and decoder together to minimize the reconstruction error. At this point, encoder is actually a module of the encoder used by DTWSSE. The process of training is shown in the Fig. 6.

The encoder and decoder still used the two architectures shown in Fig. 4 and Fig. 5, but the encoder at this point is actually an encoder module in the figure. In the experiment, the dimension of hidden vector is still set to 800×1.

Table 3. The results of the comparison with the SMOTE method using the DTW metric as the distance measure, the "SMOTE(DTW)" column represents this method, which does not use autoencoder for the interpolation process.

Metrics	Datasets	SMOTE	SMOTE (DTW)	DTWSSE (CNN)	DTWSSE (Fully-connected)
Top-1 accuracy (%)	Dis.TW	69.06	69.06	69.06	**74.10**
	Dis.A.G.	75.54	76.26	**76.98**	76.26
	Dis.C.	79.71	78.26	**80.07**	77.90
	Mid.TW	52.60	51.30	56.49	**57.14**
	Mid.A.G.	56.49	54.55	62.34	**62.99**
	Mid.C.	83.85	81.44	**84.19**	83.16
	Pro.TW	79.02	80.49	**80.98**	80.49
	Pro.A.G.	87.80	86.34	**88.29**	87.32
	Pro.C.	91.07	91.07	**91.75**	**91.75**
	Pha	83.45	**83.92**	83.68	82.98
Worst accuracy (%)	Dis.TW	**63.31**	58.99	60.43	**63.31**
	Dis.A.G.	**67.63**	62.59	**67.63**	66.91
	Dis.C.	72.83	73.19	**73.55**	71.01
	Mid.TW	45.45	46.75	46.75	**50.00**
	Mid.A.G.	46.10	44.81	**50.65**	46.10
	Mid.C.	59.11	58.76	74.57	**74.91**
	Pro.TW	74.15	69.27	**74.63**	72.68
	Pro.A.G.	80.98	80.98	**82.44**	80.00
	Pro.C.	81.10	79.38	82.82	**85.22**
	Pha	79.60	**80.77**	79.60	78.67
Average accuracy (%)	Dis.TW	65.20	63.76	66.19	**67.72**
	Dis.A.G.	71.04	71.13	**73.29**	72.57
	Dis.C.	76.18	75.77	**76.95**	75.27
	Mid.TW	49.11	49.19	52.60	**52.84**
	Mid.A.G.	51.22	49.27	**57.63**	56.25
	Mid.C.	79.38	77.71	**79.98**	79.73
	Pro.TW	76.89	76.95	**78.90**	76.95
	Pro.A.G.	**85.55**	84.63	85.06	85.18
	Pro.C.	87.41	**89.69**	88.92	87.46
	Pha	81.15	**81.95**	81.22	80.36

The results are shown in the Table 4. We find that this method outperforms the classical SMOTE method in most cases. This phenomenon suggests that interpolation on the deep feature space generated through the encoder can provide some improvement in performance. Compared to our proposed DTWSSE method, this method generally performs slightly worse. We note that when using autoencoder with CNN architecture, the method yields a worst accuracy of 34.42% for the classifier after processing the *MiddlePhalanxOutlineAgeGroup* dataset and a worst accuracy of 36.59% for the classifier after processing the *ProximalPhalanxOutlineAgeGroup* Dataset. This suggests that interpolating only on the deep feature space may cause the model to converge at a large local minimum of the loss function during training. In addition our proposed method DTWSSE method

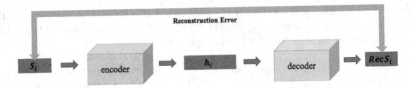

Fig. 6. An overview of the naive autoencoder training process. This approach does not use the siamese network as the encoder architecture, and the encoder does not have to learn any special mapping relations. In this ablation study, we only minimize the reconstruction error of autoencoder.

Table 4. The comparative results of the SMOTE method using the DTW metric as a distance measure and interpolation using a naive autoencoder. The column "SMOTE+AE" represents this approach, which uses autoencoder with CNN architecture and Fully-connected Neural Network architecture for comparison with DTWSSE, respectively.

Metrics	Datasets	SMOTE	SMOTE+AE (CNN)	DTWSSE (CNN)	SMOTE+AE (Fully-connected)	DTWSSE (Fully-connected)
Top-1 accuracy (%)	Dis.TW	64.75	**69.06**	**69.06**	70.50	**74.10**
	Dis.A.G.	74.82	**76.98**	**76.98**	74.10	**76.26**
	Dis.C	79.71	79.35	**80.07**	77.54	**77.90**
	Mid.TW	53.90	55.19	**56.49**	56.49	**57.14**
	Mid.A.G.	**64.94**	59.09	62.34	**64.94**	62.99
	Mid.C.	84.19	**84.54**	84.19	82.13	**83.16**
	Pro.TW	80.98	80.49	80.98	**83.41**	80.49
	Pro.A.G.	87.32	**88.29**	88.29	87.32	**87.32**
	Pro.C	91.41	91.41	**91.75**	91.07	**91.75**
	Pha	83.10	82.63	**83.68**	82.28	**82.98**
Worst accuracy (%)	Dis.TW	51.80	51.80	60.43	63.31	**63.31**
	Dis.A.G.	47.48	66.19	67.63	**71.94**	66.91
	Dis.C.	63.41	72.83	**73.55**	72.10	71.01
	Mid.TW	28.57	**46.75**	46.75	48.05	**50.00**
	Mid.A.G.	42.86	34.42	**50.65**	44.81	46.10
	Mid.C.	52.58	64.26	**74.57**	62.20	**74.91**
	Pro.TW	48.29	71.71	**74.63**	71.71	72.68
	Pro.A.G.	73.66	36.59	**82.44**	79.02	80.00
	Pro.C	68.73	81.44	82.82	79.04	**85.22**
	Pha	55.13	77.97	**79.60**	77.74	78.67
Average accuracy (%)	Dis.TW	59.44	64.57	66.19	66.46	**67.72**
	Dis.A.G.	66.64	72.75	**73.29**	72.48	72.57
	Dis.C.	72.51	**76.95**	76.95	75.72	75.27
	Mid.TW	46.35	49.68	52.60	52.11	**52.84**
	Mid.A.G.	54.46	48.13	**57.63**	56.09	56.25
	Mid.C.	77.41	79.47	**79.98**	76.85	79.73
	Pro.TW	77.38	76.83	**78.90**	**77.74**	76.95
	Pro.A.G.	83.78	82.62	85.06	83.72	**85.18**
	Pro.C.	83.93	**89.48**	88.92	86.64	87.46
	Pha	73.86	**81.47**	81.22	81.19	80.36

performs better compared to this method in most cases. This phenomenon confirms the effectiveness of the component of the DTWSSE method that trains the encoder to learn the mapping relations from the DTW hidden space to the Euclidean deep feature space.

4.3   Apply to Balanced Datasets

We first conducted experiments on two traffic time series datasets, *Chinatown* and *MelbournePedestrian*[1]. These datasets were recorded by automated pedestrian counting sensors located at various locations throughout the city of Melbourne, Australia. *Hoang Anh Dau* edited the system-generated data over 12 months of 2017 to create these two datasets. Each sample has 24 features, representing the variation in the number of pedestrians in a day. The number on each dimension in sample represents the number of people captured by the sensor in one hour. In addition these datasets have been pre-segmented into training and test sets.

The samples in *Chinatown* were recorded by the sensor at Chinatown-Swanston St. The dataset is divided into two classes, one from weekday and the other from weekend. The training set is balanced, with 10 samples for each of class, this is a typical few-shot learning problem. The test set size is 345.

The samples in *MelbournePedestrian* were recorded by sensors located in different locations. Each class represents a location, and there are 10 classes in the dataset. The amount of samples for each class in the training set is about 120, and there are 1194 samples in total. There are 2439 samples in the test set.

With the expansion multiplier T of 10, we conducted two comparison experiments and the results are shown in Table 5 and Table 6. It can be observed that our proposed method still performs significantly better than the SMOTE on both datasets. In addition, for the *Chinatown* dataset with a very small training sample size, the worst accuracy of the classifier is significantly lower than that without data augmentation as long as the data augmentation method is used. This may be because the synthetic samples make it more difficult for the downstream classifier to learn the true data distribution. However, since DTWSSE

Table 5. The Performance results on the *Chinatown* dataset.

Methods	Top-1 accuracy (%)	Worst accuracy (%)	Average accuracy (%)
No data augmentation	98.54	**97.38**	98.03
SMOTE	98.83	74.64	95.85
DTWSSE (CNN)	**99.13**	89.21	**98.25**
DTWSSE (DNN)	**99.13**	84.84	98.07

Table 6. The Performance results on the *MelbournePedestrian* dataset.

Methods	Top-1 accuracy (%)	Worst accuracy (%)	Average accuracy (%)
No data augmentation	96.27	87.25	95.34
SMOTE	96.76	84.26	92.45
DTWSSE (CNN)	**97.13**	91.72	**96.26**
DTWSSE (DNN)	96.72	**95.61**	96.20

---

[1] These datasets are available at http://www.timeseriesclassification.com/.

performs better on both the Top-1 accuracy metric and the average accuracy metric, this suggests that DTWSSE reduces the impact of this problem.

We then conducted an experiment on the *Libras* sign language dataset. *Libras* Sign Language Movement Dataset is a dataset in the UC Irvine Machine Learning Repository [6], which is a multivariate dataset. There are 15 classes in the dataset, each class represents a hand movement type. There are 24 samples in each class and the total number of samples is 360. We randomly selected half of the samples from each class to form the training set, the rest of the samples to form the test set. Each sample is obtained from one video of the hand movement curve. During each recorded hand movement curves, 45 frames are selected and a time series sample is formed based on the two-dimensional coordinates of the hand center. In addition, each sample was subjected to time normalization in the unitary space. The experimental results are shown in the Table 7. The results of this experiment also show that DTWSSE has better performance compared to SMOTE. These experiments also demonstrate the effectiveness of DTWSSE on balanced datasets.

Table 7. The performance results on the *Libras* dataset.

Methods	Top-1 accuracy (%)	Worst accuracy (%)	Average accuracy (%)
No data augmentation	95.56	85.00	92.36
SMOTE	94.44	87.22	91.67
DTWSSE (CNN)	**96.67**	85.56	93.33
DTWSSE (DNN)	95.56	**91.11**	**93.40**

5 Conclusion

Data augmentation of time series is challenging due to the high dimensionality of data, the temporal correlation of each dimension, and the difficulty of comparing time series similarity. In this study, we propose a synthetic minority oversampling technique based on the DTW metric, which uses an autoencoder that is unsupervisedly self-trained to adapt the DTW metric for interpolation. To accommodate the phase shift and amplitude change of the time series, we use DTW as the distance metric. To adapt the interpolation to the DTW distance metric, we use an unsupervised trained siamese network as an encoder so that it can map the time series to the Euclidean deep feature space. After that, we interpolate in the Euclidean deep feature space and use a decoder to form the new synthetic data. We evaluated the effectiveness of DTWSSE on a number of datasets and find that DTWSSE performs better than classical SMOTE in most cases and both the DTW distance metric and the use of interpolation with DTW-adapted autoencoder are essential to obtain better performance.

Acknowledgements. Zixuan Li from Tianjin University and Pengfei Liu from Zhejiang University contributed to this work by providing advice and assistance. This work is supported by the school-enterprise cooperation project of Yanbian University [2020-15], State Language Commission of China under Grant No. YB135-76 and Doctor Starting Grants of Yanbian University [2020-16].

References

1. Abid, A., Zou, J.: Autowarp: Learning a warping distance from unlabeled time series using sequence autoencoders. arXiv preprint arXiv:1810.10107 (2018)
2. Chawla, N.V., Bowyer, K.W., Hall, L.O., Kegelmeyer, W.P.: Smote: synthetic minority over-sampling technique. J. Artif. Intell. Res. **16**, 321–357 (2002)
3. Chicco, D.: Siamese neural networks: an overview. Artificial Neural Networks, pp. 73–94 (2021)
4. Davis, L.M.: Predictive modelling of bone ageing. Ph.D. thesis, University of East Anglia (2013)
5. DeVries, T., Taylor, G.W.: Dataset augmentation in feature space. arXiv preprint arXiv:1702.05538 (2017)
6. Dua, D., Graff, C.: UCI machine learning repository (2017). http://archive.ics.uci. edu/ml
7. Fawaz, H.I., Forestier, G., Weber, J., Idoumghar, L., Muller, P.A.: Data augmentation using synthetic data for time series classification with deep residual networks
8. Ismail Fawaz, H., Forestier, G., Weber, J., Idoumghar, L., Muller, P.-A.: Deep learning for time series classification: a review. Data Mining Knowl. Discovery **33**(4), 917–963 (2019). https://doi.org/10.1007/s10618-019-00619-1
9. Fernández, A., Garcia, S., Herrera, F., Chawla, N.V.: Smote for learning from imbalanced data: progress and challenges, marking the 15-year anniversary. J. Artif. Intell. Res. **61**, 863–905 (2018)
10. Fu, T.C.: A review on time series data mining. Eng. Appl. Artif. Intell. **24**(1), 164–181 (2011)
11. Gamboa, J.C.B.: Deep learning for time-series analysis. arXiv preprint arXiv:1701.01887 (2017)
12. Jiang, W., Hong, Y., Zhou, B., He, X., Cheng, C.: A gan-based anomaly detection approach for imbalanced industrial time series. IEEE Access **7**, 143608–143619 (2019)
13. Lemley, J., Bazrafkan, S., Corcoran, P.: Smart augmentation learning an optimal data augmentation strategy. IEEE Access **5**, 5858–5869 (2017)
14. Rakthanmanon, T., et al.: Searching and mining trillions of time series subsequences under dynamic time warping. In: Proceedings of the 18th ACM SIGKDD International Conference on Knowledge Discovery and Data Mining, pp. 262–270 (2012)
15. Upchurch, P., Gardner, J., Pleiss, G., Pless, R., Snavely, N., Bala, K., Weinberger, K.: Deep feature interpolation for image content changes. In: Proceedings of the IEEE Conference on Computer Vision and Pattern Recognition, pp. 7064–7073 (2017)
16. Utkin, L.V., Kovalev, M.S., Kasimov, E.M.: An explanation method for siamese neural networks. arXiv preprint arXiv:1911.07702 (2019)
17. Wang, Z., Yan, W., Oates, T.: Time series classification from scratch with deep neural networks: a strong baseline. In: 2017 International Joint Conference on Neural Networks (IJCNN), pp. 1578–1585. IEEE (2017)
18. Wen, Q., Sun, L., Song, X., Gao, J., Wang, X., Xu, H.: Time series data augmentation for deep learning: a survey. arXiv preprint arXiv:2002.12478 (2020)
19. Zhu, T., Lin, Y., Liu, Y.: Oversampling for imbalanced time series data. arXiv e-prints pp. arXiv-2004 (2020)

PT-LSTM: Extending LSTM for Efficient Processing Time Attributes in Time Series Prediction

Yongqiang Yu, Xinyi Xia[✉], Bo Lang, and Hongyu Liu

Beihang University, Beijing, China
xiaxinyi@buaa.edu.cn

Abstract. Long Short-Term Memory (LSTM) has been widely applied in time series predictions. Time attributes are important factors in time series prediction. However, existing studies often ignore the influence of time attributes when splitting the time series data, and seldom utilize the time information in the LSTM models. In this paper, we propose a novel method named Position encoding and Time gate LSTM (PT-LSTM). We first propose a position-encoding based time attributes integration method, which obtains the vector representation of time attributes through position encoding, and integrate it with the observed value vectors of the data. Moreover, we propose a LSTM variant by adding a new time gate which is specially designed to process time attributes. Therefore, PT-LSTM can make good use of time attributes in the key phases of data prediction. Experimental results on three public datasets show that our PT-LSTM model outperforms the state-of-the-art methods in time series prediction.

Keywords: Time series prediction · LSTM · Position encoding · Time attribute processing

1 Introduction

Time series prediction plays an important role in many fields, such as stock price prediction [1], electricity demand forecasting [2] and Air Pollution Forecasting [3]. The classic time series prediction method is the autoregressive integrated moving average (ARIMA) model [1,4]. However, ARIMA model suffers from strict restrictions on the type of time series, and only works well on linear data. Those shortages make the model allways a component of an entire prediction system [5].

In recent years, many researchers begin to apply recurrent neural networks (RNNs) to time series prediction problems, and achieve good results. Compared with ARIMA model, RNNs have a stronger nonlinear fitting ability and can capture the relation between sequence values, which is suitable for various types of time series. Long short-term memory (LSTM) [6] and gated recurrent units (GRUs) [7] are two of common RNN structures. In general, records in real time

© Springer Nature Switzerland AG 2021
L. H. U et al. (Eds.): APWeb-WAIM 2021, LNCS 12858, pp. 450–464, 2021.
https://doi.org/10.1007/978-3-030-85896-4_35

series data consist of two parts. The first part is attributes related to specific tasks, such as stock price, network traffic and traffic flow, which are called observation values. The second part is the properties related to time, which are called time attributes. According to the feature processing method used, previous studies can be divided into two categories. One category addresses only observed values [8–11]. For instance, Bao et al. [9] processed observed values by wavelet denoising and stacked autoencoders and then fed the results into an LSTM network. The other category addresses both the observed values and time attributes [2,12–14]. For instance, Kong et al. [2] fed a matrix of the concatenated energy consumption and corresponding time attributes (hours, weeks, holidays) into LSTM network.

Almost all existing studies based on RNNs apply standard RNN models, which based on sequence values without special processing for the temporal information. In fact, affected by people's regular work and leisure, many actual time series [2,14] are closely related to time, in which time attributes can play a guiding role in prediction. For example, electricity consumption is expected to increase at 8 pm, which cannot be exploited by a RNN. In addition, real time series data are often too long to be fed into RNN, so they need to be divided into subsequences. However, the influence on data may varies from different period, which results in inconsistencies between the observed data and the modeled results.

To eliminate the influence of subsequences and use time attributes, we propose a novel method named Position encoding and Time gate LSTM (PT-LSTM). We first obtain the vector representation of time attributes through position encoding, and integrate it with the observed value vector of the data. Moreover, we propose a LSTM variant by adding a new time gate which is specially designed to process time attributes. Experimental results show that the proposed method has the best performance on three popular public datasets. The contributions of this paper are as follows:

- We obtain the representation of time series data based on position encoding. Position encoding is used to obtain vector representation of time attributes, then this vector is added to the observed value vector element by element to form a unified representation of time series data.
- We propose a new LSTM variant, i.e., PT-LSTM. PT-LSTM adds a specifically designed time gate in the LSTM network to effectively exploit the property of time series, which can partly control input data acquisition, update the internal state and output the final results of the model.
- PT-LSTM achieves superior experimental results compared with existing models on the Pollution, BikeSharing, and Tasmania (TAS) 2016 datasets.

The rest of this paper is organized as follows. Section 2 summarizes related work on LSTM in time series prediction, time attributes utilization and position encoding. Section 3 describes Details of the proposed methods. Section 4 presents the experiments and discussion. At last, our study is concluded in Sect. 5.

2 Related Work

RNNs add intralayer connections on the basis of a feedforward neural network, which can theoretically process sequence data of any length. Nevertheless, when the input sequence is too long, RNNs suffer from the exploding or vanishing gradient problem. To address the problem, LSTM [6,15] introduces three types of gating units to control the flow of messages within the model. Existing time series prediction methods basing on LSTM can be divided into four types based on the feature selection method: (1) Directly using the original time series. For instance, Azzouni et al. [8] directly chose the traffic matrix of each moment as the time series feature in prediction. (2) Time series transformation and feature selection [16]. For instance, Bedi et al. [16] first used empirical mode decomposition (EMD) to decompose a load time series signal into several components, then trained LSTM models separately for each component. The final results is the combination of all components. (3) Generating high-level features through deep learning and then utilizing feature selection [9,10]. For instance, to predict traffic flow, Wei et al. [10] first extracted features from traffic flow data by an autoencoder and then combined it with the traffic flow data as sequence features. (4) Introducing time attributes [2,14]. To predict traffic flow, Mou et al. [14] concatenated observed values and time attributes as sequence features. Then sliding window is used to split the sequences into subsequences, including input subsequences and predicted subsequences. The length of the input features window and the step length of window sliding are determined by experiments, while the length of the feature window needs to be predicted is determined by the prediction task. The feature subsequences is the input and prediction values is the output in the LSTM model.

In the fields which relationship between time attributes greatly impacts tasks, researchers modify the internal structure of the LSTM model to utilize temporal information. For example, Baytas et al. [17] proposed the time-aware LSTM model to handle irregular time intervals between patient records. The proposed model decomposes the previous memory into long-term or short-term components and utilizes the time interval to discount short-term memory. Zhu et al. [18] proposed three different structure Time-LSTM models using time intervals in user sequential actions modeling. In Time-LSTM1, they added a time gate based on the time interval and used the time gate and input gate to filter the candidate state. In Time-LSTM2, they added two time gates based on time intervals, which had the same parameters as those used to control the time gate in Time-LSTM1. The first gate was used to control the influence of the last consumed item, and the second gate was used to model users' long-term interest. Time-LSTM3 is similar to Time-LSTM2, but it is modified based on a GRU.

Position encoding is a representative method that supplies the position information of words in natural language processing. The common practice is to encode position information into a vector, add it to word embeddings, and use the addition results as input data. There are multiple ways to encode position [19–21]. For instance, Vaswani et al. [19] substituted an RNN with a Transformer and adopted an absolute position encoding method based on the sine and cosine functions of different frequencies to process the positional information of words. Gehring et al. [20] used a convolutional neural network for a machine translation task, and they used the fully connected layer to learn the vector representation of a word's position.

3   Method

3.1   Problem Description

Suppose $x_1, x_2, \ldots, x_t, \ldots, x_T$ is time series data arranged in chronological order, where $x_t \in \mathbb{R}^N$ and $t = 1, 2, \ldots, T$ stand for observed value as time. Time series prediction are as formula (1),

$$\hat{Y} = f(x_t, x_{t-1}, \cdots x_{t-w}) \tag{1}$$

where $\hat{Y} = \hat{x}_{t+1}, \hat{x}_{t+2}, \ldots, \hat{x}_{t+m}$ stands for prediction values of next m moments. $f()$ is the prediction model, whose inputs are the observed values (ranging from t to $t - w$), and the output is $\hat{Y}$.

Prediction effect can be expressed by formula (2), where $Y = x_{t+1}, x_{t+2}, \ldots, x_{t+m}$ stands for actual values corresponding to $\hat{Y}$. $Loss()$ is the loss function. The goal of model $f()$ is to minimize gap.

$$gap = Loss(Y, \hat{Y}) \tag{2}$$

When LSTM is used as a time series prediction model, according to $f()$ in formula (1), the prediction model structure can be illustrated as in Fig. 1.

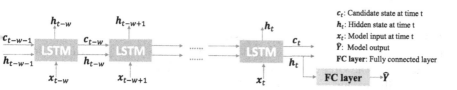

Fig. 1. Time series prediction model based on LSTM

In Fig. 1, LSTM network is mainly composed of input gates, forget gates and output gates. The next candidate state c_t is decided by the input and forget gates, in which input gate controls the new information need to be added to c_t and forget gate controls the information needs to be discard. Output gate controls the update of the hidden state h_{t-1} to h_t, depends on c_t and input data.

From the above discription, there is no special processing for time attributes in LSTM models. When the input sequence contains time attributes, these time attributes are also treated as common features. Therefore, existing LSTM model fails to take advantage of the temporal properties of the time series data. In fact, many time series are closely related to time, and time usually plays a guiding role in prediction.

In order to enable LSTM to fully use the properties of time series data in prediction, it is necessary to design and optimize from model input and model structure.

3.2   Position Encoding of Time Attributes

In this part, we first define time attributes, and then provide the formulas for the position encoding of the time attributes.

Definition 1. ***Time attributes****: A subset of time-related attributes in time series data is defined by formula (3), where $tp_t \in \mathbb{R}^P$ stands for the time attributes and $t_a \in \mathbb{R}^I$ represents all the time-related attributes in the data.*

$$tp_t = \{t \mid t \in t_e \wedge t_e \subseteq t_a \wedge t_e \ may \ affect \ the \ observed \ values\} \qquad (3)$$

The subset concept is emphasized in Definition 1 because we focus on only the properties that may affect the observed values, such as the hour in network traffic data sampled by hour.

Position encoding of time attributes can be discribed using a function $PE()$ defined by formula (4):

$$te_t = PE(tp_t) \qquad (4)$$

where tp_t stands for time attribute and te_t stands for the position encoding result. $PE()$ is divided into three parts as follows:

(1) Time Attributes Preprocessing. This step is the first step of position encoding for the time attributes. The purpose is to perform preprocessing work on the time attributes under actual circumstances, such as selecting time attributes and normalization. Preprocessing can be expressed by formula (5), where $r()$ is a mapping function and ts_t represents the preprocessed time attributes.

$$ts_t = r(tp_t) \qquad (5)$$

(2) Fully Connected Layer. This step is the main part of position encoding for time attributes. We use fully connected (FC) neural network to learn the vector representation of the time attributes, which can eliminate the inconsistency of dimension between the time attributes and the observed values. The input of the FC layer is ts_t, and we mark its output as tv_t.

(3) Time Attributes Postprocessing. This step is the last of position encoding for time attributes. Postprocessing increases the nonlinearity of the time attribute dimension transformation for better expression ability. The postprocessing step is shown in formula (6), where $d()$ is a mapping function. $\boldsymbol{te}_t$ is the final encoding vector of the time attributes and $\boldsymbol{tv}_t$ is the output of the FC layer.

$$\boldsymbol{te}_t = d(\boldsymbol{tv}_t) \tag{6}$$

3.3 PT-LSTM Model

Time series data is closely related to time, but existing models do not make full use of the temporal characteristics of the time series data. Considering that time often provides guidance in series prediction, it should play an important role in the stages of obtaining the input data, updating the internal state and exporting the final results. Moreover, such a role should be an addition to the model rather than a replacement for some existing components in the model. Based on the above items, we propose a new network structure, namely PT-LSTM, which contains two parts: position-encoding based on input data representation and the time gate extended LSTM, i.e., T-LSTM, as illustrated in Fig. 2.

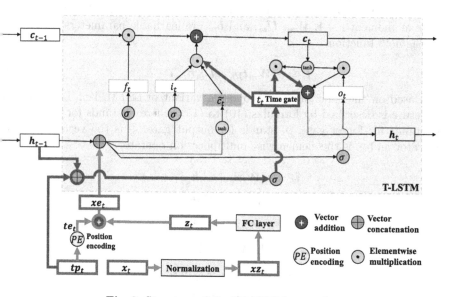

Fig. 2. Structure of the PT-LSTM network

In Fig. 2, The bold color lines represent the new components of the model: input data representation and model structure optimization.

Input Data Representation. First, position encoding result te_t is obtained through $PE()$, which is shown in formula (4). Then the observed value x_t is normalized using formula (7),

$$xz_t = scale(x_t) \tag{7}$$

where $scale()$ stand for the min-max normalization function, which is shown in formula (8).

$$scale(v) = \frac{v - \min(v)}{\max(v) - \min(v)} \tag{8}$$

xz_t is fed into the FC layer of the neural network to obtain its vector representation which has the same dimension as te_t, and its output is represented as z_t. The input data representation xe_t is obtained by adding te_t and z_t element by element.

This representation has two advantages. The first is to explicitly add time information to the input data, and the second is to reduce the interference of the sliding window on the semantics of the subsequence.

Model Structure Optimization. We design a new gate unit based on tp_t, namely, time gate t_t, as shown in formula (9), where h_{t-1} stands for the hidden state at moment $t - 1$. W_m, U_m, and b_m are learnable parameters, while σ is the sigmoid function.

$$t_t = \sigma(W_m tp_t + U_m h_{t-1} + b_m) \tag{9}$$

Based on the time gate, we propose a variant of LSTM, i.e., T-LSTM. Its structure is described by formulas (10) to (15), where i_t stands for input gate, f_t stands for forget gate, o_t stands for output gate, $+$ is the vector addition operator and $\odot$ is the elementwise multiplication operator.

$$i_t = \sigma(W_i x_t + U_i h_{t-1} + b_i) \tag{10}$$

$$f_t = \sigma(W_f x_t + U_f h_{t-1} + b_f) \tag{11}$$

$$o_t = \sigma(W_o x_t + U_o h_{t-1} + b_o) \tag{12}$$

$$\tilde{c}_t = \tanh(W_c x_t + U_c h_{t-1} + b_c) \tag{13}$$

$$c_t = f_t \odot c_{t-1} + t_t \odot i_t \odot \tilde{c}_t \tag{14}$$

$$h_t = o_t \odot \tanh(c_t) + t_t \odot \tanh(c_t) \tag{15}$$

The effect of time gate t_t in the model is achieved by formulas (14) and (15), where c_t is the internal state at moment t and $\tilde{c}_t$ is the candidate state at moment t.

Specifically, time gate t_t has three functions. First, time gate t_t controls the input information at time t. Candidate states are filtered by not only the input gate i_t but also the time gate t_t. Second, time gate t_t contributes to the internal states to store the time attributes. The time attributes are first stored in t_t and then transferred to c_t. Third, time gate t_t also controls the output information at time t. The final output is the sum of the two parts, as shown in formula (15); i.e., the first part is controlled by the output gate o_t, and the second part is controlled by the time gate t_t. Inspired by ResNet [22], formula (15) realizes the complementary role of time.

Discussion. In the PT-LSTM model, position encoding not only makes the input data carry temporal information but also eliminates, to some extent, the negative effects caused by parameter selection of the sliding window. In the new model structure where the time gate is added, time attributes play a control roles in the stages of acquiring input data, updating the internal state and outputing the result, which helps the model sufficiently exploit time attributes. Among LSTM-based time series prediction methods that considered time attributes, Kong et al. [2] and Mou et al. [14] concatenated time attributes and the observed values to form an input vector and used an LSTM model that has no specific processing step for time attributes. Zhu et al. [18] directly controlled the time gate with observed values and the time attributes at moment t, whereas the PT-LSTM model replaces the observed value at moment t with the hidden state at moment $t-1$, which can provide the correlation between the input series. In addition, compared with the time gate exploited by Zhu et al. [18], the time gate in the PT-LSTM network also has control over the output of the model.

3.4   Time Series Prediction Based on PT-LSTM

The time series prediction based on PT-LSTM is illustrated in Fig. 3, where tp_i represents the moment i and x_i represents the observed value at moment i. The prediction process mainly includes three parts: sequence preprocessing, position encoding and model prediction.

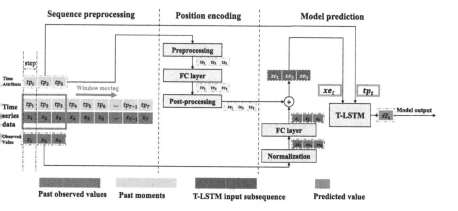

Fig. 3. Time series prediction based on PT-LSTM

Sequence Preprocessing. The purpose of sequence preprocessing is to divide time series data according to the prediction task. We divide time series data into three types of subsequences: past observed values, past moments, and future observed values. The window length of the past moments and the past observed values is $w + 1$, and the window length of the future observed values is m. The three types of windows slide synchronously, and the sliding step length is determined by the 'step' parameter in Fig. 3. After partitioning, available samples will be formed.

Position Encoding. The purpose of position encoding module is to obtain a vector representation of past moments subsequence. Figure 3 shows the processing of a single sample. Firstly, past moments subsequences (grey parts) is preprocessed by formula (5). Then it is fed into the FC layer. Finally, it is handled by formula (6) and the result is represented as te_t.

Model Prediction. We first use time series sample data to train the PT-LSTM model. The purpose of model training is to learn the parameters, including W, U, M, and b, as shown in formulas (9) to (13), and the weights of FC layer. We calculate the loss of the predicted values and the future observed values using formula (2) and choose the mean squared error as the loss function. The parameters of the PT-LSTM network are updated by using mini-batch gradient descent. In the prediction process, as shown in Fig. 3, the past observed values subsequences (green parts) is handled by normalization and FC layer. Then, the result z_t and te_t are added element by element to obtain input subsequence xe_t for the model. The other input is the past moment subsequences tp_t. The input gate, forget gate, output gate and candidate state of the model are mainly controlled by the input subsequences. The output of the model is the predicted values.

4   Experiments

4.1   Datasets and Metrics

We conducted comparative experiments on the following publicly available time series datasets.

1. Pollution [23]: This is a Beijing fine particulate matter with diameter less than 2.5 μm (PM2.5) dataset, which was collected by the US Embassy in China from 2010 to 2014. The sampling frequency is once per hour. PM2.5 and hour attributes are chose to predict PM2.5.
2. BikeSharing [24]: This dataset contains the number of bikes rented between 2011 and 2012 in the Capital Bikeshare system in America. The sampling frequency is once per hour. Total number of rental bikes (CNT) and hour (HR) attributes are chose to predict CNT.

3. TAS 2016 [25]: This dataset is the annual electricity demand of Tasmania (TAS), Australia, in 2016. The sampling frequency is twice per hour. To maintain the consistency of the sampling frequency, demand attribute is aggregated by hour. Total demand and hour attributes are chose to predict total demand.

The length of the time series and sampling frequency of each dataset are shown in Table 1.

Table 1. Time series length and sampling frequency

Dataset	Length of the time series	Sampling frequency
Pollution	43,800	Hourly
BikeSharing	17,379	Hourly
TAS 2016	8785	Hourly

Four evolution metrics, Root Mean Square Error (RMSE), Mean Absolute Error (MAE), Mean Absolute Percentage Error(MAPE) and Symmetric Mean Absolute Percentage Error (SMAPE) are used to evaluate the performance of the forecast model.

$$RMSE = \sqrt{\frac{1}{n} \sum_{i=1}^{n} (\hat{y}_i - y_i)^2} \tag{16}$$

$$MAE = \frac{1}{n} \sum_{i=1}^{n} |\hat{y}_i - y_i| \tag{17}$$

$$MAPE = \frac{100\%}{n} \sum_{i=1}^{n} |\frac{\hat{y}_i - y_i}{y_i}| \tag{18}$$

$$SMAPE = \frac{100\%}{n} \sum_{i=1}^{n} |\frac{\hat{y}_i - y_i}{\frac{|\hat{y}_i| + |y_i|}{2}}| \tag{19}$$

4.2   Experimental Settings

1) Experiment 1. Effect of the PT-LSTM Model. In this experiment, we validate the effectiveness of the PT-LSTM model. The comparison methods include LSTM, ARIMA [1], support vector regression (SVR) [26,27], LSTM-F [2], and LSTM-T1 [18], Attention-LSTM, MLP, RNN, LSTM and GRU. ARIMA is the commonly used prediction method in the field of time series. SVR is a commonly used regression method in the field of machine learning. LSTM-F refers to the model that uses time attributes as common features and uses LSTM to execute prediction tasks. LSTM-T1 is based on the Time-LSTM1 model proposed by Zhu et al. [18], which adds a time gate to the internal structure of LSTM. We replace the time interval in Time-LSTM1 with time attributes and ignore the peephole technique for LSTM [28]. Attention-LSTM refers to the LSTM model that has the attention mechanism. MLP stands for Multilayer Perceptron, and this paper uses ReLU as its activation function. RNN, GRU and LSTM are commonly used recurrent neural networks.

(2) Experiment 2. Individual Effects of Position Encoding and the Time Gate. The purpose of this experiment is to validate the effectiveness of the new components related to input data representation and model structure optimization in the PT-LSTM model. The comparison method is LSTM.

(3) Experiment 3. Impact of Different Processing Methods on the Time Attributes. This experiment aims to explore the influence of different time attributes processing methods on the prediction results. The processing methods of time attributes in PT-LSTM include pre-processing function $r()$ described by formula (5) and postprocessing function $d()$ described by formula (6). The former is mainly used to perform some necessary preprocessing for the time attribute, such as normalization, while the latter is mainly used to increase the nonlinearity of the position encoding process. The preprocessing operation in this experiment mainly used the $scale()$ function. The comparison method is identity function $idf()$, which is shown in formula (20).

$$idf(c) = c \tag{20}$$

The postprocessing operation mainly uses common activation functions in deep learning, including $sin()$, $tanh()$, $sigmoid()$, and the comparison method is also the identity function $idf()$.

4.3 Experimental Results

(1) Result of Effect of the PT-LSTM Model. In the experiments, parameters w and m are set to 4 and 1, respectively, indicating that the observed values for the past 5 moments are used to predict the observed value at the next moment. The sliding step length is set to 1. 64% of each dataset is used for training, 16% is used for verification, and 20% is used for testing. The LSTM-related models are built using PyTorch 1.1 and trained on a machine equipped with a Tesla V100 GPU. Validation errors are recorded in each training epoch, and the model parameters used in the test phase are the model parameters corresponding to the minimum validation errors. SVR uses grid search to determine the parameters, and ARIMA(p, d, q) uses the Bayesian information criterion (BIC) to determine the parameters. Based on the above settings, the experimental results are shown in Table 2.

Table 2 shows that PT-LSTM achieves best prediction results under each evaluation metric on the BikeSharing dataset and TAS2016 dataset, and achieves best prediction results on RMSE and MAE on all three datasets, which show the

Table 2. The prediction results of different models

Model	Pollution				BikeSharing				TAS2016			
	RMSE	MAE	MAPE	SMAPE	RMSE	MAE	MAPE	SMAPE	RMSE	MAE	MAPE	SMAPE
MLP	24.311	13.203	4.11E+08	**20.434**	70.198	46.833	52.479	48.369	70.328	50.59	2.463	2.422
RNN	24.775	14.084	**3.52E+08**	25.301	67.161	44.296	42.854	43.252	69.061	48.878	2.389	2.363
GRU	24.404	13.704	3.84E+08	22.607	58.896	38.59	33.74	31.311	66.296	47.604	2.318	2.317
LSTM	24.215	13.013	3.84E+08	22.356	60.616	39.686	37.633	40.329	70.702	52.569	2.592	2.535
Attention-LSTM	24.046	13.014	4.43E+08	22.354	58.576	37.616	32.854	26.901	63.334	44.598	2.175	2.146
LSTM-T1	23.848	12.861	4.73E+08	22.253	50.397	31.919	26.908	23.02	60.117	42.746	2.078	2.071
LSTM-F	26.442	16.189	3.81E+08	25.35	51.314	33.438	27.016	26.541	62.367	44.609	2.169	2.162
SVR	41.389	34.355	8.42E+08	55.073	87.784	61.844	135.699	46.775	95.208	77.999	3.860	3.75
ARIMA	93.634	68.095	1.054E+09	76.281	232.44	175.003	475.372	86.048	207.043	165.499	8.298	7.958
PT-LSTM	**23.346**	**12.757**	4.39E+08	22.428	**47.35**	**29.827**	**24.39**	**20.744**	**56.635**	**39.49**	**1.931**	**1.9**

effectiveness of PT-LSTM. In terms of RMSE, the prediction result of the LSTM model on the Pollution dataset is only 0.869 higher than that of the PT-LSTM model. This may because the data in the Pollution dataset have a complicated relationship with time and no periodic pattern, which is significantly different from the BikeSharing and TAS 2016 datasets.

(2) Result of Individual Effects of Position Encoding and the Time Gate. The prediction results of the PT-LSTM model and the two other models that can process time attributes are shown in Table 3. LSTM with only positional encoding is denoted as LSTM-PE. Model with only the new LSTM structure is denoted as T-LSTM.

Table 3. The prediction results of the LSTM-PE and T-LSTM models

Model	Pollution				BikeSharing				TAS2016			
	RMSE	MAE	MAPE	SMAPE	RMSE	MAE	MAPE	SMAPE	RMSE	MAE	MAPE	SMAPE
LSTM	24.215	13.013	3.84E+08	22.356	60.616	39.686	37.633	40.329	70.702	52.569	2.592	2.535
LSTM-PE	24.199	13.025	**3.80E+08**	21.949	50.935	33.624	30.789	27.943	64.608	48.31	2.356	2.361
T-LSTM	24.115	**12.447**	5.25E+08	**20.258**	47.723	30.172	27.71	21.591	59.419	41.866	2.038	2.007
PT-LSTM	**23.346**	12.757	4.39E+08	22.428	**47.35**	**29.827**	**24.39**	**20.744**	**56.635**	**39.49**	**1.931**	**1.9**

Table 3 shows compared with the LSTM model, the prediction effects improve on T-LSTM and LSTM-PE models, especially on the BikeSharing and TAS 2016 datasets. In terms of RMSE, PT-LSTM model achieves best prediction effect. These results demonstrate the effectiveness of position encoding and time gate extension of LSTM proposed in our paper.

(3) Result of Impact of Different Time Attributes Processing Methods. As described in Sect. 3.2, the preprocessing function $r()$ and postprocessing funtion $d()$ are used in the position encoding stage. The experimental results for the influence on different $r()$ and $d()$ in PT-LSTM prediction is shown in Table 4, 5 and 6.

Table 4. The influence of different $r()$ and $d()$ functions on the results on the Pollution dataset

$r()$	$d()$							
	scale()				idf()			
	RMSE	MAE	MAPE	SMAPE	RMSE	MAE	MAPE	SMAPE
tanh()	24.143	13.025	5.28E+08	23.365	**24.466**	**13.894**	5.14E+08	**26.16**
sin()	23.754	13.245	4.64E+08	24.109	69.65	58.649	1.06E+09	73.964
$sigmoid()$	24.573	14.738	4.99E+08	27.402	24.798	14.479	5.27E+08	26.857
$idf(x)$	**23.346**	**12.757**	**4.40E+08**	**22.428**	25.095	14.223	**5.04E+08**	26.939

Table 5. The influence of different $r()$ and $d()$ functions on the results on the Bike-Sharing dataset

$r()$	$d()$							
	scale()				idf()			
	RMSE	MAE	MAPE	SMAPE	RMSE	MAE	MAPE	SMAPE
tanh()	**47.35**	29.827	24.39	**20.744**	51.902	33.816	**26.876**	24.706
sin()	47.359	29.826	24.339	20.757	**49.771**	**32.578**	27.833	**24.286**
$sigmoid()$	66.775	46.051	57.181	32.883	49.802	32.835	29.933	29.688
$idf(x)$	47.366	**29.824**	**24.288**	20.777	51.725	33.361	29.136	28.07

Table 6. The influence of different $r()$ and $d()$ functions on the results on the TAS2016 dataset

$r()$	$d()$							
	scale()				idf()			
	RMSE	MAE	MAPE	SMAPE	RMSE	MAE	MAPE	SMAPE
tanh()	56.652	39.496	1.931	1.9	**69.505**	**52.382**	**2.528**	**2.543**
sin()	56.647	39.495	1.931	1.9	72.233	55.69	2.683	2.7
$sigmoid()$	63.359	45.601	2.228	2.197	74.85	55.57	2.696	2.629
$idf(x)$	**56.635**	**39.49**	**1.931**	**1.9**	97.315	81.591	3.918	3.993

It can be seen from Table 4, 5 and 6 that the choices of $r()$ and $d()$ do have impacts on the prediction results of the PT-LSTM model. The PT-LSTM model achieves best performance on the Pollution and TAS2016 datasets when the min-max normalization $scale()$ and no nonlinear mapping $idf()$ are used. On the BikeSharing dataset, in terms of RMSE, the PT-LSTM achieves best performance, when $scale()$ and tanh() are used.

From Table 4, 5 and 6 under the same conditions, the preprocessing operation $scale()$ can obtain better results than the preprocessing operation $idf()$. When the time attributes are normalized, various postprocessing operations have little change on prediction results. The reason may be that if the observed value has been normalized, the time attributes should also be normalized, by which the adverse effect caused by the dimension difference between the time attribute and observed value can be avoided. The output values of tanh(), sin() and $sigmoid()$ on interval $[0,1]$ are relatively close to each other.

Therefore, time attributes should be preprocessed, using methods such as max-min normalization. With the normalized time attributes, postprocessing operations, i.e., nonlinear mappings, are not necessary.

5   Conclusion

To make full use of the time attributes in time series data to achieve better prediction results, we propose a novel method called position encoding and time gate long short-term memory(PT-LSTM) in this paper. We first obtain a vector representation of the time attributes through position encoding. Then, we integrate this vector with the observed values vector by elementwise addition. Furthermore, to utilize the time information in the prediction model, we extend the LSTM model by adding a specifically designed time gate. This time gate is mainly controlled by the time attributes and can affect the processes of acquiring the input data, updating the internal state, and outputting the results of the model. The experimental results on three datasets show that the PT-LSTM model outperforms the existing methods. Future work may include further exploring the relationship between time and the observed values, as well as other ways to add mechanisms that handle time to the LSTM model.

References

1. Ariyo, A.A., Adewumi, A.O., Ayo, C.K.: Stock price prediction using the arima model. In: 2014 UKSim-AMSS 16th International Conference on Computer Modelling and Simulation, pp. 106–112 (2014)
2. Kong, W., Dong, Z.Y., Jia, Y., Hill, D.J., Xu, Y., Zhang, Y.: Short-term residential load forecasting based on lstm recurrent neural network. IEEE Trans. Smart Grid **10**(1), 841–851 (2019)
3. Tsai, Y., Zeng, Y., Chang, Y.: Air pollution forecasting using RNN with LSTM. In: International Conference on Dependable, Autonomic and Secure Computing, pp. 1074–1079 (2018)
4. Box, G.E.P., Jenkins, G.M.: Time Series Analysis: Forecasting and Control. Prentice Hall PTR (1994)
5. Wang, H., Lu, L., Dong, S., Qian, Z., Wei, H.: A novel work zone short-term vehicle-type specific traffic speed prediction model through the hybrid emd-arima framework. Transportmetrica B-Transp. Dyn. **4**(3), 159–186 (2016)
6. Hochreiter, S., Schmidhuber, J.: Long short-term memory. Neural Comput. **9**(8), 1735–1780 (1997)
7. Chung, J., Gulcehre, C., Cho, K., Bengio, Y.: Empirical evaluation of gated recurrent neural networks on sequence modeling. arXiv preprint arXiv:1412.3555 (2014)
8. Azzouni, A., Pujolle, G.: A long short-term memory recurrent neural network framework for network traffic matrix prediction. arXiv: Networking and Internet Architecture (2017)

9. Bao, W., Yue, J., Rao, Y.: A deep learning framework for financial time series using stacked autoencoders and long-short term memory. PLoS One **12**(7) (2017)

10. Wei, W., Honghai, Wu., Ma, H.: An autoencoder and LSTM-based traffic flow prediction method. Sensors **19**(13), 2946 (2019)

11. Qin, D., Yu, J., Zou, G., Yong, R., Zhao, Q., Zhang, B.: A novel combined prediction scheme based on CNN and LSTM for urban pm2.5 concentration. IEEE Access **7**, 20050–20059 (2019)

12. Wang, Yi., Gan, D., Sun, M., Zhang, N., Zongxiang, Lu., Kang, C.: Probabilistic individual load forecasting using pinball loss guided LSTM. Appl. Energy **235**, 10–20 (2019)

13. Choi, E., Bahadori, M.T., Schuetz, A., Stewart, W.F., Sun, J.: Doctor AI: predicting clinical events via recurrent neural networks. In: Machine Learning for Healthcare Conference, pp. 301–318 (2015)

14. Mou, L., Zhao, P., Xie, H., Chen, Y.: T-LSTM: a long short-term memory neural network enhanced by temporal information for traffic flow prediction. IEEE Access **7**, 98053–98060 (2019)

15. Gers, F.A., Schmidhuber, J., Cummins, F.: Learning to forget: continual prediction with LSTM. Neural Comput. **12**(10), 2451–2471 (2000)

16. Bedi, J., Toshniwal, D.: Empirical mode decomposition based deep learning for electricity demand forecasting. IEEE Access **6**, 49144–49156 (2018)

17. Baytas, I.M., Xiao, C., Zhang, X., Wang, F., Jain, A.K., Zhou, J.: Patient subtyping via time-aware LSTM networks. In: ACM Knowledge Discovery and Data Mining, pp. 65–74 (2017)

18. Zhu, Y., et al.: What to do next: Modeling user behaviors by time-LSTM. In: International Joint Conferences on Artificial Intelligence, pp. 3602–3608 (2017)

19. Vaswani, A., et al.: Attention is all you need. In: Annual Conference on Neural Information Processing Systems, pp. 5998–6008 (2017)

20. Gehring, J., Auli, M., Grangier, D., Yarats, D., Dauphin, Y.N.: Convolutional sequence to sequence learning. In: International Conference on Machine Learning, pp. 1243–1252 (2017)

21. Shaw, P., Uszkoreit, J., Vaswani, A.: Self-attention with relative position representations. In: Annual Conference of the North American Chapter of the Association for Computational Linguistics, vol. 2, pp. 464–468 (2018)

22. He, K., Zhang, X., Ren, S., Jian, S.: Deep residual learning for image recognition. In: IEEE Conference on Computer Vision and Pattern Recognition, pp. 770–778 (2016)

23. Liang, X., et al.: Assessing beijing's pm2.5 pollution: severity, weather impact, apec and winter heating. Proc. Roy. Soc. A Math. Phys. Eng. Sci. **471**(2182), 20150257 (2015)

24. Fanaeet, H., Gama, J.: Event labeling combining ensemble detectors and background knowledge. Progress Artif. Intell. **2**(2), 113–127 (2014)

25. AEMO. Aggregated price and demand data (2016). https://www.aemo.com. au/energy-systems/electricity/national-electricity-market-nem/data-nem/ aggregated-data

26. Castro-Neto, M., Jeong, Y.-S., Jeong, M.-K., Han, L.D.: Online-svr for short-term traffic flow prediction under typical and atypical traffic conditions. Expert Syst. Appl. **36**(3, Part 2), 6164–6173 (2009)

27. Wu, C., Ho, J., Lee, D.T.: Travel-time prediction with support vector regression. IEEE Trans. Intell. Transp. Syst. **5**(4), 276–281 (2004)

28. Gers, F.A., Schmidhuber, J.: Recurrent nets that time and count. In: International Joint Conference on Neural Networks, vol. 3, pp. 189–194 (2000)

Loss Attenuation for Time Series Prediction Respecting Categories of Values

Jialing Zhang[1], Zheng Liu[1(✉)], Yanwen Qu[2], and Yun Li[1]

[1] Jiangsu Key Laboratory of BDSIP, Nanjing University of Posts
and Telecommunications, Nanjing, China
{b18031606,zliu,liyun}@njupt.edu.cn
[2] School of Computer Information and Engineering, Jiangxi Normal University,
Nanchang, China
qu_yw@jxnu.edu.cn

Abstract. Forecasting future values is a core task in many applications dealing with multivariate time series data. In pollution monitoring, for example, forecasting future $PM_{2.5}$ values in air is very common, which is a crucial indicator of the air quality index (AQI). These values in time series are sometimes affiliated with category information for easy understanding. As an illustration, it is often to categorize the $PM_{2.5}$ values to indicate the levels of health concern or health risk based on predefined category intervals. Forecasting future values without considering the categories leads to potential inconsistency between the categories of predicted values and real values. The underlying reason is that the objective during training is to minimize the overall prediction error, e.g., mean square error, which does not respect the category information. We propose a category adaptive loss attenuation method with respect to training samples in stochastic gradient descent for multi-horizon time series forecasting. The proposed weighting strategy considers training samples' closeness to category boundaries in a parameterized cost-sensitive manner. The results from extensive experiments demonstrate that the weighting method can improve the overall performance of category-aware time series prediction.

Keywords: Loss attenuation · Sample weighting · Category-aware time series prediction · Temporal convolutional networks

1 Introduction

Predicting values in the near future is necessary in many applications dealing with multivariate time series data, such as pollution monitoring [20], energy

This work is supported in part by the National Key Research and Development Program of China under Grant 2018YFB1003702 and Nanjing University of Posts and Telecommunications under Grant NY219084.

Forecast	Friday 3/19/21	Saturday 3/20/21	Sunday 3/21/21
OKC	PM Good	PM Good	Ozone Good
Tulsa	PM Good	PM Moderate	PM Moderate
Lawton	PM Good	PM Good	Ozone Good

(a) Current air quality in New York[a]   (b) Air quality forecasts in Oklahoma[b]

Fig. 1. Air qualities in various cities ([a]https://www.airnow.gov/?city=NewYork&state=NY&country=USA) ([b]https://www.deq.ok.gov/air-quality-division/ambient-monitoring/current-air-quality-forecasts/)

scheduling [10], and financial management [25]. Take the air quality index (AQI) in pollution monitoring as an example. AQI shows the current or forecasted air pollution level, which is calculated based on the concentrations of certain pollutants, e.g., $PM_{2.5}$[1], PM_{10}, SO_2, NO_2, etc. An accurate estimation of AQI can provide practical suggestions for citizens and help the government make better decisions on pollution control, making it an essential task to forecast the density of these pollutants in the air.

It is common for the values in time series to be categorized based on certain pre-defined intervals for ease of understanding for the public, and so is the case with AQI. The AQI values, as well as the pollutant measurements, are categorized into different levels to indicate the level of health concerns or health risks, while the categorization standards are variable among different countries. Figure 1 shows two Web page screenshots about current air quality and forecasted air qualities in various cities in the United States. As we can see in Fig. 1 that the category information is more notable than the values. Both the government and the public even care more about these categories than the real values.

Many other applications also involve similar category information. In energy scheduling, the category of predicted energy consumption indicates energy efficiency level, which provides a direct indicator of the energy consumption status. In financial management, the category of forecasted stock volatility reveals financial risk status which is more understandable to investors, although the detailed risk score might benefit the investment decisions.

Unfortunately, the categorization might bring a potential issue that when the forecasted values lie around the category interval's boundaries, the

---

[1] The measurements of $PM_{2.5}$ are the density values ($\mu g/m^3$) of particles with an aerodynamic diameter smaller than 2.5 μm. The measurements of PM_{10} are similar.

corresponding categories would be highly probably incorrect, even if the residuals[2] of the predicted values are small. The underlying reason is that the training objective of prediction models is to minimize the overall prediction error, i.e., the differences between the predicted values and the real values, not the category misclassified error. This leads to the potential inconsistency between the categories of predicted values and real values.

It seems that formulating the category prediction as a separate classification problem could solve the issue. But there is no guarantee that the predicted categories will be consistent with the predicted values, i.e., a predicted value is within the interval of its corresponding category. When inconsistency happens, by ignoring the predicted categories and using the category of the predicted values, we are back to the start.

Another promising way is to elevate the prediction precision. With the speedup of parallel computing on powerful GPUs [5], a motley collection of neural architectures, such as Recurrent Neural Networks (RNN) [11], Long Short-Term Memory network (LSTM) [14], Gated Recurrent Unit (GRU) [6], and Residual Network (ResNet) [13], are constructed to advance the time series prediction in many fields [7,27]. Compared with traditional methods [2,9,23,26,29], approaches based on deep learning conquer the nonlinearity and the complexity of multivariate time series by extracting latent features and combining both long-term and short-term dependencies. However, advanced prediction models aim at lowering prediction errors. These models cannot solve incorrect category prediction with the ignorance of the pre-defined intervals of categories. The overall prediction error is dominated by training samples with small marginal benefits.

In this paper, we contribute to solving this problem from the perspective of data characteristics and the training process. We design an adaptive loss attenuation strategy with respect to category information to weight training samples during stochastic gradient descent (SGD) for better category prediction without relaxing the prediction residuals. The strategy emphasizes promising samples by adaptively weighting the samples' residuals, which could boost the category accuracy substantially. As we will see soon, the category prediction accuracy is sensitive to those samples close to the interval boundaries of categories. We attenuate the loss adaptively and asymmetrically in a parameterized cost-sensitive manner during the dynamic training process, intending to reduce the prediction residuals of those samples for better category prediction. The prediction model with loss attenuation also discourages samples with large prediction residuals. These large residuals could dominate the model loss, resulting in unstable prediction performance.

For simplicity, we concentrate on $PM_{2.5}$ forecasting to demonstrate the proposed adaptive loss attenuation method. We construct temporal convolutional

---

[2] The error of an observed value is the deviation of the observed value from the (unobservable) true value of a quantity of interest, and the residual of an observed value is the difference between the observed value and the estimated value of the quantity of interest. In this paper, sometimes, we use error to indicate residual for ease of explanation when there is no misunderstanding.

networks (TCN) [1] serving as the prediction model, which can capture long-term dependency in multivariate time series for predicting future values. We performed extensive experiments, whose results show improved category prediction performance and substantiate the effectiveness.

The rest of this paper is organized as follows. First, we formulate the problem of multivariate time series forecasting with categories in Sect. 3. We explain the proposed adaptive loss attenuation strategy in Sect. 4 and report the experimental results in Sect. 5. Finally, we conclude this paper in Sect. 6.

2 Related Work

Time series prediction has been studied for decades, from traditional autoregressive integrated moving average (ARIMA) [2] and support vector regression (SVR) [23], to newly proposed modular regression model fbprophet [26]. In this paper, we concentrate on neural prediction models, so we do not include non-neural models in this section to avoid redundancy. Interested readers can refer to many nice surveys and books like [9] and [29].

2.1 Loss Functions and Their Weights

Loss functions measure how good a prediction model is during the training process in terms of whether the model can output the expected outcomes. Accessible loss functions in regression analysis include square loss, absolute loss, Huber loss, ϵ-insensitive loss, etc. [28].

Square loss is the most common loss in regression problems, which measures the square of the errors between real values and predicted values. However, square loss is sensitive to outliers, so training prediction models with square loss pay more attention to outliers and deteriorate the overall prediction performance. Absolute loss is more robust to outliers than square loss since it does not increase rapidly with increasing errors. Absolute loss is not smooth when the errors approach 0, and it has a fixed gradient, which is large for small losses. Huber loss is a combination of square loss and absolute loss where a parameter δ serves as the segment point. Huber loss is quadratic for small errors within this segment point and linear for large errors beyond this segment point. Several other loss functions, such as ϵ-insensitive loss, quantile loss, and log-cosh loss, are used in practice. ϵ-insensitive loss is often used in support vector regression (SVR). Quantile loss is an extended form of absolute loss for forecasting quantile values. Log-cosh loss is the logarithm of the hyperbolic cosine of the errors.

Researchers recently proposed several new loss functions to handle the imbalanced data in classifications [3,8,17]. Most of them reweight samples based on existing loss functions. Focal loss [17] is a weighted version of cross entropy loss based on the classification probabilities. Active bias [3] reweights samples with high prediction variance or near the threshold of classification. Class-balanced loss [8] introduces a weighting factor that is inversely proportional to the effective number of samples. Lu et al. [19] proposed shrinkage loss for deep regression, which is based on shrinkage estimators and the absolute distances between predicted values and real values. Chen et al. [4] proposed a cost-sensitive loss based on interval error evaluation. They enlarged the cost of intervals with small ranges and proposed a piecewise loss function and a corresponding continuous version based on a logarithmic function.

2.2 Time Series Prediction Based on Neural Networks

The nonlinearity and the complexity of multivariate time series bring challenges for traditional time series prediction methods. Researchers recently addressed this issue with the help of deep learning based approaches for better performance, where a motley collection of neural architectures is constructed to simulate the nonlinearity structure in multivariate time series.

Among various neural architectures, recurrent neural networks (RNN) are the most popular approach for sequence modeling by far. Traditional RNN has issues like gradient vanishing and gradient explosion when training with stochastic gradient descent (SGD) [21]. Long short-term memory (LSTM) [14] and gated recurrent unit (GRU) [6] are two popular RNN-based approaches. LSTM has a selective memory function and can solve gradient-related issues, while training RNNs with LSTM blocks requires careful design of the optimization process [22]. GRU is a simplified version of LSTM with comparable performance, which has fewer parameters than LSTM. GRU includes a forget gate and has no output gate. Residual network (ResNet) [13] inspires RNNs by incorporating the residual connection mechanism with RNNs, whose advantages are fewer hidden units, reduced training time, and improved prediction accuracy.

The recently proposed temporal convolutional networks (TCN) [1] can overcome the disadvantages of RNNs and obtain excellent prediction results, which we will discuss in Sect. 4.2. Compared with traditional time series prediction methods, deep learning based approaches can extract latent features from multivariate time series and combine long-term and short-term dependencies for improved prediction performance.

3 Time Series Forecasting with Categories

Let $X_i = (x_i^1, x_i^2, \cdots, x_i^m)$ be the measurements of the time series at time i, where x_i^j is the measurement of variable j at time i. Let $X = (X_1, X_2, ..., X_T) \in \mathbb{R}^{m \times T}$ denote the multivariate time series. Multivariate time series forecasting with categories is to predict future values and their categories up to a particular time horizon, which is called as *lead time* or *prediction horizon* in some applications. We denote the predicted values in future as $Y = (Y_{T+1}, Y_{T+2}, ..., Y_{T+p}) \in \mathbb{R}^{m' \times p}$, where p is the prediction horizon and usually $m' \leq m$. $Y_j = (y_j^1, y_j^2, \cdots, y_j^{m'})$ is the predicted measurements of the multivariate time series at time j. It is known as p-step-ahead prediction problem or multi-horizon prediction problem when $p > 1$. Since the categories are decided based on pre-defined intervals, we use function $\mathcal{C}(\cdot)$ to denote the categories of predicted values according to intervals.

4   Category-Aware Adaptive Loss Attenuation

Categorizing predicted values based on pre-defined intervals may lead to potential inconsistency between the prediction value category and the real value category. We focus on neural prediction models in this paper. The objective of neural prediction models is to minimize certain loss functions, one of the key components is the prediction residuals. Accessible loss functions include square loss, absolute loss, Huber loss, etc. All are distance-based loss functions [24, 28], along with many other similar ones, because the prediction residuals are measured by the overall distances between predicted values and real values empirically.

Stochastic gradient descent (SGD) plays the most important role in training neural networks, which optimizes the loss function by approximating the gradient descents [21, 22]. It randomly samples a small number of training instances, called a "mini-batch", and updates the model parameters by evaluating their gradients. This process is iteratively performed until an approximate minimum is obtained. Most training algorithms sample training instances uniformly, i.e., each sample has the same probability of being included in a mini-batch. In practice, this sampling process is done by generating a random perturbation of all training instances and scanning the perturbation sequentially to ensure that the training algorithms can see all the training instances.

There are a few existing research efforts on weighting samples under the context of classifications or regression [3, 4, 8, 17, 19]. Suppose L is a popular loss for regression problems, let s_i denote a single training instance, then the new loss function is

$$\mathcal{L} = \sum_i w_i L(\boldsymbol{\theta}; \boldsymbol{s}_i) + \lambda \Omega(\boldsymbol{\theta}), \tag{1}$$

where w_i is the weight for $\boldsymbol{s}_i$. λ and $\Omega(\cdot)$ are the regularization parameter and the regularization term, respectively. As introduced in Sect. 2, most of the above approaches do not consider categories and are not suitable for use in forecasting with categories. We will discuss the characterizes of the training process for time series forecasting with categories and introduce our category-aware adaptive loss attenuation for weighting samples during SGD in the following section.

4.1   Boundary Closeness of Samples to Category Effective Areas

During training, the optimizer continuously minimizes the loss function, e.g., the mean prediction errors. It has no idea about how reducing the mean prediction error will contribute to a higher category prediction accuracy. Although it is intuitive that categories with high prediction accuracy should have low prediction residuals. In this paper, we propose to emphasize the optimization of the samples that can boost the category prediction accuracy, as demonstrated by the example in Fig. 2.

Suppose we employ a time series prediction model to forecast the future values based on the $PM_{2.5}$ data set used in the later section about experiments. We can reveal the relationship between predicted values and real values in Fig. 2,

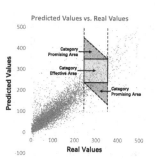

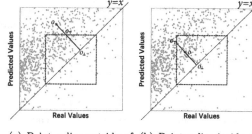

(a) Point o lies outside of the Category effective area.

(b) Point o lies inside the Category effective area.

Fig. 2. Category effective area and category promising area (Color figure online)

Fig. 3. Boundary closeness examples

where the horizontal axis represents the real values, and the vertical axis represents their corresponding predicted values. Each point represents a sample in the data set. It is easy to see that in the ideal but unrealistic case of time series prediction, all points in Fig. 2 should lie on the line $y = x$, indicating that residuals are all zero. The green square area in Fig. 2 corresponds to the category c whose interval is 250 to 350, indicating severely polluted air quality. The coordinates of the lower left corner are $(250, 250)$, and the coordinates of the upper right corner are $(350, 350)$. All points lying inside the green square area have consistent predicted categories and real categories, so we call this area the category effective area. All points between the two dotted lines but not in the category effective area are points with wrong predicted categories. To improve the category prediction accuracy, we should focus on these points to lower their residuals, i.e., to push them towards line $y = x$. It is not hard to see that points outside of the category effective area and close to its upper or lower boundaries could have a chance to belong to the correct category in the later training iterations, while points inside the category effective area but close to its upper or lower boundaries could escape from the area. Although the accurate probabilities of these promising points are difficult to estimate, we can tell based on Fig. 2 that points with the same closeness to the boundaries of the category effective area may not be equally promising because their prediction residuals are not equal. Points with reasonable prediction residuals are likely to lower their residuals during later training iterations, while points with small prediction residuals have difficulties to further reduce their residuals. On the other hand, points always having large residuals are considered to be highly uncertain and should be ignored [3]. Inspired by the concept of instance hardness in curriculum learning [31], we propose boundary closeness as a measurement of how promising the points can boost the category accuracy. We first introduce the definition of category promising area. As shown by the red areas in Fig. 2, category promising area contains the points whose prediction residuals are at most twice of the maximum allowable residuals. Maximum allowable residual of a point is the maximum possible value of its residual with respect to a certain prediction model when the predicted category of the point is correct. The dotted line indicates the category effective areas in Fig. 3. Figure 3a and Fig. 3b demonstrate the above two circumstances of boundary closeness, whether a point is in the category promising area or the category effective area. We have to consider both the boundaries closeness and the prediction residuals in the way of emphasizing points close to boundaries of category effective area and ignoring points with large prediction residuals. Let o denote the point in red, and $o_\perp$ denote the intersection point between line $y = x$ and the line passing through o and perpendicular to $y = x$. Let $o_\top$ denote the intersection point between the same line and the boundary of the category effective area. Let d be the Euclidean distance function. Then we define the boundary closeness of o as follows:

$$Boundary\,Closeness(o) = \frac{d(o, o_\top)}{d(o_\perp, o_\top)}. \tag{2}$$

Figure 3a shows an example where o is outside of the category effective area, and Fig. 3b presents an example when o is inside. In both cases, when o is moving close to the boundaries, $BoundaryCloseness(o)$ approaches to zero. When a point lies outside of category promising areas, the perpendicular line does not intersect with the boundaries, and we can set the undefined boundary closeness using the maximum value of available ones. To avoid the fluctuations, we can use the mean value of boundary closeness from the last few epochs since their variance reveals the model uncertainty [12]. We should optimize the promising points close to the boundary of categories whose category predictions are sensitive to their prediction residuals. We propose to use a generalized sigmoid function as the modulating function based on boundary closeness in the manner of the cost-sensitive weighting strategy [15, 30]. The loss is attenuated adaptively and asymmetrically, which intends to focus on those promising samples and reduce their prediction residuals. The generalized sigmoid function is defined as follows:

$$w_i = \max(1 - \frac{1}{1 + e^{\beta*(\alpha - \frac{d(i, i_\top)}{d(i_\perp, i_\top)})}}, \varepsilon_m) = \max(\frac{1}{1 + e^{\beta*(\frac{d(i, i_\top)}{d(i_\perp, i_\top)} - \alpha)}}, \varepsilon_m), \tag{3}$$

where ε_m is a smoothness constant. ε_m is 0.25 in this paper. The smoothness constant is used to prevent weights from approaching to zero, because when the weights approach to zero, the corresponding samples do not contribute to the training process. Such penalty should be avoided. To summarize, given a loss function L such as square loss, the category-aware loss function with attenuation is Eq. 1 in which weights are calculated by Eq. 3.

4.2 The Prediction Framework

Our proposed adaptive loss attenuation method is model agnostic and can incorporate with the state-of-the-art neural prediction architectures. There is no special reason that we adopt Temporal convolutional networks (TCN) as the prediction model. To make this paper self-contained, we briefly introduce the neural architecture of TCNs.

Temporal convolutional networks [1] deal with sequence modeling problems by using convolutional architectures. Unlike RNNs, TCNs avoid the time-consuming training and predicting process due to the benefits from the parallelization of convolution operations. By combining deep residual networks and dilated convolution, TCNs acquire historical information flexibly. There are two design concepts related to TCNs: (1) Using casual convolution operation can prevent temporal information from leakage, (2) Using a 1D fully-convolutional network (1D FCN) can map a sequence of arbitrary length to a sequence of fixed length [18]. TCNs consist of four main components:

Causal Convolution can only convolute the information from previous time steps; that is, a filter at time step t can only see inputs that are not later than t. Similar to time-delay neural networks, Causal convolution avoids information leakage.

1D FCN outputs a sequence of the same length as the input sequence by using a zero-padding strategy. 1D FCN can make intensive predictions by making full use of the entire time series. The receptive field of high-level convolution widens when the network deepens, which builds up long-term memory dependency of the input sequence. Compared with fully connected networks, 1D FCN can reduce the connective parameters between layers significantly and speed up the model convergence.

Dilated Convolution overcomes the narrow receptive field problem of causal convolutions. While the interval between convolution units increases exponentially to acquire long-term information, the convolution kernel's size remains the same. Formally, the 1D dilated convolutional operation on the element of a sequence is defined in Eq. 4.

$$F(t) = (s *_d f)(t) = \sum_{i=0}^{k-1} f(i) \cdot s_{t-d \cdot i}, \tag{4}$$

where $f : \{0, ..., k-1\} \to \mathbb{R}$ is the convolution kernel, k is the kernel size, d is the dilation factor and $s - d \cdot i$ represents the data of the past. d increases as the network gets deeper, which is calculated by $d_l = 2^l$ at level l of the network. Convolutions are applied on two time stamps, t and $t - d$.

Residual Temporal Block stacks two dilated causal convolution layers, the weight normalizing layer and the spatial dropout layer for regularization. The final outputs of the block are the sum of the inputs and the results from the final convolution [13]. TCN's receptive field depends on the network depth, kernel size, and the dilation factor. Thus, the output o of a residual block is:

$$o = \sigma(\boldsymbol{x} \oplus \mathcal{F}(\boldsymbol{x})), \tag{5}$$

where σ denotes the activation function. The residual layers can learn the modifications to the identity mapping rather than the entire transformation. The length of $\boldsymbol{x}$ and the length of $\mathcal{F}(\boldsymbol{x})$ may be unequal in TCN. An additional 1×1 convolutional network is employed to handle this issue.

TCNs have several advantages against RNNs. TCNs have flexible receptive fields that change according to the kernel size, the dilation factor, and the network depth. TCNs have a stable gradient during the training process, while RNNs often face gradient vanishing and explosion. TCNs have high parallelism since convolution operations can be conducted without waiting for other convolution operations. So in this paper, we adopt TCNs as the prediction model for multivariate time series prediction.

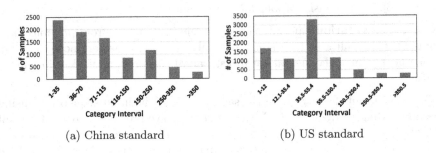

(a) China standard   (b) US standard

Fig. 4. Number of samples in each category

5   Experimental Evaluation

5.1   Data Set

We conducted extensive experiments with various loss functions, and the proposed loss attenuation method on Beijing $PM_{2.5}$ data set [16]. Beijing $PM_{2.5}$ data set contains the records of hourly $PM_{2.5}$ measurements and weather conditions, including dew point, temperature, pressure, combined wind direction, cumulated wind speed, cumulated hours of snow, and cumulated hours of rain. The size of the Beijing $PM_{2.5}$ data set is 43824. The number of samples in each category is shown in Fig. 4, according to both the China standard and the US standard of the category criteria. In the experiments, China standard of AQI is employed to be the category criterion[3]. The continuous variables in Beijing $PM_{2.5}$ data set are normalized, and the enumerated variables are encoded by one-hot vectors.

5.2   Experiment Settings

We use the records of hourly $PM_{2.5}$ data and weather conditions in the previous three days to predict $PM_{2.5}$ values of the next six hours. The data set is split into three parts randomly, i.e., the training set (60%), the validation set (20%), and the test set (20%). We evaluated the effectiveness of the proposed category-aware

---

[3] https://en.wikipedia.org/wiki/Air_quality_index#Mainland_China.

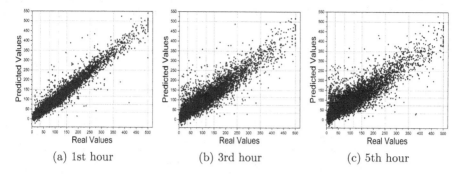

(a) 1st hour   (b) 3rd hour   (c) 5th hour

Fig. 5. The hourly prediction results using square loss with attenuation

adaptive loss attenuation method with respect to four loss functions: square loss, absolute loss, Huber loss [28], and the cost-sensitive loss (IEEM loss) [4]. IEEM loss does not support categories with non-monotonic interval length, and this is the reason that we employ the China standard in the experiments. In the US standard, the length of the second category interval is larger than the third one. We constructed temporal convolutional networks [1] with four hidden layers as the prediction model. The number of hidden units is 60, and the dropout rate is 0.15. The optimizer is Adam, and the learning rate is 0.05. We found all loss functions could achieve their best performance within 200 training epochs. We performed a grid search of values for hyper-parameters, and the best options of α and β in Eq. 3 are 0.65 and 20. Huber loss has a hyper-parameter δ to decide the segment point, and its best value is 0.12. For the forecasted categories, the evaluation measure is category accuracy which is the percentage of the samples with consistent predicted categories and real categories. For the forecasted values, the measure is Mean Square Error (MSE), which is defined as $\frac{1}{n} \sum_{t=1}^{n} (\hat{y}_t - y_t)^2$. y_t and $\hat{y}_t$ denote the real and the predicted values at time t, respectively.

5.3   Experimental Results

All figures in this paper are in color. Figure 5 shows the predicted values for the 1st hour, the 3rd hour and the 5th hour. The loss function is square loss with the proposed category-aware adaptive loss attenuation. To make the results informative, we illustrate the predicted values versus the real values. As discussed in the previous sections, it is ideal that all points $(y_t, \hat{y}_t)$ deviate very small from line $y = x$, which means small prediction residuals. When the prediction horizon increases, the accumulated uncertainty and errors also increase, which we can see from the enlarged deviation trend in Fig. 5a to 5c.

The detailed evaluation results of all loss functions are summarized in Table 1, which shows the individual category accuracy and mean square errors in each category. We report only results for the 1st hour due to the lack of space. Overall, loss functions with attenuation outperform the one without attenuation in more categories, demonstrating that the proposed loss attenuation by weighting

Table 1. The prediction results (1st hour) of various loss functions

Loss function	Interval	(0,35]	(35,75]	(75,115]	(115,150]	(150,250]	(250,350]	(350,500]
Square loss	Accuracy	**0.9249**	0.7269	0.5372	0.4968	0.7066	0.6734	0.7887
	MSE	**104.09**	274.65	566.1	666.74	1008.32	1757.46	2921.43
Square loss with attenuation	Accuracy	0.9098	**0.7554**	**0.6424**	**0.5947**	**0.7806**	**0.7462**	**0.8247**
	MSE	123.69	**247.49**	**475.09**	**538.61**	**837.4**	**1408.35**	**2132.55**
Absolute loss	Accuracy	0.872	**0.848**	0.6708	0.6137	0.7934	0.7663	**0.9072**
	MSE	**132.29**	**229.19**	508.53	537.14	926.93	1488.44	**1861.62**
Absolute loss with attenuation	Accuracy	**0.8904**	0.7903	**0.7283**	**0.6341**	**0.824**	**0.7688**	0.8608
	MSE	141.36	261.42	**486.04**	**518.86**	**828.33**	**1404.24**	1866.81
Huber loss ($\delta = 0.12$)	Accuracy	**0.8975**	**0.8114**	0.6554	0.5947	0.7551	0.7387	0.7835
	MSE	**121.57**	**214.19**	455.44	552.32	919.11	1502.49	2492.27
Huber loss with attenuation ($\delta = 0.12$)	Accuracy	0.8621	0.8074	**0.7091**	**0.6277**	**0.807**	**0.7638**	**0.8608**
	MSE	130.67	232.5	**436.92**	**488.32**	**773.62**	**1476.9**	**2043.72**
IEEM loss	Accuracy	**0.9447**	0.7509	0.6232	0.5388	**0.7313**	0.6533	0.799
	MSE	98.48	226.39	479.68	598.79	**990.25**	**1706.90**	2380.88
IEEM loss with attenuation	Accuracy	0.9329	**0.7623**	**0.6639**	**0.5654**	0.7296	**0.6859**	**0.8247**
	MSE	**96.30**	**215.58**	**451.67**	**542.87**	1018.34	1757.31	**2327.33**

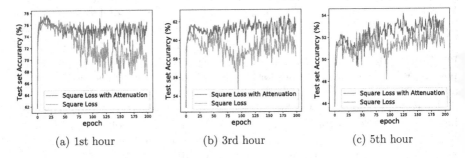

(a) 1st hour   (b) 3rd hour   (c) 5th hour

Fig. 6. Overall category accuracy versus epoch

samples adaptively and asymmetrically does improve the overall category prediction performance. For the widely used square loss, loss attenuation improved the category accuracy up to 10% points except the first category. A similar situation is observed for absolute loss, Huber loss and IEEM loss. Interestingly, the MSE of loss functions with attenuation in most categories are better than the one without attenuation. This is because we optimize the residuals of promising samples, and at the same time, we discourage the samples with large prediction residuals.

Figure 6 shows the volatility of category accuracy of the test set during the training process. We report the results in the 1st hour, the 3rd hour, and the 5th hour with respect to the square loss. At the beginning of the training process, Fig. 6a to 6c show that the category accuracy of square loss is comparable with the one with loss attenuation. After some epochs, since the loss attenuation emphasizes those promising samples to boost the category accuracy, the category

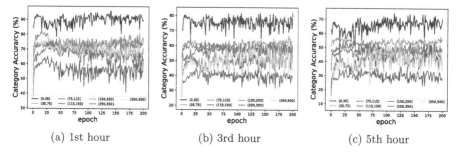

(a) 1st hour   (b) 3rd hour   (c) 5th hour

Fig. 7. Individual category accuracy using square loss with attenuation versus epoch

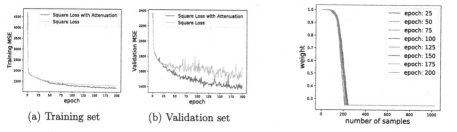

(a) Training set   (b) Validation set

Fig. 8. Training loss and validation loss

Fig. 9. Weight distribution in loss attenuation

accuracy of square loss with attenuation is always better than the one without attenuation. Although the accuracy without loss attenuation is improving due to the decreasing MSE, it cannot achieve comparable performance. Figure 7 shows the individual category accuracy using square loss with attenuation during the training process. Referring to Table 1, we found that the categories with large MSE values tend to have fairly volatile category accuracy.

Figure 8 presents the MSE of the training set and validation set in each epoch during training. As we can see, square loss with attenuation is superior to the one without attenuation and can achieve a smaller overall MSE. The results of the validation set in Fig. 8b show that not only the MSE of loss function with attenuation is always smaller than the one without attenuation, but also the MSE of loss function with attenuation fluctuates less, revealing a more stable optimization process.

We report the weight distribution every 25 epochs during the training process in Fig. 9. With the existence of the smoothness constant ε_m, the sigmoid-style curve is intercepted. About 1/5 of all samples are promising samples during training whose weights are large than ε_m.

6   Conclusion

We contribute a category-aware adaptive loss attenuation method for time series prediction respecting categories of values during SGD. The proposed weighting strategy attends the promising samples close to the category boundaries during the training process. We demonstrate that loss attenuation can improve the overall category prediction performances by extensive experimental results with the application of air quality forecasting.

References

1. Bai, S., Kolter, J.Z., Koltun, V.: An empirical evaluation of generic convolutional and recurrent networks for sequence modeling. CoRR abs/1803.01271 (2018)
2. Box, G.E.P., Pierce, D.A.: Distribution of residual autocorrelations in autoregressive-integrated moving average time series models. J. Am. Stat. Assoc. **65**(332), 1509–1526 (1970)
3. Chang, H.S., Learned-Miller, E., McCallum, A.: Active bias: training more accurate neural networks by emphasizing high variance samples. In: Advances in Neural Information Processing Systems, vol. 30, pp. 1002–1012. Curran Associates, Inc. (2017)
4. Chen, S., Liu, X., Li, B.: A cost-sensitive loss function for machine learning. In: Liu, C., Zou, L., Li, J. (eds.) DASFAA 2018. LNCS, vol. 10829, pp. 255–268. Springer, Cham (2018). https://doi.org/10.1007/978-3-319-91455-8_22
5. Cheng, J.R., Gen, M.: Accelerating genetic algorithms with GPU computing: a selective overview. Comput. Ind. Eng. **128**, 514–525 (2019)
6. Chung, J., Gülçehre, Ç., Cho, K., Bengio, Y.: Empirical evaluation of gated recurrent neural networks on sequence modeling. CoRR abs/1412.3555 (2014)
7. Cirstea, R., Micu, D., Muresan, G., Guo, C., Yang, B.: Correlated time series forecasting using deep neural networks: a summary of results. CoRR abs/1808.09794 (2018)
8. Cui, Y., Jia, M., Lin, T.Y., Song, Y., Belongie, S.: Class-balanced loss based on effective number of samples. In: 2019 IEEE/CVF Conference on Computer Vision and Pattern Recognition (CVPR), pp. 9260–9269 (2019)
9. Das, M., Ghosh, S.K.: Data-driven approaches for meteorological time series prediction: a comparative study of the state-of-the-art computational intelligence techniques. Pattern Recogn. Lett. **105**, 155–164 (2018). Machine Learning and Applications in Artificial Intelligence
10. Dong, Z., Liu, N., Rojas-Cessa, R.: Greedy scheduling of tasks with time constraints for energy-efficient cloud-computing data centers. J. Cloud Comput. **4**(1), 5 (2015)
11. Elman, J.L.: Distributed representations, simple recurrent networks, and grammatical structure. Mach. Learn. **7**, 195–225 (1991)
12. Gal, Y., Ghahramani, Z.: Dropout as a bayesian approximation: representing model uncertainty in deep learning. In: Proceedings of Machine Learning Research, 20–22 June 2016, vol. 48, pp. 1050–1059. PMLR, New York (2016)
13. He, K., Zhang, X., Ren, S., Sun, J.: Deep residual learning for image recognition. In: 2016 IEEE Conference on Computer Vision and Pattern Recognition, CVPR 2016, Las Vegas, NV, USA, 27–30 June 2016, pp. 770–778. IEEE Computer Society (2016)

4. Hochreiter, S., Schmidhuber, J.: LSTM can solve hard long time lag problems. In: Mozer, M., Jordan, M.I., Petsche, T. (eds.) Advances in Neural Information Processing Systems 9, NIPS, Denver, CO, USA, 2–5 December 1996, pp. 473–479. MIT Press (1996)

5. Kukar, M., Kononenko, I.: Cost-sensitive learning with neural networks. In: Proceedings of the 13th European Conference on Artificial Intelligence (ECAI-98), pp. 445–449. Wiley (1998)

6. Liang, X., et al.: Assessing Beijing's PM 2.5 pollution: severity, weather impact, APEC and winter heating. Proc. Roy. Soc. A Math. Phys. Eng. Sci. **471**, 20150257 (2015)

7. Lin, T., Goyal, P., Girshick, R., He, K., Dollár, P.: Focal loss for dense object detection. In: 2017 IEEE International Conference on Computer Vision (ICCV), pp. 2999–3007 (2017)

8. Long, J., Shelhamer, E., Darrell, T.: Fully convolutional networks for semantic segmentation. In: The IEEE Conference on Computer Vision and Pattern Recognition (CVPR), June 2015

9. Lu, X., Ma, C., Ni, B., Yang, X., Reid, I., Yang, M.-H.: Deep regression tracking with shrinkage loss. In: Ferrari, V., Hebert, M., Sminchisescu, C., Weiss, Y. (eds.) Computer Vision – ECCV 2018. LNCS, vol. 11218, pp. 369–386. Springer, Cham (2018). https://doi.org/10.1007/978-3-030-01264-9_22

0. Nam, T., Pardo, T.A.: Conceptualizing smart city with dimensions of technology, people, and institutions, pp. 282–291 (2011)

1. Pascanu, R., Mikolov, T., Bengio, Y.: Understanding the exploding gradient problem. CoRR abs/1211.5063 (2012)

2. Pascanu, R., Mikolov, T., Bengio, Y.: On the difficulty of training recurrent neural networks. In: Proceedings of the 30th International Conference on Machine Learning. Proceedings of Machine Learning Research, Atlanta, Georgia, USA, vol. 28, 17–19 June 2013, pp. 1310–1318. PMLR (2013)

3. Smola, A.J., Schölkopf, B.: A tutorial on support vector regression. Stat. Comput. **14**(3), 199–222 (2004)

4. Steinwart, I., Christmann, A.: Support Vector Machines. Springer, New York (2008). https://doi.org/10.1007/978-0-387-77242-4

5. Tang, N., Shen, Y., Yao, J.: Learning to fuse multiple semantic aspects from rich texts for stock price prediction. In: Cheng, R., Mamoulis, N., Sun, Y., Huang, X. (eds.) WISE 2020. LNCS, vol. 11881, pp. 65–81. Springer, Cham (2019). https://doi.org/10.1007/978-3-030-34223-4_5

6. Taylor, S.J., Letham, B.: Forecasting at scale. Peer J PrePrints **5**, e3190 (2017)

7. Wang, B., Huang, H., Wang, X.: A novel text mining approach to financial time series forecasting. Neurocomputing **83**, 136–145 (2012)

8. Wang, Q., Ma, Y., Zhao, K., Tian, Y.: A comprehensive survey of loss functions in machine learning. Ann. Data Sci. (2020). https://doi.org/10.1007/s40745-020-00253-5

9. Weigend, A., Gershenfeld, N.: Time Series Prediction: Forecasting the Future and Understanding the Past. Addison-Wesley (1993)

0. Zhou, Z.-H., Liu, X.-Y.: Training cost-sensitive neural networks with methods addressing the class imbalance problem. IEEE Trans. Knowl. Data Eng. **18**(1), 63–77 (2006)

1. Zhou, T., Wang, S., Bilmes, J.: Curriculum learning by dynamic instance hardness. In: Larochelle, H., Ranzato, M., Hadsell, R., Balcan, M.F., Lin, H. (eds.) Advances in Neural Information Processing Systems, vol. 33, pp. 8602–8613. Curran Associates, Inc. (2020)

PFL-MoE: Personalized Federated Learning Based on Mixture of Experts

Binbin Guo, Yuan Mei, Danyang Xiao, and Weigang Wu[✉]

School of Computer Science and Engineering, Sun Yat-sen University,
Guang Zhou, China
{guobb5,meiy7,xiaody}@mail2.sysu.edu.cn, wuweig@mail.sysu.edu.cn

Abstract. Federated learning (FL) is an emerging distributed machine learning paradigm that avoids data sharing among training nodes so as to protect data privacy. Under the coordination of the FL server, each client conducts model training using its own computing resource and private data set. The global model can be created by aggregating the training results of clients. To cope with highly non-IID data distributions, personalized federated learning (PFL) has been proposed to improve overall performance by allowing each client to learn a personalized model. However, one major drawback of a personalized model is the loss of generalization. To achieve model personalization while maintaining better generalization, in this paper, we propose a new approach, named PFL-MoE, which mixes outputs of the personalized model and global model via the MoE architecture. PFL-MoE is a generic approach and can be instantiated by integrating existing PFL algorithms. Particularly, we propose the PFL-MF algorithm which is an instance of PFL-MoE based on the freeze-base PFL algorithm. We further improve PFL-MF by enhancing the decision-making ability of MoE gating network and propose a variant algorithm PFL-MFE. We demonstrate the effectiveness of PFL-MoE by training the LeNet-5 and VGG-16 models on the Fashion-MNIST and CIFAR-10 datasets with non-IID partitions.

Keywords: Federated Learning · Personalization · Mixture of experts · Fine-tuning · Distributed machine learning

1 Introduction

Federated Learning (FL) allows a large number of clients (e.g., mobile phones and IoT devices) to learn a global model together without data sharing [3]. The distribution of data across clients is natural inconsistency and non-IID. The non-IID characteristic may largely affect the convergence behaviors of the global model trained, because non-IID data may cause the model parameters fluctuates largely and delay or even destroy the convergence. Personalization of the global model is necessary to handle the statistic heterogeneity of the distributed data. In personalized federated learning (PFL), each client learns a

© Springer Nature Switzerland AG 2021
L. H. U et al. (Eds.): APWeb-WAIM 2021, LNCS 12858, pp. 480–486, 2021.
https://doi.org/10.1007/978-3-030-85896-4_37

personalized model suitable for its own data distribution, which is more flexible than a single global model. However, personalization is always accompanied by the loss of generalization, which is manifested in the increases of generalization error of the personalized model. How to achieve better personalization while maintaining good generalization is the current research focus of PFL.

A large and growing body of literature has investigated to achieve personalization through various methods. Based on the MAML algorithm, Alireza et al. [1] proposed a variant of FedAvg named Per-FedAvg which turns the goal into learning a better initial global model for each client. The personalized model was fine-tuned from the initial global model, so that clients can get a better personalized model. Smith et al. [5] observed that multi-task learning is naturally suitable for federated learning. They treated each client as a individual task in multi-task learning literature, and investigated a system-aware approach called MOECHA that takes into account communication costs, straggles, and fault tolerance. FL+DE [4] use privacy-preserving FL to train a generic model and mixes it with each user's private domain model to improve model performance.

In this paper, we propose a personalized federated learning approach PFL-MoE that considers the personalized model as local expert and combines it with the federated global model via MoE architecture to achieve better personalization for each client. PFL-MoE is a generic approach and can be instantiated by existing PFL algorithms. Particularly, we propose PFL-MF algorithm, which is an instance of PFL-MoE based on the freeze-based PFL algorithm [7]. Moreover, we find that the MoE architecture cannot work well with complex input data, such as the color images, because it is difficult for the gating network to extract useful features from high-dimensional input data for decision-making. To enhance the decision-making ability of MoE gating network, we modify the model structure of PFL-MF and propose an extended algorithm PFL-MFE. We conduct experiments to evaluate our approach. An overall evaluation of PFL-MF and PFL-MFE algorithms is provided. The experiment results confirm the advantage of our design.

2 Methodology

2.1 PFL-MoE

PFL-MoE is a generic approach for personalization, which mainly contains the following three stages:

- *Federated Learning Stage:* Following the traditional FL framework, each client participates in FL training. The global model is created by repeatedly aggregating model updates from small subsets of clients. This stage is agnostic about the aggregation methods or privacy-preserving techniques of federated learning. It only needs the final global model for the next personalization.
- *Personalization Stage:* Each client downloads the latest global model from the FL server, and then conducts local adaption to get a personalized model based on the global model and local data.

– *Mixing Stage:* Via the previous two stages, the client gets two models, one is the personalized model, and the other is the global model. Based on the MoE architecture, the parameters of the gating network are trained to combine the models and make them work together.

The proposed PFL-MoE mixes the output of the personalized model and the global model using MoE architecture. More formally, in MoE architecture, the mixed output $\tilde{y} = \sum_{i=1}^{n} G(x)_i \cdot M_i(x)$, where $\sum_{i=1}^{n} G(x)_i = 1$ and $M_i, i = 1, ..., n$ are n experts (neural networks). In our method, there are $n = 2$ experts: the personalized model is viewed as the local expert, while the global model is viewed as the global expert. Their outputs are mixed by the gating network. The gating is a linear neural network, and can also be trained with SGD. The mixed predict label $\tilde{y}$ is given by Eq. 1 when the input is x:

$$\tilde{y} = g \cdot M_G(\theta; x) + (1 - g) \cdot M_G(\theta_i; x), \tag{1}$$

where $g = sigmoid(G(w_i; x))$ and the G is a linear neural network. The term g represents the mixing ratio of the expert models.

2.2 PFL-MF and PFL-MFE

Following the three stages of PFL-MoE, we propose the PFL-MF algorithm by using the local expert generated by the PFL-FB algorithm. PFL-FB is a variant of PFL-FT [6], where the global model structure M_G is divided into two parts: feature extractor M_E and classifier M_C. In personalization stage of PFL-MF, $\theta_i := [\theta_E, \theta_{C_i}]$ is partially frozen, only the θ_{C_i} can be updated. In the PFL-MF algorithm, the mixed predict label $\tilde{y}$ corresponding to x is written as:

$$\tilde{y} = g \cdot M_C(\theta_C; a) + (1 - g) \cdot M_C(\theta_{C_i}; a), \tag{2}$$

where $g = sigmoid(G(w_i; x))$ and $a = M_E(\theta_E, x)$.

To enhence the decision-making ability of the gating model, we propose PFL-MFE algorithm that using features as the input of gating. The features are a better choice for the gating input compared to raw data. Based on this idea, in the PFL-MFE algorithm, we modify the model structure of the PFL-MF algorithm, and use the activations a as the gating input:

$$g = sigmoid(G(w_i; a)), \tag{3}$$

where the number of the input neurons of G is equal to the dimension of a instead of x. Algorithm 1 describes the implementation details of the PFL-MF and PFL-MFE algorithms for each client i.

Algorithm 1. PFL-MF(E) Algorithm

Input: global extractor model structure M_E and its parameter θ_E, global classifier
model structure M_C and its parameter θ_C, client's data D_i, θ_{C_i}'s learning rate α,
w_i's learning rate β, local adaptation epochs E, loss function L, if variant flag v

Output: personalized classifier parameter θ_{C_i}, gating network parameter w_i

1: divide D_i to D_i^{per}, D_i^{gate}
2: **for** epoch $e = 1$ to E **do**
3:    **for** batch $(x, y) \subset D_i^{per}$ **do**
4:        $\widehat{y} \leftarrow M_C(\theta_{C_i}; M_E(\theta_E; x))$
5:        $\theta_{C_i} \leftarrow \theta_{C_i} - \alpha \cdot \nabla_{\theta_{C_i}} \ell(\widehat{y}, y)$
6:    **end for**
7:    **for** batch $(x, y) \subset D_i^{gate}$ **do**
8:        $a \leftarrow M_E(\theta_E; x)$
9:        **if** v **then**
10:            $g \leftarrow sigmoid(G(w_i; a))$ # PFL-MFE
11:        **else**
12:            $g \leftarrow sigmoid(G(w_i; x))$ # PFL-MF
13:        **end if**
14:        $\tilde{y} \leftarrow g \cdot M_C(\theta_C; a) + (1 - g) \cdot M_C(\theta_{C_i}; a)$
15:        $w_i \leftarrow w_i - \beta \cdot \nabla_{w_i} \ell(\tilde{y}, y)$
16:    **end for**
17: **end for**

---

5 Experimental Evaluation

5.1 Experimental Setup

Datasets and Models. In our experiments[1], we use two image recognition
datasets to conduct model training: Fashion-MNIST and CIFAR-10. With two
network models trained, we have three combinations: Fashion-MNIST + LeNet-
5, CIFAR-10 + LeNet-5, and CIFAR-10 + VGG-16. Similar to Hsu et al. [2],
we use Dirichlet distribution with α to simulate the non-IID data distributions.
The larger the α, the higher the similarity between the distributions.

Baselines. To verify the effectiveness of the proposed personalization algorithms PFL-MF and PFL-MFE, we compare them with three baselines: Local,
FedAvg, and PFL-FB. Each client has two types of tests, including local test and
global test. The accuracy of the local test and global test is used as a measure
of personalization and generalization.

5.2 Personalization Effect of PFL-MF and PFL-MFE

Comparing PFL-FB with PFL-MF in Table 1 and Table 2, for each client, the
increase of the local test accuracy of PFL-FB comes at the cost of a significant

---

[1] https://github.com/guobbin/PFL-MoE.

Table 1. The average value of **local test** accuracy of all clients in three baselines and proposed algorithms. Bold means the best in all algorithms.

	α	Local(%)	FedAvg(%)	PFL-FB(%)	PFL-MF(%)	PFL-MFE(%)
Fashion-MNIST &LeNet-5	0.5	84.87	90	92.84	92.85	**92.89**
	0.9	82.23	90.31	91.84	**92.02**	92.01
	2	78.63	90.5	90.47	**90.97**	90.93
CIFAR-10 &LeNet-5	0.5	65.58	68.92	**77.46**	75.49	77.23
	0.9	61.49	70.7	74.7	74.1	**74.74**
	2	55.8	72.69	72.5	73.24	**73.44**
CIFAR-10 &VGG-16	0.5	52.77	88.16	**91.92**	90.63	91.71
	0.9	45.24	88.45	**91.34**	90.63	91.18
	2	34.2	89.17	**90.4**	90.15	**90.4**

Table 2. The average value of **global test** accuracy of all clients. Bold means the best in all personalization algorithms.

	α	Local(%)	FedAvg(%)	PFL-FB(%)	PFL-MF(%)	PFL-MFE(%)
Fashion-MNIST &LeNet5	0.5	57.77	90	83.35	**85.45**	85.3
	0.9	65.28	90.31	85.91	**87.69**	87.67
	2	71.06	90.5	87.77	**89.37**	89.18
CIFAR-10 &LeNet5	0.5	28.89	68.92	54.28	**62.33**	58.27
	0.9	32.1	70.7	59.93	**65.78**	64.13
	2	35.32	72.69	66.06	**69.79**	69.78
CIFAR-10 &VGG-16	0.5	21.53	88.16	82.39	**85.81**	84.05
	0.9	22.45	88.45	82.62	**88.15**	87.9
	2	21.27	89.17	88.77	**89.3**	**89.3**

drop in global test accuracy. For example, in the CIFAR-10 + LeNet-5 experiment with $\alpha = 0.5$, the average global test accuracy of PFL-FB dropped by 15%, from 68.92% to 54.56%. PFL-MF achieves the average global test accuracy with 1%–8% higher than that of PFL-FB in all experiments. Table 2 shows that the global test accuracy of these three personalization algorithms are all higher than that of Local, which means that personalized federated learning can effectively improve the generalization ability of the model on client. In the proposed PFL-MF algorithm, if the personalized model deteriorates, it will be directly discarded by the gating network. Moreover, the gating network has learned which data is appropriate to use the personalized model and which data needs to be weighted more toward the global model. Consequently, PFL-MF is more stable the traditional PFL algorithms.

As shown in Table 1 and Table 2, in experiments on Fashion-MNIST, the proposed PFL-MF algorithm performs better than PFL-FB on the two tests, which indicates that PFL-MF achieves better personalization and better

eneralization than PFL-FB. However, in experiments on CIFAR-10, the average local test accuracy of PFL-MF is lower than that of PFL-FB. In PFL-MF,
he gating network can only recognize and make the decisions for simple data,
uch as the Fashion-MNIST dataset. But for the more complex color image
dataset CIFAR-10, the gating network needs to be improved. In the experiments on CIFAR-10, PFL-MFE is more effective than PFL-MF, because the
gating network can make better decisions indirectly by using the abstract fea-
ures. For the simple Fashion-MNIST dataset, PFL-MF is enough. PFL-MFE
an better recognize complex input data while maintaining the advantages of
PFL-MF. In all experiments, overall, PFL-MFE achieves the best average local
est accuracy among three personalization algorithms, and it is much better than
PFL-FB in the average global test accuracy. In a word, the proposed PFL-MFE
algorithm can realize personalization more effectively while maintaining better
generalization.

4   Conclusion and Future Work

We propose PFL-MoE, an MoE based approach for personalized federated learn-
ng. PFL-MoE can combine advantages of the personalized model and the global
model and achieve both better generalization and better personalization. PFL-
MF, an instance of PFL-MoE, performs better than existing algorithm PFL-FB
in both local test and global test. We also show that PFL-MFE strengthens
he decision-making ability of the MoE gating network and can be effective
when processing more complex data. In the future, we will explore the instance
of PFL-MoE of other personalized federated learning algorithms and compare
their overall performance.

Acknowledgement. This work is supported by The National Key Research and
Development Program of China (2018YFB0204303), National Natural Science Foundation of China (U1801266, U1811461), Guangdong Provincial Natural Science Foundation of China (2018B030312002).

References

1. Fallah, A., Mokhtari, A., Ozdaglar, A.E.: Personalized federated learning with theoretical guarantees: A model-agnostic meta-learning approach. In: Annual Conference
   on Neural Information Processing Systems. MIT Press (2020)
2. Hsu, H., Qi, H., Brown, M.: Measuring the effects of non-identical data distribution
   for federated visual classification. In: NIPS Workshop on Federated Learning for
   Data Privacy and Confidentiality (2019)
3. McMahan, B., Moore, E., Ramage, D., Hampson, S., y Arcas, B.A.: Communication-
   efficient learning of deep networks from decentralized data. In: International Conference on Artificial Intelligence and Statistics, vol. 54, pp. 1273–1282. PMLR (2017)
4. Peterson, D., Kanani, P., Marathe, V.J.: Private federated learning with domain
   adaptation. In: NIPS Workshop on Federated Learning for Data Privacy and Confidentiality (2019)

5. Smith, V., Chiang, C.K., Sanjabi, M., Talwalkar, A.S.: Federated multi-task learning. In: Annual Conference on Neural Information Processing Systems, pp. 4424–4434. MIT Press (2017)
6. Wang, K., Mathews, R., Kiddon, C., Eichner, H., Beaufays, F., Ramage, D.: Federated evaluation of on-device personalization. arXiv preprint arXiv:1910.10252 (2019)
7. Yu, T., Bagdasaryan, E., Shmatikov, V.: Salvaging federated learning by local adaptation. arXiv preprint arXiv:2002.04758 (2020)

A New Density Clustering Method Using Mutual Nearest Neighbor

Yufang Zhang, Yongfang Zha$^{(\boxtimes)}$, Lintao Li, and Zhongyang Xiong

Key Laboratory of Dependable Service Computing in Cyber Physical Society, Ministry of Education, Chongqing University, Chongqing 400044, China
{zhangyf,zhayf,lilt,xiongzy}@cqu.edu.cn

Abstract. Density-based clustering algorithms have become a popular research topic in recent years. However, most these algorithms have difficulties identifying all clusters with greatly varying densities and arbitrary shapes or have considerable time complexity. To tackle this issue, we propose a novel density assessment method by using mutual nearest neighbor, and then propose a relative density clustering algorithm (RDC). RDC can get the right number of clusters for the datasets, which include varying densities and arbitrary shapes; in addition, the time complexity of it is O($n\log n$).

Keywords: Mutual nearest neighbors · Relative density · Clustering

Introduction

As a method of unsupervised classification, clustering analysis is widely used in data analysis and machine learning [1]. It aims to divide data objects into certain number of clusters, which satisfy high intra-cluster similarity and low inter-cluster similarity [2]. Clustering analysis has been widely applied in many fields [3], such as image segmentation, pattern recognition, document clustering, and social networks [4]. Generally, clustering algorithms can be divided into four categories [5]: partitioning algorithms [6,7], hierarchical algorithms [8], density-based algorithms [9], and grid-based algorithms [10]. Partitioning algorithms and density-based algorithms are the most popular two.

Density peak clustering (DPC) [11] algorithm is one of the most popular density-based clustering algorithms. The parameter setting of DPC does not need to know the relevant information of the data in advance. However, DPC still has some defects. On the one hand, it can't deal with clusters containing manifold distributions [12]. On the other hand, DPC faces the challenge of shape loss, false distance, and false peaks [13]. DCore [13] considers that a cluster consists of a density core, retaining the main shape of the cluster; and consists of borders that are distributed out of the core. It makes DCore can overcome these problems, but it needs five parameters, which is hard to be set for users.

© Springer Nature Switzerland AG 2021
L. H. U et al. (Eds.): APWeb-WAIM 2021, LNCS 12858, pp. 487–494, 2021.
https://doi.org/10.1007/978-3-030-85896-4_38

2   The RDC Algorithm

2.1   Related Work: Natural Neighbor Structure

The Natural Neighbor Stable Structure [14] is a new concept coming from the objective reality, which is inspired by interpersonal relationships in human society. If object p is a neighbor of object q and object q is a neighbor of object p at the same time, object q is a natural neighbor of object p, vice versa.

The searching process of the Natural Neighbor Stable Structure is performed as follows: we expand k increasing from 1 to search each data object's k-nearest neighbors and reverse neighbors (a set of points consider the objective point as its k-nearest neighbors) and compute the number of reverse neighbors until all objects have at least one reverse neighbor or the number of objects without reverse neighbors doesn't change anymore. In this time, the search range k is the natural neighbor characteristic value λ [15]. For each object, the mutual nearest neighbors are the intersection of k-nearest neighbors and reverse neighbors.

2.2   Relative Density

Because the number of the mutual nearest neighbors of an object with high density (called core object) is bigger than an object with low density' (called core object). Thus, the number of the mutual nearest neighbors of an object can be used to represent its density. We used three synthetic datasets (Fig. 1) to illustrate the performance of relative density.

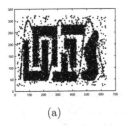 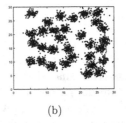 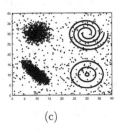

(a)   (b)   (c)

Fig. 1. Three original synthetic datasets.

Definition 1. *(Density of Object). The density of object x_i, is defined as the number of mutual nearest neighbors of x_i, which is $\rho(i) = |MNN(x_i)|$.*

The greater ρ of an object, the more likely it belongs to the core objects. In terms of some simple datasets, ρ can well both extract the optimal core objects and obtain the right number of clusters. It is hard to get the right number of clusters. Thus, we define relative density to extract the core objects.

Definition 2. *(Relative Density of Object). The relative density of object x_i, $\rho_r(i)$, is defined as follows:*

$$\rho_r(i) = \rho(i)/dist_{max} \tag{1}$$

where $dist_{max}$ is the maximum Euclidean distance from x_i to its mutual nearest neighbors, namely, $\rho_r(i)$ represents the number of mutual nearest neighbors at a unit scanning radius.

As shown in Fig. 2, the relative density (ρ_r) of the objects linking two different clusters is less than the core objects'. That is to say, ρ_r can be used for extracting the optimal core objects for recognizing the clusters with complex patterns.

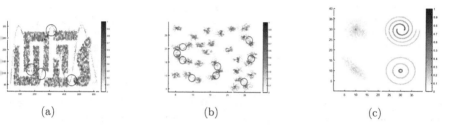

(a)   (b)   (c)

Fig. 2. The normalized relative density (ρ_r) map of the original datasets, the ρ_r of the objects in blue circles are less than the core objects', which shows that ρ_r can extract the optimal core objects to identify every cluster. (Color figure online)

2.3   The RDC Clustering Algorithm

Relative density (ρ_r) is able to distinguish the noise, the objects linking two clusters, and the overlapping objects between two clusters well. Thus, we apply ρ_r to extract the optimal core objects of the original dataset. Because a core object should have a relatively large ρ_r, then its definition is given as follows:

Definition 3. *(Core Object). The ρ_r of a core object must be the first top $100-p$ percent.*

where p is chosen from $\{5, 10, 20, 30, 40\}$ for different datasets.

Definition 4. *(Core Set). Core set is generated by the whole core objects of the original dataset.*

As shown in Fig. 3, core sets are extracted by using Definition 4 with p is chosen as 20, 40 and 10, respectively. The core sets indicate the mainframe structure of the original datasets, which is better to be separated, and then easy to cluster. The results of this process of the three datasets are shown in Fig. 4.

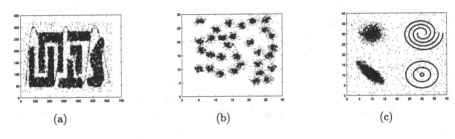

Fig. 3. The core sets (blue objects) of the three datasets. (Color figure online)

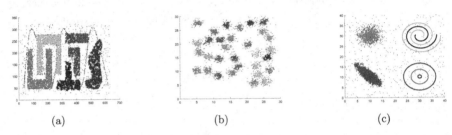

Fig. 4. The core sest clustering results of the three datasets. Different colors represent different clusters, and unassigned objects are marked as black points. (Color figure online)

Algorithm 1. Relative density clustering algorithm (RDC)

Require: D(the data set), p(ratio of non-core objects)
Ensure: $labels$(clustering results)
1: Initial $labels = 0$ for every object;
2: MNN=MNN-searching(D);
3: ρ_r = Computing relative density(D,MNN);
4: extract the first $(1\text{-}p)\%$ of the ρ_r as $CoreSet$, the other as $non-core\ set$;
5: $labels(CoreSet)$ = Core set clustering($CoreSet$);
6: eliminate erroneous clusters, reset its $labels$ and add it to $non-core\ set$;
7: **for** each object x_i in $non-core\ set$ **do**
8:     $labels(i)$ = the label of x_i's nearest labeld object;
9: **end for**
10: **Return** $labels$;

In this section, we introduce a relative density clustering algorithm based on mutual nearest neighbor (called RDC). The main processes are that: firstly, searching the mutual nearest neighbors; secondly, computing the relative density of each object; thirdly, extracting core set according to Definition 4 to get the main structure of the original dataset; fourthly, clustering core set based on mutual nearest neighbor of each core object; fifthly, eliminating outlier clusters [16]; lastly, allocating the rest objects to their nearest core object to obtain the final clustering result. The main steps of RDC are presented in Algorithm 1, and Fig. 5 are the final clustering results of the three datasets.

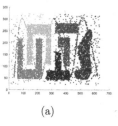
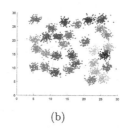
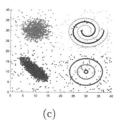

(a)   (b)   (c)

Fig. 5. The final clustering results of the three datasets.

2.4   Complexity Analysis

In this section, we will analyze the time complexity of RDC and assume the number of objects is n. It depends on four parts: (1) the time complexity for mutual nearest neighbor search by using KD-tree is $O(n\log n)$; (2) the time complexity for computing relative density and using relative density to extract core set are $O(n)$; (3) the time complexity of clustering core set by the hierarchical traversal of MNN is $O(n\log n)$; (4) the time complexity of allocating non-core objects is $O(l)$. Therefore, the overall time complexity of RDC is $O(n\log n)$.

3   Experiments and Results Analysis

To test the effectiveness of RDC, our method was compared with related algorithms including k-means [7], DBSCAN [17], DPC [11], SC [18] and DCore [13]. The experiments ran on a laptop with an Intel i5-8300H CPU, 8G RAM, Windows 10 64-bit OS, and the MATLAB 2016a programming environment.

Three evaluation indices, the accuracy (ACC), F-measure (F1) and normalized mutual information (NMI), were applied to evaluate the performances of the clustering results. These evaluation indices all range from 0 to 1, and the greater value of them, the better performance of the algorithm.

We applied six UCI [19] datasets to test the performance, including Thyroid, Seeds, Popfailures, Segmentation, and Pageblocks. Table 1 displays the characteristics of six real datasets. The parameters setting of each method in six real-world datasets of UCI are shown in Table 2. The results of ACC, F1, and NMI are shown in Table 3, 4 and 5. In these tables, the best results are boldfaced, and the second-best results are marked by the star (*) notation.

Table 1. The characteristics of six real datasets

Datasets	Number of instances	Number of attributes	Number of clusters
Thyroid	215	5	3
Seeds	210	7	3
Popfailures	540	18	2
Segmentation	2310	19	7
Pageblocks	5473	10	5

Table 2. The parameter settings of each clustering method in six real datasets

Datasets	k-means	DBSCAN	DPC	SC	DCore	RDC
Thyroid	N = 3	Eps = 5 Minpts = 3	dc = 2%	k = 8 σ = 1 N = 3	r1 = 2 r2 = 1 R = 4 T1 = 8 Tn = 3	p = 5%
Seeds	N = 3	Eps = 0.8 Minpts = 3	dc = 2%	k = 12 σ = 1 N = 3	r1 = 15 r2 = 10 R = 18 T1 = 20 Tn = 3	p = 65%
Popfailures	N = 2	Eps = 1.2 Minpts = 5	dc = 2%	k = 10 σ = 1 N = 2	r1 = 1 r2 = 0.5 R = 1 T1 = 5 Tn = 2	p = 0%
Segmentation	N = 7	Eps = 10 Minpts = 3	dc = 2%	k = 15 σ = 10 N = 7	r1 = 15 r2 = 10 R = 18 T1 = 20 Tn = 3	p = 35%
Pageblocks	N = 5	Eps = 5 Minpts = 3	dc = 2%	k = 10 σ = 1 N = 5	r1 = 12 r2 = 10 R = 15 T1 = 18 Tn = 3	p = 50%

Table 3. The value of ACC of each method on the real datasets

Datasets	k-means	DBSCAN	DPC	SC	DCore	RDC
Thyroid	0.7535*	**0.8093**	0.7302	0.7070	0.6977	**0.8093**
Seeds	0.8905*	0.6476	0.8857	0.8810	0.3810	**0.9095**
Popfailures	0.8905	0.9148*	0.9148*	0.9148*	0.9148*	**0.9167**
Segmentation	0.4732	0.6476	0.4883	**0.7390**	0.4537	0.7134*
Pageblocks	0.8999	0.9125*	0.8993	0.8977	0.9057	**0.9202**

Table 4. The value of F1 of each method on the real datasets

Datasets	k-means	DBSCAN	DPC	SC	DCore	RDC
Thyroid	0.6515	**0.7822**	0.6714	0.6574	0.6593	0.7510*
Seeds	**0.8897**	0.6983	0.8822*	0.8815	0.4938	0.8494
Popfailures	0.6346	0.8206*	0.7101	0.8179	0.8206*	**0.8854**
Segmentation	0.4878	0.2943	0.5499	**0.7477**	0.4016	0.6929*
Pageblocks	0.8185	0.8135	0.8597	0.7160	0.8796*	**0.8990**

Table 5. The value of NMI of each method on the real datasets

Datasets	k-means	DBSCAN	DPC	SC	DCore	RDC
Thyroid	0.2227	0.4244*	0.1376	0.0422	0.1189	**0.4410**
Seeds	**0.7101**	0.4592	0.6982*	0.6472	0.0849	0.6560
Popfailures	0.0014	0.0189*	1.4979e−04	0.0131	0.0016	**0.0293**
Segmentation	0.4232	0.4281	0.5206	**0.6686**	0.3282	0.6647*
Pageblocks	0.0570	0.1171	0.0328	0.0376	0.1300	**0.2594**

Table 6. The consuming time of each method on the real datasets (unit: second)

Datasets	k-means	DBSCAN	DPC	SC	DCore	RDC
Thyroid	0.170	0.046	0.541	0.241	0.223	0.356
Seeds	0.192	0.041	0.457	0.248	0.336	0.362
Popfailures	0.145	0.039	0.677	0.489	0.430	0.472
Segmentation	0.158	0.238	11.095	10.429	1.998	1.998
Pageblocks	0.191	0.675	104.722	192.631	3.588	6.306

Regarding the ACC, as displayed in Table 3, RDC obtained the best results on Thyroid, Seeds, Popfailures, and Pageblocks and the second-best results in Haberman and Segmentation. In terms of F1, as shown in Table 4, RDC gets the best results or the second-best results on all datasets except the Seeds dataset. Regarding the NMI, as demonstrated in Table 5, RDC gets the best results in Thyroid, Popfailures, and Pageblocks and the second-best results in Harberman and Segmentation. Regarding the F1 and NMI, RDC fails to achieve the best or second-best results on every real dataset, but it is still better than DBSCAN and DCore.

According to Table 6, RDC runs slower than k-means and DBSCAN, but it runs faster than DPC and SC. In these six real datasets, the consuming time of RDC is similar to DCore.

4 Conclusions

The results of experiments prove that RDC can deal with extremely complex patterns with large variations in density and shape. The parameter setting of RDC is easier than DCore, and RDC runs faster than DPC. However, it also has the disadvantage of detecting noise objects.

Acknowledgment. Thanks for the guidance and suggestions of my tutor. This work is funded by the Science and Technology Development Fund Macau (SKL-IOTSC-021-2023) and Graduate Scientific Research and Innovation Foundation of Chongqing, China (no. CYS20067).

References

1. Li, X., Yin, H., Zhou, K., Zhou, X.: Semi-supervised clustering with deep metric learning and graph embedding. World Wide Web **23**(2), 781–798 (2019). https://doi.org/10.1007/s11280-019-00723-8
2. Liu, X., Liu, Y., Xie, Q., Li, L., Li, Z.: A potential-based clustering method with hierarchical optimization. World Wide Web **21**(6), 1617–1635 (2017). https://doi.org/10.1007/s11280-017-0509-2
3. Reza, G., Nasir, S., Norwati, M.: A survey: clustering ensembles techniques. World Acad. Sci. Eng. Technol. **30**, 644–653 (2009)

4. Pei, X., Wu, T., Chen, C.: Automated graph regularized projective nonnegative matrix factorization for document clustering. IEEE Trans. Cybern. **44**, 1821–1831 (2014)

5. Han, J., Pei, J.: Data Mining: Concepts and Techniques. Morgan Kaufmann, California (2011)

6. Nanda, S., Panda, G.: A survey on nature inspired metaheuristic algorithms for partitional clustering. Swarm Evol. Comput. **44**, 1–18 (2014)

7. Jain, A.: Data clustering: 50 years beyond K-means. Pattern Recogn. Lett. **31**(8), 651–666 (2010)

8. Zhou, S., Xu, Z., Liu, F.: Method for determining the optimal number of clusters based on agglomerative hierarchical clustering. IEEE Trans. Neural Netw. Learn. Syst. **28**, 3007–3017 (2017)

9. Ester, M., Kriegel, H., Xu, X.: A density-based algorithm for discovering clusters in large spatial databases with noise. In: Proceedings of the Second International Conference on Knowledge Discovery and Data Mining, vol. 3, pp. 226–231 (1996)

10. Wang, W., Lou, B., Li, X., Lou, X., Jin, N., Yan, K.: Intelligent maintenance frameworks of large-scale grid using genetic algorithm and K-Mediods clustering methods. World Wide Web **23**(2), 1177–1195 (2019). https://doi.org/10.1007/s11280-019-00705-w

11. Alex, R., Alessandro, L.: Clustering by fast search and find of density peaks. Science **344**(6191), 1492–1496 (2014)

12. Xie, J., Xiong, Z., Ma, J.: Density core-based clustering algorithm with dynamic scanning radius. Knowl.-Based Syst. **142**, 58–70 (2018)

13. Chen, Y., Tang, S., Pei, S.: Decentralized clustering by finding loose and distribute density cores. Inf. Sci. **433**, 510–526 (2018)

14. Zhu, Q., Feng, J., Huang, J.: A self-adaptive neighborhood method without parameter k. Pattern Recogn. Lett. **80**, 30–36 (2016)

15. Huang, J., Zhu, Q., Yang, L.: A non-parameter outlier detection algorithm based on natural neighbor. Knowl.-Based Syst. **92**, 71–77 (2016)

16. Huang, J.: A novel outlier cluster detection algorithm without top-n parameter. Knowl.-Based Syst. **121**, 32–40 (2017)

17. Ester, M., Kriegel, H., Xu, X.: A density-based algorithm for discovering clusters in large spatial databases with noise. In: International Conference on Knowledge Discovery and Data Mining, vol. 96, pp. 226–231 (1996)

18. Jordan, M., Weiss, Y.: On spectral clustering: analysis and an algorithm. Adv. Neural Inf. Process. Syst. **1**, 849–856 (2001)

19. UC Irvine Machine Learning Repository Homepage. http://archive.ics.uci.edu/ml. Accessed 4 Apr 2013

Correction to: Web and Big Data

Leong Hou U, Marc Spaniol, Yasushi Sakurai,
and Junying Chen

Correction to:
L. H. U et al. (Eds.): *Web and Big Data*, LNCS 12858,
https://doi.org/10.1007/978-3-030-85896-4

For Chapter 6:
The original version of this chapter was revised. Affiliations 1 and 2 have been corrected.

For Chapter 13:
In an older version of this paper, the presentation of figures 1 and 3 was incorrect. This has been corrected.

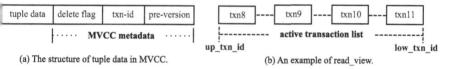

(a) The structure of tuple data in MVCC.   (b) An example of read_view.

Fig. 1. MVCC implementation.

The updated version of these chapters can be found at
https://doi.org/10.1007/978-3-030-85896-4_6
https://doi.org/10.1007/978-3-030-85896-4_13

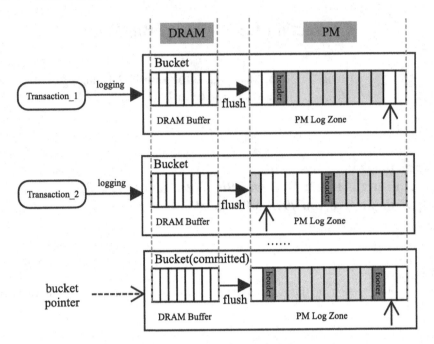

Fig. 3. The architecture of BKL.

Author Index

Printed in the United States
by Baker & Taylor Publisher Services